D1410534

PEOPLE, PLACES,
AND CHANGE

An Introduction to World Studies

HOLT, RINEHART AND WINSTON

A Harcourt Education Company

Orlando • **Austin** • New York • San Diego • Toronto • London

THE AUTHORS

Prof. David M. Helgren is Director of the Center for Geographic Education at San Jose State University in California, where he is also Chair of the Department of Geography. Prof. Helgren received his Ph.D. in geography from the University of Chicago. He is the coauthor of several geography textbooks and has written many articles on the geography of Africa. Awards from the National Geographic Society, the National Science Foundation, and the L. S. B. Leakey Foundation have supported his many field research projects. Prof. Helgren is a former president of the California Geographical Society and a founder of the Northern California Geographic Alliance.

Prof. Robert J. Sager is Chair of Earth Sciences at Pierce College in Lakewood, Washington. Prof. Sager received his B.S. in geology and geography and M.S. in geography from the University of Wisconsin and holds a J.D. in international law from Western State University College of Law. He is the coauthor of several geography and earth science textbooks and has written many articles and educational media programs on the geography of the Pacific. Prof. Sager has received several National Science Foundation study grants and has twice been a recipient of the University of Texas NISOD National Teaching Excellence Award. He is a founding member of the Southern California Geographic Alliance and former president of the Association of Washington Geographers.

Prof. Alison S. Brooks is Professor of Anthropology at George Washington University and a Research Associate in Anthropology at the Smithsonian Institution. She received her A.B., M.A., and Ph.D. in Anthropology from Harvard University. Since 1964, she has carried out ethnological and archaeological research in Africa, Europe, and Asia and is the author of more than 300 scholarly and popular publications. She has served as a consultant to Smithsonian exhibits and to National Geographic, Public Broadcasting, the Discovery Channel, and other public media. In addition, she is a founder and editor of *Anthro Notes: The National Museum of Natural History Bulletin for Teachers* and has received numerous grants and awards to develop and lead in-service training institutes for teachers in grades 5–12. She served as the American Anthropological Association's representative to the NCSS task force on developing Scope and Sequence guidelines for Social Studies Education in grade K–12.

While the details of the young people's stories in the chapter openers are real, their identities have been changed to protect their privacy.

Cover and Title Page photographs: Dancer in traditional costume, Bali.
Cover and Title Page Photo Credits: Nawrocki Stock Photo

Printed in the United States of America

ISBN 0-03-036707-7

2 3 4 5 6 7 8 9 032 07 06 05 04

CONTENT REVIEWERS

EDUCATIONAL REVIEWERS

PEOPLE, PLACES, AND CHANGE

CONTENTS

UNIT 2 United States and Canada

UNIT 3 Middle and South America

UNIT 4 Europe 222

Notes from the Field

UNIT 5

Russia and Its Western Neighbors 314

Notes from the Field

UNIT 6 Southwest and Central Asia 364

UNIT 8 **South Asia** **538**

Notes from the Field

UNIT 9 East and Southeast Asia 588

Notes from the Field

UNIT 10 The Pacific World and Antarctica 666

Notes from the Field

REFERENCE SECTION

FEATURES

CASE STUDY

COULD YOU SURVIVE?

FEATURES

FEATURES

FEATURES

DIAGRAMS, CHARTS, and TABLES

ATLAS CONTENTS

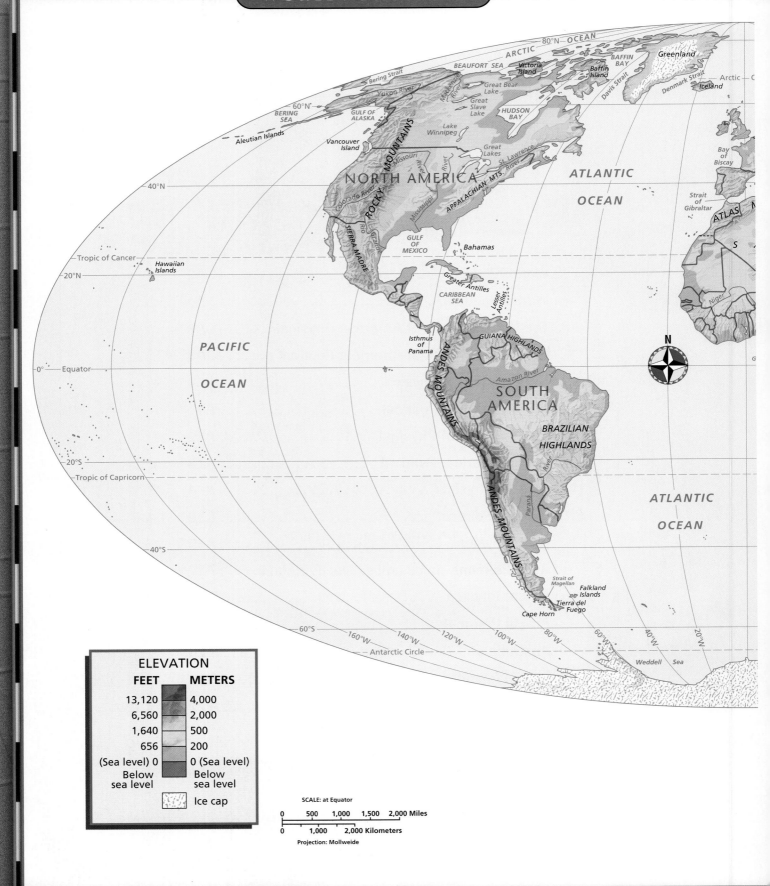

ELEVATION

FEET	METERS
13,120	4,000
6,560	2,000
1,640	500
656	200
(Sea level) 0	0 (Sea level)
Below sea level	Below sea level

Ice cap

SCALE: at Equator

0   500   1,000   1,500   2,000 Miles

0   1,000   2,000 Kilometers

Projection: Mollweide

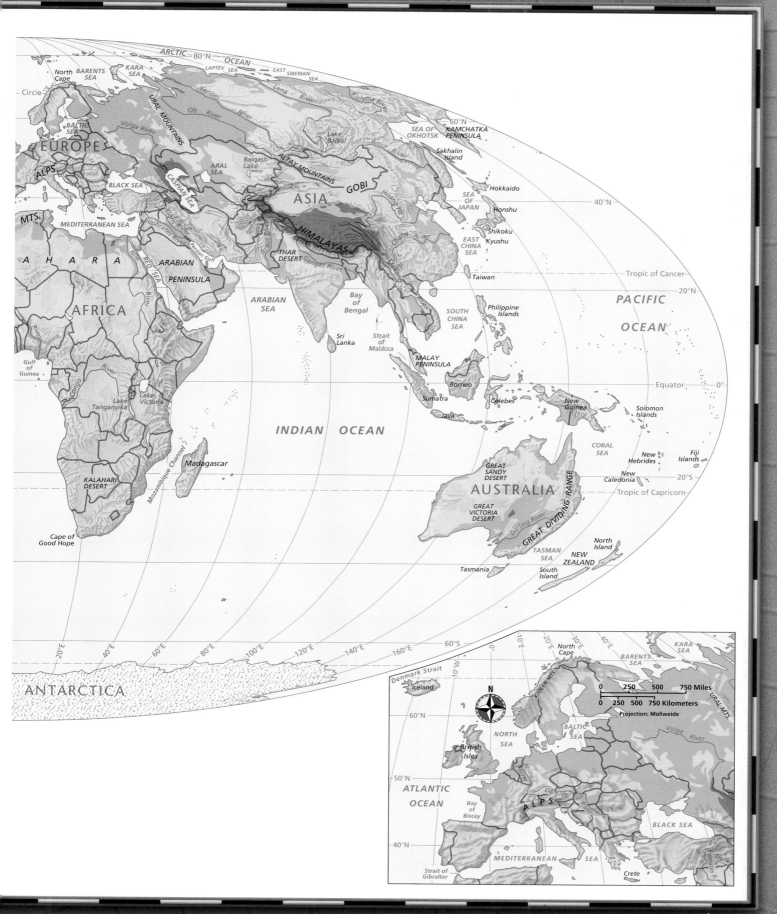

ARCTIC 80°N OCEAN
North Cape
BARENTS SEA
KARA SEA
LAPTEV SEA
EAST SIBERIAN SEA
Circle
URAL MOUNTAINS
Yenisey River
Ob River
Lena River
Kolyma Riv.
60°N
SEA OF OKHOTSK
KAMCHATKA PENINSULA
BALTIC SEA
EUROPE
Volga River
Lake Baikal
Baiqash Lake
ARAL SEA
ALTAY MOUNTAINS
Sakhalin Island
ALPS
CASPIAN SEA
ASIA
GOBI
Amur River
Hokkaido
SEA OF JAPAN
40°N
BLACK SEA
Huang He
Honshu
MTS.
Euphrates River
Tigris River
HIMALAYAS
Chang River
Shikoku
Kyushu
MEDITERRANEAN SEA
Persian Gulf
THAR DESERT
EAST CHINA SEA
SAHARA
Nile River
ARABIAN PENINSULA
RED SEA
Indus River
Ganges River
Mekong River
Taiwan
Tropic of Cancer
AFRICA
ARABIAN SEA
Bay of Bengal
20°N
SOUTH CHINA SEA
Philippine Islands
PACIFIC
Sri Lanka
Strait of Malacca
OCEAN
Gulf of Guinea
Congo River
MALAY PENINSULA
Lake Tanganyika
Lake Victoria
Borneo
Equator
0°
Sumatra
Celebes
New Guinea
Solomon Islands
Java
INDIAN OCEAN
CORAL SEA
New Hebrides
Fiji Islands
Madagascar
GREAT SANDY DESERT
New Caledonia
20°S
KALAHARI DESERT
Mozambique Channel
AUSTRALIA
GREAT VICTORIA DESERT
Tropic of Capricorn
Darling River
GREAT DIVIDING RANGE
North Island
Cape of Good Hope
TASMAN SEA
NEW ZEALAND
Tasmania
South Island
20°E 40°E 60°E 80°E 100°E 120°E 140°E 160°E
60°S
ANTARCTICA

Denmark Strait
10°W
0°
10°E
20°E
30°E
40°E
North Cape
KARA SEA
BARENTS SEA
Iceland
60°N
KJÖLEN MTS.
N
0 250 500 750 Miles
0 250 500 750 Kilometers
Projection: Mollweide
URAL MTS.
British Isles
NORTH SEA
BALTIC SEA
Volga River
ATLANTIC OCEAN
50°N
Rhine
ALPS
Danube River
BLACK SEA
Bay of Biscay
40°N
MEDITERRANEAN SEA
Strait of Gibraltar
Crete
Tigris R.
Euphrates R.

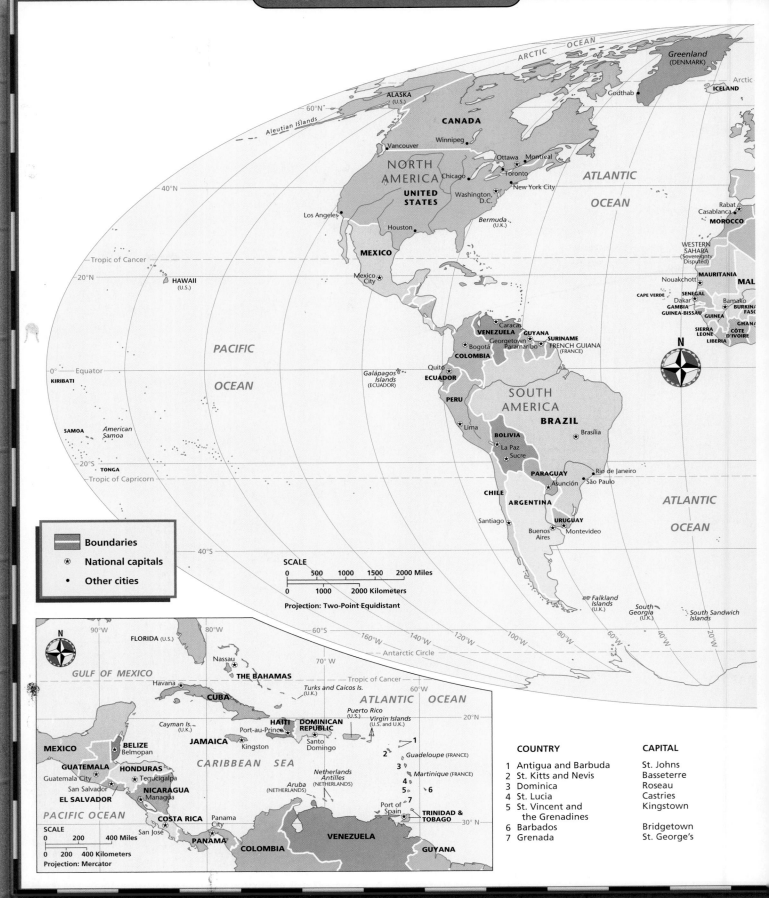

Boundaries

⊛ National capitals

• Other cities

SCALE

| 0 | 500 | 1000 | 1500 | 2000 Miles |

| 0 | 1000 | 2000 Kilometers |

Projection: Two-Point Equidistant

SCALE

| 0 | 200 | 400 Miles |

| 0 | 200 | 400 Kilometers |

Projection: Mercator

COUNTRY	CAPITAL
1 Antigua and Barbuda	St. Johns
2 St. Kitts and Nevis	Basseterre
3 Dominica	Roseau
4 St. Lucia	Castries
5 St. Vincent and the Grenadines	Kingstown
6 Barbados	Bridgetown
7 Grenada	St. George's

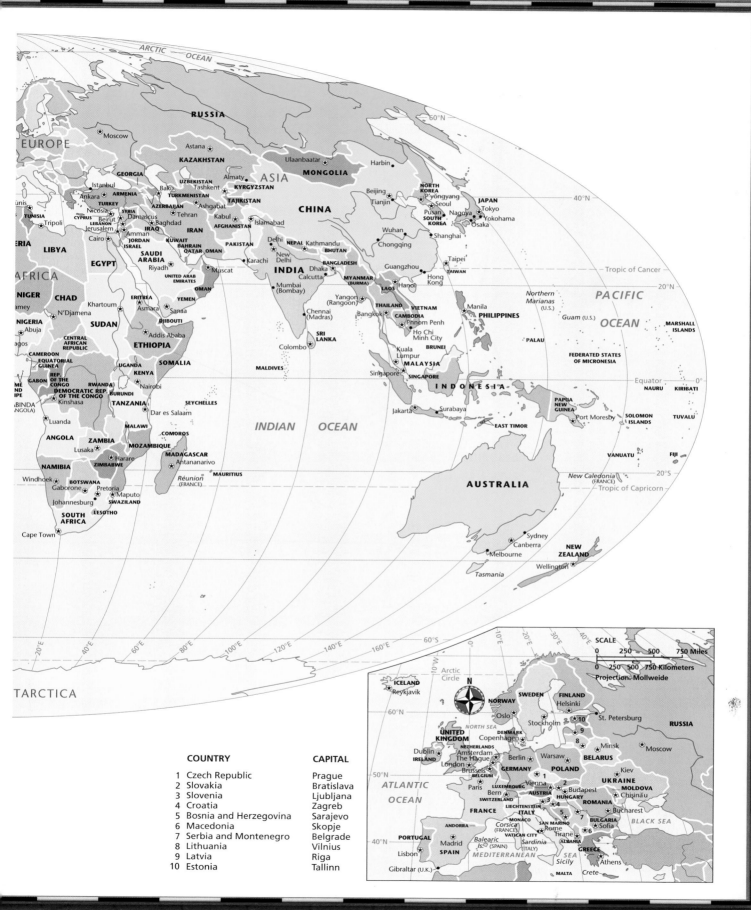

ARCTIC OCEAN

EUROPE

RUSSIA

Moscow

Astana

KAZAKHSTAN

ASIA

Ulaanbaatar

MONGOLIA

Harbin

60°N

GEORGIA

Istanbul

UZBEKISTAN

Almaty

Tashkent

KYRGYZSTAN

Beijing

NORTH
KOREA

P'yŏngyang

JAPAN

40°N

Ankara

ARMENIA

TURKEY

Baku

TURKMENISTAN

TAJIKISTAN

CHINA

Tianjin

Seoul

SOUTH
KOREA

Pusan

Nagoya

Tokyo

Yokohama

Osaka

TUNISIA

Nicosia

CYPRUS

SYRIA

AZERBAIJAN

Ashgabat

Tehran

Kabul

Tripoli

LEBANON

Beirut

Damascus

Baghdad

IRAN

AFGHANISTAN

Islamabad

Wuhan

Shanghai

Jerusalem

Amman

ISRAEL

JORDAN

IRAQ

KUWAIT

BAHRAIN

PAKISTAN

Delhi

NEPAL

Kathmandu

Chongqing

LIBYA

Cairo

EGYPT

SAUDI
ARABIA

QATAR

OMAN

New
Delhi

BHUTAN

Dhaka

Guangzhou

Taipei

Tropic of Cancer

Riyadh

UNITED ARAB
EMIRATES

Karachi

INDIA

Calcutta

BANGLADESH

MYANMAR
(BURMA)

Hong
Kong

TAIWAN

20°N

PACIFIC

AFRICA

NIGER

CHAD

Khartoum

ERITREA

Asmara

YEMEN

Sanaa

OMAN

Muscat

Mumbai
(Bombay)

Yangon
(Rangoon)

LAOS

Hanoi

Northern
Marianas
(U.S.)

OCEAN

amey

N'Djamena

NIGERIA

Abuja

SUDAN

DJIBOUTI

Addis Ababa

Chennai
(Madras)

THAILAND

Bangkok

VIETNAM

CAMBODIA

Phnom Penh

Manila

PHILIPPINES

Guam (U.S.)

MARSHALL
ISLANDS

agos

CENTRAL
AFRICAN
REPUBLIC

ETHIOPIA

SRI
LANKA

Colombo

Ho Chi
Minh City

PALAU

CAMEROON

EQUATORIAL
GUINEA

SOMALIA

UGANDA

KENYA

MALDIVES

Kuala
Lumpur

BRUNEI

FEDERATED STATES
OF MICRONESIA

ME
ND
PE

GABON

REP.
OF THE
CONGO

RWANDA

Nairobi

MALAYSIA

Singapore

SINGAPORE

Equator

0°

DEMOCRATIC REP.
OF THE CONGO

BURUNDI

NAURU

KIRIBATI

BINDA

Kinshasa

TANZANIA

SEYCHELLES

INDONESIA

PAPUA
NEW
GUINEA

ngola)

Luanda

Dar es Salaam

Jakarta

Surabaya

Port Moresby

SOLOMON
ISLANDS

TUVALU

ANGOLA

ZAMBIA

MALAWI

COMOROS

INDIAN   OCEAN

EAST TIMOR

Lusaka

MOZAMBIQUE

MADAGASCAR

Antananarivo

VANUATU

FIJI

NAMIBIA

ZIMBABWE

Harare

Réunion
(FRANCE)

MAURITIUS

New Caledonia
(FRANCE)

20°S

Windhoek

BOTSWANA

Gaborone

Pretoria

Maputo

SWAZILAND

Tropic of Capricorn

Johannesburg

LESOTHO

AUSTRALIA

SOUTH
AFRICA

Cape Town

Sydney

Canberra

NEW
ZEALAND

Melbourne

Tasmania

Wellington

20°E

40°E

60°E

80°E

100°E

120°E

140°E

160°E

60°S

TARCTICA

SCALE

0   250   500   750 Miles

0   250   500 750 Kilometers

Projection: Mollweide

10°W

Arctic
Circle

N

ICELAND

Reykjavik

0°

10°E

20°E

30°E

40°E

NORWAY

SWEDEN

FINLAND

Helsinki

60°N

Oslo

Stockholm

10

St. Petersburg

RUSSIA

9

NORTH SEA

UNITED
KINGDOM

DENMARK

Copenhagen

8

Minsk

Moscow

Dublin

IRELAND

NETHERLANDS

Amsterdam

The Hague

Berlin

Warsaw

BELARUS

50°N

London

Brussels

GERMANY

POLAND

Kiev

ATLANTIC

BELGIUM

LUXEMBOURG

1

Vienna

2

Budapest

UKRAINE

MOLDOVA

OCEAN

Paris

Bern

SWITZERLAND

AUSTRIA

HUNGARY

Chişinău

FRANCE

LIECHTENSTEIN

3

4

ROMANIA

MONACO

ITALY

5

7

Bucharest

ANDORRA

Corsica
(FRANCE)

SAN MARINO

Rome

VATICAN CITY

BULGARIA

Sofia

BLACK SEA

40°N

PORTUGAL

Madrid

Balearic
Is. (SPAIN)

Sardinia
(ITALY)

Tirane

6

ALBANIA

Lisbon

SPAIN

MEDITERRANEAN

SEA

GREECE

Athens

Gibraltar (U.K.)

Sicily

MALTA

Crete

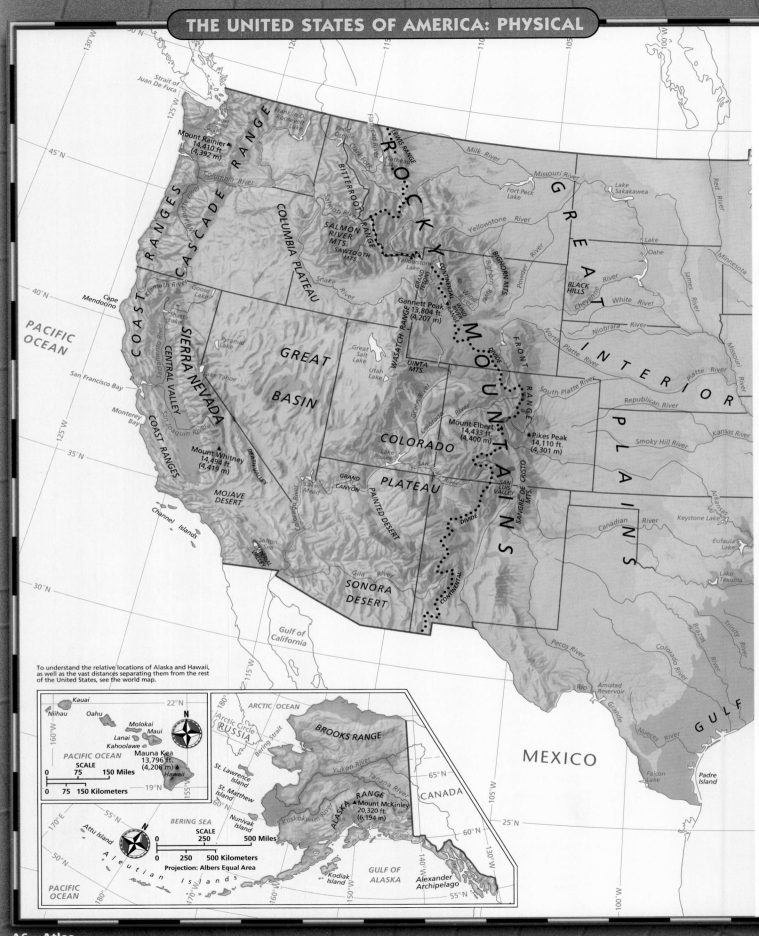

To understand the relative locations of Alaska and Hawaii, as well as the vast distances separating them from the rest of the United States, see the world map.

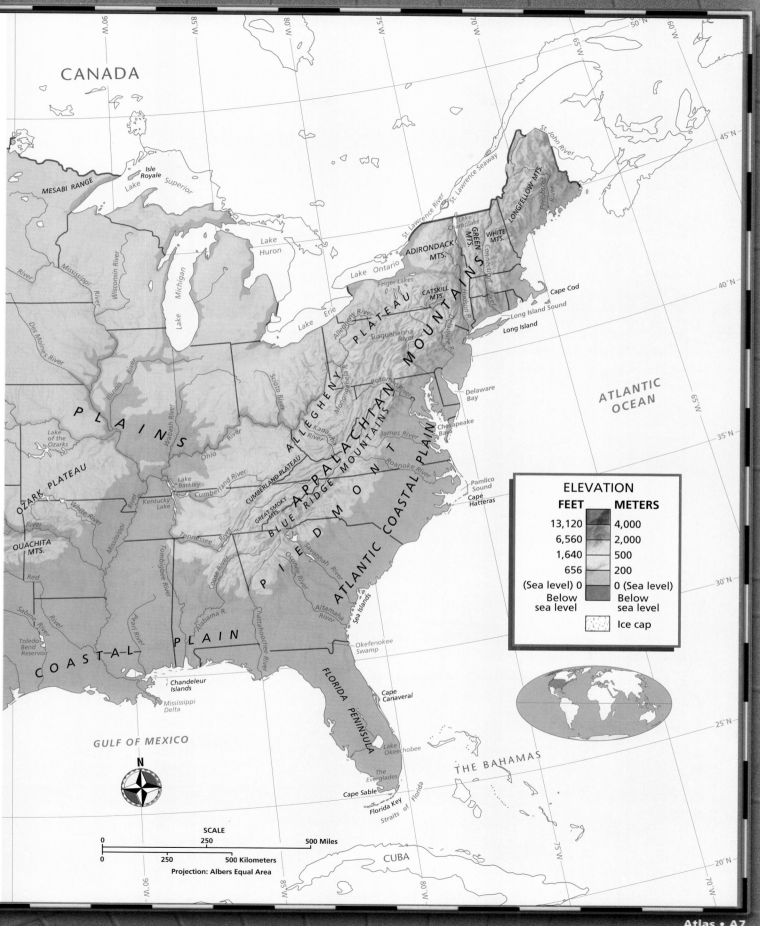

CANADA

MESABI RANGE

Isle Royale

Lake Superior

Lake Huron

Lake Michigan

Wisconsin River

Mississippi River

River

Des Moines River

P L A I N S

Lake of the Ozarks

OZARK PLATEAU

OUACHITA MTS.

Red

Sabine River

River

White River

Toledo Bend Reservoir

C O A S T A L   P L A I N

Chandeleur Islands

Mississippi Delta

GULF OF MEXICO

Illinois River

Wabash River

Ohio

Lake Barkley

Kentucky Lake

Mississippi River

Tennessee River

Tombigbee River

Pearl River

Alabama R.

Coosa River

Chattahoochee River

Scioto River

CUMBERLAND PLATEAU

Cumberland River

GREAT SMOKY MTS.

BLUE RIDGE MOUNTAINS

Oconee River

Savannah River

Altamaha River

Sea Islands

FLORIDA PENINSULA

Okefenokee Swamp

Cape Canaveral

Lake Okeechobee

The Everglades

Cape Sable

Florida Key

Straits of Florida

THE BAHAMAS

CUBA

Lake Erie

Lake Ontario

Finger Lakes

Allegheny River

ALLEGHENY

PLATEAU

Susquehanna River

Monongahela R.

Kanawha River

Potomac River

James River

Roanoke River

A P P A L A C H I A N   M O U N T A I N S

P I E D M O N T

A T L A N T I C   C O A S T A L   P L A I N

St. Lawrence River

St. Lawrence Seaway

ADIRONDACK MTS.

CATSKILL MTS.

Hudson R.

Delaware R.

GREEN MTS.

WHITE MTS.

Lake Champlain

Connecticut River

LONGFELLOW MTS.

Penobscot

St. John River

Cape Cod

Long Island Sound

Long Island

Delaware Bay

Chesapeake Bay

Pamlico Sound

Cape Hatteras

ATLANTIC OCEAN

ELEVATION

FEET		METERS
13,120		4,000
6,560		2,000
1,640		500
656		200
(Sea level) 0		0 (Sea level)
Below sea level		Below sea level

Ice cap

N

SCALE

0   250   500 Miles

0   250   500 Kilometers

Projection: Albers Equal Area

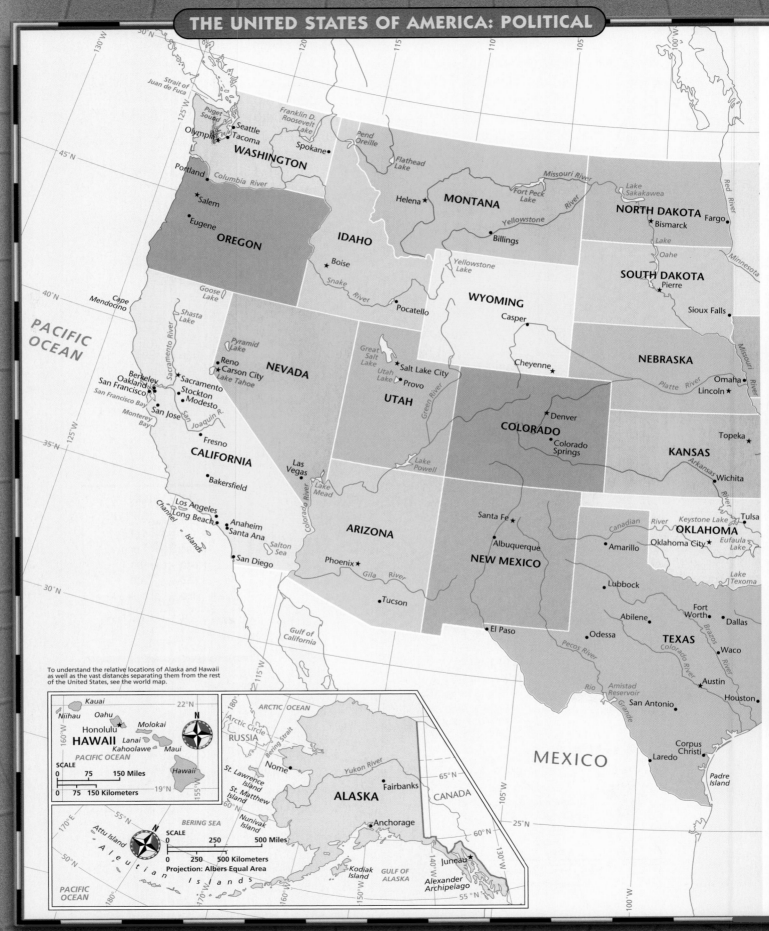

PACIFIC OCEAN

WASHINGTON
Seattle
Tacoma
Olympia ★
Spokane
Puget Sound
Strait of Juan de Fuca
Franklin D. Roosevelt Lake
Pend Oreille

Portland
Salem ★
Eugene
OREGON
Columbia River

IDAHO
Boise
Snake River
Flathead Lake

MONTANA
Helena ★
Billings
Fort Peck Lake
Yellowstone River
Missouri River

NORTH DAKOTA
Bismarck ★
Fargo
Lake Sakakawea
Red River

Cape Mendocino
Goose Lake
Shasta Lake
Sacramento River

Pyramid Lake
Reno
Carson City ★
Lake Tahoe
NEVADA

WYOMING
Yellowstone Lake
Casper
Cheyenne ★

SOUTH DAKOTA
Pierre ★
Sioux Falls
Lake Oahe
Minnesota

Great Salt Lake
Salt Lake City ★
Utah Lake
Provo
UTAH
Green River

COLORADO
Denver ★
Colorado Springs

NEBRASKA
Omaha
Lincoln ★
Missouri River
Platte River

Berkeley
Oakland
San Francisco
San Francisco Bay
Sacramento
Stockton
Modesto
San Joaquin R.
San Jose
Monterey Bay
Fresno
CALIFORNIA
Bakersfield

Las Vegas
Lake Mead
Colorado River

KANSAS
Topeka ★
Wichita
Arkansas River

Los Angeles
Long Beach
Anaheim
Santa Ana
Channel Islands
Salton Sea
San Diego

ARIZONA
Phoenix ★
Tucson
Gila River

Lake Powell

Santa Fe ★
Albuquerque
NEW MEXICO

Amarillo
Lubbock
Canadian River
Keystone Lake
OKLAHOMA
Oklahoma City ★
Eufaula Lake
Tulsa

Gulf of California

El Paso
Pecos River

Abilene
Odessa
Fort Worth
Dallas
Waco
TEXAS
Brazos River
Colorado River
Lake Texoma

MEXICO

Austin ★
San Antonio
Houston
Rio Grande
Amistad Reservoir

Corpus Christi
Laredo
Padre Island

To understand the relative locations of Alaska and Hawaii as well as the vast distances separating them from the rest of the United States, see the world map.

Kauai
Niihau
Oahu
Honolulu ★
Molokai
Lanai
Kahoolawe
Maui
HAWAII
PACIFIC OCEAN
Hawaii
22° N
19° N
N

SCALE
0   75   150 Miles
0   75   150 Kilometers

ARCTIC OCEAN
Arctic Circle
RUSSIA
Bering Strait
Nome
St. Lawrence Island
St. Matthew Island
Nunivak Island
ALASKA
Yukon River
Fairbanks
65° N
CANADA
60° N
Anchorage
25° N
Kodiak Island
GULF OF ALASKA
Juneau ★
Alexander Archipelago
55° N
130° W

BERING SEA
Attu Island
N
SCALE
0   250   500 Miles
0   250   500 Kilometers
Projection: Albers Equal Area
Aleutian Islands
PACIFIC OCEAN
55° N
50° N
170° E
180

CANADA

MINNESOTA
Duluth

Minneapolis
St. Paul

WISCONSIN

Madison
Milwaukee

IOWA
Cedar Rapids
Davenport
Des Moines

MICHIGAN
Grand Rapids
Flint
Lansing
Detroit
Ann Arbor

Rockford
Chicago
South Bend
Gary
Fort Wayne
Peoria

INDIANA
Springfield
Indianapolis

ILLINOIS

Kansas City
Kansas City
St. Louis
Jefferson City
Lake of the Ozarks

MISSOURI
Springfield

Fayetteville

ARKANSAS
Little Rock

Evansville

KENTUCKY
Louisville
Frankfort
Lexington
Ohio River

OHIO
Columbus
Dayton
Cincinnati

Cleveland
Youngstown
Akron
Toledo

NEW YORK
Buffalo
Rochester
Syracuse
Albany

PENNSYLVANIA
Allentown
Harrisburg
Pittsburgh
Philadelphia
Newark

WEST VIRGINIA
Charleston

Arlington
Alexandria
Washington, D.C.
Baltimore
Annapolis

VIRGINIA
Richmond
Roanoke
Newport News
Portsmouth
Norfolk

MD.
DELAWARE
Dover
N.J.
Trenton
Jersey City
New York City
Long Island Sound
Long Island

MAINE
Augusta
Montpelier
VT.
N.H.
Concord
MASS.
Boston
Worcester
Springfield
CONN.
Providence
R.I.
Hartford
New Haven
Bridgeport
Cape Cod

Lake Champlain
St. Lawrence River
Hudson R.
Susquehanna River
Connecticut R.

Lake Superior
Lake Huron
Lake Michigan
Lake Ontario
Lake Erie

ATLANTIC OCEAN

Chesapeake Bay
Delaware Bay

Cape Hatteras

TENNESSEE
Nashville
Knoxville
Chattanooga
Memphis
Huntsville

Lake Barkley
Kentucky Lake

NORTH CAROLINA
Winston-Salem
Greensboro
Durham
Raleigh
Charlotte

SOUTH CAROLINA
Columbia

Birmingham

MISSISSIPPI
Jackson

ALABAMA
Montgomery

GEORGIA
Atlanta
Macon
Columbus
Savannah

Chattahoochee River
Savannah River
Sea Islands

LOUISIANA
Baton Rouge
Beaumont
New Orleans
Chandeleur Islands

Shreveport
Sabine River
Red River
Toledo Bend Res.

Mobile

FLORIDA
Tallahassee
Jacksonville
Orlando
Tampa
St. Petersburg
Lake Okeechobee
Fort Lauderdale
Miami
Cape Sable
Florida Keys
Cape Canaveral

THE BAHAMAS

Straits of Florida

CUBA

GULF OF MEXICO

Mississippi River
Illinois River
Wabash River
Kentucky River

Legend:
Boundaries
⊛ National capitals
★ State capitals
• Other cities

N

SCALE
0   250   500 Miles
0   250   500 Kilometers

Projection: Albers Equal Area

NORTH AMERICA: PHYSICAL

ARCTIC OCEAN

EUROPE

ASIA

POLAR ICE PACK

North Pole

St. Lawrence Island
BERING SEA
Nunivak Island

Bering Strait

BROOKS RANGE

Mt. McKinley 20,320 ft. (6,194 m)
ALASKA RANGE

Queen Elizabeth Islands

Ellesmere Island

Greenland

Denmark Strait

Arctic Circle

BEAUFORT SEA

Banks Island

Victoria Island

Baffin Bay

Baffin Island

Davis Strait

Cape Farewell

Kodiak Island
GULF OF ALASKA

YUKON PLATEAU

Yukon River

Great Bear Lake

Mackenzie River

Southampton Island

Hudson Strait

LABRADOR SEA

Alexander Archipelago

Queen Charlotte Islands

Vancouver Island

Great Slave Lake

Coats Island
Mansel Island

Hudson Bay

PACIFIC OCEAN

R O C K Y

Peace River

Lake Athabasca

Athabasca River

C A N A D I A N

Anticosti Island

Newfoundland

Mount Rainier 14,410 ft. (4,392 m)
CASCADE RANGE

Fraser River

Saskatchewan River

Lake Winnipeg

S H I E L D

GULF OF ST. LAWRENCE

Prince Edward Island

Cape Breton Island

Columbia River

Nelson River

St. Lawrence River

Cape Mendocino

COAST RANGES

G R E A T

Snake River

Columbia River

BLACK HILLS

Missouri River

Lake Superior

Lake Michigan

Lake Huron

Lake Ontario

Lake Erie

Cape Cod

Long Island

ATLANTIC OCEAN

SIERRA NEVADA
CENTRAL VALLEY
RANGES

GREAT BASIN

DEATH VALLEY

Great Salt Lake

M O U N T A I N S

Platte River

P L A I N S

INTERIOR PLAINS

Mississippi River

Ohio River

A P P A L A C H I A N   M O U N T A I N S

PIEDMONT

Cape Hatteras

Bermuda

Mount Whitney 14,494 ft. (4,419 m)

Colorado River

COLORADO PLATEAU

Arkansas River

OZARK PLATEAU

Cumberland R.

Tennessee River

ATLANTIC COASTAL PLAIN

Guadalupe Island

BAJA CALIFORNIA

Rio Grande

Red River

Brazos River

Mississippi River

GULF COASTAL PLAIN

FLORIDA PENINSULA

Cape Canaveral

Tropic of Cancer

SIERRA MADRE OCCIDENTAL

GULF OF CALIFORNIA

SIERRA MADRE ORIENTAL

GULF OF MEXICO

Florida Keys

Straits of Florida

Bahamas

Cuba

Greater Antilles

Hispaniola

Puerto Rico

Lesser Antilles

Popocatépetl 17,887 ft. (5,452 m)

YUCATÁN PENINSULA

Jamaica

CARIBBEAN SEA

Trinidad

SIERRA MADRE DEL SUR

N

Lake Nicaragua

CENTRAL AMERICA

ISTHMUS OF PANAMA

SOUTH AMERICA

Equator 0°

ELEVATION

FEET		METERS
13,120		4,000
6,560		2,000
1,640		500
656		200
(Sea level) 0		0 (Sea level)
Below sea level		Below sea level

Ice cap

SCALE

0   250   500   750   1,000 Miles

0   250   500   750   1,000 Kilometers

Projection: Azimuthal Equal Area

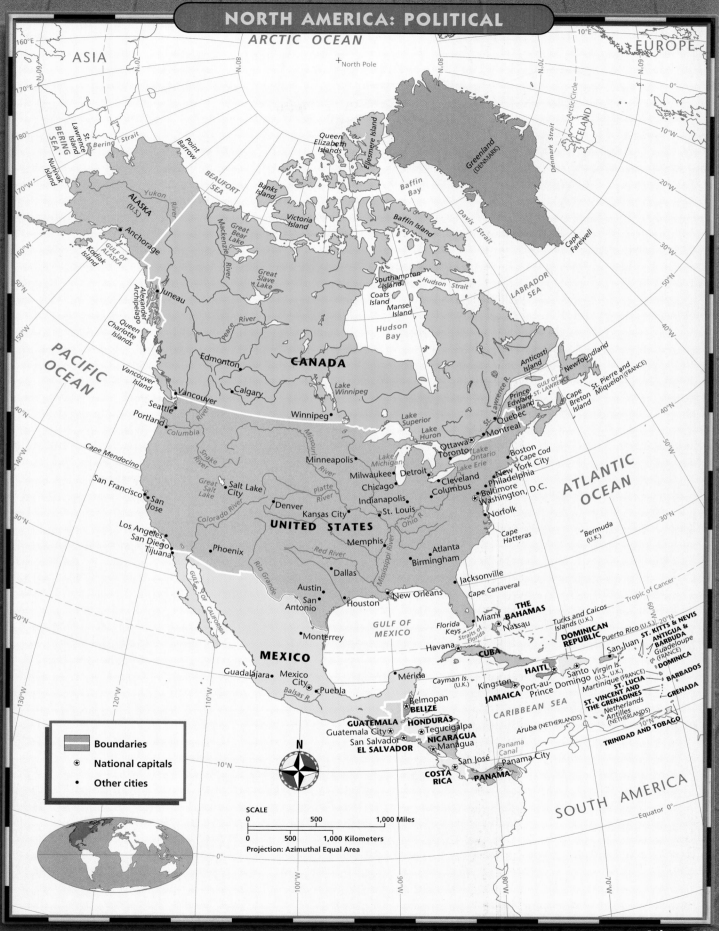

NORTH AMERICA: POLITICAL

ARCTIC OCEAN

ASIA

EUROPE

North Pole

ICELAND

BERING SEA

St. Lawrence Island

Nunivak Island

BEAUFORT SEA

Point Barrow

ALASKA (U.S.)

Yukon River

Banks Island

Queen Elizabeth Islands

Ellesmere Island

Greenland (DENMARK)

Arctic Circle

Denmark Strait

Anchorage

Gulf of Alaska

Kodiak Island

Great Bear Lake

Victoria Island

Baffin Island

Baffin Bay

Davis Strait

Cape Farewell

Juneau

Alexander Archipelago

Mackenzie River

Great Slave Lake

Southampton Island

Hudson Strait

LABRADOR SEA

Queen Charlotte Islands

Peace River

Coats Island

Mansel Island

Edmonton

CANADA

Hudson Bay

PACIFIC OCEAN

Vancouver Island

Vancouver

Calgary

Lake Winnipeg

Anticosti Island

Newfoundland

Seattle

Winnipeg

St. Lawrence R.

GULF OF ST. LAWRENCE

St. Pierre and Miquelon (FRANCE)

Portland

Columbia River

Lake Superior

Prince Edward Island

Cape Breton Island

Snake River

Missouri River

Lake Huron

Lake Michigan

Quebec

Montreal

Minneapolis

Milwaukee

Detroit

Ottawa

Toronto

Lake Ontario

Boston

Cape Cod

San Francisco

Cape Mendocino

Great Salt Lake

Salt Lake City

Chicago

Cleveland

Lake Erie

New York City

San Jose

Denver

Platte River

Indianapolis

Columbus

Philadelphia

Baltimore

Washington, D.C.

ATLANTIC OCEAN

UNITED STATES

Kansas City

St. Louis

Ohio R.

Norfolk

Colorado River

Los Angeles

San Diego

Tijuana

Phoenix

Memphis

Red River

Mississippi River

Atlanta

Birmingham

Cape Hatteras

Bermuda (U.K.)

Dallas

Austin

San Antonio

Houston

New Orleans

Jacksonville

Cape Canaveral

Rio Grande

GULF OF MEXICO

Florida Keys

Straits of Florida

THE BAHAMAS

Nassau

Turks and Caicos Islands (U.K.)

Tropic of Cancer

Puerto Rico (U.S.)

ST. KITTS & NEVIS

GULF OF CALIFORNIA

Monterrey

Havana

CUBA

DOMINICAN REPUBLIC

San Juan

ANTIGUA & BARBUDA

Guadeloupe (FRANCE)

MEXICO

Guadalajara

Mexico City

Puebla

Mérida

Cayman Is. (U.K.)

HAITI

Kingston

Port-au-Prince

Santo Domingo

Virgin Is. (U.S., U.K.)

Martinique (FRANCE)

DOMINICA

ST. LUCIA

BARBADOS

Balsas R.

JAMAICA

ST. VINCENT AND THE GRENADINES

GRENADA

Netherlands Antilles (NETHERLANDS)

Belmopan

BELIZE

CARIBBEAN SEA

GUATEMALA

HONDURAS

Aruba (NETHERLANDS)

TRINIDAD AND TOBAGO

Guatemala City

Tegucigalpa

San Salvador

NICARAGUA

Managua

EL SALVADOR

Panama Canal

San José

Panama City

COSTA RICA

PANAMA

SOUTH AMERICA

Equator 0°

Legend
- Boundaries
- ✪ National capitals
- • Other cities

N

SCALE

0   500   1,000 Miles

0   500   1,000 Kilometers

Projection: Azimuthal Equal Area

SOUTH AMERICA: PHYSICAL

CENTRAL AMERICA

CARIBBEAN SEA

N

ATLANTIC OCEAN

Panama Canal

GULF OF PANAMA

Malpelo Island

Margarita Island

Tobago
Trinidad

Lake Maracaibo

LLANOS

Orinoco River Delta

Devil's Island
Cape Orange

Cauca River

Magdalena River

▲ Mount Tolima
18,425 ft. (5,616 m)

Meta River

Angel Falls

GUIANA

HIGHLANDS

Orinoco River

Amazon River Delta

Galápagos Islands

0° Equator

GULF OF GUAYAQUIL

▲ Mount Chimborazo
20,561 ft. (6,267 m)

Caquetá River

Japurá River

Rio Negro

AMAZON

BASIN

Amazon River

Equator 0°

A N D E S

Marañón River

Juruá River

Ucayali River

Amazon River

Tapajós River

Madeira

Tocantins River

Purus

Parnaíba

Mount Huascarán
22,205 ft. (6,768 m)

Xingu River

Araguaia River

São Francisco

BRAZILIAN

HIGHLANDS

10°S

PACIFIC OCEAN

Beni River

Mamoré River

Ancohuma Peak
20,958 ft. (6,388 m)

MATO GROSSO PLATEAU

Lake Titicaca

Pilcomayo River

Lake Poopó

ATACAMA DESERT

C H A C O

Paraguay River

BRAZILIAN PLATEAU

20°S

Tropic of Capricorn

San Ambrosio Island

San Félix Island

Salado River

Paraná River

Uruguay River

Tropic of Capricorn

Juan Fernández Islands

30°S

A N D E S

▲ Mount Aconcagua
22,834 ft. (6,960 m)

Rio de la Plata

ATLANTIC OCEAN

30°S

PAMPAS

Salado River

Colorado River

Chiloé Island

GULF OF SAN MATÍAS

40°S

CHONOS ARCHIPELAGO

PATAGONIA

GULF OF SAN JORGE

Cape Tres Puntas

Bahía Grande

Strait of Magellan

Falkland Islands

South Georgia Islands

TIERRA DEL FUEGO

CAPE HORN

50°S

ELEVATION

FEET		METERS
13,120		4,000
6,560		2,000
1,640		500
656		200
(Sea level) 0		0 (Sea level)
Below sea level		Below sea level

SCALE

0   250   500   750   1,000 Miles

0   250   500   750   1,000 Kilometers

Projection: Azimuthal Equal Area

SOUTH AMERICA: POLITICAL

CENTRAL
AMERICA

CARIBBEAN SEA

ATLANTIC
OCEAN

Barranquilla
Cartagena

Caracas
Lake
Maracaibo

VENEZUELA

Georgetown
Paramaribo

Medellín

Orinoco River

GUYANA

Cayenne

Bogotá

COLOMBIA

SURINAME

FRENCH
GUIANA
(FRANCE)

Cali

Malpelo Island (COLOMBIA)

Rio Negro

Quito

Amazon River

Equator 0°

ECUADOR

Amazon River

Belém

Guayaquil

Galápagos Islands (ECUADOR)

0° Equator

Marañón River

BRAZIL

Trujillo

PERU

Ucayali River

Recife

Callao

Lima

Salvador

10°S

**PACIFIC
OCEAN**

Lake
Titicaca

Arequipa

La Paz

BOLIVIA

Brasília

São Francisco River

Lake
Poopó

Sucre

Belo Horizonte

20°S

Tropic of Capricorn

San Félix Island (CHILE)

San Ambrosio Island (CHILE)

PARAGUAY

Paraguay River

Campinas

São Paulo

Rio de Janeiro

Asunción

Curitiba

Tropic of Capricorn

Paraná River

Pôrto Alegre

Juan Fernández Islands (CHILE)

CHILE

Córdoba

Uruguay River

30°S

Valparaíso

Rosario

URUGUAY

**ATLANTIC
OCEAN**

Santiago

Buenos Aires

Montevideo

Rio de la Plata

ARGENTINA

Legend
▭	Boundaries
⊛	National capitals
•	Other cities

SCALE

| 0 | 250 | 500 | 750 | 1,000 Miles |

| 0 | 250 | 500 | 750 | 1,000 Kilometers |

Projection: Azimuthal Equal Area

Strait of
Magellan

Falkland
Islands (U.K.)

Tierra del
Fuego

South Georgia
Island (U.K.)

EUROPE: PHYSICAL

ASIA

URAL MOUNTAINS

NORTHERN EUROPEAN PLAIN

BALTIC PLAINS

KOLA PENINSULA

Pechora River

Ural River

Belaya River

Kama River

Volga River

Don River

Dnipro River

Dniester River

Nistru River

Vistula River

Oder River

Elbe River

BARENTS SEA

White Sea

Lake Onega

Lake Ladoga

Rybinsk Reservoir

North Dvina River

Dvina River

GULF OF FINLAND

Daugava R.

GULF OF BOTHNIA

BALTIC SEA

North Cape

KJØLEN MOUNTAINS

ARCTIC OCEAN

NORWEGIAN SEA

Lake Vänern

Lake Vättern

Kattegat

Skagerrak

N

NORTH SEA

Shetland Islands

Orkney Islands

PENNINES

British Isles

Hebrides

IRISH SEA

Faeroe Islands

Iceland

Arctic Circle

Thames River

English Channel

Seine River

Loire River

Garonne River

Bay of Biscay

Rhine River

Danube River

Po River

Lake Geneva

15,781 ft. Mont Blanc (4,810 m)

ALPS

PYRENEES

Ebro River

IBERIAN PENINSULA

Douro River

Tagus River

Guadiana River

Guadalquivir River

Cape Finisterre

Strait of Gibraltar

ATLANTIC OCEAN

CARPATHIAN MTS.

TRANSYLVANIAN ALPS

DINARIC ALPS

BALKAN PENINSULA

ADRIATIC SEA

APENNINES

Tiber River

TYRRHENIAN SEA

Corsica

Sardinia

Balearic Islands

Sicily

Malta

MEDITERRANEAN SEA

AFRICA

AEGEAN SEA

SEA OF MARMARA

Rhodes

Crete

SOUTHWEST ASIA

BLACK SEA

CRIMEAN PENINSULA

SEA OF AZOV

CASPIAN SEA

Mt. Elbrus (5,642 m) 18,510 ft.

CAUCASUS MTS.

Danube River

ELEVATION

FEET	METERS
13,120	4,000
6,560	2,000
1,640	500
656	200
0 (Sea level)	0 (Sea level)
Below sea level	Below sea level

Ice cap

SCALE

0   250   500 Miles

0   250   500 Kilometers

Projection: Azimuthal Equal Area

ASIA

URAL MOUNTAINS

URAL

RUSSIA

CASPIAN SEA

Nizhny Novgorod

Volga River

Ural River

Moscow

Don River

BARENTS SEA

WHITE SEA

GULF OF FINLAND

St. Petersburg

SOUTHWEST ASIA

BLACK SEA

Dnipro River

Kiev

UKRAINE

MOLDOVA

Chişinău

Minsk

BELARUS

Bucharest

RHODES

Crete

AEGEAN SEA

North Cape

FINLAND

Helsinki

Tallinn

ESTONIA

Riga

LATVIA

Vilnius

LITHUANIA

RUSSIA

Warsaw

POLAND

Kraków

ROMANIA

Belgrade

Danube River

BULGARIA

Sofia

Skopje

MACEDONIA

Tiranë

ALBANIA

GREECE

Athens

NORWAY

SWEDEN

Stockholm

Göteborg

BALTIC SEA

SLOVAKIA

Bratislava

Budapest

HUNGARY

Zagreb

CROATIA

SERBIA AND MONTENEGRO

Sarajevo

BOSNIA & HERZEGOVINA

ADRIATIC SEA

SEA

MALTA

Valletta

Oslo

Bergen

DENMARK

Copenhagen

Hamburg

Elbe River

Berlin

Dresden

Prague

CZECH REPUBLIC

Vienna

AUSTRIA

LIECHTENSTEIN

Vaduz

SLOVENIA

Ljubljana

SAN MARINO

San Marino

ITALY

Rome

VATICAN CITY

Naples

Sicily

Sardinia (ITALY)

Corsica (FRANCE)

ARCTIC OCEAN

ARCTIC OCEAN

NORTH SEA

GERMANY

Cologne

Bonn

Amsterdam

THE NETHERLANDS

The Hague

Brussels

BELGIUM

Luxembourg

LUXEMBOURG

Munich

Danube River

Rhine River

SWITZERLAND

Bern

Geneva

Lake Geneva

ALPS

Milan

Po River

MONACO

Monaco

Marseilles

Rhône River

Barcelona

Balearic Islands (SPAIN)

MEDITERRANEAN SEA

N

Faeroe Islands (DENMARK)

Shetland Islands

ICELAND

Reykjavík

SCOTLAND

Edinburgh

UNITED KINGDOM

Liverpool

Belfast

NORTHERN IRELAND

WALES

ENGLAND

London

Thames R.

Dublin

IRELAND

British Isles

Channel Islands (U.K.)

English Channel

Paris

Seine River

Loire River

FRANCE

Lyons

Bay of Biscay

PYRENEES

Andorra la Vella

ANDORRA

Valencia

SPAIN

Madrid

Seville

Gibraltar (U.K.)

Strait of Gibraltar

PORTUGAL

Lisbon

Tagus River

AFRICA

ATLANTIC OCEAN

Arctic Circle

EUROPE: POLITICAL

Boundaries
National capitals
Other cities

SCALE

0   250   500 Miles

0   250   500 Kilometers

Projection: Azimuthal Equal Area

Atlas • A15

ELEVATION

FEET	METERS
13,120	4,000
6,560	2,000
1,640	500
656	200
(Sea level) 0	0 (Sea level)
Below sea level	Below sea level

Ice cap

PACIFIC OCEAN

AUSTRALIA

New Guinea

MAOKE MOUNTAIN

ARAFURA SEA

BANDA SEA

Moluccas

CELEBES SEA

Celebes

Mindanao

Philippines

SOUTH CHINA SEA

Luzon

Luzon Strait

Taiwan

JAVA SEA

Borneo

Bangka

Java

Sumatra

Mentawai Islands

Hainan

GULF OF TONKIN

INDOCHINA PENINSULA

Xi River

Hong River

Mekong River

MALAY PENINSULA

Strait of Malacca

GULF OF THAILAND

Chao Phraya River

ANDAMAN SEA

Andaman Islands

Nicobar Islands

Irrawaddy River

BOHAI HILLS

EAST CHINA SEA

Ryukyu Islands

Okinawa

Korea Strait

Shikoku

Kyushu

Honshu

Hokkaido

SEA OF JAPAN

Kuril Islands

Sakhalin Island

SEA OF OKHOTSK

CENTRAL RANGE

KAMCHATKA PENINSULA

BERING SEA

Aleutian Islands

NORTH AMERICA

Wrangel Island

New Siberian Islands

KOLYMA MTS.

CHERSKIY RANGE

VERKHOYANSKIY RANGE

STANOVOY MOUNTAINS

Aldan River

Amur River

Lena River

Lake Baikal

YABLONOVY RANGE

Shilka River

MONGOLIAN PLATEAU

GREATER KHINGAN RANGE

NORTH CHINA PLAIN

GREAT WALL

QIN LING

Huang He

Chang Jiang

YELLOW SEA

CHINA

GOBI

GOBI

ALTAI MOUNTAINS

SAYAN MOUNTAINS

Yenisei

Lower Tunguska River

Angara River

CENTRAL SIBERIAN PLATEAU

TAYMYR PENINSULA

North Land

LAPTEV SEA

KARA SEA

Novaya Zemlya

Franz Josef Land

BARENTS SEA

S I B E R I A

Ob River

Irtysh River

WEST SIBERIAN PLAIN

KAZAKH UPLANDS

Balqash Lake

TIAN SHAN

TARIM BASIN

TAKLIMAKAN DESERT

KUNLUN MOUNTAINS

PLATEAU OF TIBET

Mount Everest 29,035 ft. (8,850 m)

Nu River

HIMALAYAS

Brahmaputra River

INDO-GANGETIC PLAIN

Ganges River

DECCAN PLATEAU

Godavari

EASTERN GHATS

WESTERN GHATS

Bay of Bengal

Sri Lanka

Maldives

Lakshadweep Islands

INDIAN OCEAN

ARABIAN SEA

Socotra Island

GULF OF ADEN

RED SEA

AFRICA

RUB' AL-KHALI

AN-NAFUD

SYRIAN DESERT

SINAI PENINSULA

MEDITERRANEAN SEA

Cyprus

ANATOLIAN PLATEAU

Mount Ararat 16,945 ft. (5,165 m)

BLACK SEA

Bosporus

SEA OF AZOV

CAUCASUS MTS.

Tigris River

Euphrates River

PERSIAN GULF

ZAGROS MTS.

Strait of Hormuz

GULF OF OMAN

GREAT SALT DESERT

CASPIAN SEA

URAL MOUNTAINS

Ural River

Kama River

USTYURT PLATEAU

TURAN LOWLAND

KYZYL KUM

Syr Darya

Amu Darya

KARA KUM

HINDU KUSH

Indus River

Sutlej

THAR DESERT

EUROPE

URAL MOUNTAINS

THAR DESERT

N

SCALE

0   500   1,000 Miles

0   500   1,000 Kilometers

Projection: Modified Oblique Conic

Legend

- Boundaries
- ✪ National capitals
- • Other cities

PACIFIC OCEAN

INDIAN OCEAN

Countries and regions:

EUROPE
AFRICA
AUSTRALIA
RUSSIA
MONGOLIA
CHINA
JAPAN
NORTH KOREA
SOUTH KOREA
TAIWAN
KAZAKHSTAN
UZBEKISTAN
TURKMENISTAN
KYRGYZSTAN
TAJIKISTAN
AFGHANISTAN
PAKISTAN
INDIA
NEPAL
BHUTAN
BANGLADESH
MYANMAR (BURMA)
THAILAND
LAOS
VIETNAM
CAMBODIA
MALAYSIA
SINGAPORE
BRUNEI
INDONESIA
PHILIPPINES
EAST TIMOR
SRI LANKA
MALDIVES
IRAN
IRAQ
KUWAIT
SAUDI ARABIA
YEMEN
OMAN
UNITED ARAB EMIRATES
QATAR
BAHRAIN
JORDAN
ISRAEL
LEBANON
SYRIA
CYPRUS
TURKEY
GEORGIA
ARMENIA
AZERBAIJAN

Seas and oceans:

BERING SEA
SEA OF OKHOTSK
SEA OF JAPAN
YELLOW SEA
EAST CHINA SEA
SOUTH CHINA SEA
PHILIPPINE SEA
CELEBES SEA
JAVA SEA
ARAFURA SEA
ANDAMAN SEA
Bay of Bengal
ARABIAN SEA
PERSIAN GULF
GULF OF THAILAND
CASPIAN SEA
BLACK SEA
MEDITERRANEAN SEA
RED SEA
GULF OF ADEN
BARENTS SEA
KARA SEA
LAPTEV SEA

Capitals and cities:

Moscow, Yekaterinburg, Chelyabinsk, Omsk, Novosibirsk, Irkutsk, Yakutsk, Vladivostok, Astana, Almaty, Bishkek, Tashkent, Ashgabat, Dushanbe, Kabul, Islamabad, Lahore, Faisalabad, Karachi, New Delhi, Delhi, Jaipur, Ahmadabad, Bhopal, Nagpur, Mumbai (Bombay), Hyderabad, Bangalore, Chennai (Madras), Colombo, Male, Kathmandu, Thimphu, Dhaka, Kolkata (Calcutta), Chittagong, Yangon (Rangoon), Mandalay, Bangkok, Vientiane, Hanoi, Ho Chi Minh City, Phnom Penh, Kuala Lumpur, Singapore, Bandar Seri Begawan, Jakarta, Bandung, Semarang, Surabaya, Ujung Pandang, Medan, Manila, Taipei, Hong Kong, Macao, Guangzhou, Chongqing, Chengdu, Wuhan, Xi'an, Nanjing, Shanghai, Qingdao, Beijing, Fushun, Changchun, Harbin, Dalian, Pyongyang, Seoul, Pusan, Nagasaki, Hiroshima, Kyoto, Osaka, Nagoya, Tokyo, Yokohama, Sapporo, Ulaanbaatar, Tehran, Mashhad, Isfahan, Shiraz, Tabriz, Baghdad, Basra, Kuwait City, Riyadh, Mecca, Jidda, Sanaa, Muscat, Abu Dhabi, Doha, Manama, Damascus, Amman, Jerusalem, Tel Aviv, Beirut, Aleppo, Nicosia, Ankara, Istanbul, Izmir, T'bilisi, Yerevan, Baku

Rivers, mountains, islands:

Lena River, Ob River, Irtysh River, Yenisey River, Angara River, Amur River, Ural River, Huang He River, Chang River, Nu River, Brahmaputra River, Ganges River, Indus River, Tigris River, Euphrates River, Mekong River, Irrawaddy River, URAL MOUNTAINS, Lake Baykal, Lake Balkhash, Aral Sea, Great Wall of China, Tropic of Cancer, Equator, Arctic Circle, Aleutian Islands, Sakhalin Island, Kuril Islands (RUSSIA), Ryukyu Islands (JAPAN), Hainan (CHINA), Andaman Islands (INDIA), Nicobar Islands (INDIA), Lakshadweep Islands (INDIA), Socotra (YEMEN), New Guinea, Luzon Strait

SCALE
0 500 1000 Miles
0 500 1000 Kilometers

Projection: Two-Point Equidistant

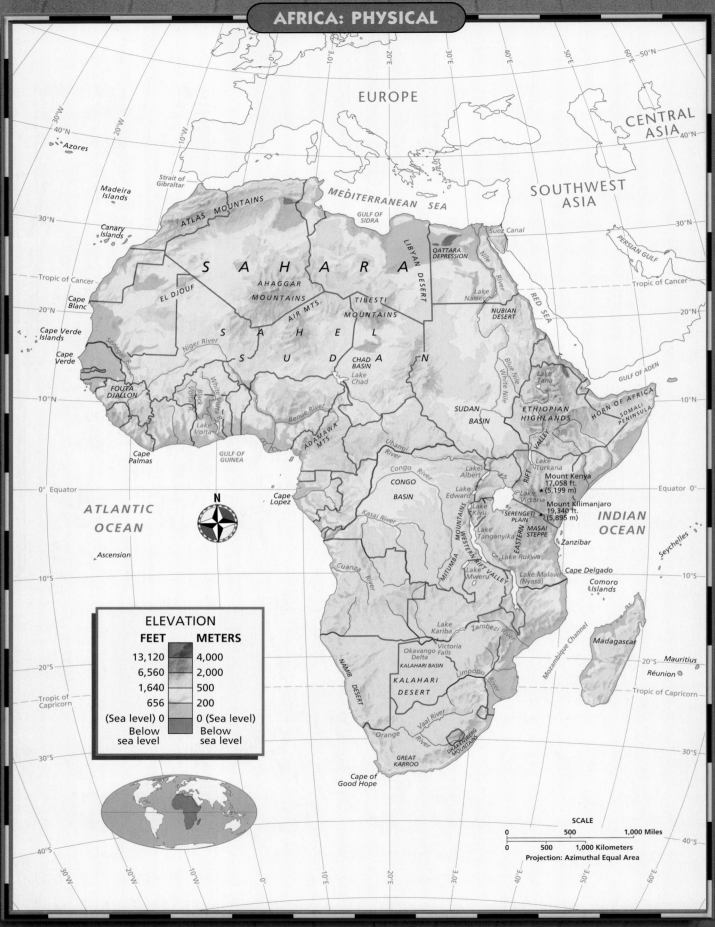

EUROPE

CENTRAL ASIA

SOUTHWEST ASIA

MEDITERRANEAN SEA

ATLAS MOUNTAINS

GULF OF SIDRA

Suez Canal

QATTARA DEPRESSION

LIBYAN DESERT

PERSIAN GULF

S A H A R A

EL DJOUF

AHAGGAR MOUNTAINS

AIR MTS.

TIBESTI MOUNTAINS

Nile River

Lake Nasser

NUBIAN DESERT

RED SEA

S A H E L

S U D A N

CHAD BASIN

Lake Chad

Blue Nile

White Nile

Lake Tana

GULF OF ADEN

ETHIOPIAN HIGHLANDS

HORN OF AFRICA

SOMALI PENINSULA

Cape Blanc

Cape Verde Islands

Cape Verde

Senegal R.

Niger River

FOUTA DJALLON

White Volta R.

Black Volta R.

Lake Volta

Benue River

ADAMAWA MTS.

SUDAN BASIN

Cape Palmas

GULF OF GUINEA

Cape Lopez

Ubangi River

Congo River

CONGO BASIN

Lake Albert

Lake Edward

Lake Victoria

Lake Turkana

RIFT VALLEY

Mount Kenya 17,058 ft. (5,199 m) ▲

Mount Kilimanjaro 19,340 ft. (5,895 m) ▲

Lake Kivu

SERENGETI PLAIN

MASAI STEPPE

Zanzibar

INDIAN OCEAN

N

ATLANTIC OCEAN

Ascension

Kasai River

MITUMBA MOUNTAINS

WESTERN RIFT VALLEY

Lake Tanganyika

EASTERN RIFT VALLEY

Lake Rukwa

Seychelles

Cape Delgado

Comoro Islands

Cuanza River

Lake Mweru

Lake Malawi (Nyasa)

Zambezi River

Lake Kariba

Victoria Falls

Mozambique Channel

Madagascar

Mauritius

Réunion

Okavango Delta

KALAHARI BASIN

Limpopo River

NAMIB DESERT

KALAHARI DESERT

Vaal River

Orange River

GREAT KARROO

DRAKENSBERG MOUNTAINS

Cape of Good Hope

Azores

Madeira Islands

Canary Islands

Strait of Gibraltar

Tropic of Cancer

40°N

30°N

20°N

10°N

Equator 0°

10°S

20°S

Tropic of Capricorn

30°S

40°S

ELEVATION

FEET		METERS
13,120		4,000
6,560		2,000
1,640		500
656		200
(Sea level) 0		0 (Sea level)
Below sea level		Below sea level

SCALE

0   500   1,000 Miles

0   500   1,000 Kilometers

Projection: Azimuthal Equal Area

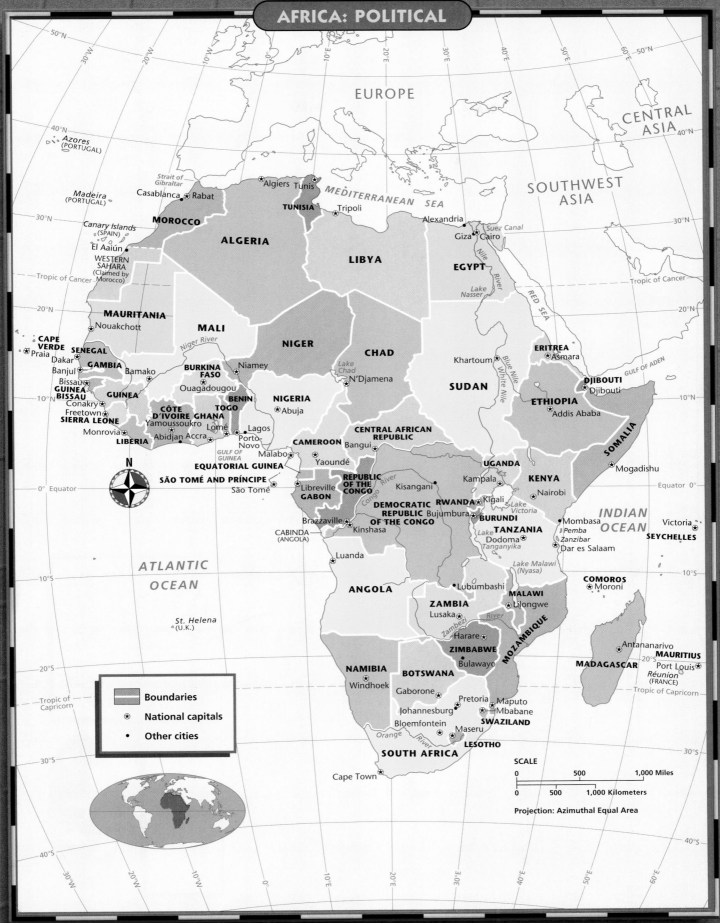

AFRICA: POLITICAL

EUROPE

CENTRAL ASIA

SOUTHWEST ASIA

MEDITERRANEAN SEA

Boundaries

⊛ **National capitals**

• **Other cities**

ATLANTIC OCEAN

INDIAN OCEAN

Azores (PORTUGAL)

Madeira (PORTUGAL)

Strait of Gibraltar

Casablanca • ⊛ Rabat

Algiers ⊛ ⊛ Tunis
TUNISIA
Tripoli ⊛

MOROCCO

Canary Islands (SPAIN)

El Aaiún •

WESTERN SAHARA (Claimed by Morocco)

Tropic of Cancer

ALGERIA

LIBYA

Alexandria •
Suez Canal
Giza • ⊛ Cairo

EGYPT

Lake Nasser

Nile River

RED SEA

GULF OF ADEN

MAURITANIA
⊛ Nouakchott

MALI

NIGER

CHAD

Khartoum ⊛

SUDAN

Blue Nile
White Nile

ERITREA
⊛ Asmara

DJIBOUTI
Djibouti ⊛

CAPE VERDE
⊛ Praia

SENEGAL
⊛ Dakar
GAMBIA
Banjul ⊛

Bamako ⊛

Niger River

Niamey ⊛

N'Djamena ⊛

Lake Chad

ETHIOPIA
Addis Ababa •

Bissau ⊛
GUINEA-BISSAU

BURKINA FASO
Ouagadougou ⊛

NIGERIA

SOMALIA

GUINEA
Conakry ⊛
Freetown ⊛
SIERRA LEONE
Monrovia •
LIBERIA

CÔTE D'IVOIRE
Yamoussoukro ⊛
Abidjan •

BENIN
TOGO
GHANA
Lomé ⊛
Accra ⊛
Porto-Novo ⊛

Abuja ⊛

Lagos •

CAMEROON
Bangui ⊛

CENTRAL AFRICAN REPUBLIC

Mogadishu •

GULF OF GUINEA

Malabo ⊛
EQUATORIAL GUINEA

Yaoundé ⊛

UGANDA
Kampala ⊛

KENYA
Nairobi ⊛

SÃO TOMÉ AND PRÍNCIPE
São Tomé ⊛

REPUBLIC OF THE CONGO
Libreville ⊛
GABON

Kisangani •

Congo River

RWANDA
Kigali ⊛

Lake Victoria

INDIAN OCEAN

Victoria ⊛
SEYCHELLES

Equator

DEMOCRATIC REPUBLIC OF THE CONGO
Brazzaville ⊛
Kinshasa ⊛

Bujumbura ⊛
BURUNDI

TANZANIA
Dodoma ⊛
Dar es Salaam •

Mombasa •
Pemba •
Zanzibar •

CABINDA (ANGOLA)

Lake Tanganyika

Luanda •

Lake Malawi (Nyasa)

COMOROS
⊛ Moroni

ATLANTIC OCEAN

St. Helena (U.K.)

ANGOLA

Lubumbashi •

ZAMBIA
Lusaka ⊛

MALAWI
Lilongwe ⊛

Zambezi River

Antananarivo ⊛

MAURITIUS
Port Louis ⊛
Réunion (FRANCE)

NAMIBIA
Windhoek ⊛

BOTSWANA
Gaborone ⊛

Harare ⊛
ZIMBABWE
Bulawayo •

MOZAMBIQUE

MADAGASCAR

Tropic of Capricorn

Pretoria ⊛
Johannesburg •
Bloemfontein ⊛

Maputo ⊛
Mbabane ⊛
SWAZILAND

Maseru ⊛
LESOTHO

SOUTH AFRICA

Orange River

Cape Town •

SCALE

0   500   1,000 Miles

0   500   1,000 Kilometers

Projection: Azimuthal Equal Area

NEW ZEALAND

North Cape
Auckland
North Island
Hamilton
Wellington
Cook Strait
Christchurch
SOUTHERN ALPS
Mount Cook 12,349 ft. (3,764 m)
South Island
Dunedin
Stewart Island

PACIFIC OCEAN

N

TASMAN SEA

CORAL SEA

GREAT BARRIER REEF

Rockhampton
Bundaberg
Brisbane
Gold Coast

GREAT DIVIDING RANGE

Sydney
Canberra
AUSTRALIAN CAPITAL TERRITORY
Mount Kosciusko 7310 ft. (2,230 m)

QUEENSLAND

NEW SOUTH WALES

Wagga Wagga
Lachlan River
Darling River
Murray River
Ballarat
Geelong
Melbourne
VICTORIA

Bass Strait

Launceston
Hobart
TASMANIA

Cape York
CAPE YORK PENINSULA
Torres Strait

GREAT

GREAT ARTESIAN BASIN

Flinders River
Cloncurry

GULF OF CARPENTARIA

ARAFURA SEA

ARNHEM LAND

Darwin

NORTHERN TERRITORY

MACDONNELL RANGES
Alice Springs

AUSTRALIA

Lake Eyre (52 ft. [16 m] below sea level)

SOUTH AUSTRALIA

Port Pirie

Adelaide
Kangaroo Island

Great Australian Bight

130°E

TIMOR SEA

ASIA

KIMBERLEY RANGE

GREAT SANDY DESERT

GIBSON DESERT

GREAT VICTORIA DESERT

WESTERN AUSTRALIA

Laverton

120°E

INDIAN OCEAN

HAMERSLEY RANGE

Broome

North West Cape
Carnarvon

Geraldton

Perth
Fremantle

ELEVATION

FEET	METERS
13,120	4,000
6,560	2,000
1,640	500
656	200
(Sea level) 0	0 (Sea level)
Below sea level	Below sea level

SCALE: At Equator
0   250   500 Miles
0   250   500 Kilometers
Projection: Lambert Conformal Conic

⊛ National capital
★ State/territorial capitals
• Other cities

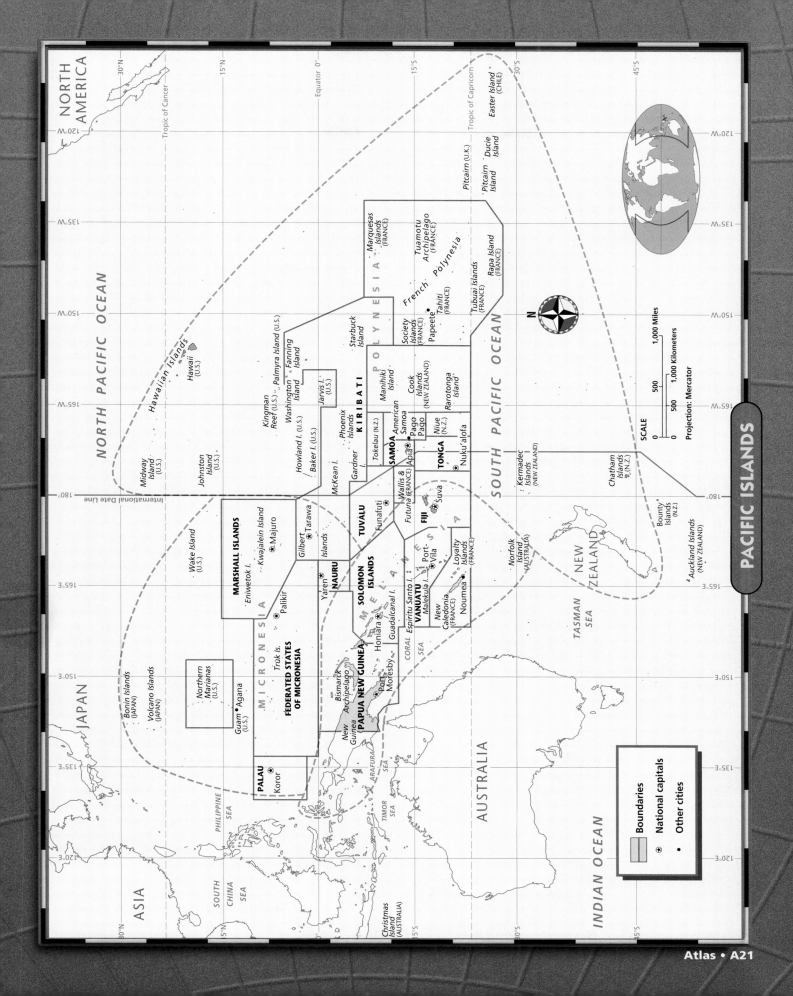

NORTH AMERICA

NORTH PACIFIC OCEAN

Tropic of Cancer

Equator 0°

Tropic of Capricorn

International Date Line

ASIA

JAPAN

Bonin Islands (JAPAN)
Volcano Islands (JAPAN)

SOUTH CHINA SEA

PHILIPPINE SEA

Northern Marianas (U.S.)

Guam ● Agana (U.S.)

MICRONESIA

FEDERATED STATES OF MICRONESIA

Truk Is.

PALAU
Koror ⊛

New Guinea

Bismarck Archipelago

PAPUA NEW GUINEA
Port Moresby ⊛

CORAL SEA

ARAFURA SEA

TIMOR SEA

Christmas Island (AUSTRALIA)

AUSTRALIA

INDIAN OCEAN

Wake Island (U.S.)

Eniwetok I.

MARSHALL ISLANDS

Kwajalein Island
⊛ Majuro

Gilbert Tarawa
Palikir ⊛

Yaren ●
NAURU

Islands

SOLOMON ISLANDS
Honiara ⊛
Guadalcanal I.

MELANESIA

Espiritu Santo I.
Malekula I. ●
VANUATU
Port-Vila ⊛

New Caledonia (FRANCE)
Noumea ⊛
Loyalty Islands (FRANCE)

TUVALU
Funafuti ⊛

Wallis & Futuna (FRANCE)
FIJI
Suva ⊛

Norfolk Island (AUSTRALIA)

TASMAN SEA

NEW ZEALAND

Auckland Islands (NEW ZEALAND)

Midway Island (U.S.)

Hawaiian Islands

Hawaii (U.S.)

Johnston Island (U.S.)

Kingman Reef (U.S.)
Washington Island (U.S.)
Fanning Island (U.S.)
Palmyra Island (U.S.)
Jarvis I. (U.S.)

Howland I. (U.S.)
Baker I. (U.S.)

McKean I.
Gardner I.

Phoenix Islands

KIRIBATI

Starbuck Island

POLYNESIA

Marquesas Islands (FRANCE)

Tuamotu Archipelago (FRANCE)

French Polynesia

Society Islands (FRANCE)
Tahiti (FRANCE)
Papeete ●

Tubuai Islands (FRANCE)

Rapa Island (FRANCE)

Manihiki Island (N.Z.)
Cook Islands (NEW ZEALAND)
Rarotonga Island (N.Z.)

Tokelau (N.Z.)
American Samoa
SAMOA
Apia ⊛
Pago Pago

Niue (N.Z.)

TONGA
Nuku'alofa ⊛

Kermadec Islands (NEW ZEALAND)

Chatham Islands (N.Z.)

Bounty Islands (N.Z.)

SOUTH PACIFIC OCEAN

Pitcairn Island (U.K.)
Ducie Island

Easter Island (CHILE)

N

SCALE

0   500   1,000 Miles

0   500   1,000 Kilometers

Projection: Mercator

30°N
15°N
15°S
30°S
45°S

120°W
135°W
150°W
165°W
180°
165°E
150°E
135°E
120°E

30°N
15°N
15°S

Boundaries
⊛ National capitals
● Other cities

PACIFIC ISLANDS

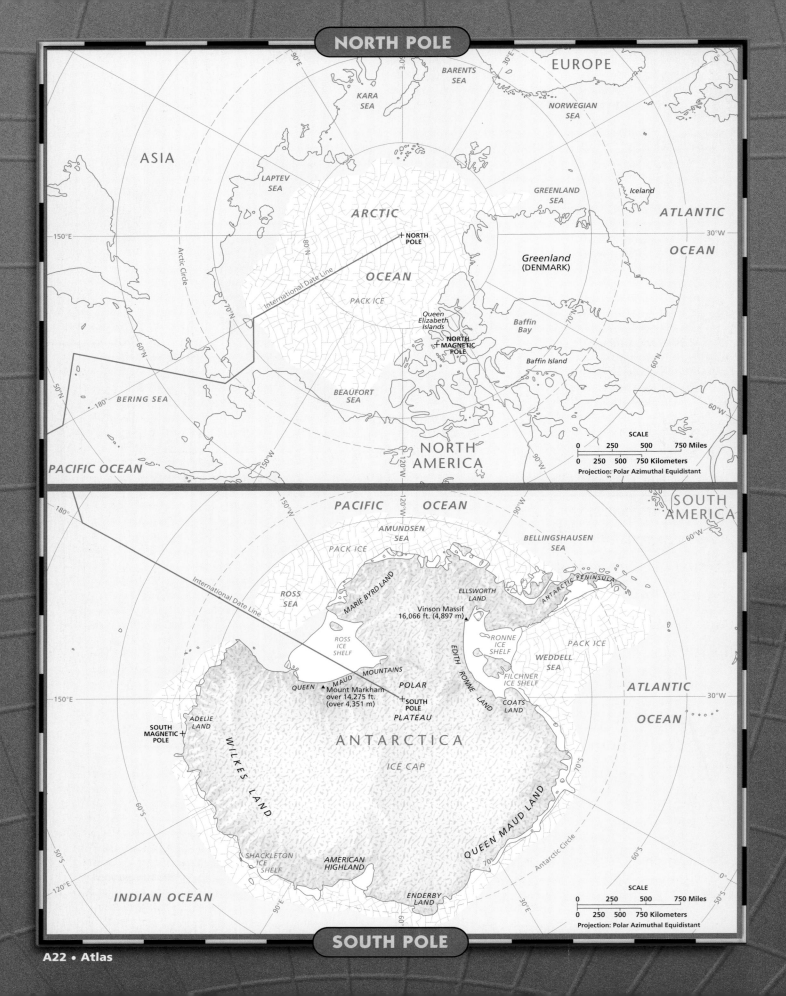

ASIA

KARA
SEA

LAPTEV
SEA

BARENTS
SEA

EUROPE

NORWEGIAN
SEA

90°E

30°E

150°E

30°W

Arctic Circle

ARCTIC

OCEAN

+ NORTH
POLE

GREENLAND
SEA

Iceland

ATLANTIC

OCEAN

Greenland
(DENMARK)

PACK ICE

International Date Line

Queen
Elizabeth
Islands

NORTH
MAGNETIC
POLE

Baffin
Bay

Baffin Island

60°N

60°W

180°

BERING SEA

BEAUFORT
SEA

NORTH
AMERICA

90°W

PACIFIC OCEAN

120°W

150°W

SCALE

0   250   500   750 Miles

0 250 500 750 Kilometers

Projection: Polar Azimuthal Equidistant

PACIFIC   OCEAN

SOUTH
AMERICA

180°

150°W

120°W

90°W

60°W

AMUNDSEN
SEA

BELLINGSHAUSEN
SEA

PACK ICE

ROSS
SEA

MARIE BYRD LAND

ELLSWORTH
LAND

ANTARCTIC PENINSULA

International Date Line

Vinson Massif
16,066 ft. (4,897 m) ▲

RONNE
ICE
SHELF

PACK ICE

ROSS
ICE
SHELF

EDITH RONNE LAND

WEDDELL
SEA

FILCHNER
ICE SHELF

ATLANTIC

MAUD MOUNTAINS

POLAR

QUEEN   ▲ Mount Markham
over 14,275 ft.
(over 4,351 m)

+ SOUTH
POLE

COATS
LAND

30°W

OCEAN

PLATEAU

SOUTH
MAGNETIC
POLE +

ADELIE
LAND

ANTARCTICA

150°E

WILKES LAND

ICE CAP

QUEEN MAUD LAND

70°S

70°S

SHACKLETON
ICE
SHELF

AMERICAN
HIGHLAND

70°S

Antarctic Circle

120°E

90°E

INDIAN OCEAN

ENDERBY
LAND

30°E

60°E

0°

50°S

SCALE

0   250   500   750 Miles

0 250 500 750 Kilometers

Projection: Polar Azimuthal Equidistant

GEOGRAPHY & MAP SKILLS

HANDBOOK

Studying geography requires the ability to understand and use various tools. This Skills Handbook explains how to use maps, charts, and other graphics to help you learn about geography and the various regions of the world. Throughout this textbook, you will have the opportunity to improve these skills and build upon them.

CONTENTS

GEOGRAPHIC

Vocabulary

- globe
- grid
- latitude
- equator
- parallels
- degrees
- minutes

- longitude
- prime meridian
- meridians
- hemispheres
- continents
- islands
- ocean

- map
- map projections
- compass rose
- scale
- legend

MAPPING
THE EARTH

The Globe

A **globe** is a scale model of Earth. It is useful for looking at the entire Earth or at large areas of Earth's surface.

The pattern of lines that circle the globe in east-west and north-south directions is called a **grid**. The intersection of these imaginary lines helps us find places on Earth.

The east-west lines in the grid are lines of **latitude**. These imaginary lines measure distance north and south of the **equator**. The equator is an imaginary line that circles the globe halfway between the North and South Poles. Lines of latitude are called **parallels** because they are always parallel to the equator. Parallels measure distance from the equator in **degrees**. The symbol for degrees is °. Degrees are further divided into **minutes**. The symbol for minutes is ´. There are 60 minutes in a degree. Parallels north of the equator are labeled with an *N*. Those south of the equator are labeled with an *S*.

The north-south lines are lines of **longitude**. These imaginary lines pass through the Poles. They measure distance east and west of the **prime meridian**. The prime meridian is an imaginary line that runs through Greenwich, England. It represents 0° longitude. Lines of longitude are called **meridians**.

Lines of latitude range from 0°, for locations on the equator, to 90°N or 90°S, for locations at the Poles. See **Figure 1**. Lines of longitude range from 0° on the prime meridian to 180° on a meridian in the mid-Pacific Ocean. Meridians west of the prime meridian to 180° are labeled with a *W*. Those east of the prime meridian to 180° are labeled with an *E*. See **Figure 2**.

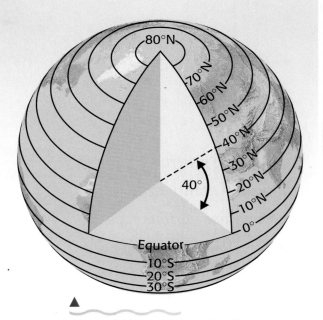

Figure 1: The east-west lines in the grid are lines of latitude.

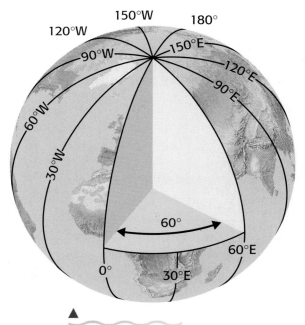

Figure 2: The north-south lines are lines of longitude.

NORTHERN HEMISPHERE

SOUTHERN HEMISPHERE

Figure 3: The hemispheres

T he equator divides the globe into two halves, called **hemispheres**. See **Figure 3**. The half north of the equator is the Northern Hemisphere. The southern half is the Southern Hemisphere. The prime meridian and the 180° meridian divide the world into the Eastern Hemisphere and the Western Hemisphere. The prime meridian separates parts of Europe and Africa into two different hemispheres. To prevent this, some mapmakers divide the Eastern and Western hemispheres at 20° W. This places all of Europe and Africa in the Eastern Hemisphere.

Our planet's land surface is organized into seven large landmasses, called **continents**. They are identified in **Figure 3**. Landmasses smaller than continents and completely surrounded by water are called **islands**. Geographers also organize Earth's water surface into parts. The largest is the world **ocean**. Geographers divide the world ocean into the Pacific Ocean, the Atlantic Ocean, the Indian Ocean, and the Arctic Ocean. Lakes and seas are smaller bodies of water.

EASTERN HEMISPHERE

WESTERN HEMISPHERE

YOUR TURN

1. Look at the Student Atlas map on page A4. What islands are located near the intersection of latitude 20° N and longitude 160° W?
2. Name the four hemispheres. In which hemispheres is the United States located?
3. Name the continents of the world.
4. Name the oceans of the world.

MAPMAKING

A **map** is a flat diagram of all or part of Earth's surface. Mapmakers have different ways of showing our round Earth on flat maps. These different ways are called **map projections**. Because our planet is round, all flat maps lose some accuracy. Mapmakers must choose the type of map projection that is best for their purposes. Many map projections are one of three kinds: cylindrical, conic, or flat-plane.

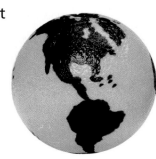

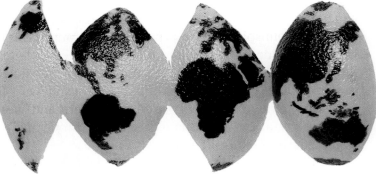

Figure 4: If you remove the peel from the orange and flatten the peel, it will stretch and tear. The larger the piece of peel, the more its shape is distorted as it is flattened. Also distorted are the distances between points on the peel.

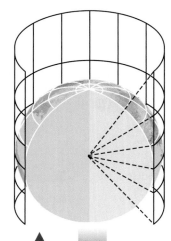

Figure 5A: Paper cylinder

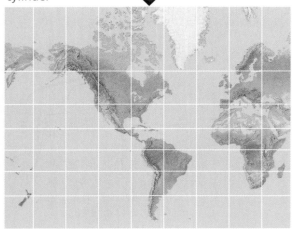

Cylindrical projections are designed from a cylinder wrapped around the globe. See **Figure 5A**. The cylinder touches the globe only at the equator. The meridians are pulled apart and are parallel to each other instead of meeting at the Poles. This causes landmasses near the Poles to appear larger than they really are. **Figure 5B** is a Mercator projection, one type of cylindrical projection. The Mercator projection is useful for navigators because it shows true direction and shape. The Mercator projection for world maps, however, emphasizes the Northern Hemisphere. Africa and South America appear smaller than they really are.

Figure 5B: A Mercator projection, although accurate near the equator, distorts distances between regions of land. This projection also distorts the sizes of areas near the poles.

Conic projections are designed from a cone placed over the globe. See **Figure 6A**. A conic projection is most accurate along the lines of latitude where it touches the globe. It retains almost true shape and size. Conic projections are most useful for areas that have long east-west dimensions, such as the United States. See the map in **Figure 6B**.

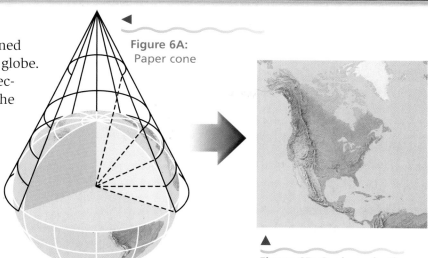

Figure 6A: Paper cone

▲ Figure 6B: Conic projection

Flat-plane projections are designed from a plane touching the globe at one point, such as at the North Pole or South Pole. See **Figures 7A** and **7B**. A flat-plane projection is useful for showing true direction for airplane pilots and ship navigators. It also shows true area. However, it distorts true shape.

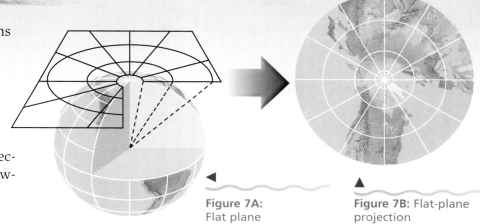

◄ Figure 7A: Flat plane

▲ Figure 7B: Flat-plane projection

The Robinson projection is a compromise between size and shape distortions. It often is used for world maps, such as the map on page 76. The minor distortions in size at high latitudes on Robinson projections are balanced by realistic shapes at the middle and low latitudes.

YOUR TURN

1. What are three major kinds of map projections?
2. Why is a Robinson projection often used for world maps?
3. What kind of projection is a Mercator map?
4. When would a mapmaker choose to use a conic projection?

MAP ESSENTIALS

In some ways, maps are like messages sent out in code. Mapmakers provide certain elements that help us translate these codes. These elements help us understand the message they are presenting about a particular part of the world. Of these elements, almost all maps have directional indicators, scales, and legends, or keys. **Figure 8**, a map of East Asia, has all three elements.

A directional indicator shows which directions are north, south, east, and west. Some mapmakers use a "north arrow," which points toward the North Pole. Remember, "north" is not always at the top of a map. The way a map is drawn and the location of directions on that map depend on the perspective of the mapmaker. Maps in this textbook indicate direction by using a **compass rose** 1. A compass rose has arrows that point to all four principal directions, as shown in **Figure 8**.

Figure 8: East and Southeast Asia—Physical

Mapmakers use scales to represent distances between points on a map. Scales may appear on maps in several different forms. The maps in this textbook provide a line **scale** 2. Scales give distances in miles and kilometers (km).

To find the distance between two points on the map in **Figure 8**, place a piece of paper so that the edge connects the two points. Mark the location of each point on the paper with a line or dot. Then, compare the distance between the two dots with the map's line scale. The number on the top of the scale gives the distance in miles. The number on the bottom gives the distance in kilometers. Because the distances are given in intervals, you will have to approximate the actual distance on the scale.

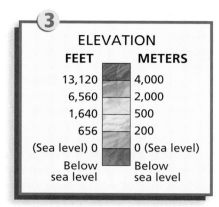

ELEVATION

FEET		METERS
13,120		4,000
6,560		2,000
1,640		500
656		200
(Sea level) 0		0 (Sea level)
Below sea level		Below sea level

The **legend** ③, or key, explains what the symbols on the map represent. Point symbols are used to specify the location of things, such as cities, that do not take up much space on a large-scale map. Some legends, such as the one in **Figure 8**, show which colors represent certain elevations. Other maps might have legends with symbols or colors that represent things such as roads. Legends can also show economic resources, land use, population density, and climate.

Size comparison of Canada to the contiguous United States

Physical maps at the beginning of each unit have size comparison maps ④. An outline of the mainland United States (not including Alaska and Hawaii) is compared to the area under study in that chapter. These size comparison maps help you understand the size of the areas you are studying in relation to the size of the United States.

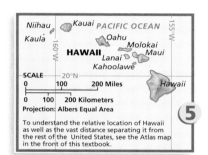

Niihau Kauai PACIFIC OCEAN
Kaula Oahu
HAWAII Molokai Maui
Lanai
Kahoolawe

SCALE 20°N
0   100   200 Miles Hawaii
0   100   200 Kilometers
Projection: Albers Equal Area

To understand the relative location of Hawaii as well as the vast distance separating it from the rest of the United States, see the Atlas map in the front of this textbook.

Inset maps are sometimes used to show a small part of a larger map. Mapmakers also use inset maps to show areas that are far away from the areas shown on the main map. Maps of the United States, for example, often include inset maps of Alaska and Hawaii ⑤. Those two states are too far from the other 48 states to accurately represent the true distance on the main map. Subject areas in inset maps can be drawn to a scale different from the scale used on the main map.

YOUR TURN

Look at the Student Atlas map on pages A4 and A5.

1. Locate the compass rose. What country is directly west of Madagascar in Africa?

2. What island country is located southeast of India?

3. Locate the distance scale. Using the inset map, find the approximate distance in miles and kilometers from Oslo, Norway, to Stockholm, Sweden.

4. What is the capital of Brazil? What other cities are shown in Brazil?

WORKING
WITH MAPS

The Atlas at the front of this textbook includes two kinds of maps: physical and political. At the beginning of most units in this textbook, you will find five kinds of maps. These physical, political, climate, population, and land use and resources maps provide different kinds of information about the region you will study in that unit. These maps are accompanied by questions. Some questions ask you to show how the information on each of the maps might be related.

Mapmakers often combine physical and political features into one map. Physical maps, such as the one in **Figure 8** on page S6, show important physical features in a region, including major mountains and mountain ranges, rivers, oceans and other bodies of water, deserts, and plains. Physical-political maps also show important political features, such as national borders, state and provincial boundaries, and capitals and other important cities. You will find a physical-political map at the beginning of most chapters.

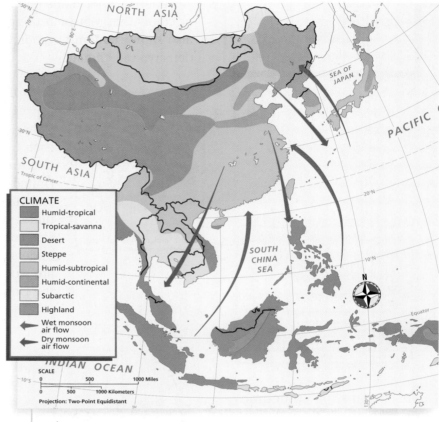

Figure 9: East and Southeast Asia—Climate

Mapmakers use climate maps to show the most important weather patterns in certain areas. Climate maps throughout this textbook use color to show the various climate regions of the world. See **Figure 9.** Colors that identify climate types are found in a legend with each map. Boundaries between climate regions do not indicate an immediate change in the main weather conditions between two climate regions. Instead, boundaries show the general areas of gradual change between climate regions.

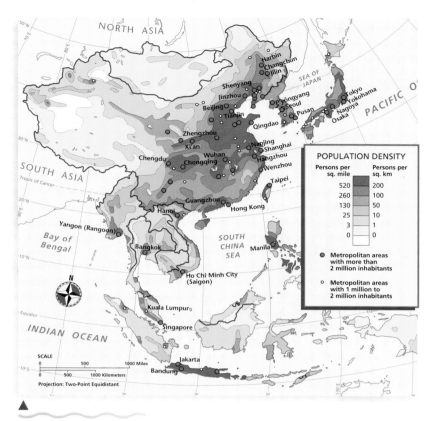

Figure 10: East and Southeast Asia—Population

Population maps show where people live in a particular region. They also show how crowded, or densely populated, regions are. Population maps throughout this textbook use color to show population density. See **Figure 10**. Each color represents a certain number of people living within a square mile or square kilometer. Population maps also use symbols to show metropolitan areas with populations of a particular size. These symbols and colors are shown in a legend.

Land Use and Resources maps show the important resources of a region. See **Figure 11**. Symbols and colors are used to show information about economic development, such as where industry is located or where farming is most common. The meanings of each symbol and color are shown in a legend.

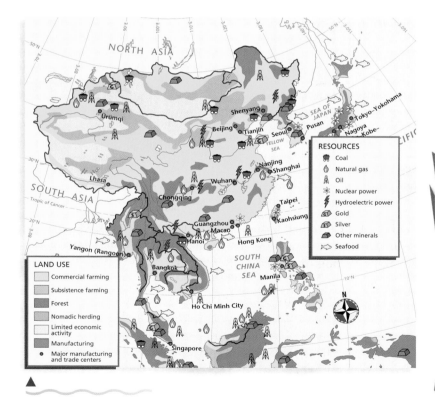

Figure 11: East and Southeast Asia—Land Use and Resources

YOUR TURN

1. What is the purpose of a climate map?

2. Look at the population map. What is the population density of the area around Qingdao in northern China?

3. What energy resource is found near Ho Chi Minh City?

USING

GRAPHS, DIAGRAMS, CHARTS, AND TABLES

Bar graphs are a visual way to present information. The bar graph in **Figure 12** shows the imports and exports of the countries of southern Europe. The amount of imports and exports in billions of dollars is listed on the left side of the graph. Along the bottom of the graph are the names of the countries of southern Europe. Above each country or group of countries is a vertical bar. The top of the bar corresponds to a number along the left side of the graph. For example, Italy imports $200 billion worth of goods.

Figure 12: Reading a bar graph

Often, line graphs are used to show such things as trends, comparisons, and size. The line graph in **Figure 13** shows the population growth of the world over time. The information on the left shows the number of people in billions. The years being studied are listed along the bottom. Lines connect points that show the population in billions at each year under study. This line graph projects population growth into the future.

A pie graph shows how a whole is divided into parts. In this kind of graph, a circle represents the whole. The wedges represent the parts. Bigger wedges represent larger parts of the whole. The pie graph in **Figure 14** shows the percentages of the world's coffee beans produced by various groups of countries. Brazil is the largest grower. It grows 25 percent of the world's coffee beans.

Major Producers of Coffee

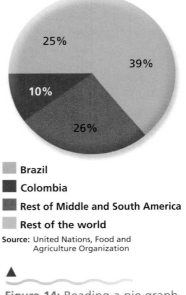

- Brazil
- Colombia
- Rest of Middle and South America
- Rest of the world

Source: United Nations, Food and Agriculture Organization

Figure 14: Reading a pie graph

Figure 13: Reading a line graph

Age structure diagrams show the number of males and females by age group. These diagrams are split into two sides, one for male and one for female. Along the bottom are numbers that show the number of males or females in the age groups. The age groups are listed on the side of the diagram. The wider the base of a country's diagram, the younger the population of that country. The wider the top of a country's diagram, the older the population.

Some countries have so many younger people that their age structure diagrams are shaped like pyramids. For this reason, these diagrams are sometimes called population pyramids. However, in some countries the population is more evenly distributed by age group. For example, see the age structure diagram for Germany in **Figure 15**. Germany's population is older. It is not growing as fast as countries with younger populations.

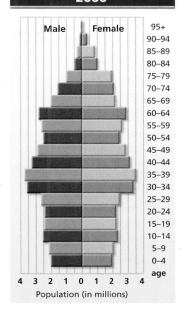

Source: U.S. Census Bureau

Figure 15: Reading an age structure diagram

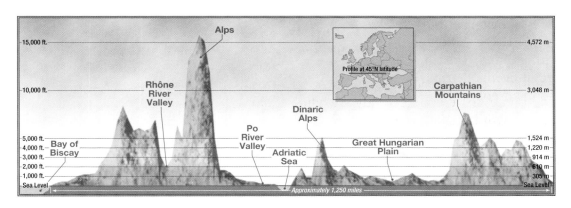

Figure 16: Reading an elevation profile

Each unit atlas includes an elevation profile. See **Figure 16**. It is a side view, or profile, of a region along a line drawn between two points.

Vertical and horizontal distances are figured differently on elevation profiles. The vertical distance (the height of a mountain, for example) is exaggerated when compared to the horizontal distance between the two points. This technique is called vertical exaggeration. If the vertical scale were not exaggerated, even tall mountains would appear as small bumps on an elevation profile.

In each unit and chapter on the various regions of the world, you will find tables that provide basic information about the countries under study.

The countries of Spain and Portugal are listed on the left in the table in **Figure 17**. You can match statistical information on the right with the name of each country listed on the left. The categories of information are listed across the top of the table.

Graphic organizers can help you understand certain ideas and concepts. For example, the diagram in **Figure 18** helps you think about the uses of water. In this diagram, one water use goes in each oval. Graphic organizers can help you focus on key facts in your study of geography.

Time lines provide highlights of important events over a period of time. The time line in **Figure 19** begins at the left with 5000 B.C., when rice was first cultivated in present-day China. The time line highlights important events that have shaped the human and political geography of China.

Spain and Portugal

COUNTRY	POPULATION/ GROWTH RATE	LIFE EXPECTANCY	LITERACY RATE	PER CAPITA GDP
Portugal	10,102,022 0.1%	72, male 80, female	93%	$18,000
Spain	40,217,413 0.1%	75, male 82, female	97%	$20,700
United States	290,342,554 0.9%	74, male 80, female	97%	$37,600

Source: Central Intelligence Agency, *The World Factbook 2003*

Figure 17: Reading a table

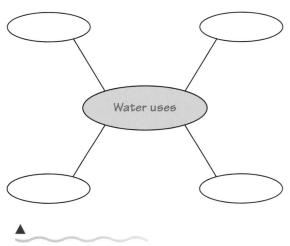

Figure 18: Graphic organizer

Historic China: A Time Line

Qin becomes China's first dynasty
200s B.C.

Rise of Ming dynasty
1368

Cultural Revolution
1966–1976

5000 B.C.	A.D. 1	1000	1200	1400	1600	1800	2000

5000 B.C.
First rice farmers cultivate the area near the Chang River

206 B.C. – A.D. 220
Han dynasty dominates China

1200s
Mongols invade China

1912
Republic is established with the overthrow of the Manchu dynasty

1989
Government troops crush protesters in Tiananmen Square

Figure 19: Reading a time line

Corn: From Field to Consumer

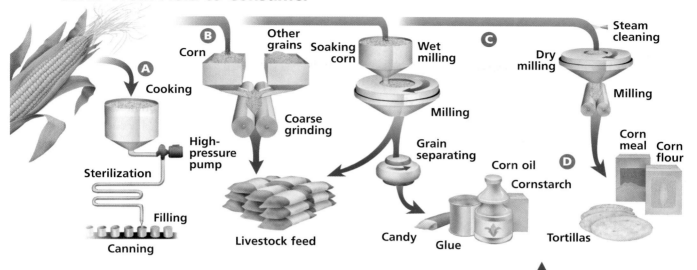

A Corn can be processed in a variety of ways. Some corn is cooked and then canned.

B Corn is ground and used for livestock feed.

C Corn also might be wet-milled or dry-milled. Then grain parts are used to make different products.

D Corn by-products, such as cornstarch and corn syrup, are used to make breads, breakfast cereals, puddings, and snack foods. Corn oil is used for cooking.

Figure 20: Reading a flowchart

Flowcharts are visual guides that explain different processes. They lead the reader from one step to the next, sometimes providing both illustrations and text. The flowchart in **Figure 20** shows the different steps involved in harvesting corn and preparing it for use by consumers. The flowchart takes you through the steps of harvesting and processing corn. Captions guide you through flowcharts.

YOUR TURN

1. Look at the statistical table for Spain and Portugal in Figure 17. Which countries have the highest literacy rate?

2. Look at the China time line in Figure 19. Name two important events in China's history between 1200 and 1400.

3. Look at Figure 20. What are three corn products?

READING
A TIME-ZONE MAP

The sun is not directly overhead everywhere on Earth at the same time. Clocks are set to reflect the difference in the sun's position. Our planet rotates on its axis once every 24 hours. In other words, in one hour, it makes one twenty-fourth of a complete rotation. Since there are 360 degrees in a circle, we know that the planet turns 15 degrees of longitude each hour. ($360° \div 24 = 15°$) We also know that the planet turns in a west-to-east direction. Therefore, if a place on Earth has the sun directly overhead at this moment (noon), then a place 15 degrees to the west will have the sun directly overhead one hour from now. During that hour the planet will have rotated 15 degrees. As a result, Earth is divided into 24 time zones. Thus, time is an hour earlier for each 15 degrees you move westward on Earth. Time is an hour later for each 15 degrees you move eastward on Earth.

By international agreement, longitude is measured from the prime meridian. This meridian passes through the Royal Observatory in Greenwich, England. Time also is measured from Greenwich and is called Greenwich mean time (GMT). For each time zone east of the prime meridian, clocks must be set one hour ahead of GMT. For each time zone west of Greenwich, clocks are set back one hour from GMT. When it is noon in London, it is 1:00 P.M. in Oslo, Norway, one time zone east. However, it is 7 A.M. in New York City, five time zones west.

WORLD TIME ZONES

As you can see by looking at the map below, time zones do not follow meridians exactly. Political boundaries are often used to draw time-zone lines. In Europe and Africa, for example, time zones follow national boundaries. The mainland United States, meanwhile, is divided into four major time zones: Eastern, Central, Mountain, and Pacific. Alaska and Hawaii are in separate time zones to the west of the mainland.

Some countries have made changes in their time zones. For example, most of the United States has daylight savings time in the summer in order to have more evening hours of daylight.

The international date line is a north-south line that runs through the Pacific Ocean. It is located at 180°, although it sometimes varies from that meridian to avoid dividing countries.

At 180°, the time is 12 hours from Greenwich time. There is a time difference of 24 hours between the two sides of the 180° meridian. The 180° meridian is called the international date line because when you cross it, the date and day change. As you cross the date line from the west to the east, you gain a day. If you travel from east to west, you lose a day.

YOUR TURN

1. In which time zone do you live? Check your time now. What time is it in New York?

2. How many hours behind New York is Anchorage, Alaska?

3. How many time zones are there in Africa?

4. If it is 9 A.M. in the middle of Greenland, what time is it in São Paulo?

GEOGRAPHIC DICTIONARY

GULF
a large part of the ocean that extends into land

OCEAN
a large body of water

CORAL REEF
an ocean ridge made up of skeletal remains of tiny sea animals

PENINSULA
an area of land that sticks out into a lake or ocean

BAY
part of a large body of water that is smaller than a gulf

ISTHMUS
a narrow piece of land connecting two larger land areas

ISLAND
an area of land surrounded entirely by water

DELTA
an area where a river deposits soil into the ocean

STRAIT
a narrow body of water connecting two larger bodies of water

SINKHOLE
a circular depression formed when the roof of a cave collapses

WETLANDS
an area of land covered by shallow water

RIVER
a natural flow of water that runs through the land

LAKE
an inland body of water

FOREST
an area of densely wooded land

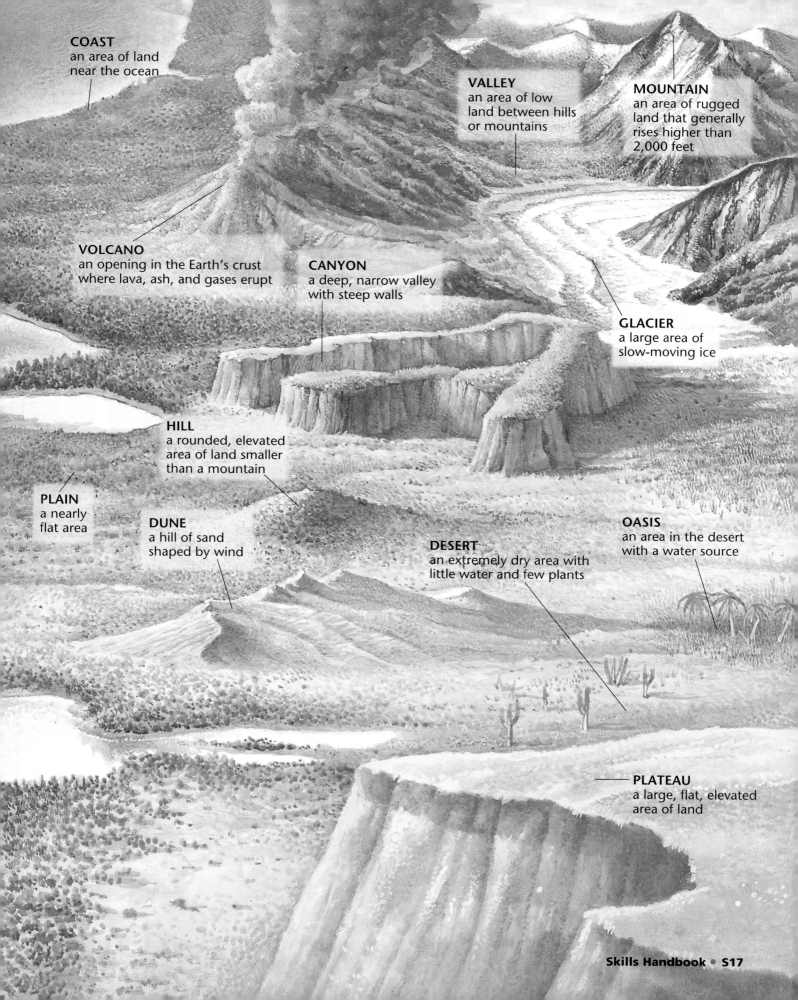

COAST
an area of land
near the ocean

VALLEY
an area of low
land between hills
or mountains

MOUNTAIN
an area of rugged
land that generally
rises higher than
2,000 feet

VOLCANO
an opening in the Earth's crust
where lava, ash, and gases erupt

CANYON
a deep, narrow valley
with steep walls

GLACIER
a large area of
slow-moving ice

HILL
a rounded, elevated
area of land smaller
than a mountain

PLAIN
a nearly
flat area

DUNE
a hill of sand
shaped by wind

DESERT
an extremely dry area with
little water and few plants

OASIS
an area in the desert
with a water source

PLATEAU
a large, flat, elevated
area of land

UNIT 1

An Introduction to World Geography and Cultures

Iceberg in sea ice, Antarctica

Carnival parade in Valletta, Malta

A Physical Geographer in Mountain Environments

Professor Francisco Pérez studies tropical mountain environments. He is interested in the natural processes, plants, and environments of mountains. **WHAT DO YOU THINK?** *What faraway places would you like to study?*

I became attracted to mountains when I was a child. While crossing the Atlantic Ocean in a ship, I saw snow-capped Teide Peak in the Canary Islands rising from the water. It was an amazing sight.

As a physical geographer, I am interested in the unique environments of high mountain areas. This includes geological history, climate, and soils. The unusual conditions of high mountain environments have influenced plant evolution. Plants and animals that live on separate mountains sometimes end up looking similar. This happens because they react to their environments in similar ways. For example, several types of tall, weird-looking plants called giant rosettes grow in the Andes, Hawaii, East Africa, and the Canary Islands. Giant rosettes look like the top of a pineapple at the end of a tall stem.

I have found other strange plants, such as rolling mosses. Mosses normally grow on rocks. However, if a moss plant falls to the ground, ice crystals on the soil surface lift the moss. This allows it to "roll" downhill while it continues to grow in a ball shape!

I like doing research in mountains. They are some of the least explored regions of our planet. Like most geographers, I cannot resist the attraction of strange landscapes in remote places.

Rosette plants, Ecuador

La Digue Island, Seychelles

Understanding Primary Sources

1. What are three parts of the environment that Francisco Pérez studies?

2. Why do some plants that live on separate mountains look similar?

Sturgeonfish

A Geographer's World

Hand-held compass

Chart of the
Mediterranean
and Europe, 1559

GPS (global
positioning
satellite)
receiver

Section 1 Developing a Geographic Eye

Read to Discover

1. What role does perspective play in the study of geography?
2. What are some issues or topics that geographers study?
3. At what three levels can geographers view the world?

Vocabulary

perspective
spatial perspective
geography
urban
rural

Reading Strategy

VISUALIZING INFORMATION Look at the photographs in this section. What do you see in the photographs that would tell you about some of the topics geographers study? Write your answers on a sheet of paper.

Perspectives

People look at the world in different ways. Their experiences shape the way they understand the world. This personal understanding is called **perspective**. Your perspective is your point of view. A geographer's point of view looks at where something is and why it is there. This point of view is known as **spatial perspective**. Geographers apply this perspective when they study the arrangement of towns in a state. They might also use this perspective to examine the movement of cars and trucks on busy roads.

Geographers also work to understand how things are connected. Some connections are easy to see, like highways that link cities. Other connections are harder to see. For example, a dry winter in Colorado could mean that farms as far away as northern Mexico will not have enough water.

Geography is a science. It describes the physical and cultural features of Earth. Studying geography is important. Geographically informed people can see meaning in the arrangement of things on Earth. They know how people and places are related. Above all, they can apply a spatial perspective to real life. In other words, people familiar with geography can understand the world around them.

This fish-eye view of a large city shows highway patterns.

▼

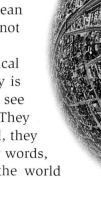

✓ **READING CHECK:** *The World in Spatial Terms* What role does perspective play in the study of geography?

The movement of people is one issue that geographers study. For example, political and economic troubles led many Albanians to leave their country in 1991. Many packed onto freighters like this one for the trip. Geographers want to know how this movement affects the environment and other people.

Interpreting the Visual Record

Movement How do you think Albania has been affected by so many people leaving the country?

Geographic Issues

Issues geographers study include Earth's processes and their impact on people. Geographers study the relationship between people and environment in different places. For example, geographers study tornadoes to find ways to reduce loss of life and property damage. They ask how people prepare for tornadoes. Do they prepare differently in different places? When a tornado strikes, how do people react?

Geographers also study how governments change and how those changes affect people. Czechoslovakia, for example, split into Slovakia and the Czech Republic in 1993. These types of political events affect geographic boundaries. People react differently to these changes. Some people are forced to move. Others welcome the change.

Other issues geographers study include religions, diet (or food), **urban** areas, and **rural** areas. Urban areas contain cities. Rural areas contain open land that is often used for farming.

✓ **READING CHECK:** The Uses of Geography What issues or topics do geographers study?

Local, Regional, and Global Geographic Studies

With any topic, geographers must decide how large an area to study. They can focus their study at a local, regional, or global level.

Local Studying your community at the local, or close-up, level will help you learn geography. You know where homes and stores are located. You know how to find parks, ball fields, and other fun places. Over time, you see your community change. New buildings are constructed. People move in and out of your neighborhood. New stores open their doors, and others go out of business.

internet connect

GO TO: go.hrw.com
KEYWORD: SG5 CH1
FOR: Web sites about the geographer's world

▲

Regional Regional geographers organize the world into convenient parts for study. For example, this book separates the world into big areas like Africa and Europe. Regional studies cover larger areas than local studies. Some regional studies might look at connections like highways and rivers. Others might examine the regional customs.

Global Geographers also work to understand global issues and the connections between events. For example, many countries depend on oil from Southwest Asia. If those oil supplies are threatened, some countries might rush to secure oil from other areas. Oil all over the world could then become much more expensive.

Region The southwest is a region within the United States. One well-known place that characterizes the landscape of the southwest is the Grand Canyon. The Grand Canyon is shown in the photo at left and in the satellite image at right.

✓ **READING CHECK:** (**The World in Spatial Terms**) What levels do geographers use to focus their study of an issue or topic?

go.hrw.com
Homework Practice Online
Keyword: SG5 HP1

Define and explain: perspective, spatial perspective, geography, urban, rural

Reading for the Main Idea

1. How can a spatial perspective be used to study the world?

2. Why is it important to study geography?

Critical Thinking

3. **Drawing Inferences and Conclusions** How do threatening weather patterns affect people, and why do geographers study these patterns?

4. **Drawing Inferences and Conclusions** Why is it important to view geography on a global level?

Organizing What You Know

5. **Finding the Main Idea** Copy the following graphic organizer. Use it to examine the issues geographers study. Write a paragraph on one of these issues.

Themes and Essential Elements of Geography

Read to Discover

1. What tools do geographers use to study the world?
2. What shapes Earth's features?
3. How do humans shape the world?
4. How does studying geography help us understand the world?

Vocabulary

absolute location
relative location
place
region

movement
diffusion
human-environment interaction

Reading Strategy

TAKING NOTES Taking notes while you read will help you understand and remember the information in this section. Write down the headings in the section. As you read, fill in notes under each heading. Underline the most important details you find.

Libya — Giza — Saudi Arabia — Egypt — Sudan

▲
The location of a place can be described in many ways.

Interpreting the Visual Record

(Location) **Looking at the photo of this hotel in Giza, Egypt, and at the map, how would you describe Giza's location?**

Learning Geography

The study of geography has long been organized according to five important themes, or topics of study. One theme, location, deals with the exact or relative spot of something on Earth. Place includes the physical and human features of a location. Human-environment interaction covers the ways people and environments affect each other. Movement involves how people change locations and how goods are traded as well as the effects of these movements. For example, when people move they may bring animals, diseases, and their own culture to a new place. Region organizes Earth into geographic areas with one or more shared characteristics.

Another way to look at geography, however, is to study its essential elements, or most important parts. In 1994, several geographers and teachers created national geography standards called *Geography For Life*. The six essential elements they created to organize the study of geography are The World in Spatial Terms, Places and Regions, Physical Systems, Human Systems, Environment and Society, and The Uses of Geography. Because the six essential elements and the five themes share many of the same properties, both will be used throughout this textbook. Look for labels on questions, photographs, maps, graphs, and charts that show which geography theme or essential element is the main focus. In this section we discuss several topics related to the geography themes and essential elements. Here you will discover the relationship between these two ways of learning about our world.

✓ **READING CHECK:** (*The Uses of Geography*) What are the five themes of geography? What are the six essential elements?

The World in Spatial Terms

This element focuses on geography's spatial perspective. As you learned in Section 1, geographers apply spatial perspective when they look at the location of something and why it is there.

Location The term location can be used in two ways. **Absolute location** defines an exact spot on Earth. For example, the address of the Smithsonian American Art Museum is an absolute location. The address is at 8th and G Streets, N.W., in Washington, D.C. City streets often form a grid. This system tells anyone looking for an address where to go. The grid formed by latitude and longitude lines also pinpoints absolute location. Suppose you asked a pilot to take you to 52° north latitude by 175° west longitude. You would land at a location on Alaska's Aleutian Islands.

Relative location describes the position of a place in relation to another place. Measurements of direction, distance, or time can define relative location. For example, the following sentences give relative location. "The hospital is one mile north of our school." "Canada's border is about an hour's drive from Great Falls, Montana."

A geographer must be able to use maps and other geographic tools and technologies to determine spatial perspective. A geographer must also know how to organize and analyze information about people, places, and environments using geographic tools.

✓ **READING CHECK:** (*The World in Spatial Terms*) What two ways describe location?

Places and Regions

To help explain why many areas of the world are similar to or different from one another, geographers organize Earth's surface into different places and regions. The Places and Regions essential element deals with how people have created regions based on Earth's features and how culture and other factors affect how we see places and regions.

Place Our world has a vast number of unique places and regions. A **place** can be described both by its physical location and by its physical and human features. Physical features include coastlines and landforms. They can also include lakes, rivers, or soil types. For example, Colorado is flat in the east but mountainous in the west. This is an example of a place being described in terms of its landforms. A place can also be described by its climate. For example, Greenland has long, cold winters. Florida has mild winters and hot, humid summers.

▲

(*Place*) Places can be described by what they do not have. This photo shows the result of a long period without rain.

Region A **region** is an area of Earth's surface with one or more shared characteristics. Many of the characteristics that describe places can also be used to describe regions. Regions vary in size. Some are very large, like North America. Others are much smaller, like the Florida Keys. Regions are also different from the surrounding areas. For example, Silicon Valley is a region in California that is known for its many computer companies and engineers.

What defines a region? Some regions have boundaries that are easy to define. For example, natural vegetation regions have similar plants. Deserts, forests, and grasslands are examples of natural regions with fairly clear boundaries. A region can also be described as cultural, economic, or political.

✓ **READING CHECK:** (*Places and Regions*) What features can you use to describe a place?

Physical Systems

Physical systems shape Earth's features. Geographers study earthquakes, mountains, rivers, volcanoes, weather patterns, and similar topics and how these physical systems have affected Earth's characteristics. For example, geographers might study how volcanic eruptions in the Hawaiian Islands spread lava, causing landforms to change. They might note that southern California's shoreline changes yearly, as winter and summer waves move beach sand.

Geographers also study how plants and animals relate to these nonliving physical systems. For example, deserts are places with cactus and other plants, as well as rattlesnakes and other reptiles, that can live in very dry conditions. Geographers also study how different types of plants, animals, and physical systems are distributed on Earth.

✓ **READING CHECK:** (*Physical Systems*) What types of physical systems do geographers study?

(*Movement*) People travel from place to place on miles of new roadway.

▼

Men in rural Egypt wear a long shirt called a *galabia*. This loose-fitting garment is ideal for people living in Egypt's hot desert climate. In addition, the galabia is made from cotton, an important agricultural product of Egypt.

Interpreting the Visual Record

(*Human-Environment Interaction*) **How does the *galabia* show how people have adapted to their environment?**

▶

Human Systems

People are central to geography. Geographers study human systems, or the human activities, movements, and settlements that shape Earth's surface. Human systems also include peoples' customs, history, languages, and religions.

Movement Geographers study the **movement** of people and ideas. When people move, they may go to live in other countries or move within a country. Geographers want to know how and why people move from place to place.

People move for many reasons. Some move to start a new job. Some move to attend special schools. Others might move to be closer to family. People move either when they are pushed out of a place or when they are pulled toward another place. In the Dust Bowl, for example, crop failures pushed people out of Oklahoma in the 1930s. Many were pulled to California by their belief that they would find work there.

Geographers also want to know how ideas or behaviors move from one region to another. The movement of ideas occurs through communication. There are many ways to communicate. People visit with each other in person or on the phone. New technology allows people to communicate by e-mail. Ideas are also spread through films, magazines, newspapers, radio, and television. The movement of ideas or behaviors from one region to another is known as **diffusion**.

The things we produce and trade are also part of the study of human systems. Geographers study trading patterns and how countries depend on each other for certain goods. In addition, geographers look at the causes and results of conflicts between peoples. The study of governments we set up and the features of cities and other settlements we live in are also part of this study.

✓ **READING CHECK:** (*Human Systems*) What are some reasons why people move?

▲
A satellite dish brings different images and ideas to people in a remote area of Brazil.
Interpreting the Visual Record How might resources have affected the use of technology here?

▲
This woman at a railway station in Russian Siberia sells some goods that were once unavailable in her country.

Environment and Society

Human actions, such as using oil or water, affect the environment. At the same time, Earth's physical systems, such as climate or natural hazards, affect human activities. Our survival depends on what Earth provides. Many geographers consider the relationship between people and the environment a central focus of geography.

Human-Environment Interaction Geographers study how people and their surroundings affect each other. This relationship between people and the environment, or **human-environment interaction**, can be examined in three ways. First, geographers study

▲

Open-air markets like this one in Mali provide opportunities for farmers to sell their goods.

how humans depend on their physical environment to survive. Human life requires certain living and nonliving resources, such as freshwater and fertile soil for farming.

Geographers also study how humans change their behavior to be better suited to an environment. These changes or adaptations include the kinds of clothing, food, and shelter that people create. These changes help people live in harsh climates.

Finally, humans change the environment. For example, farmers who irrigate their fields can grow fruit in Arizona's dry climate. People in Louisiana have built levees, or large walls, to protect themselves when the Mississippi River floods.

✔ **READING CHECK:** (*Environment and Society*) How might people change to live in certain environments?

The Uses of Geography

Geography helps us understand the relationships among people, places, and the environment over time. Understanding how a relationship has developed can help in making plans for the future. For example, geographers can study how human use of the soil in a farming region has affected that region over time. Such knowledge can help them determine what changes have been made to the soil and whether any corrective measures need to be taken.

✔ **READING CHECK:** (*The Uses of Geography*) How can studying geography help plan for the future?

go.hrw.com
Homework Practice Online
Keyword: SG5 HP1

Section Review 2

Define and explain: absolute location, relative location, place, region, movement, diffusion, human-environment interaction

Reading for the Main Idea

1. (*The World in Spatial Terms*) How do geographers study the world?

2. (*Physical Systems*) What shapes Earth's features? Give examples.

Critical Thinking

3. Finding the Main Idea How do humans shape the world in which they live?

4. Analyzing Information What benefits can studying geography provide?

Organizing What You Know

5. Summarizing Copy the following graphic organizer. Use it to identify and describe all aspects of each of the six essential elements.

Element	Description

Section 3 Being a Geographer

Read to Discover

1. What is included in the study of human geography?
2. What is included in the study of physical geography?
3. What types of work do geographers do?

Vocabulary

human geography
physical geography
cartography
meteorology
climatology

Reading Strategy

READING ORGANIZER   Before you read this section, create a three column chart. Title the columns Human Geography, Physical Geography, and Working as a Geographer. As you read, write information that you learn about each topic on your chart.

Human Geography

The study of people, past or present, is the focus of **human geography**. People's location and distribution over Earth, their activities, and their differences are studied. For example, people living in different countries create different kinds of governments. Political geographers study those differences. Economic geographers study the exchange of goods and services across Earth. Cultural geography, population geography, and urban geography are some other examples of human geography. A professional geographer might specialize in any of these branches.

✓ **READING CHECK:** (*Human Systems*) How is human geography defined?

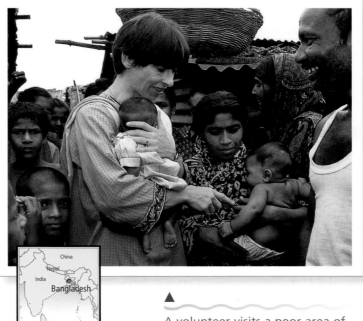

▲
A volunteer visits a poor area of Bangladesh. Geographers study economic conditions in regions to help them understand human geography.

Physical Geography

The study of Earth's natural landscapes and physical systems, including the atmosphere, is the focus of **physical geography**. The world is full of different landforms such as deserts, mountains, and plains. Climates affect these landscapes. Knowledge of physical systems helps geographers understand how a landscape developed and how it might change.

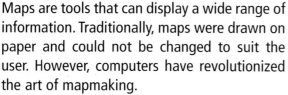

A mapmaker creates a digital map.

Maps are tools that can display a wide range of information. Traditionally, maps were drawn on paper and could not be changed to suit the user. However, computers have revolutionized the art of mapmaking.

Today, mapmakers use computers to create and modify maps for different uses. They do this by using a geographic information system, or GIS. A GIS is a computer system that combines maps and satellite photographs with other kinds of spatial data—information about places on the planet. This information might include soil types, population figures, or voting patterns.

Using a GIS, mapmakers can create maps that show geographic features and relationships. For example, a map showing rainfall patterns in a particular region might be combined with data on soil types or human settlement to show areas of possible soil erosion.

The flexibility of a GIS allows people to seek answers to specific questions. Where should a new road be built to ease traffic congestion? How are changes in natural habitat affecting wildlife? These and many other questions can be answered with the help of computer mapping.

Computer Mapping

Understanding What You Read

1. How could a GIS help people change their environment?
2. What social, environmental, or economic consequences might future advances in GIS technology have?

Knowledge of physical and human geography will help you understand the world's different regions and peoples. In your study of the major world regions, you will see how physical and human geography connect to each other.

✔ **READING CHECK:** (*Physical Systems*) What is included in the study of physical geography?

Working as a Geographer

Geography plays a role in almost every occupation. Wherever you live and work, you should know local geography. School board members know where children live. Taxi drivers are familiar with city streets. Grocery store managers know which foods sell well in certain areas.

They also know where they can obtain these products throughout the year. Local newspaper reporters are familiar with town meetings and local politicians. Reporters also know how faraway places can affect their communities. Doctors must know if their towns have poisonous snakes or plants. City managers know whether nearby rivers might flood. Emergency workers in mountain towns check snow depth so they can give avalanche warnings. Local weather forecasters watch for powerful storms and track their routes on special maps.

Some specially trained geographers practice in the field of **cartography**. Cartography is the art and science of mapmaking. Today, most mapmakers do their work on computers. Geographers also work as weather forecasters. The field of forecasting and reporting rainfall, temperature, and other atmospheric conditions is called **meteorology**. A related field is **climatology**. These geographers, known as climatologists, track Earth's larger atmospheric systems. Climatologists want to know how these systems change over long periods of time. They also study how people might be affected by changes in climate.

Governments and a variety of organizations hire geographers to study the environment. These geographers might explore such topics as pollution, endangered plants and animals, or rain forests. Some geographers who are interested in education become teachers and writers. They help people of all ages learn more about the world. Modern technology allows people all over the world to communicate instantly. Therefore, it is more important than ever to be familiar with the geographer's world.

▲

Experts examine snow to help forecast avalanches. They study the type of snow, weather conditions, and landforms.

✓ **READING CHECK:** (*The Uses of Geography*) What types of work do geographers perform?

Define and explain: human geography, physical geography, cartography, meteorology, climatology

Reading for the Main Idea

1. (*Human Systems*) What topics are included in the study of human geography?

2. (*The Uses of Geography*) How do people who study the weather use geography?

Critical Thinking

3. Finding the Main Idea Why is it important to study physical geography?

4. Making Generalizations and Predictions How might future discoveries in the field of geography affect societies, world economies, or the environment?

Organizing What You Know

5. Categorizing Copy the following graphic organizer. Use it to list geographers' professions and their job responsibilities.

Cartographer —makes maps —studies maps		

CASE STUDY

HOW GEOGRAPHERS TRACK HURRICANES

As you learned in Chapter 1, geographers called climatologists study Earth's atmosphere. Sometimes large circulating storms called hurricanes develop in the atmosphere above tropical oceans. Hurricanes often move over land and into populated areas. When a hurricane approaches land, it brings strong winds, heavy rains, and large ocean waves.

Climatologists try to predict where these storms will travel. They want to be able to warn people in the hurricane's path. Early warnings can help people be better prepared for the deadly winds and rain. It is a difficult job because hurricanes can change course suddenly. Hurricanes are one of the most dangerous natural hazards.

The map below shows the path of Hurricane Fran in 1996. Notice how Fran moved to the west and became stronger until it reached land. It began as a tropical depression and became a powerful hurricane as it passed over warm ocean waters.

One way of determining a hurricane's strength is by measuring the atmospheric pressure inside it. The lower the pressure, the stronger the storm. Hurricanes are rated on a scale of one to five. Study Table 1 to see how wind speed and air pressure are used to help determine the strength of a hurricane.

Hurricane Mitch formed in October 1998. The National Weather Service (NWS) recorded Mitch's position and strength. They learned that Mitch's pressure was one of the lowest ever recorded. The

Table 1: Saffir-Simpson Scale

Hurricane Type	Wind Speed MPH	Air Pressure MB (inches)
Category 1	74–95	more than 980 (28.94)
Category 2	96–110	965–979 (28.50–28.91)
Category 3	111–130	945–964 (27.91–28.47)
Category 4	131–155	920–944 (27.17–27.88)
Category 5	more than 155	less than 920 (27.17)

Source: Florida State University, <http://www.met.fsu.edu/explores/tropical.html>

Path of Hurricane Fran, 1996

SCALE
0   300   600 Miles
0   300   600 Kilometers
Projection: Miller Cylindrical

30 mph — Wind speed (in miles per hour)
1006 mb — Atmospheric pressure (in millibars)
○ Tropical depression
◎ Tropical storm
🌀 Hurricane
━━ Fran's path

GULF OF MEXICO
ATLANTIC OCEAN
CARIBBEAN SEA
PACIFIC OCEAN

Sept. 6 — 989 mb — 35 mph
Sept. 5 — 954 mb — 100 mph
Sept. 4 — 956 mb — 100 mph
Sept. 3 — 977 mb — 75 mph
Sept. 2 — 976 mb — 70 mph
Sept. 1 — 982 mb — 65 mph
Aug. 31 — 984 mb — 61 mph
Aug. 30 — 990 mb — 65 mph
Aug. 29 — 984 mb — 65 mph
Aug. 28 — 997 mb — 52 mph
Aug. 27 — 1006 mb — 30 mph
Aug. 26 — 1007 mb — 30 mph
Aug. 25 — 1007 mb — 30 mph
Aug. 24 — 1007 mb — 30 mph

Table 2: Hurricane Mitch, 1998 Position and Strength

Date	Latitude (Degrees)	Longitude (Degrees)	Wind Speed (MPH)	Pressure (Millibars)	Storm Type
10/22	12 N	78 W	30	1002	Tropical depression
10/24	15 N	78 W	90	980	Category 2
10/26	16 N	81 W	130	923	Category 4
10/27	17 N	84 W	150	910	Category 5
10/31	15 N	88 W	40	1000	Tropical storm
11/01	15 N	90 W	30	1002	Tropical depression
11/03	20 N	91 W	40	997	Tropical storm
11/05	26 N	83 W	50	990	Tropical storm

Source: <http://www.met.fsu.edu/explores/tropical.html>

NWS estimated that Mitch's maximum sustained surface winds reached 180 miles per hour.

Hurricanes like Mitch cause very heavy rains in short periods of time. These heavy rains are particularly dangerous. The ground becomes saturated, and mud can flow almost like water. The flooding and mudslides caused by Mitch killed an estimated 10,000 people in four countries. Many people predicted that the region would not recover without help from other countries.

In the southeastern United States, many places have emergency preparedness units. The people assigned to these groups organize their communities. They provide food, shelter, and clothing for those who must evacuate their homes.

You Be the Geographer

1. Trace a map of the Caribbean. Be sure to include latitude and longitude lines.

2. Use the data about Hurricane Mitch in Table 2 to plot its path. Make a key with symbols to show Mitch's strength at each location.

3. What happened to Mitch when it reached land?

▲

This satellite image shows the intensity of Hurricane Mitch. With advanced technology, hurricane tracking is helping to save lives.

CHAPTER 1 Review and Practice

Define and Identify

Identify each of the following:

1. perspective
2. spatial perspective
3. geography
4. urban
5. rural
6. absolute location
7. relative location
8. place
9. region
10. movement
11. diffusion
12. human-environment interaction
13. human geography
14. physical geography
15. cartography
16. meteorology
17. climatology

Review the Main Ideas

18. What is geography?
19. What do urban areas contain? What do rural areas contain?
20. What are three ways to study geography? Give an example of when each type could be used.
21. What kind of directions would you give to indicate a place's absolute location? Its relative location?
22. How can a place be described?

23. What are some ways to define a region?
24. What are some reasons why people move?
25. How do some people adapt to better suit their environment?
26. Why is cartography important?
27. What types of jobs do geographers do?

Think Critically

28. **Analyzing Information** How can a geographer use spatial perspective to explain how things in our world are connected?
29. **Drawing Inferences and Conclusions** When and how do humans relate to the environment? Provide some examples of this relationship.
30. **Summarizing** How are patterns created by the movement of goods, ideas, and people?
31. **Finding the Main Idea** How are places and regions defined?
32. **Finding the Main Idea** How does studying geography help us understand the world?

Map Activity

33. On a separate sheet of paper, match the letters on the map with their correct labels.

   Africa
   Antarctica
   Asia
   Australia

   Europe
   North America
   South America

Writing Activity

Write a letter persuading another student to enroll in a geography class. Include examples of professions that use geography and relate that information to the everyday life of a student. Be sure to use standard grammar, spelling, sentence structure, and punctuation.

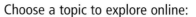

internet connect

Internet Activity: **go.hrw.com**
KEYWORD: **SG5 GT1**

Choose a topic to explore online:
- Learn to use online maps.
- Be a virtual geographer for a day.
- Compare regions around the world.

Social Studies Skills Practice

Interpreting Maps

Study the following map of the state of California. Use what you know about location to answer the questions.

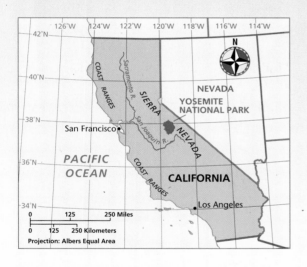

1. How would you describe the relative location of Los Angeles?

2. If you were in San Francisco, how would you describe the relative location of Yosemite National Park?

3. What would you use on this map to find the absolute location of places?

4. What is the absolute location of Los Angeles?

Analyzing Primary Sources

Read the following quote from geographer Dr. Reginald G. Golledge. Then answer the questions.

"As I was growing up in Australia, my family moved frequently, largely from one small town to another . . . The small-town environment and the surrounding countryside favored the development of a state of mind that constantly asked, 'What's over the next hill? How far is it to the river? Where are the wild berries and fruits located?'"

Source: *Geographical Voices: Fourteen Autobiographical Essays*

1. Did Dr. Golledge grow up in a rural area or an urban area?

2. How do you think Dr. Golledge's childhood experiences led him to become a geographer?

3. As a child, was Golledge interested more in human geography or physical geography?

4. Which two of the five geography themes best describes the questions Dr. Golledge asks?

CHAPTER 2

Planet Earth

Diver, coral, and fish, Fiji Islands

Quartz crystals

Erupting volcano

Tornado in Saskatoon, Canada

Section 1 — The Land

Read to Discover

1. What processes build up the land?
2. What processes shape Earth's surfaces?
3. How has topography affected human history and culture?

Vocabulary

landforms
topography
plate tectonics
subduction
earthquakes
lava
fault
weathering

erosion
plain
alluvial fan
floodplain
delta
glaciers
terraces

Reading Strategy

TAKING NOTES Taking notes while you read will help you understand and remember the information in this section. Write down the headings in the section. As you read, fill in notes under each heading. Underline the most important details you find.

Building Up the Land

Landforms are shapes on Earth's surface. The shape, height, and arrangement of landforms in a certain place is called **topography**. The theory of **plate tectonics** helps explain how Earth's topography formed and how it changes. According to this theory, Earth's surface is divided into several large plates, or pieces. There are also a number of smaller plates. These plates move very slowly—just inches per year.

Plate Tectonics

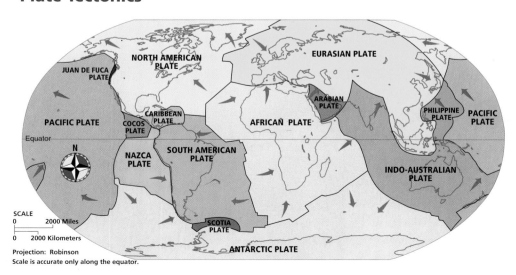

The plates that make up Earth's crust are moving, usually a few inches per year. This map shows the plates and the direction of their movement.

Colliding Plates Some of the plates collide as they move, and one plate may move underneath the other. This process is called **subduction**. In subduction zones, volcanoes and **earthquakes** are common. An earthquake is a sudden, violent movement along a break within the outer layers of Earth's crust.

Look at the Plate Tectonics map on the previous page and find the Pacific plate. Where the Pacific plate moves against neighboring plates, volcanoes and earthquakes are common. In fact, the edge of the Pacific plate is called the Ring of Fire because it is rimmed by active volcanoes. The region's earthquakes and volcanoes have killed thousands of people and caused terrible destruction. Several major earthquakes have hit California in recent years. Local authorities along the West Coast are constantly preparing for future earthquakes. Scientists predict that one of the strongest earthquakes in U.S. history may occur in the San Francisco Bay area within the next 30 years.

In some places, colliding plates have other results. Instead of sinking, one of the plates may crumple up and form a mountain range. The Andes in South America and the Himalayas in Asia formed in this way.

Other Plate Movements In other parts of the world, plates move away from each other. From the gap, hot **lava**, or melted rock from deep in the Earth, may emerge. The lava may build up, forming a mountain range. This process is happening in the Atlantic Ocean where the Eurasian plate and the North American plate are moving away from each other.

Tectonic plates can also slide past each other. Earthquakes occur from these sudden changes in Earth's crust. In California the Pacific plate is sliding northwestward along the edge of the North American plate. This movement has created the San Andreas Fault zone. A **fault** is a fractured surface in Earth's crust where a mass of rock is in motion.

✓ **READING CHECK:** (*Physical Systems*) What are three ways that tectonic plates move?

These steep peaks in Chile are part of the Andes. **Interpreting the Visual Record** (*Place*) **How do these mountains show the effects of colliding plates?**

Shaping Earth's Surface

The forces of plate tectonics build up the land. At the same time, water, wind, and ice constantly break down rock and move rocky material. This process of breaking down landforms and creating new ones is called **weathering**.

Heat, Water, and Chemical Action Weathering breaks rocks into smaller pieces in several ways. Heat can cause rocks to crack. Water may then get into the cracks. If the water freezes, the ice expands with a force great enough to break the rock. Water can also work its way underground and slowly dissolve minerals such as limestone. This process sometimes carves out caves. In some areas small plants called lichens attach to bare rock. Chemicals in the lichens gradually break down the stone. All these processes eventually break rock down into sediment, in the form of gravel, sand, silt, or clay. Then water, ice, or wind can move the sediment and create new topography with it. This process of moving rocky material or sediment to another place is called **erosion**.

Moving water is the most common force that erodes the land. Flowing water carries sediment. This sediment eventually forms different kinds of landforms depending on where it is deposited. For example, a river flowing from a mountain range onto a flat area, or **plain**, may deposit sediment there. The sediment sometimes builds up into a fan-shaped form called an **alluvial fan**. A **floodplain** is created when rivers flood their banks and deposit sediment. A **delta** forms where a river carries sediment all the way to the ocean. The sediment settles to the bottom where the river meets the ocean. The Nile and Mississippi Rivers have two of the world's largest deltas.

Waves in the ocean or lakes also shape the land they touch. Waves can shape beaches into great dunes, such as on the shore of Long Island. Oregon's jagged coastline also shows how waves can erode land.

▲

Erosion wears away Earth's surface at an island beach off the Florida coast. **Interpreting the Visual Record** (*Place*) **What physical process is causing erosion on this beach?**

Ocean water turns muddy as the Mississippi River pushes sediment out of its delta.

▼

Ice and Wind Action In high mountain settings and in the coldest places on Earth one finds **glaciers**. These large, slow-moving rivers of ice can move tons of rock.

Glaciers covered most of Canada and the United States during the last ice age — or period of extreme cold. As they advanced, the glaciers carved out gashes in Earth's surface. Glaciers dug the Great Lakes. As the ice melted and retreated, tons of rock and sediment were left behind.

Wind also shapes the land. Strong winds can lift soil into the air and carry it far away. On beaches and in deserts, wind drops sand, which piles up into dunes. In addition, blowing sand can wear away rock. The sand acts like sandpaper to polish jagged edges and rough surfaces.

Erosion and Soil These processes of breaking down Earth's surface create deposits of soil. People need soil to grow food. Erosion, however, can also remove soil from farmers' fields. Heavy rainfall can wash away soil. Strong winds can blow it away.

Over the centuries, however, people have developed ways to conserve our precious soil. Some farmers plant rows of trees to block the wind. Others who farm on steep hillsides build **terraces** into the slope. Terraces are horizontal ridges like stair steps. By slowing the downhill rush of water the terraces keep the soil in place. They also provide more space for growing crops.

✓ **READING CHECK:** (*Physical Systems*) What forces cause erosion?

Rice paddies like these in Indonesia are common throughout island Southeast Asia.

Interpreting the Visual Record

(*Human-Environment Interaction*)

How have farmers limited erosion in the rice paddies pictured below?

People and Topography

Topography has quite a bit to do with human history and culture. Those effects are so big, however, that we may not see them easily.

Landforms and Life Why do you live where you live? Perhaps your parents moved to your city to take jobs in the tourist industry. Do tourists visit your area partly because of its landforms, such as mountains? Or maybe your town grew up on a river delta. People could farm the delta's fertile soil. They could also use either the river or the sea for trade and travel. What are some more ways that your area's topography may have influenced its growth?

Reading a Topographic Map

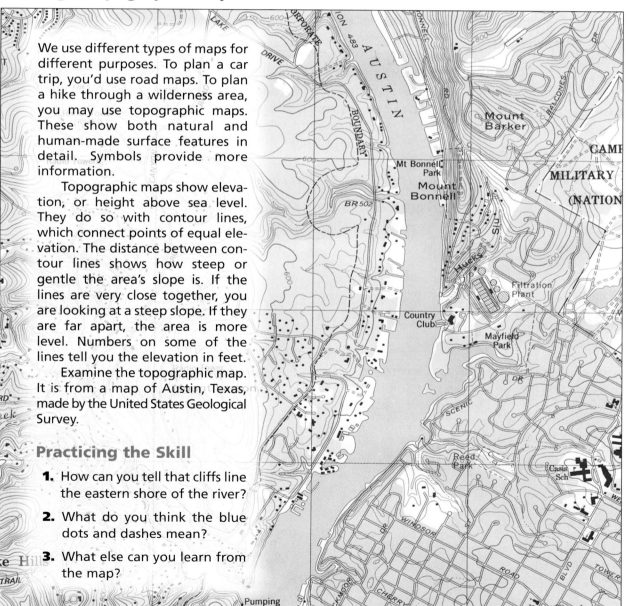

We use different types of maps for different purposes. To plan a car trip, you'd use road maps. To plan a hike through a wilderness area, you may use topographic maps. These show both natural and human-made surface features in detail. Symbols provide more information.

Topographic maps show elevation, or height above sea level. They do so with contour lines, which connect points of equal elevation. The distance between contour lines shows how steep or gentle the area's slope is. If the lines are very close together, you are looking at a steep slope. If they are far apart, the area is more level. Numbers on some of the lines tell you the elevation in feet.

Examine the topographic map. It is from a map of Austin, Texas, made by the United States Geological Survey.

Practicing the Skill

1. How can you tell that cliffs line the eastern shore of the river?

2. What do you think the blue dots and dashes mean?

3. What else can you learn from the map?

In 1914 an enormous canal was completed across the Isthmus of Panama, linking the Pacific and Atlantic Oceans. Workers used millions of pounds of explosives and steam-powered shovels to cut through much of the landscape.

Interpreting the Visual Record

Through what landforms did the Panama Canal workers have to dig?

Landforms affect the history of entire countries. For one example, start by looking at a map of India. You will see that the Ganges River crosses a broad plain before emptying into the Bay of Bengal. This river has brought sediment down from the Himalayas for countless centuries. It dropped the sediment on the plain, forming a vast area of excellent farmland. Many invaders have attacked India, trying to win this rich plain for themselves.

Here is an example of how landforms affected language. Find the island of New Guinea on a map of Southeast Asia. Notice how mountainous it is. These mountains have isolated New Guinea's peoples so much that many languages developed. In fact, more than 700 different languages are spoken on the island today.

Changing Landforms For thousands of years, people have changed Earth's surface to suit their needs. They have dug canals for irrigation ditches and carved terraces for farms. They have created artificial hills on which to build temples. People have even held back the sea to claim more dry land. Today, engineers build dams to control river flooding. They drill tunnels through mountains instead of laying roads over the mountains. Thus, while earthquakes, volcanoes, weathering, and erosion change Earth's surface, people do so also.

✓ **READING CHECK:** (**Environment and Society**) What are some landforms that could affect human history and culture?

Section Review 1

Homework Practice Online
Keyword: SG5 HP2

Define and explain: landforms, topography, plate tectonics, subduction, earthquakes, lava, fault, weathering, erosion, plain, alluvial fan, floodplain, delta, glaciers, terraces

Reading for the Main Idea

1. (*Physical Systems*) What events are common where tectonic plates collide?

2. (*Physical Systems*) How do rivers create new landforms?

Critical Thinking

3. **Comparing and Contrasting** How are weathering and erosion different?

4. **Making Predictions** How may the lives of people who live in the mountains or on plains be different?

Organizing What You Know

5. **Categorizing** Copy the following graphic organizer. Use it to describe the results of each force of erosion or weathering.

heat ⇨
cold ⇨
water moving through limestone ⇨
chemicals in lichens ⇨
waves ⇨
glaciers ⇨
wind ⇨

Read to Discover

1. Where is water found on Earth?
2. What is the water cycle?
3. How do people and water affect each other?
4. What are short-term and long-term results of air pollution?

Vocabulary

tributary
groundwater
aquifers
water cycle
evaporation
water vapor

condensation
precipitation
acid rain
ozone layer
global warming
greenhouse effect

Reading Strategy

READING ORGANIZER   Before you read this section, create a spider map. Label the circle Water and Air. Create a leg for each of these topics: Geographic Distribution of Water, The Water Cycle, Water and People, and The Air We Breathe. As you read the section, fill in the map with details about each topic.

Geographic Distribution of Water

Water is essential for life. The presence or absence of water in a place affects whether people can live there. Water, therefore, is part of both physical and human geography. Throughout this book, you will see how water or its lack determines what life is like around the world.

The oceans contain about 97 percent of Earth's water. Another 2 percent is locked in the ice of Earth's polar regions and glaciers. Only about 1 percent is freshwater in lakes, streams, rivers, and below Earth's surface.

Earth's freshwater resources are not evenly distributed. Some places are extremely dry. Dry states such as Nevada have few natural lakes. Others have many lakes and rivers. For example, in the United States, Minnesota has more than 11,000 lakes. Some areas have too much water. Floods can make survival difficult in places where rainfall is very heavy or where rivers burst their banks.

Mountain glaciers like this one can move slowly downhill. This photo shows the face of a glacier. Here chunks may break off, or calve, and form icebergs.

Interpreting the Visual Record   **What dangers may these kayakers face?**

▼

Groundwater

Precipitation

Runoff

Well

Groundwater

In some areas where rainfall is scarce, there is enough groundwater to support agriculture.
Interpreting the Visual Record How do people gain access to groundwater?

Pivoting sprinklers irrigate these circular cornfields in Kansas.
Interpreting the Visual Record
Human-Environment Interaction
Why may irrigation be necessary in these fields?

Surface Water Water may collect at high elevations, where rivers begin. The first and smallest streams that form are called headwaters. When these headwaters meet and join, they form larger streams. In turn, these streams join with others to form rivers. Any smaller stream or river that flows into a larger river is a **tributary**. For example, the Missouri River is a major tributary of the Mississippi River.

A lake may form where a river flows into a low-lying area. Most lakes are freshwater, but some are salty. For example, the Dead Sea in Southwest Asia is actually a lake that is much saltier than the ocean. When the lake water evaporates, it leaves behind salts and minerals, making the lake salty.

Most of Earth's water is in the oceans. The Pacific, Atlantic, Indian, and Arctic Oceans are connected. This vast body of water covers about 70 percent of Earth's surface. These oceans also include smaller areas called seas and gulfs. The Gulf of Mexico and the Mediterranean Sea are two examples of smaller ocean areas.

Groundwater Not all surface water immediately returns to the atmosphere through evaporation. Some water from rain, snow, rivers, and lakes seeps into the ground. This **groundwater** trickles down until all the tiny spaces in the soil and rock are filled. In some places, the groundwater collects in water-bearing layers of rock, sand, or gravel called **aquifers**. Some aquifers are quite large. For example, the

The Water Cycle

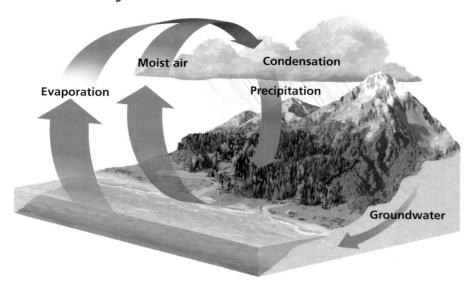

◀

The circulation of water from one part of the hydrosphere to another depends on energy from the Sun. Water evaporates, condenses, and falls to Earth as precipitation.

Interpreting the Visual Record (Place)

How would a seasonal increase in the amount of the Sun's energy received by an area change the water cycle in that area?

Ogallala Aquifer stretches across the Great Plains from Texas to South Dakota. Many Americans get their water from wells—deep holes dug down to reach an aquifer's groundwater. Elsewhere, groundwater may bubble up from an aquifer as springs.

✔ **READING CHECK:** (*Physical Systems*) Where is most of Earth's surface water found?

Flooded streets are a way of life during the wet monsoon season in Tamil Nadu, India.

▼

The Water Cycle

The circulation of water from Earth's surface to the atmosphere and back is called the **water cycle**. The total amount of water on the planet doesn't change. Water, however, does change its form and its location.

The Sun's energy drives the water cycle. **Evaporation** occurs when the Sun heats water on Earth's surface. The heated water evaporates, becoming a gas called **water vapor**. As the water vapor cools, **condensation** happens. This is the process by which water changes from a gas into tiny liquid droplets. These droplets join together to form clouds. If the droplets become heavy enough, **precipitation** occurs— that is, the water falls back to Earth. This water

can be in the form of rain, hail, sleet, or snow. The entire cycle of evaporation, condensation, and precipitation repeats over and over.

✔ **READING CHECK:** (*Physical Systems*) What are the three main steps in the water cycle?

Davenport, Iowa, located on the Missisippi River, suffered severe flooding when heavy rains caused the river to rise above its banks.

Water and People

Water plays a vital role in our survival. As a result, you will often see events and problems related to water in the news. Some of those events are natural disasters. Some of them are issues that people create.

Water Hazards Water can be extremely destructive. Thunderstorms, especially when accompanied by hail or tornadoes, can damage buildings and ruin crops. Heavy rains can cause floods, the world's deadliest natural hazard. Of every ten people who die from natural disasters, four die in floods. Some floods occur in usually dry places when a large amount of rain falls in a short amount of time. Then the water collects on the surface instead of soaking into the hard, dry ground. Normally dry creekbeds can suddenly gush with rushing water. People and livestock are sometimes caught in these flash floods.

Floods also happen in low-lying places next to rivers and on coastlines. Too much rain or snowmelt entering a river can push the water over the river's banks. Powerful storms, especially hurricanes, can cause ocean waters to surge into coastal areas. Is your region ever threatened by floods? What causes floods where you live?

Water Conservation In those places where there isn't enough water, however, many people try to use as little as possible. Scientists have developed new water management methods for saving the precious liquid. Many modern factories now recycle water. Farmers can irrigate their crops more efficiently. Cities build water treatment plants to purify water that might otherwise be wasted. Some people in dry regions use desert plants instead of grass for landscaping. As a result, they use less water in their yards.

An Omani man collects water from a local *falaj*, or aqueduct. These channels are dug to carry water from desert springs to farms and villages. **Interpreting the Visual Record**
(*Human-Environment Interaction*) **How does this method of irrigation differ from modern methods?**

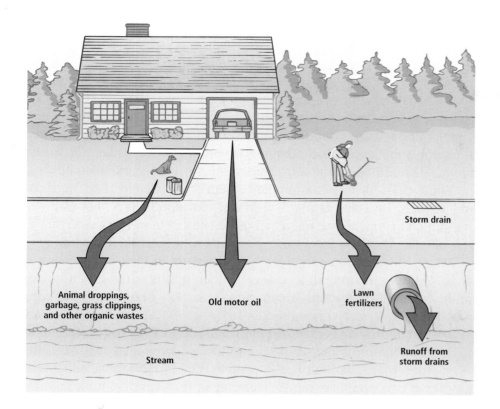

Animal droppings, garbage, grass clippings, and other organic wastes

Old motor oil

Lawn fertilizers

Storm drain

Stream

Runoff from storm drains

Most of the water that goes down drains, or wastewater, flows through pipes to a wastewater treatment plant. There the polluted water is treated before being returned to a river or a lake. Most of the waste-water from homes is easy to purify. However, industrial wastewater and storm runoff from streets and fields contain toxic substances that are difficult to purify.

Interpreting the Diagram **What are some sources of pollution created by this single home?**

Water management is often a local environmental issue. Growing cities may want to pump more groundwater from an aquifer, while farmers say they need that water for their crops. In dry areas, businesses that use large amounts of water, such as golf courses or fish farms, may draw criticism. What are the water management issues in your community?

Water Pollution Even where water is plentiful, it may not be clean enough to use. Polluted water can carry disease-causing bacteria or substances that harm people and animals.

Water pollution has many causes. Agriculture and industry are two main ones. When farmers use too many chemical fertilizers and pesticides, these chemicals ooze into local streams. Industrial waste may drain poisons or metals into the water supply. Heavy rain can wash motor oil from parking lots into groundwater. In addition, some poor communities don't have quality sewer systems for household wastes. Although most countries try to keep their water clean, sometimes the cost of doing so is higher than they can afford.

Pollution may spread far from its source. Rivers carry chemicals from distant factories to the oceans. There, pollution can sicken or kill fish and shellfish. People who eat these foods from polluted waters can get sick.

✔ **READING CHECK:** (*Environment and Society*) What are some causes of water pollution?

The Air We Breathe

Like water, air is necessary for survival. Just as human activities can pollute our water, they can also pollute our air.

Air Pollution Air pollution comes from several sources. Burning fuels for heating and running factories releases chemicals into the air. A major cause of air pollution is exhaust from the hundreds of millions of motor vehicles on the planet. Particularly in big cities, all these chemicals build up in the air. They create a mixture called smog.

Some cities have special problems with smog. Denver, Los Angeles, and Mexico City, for example, lie in bowl-shaped valleys that trap air pollution. On some days, the air in these cities gets so thick with smog that officials urge residents to stay indoors to protect their health.

When air pollution combines with moisture in the air, it can form an acid similar in strength to vinegar. When it falls to the ground, this liquid is called **acid rain**. It can damage or kill trees. Acid rain can even kill fish.

Many countries have laws to limit pollution. However, pollution is an international problem. Winds can blow polluted air away, but just to another place. Pollution can easily blow from one country to another. It can even pass across continents. As a result, countries that keep their own air clean can still suffer from other countries' pollution.

Pollution and Climate Change Smog and acid rain are short-term effects of air pollution. Air pollution may also have long-term effects by changing Earth's atmosphere. Certain kinds of pollution damage the **ozone layer** in the upper atmosphere. This ozone layer protects living things by absorbing harmful ultraviolet light from the Sun. Damage to Earth's ozone layer may cause human health problems such as skin cancer.

Another issue of growing concern is **global warming**—a slow increase in Earth's average temperature. The Sun constantly warms Earth's surface. The gases and water vapor in the atmosphere trap some of the heat. This process helps keep Earth warm. Without the atmosphere, heat would escape into space, and we would freeze. The process is called the **greenhouse effect**. In a greenhouse the Sun's heat passes through the glass roof but is then trapped inside. Evidence suggests that pollution causes the atmosphere to trap more heat. As a result, Earth would get warmer.

Heavy smog clouds the Los Angeles skyline. **Interpreting the Visual Record** *Human-Environment Interaction* **What problems do you think smog would create in everyday life?**

The Greenhouse Effect

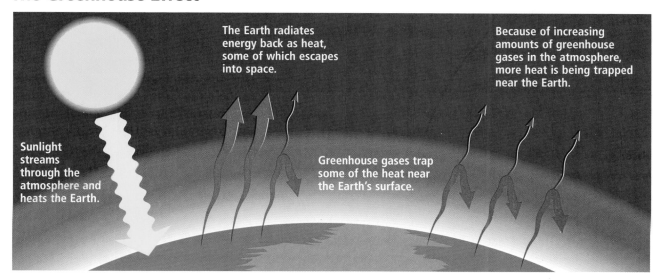

Sunlight streams through the atmosphere and heats the Earth.

The Earth radiates energy back as heat, some of which escapes into space.

Greenhouse gases trap some of the heat near the Earth's surface.

Because of increasing amounts of greenhouse gases in the atmosphere, more heat is being trapped near the Earth.

Scientists agree that Earth's climate has warmed during the last century. Not all agree, however, on the explanation. Most scientists say that air pollution caused by people has made temperatures rise. Burning fuels such as oil and coal is listed as the main culprit. Other scientists think warmer temperatures have resulted from natural causes. There is also disagreement about what has caused the thinning of the ozone layer.

✓ **READING CHECK:** *Environment and Society* How may air pollution affect Earth's climate?

 The Earth's atmosphere acts like the glass in a greenhouse. Sunlight passes through the atmosphere and heats the Earth. As heat radiates up from the Earth, some heat escapes into space. The rest of the heat is trapped by gases in the atmosphere.

Interpreting the Diagram **What is one result of an increase in greenhouse gases in the atmosphere?**

Define and explain: tributary, groundwater, aquifers, water cycle, evaporation, water vapor, condensation, precipitation, acid rain, ozone layer, global warming, greenhouse effect

Reading for the Main Idea

1. *Environment and Society* What are some hazards that water can create?

2. *Environment and Society* What are the main causes of air pollution?

go.hrw.com **Homework Practice Online** Keyword: SG5 HP2

Critical Thinking

3. Analyzing Information Why would protecting groundwater from pollution be important?

4. Making Generalizations and Predictions What may happen if air pollution continues to increase?

Organizing What You Know

5. Sequencing Copy the following graphic organizer. Use it to describe the steps in the water cycle.

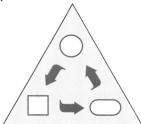

Climate, Weather, and Vegetation

Read to Discover

1. What factors create climate and weather?
2. How are climate, plants, and animal life related?

Vocabulary

weather
climate
prevailing winds

currents
rain shadow

Reading Strategy

FOLDNOTES: TRI-FOLD Create a **Tri-Fold** FoldNote as described in the Appendix. Label the columns "Know," "Want," and "Learn." Use the main ideas to write down what you know about weather and climate. Then write down what you want to know. After you study the section, write down what you learned.

Wildlife eat the summer vegetation in the Alaskan tundra.
Interpreting the Visual Record Why is there snow on the mountain peaks during summer?

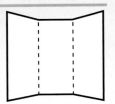

Factors Affecting Climate and Weather

Weather is the condition of the atmosphere at a certain time and place. **Climate** refers to the weather conditions in an area over a long period of time. Weather and climate then help determine what kind of plants grow in a certain place.

Several factors determine a region's climate. Some of the forces that affect whether it will be sunny or rainy today are related to what is happening on the other side of the planet. Other forces are local.

The Sun Solar heat, or heat from the Sun, makes life possible on Earth. It also affects our weather and climate. The Sun doesn't heat Earth evenly, however. Because Earth is a sphere, areas closest to the North Pole and the South Pole don't receive direct rays from the Sun. Also, because Earth is tilted on its axis, areas away from the Sun receive less heat. Regions closer to the equator receive more heat. Therefore, the higher a place's latitude, the less solar heat it gets and the colder its climate.

Each year is divided into periods of time called seasons. Each season is known for a certain type of weather, based on temperature and amount of precipitation. Winter, spring, summer, and fall are examples of seasons that are described by their average temperature. "Wet" and "dry" seasons are described by their precipitation. The seasons change as Earth orbits the Sun. As this happens, the amount of solar energy received in any given location changes.

Winds Solar heat doesn't stay in one place. It moves around the planet. Otherwise, some places would be much hotter and others much colder than they are now. Winds, created by changes in air pressure, move the heat.

You may think of air as weightless, but it isn't. Cold air weighs more than warm air. When air warms, it gets lighter and rises. Colder air then moves in to replace the rising air. Wind is the result of this process.

Winds blow in great streams of air around the planet. Winds that blow in the same direction over large areas of Earth are called **prevailing winds**. These winds then make a region warmer or colder, drier or wetter, depending on from where they blow.

Some regions on Earth, particularly in the tropics, have seasons tied to precipitation rather than temperature. Shifting wind patterns are one cause of seasonal change. For example, in January winds from the north bring dry air to India. By June the winds have shifted, coming from the southwest and bringing moisture from the Indian Ocean.

As Earth revolves around the Sun, the tilt of the poles toward and away from the Sun causes the seasons to change. The day when the Sun's vertical rays are farthest from the equator is called a solstice. Solstices occur twice a year—about June 21 and about December 22. The days when the Sun's rays strike the equator directly are called equinoxes. These days mark the beginning of spring and fall.

Interpreting the Diagram At what point is the North Pole tilted toward the Sun?

The Seasons

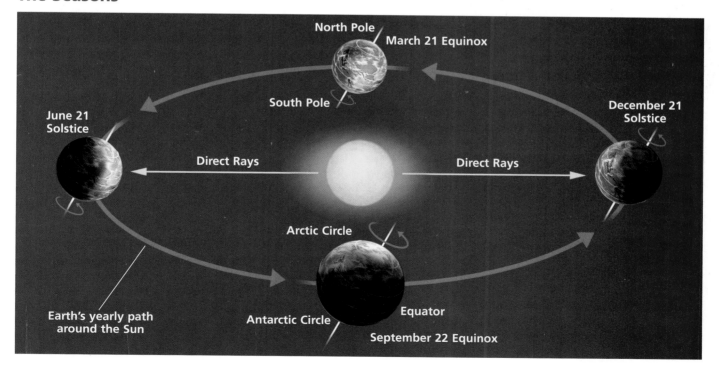

North Pole
March 21 Equinox
South Pole
June 21 Solstice
December 21 Solstice
Direct Rays
Direct Rays
Arctic Circle
Earth's yearly path around the Sun
Antarctic Circle
Equator
September 22 Equinox

This infrared satellite image shows the Gulf Stream moving warm water from lower latitudes to higher latitudes. The dark red shape alongside Florida's east coast is the Gulf Stream.

Oceans and Currents Winds move ocean water in the same general directions as the air above it moves. Warm ocean water from near the equator moves in giant streams, or **currents**, to colder areas. Cold water flows from the polar regions to the tropics. So, just as wind moves heat between places, so do ocean currents.

The Gulf Stream is an important ocean current. It moves warm water north from the Gulf of Mexico to the east coast of the United States. It then moves across the Atlantic Ocean toward Europe. The warm air that moves with it keeps winters mild. As a result, much of western Europe has warmer winters than areas in Canada that are just as far north.

Distance from the ocean also affects a region's climate. Water heats and cools more slowly than land. Therefore, coastal areas don't have the wide differences in temperature that areas in the middle of continents have. For example, Kansas City has colder winters and hotter summers than San Francisco. The cities are at about the same latitude, but Kansas City is in the continent's interior. In contrast, San Francisco lies on the Pacific Ocean.

Weather maps show atmospheric conditions as they currently exist or as they are forecast for a particular time period. Most weather maps have legends that explain what the symbols on the map mean. This map shows a cold front sweeping through the central United States. A low-pressure system is at the center of a storm bringing rain and snow to the Midwest. Notice that temperatures behind the cold front are considerably cooler than those ahead of the front.

You Be the Geographer According to this map, what region is experiencing the highest temperatures?

Reading a Weather Map

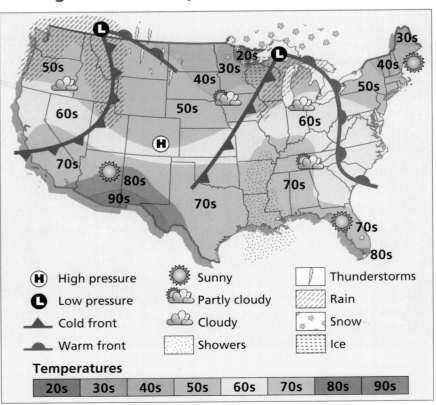

(H) High pressure	☼ Sunny	Thunderstorms
(L) Low pressure	Partly cloudy	Rain
Cold front	Cloudy	Snow
Warm front	Showers	Ice

Temperatures

| 20s | 30s | 40s | 50s | 60s | 70s | 80s | 90s |

Landforms and Precipitation

Windward (wet)

Leeward (dry)

Snow

Warming
dry air

Rain

Cooling
moist air

Rain
Shadow

Ocean

Inland

Moist air from the ocean cools as it moves up the windward side of a mountain. The water vapor in the air condenses and falls in the form of rain or snow. The drier air then moves down the leeward side of a mountain. This drier air brings very little precipitation to areas in the rain shadow.

Pictured in the bottom photo are mountains in the western part of the Sierra Nevada in Sequoia National Park. The top photo shows part of the eastern slope of the same range near Bishop, California.

(Place) **How does the vegetation of these places differ? What causes the difference?**

Elevation and Mountain Effects

Have you seen photos of Kilimanjaro, a mountain in East Africa? The mountain has snow on it all year although it is only about 250 miles from the equator. How can this be?

An increase in elevation—height on Earth's surface above sea level—causes a drop in temperature. This happens because the air is less dense at higher elevations. Thus the base of a mountain may be hot while the top is covered with ice.

Elevation has another effect on weather and climate. Warm, moist air blowing against a mountainside will rise. As it rises, it cools and forms clouds. Precipitation falls from the clouds. The side of the mountain facing the wind often gets heavy rain. By the time the air reaches the other side of the mountain it has lost most of its moisture. This can create a dry area called a **rain shadow**. Compare some of the physical maps and climate maps in the unit atlases to find examples of this effect.

✓ **READING CHECK:** (*Physical Systems*)
What are the main factors affecting climate and weather?

Climate Regions, Plants, and Animals

The chart below describes the 12 main climate types in terms of weather. Climate affects what kind of plants, or vegetation, can grow in a certain area. For example, if your region has a tundra climate, you won't be able to grow palm trees in your yard. Palm trees need a much warmer climate.

In turn, vegetation helps determine what animals are present. If you live in a desert, you won't see tree-dwelling monkeys, except in a zoo! What plants and animals live in your area?

World Climate, Plant, and Animal Regions

Climate	Major Weather Patterns	Vegetation	Animals You May See in the Climate Region (Animals Vary by Region.)
HUMID TROPICAL	warm and rainy all year	rain forest	bats, tree frogs, monkeys, jaguars, tigers, snakes, parrots
TROPICAL SAVANNA	warm all year, with rainy and dry seasons	grassland with scattered trees	anacondas, lions, elephants, gazelles, ostriches, hyenas rhinoceroses, zebras
DESERT	dry and sunny	a few hardy plants such as cacti	lizards, scorpions, snakes, bats, bobcats, coyotes
STEPPE	semiarid, hot summers with cooler winters	grassland and a few trees	antelope, wild horses, kangaroos, coyotes, camels
MEDITERRANEAN	dry, sunny, warm winters and mild, wetter winters	scrub woodland and grassland	deer, elk, mountain lions, wolves
HUMID SUBTROPICAL	hot, humid summers and mild, humid winters; rain all year	mixed forest	alligators, deer, bears, squirrels, foxes, snakes, many species of birds
MARINE WEST COAST	cloudy, mild summers and cool, rainy winters	evergreen forest	wild boars, deer, bears, seals
HUMID CONTINENTAL	four distinct seasons; long, cold winters and short, warm summers	mixed forest	wolverines, wild boars, deer, badgers, beavers, ducks
SUBARCTIC	long, cold winters and short, warm summers; low	evergreen forest	rabbits, moose, elk, wolves, lynxes, bears
TUNDRA	cold all year, little precipitation	moss, lichens, low shrubs, marshes during the summer	rabbits, reindeer, wolves, foxes
ICE CAP	freezing cold all year	no vegetation	animals that depend on the sea, such as polar bears, seals, and penguins
HIGHLAND	wide range of temperatures and precipitation amounts, depending on elevation	forest to tundra vegetation, depending on location and elevation	wide range of animals, depending on location, elevation, and vegetation

World Climate Regions

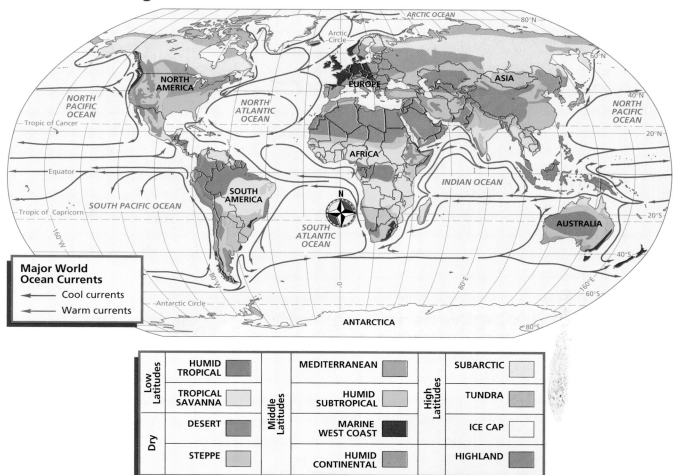

go.hrw.com
Homework Practice Online
Keyword: SG5 HP2

Define and explain: weather, climate, prevailing winds, currents, rain shadow

Reading for the Main Idea

1. (*Physical Systems*) How does the Sun's heat affect temperature and winds?

2. (*Physical Systems*) What effect does the Gulf Stream have on Europe's climates?

Critical Thinking

3. Drawing Inferences From looking at the map, why do you think central Asia is very cold in winter and often hot in the summer?

4. Finding the Main Idea Why may a mountaintop and a nearby valley have wide differences in temperature?

Organizing What You Know

5. Summarizing Copy the following graphic organizer. Use it to summarize the 12 climate types.

Climate	Weather	Vegetation	Animals

Read to Discover

1. What are the most important renewable resources?
2. How do the main energy resources differ?
3. How do we use mineral resources?
4. How do resources affect people?

Vocabulary

renewable resources
nonrenewable resources
deforestation
reforestation
fossil fuels

petroleum
hydroelectric power
geothermal energy
solar power

Reading Strategy

TAKING NOTES As you read this section, list the natural resources mentioned in the text. Beside each resource, write R if the resource is renewable and N if the resource is nonrenewable.

▲
A row of poplar trees divides farmland near Aix-en-Provence, France.

(*Human-Environment Interaction*) **What effect will these trees have on erosion?**

Using Renewable Resources

The landforms, water, climate, and weather of a place all affect the people who live there. Another factor that affects daily life is the resources available to them. A resource is any material that is part of Earth and that people need and value.

Some of Earth's resources are renewable, while others are nonrenewable. **Renewable resources**, such as soil and forests, are those that natural processes continuously replace. **Nonrenewable resources** are those that can't be replaced naturally after they have been used. Once they've been used, they're gone forever!

You read in Section 1 about the need to preserve soil, since it is essential to survival. Soil qualifies as a renewable resource because natural processes create more of it. For example, when a tree dies and falls to the forest floor, the tree decays and adds valuable nutrients to the soil. Bacteria and other organisms break down the wood and turn it into humus. However, these processes are very slow. Soil that required hundreds of years to build up can be washed away in a few seconds.

Forests Forests are renewable resources because we can plant new trees. People use trees for many products. Wood products include lumber for buildings and furniture. Plastics and some fabrics use wood in the manufacturing process. Cooking oils, medicines, nuts, and rubber are among the many products that trees supply. In addition, trees and other plants release oxygen into the atmosphere. We enjoy forests for hiking and camping. Wildlife depends on forests for food and shelter.

Like soil, forests can be destroyed much faster than they can grow. In some places, forests are not being replaced as quickly as they are cut down. This loss of forest areas is called **deforestation**. People can reverse the trend by planting new trees. This practice, called **reforestation**, is important for both people and wildlife.

Resources and Land Management The preservation of renewable resources is often part of larger land management issues. For example, suburbs spring up on what was valuable farmland. Fertile soil there can no longer grow food. Or, a developer may want to build a shopping mall in a forested area. Residents may prefer to preserve the trees within a park. These and similar local environmental issues are debated across the United States as towns and cities grow.

✔ **READING CHECK:** *Environment and Society* How can people help preserve forest resources?

▲
Human-Environment Interaction
Villagers work on a reforestation project in Cameroon.

Human-Environment Interaction
Development at the edge of Danville, California, is replacing farmland and rangeland.
▼

Human-Environment Interaction Deep underground, a miner digs coal in a narrow tunnel.

Wind turbines are just one source of electricity. Interpreting the Visual Record Human-Environment Interaction How does this photo show human adaptation to the environment?

Energy Resources

Most of the energy we use comes from the three **fossil fuels**: coal, petroleum, and natural gas. Fossil fuels were formed from the remains of ancient plants and animals. These remains gradually decayed and were covered with sediment. Over long periods of time, pressure and heat changed these materials. They became completely different solids, liquids, or gases. All fossil fuels are nonrenewable resources.

For thousands of years, people have burned coal for heat. Burning coal pollutes the air, however. Modern ways of burning coal produce less pollution, but cost more money. **Petroleum** may be the fossil fuel with which you are most familiar. When it is first pumped out of the ground, petroleum is a dark oily liquid called crude oil. It is then processed into gasoline, diesel and jet fuels, and heating oil. Burning these fuels also creates air pollution. The cleanest-burning fossil fuel is natural gas, which is usually found near petroleum deposits.

Renewable Energy Resources Energy sources besides fossil fuels exist. Their big advantage is they are cleaner, in general. Renewable energy sources aren't available everywhere, however. They may also cost more money. Some of these energy sources have other drawbacks too.

Water pours through Owen Falls Dam in Uganda. More than 99 percent of Uganda's electricity comes from hydroelectric power.
Interpreting the Visual Record **What body of water is used to produce hydroelectric power?**

France has 59 nuclear reactors like this one and depends on nuclear power for about 77 percent of its energy.

Clean Energy Sources The most commonly used renewable energy source is **hydroelectric power** — the production of electricity by waterpower. Dams harness the energy of falling water from rivers to run generators that produce electricity. Although hydroelectric power doesn't pollute the air, it does affect the environment. The lakes that form when dams block rivers may drown farmland and forests. Fish and wildlife habitats are also affected.

Wind has powered sailing ships and windmills for centuries. Now wind has a new use. It can create electricity by turning a system of fan blades called a turbine. "Wind farms" with hundreds of wind turbines have been built in windy places. The heat of Earth's interior — **geothermal energy** — is another clean source of power. People can use the energy directly to heat water, or they can generate electricity with it. **Solar power** — heat and light from the Sun — can heat water or homes. Special solar panels also absorb solar energy to make electricity.

Nuclear Power The last major renewable energy resource is nuclear power. Although operating a nuclear power plant doesn't release pollution into the air, it does produce waste materials that will be deadly for many centuries. Management of these wastes is a serious problem. In addition, some nuclear power plants have had serious accidents. A nuclear accident in Chernobyl in Ukraine killed people, caused cancer in survivors, and poisoned farmland.

✔ **READING CHECK:** (*Environment and Society*) What are the main advantages of using renewable energy sources?

Mineral Resources

Energy resources are not the only nonrenewable resources that come out of the ground. We also use solid substances called minerals. Examples include metals, rocks, and salt.

Minerals fulfill many needs. Look around you to see just a few of the ways we use minerals. Your school is probably built on steel girders made from iron. The outside walls may be granite, limestone, or other types of rock. Window glass is made from quartz, a mineral found in sand. The "lead" in your pencil is actually graphite, another mineral. Metals are everywhere—from the staples through your homework papers to the coins in your wallet and the watch on your wrist.

Because they are nonrenewable, we need to conserve mineral resources. Recycling common items, such as aluminum cans, will make the supply of these resources last longer. It also reduces the amount of energy that factories use to convert metal into useful objects.

✓ **READING CHECK:** *Environment and Society* How can people conserve mineral resources?

Stretching from north to south across Alaska, a pipeline carries oil to the port of Sitka. **Interpreting the Visual Record** *Human-Environment Interaction* **Why do you think the pipeline is above ground?**

Resources and People

Why does it matter what resources an area has, or how much it has of a resource? Actually, resources affect culture, history, and current events.

Resources and Wealth As you read this book, you will find that some places are rich in resources of many kinds. For example, the United States has fertile soil, forests, oil, metals, and many other resources. These riches have allowed our country to develop its economy. Our resources provide raw materials for various industries, from building houses to making cars. We also grow huge amounts of food. Partly because the United States has such a powerful economy, we also have great power in world affairs.

In contrast, some other countries are poor in resources. There, few industries grow, and people don't have many choices about how to earn a living. Some countries

have large amounts of some resources but not of others. For example, Saudi Arabia is rich in oil but lacks water for growing food. Saudi Arabia pays other countries for food with the profit it earns on oil.

Resources and Daily Life The resources available to people affect how they live. In this country we have many resources. We can choose among many different ways to dress, build our homes, eat, travel, and entertain ourselves. People of other cultures may have fewer choices because they have fewer resources. Or, their environments may offer resources that we don't use.

Consider people who live in a rain forest, far from any city or factory. These people depend on the resources in their environment for all their needs. They may craft containers by weaving plant fibers together or canoes by hollowing out tree trunks. Their musical instruments are not electric guitars, but perhaps flutes made from bamboo. What kinds of songs would they sing? These forest people would be more likely to sing about finding food than about new cars.

✓ **READING CHECK:**

(*Environment and Society*) How does the lack of resources affect people?

This Brazilian rain forest is being cleared by burning.

(*Human-Environment Interaction*)

How do you think the loss of land affects people who live in the rain forest?

Homework Practice Online

Keyword: SG5 HP2

Section Review 4

Define and explain: renewable resources, nonrenewable resources, deforestation, reforestation, fossil fuels, petroleum, hydroelectric power, geothermal energy, solar power

Reading for the Main Idea

1. (*Environment and Society*) What are fossil fuels, and how are they used?

2. (*Environment and Society*) What are the main renewable energy sources?

Critical Thinking

3. Analyzing Information How are preserving soil and forest resources related to resource and land management?

4. Making Generalizations and Predictions How may a country that has only one or two valuable resources develop its economy?

Organizing What You Know

5. Categorizing Copy the following graphic organizer. Use it to describe the mineral resources that may be used in a typical home.

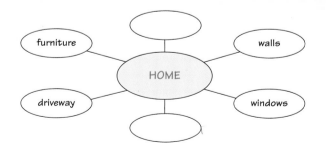

Review and Practice

Define and Identify

Idenfity each of the following:

1. topography
2. plate tectonics
3. erosion
4. tributary
5. water cycle
6. global warming
7. climate
8. rain shadow
9. nonrenewable resources
10. geothermal energy

Review the Main Idea

11. What is the theory of plate tectonics and how does it work?
12. What may occur when tectonic plates move away from each other?
13. How is water involved in erosion?
14. What methods are used to protect soil from erosion?
15. What percentage of Earth's water is freshwater? What covers 70% of Earth's surface?
16. What are the three phases of the water cycle? What drives the water cycle?
17. What are the two main causes of water pollution?
18. Why may one country suffer from another country's air pollution?
19. What parts of the Earth receive the most solar heat? Why?
20. What makes wind?
21. Explain why Kansas City has more extreme seasons than San Francisco.
22. Why may the base of a mountain be hot while the top is covered in ice?
23. Why is it important to preserve renewable resources such as soil and forests?
24. What problems are associated with fossil fuels?
25. What are some examples of renewable energy resources?
26. What are minerals used for?

Think Critically

27. **Drawing Inferences and Conclusions** Why are we developing alternative energy sources?
28. **Finding the Main Idea** How are the Earth's land, water, and atmosphere related?
29. **Understanding Cause and Effect** How may a dam affect a river and its surrounding areas?
30. **Drawing Inferences and Conclusions** How do the laws that govern and restrict pollution both help and hurt people?
31. **Making Generalizations and Predictions** Why is pollution a global concern?

Map Activity

32. Match the letters on the map with their correct labels.

    Humid subtropical
    Steppe climate
    Marine west coast climate
    Mediterranean climate
    Desert
    Humid tropical
    Tropical savanna

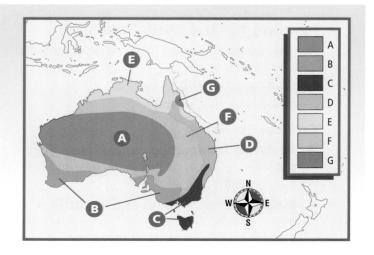

Writing Activity

Imagine you are writing a report about your region of the United States for students around the world. Use your textbook, the library, and the Internet to research the landforms, climate, resources, and history of your region. Then write a few paragraphs highlighting what you discover.

internet connect

Internet Activity: **go.hrw.com**
KEYWORD: **SG5 GT2**

Choose a topic to explore online:
- Learn more about using weather maps.
- Discover facts about Earth's water.
- Investigate earthquakes.

Social Studies Skills Practice

Interpreting Graphs

The United States uses different resources to meet its energy needs. Study the following graph and answer the questions.

Energy Consumption in the United States, 2002

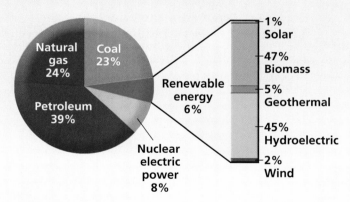

Natural gas 24%
Coal 23%
Petroleum 39%
Renewable energy 6%
Nuclear electric power 8%

- 1% Solar
- 47% Biomass
- 5% Geothermal
- 45% Hydroelectric
- 2% Wind

Source: Energy Information Administration

1. What percentage of the nation's energy consumption is renewable?
2. Which fossil fuel is used the most?
3. Based on what you have learned in this chapter, which renewable resources provide the cleanest energy?
4. Why do you think solar, wind, and geothermal energy are not commonly used resources?

Analyzing Primary Sources

In 1906, San Francisco experienced the most powerful earthquake recorded in the United States. Read the following account of the disaster from Peter Bacigalupi, one of San Francisco's shop owners. Then answer the questions.

"I was awakened from a sound slumber by a terrific trembling, which acted in the same manner as would a bucking broncho . . . My bed was going up and down in all four directions at once, while all about me I heard screams, wails, and crashing of breaking china-ware and nick-nacks. A great portion of plaster right over the head of my bed fell all around me, and caused a cloud of dust, which was very hard to breathe through . . . I started to walk downtown, and arriving within eight blocks of the business section, noted that there were hardly any panes of glass left in any of the show windows . . . Buildings were tumbled over on their sides, others looked as though they had been cut off short with a cleaver."

1. Was there any warning that the earthquake was about to occur?
2. What effect did the earthquake have on Mr. Bacigalupi's house?
3. What did he witness when he walked around the city?
4. How do you think communities can prepare for earthquakes such as this one?

CHAPTER 3

The World's People

The Colosseum,
Rome, Italy

1998 Olympic
opening
ceremony,
Nagano, Japan

Easter Island,
Chile

Section 1 — What Is Culture?

Read to Discover

1. What is culture?
2. Why are cultural symbols important?
3. What influences how cultures develop?
4. How did agriculture affect the development of culture?

Vocabulary

culture
culture region
culture traits
ethnic groups
multicultural
race
acculturation

symbol
ethnocentrism
domestication
subsistence agriculture
commercial agriculture
civilization

Reading Strategy

READING ORGANIZER Before you read, create a chart with columns titled Term, Definition, Example. Write each of the terms above in the left column. As you read write the definition and give an example in the other two columns.

Aspects of Culture

The people of the world's approximately 200 countries speak hundreds of different languages. They may dress in different ways and eat different foods. However, all societies share certain basic institutions, including a government, an educational system, an economic system, and religious institutions. These vary from society to society and are often based on that society's **culture**. Culture is a learned system of shared beliefs and ways of doing things that guides a person's daily behavior. Most people around the world have a national culture shared with people of their own country. They may also have religious practices, beliefs, and language in common with people from other countries. Sometimes a culture dominates a particular region. This is known as a **culture region**. In a culture region, people may share certain **culture traits**, or elements of culture, such as dress, food, or religious beliefs. West Africa is an example of a culture region. Culture can also be based on a person's job or age. People can belong to more than one culture and can choose which to emphasize.

Race and Ethnic Groups Cultural groups share beliefs and practices learned from parents, grandparents, and ancestors. These groups are sometimes called **ethnic groups**. An ethnic group's shared culture may include its religion, history, language, holiday traditions, and special foods.

When people from different cultures live in the same country, the country is described as **multicultural** or multiethnic. Many countries

Dance is an example of a culture trait. Dancers from central Texas perform a traditional Czech dance.

▼

World Religions

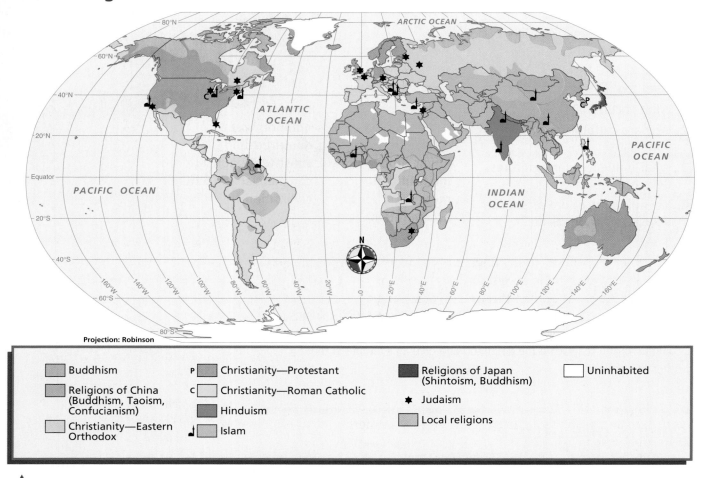

Map Legend:
- Buddhism
- Religions of China (Buddhism, Taoism, Confucianism)
- Christianity—Eastern Orthodox
- P — Christianity—Protestant
- C — Christianity—Roman Catholic
- Hinduism
- Islam
- Religions of Japan (Shintoism, Buddhism)
- ★ Judaism
- Local religions
- Uninhabited

Projection: Robinson

▲

Religion is one aspect of culture.

A disc jockey plays Cuban music for the large Cuban ethnic group of Miami, Florida.

▼

are multicultural. In some countries, such as Belgium, different ethnic groups have cooperated to form a united country. In other cases, such as in French-speaking Quebec, Canada, ethnic groups have frequently been in conflict. Sometimes, people from one ethnic group are spread over two or more countries. For example, Germans live in different European countries: Germany, Austria, and the Czech Republic. The Kurds, who are a people with no country of their own, live mostly in Syria, Iran, Iraq, and Turkey.

Race is based on inherited physical or biological traits. It is sometimes confused with ethnic group. For example, the Hispanic ethnic group in the United States includes people who look quite different from each other. However, they share a common Spanish or Latin American heritage. As you know, people vary in physical appearance. Some of these differences have developed in response to climate factors like cold and sunlight. Because people have moved from region to region throughout history, these differences are not clear-cut. Each culture defines race in its own way, emphasizing particular biological and ethnic characteristics. An example can be seen in Rwanda, a country in East Africa. In this country, the Hutu and the Tutsi have carried on a bitter civil war. Although both are East African, each one considers itself different from the other. Their definition of race involves height and facial features. Around the world, people tend to identify races based on obvious physical traits. However, these definitions of race are based primarily on attitudes, not actual biological differences.

Cultural Change Cultures change over time. Humans invent new ways of doing things and spread these new ways to others. The spread of one culture's ways or beliefs to another culture is called diffusion. Diffusion may occur when people move from one place to another. The English language was once confined to England and parts of Scotland. It is now one of the world's most widely spoken languages. English originally spread because people from England founded colonies in other regions. More recently, as communication among cultures has increased, English has spread through English-language films and television programs. English has also become an international language of science and technology.

People sometimes may borrow aspects of another culture as the result of long-term contact with another society. This process is called **acculturation**. For example, people in one culture may adopt the religion of another. As a result, they might change other cultural practices to conform to the new religion. For example, farmers who become Muslim may quit raising pigs because Islam forbids eating pork.

✓ **READING CHECK:** (*Human Systems*) What is the definition of culture?

Cultural Differences

A **symbol** is a sign that stands for something else. A symbol can be many things such as a word, a shape, a color, or a flag. People learn symbols from their culture. The sets of sounds of a language are symbols. These symbols have meaning for the people who speak that language. The same sound may mean something different to people who speak another language. The word bad means "evil" in English, "cool" to teenagers, and "bath" in German.

If you traveled to another country, you might notice immediately that people behave differently. Some people, however, may see the differences in other cultures as inferior to their own. This view is called **ethnocentrism**. Many people may even have an ethnocentric view toward the foods some cultures eat. For example, they may think it is disgusting that the Inuit of Canada eat whale blubber. To the Inuit, however, eating blubber is perfectly normal.

✓ **READING CHECK:** (*Human Systems*) How do symbols reflect differences among societies and cultures?

▲
(*Movement*) Some immigrants from China settle in New York City's Chinatown.

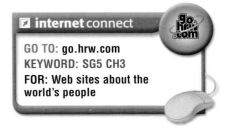

GO TO: go.hrw.com
KEYWORD: SG5 CH3
FOR: Web sites about the world's people

Fans cheer for the U.S. Olympic soccer team.

Interpreting the Visual Record Why do you think symbols such as flags create strong emotions?

▼

Development of a Culture

All people have the same basic needs for food, water, clothing, and shelter. People everywhere live in families and mark important family changes together. They usually have rituals or traditions that go with the birth of a baby, the wedding of a couple, or the death of a grandparent. All human societies need to deal with natural disasters. They must also deal with people who break the rules of behavior. However, people in different places meet these needs in unique ways. They eat different foods, build different kinds of houses, and form families in different ways. They have different rules of behavior. Two important factors that influence the way people meet basic needs are their history and environment.

History Culture is shaped by history. A region's people may have been conquered by the same outsiders. They may have adopted the same religion. They may have come from the same area and may share a common language. However, historical events may have affected some parts of a region but not others. For example, in North America French colonists brought their culture to Louisiana and Canada. However, they did not have a major influence on the Middle Atlantic region of the United States.

Cultures also shape history by influencing the way people respond to the same historical forces. Nigeria, India, and Australia were all colonized by the British. Today each nation still uses elements of the British legal system, but with important differences.

Environment The environment of a region can influence the development of culture. For example, in Egypt the Nile River is central to people's lives. The ancient Egyptians saw the fertile soils brought by the flooding of the Nile as the work of the gods. Beliefs in mountain spirits were important in many mountainous regions of the world. These areas include Tibet, Japan, and the Andes of South America.

A couple prepares for a wedding ceremony in Kazakhstan.

The layout of Marrakech, Morocco, is typical of many North African cities.

Interpreting the Visual Record _Place_

How are the streets and houses of Marrakech different from those in your community?

Culture also determines how people use and shape their landscape. For example, city plans are cultural. Cities in Spain and its former colonies are organized around a central plaza, or square, with a church and a courthouse. On the other hand, Chinese cities are oriented to the four compass points. American cities often follow a rectangular grid plan. Many French city streets radiate out from a central core.

✔ **READING CHECK:** (*Human Systems*) What are some ways in which culture traits spread?

Development of Agriculture

For most of human history people ate only wild plants and animals. When the food ran out in one place, they migrated, or moved to another place. Very few people still live this way today. Thousands of years ago, humans began to help their favorite wild plant foods to grow. They probably cleared the land around their campsites and dumped seeds or fruits in piles of refuse. Plants took root and grew. People may also have dug water holes to encourage wild cattle to come and drink. People began cultivating the largest plants and breeding the tamest animals. Gradually, the wild plants and animals changed. They became dependent on people. This process is called **domestication**. A domesticated species has changed its form and behavior so much that it depends on people to survive. Domestic sheep can no longer leap from rock to rock like their wild ancestors. However, the wool of domestic sheep is more useful to humans. It can be combed and twisted into yarn.

This ancient Egyptian wall painting shows domesticated cattle.
Interpreting the Visual Record Can you name other kinds of domesticated animals?

Domestication happened in many parts of the world. In Peru llamas and potatoes were domesticated. People in ancient Mexico and Central America domesticated corn, beans, squash, tomatoes, and hot peppers. None of these foods was grown in Europe, Asia, or Africa before the time of Christopher Columbus's voyages to the Americas. Meanwhile, Africans had domesticated sorghum and a kind of rice. Cattle, sheep, and goats were probably first raised in Southwest Asia. Wheat and rye were first domesticated in Central Asia. The horse was also domesticated there. These domesticated plants and animals were unknown in the Americas before the time of Columbus.

Our Amazing Planet

Thousands of years ago, domesticated dogs came with humans across the Bering Strait into North America. A breed called the Carolina dog may be descended almost unchanged from those dogs. The reddish yellow, short-haired breed also appears to be closely related to Australian dingoes.

Agriculture and Environment Agriculture changed the landscape. To make room for growing food, people cut down forests. They also built fences, dug irrigation canals, and terraced hillsides. Governments were created to direct the labor needed for these large projects. Governments also defended against outsiders and helped people resolve problems. People could now grow enough food for a whole year. Therefore, they stopped migrating and built permanent settlements.

Types of Agriculture Some farmers grow just enough food to provide for themselves and their own families. This type of farming is called **subsistence agriculture**. In the wealthier countries of the world, a small number of farmers can produce food for everyone. Each farm is large and may grow only one product. This type of farming is called **commercial agriculture**. In this system companies rather than individuals or families may own the farms.

Agriculture and Civilization Agriculture enabled farmers to produce a surplus of food—more than they could eat themselves. A few people could make things like pottery jars instead of farming. They traded or sold their products for food. With more food a family could feed more children. As a result, populations began to grow. More people became involved in trading and manufacturing. Traders and craftspeople began to live in central market towns. Some towns grew into cities, where many people lived and carried out even more specialized tasks. For example, cities often supported priests and religious officials. They were responsible for organizing and carrying out religious ceremonies. When a culture becomes highly complex, we sometimes call it a **civilization**.

✓ **READING CHECK:** (*Environment and Society*) In what ways did agriculture affect culture?

Go.hrw.com Homework Practice Online
Keyword: SG5 HP3

Section Review 1

Define and explain: culture, culture region, culture trait, ethnic groups, multicultural, race, acculturation, symbol, ethnocentrism, domestication, subsistence agriculture, commercial agriculture, civilization

Reading for the Main Idea

1. (*Human Systems*) How can an individual belong to more than one cultural group?

2. (*Human Systems*) What institutions are basic to all societies?

Critical Thinking

3. Drawing Inferences and Conclusions In what ways do history and environment influence or shape a culture? What examples can you find in the text that explain this relationship?

4. Analyzing Information What is the relationship between the development of agriculture and culture?

Organizing What You Know

5. Summarizing Copy the following graphic organizer. Use it to describe culture by listing shared beliefs and practices.

Culture

Section 2 Economics and Population

Read to Discover

1. What is economics?
2. How are industrialized countries different from developing countries?
3. What are the different types of economic systems?
4. Where do most people on Earth live?

Vocabulary

gross national product
gross domestic product
industrialized countries
literacy rate
developing countries
third-world countries
free enterprise
market economy
command economy
tradition-based economy
mixed economy
one-crop economy
exports
imports
interdependence
birthrate
death rate
population density
overpopulation
migration
emigrant
immigrant

Reading Strategy

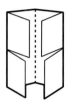

FOLDNOTES: FOUR-CORNER FOLD Create a **Four-Corner Fold** described in the Appendix. Title the flaps The Economy, Developed and Undeveloped Countries, Types of Economies, and Population. As you read, write what you learn about each topic beneath its flap.

The Economy

All of the activities that people do to earn a living are part of a system called the economy. This includes people going to work, making things, selling things, buying things, and trading services. Economics is the study of the production, distribution, and use of goods and services.

Economic Indicators A common means of measuring a country's economy is the **gross national product** (GNP). The GNP is the value of all goods and services that a country produces in one year. It includes goods and services made by factories owned by that country's citizens but located in foreign countries. Most economists use **gross domestic product** (GDP) instead of GNP. GDP includes only those goods and services produced within a country. GDP divided by the country's population is called per capita GDP. This figure shows individual purchasing power and is useful for comparing levels of economic development.

Economic Activities Economists divide economic activities into four industries—primary, secondary, tertiary, and quaternary (see chart on the next page). A country's economy is usually based on one or more of these activities.

Shoppers crowd a street in Tokyo, Japan.

Economic Activities

ECONOMIC INDUSTRIES	DESCRIPTION	TYPES OF ACTIVITIES	EXAMPLE	
Primary industry	Involves natural resources or raw materials	Farming, fishing, mining, forestry	Dairy farmer feeds his cows.	
Secondary industry	Makes finished products using natural resources or raw materials	Manufacturing and construction	Factories make cheese.	
Tertiary industry	Handles goods that are ready for sale	Trucking, restaurants, grocery stores	Grocery stores sell cheese.	
Quaternary industry	Collects information	Research and management	A technician inspects dairy products in a lab.	

▲

Interpreting the Chart Which economic industry involves selling goods?

A monorail in Sydney, Australia takes passengers throughout the city's central business district.
Interpreting the Visual Record (*Place*)
What in this photo suggests that this is a city in an industrialized country?

▼

Australia
Sydney

The World's Rich and Poor

Economists divide the countries of the world into two groups. They use various measures including GNP, GDP, per capita GDP, life expectancy, and literacy to determine a country's stage of development. Developed countries like the United States, Canada, Japan, and most European countries are the world's wealthiest. They are called **industrialized countries**.

Industrialization occurs when a country relies more on manufacturing and less on agriculture. In industrialized countries, many people work in manufacturing, service, and information industries. These countries have strong secondary, tertiary, and quaternary industries. They have good health care systems. Industrialized countries also have good systems of education. The **literacy rate**, or the percentage of people, who can read and write is high.

Most people in industrialized countries live in cities and have access to telecommunications systems—systems that allow long-distance communication. The level of technology in most countries is usually measured by how many telephones, televisions, or computers are in use.

Developing countries make up the second group. They are in different stages of moving toward development. About two thirds of the world's people live in developing countries. These countries are poor. People often work in farming or other primary industries earning low wages. Cities in developing countries are often very crowded. Many people move to cities to find work. Most people are not educated. They usually have little access to health care or telecommunications.

Some developing countries have made economic progress in recent decades. South Korea and Mexico are good examples. These countries are experiencing strong growth in manufacturing and trade. However, some of the world's poorest countries are developing slowly or not at all.

This photo shows daily life in a village in eastern Afghanistan.
Interpreting the Visual Record _Place_
What in this photo suggests that this village is in a developing country?

One Planet, Four Worlds Some people also refer to developing countries as **third-world countries**. These countries lack the economic opportunities of most industrialized countries. Some industrialized countries are called first-world and second-world countires. First-world countries include the United States, Canada, Western Europe, Japan and Australia. Second-world countries include Russia, the former Soviet republics, China, and Eastern Europe.

Third-world countries in Latin America, however, experience some economic growth. Countries like Haiti, however, show no economic growth. They are known as fourth-world countries.

✓ **READING CHECK:** What are some of the differences between industrialized and developing countries?

Interpreting the Chart **Which countries have the highest literacy rates?**

Comparing Developed and Developing Countries

COUNTRY	POPULATION	POPULATION GROWTH RATE	PER CAPITA GDP	LIFE EXPECTANCY	LITERACY RATE	TELEPHONE LINES
United States	290.3 million	0.9%	$ 37,600	77	97%	194 million
France	60.1 million	0.4%	$ 26,000	79	99%	35 million
South Korea	48.2 million	0.7%	$ 19,600	75	98%	24 million
Mexico	104.9 million	1.4%	$ 8,900	72	92%	9.6 million
Poland	38.6 million	0.0%	$ 9,700	73	99%	8 million
Brazil	182.1 million	1.1%	$ 7,600	71	86%	17 million
Egypt	74.7 million	1.8%	$ 4,000	70	57%	3.9 million
Myanmar	42 million	0.5%	$ 1,700	55	83%	250,000
Mali	11.6 million	2.8%	$ 900	45	46%	23,000

Source: Central Intelligence Agency, _The World Factbook 2003_

Making a Living

Countries organize their economies in different ways. Most developed countries have an economic system called **free enterprise**. This system is organized around the production and distribution of goods and services. The United States operates under a free enterprise system. There are many benefits of this system. Companies are free to make whatever goods they wish. Employees can seek the highest wages for their work. People, rather than the government, control the factors of production. Factors of production are the things that determine what goods are produced in an economy. They include the natural resources that are available for making goods for sale. They also include the capital, or money, needed to pay for production and the labor needed to manufacture goods. The work of entrepreneurs is another factor of production. Entrepreneurs are people who start businesses in a free enterprise system.

Business owners in a free enterprise system sell their goods in a **market economy**. In such an economy, business owners and customers make decisions about what to make, sell, and buy. In contrast, the governments of some countries control the factors of production. The government decides what, and how much, will be produced. It also sets the prices of goods to be sold. This is called a **command economy**.

Some countries with a command economy are communist. Communism is a political system where the government owns almost all the factors of production. Only five countries in the world are communist today—China, Cuba, Laos, North Korea, and Vietnam.

The third type of economy is called a **tradition-based economy**. This type of economy is based on customs and tradition. Economic activities are based on laws, rituals, religious beliefs, or habits developed by the society long ago. The Mbuti people of the Democratic Republic of the Congo practice a tradition-based economy.

Large shopping malls, such as this one in New York City's Trump Tower, are common in countries that have market economies and a free enterprise system. Shoppers here can find a wide range of stores and goods concentrated in one area.

Another economic system is called a **mixed economy**. Most countries have this type of economy. Their economy is based on at least two of the economic systems you've learned about. For example, the United States has a market economy but certain things are regulated by the government.

Finally, some countries in tropical and subtropical regions have a **one-crop economy**. Their economy is based on a single crop, such as bananas, sugarcane, or cacao.

Buying and Selling International trade plays a large role in a country's economy. A country's **exports** include products sold to other countries. On the other hand, a country's **imports** include products a country buys from other countries. Imported products are usually things that aren't produced or available in the country that is buying the item. For example, Japan must import many agricultural products from other countries. Because Japan is a relatively small island, it does not have enough land suitable for crop growing.

Getting the Goods In international trade a condition known as **interdependence** occurs between countries when they depend on each other for resources or goods and services. An industrialized country may depend on the raw materials of a developing country. However, the developing country depends on the finished goods and technology of the industrialized country. For example, Mexico exports crude oil to the United States. In return, the United States exports computer equipment to Mexico.

✓ **READING CHECK:** (*Human Systems*) What are the four types of economies?

The World's People • 57

Six Billion and Counting

In 1960, the world's population hit three billion. Since then the world's population has grown to over six billion. More than 90 percent of this population growth was in the developing countries of Africa, Latin America, and Asia. More than a quarter of the world's six billion people are between the ages of 10 and 24. About 86 percent of these young people live in developing countries.

World of People Some countries are very crowded. Others are only thinly populated. People who study these differences in the world's population are called demographers. They collect information, or demographics, which include population size, and the ages and gender of the population. They also determine **population density**, or how many people live closely together. Population density is calculated by dividing a country's population by its area—stated in either square miles or square kilometers. When a country has an extremely high population density, it may be suffering from **overpopulation**. An overpopulated country usually cannot support its people without outside help.

People are spread unevenly across Earth. Some places are crowded with people, while others are empty. Where do most of the world's people live? Asia is the world's most populated region. China and India both have more than a billion people! In addition, Indonesia, Pakistan, Japan, and Bangladesh each have over 100 million people.

The regions on this map that are shaded dark purple have a high population density.

Interpreting the Map How do you think the patterns on this map will change over the next 100 years? Why?

▼

World Population Density

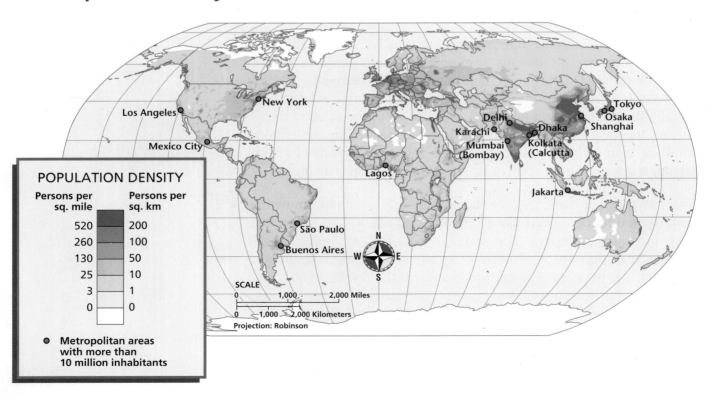

POPULATION DENSITY

Persons per sq. mile	Persons per sq. km
520	200
260	100
130	50
25	10
3	1
0	0

● Metropolitan areas with more than 10 million inhabitants

SCALE
0   1,000   2,000 Miles
0   1,000   2,000 Kilometers
Projection: Robinson

Growing Pains Births add to a country's population. Deaths subtract from it. The number of births per 1,000 people in a year is called the **birthrate**. Similarly, the **death rate** is the annual number of deaths per 1,000 people. The birthrate minus the death rate equals the rate of natural population increase. This number is expressed as a percentage. The birthrate in developing countries is more than double that of industrialized countries. For example, the birthrates of Niger and Bulgaria are very different. Niger has the world's highest birthrate. Most women in Niger have about seven children. On the other hand, Bulgaria has the world's lowest birthrate. Most Bulgarian women only have one child.

On the Move Throughout history, people have moved from place to place looking for better opportunities. People are constantly moving within their own country or across international borders. This movement of people is called **migration**. One person or a group migrate either for a short period of time or permanently. There are several different types of migration. Someone who leaves one place for another is called an **emigrant**.

On the other hand, an **immigrant** is someone arriving from another country. A migrant worker is someone looking for work by regularly moving from place to place. Some people move to other countries for opportunities they don't have in their homeland. Most people emigrate for economic reasons.

✓ **READING CHECK:** (*Human Systems*) What region of the world has the most people?

Homework Practice Online

Keyword: SG5 HP3

Define and explain: gross national product, gross domestic product, industrialized countries, literacy rate, developing countries, third-world countries, free enterprise, market economy, command economy, tradition-based economy, mixed economy, one-crop economy, exports, imports, interdependence, birthrate, death rate, population density, overpopulation, migration, emigrant, immigrant

Reading for the Main Idea

1. (*Environment and Society*) What geographic features influence population density?

2. (*Human Systems*) What characteristics do developed nations share?

Critical Thinking

3. **Finding the Main Idea** What are the different economic systems? Describe each.

4. **Drawing Inferences and Conclusions** What causes overpopulation and how can it be prevented?

Organizing What You Know

5. **Summarizing** Copy the following graphic organizer. Use it to study your local community and classify the businesses in your area.

Primary Industries	Secondary Industries	Tertiary Industries	Quaternary Industries
●	●	●	●
●	●	●	●

Section 3 Global Connections

Read to Discover

1. What is globalization? How are people around the world connected?

2. Why are refugees a global problem? What causes famine? How do people in need get help?

Vocabulary

globalization
popular culture
refugees
famine
humanitarian aid
drought

Reading Strategy

READING ORGANIZER Before you read, create a spider map. Label the center oval Global Connections. Draw seven legs and label them Technology, Cities, Travel, Trade, Sports, Refugees, and Assistance. As you read, write what you learn about these topics beneath each of the legs.

▲ A Buddhist monk in Cambodia may use this laptop computer to log on to the Internet.

Living in a Small World

In just seconds an e-mail message sent by a teenager in India beams all the way to a friend in the United States. A businesswoman in Singapore takes a call from her cell phone from an investor in New York. With just a few taps on a computer's keyboard, anyone in the world can also immediately access the Internet. These are all examples of how small our world has become with the use of cell phones, e-mail, the Internet, and satellite television.

Global Tech Thanks to these technologies, people around the world communicate and do business with each other faster than anyone ever thought possible. **Globalization** is the term most often used to describe how time and distance in the world seem to be shrinking. Globalization is also used to describe how countries are increasingly linked through **popular culture** and a global economy. Popular culture includes things people across the world share such as movies, literature, music, clothing, and food. For example, you can find the American restaurant, McDonald's, in almost every major world city today. Kids throughout the world exchange Pokemon trading cards from Japan. Millions read Harry Potter.

Speaking Globally Almost 6,000 languages are spoken today. English, however, is the language of globalization. As a result, a quarter of the world's population speaks English for global business, communications, higher education, diplomacy, aviation, the Internet, science, popular music, entertainment and international travel. American news channels and movies are seen everywhere. For example, CNN uses satellites to broadcast in English to millions of TV sets around the world.

Cultural Centers Even with fast communication, globalization wouldn't be possible without major cities. As transportation and cultural centers, cities provide the perfect place for different people to exchange goods and ideas. For example, Miami is sometimes called the "Gateway to Latin America." As an international port and multicultural city, many companies that operate in Latin America are headquartered in Miami. Many other global cities also depend on their geographical location for international business. Seattle and San Francisco have economic ties to major Asian cities located across the Pacific Ocean, such as Tokyo and Hong Kong.

▲
This restaurant in Ecuador provides visitors with Internet access.

Ships dock in Miami, Florida.
Interpreting the Visual Record
(*Movement*) What in this photo suggests that Miami is a major international city?
▼

Travel Ills There's a downside, however, to life in a well-connected world. You can board a plane at any major airport today and travel to just about anywhere in the world. Some people, however, carry more than just their luggage on to these flights. They can also carry diseases. For example, in 2003, one woman who didn't realize she was infected with the contagious disease called SARS, traveled from China to Toronto, Canada. As she made contact with several people in Toronto, they too came down with the disease. However, steps are now taken to prevent people with contagious diseases from boarding international flights.

Quick Trades Globalization not only links the world's people, it also connects businesses and countries. For centuries, people have traded. But, never as fast as today. Through the use of the Internet it is quick and simple to order goods from anywhere in the world. For example, a shoe retailer in Chicago can find a Web site that links them to someone in China who makes the sneakers they need. The order is then flown to Chicago the following day. That afternoon the sneakers are sold to customers.

Made in the USA? Check the label on your shoes, other clothing, or book bag to see where it's made. It probably doesn't say the United States. Why? Most clothing and a lot of electronic equipment are imported to the United States from other countries. Many international companies build their factories in places where workers will work for less money than American workers. By hiring cheap labor, these companies lower their manufacturing costs. As a result, these products usually have a lower price tag than products made in the United States.

World Sports You've already learned that money, ideas, and goods are traded in the global economy. But, did you also know that people could be exchanged as well? For example, more and more baseball players from Latin America and Asia are now playing professionally in the United States. In addition, many American and European soccer teams frequently trade players across the Atlantic.

✔ **READING CHECK:**

Human Systems What are some examples of globalization?

Fans of Hideki Matsui—a professional baseball player from Japan—show their support as they watch him play for the New York Yankees.

Interpreting the Visual Record

Movement **How is this sign an example of globalization?**

Helping People in Need

In a smaller world, global problems also connect the world's people. What happens in one part of the world affects the entire planet. Millions of people today suffer without life's necessities. In response to these problems, the global community tries to help as many people as possible.

Searching for Home One of the major global problems today are the 14 million people who seek refuge in other countries. These **refugees** require food, shelter, and help with finding jobs. Many international agencies help refugees start new lives. Unlike immigrants, however, refugees flee their countries because of persecution, war, or economic reasons. Some refugees even eventually become citizens in the country they settle in. For example, many Cuban refugees and their families are now United States citizens.

Hungry Planet A great shortage of food, or **famine**, affects millions of people throughout the world. International relief agencies provide **humanitarian aid** to famine areas. This aid includes medicine and millions of pounds of grain and other foods. These efforts, however, sometimes are not enough to relieve the problem. Today in Ethiopia more than 12 million people are at risk for starvation. The lack of rain, or **drought**, has prevented farmers from growing enough food to feed their country's population.

Movement In the late 1990s unrest in Kosovo, Yugoslavia, disrupted the lives of hundreds of thousands of ethnic Albanians. Many people were forced from their homes. Here, refugees in neighboring Macedonia wait to be transported to nearby transition camps.

✓ **READING CHECK:** (*Human Systems*) What are some reasons why refugees flee their homeland?

Section Review 3

Define and explain: globalization, popular culture, refugees, famine, humanitarian aid, drought

Reading for the Main Idea

1. (*Human Systems*) What are some effects of globalization?

2. (*Human Systems*) How does humanitarian aid help people?

Critical Thinking

3. Drawing Conclusions How has globalization made the world smaller?

Homework Practice Online

Keyword: SG5 HP3

4. Making Predictions What will happen if the number of refugees continues to grow?

Organizing What You Know

5. Contrasting Copy the following graphic organizer. Use it to discuss two arguments about globalization.

Good results of globalization		Bad results of globalization
	⇦⇨	

CHAPTER 3 Review and Practice

Define and Identify

Idenfity each of the following:

1. culture
2. ethnic groups
3. ethnocentrism
4. domestication
5. subsistence agriculture
6. civilization
7. gross national product
8. literacy rate
9. third-world countries
10. mixed economy
11. imports
12. birthrate
13. population density
14. migration
15. immigrant
16. globalization
17. popular culture
18. refugees
19. humanitarian aid

Review the Main Ideas

20. What is culture, and why should people study it?
21. How does diffusion occur?
22. What are two important factors that influence the way people meet basic needs?
23. What is the difference between subsistence and commercial agriculture?

24. How does gross national product differ from gross domestic product?
25. How do third-world countries differ from fourth-world nations?
26. Why do countries import products?
27. How has globalization affected how people communicate?
28. How do refugees differ from immigrants?

Think Critically

29. **Drawing Inferences and Conclusions** Why are ethnic groups sometimes confused with races?
30. **Identifying Cause and Effect** How did the development of agriculture affect the global population?
31. **Comparing and Contrasting** How do industrialized countries differ from developing countries?
32. **Summarizing** How have new technologies helped to create a global culture?
33. **Finding the Main Idea** How has globalization changed how countries trade with each other?

Map Activity

34. On a separate sheet of paper, match the letters on the map with their correct labels.
    Buddhism
    Christianity—Eastern Orthodox
    Christianity—Protestant
    Christianity—Roman Catholic
    Hinduism
    Islam

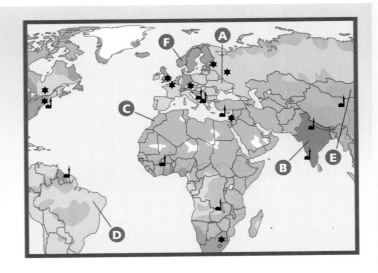

Writing Activity

Research the economy of your community. Has the economy grown or declined in the last 10 years? Why? What goods are exported from your community? What goods are imported to your community? Write about what you learn from your research. Then write about how you think your community might change in the future.

internet connect

Internet Activity: **go.hrw.com**
KEYWORD: SG5 GT3

Choose a topic to explore online:
- Visit famous buildings and monuments around the world.
- Compare facts about life in different countries.
- Examine world population growth.

Social Studies Skills Practice

Interpreting Cartoons

Study the following cartoon. Then answer the questions.

1. What is the main idea of this cartoon?
2. Why is the Earth in the middle of a maze?
3. Does the cartoonist believe it is difficult or easy to connect with people around the world by using the Internet? Why?
4. How is this cartoon an example of globalization?

Analyzing Primary Sources

Read the following quote from French-American film director Jean-Marc Barr. Then answer the questions.

"We believe Europe is going to exist because the English language allows it to culturally. Never on this continent has there been a language that all the classes can speak, from a Polish man to a Spaniard to an Icelandic. My biggest and most rewarding events in my life have been because I have been able to speak English with people all over the world."

1. What advantage does Barr see for Europe as English is used more?
2. Why would a film director such as Barr be especially interested in language?
3. Based on your knowledge of culture, why might some Europeans resist the use of English?
4. How do you think Barr feels about globalization?

FOCUS ON REGIONS

What is a Region?

Think about where you live, where you go to school, and where you shop. These places are all part of your neighborhood. In geographic terms, your neighborhood is a region. A region is an area that has common features that make it different from surrounding areas.

What regions do you live in? You live on a continent, in a country, and in a state. These are all regions that can be mapped.

Regions can be divided into smaller regions called subregions. For example, Africa is a major world region. Africa's subregions include North Africa, West Africa, East Africa, central Africa, and southern Africa. Each subregion can be divided into even smaller subregions.

Regional Characteristics Regions can be based on physical, political, economic, or cultural characteristics. Physical regions are based on Earth's natural features, such as continents, landforms, and climates. Political regions are based on countries and their subregions, such as states, provinces, and cities. Economic regions are based on money-making activities such as agriculture or industries. Cultural regions are based on features such as language, religion, or ethnicity.

▲
East Africa is a subregion of Africa. It is an area of plateaus, rolling hills, and savanna grasslands.

Major World Regions

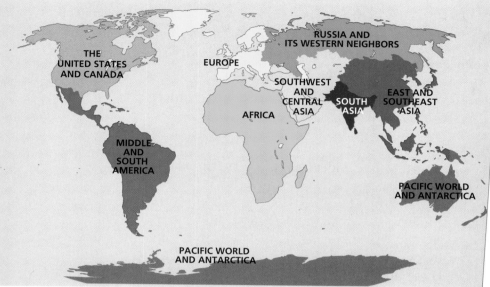

THE UNITED STATES AND CANADA

EUROPE

RUSSIA AND ITS WESTERN NEIGHBORS

SOUTHWEST AND CENTRAL ASIA

AFRICA

SOUTH ASIA

EAST AND SOUTHEAST ASIA

MIDDLE AND SOUTH AMERICA

PACIFIC WORLD AND ANTARCTICA

PACIFIC WORLD AND ANTARCTICA

The international border between Kenya and Tanzania is a clearly defined regional boundary.

Regional Boundaries All regions have boundaries, or borders. Boundaries are where the features of one region meet the features of a different region. Some boundaries, such as coastlines or country borders, can be shown as lines on a map. Other regional boundaries are less clear.

Transition zones are areas where the features of one region change gradually to the features of a different region. For example, when a city's suburbs expand into rural areas, a transition zone forms. In the transition zone, it may be hard to find the boundary between rural and urban areas.

Types of Regions There are three basic types of regions. The first is a formal region. Formal regions are based on one or more common features. For example, Japan is a formal region. Its people share a common government, language, and culture.

The second type of region is a functional region. Functional regions are based on movement and activities that connect different places. For example, Paris, France, is a functional region. It is based on the goods, services, and people that move throughout the city. A shopping center or an airport might also be a functional region.

The third type of region is a perceived region. Perceived regions are based on people's shared feelings and beliefs. For example, the neighborhood where you live may be a perceived region.

The three basic types of regions overlap to form complex world regions. The world can be divided into nine major world regions (see map above). Each has general features that make it different from the other major world regions. These differences include physical, cultural, economic, historical, and political features.

Understanding What You Read

1. Regions can be based on what types of characteristics?

2. What are the three basic types of regions?

Building Skills for Life: Drawing Mental Maps

We create maps in our heads of all kinds of places—our homes, schools, communities, country, and the world. Some of these places we know well. Others we have only heard about. These images we carry in our heads are shaped by what we see and experience. They are also influenced by what we learn from news reports or other sources. Geographers call the maps that we carry around in our heads mental maps.

We use mental maps to organize spatial information about people and places. For example, our mental maps help us move from classroom to classroom at school or get to a friend's home. A mental map of the United States helps us list the states we would pass through driving from New York City to Miami.

We use our mental maps of places when we draw sketch maps. A sketch map showing the relationship between places and the relative size of places can be drawn using very simple shapes. For example, triangles and rectangles could be used to sketch a map of the world. This quickly drawn map would show the relative size and position of the continents.

Think about some simple ways we could make our map

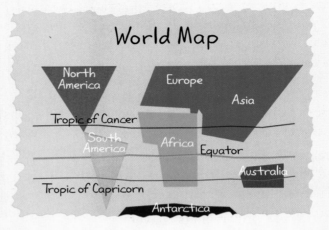

World Map

North America
Europe
Asia
Tropic of Cancer
South America
Africa
Equator
Australia
Tropic of Capricorn
Antarctica

of the world more detailed. Adding the equator, Tropic of Cancer, and Tropic of Capricorn would be one way. Look at a map of the world in your textbook's Atlas. Note that the bulge in the continent of Africa is north of the equator. Also note that all of Asia is north of the equator. Next note that the Indian subcontinent extends south from the Tropic of Cancer. About half of Australia is located north of the Tropic of Capricorn. As your knowledge of the world increases, your mental map will become even more detailed.

THE SKILL

1. Look at the maps in your textbook's Atlas. Where does the prime meridian fall in relation to the continents?

2. On a separate sheet of paper, sketch a simple map of the world from memory. First draw the equator, Tropic of Cancer, Tropic of Capricorn, and prime meridian. Then sketch in the continents. You can use circles, rectangles, and triangles.

3. Draw a second map of the world from memory. This time, draw the international date line in the center of your map. Add the equator, Tropic of Cancer, and Tropic of Capricorn. Now sketch in the continents. What do you notice?

HANDS on GEOGRAPHY

Mental maps are personal. They change as we learn more about the world and the places in it. For example, they can include details about places that are of interest only to you.

What is your mental map of your neighborhood like? Sketch your mental map of your neighborhood. Include the features that you think are important and that help you find your way around. These guidelines will help you get started.

1. Decide what your map will show. Choose boundaries so that you do not sketch more than you need to.

2. Determine how much space you will need for your map. Things that are the same size in reality should be about the same size on your map.

3. Decide on and note the orientation of your map. Most maps use a directional indicator. On most maps, north is at the top.

4. Label reference points so that others who look at your map can quickly and easily figure out what they are looking at. For example, a major street or your school might be a reference point.

5. Decide how much detail your map will show. The larger the area you want to represent, the less detail you will need.

6. Use circles, rectangles, and triangles if you do not know the exact shape of an area.

7. As you think of them, fill in more details, such as names of places or major land features.

Lab Report

1. What are the most important features on your map? Why did you include them?

2. Compare your sketch map to a published map of the area. How does it differ?

3. At the bottom, list three ways that you could make your sketch map more complete.

UNIT 2

United States and Canada

CHAPTER 4
The United States

CHAPTER 5
Canada

Canadian Rocky Mountains

CN Tower and SkyDome, Toronto, Canada

An Englishman in Texas

Jon Hall grew up in the London suburbs. He studied Greek and Latin as a student in Texas. Here he contrasts what he sees as the British and Texan attitudes toward personal space and sports. **WHAT DO YOU THINK?** *How do you think people in your community feel about these topics?*

As an Englishman, the absence in Texas of fences and walls and clearly marked boundaries made me rather nervous at first. In London, with thousands of people in a small space, everyone is uptight about fencing off *their* little bit of land. In Texas, front yards and parks and parking lots sprawl casually without boundaries. And Texans really are more open and friendly than others. On the street, in a store, in a restaurant, greeting strangers is just the thing to do.

Brits and Texans support sports differently. In Britain, the spectators tend to be males between 15 and 45 years old—definitely not a family atmosphere. But at Texas football games, you'll see grandparents with their grandkids and guys and gals on dates. At the high school level too, there is much wider participation: the band, cheerleaders, parents, fans. I played soccer for my high school and most Saturdays we'd have a crowd of about seven.

◄ *American teenagers*

Street scene in Austin, Texas

Understanding Primary Sources

1. Why does Jon Hall think the people of London are more concerned about boundaries than Texans?

2. According to Jon Hall, what gives Texas football games a "family atmosphere"?

American buffalo

The United States and Canada

Elevation Profile

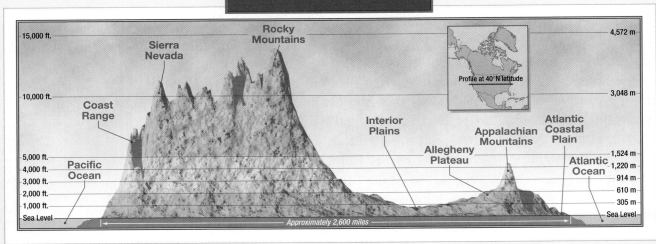

15,000 ft. — 4,572 m

Rocky Mountains

Sierra Nevada

10,000 ft. — 3,048 m

Coast Range

Profile at 40°N latitude

Interior Plains

Atlantic Coastal Plain

Appalachian Mountains

Allegheny Plateau

5,000 ft. — 1,524 m
4,000 ft. — 1,220 m

Pacific Ocean

Atlantic Ocean

3,000 ft. — 914 m
2,000 ft. — 610 m
1,000 ft. — 305 m
Sea Level — Sea Level

Approximately 2,600 miles

The United States and Canada:
Comparing Sizes

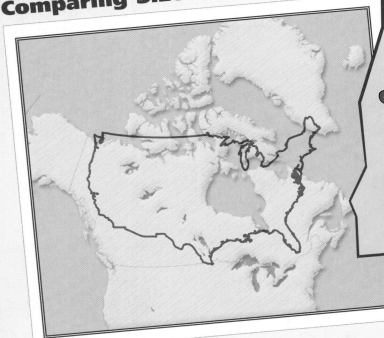

GEOSTATS:

Highest point in North America: Mount McKinley, Alaska—20,320 ft. (6,194 m)

Lowest point in North America: Death Valley, California—282 ft. below sea level (86 m below sea level)

Largest lake in North America: Lake Superior—31,800 sq. mi. (82,362 sq km)

World's highest tides: Bay of Fundy, Nova Scotia, Canada—as high as 70 ft. (21 m)

United States and Canada:
Physical

RUSSIA

ARCTIC OCEAN

Bering Strait

Arctic Circle

Aleutian Islands

BERING SEA

BROOKS RANGE

Mount McKinley 20,320 ft. (6194 m)

ALASKA RANGE

Yukon River

GULF OF ALASKA

Mount Logan 19,524 ft. (5951 m)

COAST MOUNTAINS

BEAUFORT SEA

Ellesmere Island

Greenland (DENMARK)

ICELAND

Arctic Circle

Baffin Bay

Baffin Island

Victoria Island

Great Bear Lake

Mackenzie River

Liard River

Peace River

Great Slave Lake

CANADA

Hudson Strait

LABRADOR SEA

Hudson Bay

James Bay

LABRADOR PENINSULA

Newfoundland

GULF OF ST. LAWRENCE

Athabasca R.

Nelson River

CANADIAN SHIELD

Saskatchewan River

ROCKY MOUNTAINS

GREAT

Vancouver Island

Fraser River

Columbia

COLUMBIA PLATEAU

Mount Rainier 14,410 ft. (4392 m)

Mount St. Helens 8366 ft. (2550 m)

Snake River

CASCADE RANGE

St. Lawrence River

Lake Superior

Lake Michigan

Lake Huron

Missouri River

Mississippi R.

Lake Ontario

Niagara Falls

Lake Erie

INTERIOR PLAINS

UNITED STATES

PLAINS

Mount Shasta 14,162 ft. (4317 m)

GREAT BASIN

SIERRA NEVADA

CENTRAL VALLEY

COAST RANGES

Great Salt Lake

N. Platte River

S. Platte River

DEATH VALLEY

Colorado River

Arkansas River

OZARK PLATEAU

Red River

MOJAVE DESERT

COLORADO PLATEAU

Rio Grande

Pecos River

Ohio River

CUMBERLAND PLATEAU

ALLEGHENY PLATEAU

APPALACHIAN MOUNTAINS

PIEDMONT

Chesapeake Bay

ATLANTIC COASTAL PLAIN

ATLANTIC OCEAN

GULF COASTAL PLAIN

Mississippi River

Rio Grande

MEXICO

GULF OF MEXICO

Tropic of Cancer

PACIFIC OCEAN

HAWAII

Niihau
Kauai
Kaula
PACIFIC OCEAN
Oahu
Molokai
Maui
Lanai
Kahoolawe
Hawaii

SCALE
0   100   200 Miles
0   100   200 Kilometers
Projection: Albers Equal Area

To understand the relative location of Hawaii as well as the vast distance separating it from the rest of the United States, see the Atlas map in the front of this textbook.

ELEVATION

FEET	METERS
13,120	4,000
6,560	2,000
1,640	500
656	200
(Sea level) 0	0 (Sea level)
Below sea level	Below sea level
	Ice caps

SCALE
0   500   1000 Miles
0   500   1000 Kilometers
Projection: Azimuthal Equal Area

N

1. **Place** Where is the highest point in North America? Which southwestern desert includes an area below sea level?

2. **Region** Which two large lakes are entirely within Canada?

3. **Region** What are four tributaries of the Mississippi River?

Critical Thinking

4. **Human-Environment Interaction** Compare this map to the **population map** of the region. What is one physical feature that many of the largest cities have in common? What is the connection between the cities' locations and these physical features?

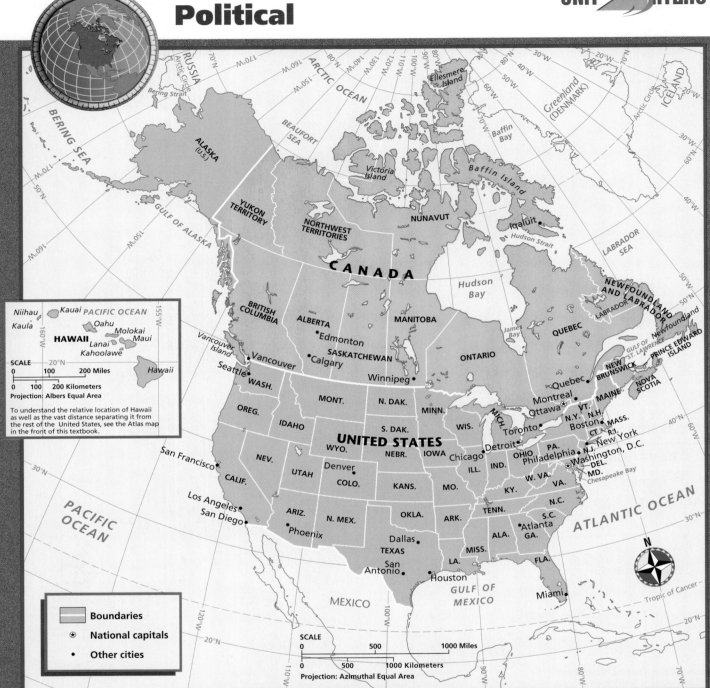

Boundaries

⊛ **National capitals**

• **Other cities**

SCALE
0   500   1000 Miles

0   500   1000 Kilometers
Projection: Azimuthal Equal Area

1. (Place) Compare this map to the **physical map** of the region. What physical feature forms part of the border between the United States and Mexico?

Critical Thinking

2. (Movement) Compare this map to the **climate** and **population maps**. Which U.S. border—the Canadian or Mexican—has a denser population? Why?

3. (Region) Which Canadian province or territory appears to be the largest? the second largest? Why is it hard to compare their sizes?

Climate

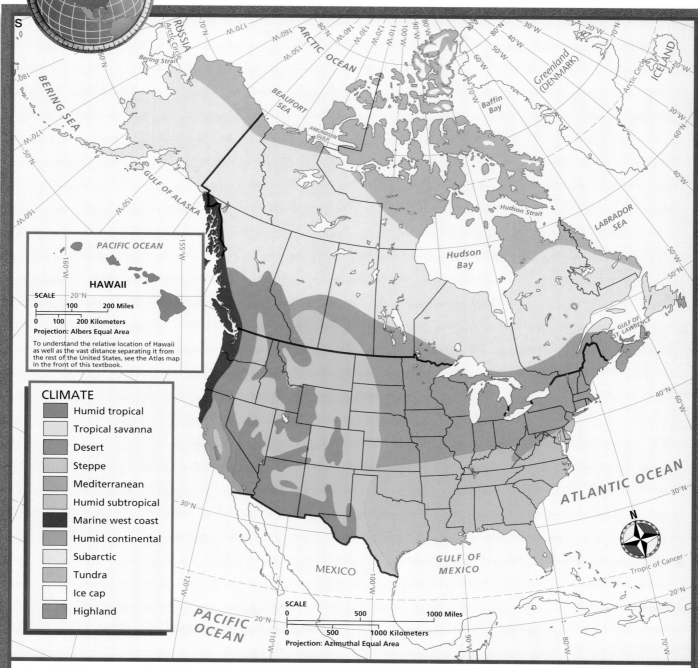

CLIMATE
- Humid tropical
- Tropical savanna
- Desert
- Steppe
- Mediterranean
- Humid subtropical
- Marine west coast
- Humid continental
- Subarctic
- Tundra
- Ice cap
- Highland

HAWAII

SCALE   20°N
0   100   200 Miles
0   100   200 Kilometers
Projection: Albers Equal Area

To understand the relative location of Hawaii as well as the vast distance separating it from the rest of the United States, see the Atlas map in the front of this textbook.

SCALE
0   500   1000 Miles
0   500   1000 Kilometers
Projection: Azimuthal Equal Area

1. (Region) Which U.S. state has the greatest diversity of climates? What are three states that have only one climate type?

2. (Human-Environment Interaction) Compare this map to the **physical** and **population maps** of the region. Which climate region contains the most big cities? Which climate regions do not have big cities?

Critical Thinking

3. (Movement) Compare this map to the **physical map**. What may have limited settlement of the U.S. Great Plains?

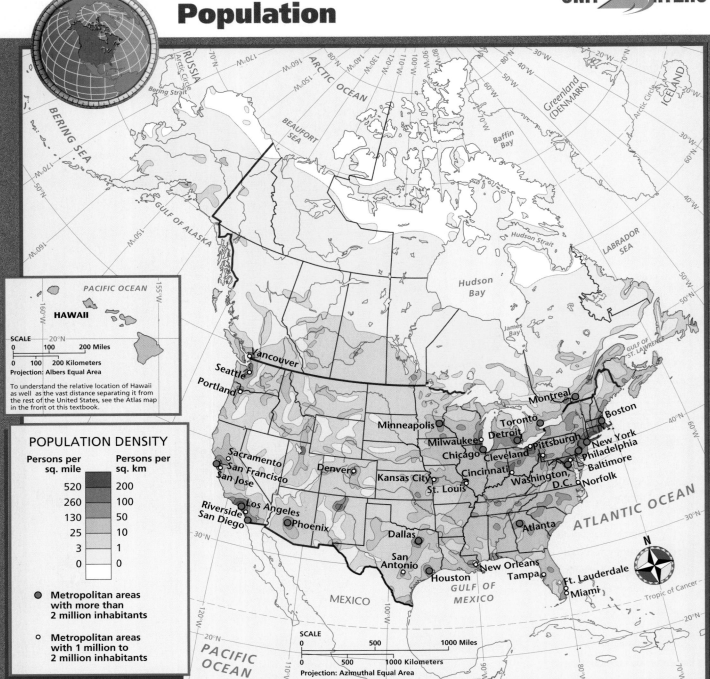

HAWAII

PACIFIC OCEAN

SCALE   20°N
0   100   200 Miles
0   100   200 Kilometers
Projection: Albers Equal Area

To understand the relative location of Hawaii as well as the vast distance separating it from the rest of the United States, see the Atlas map in the front of this textbook.

POPULATION DENSITY

Persons per sq. mile	Persons per sq. km
520	200
260	100
130	50
25	10
3	1
0	0

● Metropolitan areas with more than 2 million inhabitants

○ Metropolitan areas with 1 million to 2 million inhabitants

SCALE
0   500   1000 Miles
0   500   1000 Kilometers
Projection: Azimuthal Equal Area

1. (Region) Which country appears to have a larger population?

2. (Place) What are Canada's two largest cities?

3. (Region) Based on the map, which area of the United States do you think was settled first? Why?

Critical Thinking

4. (Place) Compare this map to the **climate map** of the region. Although Seattle and Montreal lie at about the same latitude, Montreal has a colder climate. What may account for this difference?

United States and Canada:
Land Use and Resources

UNIT 2 ATLAS

LAND USE
Livestock raising
Commercial farming
Forests
Manufacturing
Limited economic activity
Major manufacturing and trade centers
RESOURCES
Coal
Natural gas
Oil
Nuclear power
Hydroelectric power
Gold
Silver
Uranium
Other minerals
Seafood
RUSSIA
Arctic Circle
Bering Strait
BERING SEA
ARCTIC OCEAN
BEAUFORT SEA
Baffin Bay
Hudson Strait
LABRADOR SEA
Hudson Bay
James Bay
PACIFIC OCEAN
Honolulu
HAWAII
SCALE
0 100 200 Miles
0 100 200 Kilometers
Projection: Albers Equal Area
To understand the relative location of Hawaii as well as the vast distance separating it from the rest of the United States, see the Atlas map in the front of this textbook.
Anchorage
Edmonton
Calgary
Vancouver
Seattle
Portland
Spokane
Regina
Winnipeg
WHEAT BELT
Minneapolis-St. Paul
DAIRY BELT
Toronto
Detroit
Quebec
Montreal
Halifax
Boston
New York
Philadelphia
Washington, D.C.
Chicago
CORN BELT
Pittsburgh
Cincinnati
St. Louis
Salt Lake City
Denver
WHEAT BELT
San Francisco
San Jose
Los Angeles
San Diego
Phoenix
Nashville
Charlotte
Dallas-Ft. Worth
Atlanta
ATLANTIC OCEAN
San Antonio
Houston
New Orleans
Tampa-St. Petersburg
Miami
MEXICO
GULF OF MEXICO
Tropic of Cancer
PACIFIC OCEAN
SCALE
0 500 1000 Miles
0 500 1000 Kilometers
Projection: Azimuthal Equal Area
N

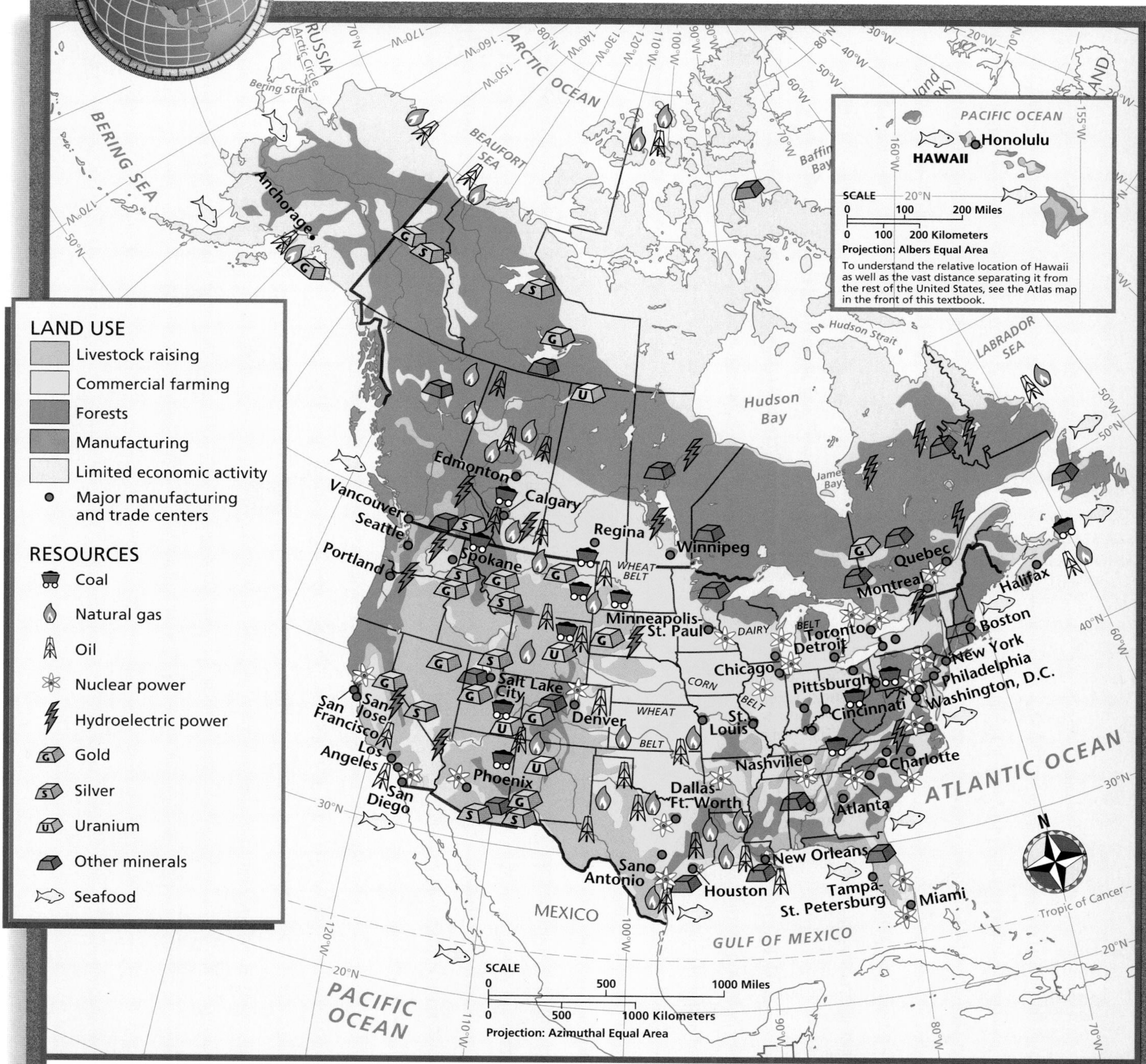

1. *Human-Environment Interaction* Look at the **physical map**. In which area of North America are gold, silver, and uranium found?

2. *Human-Environment Interaction* Which two states on the Gulf of Mexico produce large amounts of oil and natural gas?

3. *Human-Environment Interaction* Which type of land use is most common throughout Canada?

Critical Thinking

4. *Region* Compare this map to the **population map**. Why do you think most nuclear power plants are in eastern North America?

Fast FACTS

The United States

UNITED STATES

CAPITAL:
Washington, D.C.

AREA:
3,717,792 sq. mi.
(9,629,091 sq km)

POPULATION: 290,342,554

MONEY:
U.S. dollar

LANGUAGES:
English, Spanish (spoken by a large minority)

 **Iowa**
CAPITAL: Des Moines
NICKNAME:
Hawkeye State

 **Mississippi**
CAPITAL: Jackson
NICKNAME:
Magnolia State

 Kansas
CAPITAL: Topeka
NICKNAME:
Sunflower State

Missouri
CAPITAL: Jefferson City
NICKNAME:
Show Me State

 Alabama
CAPITAL: Montgomery
NICKNAME:
Heart of Dixie,
Camellia State

  Delaware
CAPITAL: Dover
NICKNAME:
First State,
Diamond State

Kentucky
CAPITAL: Frankfort
NICKNAME:
Bluegrass State

Montana
CAPITAL: Helena
NICKNAME:
Treasure State

Alaska
CAPITAL: Juneau
NICKNAME:
The Last Frontier
(unofficial)

Florida
CAPITAL: Tallahassee
NICKNAME:
Sunshine State

 Louisiana
CAPITAL: Baton Rouge
NICKNAME:
Pelican State

Nebraska
CAPITAL: Lincoln
NICKNAME:
Cornhusker State

Arizona
CAPITAL: Phoenix
NICKNAME:
Grand Canyon State

 Georgia
CAPITAL: Atlanta
NICKNAME:
Peach State, Empire
State of the South

 Maine
CAPITAL: Augusta
NICKNAME:
Pine Tree State

Nevada
CAPITAL: Carson City
NICKNAME:
Sagebrush State,
Battle Born State, Silver State

 Arkansas
CAPITAL: Little Rock
NICKNAME:
Natural State,
Razorback State

 Hawaii
CAPITAL: Honolulu
NICKNAME:
Aloha State

 Maryland
CAPITAL: Annapolis
NICKNAME:
Old Line State,
Free State

New Hampshire
CAPITAL: Concord
NICKNAME:
Granite State

 California
CAPITAL: Sacramento
NICKNAME:
Golden State

Idaho
CAPITAL: Boise
NICKNAME:
Gem State

 **Massachusetts**
CAPITAL: Boston
NICKNAME:
Bay State, Old Colony

New Jersey
CAPITAL: Trenton
NICKNAME:
Garden State

 Colorado
CAPITAL: Denver
NICKNAME:
Centennial State

 Illinois
CAPITAL: Springfield
NICKNAME:
Prairie State

  Michigan
CAPITAL: Lansing
NICKNAME:
Great Lakes State,
Wolverine State

 New Mexico
CAPITAL: Santa Fe
NICKNAME:
Land of Enchantment

 Connecticut
CAPITAL: Hartford
NICKNAME:
Constitution State,
Nutmeg State

 Indiana
CAPITAL: Indianapolis
NICKNAME:
Hoosier State

 Minnesota
CAPITAL: St. Paul
NICKNAME:
Gopher State,
North Star State

 New York
CAPITAL: Albany
NICKNAME:
Empire State

Countries, states, provinces, and territories not drawn to scale.

 North Carolina
CAPITAL: Raleigh
NICKNAME: Tar Heel State, Old North State

 **Pennsylvania**
CAPITAL: Harrisburg
NICKNAME: Keystone State

 Texas
CAPITAL: Austin
NICKNAME: Lone Star State

 North Dakota
CAPITAL: Bismarck
NICKNAME: Peace Garden State

 **Rhode Island**
CAPITAL: Providence
NICKNAME: Little Rhody, Ocean State

 Utah
CAPITAL: Salt Lake City
NICKNAME: Beehive State

 West Virginia
CAPITAL: Charleston
NICKNAME: Mountain State

 Ohio
CAPITAL: Columbus
NICKNAME: Buckeye State

 South Carolina
CAPITAL: Columbia
NICKNAME: Palmetto State

 Vermont
CAPITAL: Montpelier
NICKNAME: Green Mountain State

 Wisconsin
CAPITAL: Madison
NICKNAME: Badger State

 Oklahoma
CAPITAL: Oklahoma City
NICKNAME: Sooner State

 **South Dakota**
CAPITAL: Pierre
NICKNAME: Coyote State, Mount Rushmore State

 Virginia
CAPITAL: Richmond
NICKNAME: Old Dominion

 Wyoming
CAPITAL: Cheyenne
NICKNAME: Equality State, Cowboy State

 Oregon
CAPITAL: Salem
NICKNAME: Beaver State

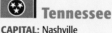 **Tennessee**
CAPITAL: Nashville
NICKNAME: Volunteer State

 **Washington**
CAPITAL: Olympia
NICKNAME: Evergreen State

Canada

CANADA
CAPITAL: Ottawa
AREA: 3,890,695 sq. mi. (9,976,140 sq km)
POPULATION: 32,207,113

MONEY: Canadian dollar
LANGUAGES: English (official), French (official)

 Nova Scotia
CAPITAL: Halifax

 Saskatchewan
CAPITAL: Regina

 Nunavut
CAPITAL: Iqaluit

 Yukon Territory
CAPITAL: Whitehorse

 Alberta
CAPITAL: Edmonton

 New Brunswick
CAPITAL: Fredericton

 Ontario
CAPITAL: Toronto

 British Columbia
CAPITAL: Victoria

 **Newfoundland and Labrador**
CAPITAL: St. John's

 **Prince Edward Island**
CAPITAL: Charlottetown

 **Manitoba**
CAPITAL: Winnipeg

 Northwest Territories
CAPITAL: Yellowknife

 Quebec
CAPITAL: Quebec

internet connect
COUNTRY STATISTICS
GO TO: **go.hrw.com**
KEYWORD: **SG5 FactsU2**
FOR: **more facts about the United States and Canada**

Sources: Central Intelligence Agency, *The World Factbook 2003*; *The World Almanac and Book of Facts 2003*

CHAPTER 4

The United States

Before we study the world's other countries, we will look at the United States. What do you already know about the people and geography of the United States?

In this book you will meet people from all over the world. Each of them has cultural traditions that are different from yours. However, each has many things in common.

What is culture? As you learned in Chapter 3, culture is a learned system of shared beliefs and behaviors. To learn about American culture, we are going to start by meeting an American: you. What beliefs do you have? What do you like to eat? How old will you be when you finish school? What kind of music do you like? What language do you speak at home? Do you practice a religious faith? Which holidays do you celebrate? All of these things reflect something about our American culture, as well as our diversity.

Section 1 Physical Geography

Read to Discover

1. What are the major physical features of the United States?
2. What climate regions are found in the United States?
3. What natural resources does the United States have?

Vocabulary

contiguous
Continental Divide
basins

Places

Coastal Plain
Appalachian Mountains
Interior Plains
Rocky Mountains
Great Lakes
Mississippi River

Great Plains
Columbia River
Great Basin
Colorado Plateau
Sierra Nevada
Cascade Range
Aleutian Islands

Reading Strategy

FOLDNOTE: PYRAMID Create a **Pyramid** FoldNote as described in the Appendix. Label the sides of the pyramid "Physical Features," "Climate," and "Natural Resources." As you read the section, write what you learn about each topic on the appropriate pyramid side.

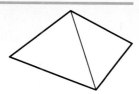

The United States: Physical-Political

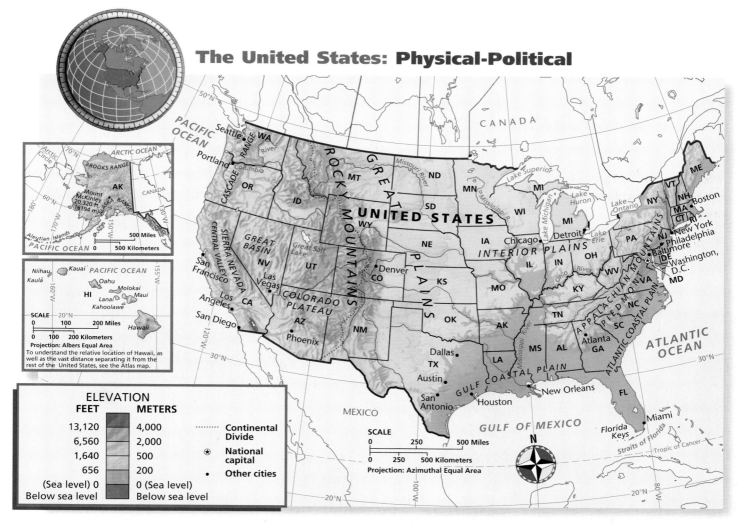

Physical Features

The 48 **contiguous** American states and the District of Columbia lie between the Atlantic and Pacific Oceans. Contiguous states are those that border each other. Two states are not contiguous: Alaska, to the northwest of Canada, and Hawaii, in the Pacific Ocean. The United States also has territories in the Pacific Ocean and the Caribbean Sea. We will now look at the physical features of the 50 states. You can use the map on the next page to follow along.

The East The eastern United States rises from the Coastal Plain to the Appalachian Mountains. The Coastal Plain is a low region that lies close to sea level. It rises gradually inland. The Coastal Plain stretches from New York to Mexico along the Atlantic and Gulf of Mexico coasts.

The Appalachians include mountain ranges and river valleys from Maine to Alabama. The mountains are very old. Erosion has lowered and smoothed the peaks for more than 300 million years. The highest mountain in the Appalachians rises to just 6,684 feet (2,037 m).

At the foot of the Appalachians, between the mountains and the Coastal Plain, is the Piedmont. The Piedmont is a region of rolling plains. It begins in New Jersey and extends as far south as Alabama.

The Interior Plains Vast plains make up most of the United States west of the Appalachians. This region is called the Interior Plains. The Interior Plains stretch westward to the Rocky Mountains.

After the last ice age, glaciers shrank. They left rolling hills, lakes, and major river systems in the northern Interior Plains. The Great Lakes were created by these retreating ice sheets. From west to east, the Great Lakes are Lake Superior, Lake Michigan, Lake Huron, Lake Erie, and Lake Ontario.

The Mississippi River and its tributaries drain the Interior Plains. Along the way, they deposit rich soils that produce fertile farmlands. A tributary is a stream or river that flows into a larger stream or river. Tributaries of the Mississippi include the Missouri and Ohio Rivers.

The Great Smoky Mountains of Tennessee are a range of the Appalachian Mountains.

Interpreting the Visual Record *Place*
What clues from this photograph might tell you that these mountains are very old?

Physical Regions of the United States and Canada

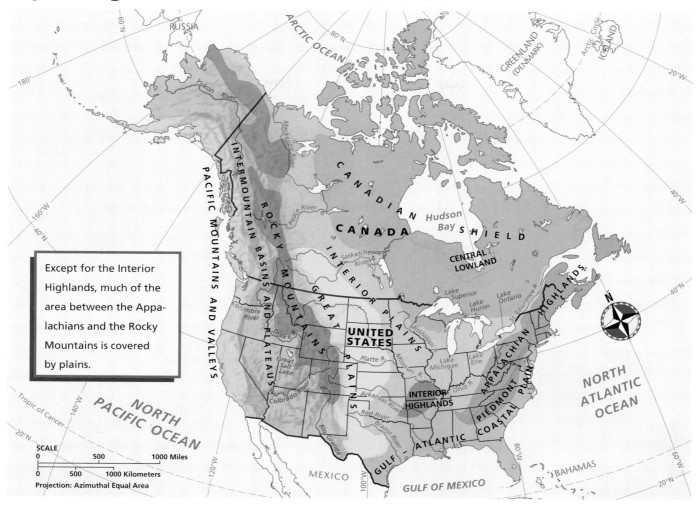

Except for the Interior Highlands, much of the area between the Appalachians and the Rocky Mountains is covered by plains.

In some places on its way to the Gulf of Mexico, the great Mississippi River is 1.5 miles (2.4 km) wide!

The flattest part of the Interior Plains is the Great Plains region. It lies closest to the Rocky Mountains. The region has a higher elevation than the rest of the Interior Plains. The Great Plains extend from Mexico in the south into Canada in the north.

The West As we continue westward, we reach the Rocky Mountains. The Rockies include a series of mountain ranges separated by high plains and valleys. They extend from Mexico to the cold Arctic. Many Rocky Mountain peaks reach more than 14,000 feet (4,267 m).

Running along the crest of the Rockies is the **Continental Divide**. It divides the flow of North America's rivers. Rivers east of the divide, such as the Missouri, flow eastward. Rivers west of the divide, such as the Columbia, flow westward.

West of the Rockies is a region of plateaus and **basins**. A basin is a region surrounded by higher land, such as mountains. The Great Basin in Nevada and Utah,

The Rio Grande cuts through Big Bend National Park.

Interpreting the Visual Record (Place)

What landforms are found in this area?

for example, is surrounded by high mountains. Southeast of the Great Basin is the Colorado Plateau. The Colorado Plateau lies in Utah, Colorado, New Mexico, and Arizona. West of the Great Basin lie the Sierra Nevada, the Coast Ranges, and many valleys. The Cascade Range in the Pacific Northwest was formed by volcanic eruptions. Volcanic eruptions and earthquakes are a danger in the Pacific states. In this area, the North American plate is colliding with the Pacific plate.

Hawaii and Alaska Farther west, Hawaii and Alaska also experience tectonic activity. The Hawaiian Islands were formed by large volcanoes that have risen from the floor of the Pacific Ocean. Alaska's Aleutian (uh-loo-shuhn) Islands also have volcanic origins.

Southeastern and south-central Alaska are very mountainous. The highest mountain in North America is Mount McKinley, in the Alaska Range. The American Indian name for Mount McKinley is Denali. It soars to a height of 20,320 feet (6,194 m).

✓ **READING CHECK:** *Places and Regions* What are the major physical features of the United States?

A Winter in Massachusetts
B Spring in California
C Summer in Florida
D Fall in Colorado

Climate

The climates of the United States are varied. The country has 11 climate types—the greatest variety of climates of any country.

The East Most of the eastern United States is divided into two climate regions. In the north is a humid continental climate with snowy winters and warm, humid summers. Southerners experience the milder winters and warm, humid summers of a humid subtropical climate. Coastal areas often experience tropical storms. Southern Florida, with a tropical savanna climate, is warm all year.

The Interior Plains Humid continental, humid subtropical, and steppe climates meet in the interior states. People there sometimes experience violent weather, such as hail and tornadoes. The steppe climate of the Great Plains supports wide grasslands. Summers are hot, and droughts can be a problem. Blinding snowstorms called blizzards sometimes occur during winters, which can be very cold.

The West Climates in the West are mostly dry. Steppe and varied highland climates dominate much of the Rocky Mountain region. Temperatures and the amount of rain and snow vary.

Much of the Southwest has a desert climate. The West Coast has two climate types. The forested north has a wet and mild marine west coast climate. A drier Mediterranean climate is found in the south.

Except in the southeast, most of Alaska has very cold subarctic and tundra climates. Hawaii is the only state within the tropics. Northeasterly trade winds bring rain to eastern sides of the islands. Hawaii's western slopes have a drier tropical savanna climate.

✓ **READING CHECK:** (*The World in Spatial Terms*) What climate regions are found in the United States?

Natural Resources

The United States has many resources. Some of the most productive farmlands in the world are found in the Interior Plains. Ranches and farms produce beef, wheat, corn, and soybeans. California, Florida, Texas, and other areas grow fruit, vegetables, and cotton.

Alaska, California, Texas, and other states supply oil and natural gas. Coal and other minerals are found in Appalachian and western states. Gold and silver mines also operate in some western states.

Forests, especially in the Northwest and the Southeast, are important sources of lumber. The Atlantic Ocean, Gulf of Mexico, and Pacific Ocean are rich sources of fish and other seafood. The natural beauty of the country is also a valuable resource for tourism. All these resources help support industry and other economic activities.

✓ **READING CHECK:** (*Places and Regions*) What natural resources does the United States have?

Redwoods, the tallest trees in the world, grow in California and Oregon. They can grow well over 300 feet (90 m) high with trunks 20 feet (6 m) in diameter. Some redwood trees are more than 1,500 years old!

Homework Practice Online
Keyword: SG5 HP4

Section Review 1

Define and explain: contiguous, Continental Divide, basins

Working with Sketch Maps On a map of the United States that you draw or that your teacher provides, label the following: Coastal Plain, Appalachian Mountains, Interior Plains, Rocky Mountains, Great Lakes, Mississippi River, Great Plains, Columbia River, Great Basin, Colorado Plateau, Sierra Nevada, Cascade Range, and Aleutian Islands.

Reading for the Main Idea

1. (*Places and Regions*) What are the two major mountain regions in the United States? What major landform region lies betweeen them?

2. (*Places and Regions*) What resources are found in the country? Why are they important for the economy?

3. (*Places and Regions*) What parts of the United States have particularly rich farmlands?

Critical Thinking

4. Drawing Inferences and Conclusions The Rockies are higher than the Appalachians. How is this fact a clue to the relative age of the two mountain systems?

Organizing What You Know

5. Categorizing Copy the following graphic organizer. Use it to categorize the major physical features and climates of the East, Interior Plains, and West.

	Physical Features	Climates
East		
Interior Plains		
West (including Alaska and Hawaii)		

The History and Culture of the United States

Read to Discover

1. What was the history of the United States?
2. What rights and responsibilities do U.S. citizens have?
3. How have different groups of people added to the cultural diversity of the United States?

Vocabulary

colonies
plantations
annexed

textiles
bilingual

Places

Boston
New York

Reading Strategy

READING ORGANIZER Create a two-column chart. Title the first column History and Government, and the second column A Diverse People. As you read this section, list the details you learn about the history, government, and cultures of the United States.

▲
Anasazi homes were built of stone and sun-dried clay bricks. They were built in openings in high cliffs.

History and Government

There are more than 2 million American Indians living in the United States today. They are the descendants of the first people in the Americas. Scientists believe people first crossed into North America from Asia at least 20,000 years ago. Over time, these peoples spread throughout the Americas. They developed many different cultures and civilizations. These cultures included the Maya, Aztec, and Inca.

A variety of cultures developed in North America. For example, after about A.D. 700, the Anasazi in the southwestern United States developed a complex irrigation system. This system made it possible for the Anasazi to grow crops in a dry region. Some people in the Mississippi River and Ohio River valleys farmed. They also built large mounds. These mounds were built for different purposes, including burials.

There also were various peoples in the Northeast, such as the Iroquois and Algonquian. These peoples hunted and gathered wild foods and grew some crops.

The Metropolitan Museum of Art, Gift of Edgar William and Bernice Chrysler Garbisch, 1963 (63.201.3)

Colonial Era Europeans began settling in North America in the 1500s. The Spanish, French, English, Dutch, and others established **colonies**. A colony is a territory controlled by people from a foreign land. By the mid-1700s the British Empire included more than a dozen colonies along the Atlantic coast. New cities such as Boston and New York became major seaports in the British colonies. Spain and France claimed much of the land west of the British colonies.

Some settlers established **plantations**. A plantation is a large farm that grows mainly one crop to sell. Plantations were particularly common in the rich soils and mild climates of the southern British colonies. Many of the colonial plantations produced cotton or tobacco.

Beginning in the 1600s, thousands of enslaved Africans were brought to the colonies. Most were put to work on plantations. Slavery continued in the United States until after the Civil War in 1865. About 13 percent of Americans today are descended from Africans brought to this country by force.

Expansion The American colonies declared independence from the British Empire in 1776. Gradually, the United States expanded. By 1850 the United States stretched from the Atlantic Ocean to the Pacific Ocean. The United States bought Alaska from Russia in 1867. In 1898 Hawaii was **annexed**, or formally added to, the United States.

Industrial Growth The economy of the United States grew rapidly in the 1800s. By the late 1800s, important industries included steel, oil, and **textiles**, or cloth products. The steel industry grew around cities that were near coal and iron ore deposits. Most of those new industrial cities were in Appalachian and Midwest states.

The development of waterways and railroads helped industry and people move farther into the interior. The chance for a better life also attracted millions of immigrants. Immigration was particularly heavy in the late 1800s and early 1900s. The cultural diversity of the United States is a result of this historical pattern of immigration.

New York's Erie Canal was built in the early 1800s. It allowed barges to move goods to and from farms and factories.

Interpreting the Visual Record

Human-Environment Interaction How did the canal influence the economic development of New York farmland?

War and Peace Despite two world wars and other conflicts in the 1900s, the United States continued to prosper. Many Americans died in World Wars I and II. However, no battles were fought on the U.S. mainland. This spared the country the terrible damage seen in Europe, Asia, and the Pacific. After World War II, the United States and the Soviet Union became rivals in what was known as the Cold War. The Cold War lasted until the 1990s. U.S. troops served in several foreign wars in the last half of the 1900s. Today, the United States is a leading member of many international organizations.

Government The United States has a limited, democratic government based on the U.S. Constitution. This document spells out the powers and functions of the branches of the federal government. The national government includes an elected president and Congress. In general, the national government handles issues affecting the whole country. Many powers are left to the 50 state governments.

Rights and Responsibilities American citizens have many rights and responsibilities, including the right to vote. They are encouraged to play an active role in government. Without such participation, the democratic system suffers. In this regard, the United States is similar to other democratic countries, like Germany and Great Britain. It differs from countries with minority rule, like China, where the government limits political rights.

✓ **READING CHECK:** (*Human Systems*) What were some major events in the history of the United States?

The U.S. Constitution has served as a model for governments in other countries.

The Granger Collection, New York

A Diverse People

The United States is home to people who speak many languages. About 17 million people in this country speak Spanish. Many of these people live in areas near Spanish-speaking countries like Mexico and Cuba.

Some people are **bilingual**. Bilingual means having the ability to speak two languages. By the 1990s more than 30 million U.S. residents spoke a language other than English. These languages include Spanish, French, Chinese, Russian, Arabic, and Navajo.

The United States is also home to many religious faiths. Most people are Protestant Christians or Roman Catholics. However, many cities have Jewish synagogues and Islamic mosques, as well as places of worship for other religions. This religious variety adds to cultural diversity by contributing distinct ideas and customs to American life.

America's food is as diverse as its people. Chinese, Mexican, and Arab dishes are now part of the American diet. They join traditional foods such as fried chicken.

Americans have varied traditions and enjoy many different forms of entertainment. They celebrate a variety of holidays, such as *Cinco de Mayo* or Saint Patrick's Day. Many Americans celebrate Independence Day on July 4 with fireworks, concerts, and picnics.

Many religious holidays are also celebrated in the United States. These include the Christian holidays of Christmas and Easter and the Jewish celebrations of Hanukkah, Yom Kippur, and Rosh Hashanah. Some African Americans also celebrate Kwanzaa. Kwanzaa is based on a traditional African festival.

The United States has been home to many noted artists and writers. You might, for example, be familiar with the art of Georgia O'Keeffe. American writers include Mark Twain, Emily Dickinson, and Langston Hughes. In addition, musical forms such as blues, jazz, and rock 'n' roll have origins in this country.

American movies, television programs, and sports also are popular elsewhere. In many ways the United States influences the rest of the world through its culture.

Many people visit New Orleans, Louisiana, to listen to the city's popular jazz bands.

Interpreting the Visual Record *Place*
What can you learn about the climate of New Orleans by looking at the building in this picture?

✓ **READING CHECK:** (*Human Systems*) How has cultural diversity enriched life in the United States?

Define and explain: colonies, plantations, annexed, textiles, bilingual

Working with Sketch Maps On the map that you created in Section 1, label Boston and New York. In a box in the margin, identify the location of the thirteen British colonies that became the United States.

Reading for the Main Idea

1. (*Human Systems*) How long did it take for the United States to expand from the Atlantic Ocean to the Pacific Ocean?

2. (*Human Systems*) What are the roles and responsibilities of citizens of the United States?

go. hrw .com
Homework Practice Online
Keyword: SG5 HP4

Critical Thinking

3. Drawing Inferences and Conclusions How do you think American culture has been able to influence people and culture around the world? What affect has it had?

4. Analyzing Information How are the many cultural traditions of the United States reflected in its religious holidays? Give examples.

Organizing What You Know

5. Sequencing Copy the following time line. Use it to list important events that took place in North America during the centuries shown. The time line has been started for you.

1500s	1600s	1700s	1800s	1900s

1500s
Europeans begin to settle North America.

Art and Memories

Throughout history, people have created statues to help them remember past events. Some of these monuments remind us of tragedies and of the sacrifices made by our fellow citizens. For hundreds, even thousands of years, most of these memorial works of art have been fairly realistic statues of people. For example, the ancient Greeks and Romans carved statues of soldiers who died in battle. Your city may have a similar monument—perhaps a bronze statue dedicated to local citizens who served in World War II.

In Washington, D.C., the Vietnam Veterans Memorial honors the men and women who gave their lives during the Vietnam War. A college student named Maya Lin designed the main feature of the memorial—a wall made of two black granite panels. Each panel is more

than 246 feet long. Etched into the dark rock are the names of the 58,226 Americans who died in Vietnam. The monument was controversial at first because it was very different from the traditional style for memorials. Since then, millions of Americans have come to appreciate the new design. In fact, they have made it their own by leaving mementos at the wall. Among the thousands of items that have been left there are children's toys, family photographs, birthday cards, and battered combat boots.

On April 19, 1995, 168 Americans died in a terrorist attack on the Murrah Building in Oklahoma City, Oklahoma. Like the Vietnam wall, the design for the Oklahoma City National Memorial didn't follow traditional styles. Instead, nine rows of chairs, one for each of the victims, are silent

Memorial Day and Veterans Day draw many visitors to the Vietnam Veterans Memorial.

The empty chairs of the Oklahoma City National Memorial symbolize the loss felt by the victims' families and friends. Each bronze, stone, and glass chair bears the name of one of the Murrah Building victims.

This picture shows what designers and architects have planned for the World Trade Center site in New York City. The view is from the southeast.

reminders of the horror. To commemorate the children who died in the tragedy, 19 of the chairs are smaller than the others.

The United States experienced another tragedy with the terrorist attacks on the World Trade Center in New York City on September 11, 2001. Soon after that terrible day, visitors began leaving candles, notes, flowers, and other tributes on a nearby fence. To create a permanent memorial, thousands of people would also participate. Artists around the world submitted designs for the memorial to the lives lost. In 2004, a panel of experts that included Maya Lin announced the winner from over 5,200 entries.

The winning design, called *Reflecting Absence*, will be built on the site where the World Trade Center Twin Towers once stood. The memorial includes two reflecting pools and the names of those who died in the attack.

Understanding What You Read

1. How do memorial designs of recent years differ from traditional designs?
2. How have Americans shown their respect for the people who lost their lives in the Vietnam War and the terrorist attacks?

Read to Discover

1. What are the major economic characteristics of the five regions of the United States?
2. What are some of the challenges the United States faces today?

Vocabulary

second-growth forests
megalopolis
diversify
Corn Belt
Dairy Belt
Wheat Belt
center-pivot irrigation
strip mining
trade deficit

Places

Washington, D.C.
Philadelphia
Baltimore
Atlanta
Houston
New Orleans
Miami
Dallas
Chicago
Detroit
Phoenix
Las Vegas
San Diego
San Francisco
Seattle
Portland

Reading Strategy

TAKING NOTES Taking notes while you read will help you understand and remember information in this section. Write down the headings in this section. As you read, fill in what you learn about the five regions of the United States under each heading.

▲ Small towns and beautiful scenery can be found throughout Vermont and the rest of New England.

A Prosperous Country

The United States is the richest country in the world. The value of all American products and services exceeds that of any other country. Now we will examine how each American region contributes to this powerful economy. These five regions are the Northeast, the South, the Midwest, the Interior West, and the Pacific.

The Northeast

The Northeast includes 12 states and shares a border with Canada. First we will look at the New England states. These are Maine, New Hampshire, Vermont, Massachusetts, Rhode Island, and Connecticut. Then we will turn to the Middle Atlantic states. They are New York, Pennsylvania, New Jersey, Delaware, Maryland, and West Virginia.

New England A short growing season and rocky terrain limit farming in New England. As a result, most farms in this region are small. Some are now used as second homes or retirement retreats for people living in cities.

Cool, shallow waters off the coast are good fishing areas. Cod and shellfish are the most valuable seafood. The U.S. government has set rules to prevent overfishing in some areas.

The early shipbuilding industry in New England used wood from the region's forests. Nearly all of New England's forests today are **second-growth forests**. These are the trees that cover an area after the original forest has been cut. In the fall New England's forests burst into color. The beautiful fall scenery draws many tourists.

New England was the country's first industrial area. Textile mills and shoe factories were built along rivers and swift streams. The flowing water provided power for the mills. Today, many banks, investment houses, and insurance companies are based in the region. In addition, the area has many respected colleges and universities. These schools include Harvard, Yale, the Massachusetts Institute of Technology, and many others.

Middle Atlantic States
Soils are better for farming in the Middle Atlantic states. However, the region's expanding cities have taken over more and more farmland.

Major coal-mining areas are found in the Appalachians, particularly in West Virginia and Pennsylvania. Coal is used in the steelmaking process. The steel industry helped make Pittsburgh, in western Pennsylvania, the largest industrial city in the Appalachians.

Today nearly every kind of manufacturing and service industry can be found in the Middle Atlantic states. Major seaports allow farmers and companies to ship their products to markets around the world. In addition, tourists visit natural and historical sites. These sites include Niagara Falls between New York and Canada and Gettysburg, a major Civil War battleground in Pennsylvania.

United States

Country	Population/ Growth Rate	Life Expectancy	Literacy Rate	Per Capita GDP
United States	290,342,554 0.9%	74, male 80, female	97%	$37,600

Source: Central Intelligence Agency, *The World Factbook 2003*

Interpreting the Chart **What is the U.S. per capita GDP?**

New York City is an important seaport.

Interpreting the Visual Record

Movement **Why do you suppose shipping helped the major cities of the Northeast grow?**

▼

Megalopolis Overlapping the two areas of the Northeast is a huge, densely populated urban area. This area is called a **megalopolis**. A megalopolis is a string of cities that have grown together. Here it stretches along the Atlantic coast from Boston to Washington, D.C. D.C. stands for District of Columbia. The three other major cities are New York City, Philadelphia, and Baltimore. At least 40 million people live in this urban area.

Except for Washington, D.C., all of these cities were founded during the colonial era. They grew because they were important seaports. Today, they are major industrial and financial centers as well. These cities are connected by roads, railroads, and airline routes. Many of the world's largest companies have home offices there. Washington, D.C., is the country's capital and the center for government offices.

✓ **READING CHECK:** (*Places and Regions*) What are some of the major economic features of the Northeast?

The South

The South includes 12 states. They are Virginia, North Carolina, South Carolina, Georgia, Florida, Alabama, Mississippi, Tennessee, Kentucky, Arkansas, Louisiana, and Texas. The region has long coastlines along the Atlantic Ocean and the Gulf of Mexico. Texas shares a long border with Mexico.

Agriculture Historically, the South was rural and agricultural. Many small towns and farming areas still stretch across the region. The South has long been a major producer of cotton, tobacco, and citrus fruit. In recent years, some farmers have decided to **diversify**. This means those farmers are producing a variety of crops instead of just one.

Many visitors to San Antonio, Texas, enjoy dining along the Riverwalk.

Interpreting the Visual Record (Place)
How does architecture along the Riverwalk reflect San Antonio's cultural history?

▼

Industry The South has become more urban and industrial in recent decades. The South's cities, such as Atlanta, have grown along with the economy. More than 3.5 million people live in and around Atlanta.

Today, many textile factories operate in the Piedmont areas of Georgia, the Carolinas, and Virginia. Some cities, such as Austin, Texas, also have growing computer, software, and publishing companies. The Texas Gulf Coast and the lower Mississippi River area have huge oil refineries and petrochemical plants. Their products are shipped from Houston, New Orleans, and other major seaports.

Warm weather and beautiful beaches draw many vacationers to resorts in the South. Resort areas include eastern Virginia and Florida. Many people also vacation in the coastal islands of North and South Carolina and Texas.

Many cities in the South have important links with countries in both Central and South America. This is largely because they are located close to those countries. For example, Miami is an important travel connection with Caribbean countries, Mexico, and South America. Atlanta, Houston, and Dallas also are major transportation centers.

✓ **READING CHECK:**   *Places and Regions*   How does geography affect the economic resources of the South?

▲
The Mississippi River flows past the Gateway Arch in St. Louis, Missouri. The city was known as the "gateway to the West" in the 1800s.

A Corn can be processed in a variety of ways. Some corn is cooked and then canned.
B Corn is ground and used for livestock feed.
C Corn also might be wet-milled or dry-milled. Then grain parts are used to make different products.
D Corn by-products, such as cornstarch and corn syrup, are used to make breads, breakfast cereals, and snack foods.

The Midwest

The Midwest includes eight states: Ohio, Michigan, Indiana, Illinois, Wisconsin, Minnesota, Iowa, and Missouri. All but Iowa and Missouri have shorelines on the Great Lakes.

Corn: From Field to Consumer

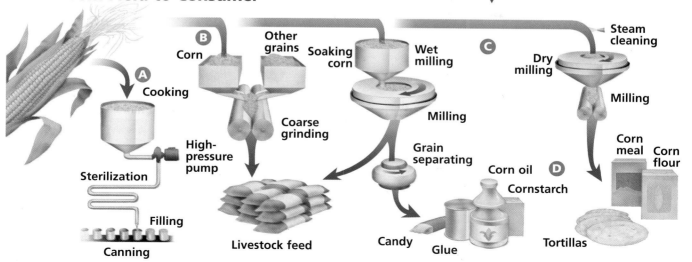

CONNECTING TO Technology

The Great Lakes and St. Lawrence Seaway

The St. Lawrence Seaway permits ships to go between the Great Lakes and the Atlantic Ocean. This waterway's canals and locks allow ships to move from one water level to another. The difference in water levels is significant. For example, Lake Erie is about 570 feet (174 m) above sea level. Farther to the east, Montreal is about 100 feet (30 m) above sea level. Ships moving from one water level to another enter a lock. The water level inside the lock is raised or lowered. It is changed to match the water level in the waterway ahead of the ship. From there, the ship can move on to the next lock.

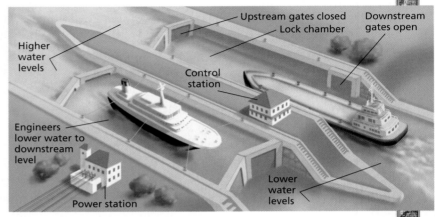

Moving through a canal lock

Labels: Higher water levels; Engineers lower water to downstream level; Power station; Control station; Upstream gates closed; Lock chamber; Downstream gates open; Lower water levels

Understanding What You Read

1. What U.S. cities are located along the shores of the Great Lakes? Why might they have been established here?

2. Which of the Great Lakes lies at the highest elevation? Which lies at the lowest elevation?

Agriculture Good soils and flat land have helped make the Midwest one of the world's great farming regions. Farmers produce corn, dairy products, and soybeans and raise livestock.

The core of the Midwest's corn-growing region is the **Corn Belt**. It stretches from central Ohio to central Nebraska. Much of the corn is used to feed livestock, such as beef cattle and hogs. Soybean production has also become important.

States in the **Dairy Belt** are major producers of milk, cheese, and other dairy products. The Dairy Belt lies north of the Corn Belt. This area includes Wisconsin and most of Minnesota and Michigan. Much of the Dairy Belt is pasture. Farmers also grow crops to feed dairy cows.

Many of the Midwest's farm and factory products are shipped to markets by water. One route is along the Mississippi River to the Gulf of Mexico. The other is through the Great Lakes. This route continues through the St. Lawrence Seaway to the Atlantic Ocean.

Industry One of the busiest shipping ports on the Great Lakes is Chicago, Illinois. This city also has one of the world's busiest airports. Chicago is linked to the rest of the region by highways and railroads. Its industries attracted many immigrants in the late 1800s. They moved there to work in steel mills, meat-packing plants, and other businesses. Today, Chicago is the third-largest city in the United States.

Other Midwest cities were also founded on important transportation routes on the Great Lakes and major rivers. The locations of these cities gave industries access to nearby farm products, coal, and iron ore. Those resources have supported thriving industries. These industries include food processing, iron, steel, machinery, and automobile manufacturing. Detroit, Michigan, has been the nation's leading automobile producer since the early 1900s.

The Midwest's traditional industries declined in the late 1900s. In addition, industrial pollution threatened the Great Lakes and surrounding areas. In response, companies have modernized their plants and factories. The region has also attracted new industries. Many produce high-technology products. The Midwest is again a prosperous region. Also, stricter pollution laws have made many rivers and the Great Lakes much cleaner.

Natural sandstone pillars, arches, and other unusual formations draw many visitors to Monument Valley in Arizona and Utah.

Interpreting the Visual Record What natural force do you think may have created sandstone structures like this one?

▼

✔ **READING CHECK:** *Places and Regions*
What are the major economic activities of the Midwest? What resources support them?

The Interior West

The Interior West includes 13 states. They stretch from Idaho, Montana, and North Dakota southward to Arizona, New Mexico, and Oklahoma. West Texas might also be considered part of this region. The Interior West includes the Great Plains and the Rocky Mountains.

Canada

United States
Monument
Valley

Mexico

Yellowstone's natural beauty makes it one of the most popular national parks in the United States.

Agriculture Ranching became important in the region in the 1800s. Great herds of cattle and flocks of sheep roamed the Great Plains. Today, ranching in the region is often combined with wheat farming.

The greatest wheat-growing area is known as the **Wheat Belt**. It stretches across the Dakotas, Montana, Nebraska, Oklahoma, Colorado, and Texas. Much of the farmland in the Interior West must be irrigated. One method of irrigation uses long sprinkler systems mounted on huge wheels. The wheels rotate slowly. In this way the sprinkler irrigates the area within a circle. This is called **center-pivot irrigation**. From the air, parts of the irrigated Great Plains resemble a series of green circles.

Mining and Industry The Interior West also has rich deposits of coal, oil, gold, silver, copper, and other minerals. However, mining can cause problems. For example, coal miners in parts of the Great Plains strip away soil and rock. This process is called **strip mining**. This kind of mining leads to soil erosion and other problems. Today, laws require miners to restore mined areas.

One of the Interior West's greatest resources is its natural beauty. Parks, such as Yellowstone, are scattered throughout the region. Warm, sunny cities like Phoenix and Las Vegas are growing rapidly.

✔ **READING CHECK:** (*Places and Regions*) How does geography affect the major resources of the Interior West?

The Pacific States

The Pacific states are California, Oregon, Washington, Alaska, and Hawaii. Alaska is separated from the 48 contiguous states by Canada and the Pacific Ocean. Hawaii is a series of islands far to the west in the Pacific.

California More than 10 percent of all Americans live in California, in large part because of its mild climate and wealth of resources. More than 90 percent of the people in California live in urban areas. The Los Angeles, San Diego, and San Francisco Bay urban areas are among the largest in the country. California is the leading agricultural producer and leading industrial state. Big companies own many farms in central and southern areas. Crops include cotton, nuts, vegetables, and fruit. Aerospace, construction, entertainment, computers, software, and tourism are important industries in the state.

Northwest States Forests and fish are two of the most important resources in Oregon and Washington. Both resources have been the focus of environmental debates, and environmentalists and industry leaders continue to work on ways to resolve their differences.

Seattle is Washington's largest city. It is home to many important industries, including a major computer software company. More than half of the people in Oregon live in and around Portland.

San Francisco, California, lies across the Bay Bridge from Oakland.
Interpreting the Visual Record What does the fact that this bridge connects two large cities tell you about the San Francisco Bay area?

Alaska and Hawaii Alaska's economy is largely based on oil, forests, and fish. As in Washington and Oregon, there are debates over developing these resources. For example, some people want to limit oil drilling in wild areas of Alaska. Others want to expand drilling.

Hawaii's natural beauty, mild climate, and fertile soils are its most important resources. Millions of tourists visit the islands each year.

✓ **READING CHECK:** (*Places and Regions*) What are the economic features of the Pacific states?

Challenges Today

The United States faces many challenges today. For example, other countries look to the United States for help in resolving international conflicts. Also, U.S. soldiers have fought in several conflicts overseas.

Another challenge is trade. The United States has a **trade deficit**. This means the value of American exports is lower than the value of its imports. People have debated the best way to help American companies sell their goods abroad. Some feel the government should play an active role in promoting exports and protecting American industries. Others think that the market should be allowed to work on its own.

The United States also faces challenges at home. These have long included fighting poverty, crime, and pollution. Many people are also concerned about urban sprawl around rapidly growing cities. These are likely to remain difficult challenges during the new century.

✓ **READING CHECK:** (*Human Systems*) What are some of the challenges the United States faces today?

Our Amazing Planet

Pacific salmon return from the sea to deposit their eggs in the same rivers or streams in which they were hatched. Some species of salmon swim against the current through rapids and even waterfalls for more than 2,000 miles (3,200 km) up Alaska's Yukon River!

Section Review 3

go.hrw.com **Homework Practice Online** Keyword: SG5 HP4

Define and explain: second-growth forests, megalopolis, diversify, Corn Belt, Dairy Belt, Wheat Belt, center-pivot irrigation, strip mining, trade deficit

Working with Sketch Maps On the map you created for Section 2, label the 50 states and the following places: Washington, D.C., Philadelphia, Baltimore, Atlanta, Houston, New Orleans, Miami, Dallas, Chicago, Detroit, Phoenix, Las Vegas, San Diego, San Francisco, Seattle, and Portland. In a box in the margin, identify major U.S. seaports on your map.

Reading for the Main Idea

1. (*Places and Regions*) What five major cities make up the Northeast's megalopolis?

2. (*Human Systems*) How has the economy of the South changed in recent years?

3. **Human Systems** How do farm and industrial products from the Midwest get to markets elsewhere?

Critical Thinking

4. **Drawing Inferences and Conclusions** Why do you think a trade deficit can be a problem for a country?

Organizing What You Know

5. **Categorizing** Copy the following graphic organizer. Use it to list important economic characteristics and cities of the five regions of the United States.

Northeast	South	Midwest	Interior West	Pacific States

Review and Practice

Define and Identify

Identify each of the following:

1. contiguous
2. Continental Divide
3. basins
4. colonies
5. plantations
6. annexed
7. textiles
8. bilingual
9. second-growth forests
10. megalopolis
11. diversify
12. Corn Belt
13. center-pivot irrigation
14. strip mining
15. trade deficit

Review the Main Ideas

16. What are the two major mountain regions of the United States?
17. Where are the dry climate regions located in the United States?
18. Where was the first industrial area located in the United States?
19. Where are the Corn Belt, Dairy Belt, and Wheat Belt located?
20. Where did the steel industry grow in the late 1800s?
21. What water routes are used to transport products from the Midwest to markets outside the region?
22. What state is more than 90 percent urban?

Think Critically

23. **Contrasting** How is the physical geography of the Appalachians different from that of the Rocky Mountains? Why is this true?
24. **Drawing Inferences and Conclusions** How has climate affected agriculture in the Interior West?
25. **Finding the Main Idea** Explain the relationship between rights and responsibilities in the United States. How do you think this relationship might be different in other nations?
26. **Finding the Main Idea** What cities were supported in their development by nearby mineral resources? How?
27. **Analyzing Information** Why does the United States play a leading role in world affairs?

Map Activity

28. On a separate sheet of paper, match the letters on the map with their correct labels.

Atlantic Ocean	Great Lakes
Pacific Ocean	New York City
Alaska	Los Angeles
Hawaii	Miami
Gulf of Mexico	Chicago

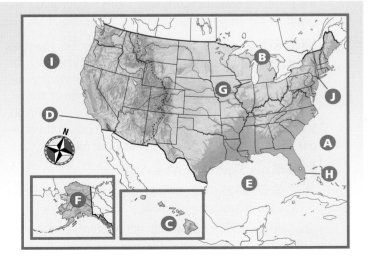

Writing Activity

You might be familiar with the song "America the Beautiful." It reminds the listener of the physical beauty of the United States—"from sea to shining sea." Write a short poem, song, or rap describing the physical geography of the eastern, interior, or western United States. Be sure to use standard grammar, spelling, sentence structure, and punctuation.

internet connect

Internet Activity: **go.hrw.com**
KEYWORD: SG5 GT4

Choose a topic to explore about the United States:
- Visit America's national parks.
- Experience life in the early colonies.
- Learn about holidays celebrated in the United States.

Social Studies Skills Practice

Interpreting Highway Maps

Study this highway map of southern Florida. Then answer the questions.

1. How can you tell the interstates from other national and state highways?

2. About how far is it between the Highway 27 and Highway 41 intersections on Florida's Turnpike?

3. What symbol indicates that drivers can enter the highways only at certain points?

4. What is the most direct route from South Miami to Hialeah? In what general direction would you be traveling?

Interpreting Primary Sources

Read the following excerpt from a letter written by Al Wurth of the Sierra Club about an old-growth forest in Pennsylvania. Then answer the questions below.

"The presence of . . . standing dead trees . . . with ample numbers of rotting logs indicates this forest has not been logged for many decades. This abundance [large amount] of decaying wood on the forest floor provides good cover for amphibians. . . . Some of the greatest concentrations of native wildflowers in the Lehigh Valley can be found in areas of this forest where outdoor recreation has not compacted its soil."

1. What are some signs that this forest has not been disturbed for a long time?

2. What use do the dead trees and decaying material serve?

3. What is the connection between outdoor recreation and damage to the forest?

4. Why do you think some people may not enjoy the old-growth forest that Wurth describes?

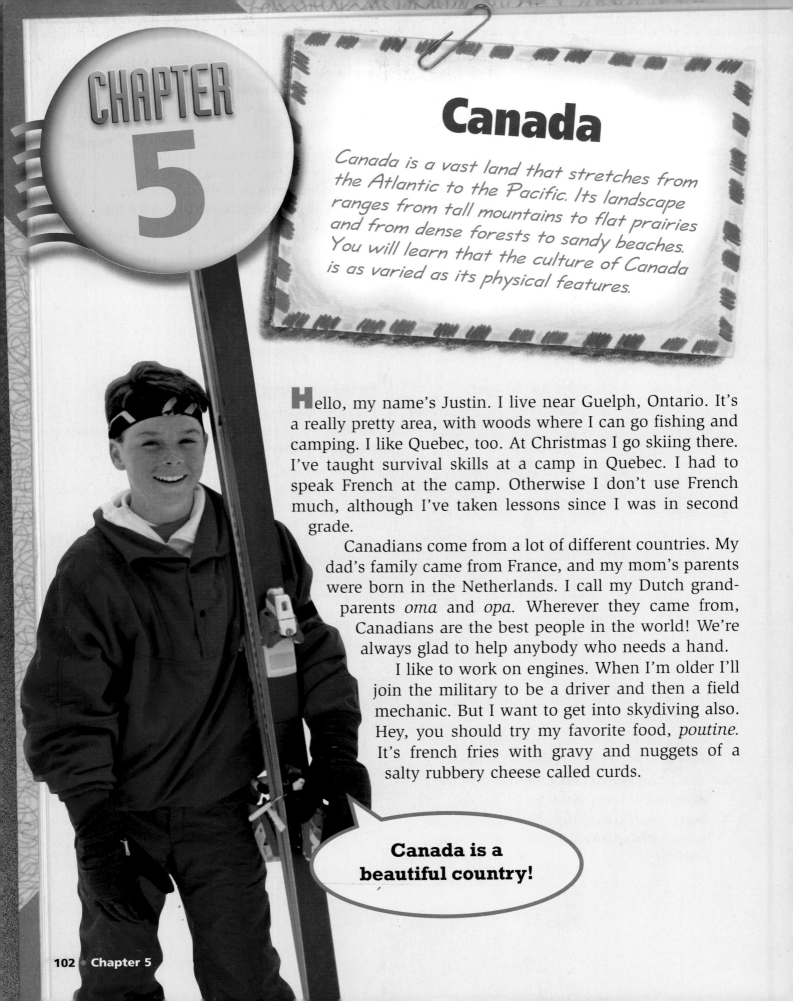

CHAPTER 5

Canada

Canada is a vast land that stretches from the Atlantic to the Pacific. Its landscape ranges from tall mountains to flat prairies and from dense forests to sandy beaches. You will learn that the culture of Canada is as varied as its physical features.

Hello, my name's Justin. I live near Guelph, Ontario. It's a really pretty area, with woods where I can go fishing and camping. I like Quebec, too. At Christmas I go skiing there. I've taught survival skills at a camp in Quebec. I had to speak French at the camp. Otherwise I don't use French much, although I've taken lessons since I was in second grade.

Canadians come from a lot of different countries. My dad's family came from France, and my mom's parents were born in the Netherlands. I call my Dutch grandparents *oma* and *opa*. Wherever they came from, Canadians are the best people in the world! We're always glad to help anybody who needs a hand.

I like to work on engines. When I'm older I'll join the military to be a driver and then a field mechanic. But I want to get into skydiving also. Hey, you should try my favorite food, *poutine*. It's french fries with gravy and nuggets of a salty rubbery cheese called curds.

Canada is a beautiful country!

Section 1 Physical Geography

Read to Discover

1. What are Canada's major landforms, rivers, and lakes?
2. What are the major climate types and natural resources of Canada?

Vocabulary

potash
pulp
newsprint

Places

Rocky Mountains
Appalachian Mountains
Canadian Shield
Hudson Bay
Great Lakes
St. Lawrence River
Great Bear Lake
Great Slave Lake

Reading Strategy

READING ORGANIZER Before you read, create four boxes on a sheet of paper by drawing a line down the center and a line across the middle of the page. Label the boxes Land, Water, Climate, and Resources. As you read the section, write down what you learn.

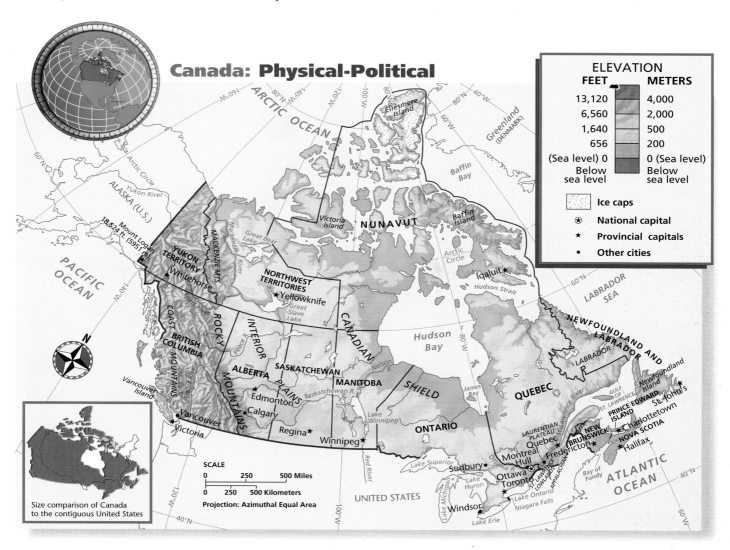

Canada: Physical-Political

ELEVATION	
FEET	METERS
13,120	4,000
6,560	2,000
1,640	500
656	200
(Sea level) 0	0 (Sea level)
Below sea level	Below sea level

Ice caps
⊛ National capital
★ Provincial capitals
• Other cities

SCALE
0   250   500 Miles
0   250   500 Kilometers
Projection: Azimuthal Equal Area

Size comparison of Canada to the contiguous United States

Physical Features

The physical geography of Canada has much in common with that of the United States. Both countries share some major physical regions. For example, the Coast Mountains and the Rocky Mountains extend into western Canada. Broad plains stretch across the interiors of both countries. Also, the Appalachian Mountains extend into southeastern Canada.

The Canadian Shield, a region of rocky uplands, borders Hudson Bay. To the south are some of Canada's most fertile soils, in the St. Lawrence River Valley and the Great Lakes region. The Great Lakes are Lake Erie, Lake Huron, Lake Michigan, Lake Ontario, and Lake Superior.

Canada has thousands of lakes and rivers. Many of Canada's lakes were carved out by Ice Age glaciers. The Great Bear and Great Slave are two of Canada's larger lakes. The most important river is the St. Lawrence. The St. Lawrence River links the Great Lakes to the Atlantic Ocean.

✓ **READING CHECK:** (*Places and Regions*) What are the major physical features of Canada?

Climate

The central and eastern parts of southern Canada have a humid continental climate. The mildest area of Canada is in the southwest. This region has a marine west coast climate. Here, winters are rainy and heavy snow falls in the mountains. Much of central and northern Canada has a subarctic climate. The far north has tundra and ice-cap climates. Permafrost underlies about half of Canada.

✓ **READING CHECK:** (*Places and Regions*) What are Canada's climates?

Banff National Park is Canada's oldest and most famous national park. The park has spectacular views of Canada's Rocky Mountains.

Interpreting the Visual Record (*Place*)
What types of climate would you expect to find here?

▼

Resources

Canada's Atlantic and Pacific coastal waters are among the world's richest fishing areas. Canada's many lakes and streams provide freshwater fish and attract tourists as well. Wheat farmers and cattle producers benefit from Canada's fertile soil.

Minerals are the most valuable of Canada's natural resources. The Canadian Shield contains many mineral deposits. Canada is a leading source of the world's nickel, zinc, and uranium. Lead, copper, gold, silver, and coal are also present. Saskatchewan has the world's largest deposits of **potash**, a mineral used to make fertilizer. Alberta produces most of Canada's oil and natural gas.

A belt of coniferous forests stretches across Canada from Labrador to the Pacific coast. These trees provide lumber and **pulp**. Pulp—softened wood fibers—is used to make paper. The United States, the United Kingdom, and Japan get much of their **newsprint** from Canada. Newsprint is cheap paper used mainly for newspapers.

✓ **READING CHECK:** *Environment and Society* How do Canada's major resources affect its economy?

Canada's resources can be shipped to markets through Vancouver.

Logs are floated down British Columbia's rivers to sawmills. Timber is a major resource.

Homework Practice Online
Keyword: SG5 HP5

Section Review 1

Define and explain: potash, pulp, newsprint

Working with Sketch Maps On a map of Canada that you draw or that your teacher provides, label the following: Rocky Mountains, Appalachian Mountains, Canadian Shield, Hudson Bay, Great Lakes, St. Lawrence River, Great Bear Lake, and Great Slave Lake.

Reading for the Main Idea

1. (*Places and Regions*) What are Canada's major landforms?

2. (*Places and Regions*) What river links the Great Lakes to the Atlantic Ocean?

Critical Thinking

3. **Drawing Inferences and Conclusions** Why do you think there are so many lakes in Canada?

4. **Drawing Inferences and Conclusions** Where would you expect to find Canada's mildest climate? Why?

Organizing What You Know

5. **Finding the Main Idea** Use the following graphic organizer to identify Canadian resources and their economic benefits.

Natural Resources

Read to Discover

1. How did France and Britain affect Canada's history?
2. How have immigrants influenced Canadian culture?

Vocabulary

provinces
dominion
Métis

People

Samuel de Champlain

Places

Quebec
Ontario
Nova Scotia
New Brunswick
Newfoundland
Prince Edward Island
British Columbia
Manitoba
Alberta
Saskatchewan

Reading Strategy

TAKING NOTES As you read, create an outline by using the headings in this section. Fill in notes beneath each heading. Include dates of important events in your notes.

▲
A French artist shows an early expedition in Canada led by French explorer Jacques Cartier. Cartier explored the St. Lawrence River area up to present-day Montreal in the 1500s.

History

As the ice sheets of the ice ages melted, people moved into all areas of what is now Canada. As they did elsewhere in the Americas, Native Canadians adapted to the physical environment.

Over the years, these first Canadians divided into groups known as the First Nations. Cree, Déné, Mohawk, Ojibwa, Oneida, and Kwakiutl are a few of their names. In the far north the Inuit adapted to the region's extreme cold, where farming was impossible. By hunting seals, whales, walruses, and other animals, the Inuit could feed, clothe, and house themselves.

European Settlement The first Europeans in Canada were the Vikings, or Norse. They landed on Newfoundland Island in about A.D. 1000. Norse settlement either failed or was abandoned. European exploration began again in the late 1400s. Explorers and fishers from western Europe began crossing the Atlantic.

Europeans valued the furs that Native Canadians supplied. The Canadians wanted European metal goods like kettles and axes. Both groups began to adopt aspects of each other's culture, including foods, clothing, and travel methods.

The French built the Fortress of Louisbourg in Nova Scotia. The British captured the fortress in 1758.

New France France was the first European country to successfully settle parts of what would become Canada. Quebec City was founded in 1608. The French called their new territories in North America New France. At its height, New France included much of eastern Canada and the central United States. New France was important for several reasons. It was part of the French Empire. It was a base that could be used to spread France's religion and culture. It was also an important commercial area for France's empire.

France and Britain were rival colonial powers. Part of their competition included building and defending their empires around the world. The French built trade and diplomatic relations with the First Nations people. The French did this to increase their power and influence on the continent. Furs, fish, and other products were traded between New France and other parts of the French Empire. Manufactured goods from France and other countries in Europe became the main imports to New France. French missionaries tried to convert native people to Christianity. Some did become Christians, while others held to their traditional beliefs.

New France lasted a century and a half before it was conquered by the British. During that time, it shaped the geography of Canada in important ways. The descendants of French settlers form one of Canada's major ethnic groups today. Almost a quarter of present-day Canadians are of French ancestry. This has deeply affected Canada's culture and politics.

British Conquest and American Revolution The Seven Years' War (1756–63) was mainly fought in Europe. This same period of conflict in the American colonies was called the French and Indian War. As a result of that war the British took control of New France. A

BIOGRAPHY

Samuel de Champlain
(1567–1635)

Character Trait: Pursuit of Excellence

Known as the Father of New France, Samuel de Champlain established the first permanent French colony in North America in 1604 in Nova Scotia. He later moved the colony to Quebec City. In 1629, English forces captured Quebec and put Champlain in prison. When France regained control of Quebec, Champlain returned to New France to serve as governor.

How did Champlain pursue excellence?

Canada • 107

small number of French went back to France. However, the great majority of the *habitants* (inhabitants) stayed. For most of them, few changes occurred in their daily activities. They farmed the same land, prayed in the same churches, and continued to speak French. Few English-speaking settlers came to what is now called Quebec.

The American Revolution pushed new groups of people into other areas of British North America. Many United Empire Loyalists—Americans who remained loyal to the king of England—fled north. Most Loyalists either could not stay in the new United States or were too afraid to remain. For some, their political views may have led them to move to British-controlled territories. For many others, it was the desire to get free land. This movement of people was part of a larger westward migration of pioneers.

After the American Revolution, the borders of British North America were redrawn. Quebec was divided into two colonies. Lower Canada was mostly French-speaking, and Upper Canada was mostly English-speaking. The boundary between Upper and Lower Canada forms part of the border between the **provinces** of Quebec and Ontario today. Provinces are administrative divisions of a country. To the east, Nova Scotia (noh-vuh skoh-shuh) was also divided. A new province called New Brunswick was created where many of the British Loyalists lived.

Creation of Canada   For two generations these colonies developed separately. The British also maintained colonies in Newfoundland, Prince Edward Island, the western plains, and the Pacific coast. The colonies viewed themselves as different from other parts of the British Empire. Therefore, the British Parliament created the Dominion of Canada in 1867. A **dominion** is a territory or area of influence. For Canadians, the creation of the Dominion was a statement of independence. They saw a future separate from that of the United States. The motto of the new Dominion was "from sea to sea."

The British flag flies alongside the provincial flag at government buildings in Victoria, British Columbia. Canada is a member of the British Commonwealth of Nations. In fact, the British monarch also is Canada's.

However, it included only New Brunswick, Nova Scotia, and the southern parts of Ontario and Quebec.

How would Canadians create a nation from sea to sea? With railroads. The Canadian heartland in Ontario and Quebec was already well served by railroads. From the heartland the Intercolonial Railway would run east to the Atlantic Ocean. The Canadian Pacific Railroad would be the first of three transcontinental railroads running west to the Pacific Ocean. It was completed in 1885. Both British Columbia and Prince Edward Island were quickly added to the Dominion.

Canada also acquired vast lands between the original provinces and British Columbia. It also expanded to the north. Much of this land was bought from the Hudson's Bay Company, a British fur-trading business. Most of the people in this area were Canadian Indians and **Métis** (may-TEES). Métis, people of mixed European and native ancestry, considered themselves a separate group. With the building of the railroads and the signing of treaties with Native Canadians, the way was opened for settlement of the area. Manitoba became a province in 1870. Alberta and Saskatchewan followed in 1905.

Government Canada is a federation today. It has a central government led by a prime minister. Its 10 provincial governments are each led by a premier. Canada's central government is similar to our federal government. Its provincial governments are much like our state governments. A federal system lets people keep their feelings of loyalty to their own province. At the same time they remain part of a larger national identity.

✔ **READING CHECK:** (*Human Systems*) How is Canada's government similar to that of the United States?

This train follows the Bow River in Alberta.

Interpreting the Visual Record

(*Human-Environment Interaction*) **How did railroad technology help people change their environment?**

▼

Culture

A history of colonial rule and waves of immigration have shaped Canada today. The country is home to a variety of ethnic groups and cultures. They have combined to form a single country and Canadian identity.

Immigration During the late 1800s and early 1900s, many immigrants from Europe came to Canada. Many farmed, but others worked in mines, forests, and factories. British Columbia became the first Canadian province to have a substantial Asian minority. Many Chinese Canadians helped build the railroads.

These immigrants played an important part in the economic boom that Canada experienced in the early 1900s. Quebec, New Brunswick,

	Canada			
COUNTRY	**POPULATION/ GROWTH RATE**	**LIFE EXPECTANCY**	**LITERACY RATE**	**PER CAPITA GDP**
Canada	32,207,113 0.94%	76, male 83, female	97%	$29,400
United States	290,342,554 0.9%	74, male 80, female	97%	$37,600

Source: Central Intelligence Agency, *The World Factbook 2003*

Interpreting the Chart **Which country has the greater growth rate?**

Visitors enjoy the sights and sounds of a children's festival in Vancouver. Vancouver and other Canadian cities are home to large and increasingly diverse populations.

and Ontario produced wheat, pulp, and paper. British Columbia and Ontario supplied minerals and hydroelectricity. By the 1940s Canadians enjoyed one of the highest standards of living in the world.

Movement to Cities In recent years Canadians have moved from farms to the cities. Some settlements in Newfoundland—which became Canada's 10th province in 1949—and rural Saskatchewan disappeared because the people left. Many Canadians have moved to Ontario to find jobs. Others moved to British Columbia for its mild climate. Resources such as oil, gas, potash, and uranium have changed the economies of the western provinces. The economic center of power remains in the cities of southern Ontario and southwestern Quebec. Toronto is now Canada's largest city. Many Canadian businesses have their main offices there.

After World War II, another wave of immigrants from Europe came to Canada. They were joined by other people from Africa, the Caribbean, Latin America, and particularly Asia. Asian businesspeople have brought a great deal of wealth to Canada's economy. Most immigrants have settled in Canada's large cities. Toronto has become one of the most culturally diverse cities in the world. Many Canadians now enjoy Thai, Vietnamese, and other Asian foods. Chinese New Year parades and other colorful festivals attract tourists.

✓ **READING CHECK:** *Human Systems* How has immigration changed Canada?

Section Review 2

Define or identify: Samuel de Champlain, provinces, dominion, Métis

Working with Sketch Maps On the map you created in Section 1, label Quebec, Ontario, Nova Scotia, New Brunswick, Newfoundland, Prince Edward Island, British Columbia, Manitoba, Alberta, and Saskatchewan. Which provinces seem to use lines of latitude as boundaries?

Reading for the Main Idea

1. *Human Systems* How did French and British colonization influence Canada's history?

2. *Human Systems* How did immigrants contribute to Canada?

Critical Thinking

3. Identifying Cause and Effect Why did Europeans come to Canada? What was the effect of the arrival of Europeans on the First Nations?

4. Summarizing How and why was the country of Canada created?

Organizing What You Know

5. Sequencing Copy the following graphic organizer. Use it to explain how the Dominion of Canada developed. Add boxes as needed.

Quebec	⇨	Ontario	⇨	

Read to Discover

1. How has regionalism affected Canada?
2. Into what major areas and provinces is Canada divided?

Vocabulary

regionalism
maritime
Inuit

Places

Gulf of St. Lawrence
Labrador
Halifax
Windsor
Quebec City
Montreal
Toronto
Ottawa
Edmonton
Calgary
Winnipeg
Vancouver
Yukon Territory
Northwest Territories
Nunavut

Reading Strategy

MNEMONIC DEVICE Use the chapter map or skim the section to find the names of Canada's provinces. Write down the names. As you read, create a mnemonic device, or memory game, that helps you remember an important fact about each province.

Regionalism

English is the main language in most of Canada. In Quebec, however, French is the dominant language. The cultural differences between English and French Canada have created problems. When Canadians from different regions discuss important issues, they are often influenced by **regionalism**. Regionalism refers to the strong connection that people feel toward their region. Sometimes, this connection is stronger than their connection to their country as a whole.

Regionalism was very important in America during the 1800s. At that time the United States split into the North and the South as its citizens fought the Civil War. The country was divided over issues such as slavery. People supported whichever group shared their beliefs. In Canada many residents of Quebec, or Quebecois (kay-buh-kwah), believe their province should be given a special status. Quebecois argue that this status would recognize the cultural differences between their province and the rest of Canada. Some even want Quebec to become independent.

On the other hand, many English-speaking Canadians think Quebec already has too many privileges. Others, especially in western Canada, want the provinces to have more freedom from national control. Most Canadians, however, still support a united Canada. Strong feelings of regionalism will continue to be an important issue in Canada's future.

▲ Residents of Quebec demonstrate for independence. The sign reads "Yes, it becomes possible."

✓ **READING CHECK:** (*Human Systems*) Why do some people in Quebec want independence from the rest of Canada?

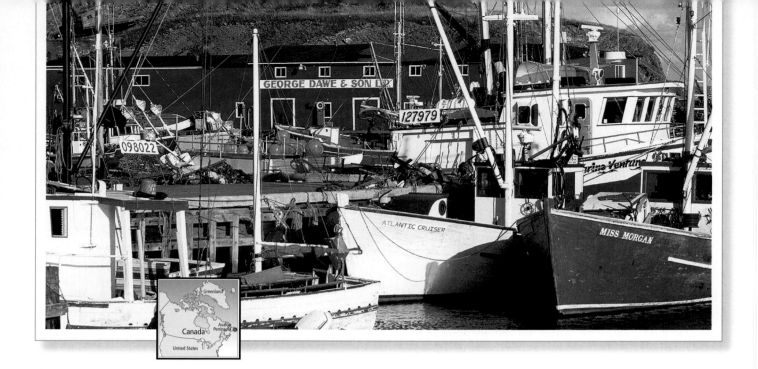

The harbor at Avalon Peninsula is home to many fishing boats.

Interpreting the Visual Record (Place)
Why do you think most people in the Maritime Provinces live in coastal cities?

Our Amazing Planet

Canada's Bay of Fundy has some of the highest tides in the world — up to 70 feet (21 m). The tide brings water from the North Atlantic into the narrow bay. The bore, or leading wave of the incoming water, can roar like a big truck as the tide rushes in.

The Eastern Provinces

New Brunswick, Nova Scotia, and Prince Edward Island are often called the Maritime Provinces. **Maritime** means "on or near the sea." Each of these provinces is located near the ocean. Prince Edward Island is a small island, and Nova Scotia occupies a peninsula. New Brunswick has coasts on the Gulf of St. Lawrence and on the Bay of Fundy. Newfoundland and Labrador is usually not considered one of the Maritime Provinces. It includes the island of Newfoundland and a large region of the mainland called Labrador.

A short growing season and poor soils make farming difficult in the eastern provinces. Most of the region's economy is related to forestry and fishing.

Many people in the eastern provinces are descendants of families that emigrated from the British Isles. In addition, many French-speaking families have moved from Quebec to New Brunswick. Most of the region's people live in coastal cities. The cities have industrial plants and serve as fishing and shipping ports. Halifax, Nova Scotia, is the region's largest city.

✔ **READING CHECK:** (*Places and Regions*) Why are most of the eastern provinces called the Maritime Provinces?

The Heartland

Inland from the eastern provinces are Quebec and Ontario. More than half of all Canadians live in these heartland provinces. In fact, the chain of cities that extends from Windsor, Ontario, to the city of Quebec is the country's most urbanized region.

CONNECTING TO *Literature*

Anne of Green Gables
by Lucy Maud Montgomery

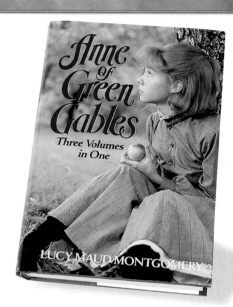

Canada's smallest province, Prince Edward Island, was the birthplace (in 1874) of one of the country's best-loved writers. Lucy Maud Montgomery based her Anne of Green Gables *series on the island she loved. She created characters and situations that lived in the minds of readers. Since its publication in 1908,* Anne of Green Gables *put the tiny island on the map, inspiring tours and festivals. It has even drawn tourists from as far away as Japan. They come to capture the spirit of the brave orphan. In this passage, young Anne is being driven to Green Gables by her new guardian, Matthew. He is kind but hardly imaginative!*

Anne says, "When I don't like the name of a place or a person I always imagine a new one and always think of them so. There was a girl at the asylum [orphanage] whose name was Hepzibah Jenkins, but I always imagined her as Rosalia DeVere." . . .

They had driven over the crest of a hill. Below them was a pond. . . . A bridge spanned it midway and from there to its lower end, where an amber-hued belt of sand hills shut it in from the dark-blue gulf beyond, the water was a glory of many shifting hues. . . .

"That's Barry's pond," said Matthew.

"Oh, I don't like that name, either. I shall call it—let me see—the Lake of Shining Waters. Yes, that is the right name for it. I know because of the thrill. When I hit on a name that suits exactly it gives me a thrill. Do things ever give you a thrill?"

Matthew ruminated.[1] "Well now, yes. It always kind of gives me a thrill to see them ugly white grubs[2] that spade up in the cucumber beds. I hate the look of them."

"Oh, I don't think that can be exactly the same kind of thrill. Do you think it can? There doesn't seem to be much connection between grubs and lakes of shining waters, does there? But why do other people call it Barry's pond?"

"I reckon because Mr. Barry lives up there in that house."

Analyzing Primary Sources
1. Why is *Anne of Green Gables* popular outside of Prince Edward Island?
2. How does imagination affect a person's view of the world?

Definitions ¹ruminate: to think over in the mind slowly   ²grubs: wormlike insect larvae

Day draws to a close in Toronto, Ontario. The city is located at the site of a trading post from the 1600s. Today Toronto is one of North America's major cities.

Quebec The city of Quebec is the capital of the province. The city's older section has narrow streets, stone walls, and French-style architecture. Montreal is Canada's second-largest city and one of the largest French-speaking cities in the world. About 3.5 million people live in the Montreal metropolitan area. It is the financial and industrial center of the province. Winters in Montreal are very cold. People in the city center use underground passages and overhead tunnels to move between buildings.

Ontario Ontario is Canada's leading manufacturing province. It is also Canada's most populous province. About 4.7 million people live in the metropolitan area of Toronto, Ontario's capital. Toronto is a major center for industry, finance, education, and culture. Toronto's residents have come from many different regions, including China, Europe, and India. Between Toronto and Montreal lies Ottawa, Canada's capital. In Ottawa many people speak both English and French. It has grand government buildings, parks, and several universities.

✔ **READING CHECK:** (*Places and Regions*) What are the major cities of Canada's heartland?

Canada's Prairie Provinces are home to productive farms like this one near Brandon, Manitoba.

Interpreting the Visual Record (*Place*) **What can you tell about the physical geography of this region of Canada?**

▼

The Western Provinces

Farther to the west are the major farming regions of Manitoba, Saskatchewan, and Alberta. These three provinces are called the Prairie Provinces. Along the Pacific coast is British Columbia.

The Prairie Provinces More people live in Quebec than in all of the Prairie Provinces combined. The southern grasslands of these provinces are part of a rich wheat belt. Farms here produce far more wheat than Canadians need. The extra wheat is exported. Oil and natural gas production also are important in Alberta. Rocky Mountain resorts in western Alberta attract many tourists. The major cities of the Prairie Provinces are Edmonton, Calgary, and Winnipeg.

British Columbia British Columbia is Canada's westernmost province. This mountainous province has rich natural resources, including forests, salmon, and important minerals. Almost 4 million people live in British Columbia. Nearly half of them are in the coastal city of Vancouver. Vancouver is a multicultural city with large Chinese and Indian populations. It also is a major trade center.

✓ **READING CHECK:** (*Environment and Society*) How does geography affect the location of economic activities in the Prairie Provinces?

Our Amazing Planet

In the St. Elias Mountains in the Yukon Territory is the world's largest nonpolar ice field. The field covers an area of 15,822 square miles (40,570 sq km) and stretches into Alaska.

First Nations people of British Columbia created this totem pole.

▼

The Canadian North

Canada's vast northern lands include the Yukon Territory, the Northwest Territories, and Nunavut (noo-nah-vuht). Nunavut is a new territory created for the **Inuit** (Eskimos) who live there. *Nunavut* means "Our Land" in the Inuit language. Nunavut is part of Canada, but the people have their own local government. The three territories cover more than one third of Canada but are home to only about 100,000 people. Boreal forests, tundra, and frozen Arctic ocean waters separate isolated towns and villages.

✓ **READING CHECK:** Who lives in Nunavut?

Section Review 3

go. hrw .com **Homework Practice Online**
Keyword: SG5 HP5

Define and explain: regionalism, maritime, Inuit

Working with Sketch Maps On the map that you created in Section 2, locate and label the major cities of Canada's provinces and territories. Where are most of these major cities located? What may have led to their growth?

Reading for the Main Idea

1. (*Places and Regions*) How does regionalism affect Canada's culture?

2. (*The World in Spatial Terms*) Into which provincial groups is Canada divided?

Critical Thinking

3. Drawing Inferences and Conclusions What makes the heartland a good area in which to settle?

4. Finding the Main Idea Why was Nunavut created?

Organizing What You Know

5. Categorizing Use the following graphic organizer to identify Canada's regions and provinces.

Region	Provinces

Review and Practice

Define and Identify

Identify each of the following:

1. potash
2. pulp
3. newsprint
4. Samuel Champlain
5. provinces
6. dominion
7. Métis
8. regionalism
9. maritime
10. Inuit

Review the Main Ideas

11. How is the physical geography of Canada similar to that of the United States?
12. What created many of Canada's lakes?
13. What part of Canada has the mildest climate?
14. What natural resources does Canada have? Where is Canada's major wheat-farming area?
15. What are some of the First Nations called?
16. On what animals did the Inuit depend?
17. Where did the Vikings settle? Where did French colonists settle?
18. What products did the First Nations people and the French trade?
19. How did Canada come under British control?

20. How did the American Revolution affect Canada?
21. How did the railroad change Canada?
22. What kind of government does Canada have?
23. What issue causes conflict in Quebec?
24. What are the Maritime, Heartland, and Western Provinces?
25. Where is Canada's most densely populated area?
26. What are Canada's main cities?

Think Critically

27. **Comparing** How is Canada's government similar to that of the United States?
28. **Finding the Main Idea** How has immigration changed Canada?
29. **Drawing Inferences and Conclusions** How have past events shaped current conflicts in Canada?
30. **Drawing Inferences and Conclusions** If fishing and lumber are the primary industries of the Maritime Provinces, what are some likely secondary industries? List three industries.
31. **Summarizing** What geographic factors are responsible for economic activities in the Canadian provinces?

Map Activity

32. On a separate sheet of paper, match the letters on the map with their correct labels.

    Great Slave Lake
    Great Bear Lake
    Newfoundland and
      Labrador
    Prince Edward
      Island
    Manitoba

    Alberta
    Toronto
    Calgary
    Vancouver
    Nunavut

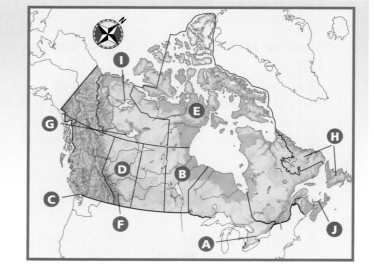

Writing Activity

Write three paragraphs explaining where in Canada you might like to live and why. Name a province and describe the geographic, climatic, political, and cultural features that make it attractive to you. Would you want to live in one of that province's cities? If so, which one, and why? Be sure to use standard grammar, sentence structure, spelling, and punctuation.

internet connect

Internet Activity: go.hrw.com
KEYWORD: SG5 GT5

Choose a topic to explore about Canada:
- Take a trip to the Yukon Territory.
- Learn about Canada's First Nations.
- Meet the people of Quebec.

Social Studies Skills Practice

Interpreting Maps

Study the map and answer the questions below.

Languages in Canada

CANADA

Concentrations of English-speaking Canadians

Concentrations of French-speaking Canadians

Source: Thomas M. Poulsen, "Nations and States: A Geographic Background to World Affairs"

1. What information does this map offer?
2. Where do most French-speaking Canadians live?
3. Why do you think large areas of the map are blank?
4. Based on your knowledge of Canada, what additional languages might be added to this map?

Analyzing Primary Sources

Read the following quote about housing problems in Nunavut. Then answer the questions.

". . . we heard . . . reports of families sleeping in shifts because there is insufficient [not enough] room for all members to sleep at once. The lack of sleep has in turn affected employee absenteeism and children's performance in school. Crowded housing conditions . . . have contributed to health problems such as respiratory [breathing] difficulties and communicable [spreadable] diseases. The shortage has also affected the economy by making it difficult to recruit employees. Quite often a job without available housing is a job unfilled. At the same time, an individual may be reluctant to change employers if it means losing their home."

1. What evidence does the report use to prove that a housing crisis exists?
2. How has the crisis affected the health of Nunavut's citizens?
3. How has the housing shortage affected the economy?
4. What effects has the housing problem had on children?

COULD YOU SURVIVE THE CANADIAN ARCTIC?

ONLINE EXPEDITIONS

GO TO: go.hrw.com
KEYWORD: SG5 CH5

A Land of Ice and Snow

Northeastern Canada is no place for the timid. It's cold! Average winter temperatures are way below zero. Ice and snow then cover the land. Even in summer the temperature seldom rises above freezing. Few plants besides mosses and lichens can survive the cold. Yet the Inuit have survived here for thousands of years. How?

SURVIVAL CHALLENGE

Now imagine that you are an explorer of the 1800s. You have bought the map pictured here from a mysterious old fellow. He told you the X marks the location of a pile of silver left long ago by Vikings. You can't wait to go in search of the treasure! However, because you don't want any competition for the loot, you don't want to draw attention to yourself by packing in lots of supplies. You decide to live off the land. What should you take with you that will help you do so? What natural resources can you use in this harsh environment? Keep in mind that almost nothing from your regular environment is available. There are no plants to eat. What would you do to replace torn or worn-out clothes? What if you needed a tool you didn't have with you?

Along with the map, the old man sold you the two diagrams shown. The information on them came from the Inuit. What do the diagrams mean? Could they help you survive?

Belcher Islands

You are here.

Learning the Land

As part of the planning for your trip, you must decide the best way to reach the treasure. If you start at the bottom left edge of the area shown on the map, what route should you take to the *X*? How will your route affect the natural resources on which you can rely?

If you reach the treasure, you will have learned an important lesson about natural resources. What do you think it is?

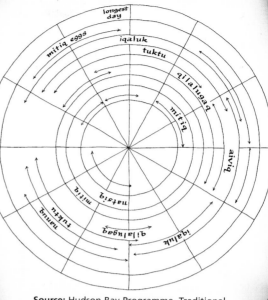

Source: Hudson Bay Programme, Traditional Ecological Knowledge of Environmental Changes in Hudson and James Bays, Part I.

Polar bears prowl the ice at the edge of Canada's Hudson Bay.

narwhal/tuugalik
skin and blubber–
Vitamins A and C;
oil–lamp oil;
sinew–thread

bowhead whale/arviq
blubber and meat–food;
bones–house roof supports,
tools, sled runners

Arctic char/iqaluk
meat–protein, calcium,
Vitamin B; bones–needles;
skin–waterproof coats

musk ox/umingmak
wool–warm clothing

dog/kringmerk
pull sleds

beluga whale/qilalugaq
blubber and skin–Vitamin C;
fat–cooking oil, lamp fuel;
meat–dried, raw, or
cooked, also for sled dogs;
skin–clothing, boats, boots

caribou/tuktu
hide–waterproof clothing,
blankets, mattresses;
tendons–thread, rope;
liver–Vitamin A

walrus/aiviq
meat–raw or boiled,
also for sled dogs;
hide–large boats,
shelter roofs, boots

polar bear/nanuq
skins–clothing;
meat–only if baked
or boiled

ringed seal/natsiq
meat–food; skins–
waterproof clothing,
boots, hayaks, tents

duck/mitiq
meat and eggs–food

Building Skills for Life: Analyzing Changing Landscapes

▲

This map from the mid-1600s shows Quebec when it was a French colony.

The world and its people are always changing. Sometimes these changes happen slowly. They may even be so slow that they are hard to notice. For example, some mountain ranges have built up over millions of years. These ranges are now slowly eroding. Because mountains look almost the same every day, it may be hard to notice changes.

Other times, the world changes quickly. Mudslides can bury villages so fast that people do not have time to escape. In less than 30 seconds, houses and crops might be completely destroyed.

Geographers want to know what the world is like today. However, they also need to know what it was like in the past. Analyzing how places have changed over time can help us better understand the world. For example, suppose you took a trip to Quebec. You would notice that most people there speak French. If you knew that Quebec used to be a French colony, it would help you understand why French is the main language today.

Understanding how places have changed in the past can also help us predict future changes. This is an important goal for people such as city planners, government officials, and transportation engineers.

As you study geography, try to remember that the world is always changing. Think about how places have changed and why these changes are important. Ask yourself how places might change in the future. Be aware that maps, photographs, newspapers, and other tools of geography can become outdated. After all, the world does not wait for geography!

PRACTICING THE SKILL

1. Find an area in your community that you think is changing quickly. Observe the changes. Are new businesses, houses, or roads being built? Are the changes big or small?

2. Talk to a parent, grandparent, or neighbor. Ask how your community, town, or city has changed during the last 20 to 30 years. What are some of the major changes? Does this person remember some old places that are no longer there?

3. Look for an old book, magazine, or map. Try to find one that is at least 30 years old. How is it different from a current book, magazine, or map?

HANDS on

GEOGRAPHY

You can analyze changing landscapes by comparing old photographs of a place to new ones. Important changes might be easy to see. For example, new buildings and new roads often stand out on the more recent photographs.

Look at the two photographs below. They show a small section of Las Vegas, Nevada. The photograph on the left was taken in 1963. The photograph on the right was taken 35 years later in 1998. Now compare the two photographs. What do you notice?

◄ Las Vegas, 1963

▲ Las Vegas, 1998

Lab Report

1. How do you know these two photographs show the same place? What evidence do you see?

2. How did this section of Las Vegas change between 1963 and 1998? Do you think these are big changes or small ones?

3. Find a street map of Las Vegas and try to figure out exactly what part of the city the photographs show. Then compare the map with the 1998 photograph. What information does the map give about this section of the city?

UNIT 3

Middle and South America

Congress Building, Brasília, Brazil

Dancer, Puerto Vallarta, Mexico

Machu Picchu, Peru, and llama

A Conservationist in Costa Rica

Sandy Wiseman works for a conservation organization in Canada. He often organizes trips to rain forests. Here Dr. Wiseman tells about a morning hike through a Costa Rican forest. **WHAT DO YOU THINK?** *Which of the animals he mentions would you like to see for yourself?*

Birds of many kinds were already active in the canopy. From high in the treetops, parrots and parakeets were squawking and feeding, not just themselves but dozens of other creatures with the fruit they dropped to the forest floor.

A tiny clear-winged butterfly floated in jerks along the path and came to rest on a leaf over the trail. Its transparent wings made it almost invisible. Later I spotted a small anteater. Only after it heard me reach for my camera did it stand up with nose held high to taste the air. The anteater spread wide its hooked forepaws as if to invite a hug, in a defensive pose. Within a minute it resumed its foraging, shuffling, and sniffing into the forest.

I now thought better of hurrying through the woods. I would sit for a while and take in my surroundings. With patient observation and quiet thought, the richness of the rain forest rekindles [renews] marvel and wonder.

Clear-winged butterfly, Costa Rica

Understanding Primary Sources

1. How do the parrots and parakeets feed other animals?

2. How does Sandy Wiseman react to seeing the creatures in the rain forest?

Blue poison dart frog

Middle and South America

Elevation Profile

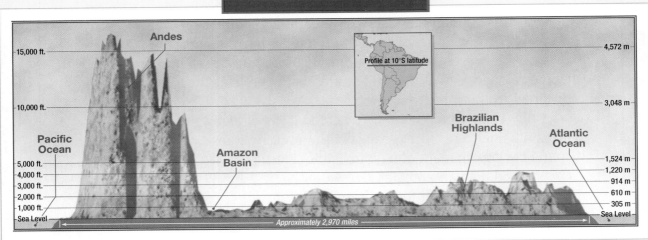

Andes

15,000 ft. — 4,572 m

Profile at 10°S latitude

10,000 ft. — 3,048 m

Pacific Ocean

Brazilian Highlands

Atlantic Ocean

Amazon Basin

5,000 ft. — 1,524 m
4,000 ft. — 1,220 m
3,000 ft. — 914 m
2,000 ft. — 610 m
1,000 ft. — 305 m
Sea Level — Sea Level

Approximately 2,970 miles

The United States and Middle and South America:
Comparing Sizes

GEOSTATS:

 World's highest waterfall: Angel Falls, Venezuela—3,212 ft. (979 m)

World's largest river system: Amazon River drains 2,053,318 square miles (5,318,094 sq km)

 World's highest capital city: La Paz, Bolivia—12,001 ft. (3,658 m)

 World's largest tropical rain forest: Amazon rain forest

 Highest mountain in South America: Mount Aconcagua, Argentina—22,834 ft. (6,960 m)

ELEVATION

FEET		METERS
13,120		4,000
6,560		2,000
1,640		500
656		200
(Sea level) 0		0 (Sea level)
Below sea level		Below sea level

SCALE

0 — 500 — 1000 Miles

0 — 500 — 1000 Kilometers

Projection: Azimuthal Equal Area

1. (Region) Which country has two highland regions and a large plateau?

2. (Region) Which country has two large peninsulas that extend into different oceans?

3. (Region) Which island groups separate the Caribbean Sea from the Gulf of Mexico and the Atlantic Ocean?

Critical Thinking

4. (Movement) Find central Mexico on the map. Why do you think east-west travel might be difficult in this area? What physical feature do you think would make travel easier in northern Brazil?

Map showing Middle and South America political boundaries, national capitals, and other cities.

SCALE

| 0 | 500 | 1000 Miles |
| 0 | 500 | 1000 Kilometers |

Projection: Azimuthal Equal Area

Legend:
- Boundaries
- ⊛ National capitals
- • Other cities

Countries and cities labeled:
UNITED STATES, GULF OF MEXICO, MEXICO, Guadalajara, Mexico City, BELIZE, Belmopan, GUATEMALA, Guatemala City, San Salvador, EL SALVADOR, HONDURAS, Tegucigalpa, NICARAGUA, Managua, COSTA RICA, San José, PANAMA, Panama City, Nassau, BAHAMAS, Havana, CUBA, CAYMAN ISLANDS (U.K.), JAMAICA, Kingston, HAITI, Port-au-Prince, DOMINICAN REPUBLIC, Santo Domingo, Puerto Rico (U.S.), ATLANTIC OCEAN, Tropic of Cancer, ANTIGUA AND BARBUDA, Guadeloupe (FRANCE), DOMINICA, ST. KITTS AND NEVIS, ST. LUCIA, ST. VINCENT AND THE GRENADINES, BARBADOS, GRENADA, TRINIDAD AND TOBAGO, Port-of-Spain, CARIBBEAN SEA, VENEZUELA, Caracas, Georgetown, GUYANA, Paramaribo, SURINAME, Cayenne, FRENCH GUIANA (FRANCE), COLOMBIA, Bogotá, GALÁPAGOS ISLANDS (ECUADOR), Quito, ECUADOR, Equator, PERU, Lima, PACIFIC OCEAN, BRAZIL, Brasília, La Paz, BOLIVIA, Sucre, Rio de Janeiro, São Paulo, PARAGUAY, Asunción, CHILE, Tropic of Capricorn, ARGENTINA, Santiago, URUGUAY, Buenos Aires, Montevideo, ATLANTIC OCEAN, FALKLAND ISLANDS (U.K.)

1. **Location** Which country connects Middle America and South America?

2. **Region** What is the largest country in Middle America? in South America?

Critical Thinking

3. **Human-Environment Interaction** Compare this map to the **physical map** of the region. What are some rivers that mark the borders between different countries in South America?

4. **Human-Environment Interaction** Compare this map to the **land use and resources** and **physical maps** of the region. Why would it be difficult to mark the boundaries where Colombia, Brazil, and Peru meet?

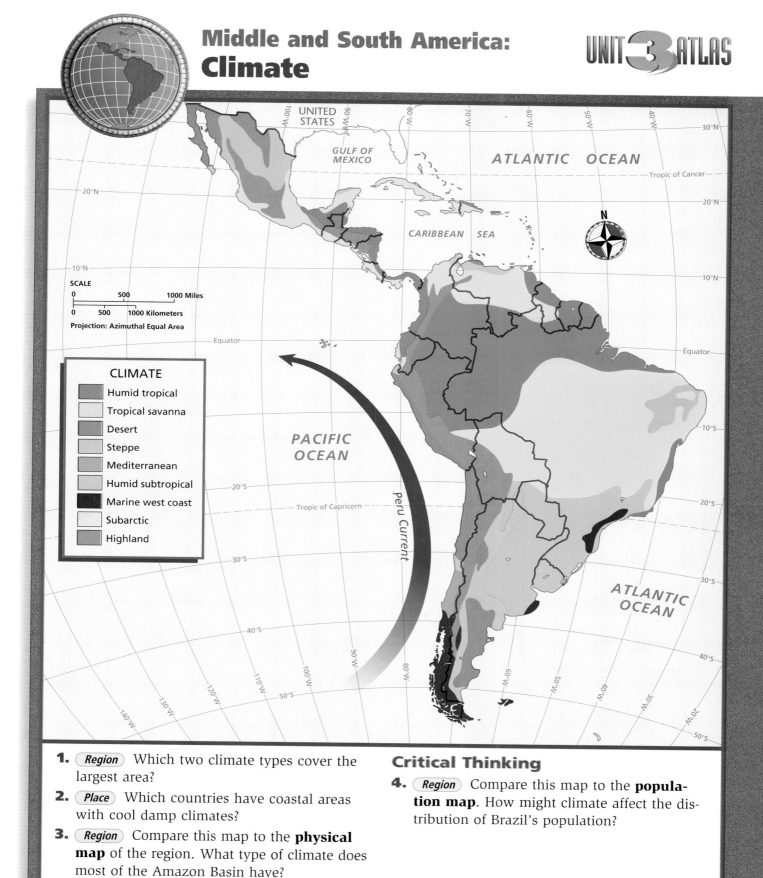

CLIMATE
- Humid tropical
- Tropical savanna
- Desert
- Steppe
- Mediterranean
- Humid subtropical
- Marine west coast
- Subarctic
- Highland

SCALE
0   500   1000 Miles
0   500   1000 Kilometers
Projection: Azimuthal Equal Area

1. (*Region*) Which two climate types cover the largest area?

2. (*Place*) Which countries have coastal areas with cool damp climates?

3. (*Region*) Compare this map to the **physical map** of the region. What type of climate does most of the Amazon Basin have?

Critical Thinking

4. (*Region*) Compare this map to the **population map**. How might climate affect the distribution of Brazil's population?

Middle and South America:
Population

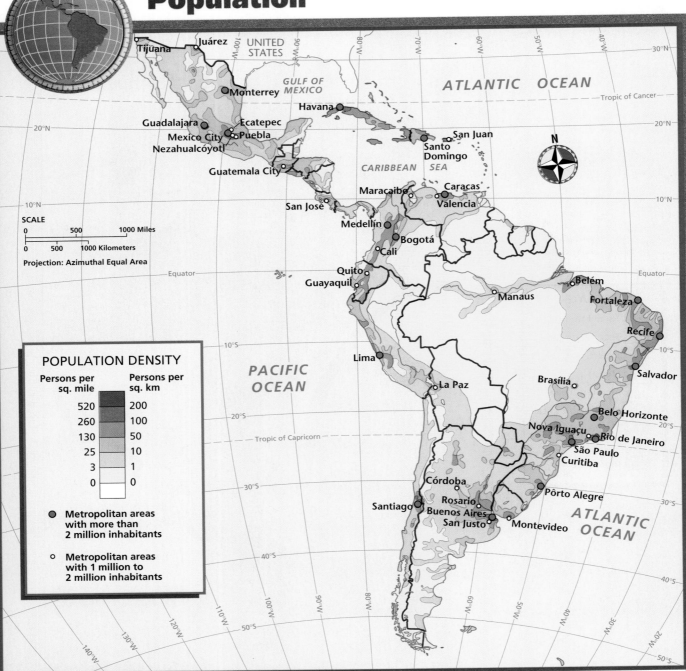

POPULATION DENSITY

Persons per sq. mile	Persons per sq. km
520	200
260	100
130	50
25	10
3	1
0	0

● Metropolitan areas with more than 2 million inhabitants

○ Metropolitan areas with 1 million to 2 million inhabitants

SCALE
0   500   1000 Miles
0   500   1000 Kilometers
Projection: Azimuthal Equal Area

1. (Place) Which area in South America has no place with more than three people per square mile?

2. (Place) Compare this map to the **physical map** of the region. Which two islands have cities with populations of more than 2 million?

Critical Thinking

3. (Movement) Compare this map to the **physical map**. Why might a major city be located deep in the rain forest?

4. (Human-Environment Interaction) Compare this map to the **physical map**. Which lakes seem to affect population density?

LAND USE

- Hunting and gathering
- Commercial farming
- Livestock raising
- Subsistence farming
- Manufacturing
- Limited economic activity
- Major manufacturing and trade centers

RESOURCES

- Coal
- Natural gas
- Oil
- Nuclear power
- Hydroelectric power
- Gold
- Silver
- Other minerals
- Timber
- Seafood

SCALE
0   500   1000 Miles
0   500   1000 Kilometers
Projection: Azimuthal Equal Area

1. (**Region**) What is the major natural resource in the small Caribbean islands?

2. (**Place**) Which two countries in Middle America have nuclear power plants? Which South American countries have them?

3. (**Interaction**) What types of agriculture are important in the Buenos Aires region?

Critical Thinking

4. (**Interaction**) Compare this map to the **climate map** of the region. How does the Peru current seem to affect the fishing industry?

5. (**Interaction**) Compare this map to the **physical map** of the region. Why do you think Cuba lacks hydroelectric power?

Middle and South America

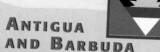

ANTIGUA AND BARBUDA

CAPITAL:
Saint John's

AREA:
171 sq. mi. (442 sq km)

POPULATION:
67,897

MONEY:
East Caribbean dollar

LANGUAGES:
English

CHILDREN BORN/WOMAN:
2.3

BELIZE

CAPITAL:
Belmopan

AREA:
8,867 sq. mi. (22,966 sq km)

POPULATION:
266,440

MONEY:
Belizean dollar

LANGUAGES:
English (official), Spanish, Mayan, Garifuna (Carib)

CHILDREN BORN/WOMAN:
3.9

ARGENTINA

CAPITAL:
Buenos Aires

AREA:
1,068,296 sq. mi. (2,766,890 sq km)

POPULATION:
38,740,807

MONEY:
Argentine peso

LANGUAGES:
Spanish (official), English, Italian, German, French

CHILDREN BORN/WOMAN:
2.3

BOLIVIA

CAPITAL:
La Paz, Sucre

AREA:
424,162 sq. mi. (1,098,580 sq km)

POPULATION:
8,586,443

MONEY:
boliviano

LANGUAGES:
Spanish, Quechua, Aymara (all official)

CHILDREN BORN/WOMAN:
3.2

BAHAMAS

CAPITAL:
Nassau

AREA:
5,382 sq. mi. (13,940 sq km)

POPULATION:
297,477

MONEY:
Bahamian dollar

LANGUAGES:
English, Creole (among Haitian immigrants)

CHILDREN BORN/WOMAN:
2.2

BRAZIL

CAPITAL:
Brasília

AREA:
3,286,470 sq. mi. (8,511,965 sq km)

POPULATION:
182,032,604

MONEY:
real

LANGUAGES:
Portuguese (official), Spanish, English, French

CHILDREN BORN/WOMAN:
2.0

BARBADOS

CAPITAL:
Bridgetown

AREA:
166 sq. mi. (430 sq km)

POPULATION:
277,264

MONEY:
Barbadian dollar

LANGUAGES:
English

CHILDREN BORN/WOMAN:
1.6

CHILE

CAPITAL:
Santiago

AREA:
292,258 sq. mi. (756,950 sq km)

POPULATION:
15,665,216

MONEY:
Chilean peso

LANGUAGES:
Spanish

CHILDREN BORN/WOMAN:
2.1

Countries not drawn to scale.

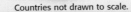

COLOMBIA

CAPITAL: Bogotá

AREA:
439,733 sq. mi.
(1,138,910 sq km)

POPULATION:
41,662,073

MONEY:
Colombian peso

LANGUAGES:
Spanish

CHILDREN BORN/WOMAN:
2.6

COSTA RICA

CAPITAL: San José

AREA:
19,730 sq. mi. (51,100 sq km)

POPULATION:
3,896,092

MONEY:
Costa Rican colon

LANGUAGES:
Spanish (official), English

CHILDREN BORN/WOMAN:
2.3

CUBA

CAPITAL: Havana

AREA:
42,803 sq. mi.
(110,860 sq km)

POPULATION:
11,263,429

MONEY:
Cuban peso

LANGUAGES:
Spanish

CHILDREN BORN/WOMAN:
1.6

DOMINICA

CAPITAL: Roseau

AREA:
291 sq. mi. (754 sq km)

POPULATION:
69,655

MONEY:
East Caribbean dollar

LANGUAGES:
English (official), French patois

CHILDREN BORN/WOMAN:
2.0

DOMINICAN REPUBLIC

CAPITAL:
Santo Domingo

AREA:
18,815 sq. mi. (48,730 sq km)

POPULATION:
8,715,602

MONEY:
Dominican peso

LANGUAGES:
Spanish

CHILDREN BORN/WOMAN:
2.9

ECUADOR

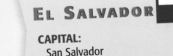

CAPITAL: Quito

AREA:
109,483 sq. mi.
(283,560 sq km)

POPULATION:
13,710,234

MONEY:
U.S. dollar

LANGUAGES:
Spanish (official), ethnic languages including Quechua

CHILDREN BORN/WOMAN:
3.0

EL SALVADOR

CAPITAL:
San Salvador

AREA:
8,124 sq. mi. (21,040 sq km)

POPULATION:
6,470,379

MONEY:
Salvadoran colon

LANGUAGES:
Spanish, Nahua

CHILDREN BORN/WOMAN:
3.2

FRENCH GUIANA

(Overseas department of France)

CAPITAL:
Cayenne

AREA:
35,135 sq. mi. (91,000 sq km)

POPULATION:
186,917

MONEY:
French franc; euro

LANGUAGES:
French

CHILDREN BORN/WOMAN:
3.0

GRENADA

CAPITAL:
St. George's

AREA:
131 sq. mi. (340 sq km)

POPULATION:
89,258

MONEY:
East Caribbean dollar

LANGUAGES:
English (official), French patois

CHILDREN BORN/WOMAN:
2.4

Source: Central Intelligence Agency, *The World Factbook 2003;* pop. figures are 2003 estimates.

GUATEMALA

CAPITAL:
Guatemala City

AREA:
42,042 sq. mi.
(108,890 sq km)

POPULATION:
13,909,384

MONEY:
quetzal

LANGUAGES:
Spanish, Quiche, Cakchiquel,
Kekchi

CHILDREN BORN/WOMAN:
4.6

GUYANA

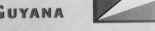

CAPITAL: Georgetown

AREA:
83,000 sq. mi.
(214,970 sq km)

POPULATION:
702,100

MONEY:
Guyanese dollar

LANGUAGES:
English, ethnic dialects

CHILDREN BORN/WOMAN:
2.1

HAITI

CAPITAL: Port-au-Prince

AREA:
10,714 sq. mi.
(27,750 sq km)

POPULATION:
7,527,817

MONEY:
gourde

LANGUAGES:
French (official), Creole

CHILDREN BORN/WOMAN:
4.9

HONDURAS

CAPITAL: Tegucigalpa

AREA:
43,278 sq. mi.
(112,090 sq km)

POPULATION:
6,669,789

MONEY:
lempira

LANGUAGES:
Spanish, ethnic languages

CHILDREN BORN/WOMAN:
4.1

JAMAICA

CAPITAL:
Kingston

AREA:
4,243 sq. mi. (10,990 sq km)

POPULATION:
2,695,867

MONEY:
Jamaican dollar

LANGUAGES:
English, Creole

CHILDREN BORN/WOMAN:
2.0

MEXICO

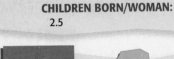

CAPITAL:
Mexico City

AREA:
761,602 sq. mi.
(1,972,550 sq km)

POPULATION:
104,907,991

MONEY:
Mexican peso

LANGUAGES:
Spanish, Mayan, Nahuatl,
ethnic languages

CHILDREN BORN/WOMAN:
2.5

NICARAGUA

CAPITAL:
Managua

AREA:
49,998 sq. mi.
(129,494 sq km)

POPULATION:
5,128,517

MONEY:
gold cordoba

LANGUAGES:
Spanish (official), English,
ethnic languages

CHILDREN BORN/WOMAN:
3.0

PANAMA

CAPITAL: Panama City

AREA:
30,193 sq. mi.
(78,200 sq km)

POPULATION:
2,960,784

MONEY:
balboa

LANGUAGES:
Spanish (official), English

CHILDREN BORN/WOMAN:
2.5

PARAGUAY

CAPITAL: Asunción

AREA:
157,046 sq. mi.
(406,750 sq km)

POPULATION:
6,036,900

MONEY:
guarani

LANGUAGES:
Spanish (official), Guarani

CHILDREN BORN/WOMAN:
4.0

PERU

CAPITAL:
Lima

AREA:
496,223 sq. mi.
(1,285,220 sq km)

POPULATION:
28,409,897

MONEY:
nuevo sol

LANGUAGES:
Spanish (official), Quechua
(official), Aymara

CHILDREN BORN/WOMAN:
2.8

Countries not drawn to scale.

PUERTO RICO (U.S. Commonwealth)

CAPITAL:
San Juan

AREA:
3,515 sq. mi. (9,104 sq km)

POPULATION:
3,937,316

MONEY:
U.S. dollar

LANGUAGES:
Spanish, English

CHILDREN BORN/WOMAN:
1.9

SAINT KITTS AND NEVIS

CAPITAL:
Basseterre

AREA: 101 sq. mi. (261 sq km)

POPULATION:
38,763

MONEY:
East Caribbean dollar

LANGUAGES: English

CHILDREN BORN/WOMAN:
2.4

SAINT LUCIA

CAPITAL:
Castries

AREA:
239 sq. mi. (620 sq km)

POPULATION:
162,157

MONEY:
East Caribbean dollar

LANGUAGES:
English (official), French patois

CHILDREN BORN/WOMAN:
2.3

SAINT VINCENT AND THE GRENADINES

CAPITAL:
Kingstown

AREA:
150 sq. mi. (389 sq km)

POPULATION:
116,812

MONEY:
East Caribbean dollar

LANGUAGES:
English, French patois

CHILDREN BORN/WOMAN:
2.0

SURINAME

CAPITAL:
Paramaribo

AREA:
63,039 sq. mi.
(163,270 sq km)

POPULATION:
433,998

MONEY:
Surinamese guilder

LANGUAGES: Dutch (official), English, Sranang Tongo

CHILDREN BORN/WOMAN:
2.5

TRINIDAD AND TOBAGO

CAPITAL:
Port-of-Spain

AREA:
1,980 sq. mi. (5,128 sq km)

POPULATION:
1,104,209

MONEY:
Trinidad and Tobago dollar

LANGUAGES:
English, Hindi, French, Spanish

CHILDREN BORN/WOMAN:
1.8

URUGUAY

CAPITAL: Montevideo

AREA:
68,039 sq. mi.
(176,220 sq km)

POPULATION:
3,413,329

MONEY:
Uruguayan peso

LANGUAGES:
Spanish, Portunol

CHILDREN BORN/WOMAN:
2.4

VENEZUELA

CAPITAL:
Caracas

AREA:
352,143 sq. mi.
(912,050 sq km)

POPULATION:
24,654,694

MONEY:
bolivar

LANGUAGES:
Spanish (official), many ethnic languages

CHILDREN BORN/WOMAN:
2.4

internet connect

COUNTRY STATISTICS
GO TO: go.hrw.com
KEYWORD: SG5 FactsU3
FOR: more facts about Middle and South America

CHAPTER 6

Mexico

Now we will study Mexico, our neighbor to the south. More than 100 million people live in Mexico. Below you will meet Ellie, a Mexican student.

Hola! My name is Ellie, and I am 14. If you are my friend, I will greet you with a fast kiss on the cheek. I live in a small village, San Francisco Acatepec, on the edge of the city of Puebla. Our house is made of adobe and has a big yard. Our house is surrounded by a big adobe wall. We have a vegetable garden, flowers, and a lot of trees. I live with my mom and dad, my older brother (he's in the ninth grade), my three cats, and two dogs.

I am in the eighth grade. School starts at 8:00 A.M. On Monday mornings, we salute the flag and sing the Mexican national anthem. School ends at 2:15 but on Friday I have to stay till 4:45 to take an additional drama class. I love drama since I want to be an actress someday and a marine biologist.

My favorite holiday is Dia de los Muertos (Day of the Dead). On that day, we make bread and put out offerings to honor the dead. We put out clothes, sugar cane, chocolate, sugar candy skulls, flowers, bread, pictures, incense, and candles.

¿Has estado alguna vez en México?

◄ Translation: Have you ever been to Mexico?

Read to Discover

1. What are the main physical features of Mexico?
2. What climate types, plants, and animals are found in Mexico?
3. What are Mexico's main natural resources?

Vocabulary

sinkholes

Places

Gulf of Mexico
Baja California
Gulf of California
Río Bravo (Rio Grande)
Mexican Plateau

Sierra Madre Oriental
Sierra Madre Occidental
Mount Orizaba
Yucatán Peninsula

Reading Strategy

VISUALIZING INFORMATION Previewing the Physical-Political map of Mexico will help you understand what you are about to read. What physical features are shown on the map? What can you predict about Mexico's climate just by studying the map? Write your answers on a sheet of paper.

Mexico: Physical-Political

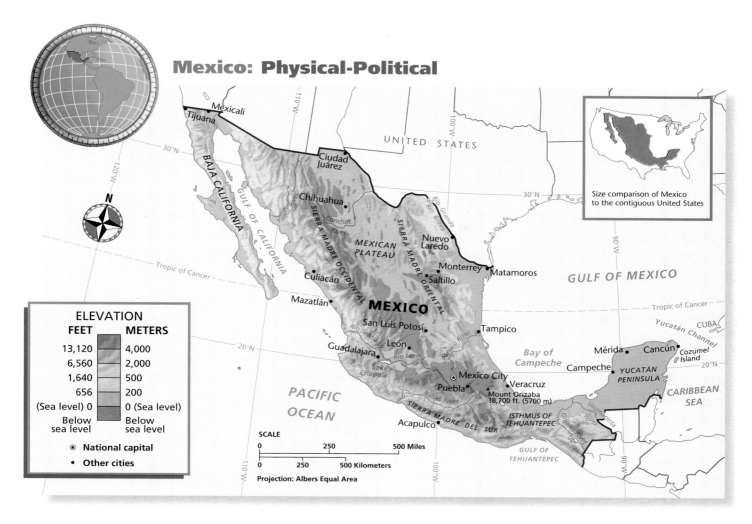

Size comparison of Mexico to the contiguous United States

ELEVATION

FEET	METERS
13,120	4,000
6,560	2,000
1,640	500
656	200
(Sea level) 0	0 (Sea level)
Below sea level	Below sea level

⊛ National capital
• Other cities

SCALE
0   250   500 Miles
0   250   500 Kilometers
Projection: Albers Equal Area

► Volcanic Mount Orizaba rises southeast of Mexico City.

Interpreting the Visual Record

(Region) **What kinds of climates do you think people living in this area might experience?**

▲ Thousands of monarch butterflies migrate south to the mountains of central Mexico for the winter.

Physical Features

Mexico is a large country. It has a long coast on the Pacific Ocean. It has a shorter one on the Gulf of Mexico. In far southern Mexico, the two bodies of water are just 137 miles (220 km) apart. This part of Mexico is called the Isthmus of Tehuantepec (tay-WAHN-tah-pek). The Caribbean Sea washes the country's sunny southeastern beaches. Beautiful Caribbean and Pacific coastal areas attract many tourists.

Baja (BAH-hah) California is a long, narrow peninsula. It extends south from Mexico's northwestern border with the United States. The peninsula separates the Gulf of California from the Pacific Ocean. One of Mexico's few major rivers, the Río Bravo, forms the Mexico-Texas border. In the United States this river is called the Rio Grande.

Plateaus and Mountains Much of Mexico consists of a rugged central region called the Mexican Plateau. The plateau's wide plains range from 3,700 feet (1,128 m) to 9,000 feet (2,743 m). Isolated mountain ridges rise much higher. Two mountain ranges form the edges of the Mexican Plateau. The Sierra Madre Oriental rise to the east. The Sierra Madre Occidental lie in the west.

At the southern end of the plateau lies the Valley of Mexico. Mexico City, the capital, is located there. The mountains south of Mexico City include towering, snowcapped volcanoes. Volcanic eruptions and earthquakes are a threat in this area. The highest peak, Mount Orizaba (oh-ree-SAH-buh), rises to 18,700 feet (5,700 m).

The Yucatán The Yucatán (yoo-kah-TAHN) Peninsula is generally flat. Limestone underlies much of the area, and erosion has created numerous caves and **sinkholes**. A sinkhole is a steep-sided depression formed when the roof of a cave collapses. The climate in the northern part of the peninsula is hot and dry. Scrub forest is the main vegetation. Farther south, rainfall becomes much heavier. Tropical rain forests cover much of the southern Yucatán.

✓ **READING CHECK:** (Places and Regions) What are Mexico's major physical features?

The States of Mexico

MAP LABELS:

UNITED STATES

BAJA CALIFORNIA
SONORA
CHIHUAHUA
COAHUILA
BAJA CALIFORNIA SUR
SINALOA
DURANGO
NUEVO LEÓN
ZACATECAS
TAMAULIPAS
NAYARIT
SAN LUIS POTOSÍ
1
GUANAJUATO
2
JALISCO
HIDALGO
COLIMA
MICHOACÁN
5 3
4 6 PUEBLA
GUERRERO
VERACRUZ
OAXACA
CHIAPAS
TABASCO
CAMPECHE
YUCATÁN
QUINTANA ROO

GULF OF CALIFORNIA
GULF OF MEXICO
PACIFIC OCEAN
Bay of Campeche
Yucatán Channel
Cozumel Island
CARIBBEAN SEA
GULF OF TEHUANTEPEC

Tropic of Cancer

1. AGUASCALIENTES
2. QUERÉTARO
3. TLAXCALA
4. MÉXICO
5. DISTRITO FEDERAL (Federal District)
6. MORELOS

N

SCALE
0   150   300 Miles
0   150   300 Kilometers
Projection: Albers Equal Area

Climate, Vegetation, and Wildlife

Mexico's climate varies by region. Its mountains, deserts, and forests also support a variety of plants and animals.

A Tropical Area Mexico extends from the middle latitudes into the tropics. It has desert, steppe, savanna, and humid tropical climates. Most of northern Mexico is dry. There, Baja California's Sonoran Desert meets the Chihuahuan (chee-WAH-wahn) Desert of the plateau. Desert scrub vegetation and dry grasslands are common. Cougars, coyotes, and deer can be found in some areas of the north.

The forested plains along Mexico's southeastern coast are hot and humid much of the year. Summer is the rainy season. Forests cover about 20 percent of Mexico's land area. Tropical rain forests provide a home for anteaters, jaguars, monkeys, parrots, and other animals.

Many varieties of cactus thrive in the Sonoran Desert.

Climate Variations In some areas changes in elevation cause climates to vary widely within a short distance. Many people have settled in the mild environment of the mountain valleys. The valleys along Mexico's southern coastal areas also have pleasant climates.

The areas of high elevation on the Mexican Plateau experience surprisingly cool temperatures. Freezing temperatures sometimes reach as far south as Mexico City.

✓ **READING CHECK:** (*Places and Regions*) What are Mexico's climate zones?

Resources

Petroleum is Mexico's most important energy resource. Oil reserves lie primarily under southern and Gulf coastal plains as well as offshore in the Gulf of Mexico. In 2001 Mexico had the world's ninth-largest crude oil reserves.

Mining is also important in Mexico. Some gold and silver mines begun centuries ago are still in operation. Fresnillo has been a silver-mining center since 1569. New mines have been developed in Mexico's northern and southern mountains. Silver is the most valuable part of Mexico's mining industry. In 2001 Mexico's silver production totaled 2,800 tons (2,520,000 kg). Mexico also produces large amounts of copper, gold, lead, and zinc.

Water is a limited resource in parts of Mexico. Water scarcity, particularly in the dry north, is a serious issue.

✓ **READING CHECK:** (*Environment and Society*) What problems might water scarcity cause for Mexican citizens?

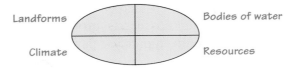

Homework Practice Online
Keyword: SG5 HP6

Section Review 1

Define and explain: sinkholes

Working with Sketch Maps On a map of Mexico that you draw or that your teacher provides, label the following: Gulf of Mexico, Baja California, Gulf of California, Río Bravo (Rio Grande), Mexican Plateau, Sierra Madre Oriental, Sierra Madre Occidental, Mount Orizaba, and Yucatán Peninsula. In a caption, describe the Yucatán.

Reading for the Main Idea

1. (*Places and Regions*) What are Mexico's major physical features?

2. (*Places and Regions*) What are the major climate zones of Mexico?

Critical Thinking

3. **Drawing Inferences and Conclusions** Based on physical features and climate, which areas of Mexico provide the best conditions for people to live?

4. **Drawing Inferences and Conclusions** How do you think Mexico's geography affects movement and communication between different parts of the country?

Organizing What You Know

5. **Summarizing** Copy the following graphic organizer. Use it to describe Mexico's physical geography.

Landforms   Bodies of water

Climate   Resources

Read to Discover

1. What early cultures developed in Mexico?
2. What was Mexico like under Spanish rule and after independence?
3. What are some important features of Mexican culture?

Vocabulary

chinampas
conquistadores
epidemic
empire
mestizos

mulattoes
missions
ejidos
haciendas

People

Maya
Aztec
Hernán Cortés
Benito Juárez

Reading Strategy

FOLDNOTES: KEY-TERM FOLD Create the FoldNote titled **Key-Term Fold** described in the Appendix. Before you read, write the vocabulary terms on the tabs of the paper. As you read the section, write down the meaning of each term underneath its tab.

Early Cultures

Mesoamerica (*meso* means "in the middle") is the cultural area including Mexico and much of Central America. Many scientists think the first people to live in Mesoamerica arrived from the north about 12,000 years ago. By about 5,000 years ago, people in Mesoamerica were growing beans, peppers, and squash. They also domesticated an early form of corn. It eventually developed into the corn that we see today.

By about 1500 B.C. many people throughout the region were living in small farming villages. Along the humid southern coast of the Gulf of Mexico lived the Olmec people. The Olmec built temples, pyramids, and huge statues. They traded carved jade and obsidian, a volcanic stone, throughout eastern Mexico.

By about A.D. 200, other complex cultures were developing in what is now Mexico. Many of these civilizations had large city centers. Those centers had apartments, great avenues, open plazas, and pyramid-shaped temples. Some temple areas throughout Mesoamerica had stone ball courts. Players on those courts competed in a game somewhat like basketball. However, this ball game was not simply a sport. It had deep religious importance. Players who lost might be sacrificed to the gods.

Maya ruins include stone carvings and pyramid-type structures. Figures such as this Chac Mool are thought to represent the rain god.

The Maya

The Maya Maya civilization developed in the tropical rain forest of southeastern Mexico, Guatemala, Belize, and Honduras. Maya city-states were at their peak between about A.D. 250 and 800. The Maya made accurate astronomical calculations and had a detailed calendar. Modern scholars can now read some Maya writing. This has helped us understand their civilization.

The Maya grew crops on terraced hillsides and on raised fields in swampy areas. They dug canals, piling the rich bottom mud onto the fields alongside the canals. This practice enriched the soil. Using this productive method of farming, the Maya supported an extremely dense population.

Sometime after A.D. 800, Maya civilization collapsed. The cities were abandoned. This decline may have been caused by famine, disease, warfare, or some combination of factors. However, the Maya did not die out. Millions of people of Maya descent still live in Mexico and Central America today.

The Aztec A people called the Aztec began moving into central Mexico from the north about A.D. 1200. They later established their capital on an island in a lake in the Valley of Mexico. Known as Tenochtitlán (tay-nawch-teet-LAHN), this capital grew into a splendid city. Its population in 1519 is estimated to have been at least 200,000. It was one of the largest cities in the world at that time. The Aztec conquered other Indian peoples around them. They forced these peoples to pay taxes and provide captives for sacrifice to Aztec gods.

The Aztec practiced a version of raised-field agriculture in the swampy lakes of central Mexico. The Aztec called these raised fields *chinampas* (chee-NAHM-pahs). There they grew the corn, beans, and peppers that most people ate. Only rich people in this society ate meat. On special occasions common people sometimes ate dog meat. The upper classes also drank chocolate.

✓ **READING CHECK:** What were the main features of Mexico's early civilizations?

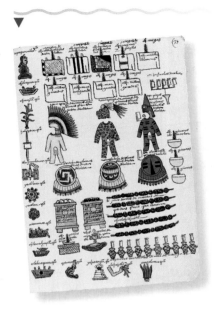

This copy of an original Aztec tax record shows items that were to be collected as tribute.

▼

The Maya ruins of Tulum, an ancient Maya ceremonial and religious center, lie on the Caribbean coast.

Interpreting the Visual Record (Place)

What natural and human-made features would have protected Tulum?

▼

TENOCHTITLÁN

Tenochtitlán—now Mexico City—was founded by the Aztec in the early 1300s. According to their legends, they saw an eagle sitting atop a cactus on a swampy island in Lake Texcoco. The eagle held a snake in its mouth. A prophecy had instructed them to build a city where they saw such an eagle.

Within 200 years this village had become an imperial capital and the largest city in the Americas. It was a city of pyramids, palaces, markets, and gardens. Canals and streets ran through the city. Stone causeways connected the island to the mainland.

Bernal Díaz, a Spanish soldier, described his first view of the Aztec capital in 1519.

❝When we saw so many cities and villages built in the water and other great towns on dry land and that straight and level Causeway going towards [Tenochtitlán], we were amazed and said that it was like the enchantments they tell of in the legend of Amadis, on account of the great towers and temples and buildings rising from the water, and all built of masonry. And some of our soldiers asked whether the things that we saw were not a dream.**❞**

The Spaniards went on to conquer the Aztec and destroy Tenochtitlán. On the ruins they built Mexico City. They also drained Lake Texcoco to allow the city to expand.

Understanding What You Read
1. Where and when was Tenochtitlán first built?
2. What was the Spaniards' reaction to Tenochtitlán?

A sketch map of the Aztec capital of Tenochtitlán

Colonial Mexico and Independence

Spanish Conquest Hernán Cortés, a Spanish soldier, arrived in Mexico in 1519 with about 600 men. These **conquistadores** (kahn-kees-tuh-DAWR-eez), or conquerors, had both muskets and horses. These were unknown in the Americas at that time. However, the most important factor in the conquest was disease. The native people of the Americas had no resistance to European diseases. The first **epidemic**, or widespread outbreak, of smallpox struck central Mexico in 1520. The death toll from disease greatly weakened the power of the Aztec. In 1521 Cortés completed his conquest of the Aztec and the other American Indian peoples of southern Mexico. They named the territory New Spain.

Colonial Mexico During this period, Spain ruled an **empire**. An empire is a system in which a central power controls a number of

BIOGRAPHY

Benito Juárez
(1806–72)

Character Trait: Citizenship

Over time, control of Mexico passed from Spaniards born in Spain to the Mexicans themselves. Benito Juárez was the country's first president of Indian heritage. He is also a national hero. A passionate political leader, Juárez stood up for the rights of all Mexicans and laid the foundation for a democratic government. *How may Juárez's heritage have affected his efforts for Mexico's citizens?*

The Spanish built many beautiful churches in Mexico, including this one in Taxco.

▼

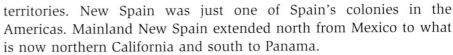

territories. New Spain was just one of Spain's colonies in the Americas. Mainland New Spain extended north from Mexico to what is now northern California and south to Panama.

After the initial conquest, Spanish and American Indian peoples and cultures mixed. This mix formed a new Mexican identity. The Spaniards called people of mixed European and Indian ancestry **mestizos** (me-STEE-zohs). When enslaved Africans were brought to Spanish America, they added to this blend of cultures. The Spaniards called people of mixed European and African ancestry **mulattoes** (muh-LA-tohs). Africans and Indians also intermarried.

Large areas of northern Mexico were left to the Roman Catholic Church to explore and to rule. Church outposts known as **missions** were scattered throughout the area. Mission priests often learned Indian languages and tried to convert the Indians to Catholicism.

Colonial Economy At first, the Spaniards were mainly interested in mining gold and silver in Mexico. Gradually, agriculture also became an important part of the colonial economy. Indians did most of the hard physical labor on farms and in mines. Many of them died from disease and overwork. Therefore, Spaniards began to bring enslaved Africans to the Americas as another source of labor.

Before the arrival of the Spaniards, Indian communities owned and worked land in groups. The lands they worked in common are called *ejidos* (e-HEE-thohs). After the conquest, the Spanish monarch granted **haciendas** (hah-see-EN-duhs), or huge expanses of farmlands, to favored people. Peasants, usually Indians, lived and worked on these haciendas. Cattle ranching operated according to a similar system.

Independence and After In 1810 a Catholic priest named Miguel Hidalgo y Costilla began a revolt against Spanish rule. Hidalgo was killed in 1811. However, fighting continued until independence was won in 1821.

Fifteen years later, Texas broke away from Mexico. Texas became part of the United States in 1845. Shortly after, the United States and Mexico argued over the location of their common border. This conflict led to a war in which Mexico lost about half its territory. Americans know this conflict as the Mexican War. Mexicans usually refer to it as the War of the North American Invasion.

In the early 1900s many Mexicans grew unhappy with the government of military leader Porfirio Díaz. As a result, in 1910 the Mexican Revolution broke out. Fighting between various leaders and groups lasted until 1920.

One of the major results of the revolution was land reform. The new government took land from the haciendas. This land was given back to peasant villages according to the old *ejido* system. Today *ejidos* make up about half of Mexico's farmland.

✓ **READING CHECK:** (*Human Systems*) How did Mexico gain independence from Spain?

Interpreting the Visual Record

Movement What celebrations in your community reflect special customs that began in other countries?

Culture and Customs

About 89 percent of Mexico's people are Roman Catholic. The Day of the Dead is an example of how cultures mix in Mexico. This holiday takes place on November 1 and 2. These are the same dates the Catholic Church celebrates All Saints' Day and All Souls' Day. The Day of the Dead honors dead ancestors. Families often place different foods on the graves of dead relatives. This recalls the Indian belief that the dead need material things just as the living do.

In Mexico ethnic identity is associated more with culture than with ancestry. One major indicator of a person's ethnic identity is language. Speaking one of the American Indian languages identifies a person as Indian. People who speak only Spanish are usually not considered Indian. This may be true even if they have Indian ancestors.

✓ **READING CHECK:** **Human Systems** What is the significance of the Day of the Dead?

Define or identify: Maya, Aztec, *chinampas,* Hernán Cortés, conquistadores, epidemic, empire, mestizos, mulattoes, missions, *ejidos,* haciendas, Benito Juárez

Working with Sketch Maps On the map you created in Section 1, shade the areas once controlled by the Maya and Aztec. Which civilization occupied the Yucatán Peninsula?

Reading for the Main Idea

1. **Human Systems** What were some notable achievements of the Maya and Aztec civilizations?

2. **Human Systems** What were the effects of Spanish rule on Mexico?

Homework Practice Online

Keyword: SG5 HP6

Critical Thinking

3. Analyzing Information What advantages did Cortés have in his conquest of the Aztec?

4. Finding the Main Idea What is a sign of a person's ethnic identity in Mexico?

Organizing What You Know

5. Identifying Cause and Effect Copy the following graphic organizer. Use it to develop a cause-and-effect chart to identify events related to the Mexican War.

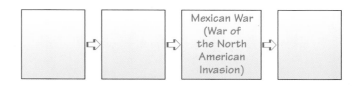

Mexican War (War of the North American Invasion)

MAQUILADORAS ALONG THE U.S.-MEXICO BORDER

Geographers are often interested in borders. Borders are more than just lines on a map. They are places where different countries, cultures, and ways of life meet. For example, the U.S.-Mexico border separates a developing country from a very rich country. This fact has had an important influence on the location of industries in the region.

On the Mexican side of the border there are many *maquiladoras* (mah-kee-lah-DOHR-ahs)—factories that can be owned by foreign companies. The first *maquiladoras* were built in the mid-1960s. Since then, their numbers have increased dramatically. There are now more than 2,000 *maquiladoras* in Mexico. They employ hundreds of thousands of workers.

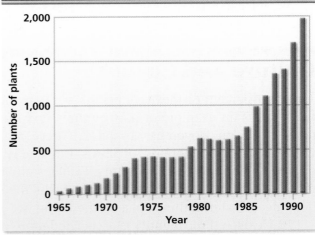

Growth in *Maquiladora* Plants

Source: Instituto Nacional de Estadistica Geografia e Informatica, Mexico

The border separates Mexicali, Mexico, from Calexico, California. The big buildings are *maquiladoras*.

Interpreting the Visual Record (*Location*) **How have each country's laws affected how land is used along the border?**

Many *maquiladoras* are owned by American companies. They produce goods such as vacuum cleaners, automobile parts, and electronics. These goods are usually exported to the United States. Most *maquiladoras* are located within about 20 miles (32 km) of the U.S.-Mexico border. Cities such as Tijuana, Ciudad Juárez, and Nuevo Laredo have many *maquiladoras*.

Why have so many American companies chosen to build factories across the border in Mexico? The location allows companies to take advantage of the difference in wealth between the two countries. Mexico has a much lower standard of living than the United States. Workers there get paid less. Therefore, factories in Mexico can produce goods more cheaply. The United States has a higher standard of living. People there have more money to buy goods. They buy the products that have been

U.S.-Mexico Border Region

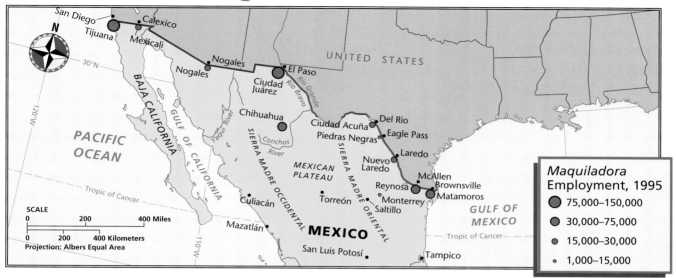

Maquiladora Employment, 1995
- ● 75,000–150,000
- ● 30,000–75,000
- ● 15,000–30,000
- · 1,000–15,000

assembled in Mexico and shipped to American stores.

American companies have other reasons for building factories in Mexico. The Mexican government has given tax breaks to foreign companies that own and operate *maquiladoras*. It has encouraged the growth of *maquiladoras*. They create jobs for Mexican citizens and bring money into the country. Also, environmental laws in Mexico are not as strict as in the United States. Therefore, companies in Mexico do not have to spend as much money to control pollution.

Maquiladoras have become an important part of the border economy. They are also a good example of how borders can influence the landscape. The U.S.-Mexico border has attracted *maquiladoras* because it is more than just a line on a map. It separates two countries with different cultures, economies, and governments. Some American companies have built factories on the Mexican side of the border that export goods to the United States. These companies benefit from the different standards of living in the two countries and the border that separates them.

◀
Trucks carrying goods from Mexico to the United States are inspected by U.S. Customs officials in Laredo, Texas.

Understanding What You Read

1. Why have some American companies built factories in Mexico?

2. What are some of the goods that are produced in *maquiladoras*?

Read to Discover

1. What kind of government and economy does Mexico have today?
2. What are the important features of Mexico's six culture regions?

Vocabulary

inflation
cash crops
smog
maquiladoras
slash-and-burn agriculture

Places

Tijuana
Ciudad Juárez
Acapulco
Mazatlán
Cancún

Mexico City
Guadalajara
Tampico
Campeche
Monterrey

Reading Strategy

TAKING NOTES As you read this section, create an outline using the headings from the section. Beneath the heading write some important details from what you learn.

Mexico

Country	Population/ Growth Rate	Life Expectancy	Literacy Rate	Per Capita GDP
Mexico	104,907,991 1.4%	69, male 75, female	92%	$9,000
United States	290,342,554 0.9%	74, male 80, female	97%	$37,600

Source: Central Intelligence Agency, *The World Factbook 2003*

Interpreting the Chart What does the per capita GDP in Mexico indicate about its economic development?

Government and Economy

Like that of the United States, Mexico's government includes an elected president and a congress. However, in Mexico one political party—the Partido Revolucionario Institucional (PRI)—controlled the Mexican government for 71 years. This control ended in 2000 when Vicente Fox of the National Action Party was sworn in as president.

For many years, Mexico operated more on the principles of a command economy in which the government controlled economic activity. In recent decades, however, Mexico has worked to reduce government control of the economy. Mexico's economy is growing and modernizing. However, living standards are much lower than in other nations.

Mexico began to export oil in 1911 and is a leading oil exporter today. However, problems began when the price of oil fell in the 1980s. Since then, Mexico has wrestled with debts to foreign banks, high unemployment, and **inflation**. Inflation is the rise in prices that occurs when currency loses its buying power.

The North American Free Trade Agreement (NAFTA) has helped Mexico's economy. NAFTA took effect in 1994. It made trade between Mexico, the United States, and Canada easier. Mexico's leaders hope increased trade will create more jobs in their country.

Agriculture Agriculture has long been an important part of the Mexican economy. In fact, farming is the traditional focus of life in the country. This is true even though just 12 percent of the land can grow crops. Rainfall supports agriculture in the southern part of the Mexican Plateau and in southern valleys. Plantations in coastal lowlands and on mountain slopes along the Gulf of Mexico also produce important crops. Those crops include coffee and sugarcane. Northern drylands are important for livestock ranching.

High demand in the United States has encouraged a shift to the growing of **cash crops**. A cash crop is produced primarily to sell, rather than for the farmer to eat. Trucks bring Mexican vegetables, fruits, and other cash crops to the United States.

Industry Many Mexicans work in primary and secondary industries. These include the oil industry, mining, and manufacturing. The country's fastest-growing industrial centers lie along the U.S. border. Tijuana (tee-HWAH-nah) and Ciudad Juárez (syoo-thahth HWAHR-es) are two of these major industrial centers.

Many U.S. and other foreign companies have built factories in Mexico. This is because wages are lower there. Mexican workers in these factories assemble products for export to other countries. (See the Case Study in this chapter.)

Tourism Tourism and other service industries are also important to Mexico's economy. Many tourists visit old colonial cities and Maya and Aztec monuments. Popular coastal cities and resorts include Acapulco, Mazatlán, and Cancún. Acapulco and Mazatlán are located on Mexico's Pacific coast. Cancún is on the Yucatán Peninsula.

✓ **READING CHECK:** (*Environment and Society*) How does geography affect the location of economic activities in Mexico?

▲
Gourds—hard-shelled ornamental fruits—are just some of Mexico's many agricultural products.

Puerto Vallarta—a popular beach resort—is on the Pacific coast.
Interpreting the Visual Record
(*Movement*) **How do you think tourism has changed settlement patterns?**

▼

Mexico's Culture Regions

Mexico's 31 states and one federal district can be grouped into six culture regions. These regions are highly diverse in their resources, climate, population, and other features.

Greater Mexico City Greater Mexico City is Mexico's most developed and crowded region. This area includes Mexico City and about 50 smaller cities. More than 20 million people live there. It is one of the most densely populated urban areas in the world.

Mexico City is also one of the world's most polluted cities. Thousands of factories and millions of automobiles release exhaust and other pollutants into the air. Surrounding mountains trap the resulting **smog**—a mixture of smoke, chemicals, and fog. Smog can cause health problems like eye irritation and breathing difficulties.

Wealth and poverty exist side by side in Mexico City. The city has very poor slums. It also has busy highways, modern office buildings, high-rise apartments, museums, universities, and old colonial cathedrals.

Central Interior Mexico's central interior region lies north of the capital. It extends toward both coasts. Many cities here began as mining or ranching centers during the colonial period. Small towns with a central square and a colonial-style church are common.

The region has many fertile valleys and small family farms. In recent years the central interior has attracted new industries from overcrowded Mexico City. As a result, cities like Guadalajara are growing rapidly.

Oil Coast The forested coastal plains between Tampico and Campeche (kahm-PAY-chay) were once lightly settled. However, the population has grown as oil production in this region has increased. In addition, large forest areas are being cleared for farming and ranching.

Mexico City was 250 miles (400 km) away from the center of the 1985 earthquake on Mexico's Pacific coast. However, the city suffered heavy damage and thousands of deaths. The city sits on a former lake bed. The loose soil under the city made the damage worse.

Smog covers Mexico City. The city continues to work toward solutions to challenges facing it as one of the world's largest cities.

Interpreting the Visual Record What two words do you think the word *smog* comes from?

Southern Mexico Many people in southern Mexico speak Indian languages. They live in the country's poorest region. It has few cities and little industry. Subsistence farming is common. Poverty and corrupt local governments have led to unrest. In the 1990s people in the state of Chiapas staged an antigovernment uprising.

Northern Mexico Northern Mexico has become one of the country's most prosperous and modern areas. NAFTA has helped the region's economy grow. Monterrey and Tijuana are important cities here. Factories called *maquiladoras* (mah-kee-lah-DORH-ahs) are located along the northern border and are often foreign owned.

American music, television, and other forms of entertainment are popular near the border. Many Mexicans cross the border to shop, work, or live in the United States. In recent decades, the U.S. government has increased its efforts to stop illegal immigration across the border.

The Yucatán Most of the Yucatán Peninsula is sparsely populated. Mérida is this region's major city. As in other parts of Mexico, some farmers in the region practice **slash-and-burn agriculture**, in which an area of forest is burned to clear it for planting. The ashes enrich the soil. After a few years of planting crops, the soil is exhausted. The farmer then moves on to a new area of forest. Farmers can return to previously farmed areas years later.

Maya ruins and sunny beaches have made tourism a major industry in this area. The popular resort of Cancún and the island of Cozumel are located here.

✓ **READING CHECK:** (*Human Systems*) What are the six culture regions of Mexico?

▲ Celebrations, such as Danza de Los Viejitos—Dance of the Old Men— are popular throughout Mexico.

Section Review 3

Define and explain: inflation, cash crops, smog, *maquiladoras*, slash-and-burn agriculture

Working with Sketch Maps On the map you created in Section 2, label Tijuana, Ciudad Juárez, Acapulco, Mazatlán, Cancún, Mexico City, Guadalajara, Tampico, Campeche, and Monterrey. Which city is the national capital? Which cities are located at or near sea level? Which are located at higher elevations?

Reading for the Main Idea

1. (*Human Systems*) What are three economic problems faced by Mexico in recent decades?

2. (*Human Systems*) What are Mexico's six culture regions? Describe a feature of each.

go.hrw.com **Homework Practice Online** Keyword: SG5 HP6

Critical Thinking

3. **Analyzing Information** How have changes in the price of oil affected Mexico?

4. **Drawing Inferences and Conclusions** Why would farmers in Mexico grow only cash crops?

Organizing What You Know

5. **Categorizing** Copy the following graphic organizer. Use it to list key facts about the population and economy of each culture region in Mexico.

	Population	Economy
Greater Mexico City		
Central interior		
Oil coast		
Southern Mexico		
Northern Mexico		
Yucatán		

Review and Practice

Define and Identify

Identify each of the following:

1. sinkholes
2. Maya
3. Aztec
4. conquistadores
5. epidemic
6. empire
7. mestizos
8. Benito Juárez
9. missions
10. haciendas
11. inflation
12. cash crops
13. smog
14. *maquiladoras*

Review the Main Ideas

15. What are the Isthmus of Tehuantepec and Baja California?
16. What is the Mexican Plateau? What forms its edges?
17. What are some animals that live in Mexico's northern deserts? in its southern rain forests?
18. What is Mexico's main energy resource? mineral resource?
19. What were some features of Olmec civilization?
20. When was the Maya civilization at its peak, and when did it decline?
21. What was the city of Tenochtitlán like?
22. How did European diseases affect the Indians in Mexico?
23. What were the main ethnic divisions in New Spain?
24. What is the Day of the Dead?
25. Why did Mexico's economy improve after 1994?
26. What are Mexico's six main culture regions?

Think Critically

27. **Drawing Inferences and Conclusions** Why do climates in southern Mexico vary so widely?
28. **Finding the Main Idea** How did the Maya and Aztec modify their environment to suit their needs?
29. **Comparing** How did land ownership in Mexico change under Spanish rule?
30. **Summarizing** What problems and hazards face the people of Mexico City?
31. **Finding the Main Idea** What is the major drawback of slash-and-burn agriculture in Mexico?

Map Activity

32. On a separate sheet of paper, match the letters on the map with their correct labels.

Río Bravo (Rio Grande)	Tijuana
Mexico City	Ciudad Juárez
Mount Orizaba	Acapulco
Yucatán Peninsula	Cancún
	Guadalajara

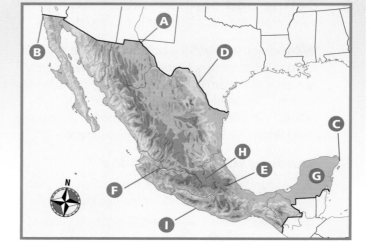

Writing Activity

Imagine that you are a Spanish soldier reporting back to Spain on the situation in Mexico. Research and write a short report on the effects of disease on the Aztec. Include a map, chart, graph, model, or database illustrating the information in your report. Be sure to use standard grammar, spelling, sentence structure, and punctuation.

internet connect

Internet Activity: **go.hrw.com**
KEYWORD: **SG5 GT6**

Choose a topic to explore about Mexico:
- Travel along Mexico's coastlines.
- See the arts and crafts of Mexico.
- Use ancient Maya hieroglyphs.

Social Studies Skills Practice

Interpreting Graphs

You have read about Mexico City's pollution problem. Most people use public transportation, but private vehicles still crowd the city's streets. Study the following graph. Then answer the questions.

Vehicles in Mexico City

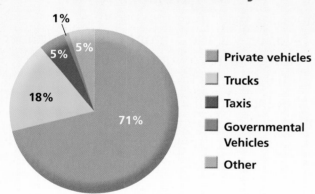

1% · 5% · 5% · 18% · 71%

- Private vehicles
- Trucks
- Taxis
- Governmental Vehicles
- Other

1. What is the largest category on the graph? the smallest?

2. If more people used public transportation, which group or groups might get smaller?

3. Why do you think trucks are listed as a separate category?

4. What does the graph tell you about the actual number of vehicles in Mexico City? Support your answer.

Analyzing Primary Sources

In 1910, Mexican president Porfirio Díaz had his political opponent Francisco Madero thrown in prison. Madero wrote a letter from prison encouraging Mexicans to revolt against the government. Read the passage from Madero's letter. Then answer the questions.

"A force of tyranny . . . oppresses us in such a manner that it has become intolerable. In exchange for . . . tyranny we are offered peace, but peace full of shame for the Mexican nation, because its basis is not law, but force; because its object is not the . . . prosperity [wealth and happiness] of the country, but to enrich a small group who . . . have converted the public charges [responsibilities] into fountains of . . . personal benefit . . . ."

1. From the context, what do you think the word *tyranny* means?

2. How does Madero feel about Mexico's being at peace?

3. Madero uses the word *fountains* to describe the wealth that a small group of people is taking from the government. Why may Madero have chosen that word?

4. How do you think Mexicans who read this letter reacted to it?

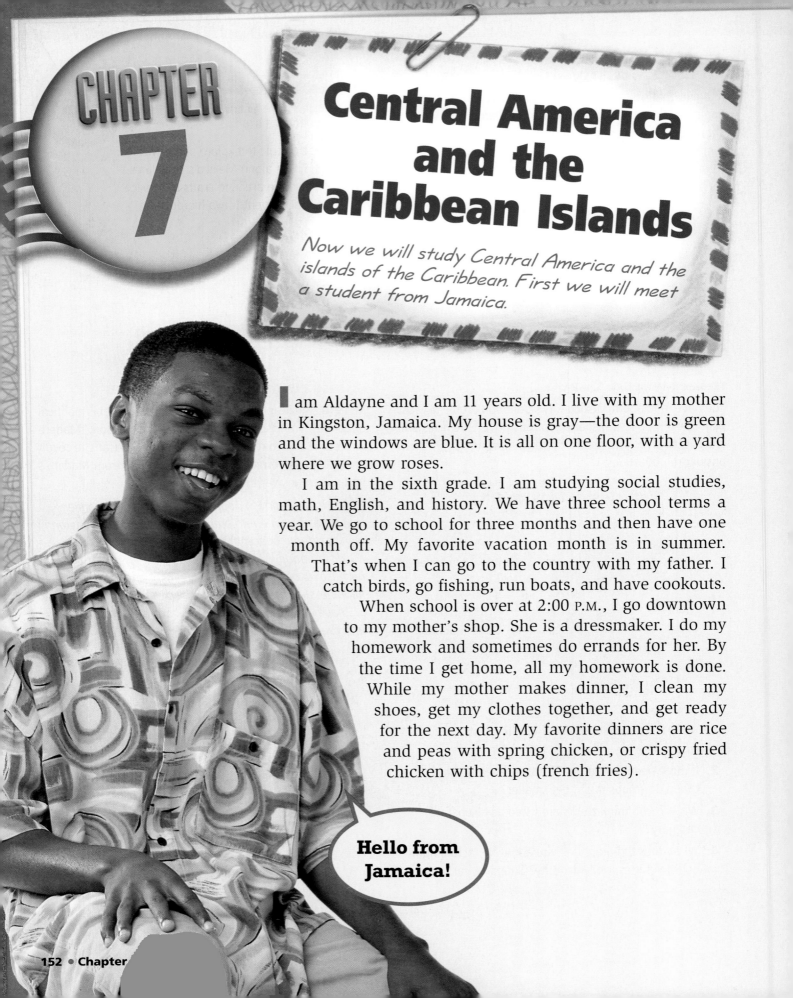

CHAPTER 7

Central America and the Caribbean Islands

Now we will study Central America and the islands of the Caribbean. First we will meet a student from Jamaica.

I am Aldayne and I am 11 years old. I live with my mother in Kingston, Jamaica. My house is gray—the door is green and the windows are blue. It is all on one floor, with a yard where we grow roses.

I am in the sixth grade. I am studying social studies, math, English, and history. We have three school terms a year. We go to school for three months and then have one month off. My favorite vacation month is in summer. That's when I can go to the country with my father. I catch birds, go fishing, run boats, and have cookouts.

When school is over at 2:00 P.M., I go downtown to my mother's shop. She is a dressmaker. I do my homework and sometimes do errands for her. By the time I get home, all my homework is done. While my mother makes dinner, I clean my shoes, get my clothes together, and get ready for the next day. My favorite dinners are rice and peas with spring chicken, or crispy fried chicken with chips (french fries).

Hello from Jamaica!

Section 1 Physical Geography

Read to Discover

1. What are the physical features of Central America and the Caribbean islands?
2. What climates are found in the region?
3. What natural resources does the region have?

Vocabulary

archipelago
cloud forest
bauxite

Places

Central America
Caribbean Sea
Cuba
Jamaica
Greater Antilles
Hispaniola

Puerto Rico
Lesser Antilles
Virgin Islands
Trinidad and Tobago
Bahamas

Reading Strategy

READING ORGANIZER Before you read, draw a large circle on a sheet of paper. Draw a line down the center of the circle and another line across it. Label the four parts Physical Features, Climate, Vegetation, and Resources. List the information you learn in each part.

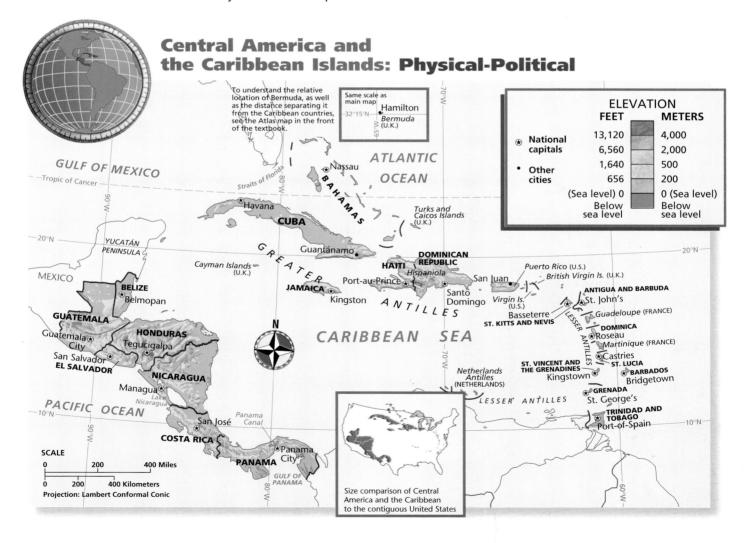

Central America and the Caribbean Islands: Physical-Political

To understand the relative location of Bermuda, as well as the distance separating it from the Caribbean countries, see the Atlas map in the front of the textbook.

Same scale as main map
Hamilton
32°15'N
Bermuda (U.K.)
65°W

ELEVATION

	FEET	METERS
⊛ National capitals	13,120	4,000
	6,560	2,000
• Other cities	1,640	500
	656	200
	(Sea level) 0	0 (Sea level)
	Below sea level	Below sea level

GULF OF MEXICO
Tropic of Cancer
ATLANTIC OCEAN
Nassau
BAHAMAS
Straits of Florida
Havana
CUBA
Turks and Caicos Islands (U.K.)
20°N
YUCATÁN PENINSULA
GREATER
Guantánamo
20°N
MEXICO
Cayman Islands (U.K.)
DOMINICAN REPUBLIC
HAITI
Hispaniola
Puerto Rico (U.S.)
British Virgin Is. (U.K.)
BELIZE
Belmopan
JAMAICA
Port-au-Prince
San Juan
ANTIGUA AND BARBUDA
GUATEMALA
Kingston
ANTILLES
Santo Domingo
Virgin Is. (U.S.)
St. John's
Guadeloupe (FRANCE)
Guatemala City
HONDURAS
Tegucigalpa
N
Basseterre
ST. KITTS AND NEVIS
LESSER ANTILLES
DOMINICA
Roseau
San Salvador
EL SALVADOR
CARIBBEAN SEA
Martinique (FRANCE)
Castries
ST. LUCIA
NICARAGUA
ST. VINCENT AND THE GRENADINES
BARBADOS
Managua
Lake Nicaragua
Netherlands Antilles (NETHERLANDS)
Kingstown
Bridgetown
GRENADA
PACIFIC OCEAN
10°N
LESSER ANTILLES
St. George's
TRINIDAD AND TOBAGO
Port-of-Spain
10°N
San José
Panama Canal
COSTA RICA
Panama City
PANAMA
GULF OF PANAMA

SCALE
0   200   400 Miles
0   200   400 Kilometers
Projection: Lambert Conformal Conic

Size comparison of Central America and the Caribbean to the contiguous United States

Physical Features

Central America and the Caribbean Sea are home to 20 countries and a number of island territories. Central America includes Guatemala, Belize, Honduras, El Salvador, Nicaragua, Costa Rica, and Panama. The Caribbean islands include Cuba, Jamaica, Haiti, and the Dominican Republic. There also are nine smaller island countries.

Central America forms a bridge between North and South America. No place on this isthmus is more than 125 miles (200 km) from the sea. Mountains separate the Caribbean and Pacific coastal plains.

The Caribbean islands form an **archipelago** (ahr-kuh-PE-luh-goh), or large group of islands. The Caribbean archipelago is arranged in a long curve. It stretches from south of Florida to South America.

There are two main island groups in the Caribbean archipelago. The four large islands of the Greater Antilles (an-TI-leez) are Cuba, Jamaica, Hispaniola, and Puerto Rico. The small islands of the Lesser Antilles stretch from the Virgin Islands to Trinidad and Tobago. Another island group, the Bahamas, lies outside the Caribbean, east of Florida. It includes nearly 700 islands and thousands of reefs.

Earthquakes and volcanic eruptions are frequent in this region. Colliding plates cause this tectonic activity. The Cocos plate collides with and dives under the Caribbean plate off Central America's western coast. Another plate boundary lies to the east. The Caribbean plate borders the North American plate there. Volcanic eruptions can cause great damage.

✔ **READING CHECK:** (*Places and Regions*) What are the physical features of Central America and the Caribbean islands?

Climate and Vegetation

Along the Caribbean coast of Central America are humid tropical plains. The area also has dense rain forests. Inland mountains rise into mild highland climates. Most of the people live there because the temperatures are more moderate. Much of the original savanna vegetation inland

Our Amazing Planet

Dominica, in the far southeast of the region, receives up to 250 inches (835 cm) of rain per year! In contrast, Miami, Florida, receives only about 56 inches (140 cm).

Forested mountains rise above Roseau, capital of the island country of Dominica. Dominica is in the Lesser Antilles.

Interpreting the Visual Record (*Place*)
What might the lush forest tell us about Dominica's climate?

has been cleared. It has been replaced by plantations and ranches. The Pacific coast has a warm and sunny tropical savanna climate.

Some of Central America's mountain areas are covered by **cloud forest**. This is a high-elevation, very wet tropical forest where low clouds are common. It is home to numerous plant and animal species.

The islands of the Caribbean have pleasant humid tropical and tropical savanna climates. Winters are usually drier than summers. The islands receive 40 to 60 inches (102 to 152 cm) of rainfall each year. On some islands the bedrock is mostly limestone. Water drains quickly. As a result, drought conditions are common.

Hurricanes are a danger in the region. Hurricanes are tropical storms that bring violent winds, heavy rain, and high seas. Most occur between June and November. They can cause great destruction and loss of life.

✔ **READING CHECK:** (*Environment and Society*) What effect do hurricanes have on people in the region?

▲ A hiker explores Costa Rica's cloud forest.

Resources

Agriculture in the region can be profitable where volcanic ash has enriched the soil. Coffee, bananas, sugarcane, and cotton are major crops. Timber is exported from the rain forests of Belize and Honduras. Tourism is the most important industry, particularly in the Caribbean islands.

The region has few mineral resources. However, Jamaica has large reserves of **bauxite**, the most important aluminum ore. There are huge copper deposits in Panama. Energy resources are limited. This makes the region dependent on energy imports and limits economic development.

✔ **READING CHECK:** (*Environment and Society*) Why do you think tourism is the most important industry in the region?

go.
hrw
.com
Homework Practice Online
Keyword: SG5 HP7

Section Review 1

Define and explain: archipelago, cloud forest, bauxite

Working with Sketch Maps On a map of the region that you draw or that your teacher provides, label the following: Central America, Caribbean Sea, Cuba, Jamaica, Greater Antilles, Puerto Rico, Hispaniola, Lesser Antilles, Virgin Islands, Trinidad and Tobago, and the Bahamas. Identify continents Central America links.

Reading for the Main Idea

1. (*Places and Regions*) What two major island groups make up the Caribbean archipelago?

2. (*Places and Regions*) In what climate region do most Central Americans live and why?

3. (*Places and Regions*) What are some of the region's crops?

Critical Thinking

4. Making Generalizations and Predictions What natural hazards do you think will continue to be a problem for the region? Why?

Organizing What You Know

5. Categorizing Copy the following graphic organizer. Use it to describe the climates, vegetation, and resources found in the region.

Climates	Vegetation	Resources

Read to Discover

1. What was Central America's early history like?
2. How is the region's history reflected in its people today?
3. What are the countries of Central America like today?

Vocabulary

cacao
dictators
cardamom
civil war
ecotourism

Places

Guatemala City
Lake Nicaragua
San José
Panama City
Panama Canal

Reading Strategy

MNEMONIC DEVICE Before you read, write the letters in the words *CENTRAL AMERICA* down the left side of a sheet of paper. As you read the section, write a fact you learn that begins with each letter.

▲ Maya ruins can be found here in Belize and in other parts of Central America and Mexico.

(map labels: Mexico, Belize, Xunantunich, Guatemala, Honduras)

History

More than 39 million people live in the countries of Central America. These countries have a shared history.

Early History The early peoples of Central America developed different cultures and societies. The Maya, for example, built large cities with pyramids and temples. People of Maya descent still live in Guatemala and parts of Mexico. Many of their ancient customs and traditions still influence modern life.

In the early 1500s European countries began establishing colonies in the region. Most of Central America came under the control of Spain. In the 1600s the British established the colony of British Honduras, which is now Belize. The British also occupied the Caribbean coast of Nicaragua.

European colonists established large plantations. They grew crops like tobacco and sugarcane. They forced the Central American Indians to work on the plantations. Some Indians were sent to work in gold mines elsewhere in the Americas. In addition, many Africans were brought to the region as slaves.

Independence Costa Rica, El Salvador, Guatemala, Honduras, and Nicaragua declared independence from Spain in 1821. They formed the United Provinces of Central America, but separated from each other in 1838–1839. Panama, once part of Colombia, became independent in 1903. The British left Nicaragua in the late 1800s. British Honduras gained independence as Belize in 1981.

✓ **READING CHECK:** (*Human Systems*) What role did Europeans play in the region's history?

Culture

Central America's colonial history is reflected in its culture today. In what ways do you think this is true?

People, Languages, and Religion The region's largest ethnic group is mestizo. Mestizos are people of mixed European and Indian ancestry. People of African ancestry make up a significant minority. Various Indian peoples also live in the region.

Spanish is the official language in most countries. However, many people speak Indian languages. In the former British colony of Belize, English is the official language.

Many Central Americans practice religions brought to the region by Europeans. Most are Roman Catholics. Spanish missionaries converted many Indians to Catholicism. However, Indian religions have influenced Catholicism in the region. Protestant Christians are a large minority in some countries, particularly Belize.

Our Amazing Planet

Lake Nicaragua was probably once part of an ocean bay. It is a freshwater lake, but it also has some oceanic animal life. This animal life includes the Lake Nicaragua shark. It grows to a length of about 8 to 10 feet (2.4 to 3 m).

Guatemalans celebrate the Christian holiday *Semana Santa*, or Holy Week. The street is covered with colored sand and flowers.

CONNECTING TO *Math*

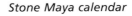

Stone Maya calendar

The Maya created one of the most advanced civilizations in the Americas. They built impressive cities of stone and invented a complex writing system. They also created calendars that allowed them to plan for the future.

The Maya based their calendar system on religion, mathematics, and astronomy. They believed that the days, months, and years were represented by different gods. Those gods had powers that helped determine the course of events. The Maya also understood the mathematical concepts of zero and numerical positioning. Numerical positioning is the idea that numbers can have different values depending on their position in a sequence, such as the 1 in 10 and 100. The Maya also calculated the length of the solar year. They predicted eclipses and lunar cycles.

MAYA CALENDAR

Based on this knowledge, the Maya created two calendars. One was a religious calendar of 260 days. The other was a solar calendar of 365 days. These two calendars were used together to record historical events and to determine future actions. Using calendars, the Maya chose the best times to plant crops, hold festivals, and crown new rulers. They even believed that their calendars would help them predict the future.

Understanding What You Read

1. What were the foundations of the calendar system developed by the Maya?
2. How did the Maya's belief systems affect their use of calendars?

Food and Festivals Central America shares many traditional foods with Mexico and South America. These foods include corn and sweet potatoes. The region is also home to tomatoes, hot peppers, and **cacao** (kuh-KOW). Cacao is a small tree on which cocoa beans grow.

As in other Catholic countries, each town and country celebrates special saints' feast days. Images of the saints are paraded through the streets. A community might sponsor a fair and have dancing or plays.

Government From time to time, Central American countries have been ruled by **dictators**. A dictator is a person who rules a country with complete authority. The opponents of dictators often are arrested or even killed. Such abuses are one reason for limiting the power of government. Today the region's countries have elected governments.

✓ **READING CHECK:** (*Human Systems*) Why should government powers be limited?

Central America Today

Now we will take a closer look at each of the countries of Central America today.

Guatemala Guatemala is the most populous country in Central America. More than 13 million people live there. Nearly half of the country's people are Central American Indians. Many speak Maya languages. A majority of Guatemala's population are mestizos.

Most Maya live in isolated villages in the country's highlands. Fighting between rebels and government forces has killed more than 100,000 Guatemalans since the 1960s. Guatemalans hope that recent peace agreements will end this conflict.

Coffee is Guatemala's most important crop. The country also is a major producer of **cardamom**, a spice used in Asian foods.

▲
A woman in the Guatemalan highlands weaves traditional fabrics.

Belize Belize is located on the Caribbean coast of the Yucatán Peninsula. It has the smallest population in Central America. Only about 266,000 people live there. The country's Maya ruins, coral reefs, and coastal resorts attract many tourists.

Honduras Honduras is a country of rugged mountains. Most people live in mountain valleys and along the northern coast. Transportation is difficult in the rugged terrain. Only 15 percent of the land is suitable for growing crops. Fruit is an important export.

El Salvador El Salvador lies on the Pacific side of Central America. Volcanic ash has made the country's soils the most fertile in the region. Important crops include coffee and sugarcane.

Most Salvadorans live in poverty. A few powerful families own much of the best land. These conditions were a major reason behind a long **civil war** in the 1980s. A civil war is a conflict between two or more groups within a country. The war killed many Salvadorans and slowed economic progress. Salvadorans have been rebuilding their country since the war ended in 1992.

Nicaragua Nicaragua is the largest Central American country. It has coasts on both the Caribbean Sea and the Pacific Ocean. Lake Nicaragua, near the Pacific coast, is the largest lake in Central America.

Nicaragua also has been rebuilding since the end of a long civil war. Its civil war ended in 1990. Free elections that year ended the rule of the Sandinistas. The Sandinistas had overthrown a dictator in 1979. They then ruled Nicaragua without elections. Today, the country is a democracy with many political voices.

Central America

Country	Population/ Growth Rate	Life Expectancy	Literacy Rate	Per Capita GDP
Belize	266,440 2.4%	65, male 69, female	94%	$4,900
Costa Rica	3,896,092 1.6%	74, male 79, female	96%	$8,500
El Salvador	6,470,379 1.8%	67, male 74, female	80%	$4,700
Guatemala	13,909,384 2.6%	64, male 66, female	70%	$3,700
Honduras	6,669,789 2.3%	65, male 68, female	76%	$2,600
Nicaragua	5,128,517 2.0%	67, male 71, female	67%	$2,500
Panama	2,960,784 1.3%	69, male 74, female	92%	$6,000
United States	290,342,554 0.9%	74, male 80, female	97%	$37,600

Source: Central Intelligence Agency, *The World Factbook 2003*

Interpreting the Chart Which two Central American countries have the highest per capita GDP? Why might this be?

Costa Rica Costa Rica has a long history of stable, democratic government. In the last half of the 1900s, the country remained at peace. During that time, many of its neighbors were torn by civil wars. Costa Rica has also made important progress in reducing poverty.

Costa Rica's capital, San José, is located in the central highlands. Many coffee farms are also located in the highlands. Coffee and bananas are important Costa Rican crops.

Many travelers are attracted to Costa Rica's rich tropical rain forests and national parks. **Ecotourism**—the practice of using an area's natural environment to attract tourists—is an important part of Central American and Caribbean economies.

Panama Panama lies between Costa Rica and Colombia. Most Panamanians live in areas near the Panama Canal. Canal fees and industries make the canal area the country's most prosperous region.

The Panama Canal links the Pacific Ocean to the Caribbean Sea and Atlantic Ocean. The United States finished the canal in 1914. The canal played an important role in U.S. economic and foreign policies. It also allowed the United States to control territory and extend its influence in the area. The United States controlled the canal until 1999. Then, as called for by a 1978 treaty, Panama took it over.

✔ **READING CHECK:** (*The Uses of Geography*) Why might Panama want control of the canal?

Homework Practice Online
Keyword: SG5 HP7

Define and explain: cacao, dictators, cardamom, civil war, ecotourism

Working with Sketch Maps On the map you created in Section 1, label the Central American countries, Guatemala City, Lake Nicaragua, San José, Panama City, and the Panama.

Reading for the Main Idea

1. (*Human Systems*) What two European powers had Central American colonies by the late 1600s?

2. (*Human Systems*) How do many Central American communities honor certain Roman Catholic saints?

Critical Thinking

3. Finding the Main Idea How do Central America's people, languages, and religions reflect the region's history?

4. Contrasting How has Costa Rica's history differed from that of its Central American neighbors?

Organizing What You Know

5. Categorizing Copy the following graphic organizer. Use it to write at least one important fact about each Central American country today. Add as many rows as needed to list all of the countries.

Guatemala	

Read to Discover

1. What was the Caribbean's history like?
2. How is the region's history reflected in its people today?
3. What are the countries of the Caribbean like today?

Vocabulary

Santería
calypso
reggae
merengue
guerrilla

refugees
cooperatives
plantains
commonwealth

Places

Havana
Port-au-Prince
Santo Domingo

Reading Strategy

READING ORGANIZER Before you read, draw a circle on a piece of paper. Write Caribbean Islands in the center. As you read, draw an arrow pointing toward the circle for each contribution to island culture made by people from around the world. Write these contributions on the arrows.

History

The Caribbean islands include 13 independent countries. All are former European colonies.

Early History Christopher Columbus first sailed into the Caribbean Sea for Spain in 1492. He thought he had reached the Indies, or the islands near India. He called the islands the West Indies and the people who lived there Indians. Spain established colonies there. Many Caribbean Indians died from disease or war.

In the 1600s and 1700s, the English, French, Dutch, and Danish also established Caribbean colonies. They built large plantations on the islands. Crops included sugarcane, tobacco, and cotton. Europeans brought Africans to work as slaves.

Independence A slave revolt won Haiti its independence from France in 1804. By the mid-1800s the Dominican Republic had also won independence. The United States took Cuba from Spain in the Spanish-American War in 1898. Cuba gained independence in 1902. Other Caribbean countries did not gain independence until the last half of the 1900s.

Tourists still visit Christophe's Citadel in Haiti. The fortress was built in the early 1800s after Haiti won independence from France.

✓ **READING CHECK:** (*Human Systems*) What was the early history of the Caribbean islands?

Caribbean Islands

Country	Population/ Growth Rate	Life Expectancy	Literacy Rate	Per Capita GDP
Antigua and Barbuda	67,897 0.6%	68, male 73, female	89%	$11,000
Bahamas	297,477 .93%	67, male 74, female	98%	$15,000
Barbados	277,264 0.5%	71, male 76, female	97%	$14,500
Cuba	11,263,429 0.4%	74, male 79, female	96%	$1,700
Dominica	69,655 -.98%	71, male 77, female	94%	$4,000
Dominican Republic	8,715,602 1.6%	71, male 76, female	82%	$5,700
Grenada	89,258 -0.06%	63, male 66, female	98%	$4,400
Haiti	7,527,817 1.4%	47, male 51, female	45%	$1,800
Jamaica	2,695,867 0.5%	74, male 78, female	85%	$3,700
St. Kitts and Nevis	38,763 0.13%	68, male 74, female	97%	$8,800
St. Lucia	162,157 1.25%	69, male 76, female	67%	$5,400
St. Vincent and the Grenadines	116,812 0.4%	71, male 74, female	96%	$2,900
Trinidad and Tobago	1,169,682 -0.51%	67, male 72, female	98%	$9,500
United States	290,342,554 0.9%	74, male 80, female	97%	$37,600

Source: Central Intelligence Agency, *The World Factbook 2003*

Interpreting the Chart **Why might life expectancy be greater in some Caribbean island countries than in others?**

Culture

Today, nearly every Caribbean island shows the signs of past colonialism and slavery. These signs can be seen in the region's culture.

People, Languages, and Religion

Most islanders are of African or European descent or are a mixture of the two. Much smaller numbers of Asians also live there. Chinese and other Asians came to work on the plantations after slavery ended in the region.

English, French, and mixtures of European and African languages are spoken on many islands. For example, Haitians speak French and Creole. Creole is a Haitian dialect of French. Spanish is spoken in Cuba, the Dominican Republic, Puerto Rico, and some small islands. Dutch is the main language on several territories of the Netherlands.

Another sign of the region's past are the religions practiced there. Protestant Christians are most numerous on islands that were British territories. Former French and Spanish territories have large numbers of Roman Catholics. On all the islands, some people practice a combination of Catholicism and traditional African religions. One of these religions is **Santería**. Santería began in Cuba and spread to nearby islands and parts of the United States. It has roots in West African religions and traditions.

Food, Festivals, and Music Caribbean cooking today relies on fresh fruits, vegetables, and fish or meat. Milk or preserved foods like cheese or pickled fish are seldom used. Cooking has been influenced by foods brought from Africa, Asia, and elsewhere. For example, the samosa—a spicy, deep-fried pastry—has its origins in India. Other popular foods include mangoes, rice, yams, and okra.

People on each Caribbean island celebrate a variety of holidays. One of the biggest and most widespread is Carnival. Carnival is a time of feasts and parties before the Christian season of Lent. It is celebrated with big parades and beautiful costumes.

The islands' musical styles are popular far beyond the Caribbean. Trinidad and Tobago is the home of steel-drum and **calypso** music. Jamaica is famous as the birthplace of **reggae** music. **Merengue** is the national music and dance of the Dominican Republic.

Caribbean musical styles have many fans in the United States. However, the United States has influenced Caribbean culture as well. For example, baseball has become a popular sport in the region. It is particularly popular in the Dominican Republic and Cuba. A number of successful professional baseball players in the United States come from Caribbean countries.

✓ **READING CHECK:** (*Human Systems*) How do the cultures of the Caribbean islands reflect historical events?

The Caribbean Islands Today

Now we will look at the largest island countries. We also will examine the island territory of Puerto Rico.

Cuba Cuba is the largest and the most populous country in the Caribbean. It is about the size of Tennessee but has more than twice the population. It is located just 90 miles (145 km) south of Florida. Havana, the capital, is the country's largest and most important city.

Cuba has had a Communist government since Fidel Castro seized power in 1959. Cuba has supported Communist **guerrilla** movements trying to overthrow other governments. A guerrilla takes part in irregular warfare, such as raids.

Many Cubans who oppose Castro have become **refugees** in the United States. A refugee is someone who flees to another country, usually for economic or political reasons. Many Cuban refugees and their families have become U.S. citizens. Most live in Florida.

The U.S. government has banned trade with Cuba. It also has restricted travel by U.S. citizens to the island since the 1960s. For years Cuba received economic aid and energy supplies from the Soviet Union. The collapse of the Soviet Union in the early 1990s has hurt Cuba's economy.

Today, private businesses remain limited in Cuba. Most farmland is organized into **cooperatives** and government-owned sugarcane

A girl joins the Carnival celebration in Trinidad and Tobago.

A worker cuts sugarcane in central Cuba. Sugarcane is Cuba's most important cash crop.

plantations. A cooperative is an organization owned by its members and operated for their mutual benefit.

Sugarcane remains Cuba's most important crop and export. Tourism has also become an important part of the economy. There has been debate in the United States over ending the ban on trade and travel to Cuba.

Haiti Haiti occupies the mountainous western third of the island of Hispaniola. It is the poorest country in the Americas. It is also one of the most densely populated. Its people have suffered under many corrupt governments during the last two centuries. Many Haitian refugees have come to the United States to escape poverty and political violence.

Port-au-Prince (pohr-toh-PRINS) is the national capital and center of industry. Coffee and sugarcane are two of the country's most important crops. Most Haitians farm small plots. Many grow **plantains**. Plantains are a type of banana used in cooking.

Dominican Republic The Dominican Republic occupies the eastern part of Hispaniola. It is a former Spanish colony. The capital is Santo Domingo. Santo Domingo was the first permanent European settlement in the Western Hemisphere.

The Dominican Republic is not a rich country. However, its economy, education, health care, and housing are more developed than Haiti's. Agriculture and tourism are important parts of the Dominican Republic's economy.

FOCUS ON CULTURE

Ice Cream Houses of Curaçao

In the southeastern Caribbean is an island where the houses look like they could melt in the sun. They are painted in colors that you see in a candy store or an ice cream shop. These are the old Dutch houses of Curaçao in the Netherlands Antilles.

When Dutch settlers came to Curaçao in the 1600s they brought their architectural styles with them. They adapted the styles for the climate. For example, the settlers added porches to their plantation homes for shade from the tropical sun. Soon they were painting their houses in much brighter colors than they used in the Netherlands. This practice may have started because the local tradition of whitewashing houses produced too bright a reflection for European tastes. Today some of the old houses have been turned into hotels or shops. Others are still private homes.

Why would Dutch settlers use traditional architectural styles in a new environment?

Puerto Rico Puerto Rico is the easternmost of the Greater Antilles. Once a Spanish colony, today it is a U.S. **commonwealth**. A commonwealth is a self-governing territory associated with another country. Puerto Ricans are U.S. citizens. However, they have no voting representation in the U.S. Congress.

Unemployment is higher and wages are lower in Puerto Rico than in the United States. Still, American aid and investment have helped make the economy of Puerto Rico more developed than those of other Caribbean islands. Puerto Ricans continue to debate whether their island should remain a commonwealth. Some want it to become an American state or an independent country.

Other Islands Jamaica, in the Greater Antilles, is the largest of the remaining Caribbean countries. The smallest country is St. Kitts and Nevis in the Lesser Antilles. The smallest U.S. state, Rhode Island, is nearly 12 times larger! For more about other Caribbean countries and the Bahamas, see this unit's Fast Facts chart.

A number of Caribbean and nearby islands are territories of other countries. These territories include the U.S. and British Virgin Islands. The Netherlands and France also have Caribbean territories. Bermuda, an Atlantic island northwest of the Caribbean, is a British territory.

▲ Ocho Rios, Jamaica, and other beautiful Caribbean resorts and beaches attract many tourists.

✓ **READING CHECK:** (*Human Systems*) How are Puerto Rican citizens' political rights different from those of other U.S. citizens?

Section Review 3

Homework Practice Online
Keyword: SG5 HP7

Define and explain: Santería, calypso, reggae, merengue, guerrilla, refugees, cooperatives, plantains, commonwealth

Working with Sketch Maps On the map you created in Section 2, label the Caribbean countries, Havana, Port-au-Prince, and Santo Domingo.

Reading for the Main Idea

1. (*Human Systems*) When did European powers establish colonies in the Caribbean islands?

2. (*Human Systems*) What ethnic groups make up the region's population today?

3. (*Human Systems*) Why have Cubans and Haitians come to the United States as refugees?

Critical Thinking

4. **Comparing/Contrasting** What do the histories of Caribbean countries have in common with the history of the United States? How are they different?

Organizing What You Know

5. **Sequencing** Copy the following graphic organizer. Use it to show important events and periods in the history of the Caribbean islands since 1492.

1492	1600	1700	1804	1902	1959

CHAPTER 7 Review and Practice

Define and Identify

Identify each of the following:

1. archipelago
2. cloud forest
3. bauxite
4. cacao
5. dictators
6. cardamom
7. civil war
8. ecotourism
9. Santería
10. calypso
11. guerrilla
12. refugees
13. cooperatives
14. plantains
15. commonwealth

Review the Main Ideas

16. What two main island groups make up the Caribbean archipelago?
17. What natural hazards often threaten Central America and the Caribbean islands?
18. Which culture dominated Central America before the Spaniards arrived?
19. How did European influence affect Central America and the Caribbean islands?
20. What was a major reason for the civil war in El Salvador during the 1980s?

21. Which is the most populous country in Central America? in the Caribbean?
22. What are some musical styles with origins in the Caribbean? What influence have they had abroad?
23. How is Cuba's government organized?
24. What is the relationship of Puerto Ricans to the United States government?

Think Critically

25. **Drawing Inferences and Conclusions** How did slavery affect the ethnic diversity of the region?
26. **Comparing** How have the governments of the Central American countries changed over time?
27. **Finding the Main Idea** Why have refugees from Cuba and Haiti come to the United States?
28. **Summarizing** What agricultural products are grown in many Central American and Caribbean countries? Why?
29. **Analyzing Information** What are some of the natural and environmental hazards in Central America and the Caribbean islands? How do you think people may have coped with these hazards?

Map Activity

30. On a separate sheet of paper, match the letters on the map with their correct labels.

    Guatemala
    Nicaragua
    Panama
    Cuba
    Jamaica

    Haiti
    Dominican Republic
    Puerto Rico
    Bahamas
    Havana

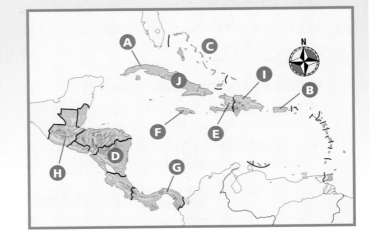

Writing Activity

Imagine that you have been asked to write a paragraph for a travel brochure about Central America and the Caribbean. Your paragraph should include information that tourists would want to know. This includes general information about the region's climates, vegetation, food, festivals, and other special celebrations. Be sure to use standard grammar, sentence structure, spelling, and punctuation.

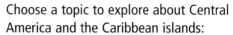

internet connect

Internet Activity: go.hrw.com
KEYWORD: SG5 GT7

Choose a topic to explore about Central America and the Caribbean islands:
- Plan an ecotour of Central America.
- Learn more about the Panama Canal.
- Hunt for hurricanes.

Social Studies Skills Practice

Interpreting Charts

Study the following chart and then answer the questions.

Country	Population Density (people per square mile)	Ranking among World Countries
Barbados	1,602	14
Cuba	261	92
Dominican Republic	433	60
Grenada	759	36
Haiti	644	47
Jamaica	617	50
Puerto Rico	1,106	21

Population Densities of Selected Caribbean Islands

1. Which country listed above has the highest population density? the lowest?
2. Which countries have densities above 1,000 people per square mile?
3. What does the chart tell you about the reasons for high population densities?

4. How do you think high population densities may affect economies? environments?

Analyzing Primary Sources

Read the quote by Henry K. Carroll, who in 1899 saw the damage caused by a hurricane in Puerto Rico. Then answer the questions.

"The gale tore up the trees, loosened the soil and the deluge of water converted the earth into a semifluid. Then followed the landslides, and thousands of acres of coffee plantations slid down into the valley . . . In such cases there is no restoration possible, for where there were smiling groves are now only bald rocks which were uncovered by the avalanche. Where the soil was not disturbed the most of the coffee trees were either uprooted, broken off, or stripped of foliage and the immature berries."

1. Based on this quote, what does the word *semifluid* mean?
2. How did the gale, or hurricane, indirectly cause the landslides?
3. Why would rebuilding many of the coffee plantations be impossible?
4. How do you think the hurricane affected Puerto Rico's economy?

CHAPTER 8

Caribbean South America

Caribbean South America is a region of varied landscapes. The fertile valleys in the Andes and the rich land near the Caribbean shore were important to Spain's empire.

My name is Jorge and I live in Armenia in northwestern Colombia. Armenia is a big city about 8 hours from the capital, Bogotá. I live in a big house in the northern part of the city with my three younger brothers, my mother and father, my grandmother, and our big black dog, Rocca. Our house has two floors around a courtyard with flowers—it is pink with yellow shutters.

My father is a merchant and a farm-owner. The farm, or hacienda, is in the country about 45 minutes away by car. About 60 people work for my father there, growing coffee, plantains, yucca, and fruits like strawberries and oranges. We also raise chickens and pigs. My dad has a fleet of five trucks to carry our produce into the city for sale to groceries and restaurants. My mom has three people to help with the cooking at the farm.

¡Hola! ¿Cómo estás?

Translation: Hello! How are you?

Section 1 Physical Geography

Read to Discover

1. What are the major landforms and rivers of Caribbean South America?
2. What climate and vegetation types are found in the region?
3. What are the natural resources of this region?

Reading Strategy

READING ORGANIZER As you read, create a concept map on a sheet of paper by using the headings in the section. List details you learn that support each heading.

Vocabulary

cordillera
tepuís
Llanos

Places

Andes
Guiana Highlands
Orinoco River

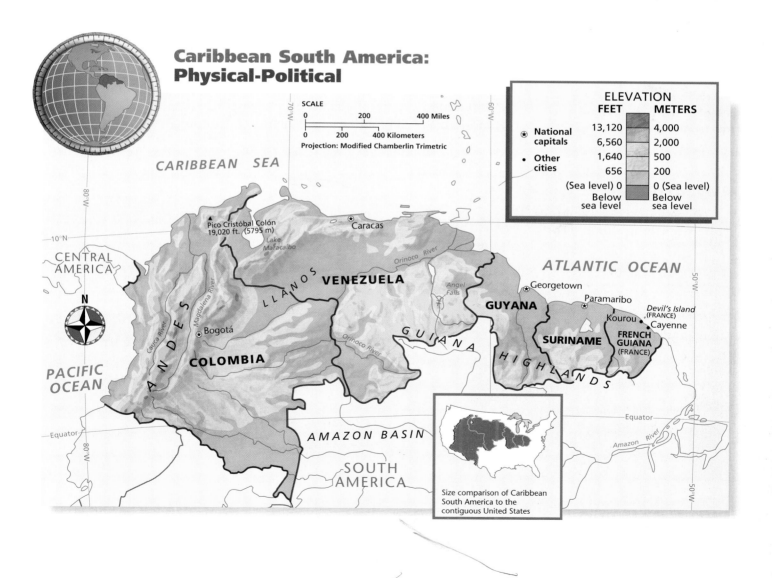

Caribbean South America: Physical-Political

SCALE
0   200   400 Miles
0   200   400 Kilometers
Projection: Modified Chamberlin Trimetric

ELEVATION

	FEET	METERS
⊛ National capitals	13,120	4,000
	6,560	2,000
• Other cities	1,640	500
	656	200
	(Sea level) 0	0 (Sea level)
	Below sea level	Below sea level

CARIBBEAN SEA

CENTRAL AMERICA

▲ Pico Cristóbal Colón 19,020 ft. (5795 m)

Lake Maracaibo

Caracas

Orinoco River

ATLANTIC OCEAN

N

LLANOS

VENEZUELA

Magdalena River

Angel Falls

⊛ Georgetown

GUYANA

Paramaribo

Devil's Island (FRANCE)

Kourou

Cauca River

⊛ Bogotá

Orinoco River

G U I A N A

SURINAME

Cayenne

FRENCH GUIANA (FRANCE)

COLOMBIA

H I G H L A N D S

PACIFIC OCEAN

Equator

AMAZON BASIN

SOUTH AMERICA

Amazon River

Equator

Size comparison of Caribbean South America to the contiguous United States

Physical Features

A rugged landscape and dense forests have often separated peoples and cultures in this region. In the west, the Andes (AN-deez) rise above 18,000 feet (5,486 m). Here the mountain range forms a three-pronged **cordillera** (kawr-duhl-YER-uh). A cordillera is a mountain system made up of parallel ranges. Many active volcanoes and earthquakes shake these mountains.

In the east the Guiana Highlands have been eroding for millions of years. However, some of the steep-sided plateaus are capped by sandstone layers that have resisted erosion. These unusual formations are called *tepuís* (tay-PWEEZ). They can reach approximately 3,000 to 6,000 feet (914 to 1,829 m) above the surrounding plains.

Between these two upland areas are the vast plains of the Orinoco (OHR-ee-NOH-koh) River basin. These plains are the **Llanos** (YAH-nohs) of eastern Colombia and western Venezuela. The northeastern edge of the Guiana Highlands slopes down to a fertile coastal plain in Guyana, Suriname, and French Guiana.

Of the region's many rivers, the Orinoco is the longest. It flows for about 1,281 miles (2,061 km) through the region on its way to the Atlantic Ocean. Large oceangoing ships can travel upriver on the Orinoco for about 225 miles (362 km).

Some remarkable animals live in and around the Orinoco. They include aggressive meat-eating fish called piranhas (puh-RAH-nuhz), 200-pound (90-kg) catfish, and crocodiles as long as 20 feet (6 m). More than 1,000 bird species live in the Orinoco River basin.

✓ **READING CHECK:** (**Places and Regions**) What are the region's major landforms?

Environments in the Andes change with elevation. Five different elevation zones are commonly recognized.

Interpreting the Visual Record

(Region) In which elevation zones can farmers grow crops?

▼

Elevation Zones in the Andes

Tierra helada

Paramo

Tree Line

Tierra fría

Tierra templada

Tierra caliente

Sea Level

☐ **Tierra helada**	☐ **Tierra fría**	◼ **Tierra caliente**
Above 16,000 feet (4,877 m) **Permanently covered with snow**	6,000 to 10,000 feet (1,829 to 3,048 m) **Potatoes, wheat, oats, barley, beans, corn, rye**	Sea Level to 3,000 feet (914 m) **Bananas, cacao, rice, sugarcane**
◼ **Paramo**	◼ **Tierra templada**	
10,000 to 16,000 feet (3,048 to 4,877 m) **Potatoes, grasslands and hardy shrubs, grazing**	3,000 to 6,000 feet (914 to 1,829 m) **Coffee, corn, wheat, cotton, potatoes, sugarcane, tobacco**	

Climate and Vegetation

The climates of the Andes are divided by elevation into five zones. The *tierra caliente* (tee-E-ruh kal-ee-EN-tee), or "hot country," refers to the hot and humid lower elevations near sea level. There is little difference between summer and winter temperatures in this region. Crops such as sugarcane and bananas are grown here.

Higher up the mountains the air becomes cooler. Moist climates with mountain forests are typical here. This zone of pleasant climates is called tierra templada (tem-PLAH-duh), or "temperate country." Coffee is a typical crop grown in this area. The next zone is the *tierra fría* (FREE-uh), or "cold country." The *tierra fría* has forests and grasslands. Farmers can grow potatoes and wheat. Bogotá, Colombia's capital, lies in the *tierra fría*. Above the tree line is a zone called the *paramo* (PAH-rah-moh). Grasslands and hardy shrubs are the usual vegetation. Frost may occur on any night of the year in this zone. The *tierra helada* (el-AH-dah), or "frozen country," is the zone of highest elevation. It is always covered with snow.

✓ **READING CHECK:** (*Places and Regions*) What are the region's climate elevation zones?

South America's capybara is the world's largest rodent. Capybaras can weigh up to 145 pounds. Also called water hogs, capybaras live along lakes and rivers in wet tropical climates.

Resources

Good soil and moderate climates help make the region a rich agricultural area. The region has other valuable resources, including oil, iron ore, and bauxite. Lowland forests provide timber. Coastal areas yield fish and shrimp. Some rivers in the region are used to produce hydroelectric power.

✓ **READING CHECK:** (*Environment and Society*) How do geographic factors affect economic activities in this region?

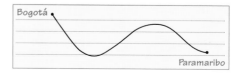

Section Review 1

Define and explain: cordillera, *tepuís*, Llanos

Working with Sketch Maps On a map of Caribbean South America that you draw or that your teacher provides, label the following: Andes, Guiana Highlands, and Orinoco River.

Reading for the Main Idea

1. (*Physical Systems*) What effect do the Andes have on the region's climate?

2. (*Environment and Society*) Why is the Orinoco River important?

go.hrw.com **Homework Practice Online** Keyword: SG5 HP8

Critical Thinking

3. **Drawing Inferences and Conclusions** How might Colombia's location affect its trade?

4. **Analyzing Information** Which physical features make farming easier in the region? Why?

Organizing What You Know

5. **Analyzing Information** Use the graphic organizer to describe the climate and vegetation found in traveling from Bogotá to Paramaribo, Suriname.

Bogotá

Paramaribo

Read to Discover

1. What are the main periods of Colombia's history?

2. What is Colombia like today?

Vocabulary

El Dorado
cassava

Places

Colombia
Bogotá
Cauca River
Magdalena River

People

Chibcha

Reading Strategy

FOLDNOTES: TRI-FOLD Create the FoldNote titled **Tri-Fold** described in the Appendix. Your Tri-Fold will be a brochure titled Colombia. Use these themes to title panels of the brochure: Location, Place, Human-Environment Interaction, Movement, and Region. As you read, record details about Colombia that support the themes. Illustrate your brochure if time permits.

Early History

Advanced cultures have lived in Colombia for centuries. Some giant mounds of earth, stone statues, and tombs found in Colombia are more than 1,500 years old.

The Chibcha In western Colombia, the Chibcha people had a well-developed civilization. The Chibcha practiced pottery making, weaving, and metalworking. Their gold objects were among the finest in ancient America.

The Chibcha had an interesting custom. New rulers were covered with gold dust and then taken to a lake to wash the gold off. Gold and emerald objects were thrown into the water as the new ruler washed. This custom inspired the legend of **El Dorado** (el duh-RAH-doh), or "the Golden One." The old legend of El Dorado describes a marvelous, rich land.

Spanish Conquest Spanish explorers arrived on the Caribbean coast of South America about 1500. They were helping to expand Spain's new empire. The Spanish conquered the Chibcha and seized much of their treasure. Spaniards and their descendants set up large estates. Powerful Spanish landlords forced South American Indians and enslaved Africans to work the land.

Giant stone figures near the headwaters of the Magdalena River are part of the San Agustín culture.

Interpreting the Visual Record What types of animals does the sculpture show?

Independence In the late 1700s people in Central and South America began struggling for independence from Spain. After independence was achieved, the republic of Gran Colombia was created. It included Colombia, Ecuador, Panama, and Venezuela. In 1830 the republic dissolved, and New Granada, now Colombia, was created. Present-day Panama was once part of New Granada.

After independence, debate raged in Colombia. People argued over how much power the central government and the Roman Catholic Church should have. Part of the problem had to do with the country's rugged geography. The different regions of Colombia had little contact with each other. They developed separate economies and identities. Uniting these different groups into one country was hard. Outbreaks of violence throughout the 1800s and 1900s killed thousands of people.

Colombia				
COUNTRY	**POPULATION/ GROWTH RATE**	**LIFE EXPECTANCY**	**LITERACY RATE**	**PER CAPITA GDP**
Colombia	41,662,073 1.6%	67, male 75, female	92%	$6,500
United States	290,342,554 0.9%	74, male 80, female	97%	$37,600

Source: Central Intelligence Agency, *The World Factbook 2003*

Interpreting the Chart How much larger is the U.S. population than that of Colombia?

✓ **READING CHECK:** (*Environment and Society*) What geographic factors influenced Colombia's ability to control its territory?

Colombia Today

Colombia is Caribbean South America's most populous country. The national capital is Bogotá, a city located high in the eastern Andes. Most Colombians live in the fertile valleys and basins among the mountain ranges because those areas are moderate in climate and good for farming. Rivers, such as the Cauca and Magdalena, flow down from the Andes to the Caribbean. They help connect settlements between the mountains and the coast. Cattle ranches are common in the Llanos. Few people live in the tropical rain forest regions in the south.

The guard tower of an old Spanish fort stands in contrast with the modern buildings of Cartagena, Colombia.

▼

CONNECTING TO Science

Botanical print of a gray cinchona

Fighting Malaria

Malaria is a disease usually transmitted by mosquitoes. It is common in the tropics. For centuries malaria was also widespread in Europe, but Europeans had no remedy. Native peoples in the South American rain forest did have a treatment, though. They used the powdered bark of the cinchona tree, which contains the drug quinine. The history of quinine and the struggle to obtain it is a story of great adventure.

The Spanish first discovered cinchona in the 1500s, when they conquered Peru. Shipments of the bark were soon arriving in Europe, where quinine was produced. Later, some countries tried to control the supply of bark. However, the Dutch smuggled cinchona seeds out of South America. They set up their own plantations in the East Indies. Before long, the Netherlands controlled most of the world's supply of quinine.

During World War II, the Axis Powers seized the Netherlands. As a result, the Allies lost their source of quinine. A crisis was prevented when some quinine was smuggled out of Germany and sold on the black market. Since then, scientists have developed synthetic drugs for the treatment of malaria. However, quinine remains an important drug. It is used to treat heart disease and is a key ingredient in tonic water.

Understanding What You Read
1. How did native peoples' use of the cinchona tree change the world?
2. How did political decisions during World War II affect the use of quinine?

Economy Colombia's economy relies on several valuable resources. Rich soil produces world-famous Colombian coffee. Only Brazil produces more coffee. Other major export crops include bananas, corn, rice, and sugarcane. **Cassava** (kuh-SAH-vuh), a tropical plant with starchy roots, is an important food crop. Colombian farms also produce flowers that are exported around the world. In fact, only the Netherlands exports more cut flowers than Colombia.

In recent years oil has become Colombia's leading export. Oil is found mainly in eastern Colombia. Other natural resources include iron ore, gold, coal, and tin. Most of the world's emeralds also come from Colombia.

Even with these rich resources, many Colombians have low incomes. Colombia faces the same types of problems as other countries in Central and South America. For example, urban poverty and rapid population growth remain a challenge in Colombia.

Cultural Life The physical geography of Colombia has isolated its regions from one another. This is one reason why the people of Colombia are often known by the area in which they live. African traditions have influenced the songs and dances of the Caribbean coast. Traditional music can be heard in some remote areas. In addition to music, many Colombians enjoy soccer. They also play a Chibcha sport called *tejo*, a type of ringtoss game. Roman Catholicism is the country's main religion.

Conflict is a serious problem in Colombia today. Border conflicts with Venezuela have gone on for many years. Many different groups have waged war with each other and with Colombia's government. These groups have controlled large areas of the country. Many farmers have been forced off of their land, and the economy has been damaged. Because of this instability, the future of Colombia is uncertain.

✓ **READING CHECK:** (**Human Systems**) How have historical events affected life in Colombia today?

Section Review 2

Homework Practice Online
Keyword: SG5 HP8

Define or identify: Chibcha, El Dorado, cassava

Working with Sketch Maps On the map you created in Section 1, label Colombia, Bogotá, and the Cauca and Magdalena Rivers.

Reading for the Main Idea

1. (**Human Systems**) Why did Spanish explorers come to Colombia?

2. (**Human Systems**) What are some characteristics of Colombia's culture?

Critical Thinking

3. Finding the Main Idea How have Colombia's varied landscapes affected its history?

4. Summarizing How have conflicts in Colombia affected its economy?

Organizing What You Know

5. Sequencing Copy the following graphic organizer. Use it to describe Colombia's historical periods.

Early history	Spanish period	Independence	Colombia today

Section 3 Venezuela

Read to Discover

1. How did the Spanish contribute to Venezuela's history?
2. What are some characteristics of Venezuela's culture?

Reading Strategy

READING ORGANIZER Before you read, create a spider map. Label the map Venezuela. Create a leg for each heading in the section. As you read the section, fill in the map with details about each heading.

Vocabulary

indigo
caudillos
llaneros
pardos

Places

Venezuela
Caracas
Lake Maracaibo

History of Venezuela

There were many small tribes of South American Indians living in Venezuela before the Spanish arrived. Most were led by chiefs and survived by a combination of hunting and farming.

Spanish Conquest Christopher Columbus landed on the Venezuelan coast in 1498. By the early 1500s the Spanish were exploring the area further. They forced South American Indians to dive for pearls and pan for gold. There was little gold, however. The settlers had to turn to agriculture. They grew **indigo** (IN-di-goh) and other crops. Indigo is a plant used to make a deep blue dye. South American Indians were forced to work the fields. When many of them died, plantation owners brought in enslaved Africans to take their place. Some slaves were able to escape. They settled in remote areas and governed themselves.

Margarita Island in Venezuela was the site of a Spanish fort in the 1500s.

Independence Partly because the colony was so poor, some people in Venezuela revolted against Spain. Simón Bolívar led the fight against the Spanish armies. Bolívar is considered a hero in many South American countries because he led wars of independence throughout the region. The struggle for independence finally ended in 1830, when Venezuela became an independent country.

Throughout the 1800s Venezuelans suffered from dictatorships and civil wars. The country's military leaders were called **caudillos** (kow-THEE-yohs). After oil was discovered, some caudillos kept the country's oil money for themselves. In 1958 the last dictator was forced out of power.

Oil Wealth By the 1970s Venezuela was earning huge sums of money from oil. This wealth allowed part of the population to buy luxuries. However, about 80 percent of the population still lived in poverty. Many of these people moved to the cities to find work. Some settled on the outskirts in shacks that had no running water, sewers, or electricity.

Venezuela's wealth drew many immigrants from Europe and from other South American countries. However, in the 1980s oil prices dropped sharply. Because Venezuela relied on oil for most of its income, the country suffered when prices decreased.

✓ **READING CHECK:** (**Human Systems**) How did the Spanish contribute to Venezuela's history?

Our Amazing Planet

Venezuela is home to the anaconda—the longest snake in the world. Adult anacondas are more than 15 feet (4.6 m) long.

Venezuela Today

Most Venezuelans live along the Caribbean coast and in the valleys of the nearby mountains. About 85 percent live in cities and towns. Caracas (kuh-RAHK-uhs), the capital, is the center of Venezuelan culture. It is a large city with a modern subway system, busy expressways, and tall office buildings. However, slums circle the city. Poverty in rural areas is also widespread. Still, Venezuela is one of South America's wealthiest countries. It is developing rapidly.

Economy Venezuela's economy is based on oil production. Lake Maracaibo (mah-rah-KY-boh) is a bay of the Caribbean Sea. The rocks under the lake are particularly rich in oil. However, the country is trying to reduce its dependence on oil income.

The Guiana Highlands in the southeast are rich in other minerals, such as iron ore for making steel. Dams on tributaries of the Orinoco River produce hydroelectricity.

Venezuela

COUNTRY	POPULATION/ GROWTH RATE	LIFE EXPECTANCY	LITERACY RATE	PER CAPITA GDP
Venezuela	24,654,694 1.5%	70, male 77, female	93%	$5,500
United States	290,342,554 0.9%	74, male 80, female	97%	$37,600

Source: Central Intelligence Agency, *The World Factbook 2003*

Interpreting the Chart **What is the average life expectancy for someone from Venezuela?**

Llaneros herd cattle on the large ranches of the Llanos.

Interpreting the Visual Record How do these *llaneros* look similar to cowboys in the United States?

Agriculture Northern Venezuela has small family farms and large commercial farms. **Llaneros** (yah-NAY-rohs)—cowboys of the Venezuelan Llanos—herd cattle on the many ranches in this region. Few people live in the Guiana Highlands. Some small communities of South American Indians practice traditional slash-and-burn agriculture there.

Cultural Life More than two thirds of Venezuela's population are **pardos**. They are people of mixed African, European, and South American Indian ancestry. Native groups make up only about 2 percent of the population. They speak more than 25 different languages. Spanish is the official language. Most of the people are Roman Catholics. Some Venezuelan Indians follow the religious practices of their ancestors.

The *joropo*, a lively foot-stomping couples' dance, is Venezuela's national dance. *Toros coleados* is a local sport. In this rodeo event, the contestant pulls a bull down by grabbing its tail. Baseball and soccer are also popular in Venezuela.

✓ **READING CHECK:** (*Human Systems*) What are some aspects of Venezuela's culture?

go.hrw.com **Homework Practice Online**
Keyword: SG5 HP8

Section Review 3

Define and explain: indigo, caudillos, *llaneros*, pardos

Working with Sketch Maps On the map you created in Section 2, label Venezuela, Caracas, and Lake Maracaibo. How does elevation affect the climate of Caracas?

Reading for the Main Idea

1. (*Environment and Society*) Why did Spanish settlers in Venezuela have to turn to agriculture?

2. (*Human Systems*) Who led Venezuela's revolt against Spain?

Critical Thinking

3. **Drawing Inferences and Conclusions** Why might Venezuela try to reduce its dependence on oil exports?

4. **Comparing** Compare the population densities of the Caribbean coast and the Guiana Highlands.

Organizing What You Know

5. **Analyzing Information** Copy the following graphic organizer. Use it to explain how oil is related to the history, urban poverty, and economy of Venezuela.

Oil	History	
	Urban poverty	
	Economy	

Read to Discover

1. Which countries influenced the early history of the Guianas?
2. How are Guyana, Suriname, and French Guiana similar today?

Vocabulary

indentured servants
pidgin languages

Places

Guyana
Suriname
French Guiana
Georgetown

Paramaribo
Devil's Island
Kourou
Cayenne

Reading Strategy

READING ORGANIZER Before you read, create a chart with these column headings: 2 facts I have already learned about the Guianas, 2 new interesting facts I learned in this section, and 2 questions I still have about the Guianas. Fill in the chart as you read.

Early History of the Guianas

Dense tropical rain forests cover much of the region east of Venezuela. Rugged highlands lie to the south. The physical environment of this region kept it somewhat isolated from the rest of South America. Thus, the three countries known as the Guianas (gee-AH-nuhz) have a history quite different from the rest of the continent.

European Settlement Spain was the first European country to claim the Guianas. The Spanish eventually lost the region to settlers from Great Britain, France, and the Netherlands. Sometimes a war fought in Europe determined which country held this corner of South America. The Europeans established coffee, tobacco, and cotton plantations. They brought Africans to work as slaves on these plantations. Sugarcane later became the main crop.

Asian Workers European countries made slavery illegal in the mid-1800s. Colonists in the Guianas needed a new source of labor for their plantations. They brought **indentured servants** from India, China, and Southeast Asia. Indentured servants agree to work for a certain period of time, often in exchange for travel expenses. As these people worked together, they developed **pidgin languages**. Pidgin languages are simple so that people who speak different languages can understand each other.

✓ **READING CHECK:** *Human Systems* What countries influenced the early history of the Guianas?

This Hindu temple is located in Cayenne, French Guiana.
▼

The Guianas

COUNTRY	POPULATION/ GROWTH RATE	LIFE EXPECTANCY	LITERACY RATE	PER CAPITA GDP
French Guiana	186,917 2.7%	73, male 80, female	83%	$6,000
Guyana	702,100 .07%	60, male 65, female	98%	$4,000
Suriname	433,449 0.3%	67, male 72, female	93%	$3,500
United States	290,342,554 0.9%	74, male 80, female	97%	$37,600

Source: Central Intelligence Agency, *The World Factbook 2003*

Interpreting the Chart (*Place*) **Why might the populations of Guyana and Suriname be growing slowly?**

The goliath bird-eating spider of northeastern South America is the largest spider in the world. The record holder had a leg span more than 11 inches (28 cm) across. That is as big as a dinner plate!

The Guianas Today

The area formerly known as British Guiana gained its independence in 1966 and became Guyana. In 1975 Dutch Guiana broke away from the Netherlands to become Suriname. French Guiana remains a part of France.

Guyana *Guyana* (gy-AH-nuh) is a South American Indian word that means "land of waters." Nearly all of Guyana's agricultural lands are located along the narrow coastal plains. Guyana's most important agricultural products are rice and sugar. The country's major mineral resource is bauxite.

Guyana has a diverse population. About half of its people are of South Asian descent. Most of these people farm small plots of land or run small businesses. About one third of the population is descended from African slaves. These people control most of the large businesses and hold most of the government positions. More than one third of the country's population lives in Georgetown, the capital.

Suriname The resources and economy of Suriname (soohr-uh-NAH-muh) are similar to those of Guyana. Many farms in Suriname are found in coastal areas. Aluminum is a major export. Interior forests also supply lumber for export to other countries.

Like Guyana, Suriname has a diverse population. There are South Asians, Africans, Chinese, Indonesians, and people of mixed heritage. Muslim, Hindu, Roman Catholic, and Protestant houses of worship line the streets of the national capital, Paramaribo (pah-rah-MAH-ree-boh). Nearly half of the country's people live there.

A woman cooks cassava cakes in Bigi Poika, Suriname.

Carnival is a time for celebration in Cayenne, French Guiana.

French Guiana French Guiana (gee-A-nuh) has a status in France similar to that of a state in the United States. It sends representatives to the French Parliament in Paris. France used to send some of its criminals to Devil's Island. This island was a prison colony just off French Guiana's coast. Prisoners there suffered terribly from overwork. Devil's Island was closed in the early 1950s.

Today, forestry and shrimp fishing are the most important economic activities. Agriculture is limited to the coastal areas. The people of French Guiana depend heavily on imports for their food and energy. France developed the town of Kourou (koo-ROO) into a space center. The European Space Agency launches satellites from this town.

More than 180,000 people live in French Guiana, mostly in coastal areas. About two thirds of the people are descended from Africans. Other groups include Europeans, Asians, and South American Indians. The national capital is Cayenne (keye-EN).

✓ **READING CHECK:** (*Human Systems*) How is French Guiana different from Guyana and Suriname?

go.hrw.com **Homework Practice Online**
Keyword: SG5 HP8

Section Review 4

Define and explain: indentured servants, pidgin languages

Working with Sketch Maps On the map you created in Section 3, label Guyana, Suriname, French Guiana, Georgetown, Paramaribo, Devil's Island, Kourou, and Cayenne.

Reading for the Main Idea

1. (*Environment and Society*) What crops did early settlers raise in the Guianas?

2. (*Human Systems*) Why did colonists in the Guianas bring indentured servants from Asia?

Critical Thinking

3. Drawing Inferences and Conclusions Why might the people of French Guiana prefer to remain a part of France?

4. Drawing Inferences and Conclusions Why do you think few people live in the interior of the Guianas?

Organizing What You Know

5. Categorizing Copy the following graphic organizer. Use it to describe the Guianas. Fill in the ovals with features of Guyana, Suriname, and French Guiana. In the center, list features they have in common.

CHAPTER 8

Review and Practice

Define and Identify

Identify each of the following:

1. cordillera
2. *tepuís*
3. Llanos
4. Chibcha
5. El Dorado
6. cassava
7. indigo
8. caudillos
9. *llaneros*
10. *pardos*
11. indentured servants
12. pidgin languages

Review the Main Ideas

13. How did the *tepuís* form?
14. What is the region's longest river? What are some animals that live in and near the river?
15. What are the five elevation zones in the Andes region?
16. Why did the Spanish conquer the Chibcha?
17. Which precious jewel is an important Colombian export?
18. What kinds of conflicts have caused problems in Colombia?
19. What resource were the Spanish explorers hoping to find in Venezuela?

20. What has happened to much of Venezuela's oil wealth throughout the country's history?
21. What are some features of Caracas?
22. Which four European countries have controlled the Guianas?
23. How does French Guiana's political status differ from that of Guyana and Suriname?

Think Critically

24. **Drawing Inferences and Conclusions** Why would different animals live in the five elevation zones?
25. **Finding the Main Idea** How has geography contributed to conflict in Colombia's history?
26. **Comparing** How are Venezuelan *llaneros* like American cowboys?
27. **Drawing Inferences and Conclusions** Why do you think most Venezuelans live along the Caribbean coast and in the valleys of the nearby mountains?
28. **Analyzing Information** How are pidgin languages in the Guianas an example of cultural cooperation?

Map Activity

29. On a separate sheet of paper, match the letters on the map with their correct labels.

Andes
Guiana Highlands
Orinoco River
Magdalena River
Lake Maracaibo
Devil's Island
Llanos

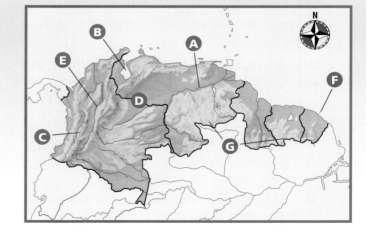

Writing Activity

Imagine that you are a teacher living in Caracas, Venezuela. Use the information in this chapter to write a quiz, with answers, for students in your geography class. Ask questions on the history, geography, economy, and people of Venezuela. Use the chapter map and the population figures in the Venezuela chart. Be sure to use standard grammar, sentence structure, spelling, and punctuation.

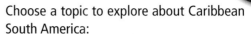

internet connect

Internet Activity: **go.hrw.com**
KEYWORD: SG5 GT8

Choose a topic to explore about Caribbean South America:
- Trek through the Guiana Highlands.
- Search for the treasures of El Dorado.
- Ride with the *llaneros* of Venezuela.

Social Studies Skills Practice

Interpreting Charts

Study the following chart comparing age structure of the populations of the Guianas and the United States. Then answer the questions.

Age Structure of the Guianas and the United States				
Age Range	**Suriname**	**Guyana**	**French Guiana**	**United States**
0–14 years	30.7%	27%	29.9%	20.9%
15–64 years	63.3%	67.9%	64.4%	66.7%
65 and over	6%	5.1%	5.7%	12.4%

Source: Central Intelligence Agency, *The World Factbook 2003*

1. Which country has the largest percentage of its population under the age of 14?
2. Which country has the largest percentage of people aged 65 and over?
3. Which age group is most equally represented in all of the countries?
4. Can you tell from the chart which country has the highest population growth rate? Why or why not?

Analyzing Primary Sources

The Chibcha custom of dusting their new chiefs with gold gave rise to the legend of El Dorado. Read the following account of the practice, written by Spanish historian Gonzalo Fernandez de Oviedo in 1535. Then answer the questions.

"He [the new chief] went about all covered with powdered gold, as casually as if it were powdered salt. For it seemed to him that to wear any other finery was less beautiful, and that to put on ornaments or arms made of gold worked by hammering, stamping, or by other means, was a vulgar [tacky] and common thing."

1. Why do you think Oviedo compared the gold to salt?
2. In the second sentence, what is a synonym that could be substituted for *arms*?
3. How did the chief feel about the other ornaments described?
4. Do you think Oviedo was impressed by the custom he described? Why or why not?

CHAPTER 9

Atlantic South America

Now we will look at the four countries of Atlantic South America. Below, Mercedes tells us about growing up in Buenos Aires, one of the region's biggest cities.

Hi! I am 13, and I live in Buenos Aires, the capital of Argentina. I live in an apartment with my mom, father, two brothers, and a sister.

I wake up at 6:30 A.M. to get ready for school. For breakfast I have a cup of tea and bread with butter and *dulce de leche* (a caramel spread). It is delicious!

In school I take 12 different classes in one year. They include math, Spanish, art, geography, biology, and language (English). School ends at 1:30 P.M. every day, and then I go home to eat lunch. My mother makes us a large meal that includes meat, pasta or potatoes, soup, and salad. At 2:00 P.M., I go back to school for English.

My favorite holiday is Christmas. My whole family goes to my grandparents' house. We barbecue *lechón* (pork) for dinner and have different types of salads. We eat *turrón,* a honey and almond bar, and a special sweet bread with fruit. At midnight everyone opens their presents.

**¡Hola!
Me llamo Mercedes.
Soy de Argentina.**

▲
Translation: Hi! My name is Mercedes. I am from Argentina.

Section 1 Physical Geography

Read to Discover

1. What landforms and rivers are found in Atlantic South America?
2. What are the region's climates, vegetation, and wildlife like?
3. What are some of the region's important resources?

Vocabulary

Pampas
estuary
soil exhaustion

Places

Amazon River
Brazilian Highlands
Brazilian Plateau
Gran Chaco
Patagonia

Tierra del Fuego
Andes
Paraná River
Paraguay River
Río de la Plata

Reading Strategy

ANTICIPATING INFORMATION Before you read, predict whether you think the following statements are true or false.

• Atlantic South America has one large river system.
• The region's climate is hot and dry.
• The region's landforms vary from coastal plains to mountains.

Check your answers while reading. Then explain why each statement is true or false.

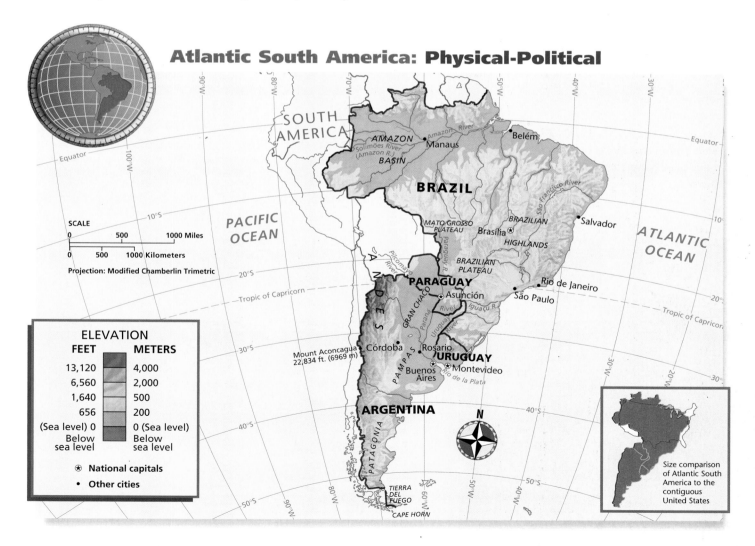

Atlantic South America: Physical-Political

SCALE
0   500   1000 Miles
0   500   1000 Kilometers

Projection: Modified Chamberlin Trimetric

ELEVATION

FEET	METERS
13,120	4,000
6,560	2,000
1,640	500
656	200
(Sea level) 0	0 (Sea level)
Below sea level	Below sea level

⊛ National capitals
• Other cities

Size comparison of Atlantic South America to the contiguous United States

internet connect

GO TO: go.hrw.com
KEYWORD: SG5 CH9
FOR: Web sites about
Atlantic South America

Physical Features

The region of Atlantic South America includes four countries: Brazil (bruh-ZIL), Argentina (ahr-juhn-TEE-nuh), Uruguay (oo-roo-GWY), and Paraguay (pah-rah-GWY). This vast region covers about two thirds of South America. Brazil alone occupies nearly half of the continent.

Plains and Plateaus This region's landforms include mainly plains and plateaus. The Amazon River basin in northern Brazil is a giant, flat flood plain. To the southeast are the Brazilian Highlands, a region of old, eroded mountains. Farther west is the Brazilian Plateau, an area of upland plains.

South of the Brazilian Plateau is a lower region known as the Gran Chaco (grahn CHAH-koh). The Gran Chaco stretches across parts of Paraguay, Bolivia, and northern Argentina. It is an area of flat, low plains covered with low trees, shrubs, and savannas.

In central Argentina are the wide, grassy plains of the **Pampas**. Patagonia, a desert region of dry plains and plateaus, is in southern Argentina. A cool, windswept island called Tierra del Fuego lies at the southern tip of the continent. Tierra del Fuego and nearby small islands are divided between Argentina and Chile.

Mountains The Andes, South America's highest mountains, extend north-south along Argentina's border with Chile. Here we find the Western Hemisphere's highest peak, Mount Aconcagua (ah-kohn-KAH-gwah). It rises to 22,834 feet (6,960 m).

River Systems The world's largest river system, the Amazon, flows eastward across northern Brazil. The Amazon River is about 4,000 miles (6,436 km) long. It extends from the Andes Mountains to the Atlantic Ocean. Hundreds of tributaries flow into it. Together they drain a vast area. This area includes parts of nearly all of the countries of northern and central South America.

Ranchers herd sheep on the Pampas of Argentina.

Interpreting the Visual Record (Region)
What other economic activities are common in flat plains regions such as this?

▼

As a result, the Amazon also carries more water than any other river. About 20 percent of the water that runs off Earth's surface flows down the Amazon. This freshwater lowers the salt level of Atlantic waters for more than 100 miles (161 km) out.

The Paraná (pah-rah-NAH) River system drains much of the central part of the region. The Paraná River is 3,030 miles (4,875 km) long. It forms part of Paraguay's borders with Brazil and Argentina. Water from the Paraná flows into the Paraguay River. It continues on to the Río de la Plata (REE-oh day lah PLAH-tah) and the Atlantic Ocean beyond. The Río de la Plata is an **estuary**. An estuary is a partially enclosed body of water where salty seawater and freshwater mix.

✓ **READING CHECK:** (*Places and Regions*) What are the region's major land-forms and rivers?

South America's tropical rain forest blankets an area of about 2.3 million square miles (nearly 6 million sq. km). That is more than two thirds the area of the contiguous United States!

Climate, Vegetation, and Wildlife

Tropical, moist climates are found in northern and coastal areas. They give way to cooler climates in southern and highland areas.

The Rain Forest The Amazon River basin's humid tropical climate supports the world's largest tropical rain forest. Rain falls almost every day in this region. The Amazon rain forest may contain the world's greatest variety of plant and animal life. Animals there include meat-eating fish called piranhas and predators such as jaguars and giant ana-condas. The sloth, a mammal related to anteaters, moves slowly through the trees. It feeds on vegetation.

Plains and Plateaus Climates in the Brazilian Highlands vary widely. In the north, the coastal region is covered mostly with tropical rain forests and savannas. Inland from the coast, the high-lands become drier and are covered with grasslands. The southeastern highlands have a mostly humid subtropical climate like the southeastern United States. These moist environments are major agricultural areas.

Southwest of the highlands, the Gran Chaco has a humid tropical climate. Because the Gran Chaco is flat, water drains slowly. Summer rains can turn areas of the region into marshlands. Wildlife there includes giant armadillos, pumas, red wolves, and at least 60 snake species.

The temperate grasslands of the Pampas stretch for almost 400 miles (644 km) southwest of the Río de la Plata. The rich soils and humid subtropical climate make the Pampas a major farming region. Farther south, warm sum-mers and cold winters cause great annual temperature ranges in the Patagonia desert. The Andes block the Pacific Ocean's rain-bearing storms from reaching the area.

✓ **READING CHECK:** (*Places and Regions*) What are the climates of the region?

A sloth makes its way along tree branches in the Amazon rain forest.

Resources

One of the region's greatest resources is the Amazon rain forest. The rain forest provides food, wood, natural rubber, medicinal plants, and many other products. However, large areas of the rain forest are being cleared for mining, ranching, and farming.

Commercial agriculture is found throughout the region. In some areas, however, planting the same crop every year has caused **soil exhaustion**. Soil exhaustion means that the soil has lost nutrients needed by plants. Overgrazing is also a problem in some places.

The region's mineral wealth includes gold, silver, copper, and iron. There are oil deposits in the region, particularly in Brazil and Patagonia. Some of the region's large rivers provide hydroelectric power. One of the world's largest hydroelectric dams is the Itaipu Dam on the Paraná River. The dam lies between Brazil and Paraguay.

✓ **READING CHECK:** (*Environment and*) (*Society*) How have humans modified the region's environment?

◄

People are clearing large areas of the Amazon rain forest by burning and by cutting.

Interpreting the Visual Record (*Human-Environment*) (*Interaction*) Why do you think someone would choose to clear rain forest areas by burning rather than by cutting?

Homework Practice Online
Keyword: SG5 HP9

Section Review 1

Define and explain: Pampas, estuary, soil exhaustion

Working with Sketch Maps On an outline map of the region that you draw or that your teacher provides, label the following: Amazon River, Brazilian Highlands, Brazilian Plateau, Gran Chaco, Patagonia, Tierra del Fuego, Andes, Paraná River, Paraguay River, and Río de la Plata.

Reading for the Main Idea

1. (*Places and Regions*) What major landforms lie between the Amazon River basin and Patagonia?

2. (*Places and Regions*) What sets the Amazon River apart from all of the world's other rivers?

3. (*Places and Regions*) Why is the Patagonia desert dry?

Critical Thinking

4. **Drawing Inferences and Conclusions** How do you think soil exhaustion in Brazil could lead to more deforestation?

Organizing What You Know

5. **Categorizing** Copy the following graphic organizer. Use it to describe Atlantic South America.

Climates	Vegetation and wildlife	Resources

Section 2 Brazil

Read to Discover

1. What is the history of Brazil?
2. What are important characteristics of Brazil's people and culture?
3. What are Brazil's four major regions like today?

Vocabulary

favelas

Places

Rio de Janeiro
São Paulo
Manaus
Belém

Salvador
São Francisco River
Mato Grosso Plateau
Brasília

Reading Strategy

FOLDNOTES: TRI-FOLD Create a **Tri-Fold** FoldNote as described in the Appendix. Write what you know about Brazil in the column labeled "Know." Then write what you want to know in the column labeled "Want." As you read the section, write what you learn about Brazil in the column labeled "Learn."

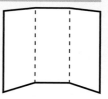

History

Most Brazilians are descended from three groups of immigrants. The first group included peoples who probably migrated to the Americas from northern Asia long ago. The second was made up of Portuguese and other Europeans who came after 1500. Africans brought as slaves made up the third group.

First Inhabitants Brazil's first human inhabitants arrived in the region thousands of years ago. They spread throughout the tropical rain forests and savannas.

These peoples developed a way of life based on hunting, fishing, and small-scale farming. They grew crops such as sweet potatoes, beans, and cassava. The root of the cassava plant is ground up and used as an ingredient in many foods in Brazil today. It also is used to make tapioca. Tapioca is a common food in grocery stores in the United States and other countries.

Europeans and Africans After 1500, Portuguese settlers began to move into Brazil. Favorable climates and soil helped make Brazil a large sugar-growing colony. Colonists brought slaves from Africa to work alongside Brazilian Indians on large sugar plantations. Sugar plantations eventually replaced forests along the Atlantic coast.

As elsewhere in the region, Brazilian Indians fought back against early European colonists. However, the Indians could not overcome powerful European forces.

Farther inland, Portuguese settlers set up cattle ranches. These ranches provided hides and dried beef for world markets. In the late 1600s and early 1700s gold and precious gems were discovered in the southeast. A mining boom drew adventurers from around the world. The coastal city of Rio de Janeiro grew during this boom. In the late 1800s southeastern Brazil became a major coffee producer. This coffee boom promoted the growth of São Paulo.

Brazil gained independence from Portugal in 1822. An emperor ruled the country until 1889. Dictators and elected governments have ruled the country at various times since then. Today, Brazil has an elected president and legislature. Like the United States, Brazil provides its citizens the opportunity to participate in the political process through voting and other political activities.

✓ **READING CHECK:** (*Human Systems*) How have different peoples influenced Brazilian history?

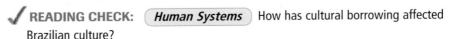

▲
Brazilian fans cheer on their country's soccer team. Soccer is very popular throughout Atlantic South America. Brazilian teams often compete in international tournaments, such as the World Cup.

People and Culture

Nearly 40 percent of Brazil's more than 180 million people are of mixed African and European descent. More than half of Brazilians are ethnic European. They include descendants of Portuguese, Spaniards, Germans, Italians, and Poles. Portuguese is the official language. Some Brazilians also speak Spanish, English, French, Japanese, and Indian languages.

Religion Brazil has the world's largest population of Roman Catholics. About 70 percent of Brazilians are Catholic. Some Brazilians also practice Macumba (mah-KOOM-bah). Macumba combines African, Indian, and Catholic religious ideas and practices.

Carnival Other aspects of Brazilian life also reflect the country's mix of cultures. For example, Brazilians celebrate Carnival before the Christian season of Lent. However, the celebration mixes traditions from Africa, Brazil, and Europe. During Carnival, Brazilians dance the samba, which was adapted from an African dance.

Food Other examples of immigrant influences can be found in Brazilian foods. In parts of eastern Brazil, an African dish called *vatapá* (vah-tah-PAH) is popular. *Vatapá* mixes seafood, sauces, and red peppers. Many Brazilians also enjoy eating *feijoada* (fay-ZHWAH-da), a stew of black beans and meat. It is traditionally served on Saturday to large groups of people. *Feijoada* has many regional varieties.

✓ **READING CHECK:** (*Human Systems*) How has cultural borrowing affected Brazilian culture?

Brazil Today

Brazil is the largest and most populous country in South America. It ranks as the fifth-largest country in the world in both land area and population. Brazil also has the region's largest economy. Many Brazilians are poor, but the country has modern and prosperous areas. We will explore these and other areas by dividing the country into four regions. Those regions are the Amazon, the northeast, the southeast, and the interior. We will start in the Amazon and move southward.

The Amazon The Amazon region covers much of northern and western Brazil. Isolated Indian villages are scattered throughout the region's dense rain forest. Some Indians had little contact with outsiders until recently.

The major inland city in the region is Manaus. More than 1 million people live there. It is the Amazon's major river port and industrial city. South of the Atlantic port of Belém is a large mining district. New roads and mining projects are bringing more people and development to this region. However, development is destroying large areas of the rain forest. It also threatens the way of life of Brazilian Indians who live there. This development has created tensions among the Indians, new settlers, and miners.

The Northeast Northeastern Brazil includes many old colonial cities, such as Salvador. It is Brazil's poorest region. Many people there cannot read, and health care is poor. The region suffers from drought and has had trouble attracting industry. Cities in the region have huge slums called **favelas** (fah-VE-lahs).

Day fades into night in Rio de Janeiro, Brazil's second-largest city. Sugarloaf Mountain stands near the entrance to Guanabara Bay. The Brazilian city is often referred to simply as Rio.

Brazil				
COUNTRY	**POPULATION/ GROWTH RATE**	**LIFE EXPECTANCY**	**LITERACY RATE**	**PER CAPITA GDP**
Brazil	182,032,604 1.1%	67, male 75, female	86%	$7,600
United States	290,342,554 0.9%	74, male 80, female	97%	$37,600

Source: Central Intelligence Agency, *The World Factbook 2003*

Major Producers of Coffee

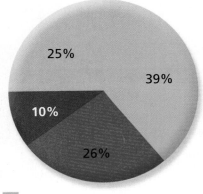

25%

39%

10%

26%

■ Brazil
■ Colombia
■ Rest of Middle and South America
■ Rest of the world

Source: United Nations, Food and Agriculture Organization

Interpreting the Chart Which single South American country produces the most coffee?

The Southeast Large favelas are also found in other Brazilian cities, particularly in the southeast. Most of Brazil's people live in the southeast. However, in contrast to the northeast, the southeast is Brazil's richest region. It is rich in natural resources and has most of the country's industries and productive farms. The southeast is one of the most productive coffee-growing regions in the world.

The giant cities of São Paulo and Rio de Janeiro are located in the southeast. More than 17.9 million people live in and around São Paulo. It is the largest urban area in South America and the fourth largest in the world. The city is also Brazil's main industrial center.

Rio de Janeiro lies northeast of São Paulo. More than 10 million people live there. The city was Brazil's capital from 1822 until 1960. Today, Rio de Janeiro remains a major seaport and is popular with tourists.

The Interior The interior region is a frontier land of savannas and dry woodlands. It begins in the upper São Francisco River basin and extends to the Mato Grosso Plateau. The region's abundant land and mild climate could one day make it an important agricultural area.

Brasília, the national capital, is located in this region. Brazil's government built the city during the 1950s and 1960s. Government officials hoped the new city would help develop Brazil's interior. It has modern buildings and busy highways. Nearly 2 million people live in Brasília, although it was designed for only 500,000.

✓ **READING CHECK:** (*Places and Regions*) What are Brazil's four main regions?

Section Review 2

Define and explain: favelas

Working with Sketch Maps On the map you created in Section 1, label Brazil, Rio de Janeiro, São Paulo, Manaus, Belém, Salvador, São Francisco River, Mato Grosso Plateau, and Brasília. In a margin box, write a caption explaining why Brazil's government built Brasília and how the city has grown over time.

Reading for the Main Idea

1. (*Human Systems*) From what major immigrant groups are many Brazilians descended?

2. (*Places and Regions*) What is Brazil's poorest region? What is its richest and most populated region?

Critical Thinking

3. **Drawing Inferences and Conclusions** Why do you think development in the Amazon has caused conflicts among miners, settlers, and Brazilian Indians?

4. **Finding the Main Idea** How did immigration influence Brazilian culture today?

Organizing What You Know

5. **Summarizing** Copy the following graphic organizer. Use it to list how early Brazilian Indians and European settlers and their descendants have used Brazil's natural resources and natural environment. Write each example in a circle radiating from the central circle. Create as many or as few circles as you need.

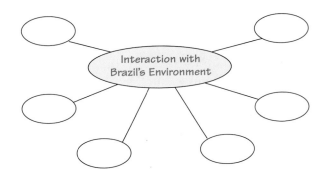

Interaction with Brazil's Environment

Read to Discover

1. What is the history of Argentina?
2. What are important characteristics of Argentina's people and culture?
3. What is Argentina like today?

Vocabulary

encomienda
gauchos
Mercosur

Places

Buenos Aires
Córdoba
Rosario

People

Eva Perón

Reading Strategy

READING ORGANIZER Before you read, create a concept map using the headings in this section. As you read, add information about the history, people, and culture of Argentina.

History

Like most of South America, what is now Argentina was originally home to groups of Indians. Groups living in the Pampas hunted wild game. Farther north, Indians farmed and built irrigation systems.

Early Argentina In the 1500s Spanish conquerors spread into southern South America. They moved into the region in search of riches they believed they would find there. They called the region Argentina, meaning "land of silver" or "silvery one."

The first Spanish settlement in Argentina was established in the early 1500s. Spanish settlements were organized under the *encomienda* system. Under that system, the Spanish monarch gave land to colonists. These landowners were granted the right to force Indians living there to work the land.

The Pampas became an increasingly important agricultural region during the colonial era. Argentine cowboys, called **gauchos** (GOW-chohz), herded cattle and horses on the open grasslands. Colonists eventually fenced off their lands into huge ranches. They hired gauchos to tend their herds of livestock. Today the gaucho, like the American cowboy, is vanishing. Still, the gaucho lives on in Argentine literature and popular culture.

In 1816 Argentina gained independence. However, a long period of instability and violence followed. Many Indians, particularly in the Pampas, were killed in wars with the Argentine

Examples of Spanish-style architecture can be seen throughout Argentina. This Roman Catholic church was built in the 1600s in Córdoba.

government. As a result, Argentina has a small Indian population today. Most of these wars had ended by the late 1870s.

Modern Argentina New waves of European immigrants came to Argentina in the late 1800s. Immigrants included Italians, Germans, and Spaniards. Exports of meat and other farm products to Europe helped make the country richer.

However, throughout much of the 1900s, Argentina struggled under dictators and military governments. These unlimited governments abused human rights. Both the country's economy and its people suffered. In 1982 Argentina lost a brief war with the United Kingdom over the Falkland Islands. Shortly afterward, Argentina's last military government gave up power to an elected government.

✔ **READING CHECK:** (*Human Systems*) How was Argentina's government organized during much of the 1900s?

People and Culture

Argentina's culture has many European ties. Most of the more than 38 million Argentines are Roman Catholic. Most also are descended from Spanish, Italian, or other European settlers. Argentine Indians and mestizos make up only about 3 percent of the population. Spanish is the official language. English, Italian, German, and French are also spoken there.

Beef is an important agricultural product and a big part of the Argentine diet. A popular dish is *parrillada*. It includes sausage and steak served on a small grill. Supper generally is eaten after 9 P.M.

✔ **READING CHECK:** (*Human Systems*) Why are so many languages spoken in Argentina?

Couples practice the Argentine tango on a Buenos Aires sidewalk. Varieties of the tango are popular in some other Middle and South American countries and in parts of Spain.

▶

CONNECTING TO *Literature*

Argentine gaucho

The Gaucho Martín Fierro

José Hernández was born in 1834. A sickly boy, he was sent to regain his health on Argentina's Pampas. The gauchos lived freely on the plains there, herding cattle. As an adult, Hernández took part in his country's political struggles. He fled to Brazil after a failed revolt. In 1872 he published his epic poem, The Gaucho Martín Fierro. *In this excerpt, Martín Fierro recalls his happier times as an Argentine cowboy.*

Ah, those times! . . . you felt proud
to see how a man could ride.
When a gaucho really knew his job,
even if the colt went over backwards,
not one of them wouldn't land on his feet
with the halter-rein in his hand. . . .

Even the poorest gaucho
had a string of matching horses;
he could always afford some amusement,
and people were ready for
  anything. . . .
Looking out across the land
you'd see nothing but cattle
  and sky.

When the branding-time came round
that was work to warm you up!
What a crowd! lassoing the running steers
and keen to hold and throw them. . . .
What a time that was! in those days surely
there were champions to be seen. . . .

And the games that would get going
when we were all of us together!
We were always ready for them,
as at times like those
a lot of neighbors would turn up
to help out the regular hands.

Analyzing Primary Sources
1. What does Martín Fierro remember about the "old days"?
2. In what ways is a gaucho's life similar to that of an American cowboy?

Argentina Today

Argentina has rich natural resources and a well-educated population. The Pampas are the most developed agricultural region. About 12 percent of Argentina's labor force works in agriculture. Large ranches and farms produce beef, wheat, and corn for export to other countries.

Much of Argentina's industry is located in and around Buenos Aires, the national capital. Buenos Aires is the second-largest urban area in South America. Its location on the coast and near the Pampas has contributed to its economic development. It is home to nearly a

Wide European-style avenues stretch through Buenos Aires. Large advertisements compete for attention in the lively city.

third of all Argentines. Other large Argentine cities include the interior cities of Córdoba and Rosario.

In 1983 Argentina returned to democracy and established an elected government. In the 1900s government leaders put economic reforms in place to help businesses grow. Argentina joined **Mercosur**—a trade organization that promotes economic cooperation among its members in southern and eastern South America. By the late 1900s and early 2000s, however, government spending and heavy debt brought Argentina into an economic and political crisis. During 2001, the government changed hands four times as its leaders tried to stop the mounting problems. By 2003, the economy had stabilized somewhat. Today, Argentines are still searching for ways to improve their economy while keeping the political freedoms gained during the 1980s.

✓ **READING CHECK:** (*Places and Regions*) What is Argentina like today?

go.hrw.com **Homework Practice Online** Keyword: SG5 HP9

Section Review 3

Define or identify: *encomienda,* gauchos, Eva Perón, Mercosur

Working with Sketch Maps On the map you created in Section 2, label Argentina, Buenos Aires, Córdoba, and Rosario.

Reading for the Main Idea

1. (*Human Systems*) What happened to Argentine Indians in the Pampas in the 1800s? How did that affect Argentine society?

2. (*Places and Regions*) Where is much of Argentina's industry located? Why?

Critical Thinking

3. **Finding the Main Idea** In what ways does Argentine culture reflect European influences? What are some examples of these influences?

4. **Analyzing Information** How does Mercosur help Argentina's economy grow today? How does location play a part in that process?

Organizing What You Know

5. **Sequencing** Copy the following time line. Use it to identify important dates, events, and periods in the history of Argentina.

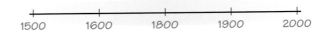

1500   1600   1800   1900   2000

Uruguay and Paraguay

Read to Discover

1. What are the people and economy of Uruguay like today?
2. What are the people and economy of Paraguay like today?

Vocabulary

landlocked

Places

Montevideo
Asunción

Reading Strategy

READING ORGANIZER Before you read, draw two overlapping circles. As you read, write characteristics about Uruguay in one circle and characteristics about Paraguay in the other. In the space where the circles overlap, write the characteristics both countries share.

Uruguay

Uruguay lies along the Río de la Plata. The Río de la Plata is the major estuary and waterway of southern South America. It stretches about 170 miles (274 km) inland from the Atlantic Ocean.

Uruguay's capital, Montevideo (mawn-tay-bee-THAY-oh), is located on the north shore of the Río de la Plata. The city is also the business center of the country.

Like its neighbors, Uruguay at times has been ruled by the military. However, in general the country has a strong democratic tradition of respect for political freedom.

Portugal claimed Uruguay during the colonial era. However, the Spanish took over the area by the 1770s. By that time, few Uruguayan Indians remained. Uruguay declared independence from Spain in 1825.

The People People of European descent make up about 88 percent of Uruguay's population. About 12 percent of the population is either mestizo, African, or Indian.

Roman Catholicism is the main religion in the country. Spanish is the official language, but many people also speak Portuguese.

More than 90 percent of Uruguayans live in urban areas. More than a third of the

Government buildings and monuments surround Independence Square in Montevideo, the capital of Uruguay.

The town of Colonia del Sacramento, Uruguay, was founded in 1680. Today it is an internationally recognized historical site.

people live in and around Montevideo. The country has a high literacy rate. In addition, many Uruguayans have good jobs and can afford a wide range of consumer goods.

Economy Uruguay's economy is tied to the economies of Brazil and Argentina. In fact, more than half of Uruguay's foreign trade is with these two Mercosur partners. In addition, many Brazilians and Argentines vacation at beach resorts in Uruguay.

Uruguay's humid subtropical climate and rich soils have helped make agriculture an important part of the economy. As in Argentina, ranchers graze livestock on inland plains. Beef is an important export.

Uruguay has few mineral resources. An important source of energy is hydroelectric power. One big challenge is developing the poor rural areas in the interior, where resources are in short supply.

✓ **READING CHECK:** *Places and Regions* What geographic factors support agriculture in Uruguay?

Uruguay and Paraguay

COUNTRY	POPULATION/ GROWTH RATE	LIFE EXPECTANCY	LITERACY RATE	PER CAPITA GDP
Paraguay	6,036,900 2.5%	71, male 77, female	94%	$4,200
Uruguay	3,413,329 0.7%	72, male 79, female	98%	$7,800
United States	290,342,554 0.9%	74, male 80, female	97%	$37,600

Source: Central Intelligence Agency, *The World Factbook 2003*

Interpreting the Chart How does Paraguay's per capita GDP compare to that of Uruguay?

Paraguay

Paraguay shares borders with Bolivia, Brazil, and Argentina. It is a **landlocked** country. Landlocked means it is completely surrounded by land, with no direct access to the ocean.

The Paraguay River divides the country into two regions. East of the river is the country's most productive agricultural land. The region west of the river is part of the Gran Chaco. This region has low trees and thorny shrubs. Ranchers graze livestock in some parts of western Paraguay.

Spanish settlers claimed Paraguay in the early 1500s. The country won independence from Spain in 1811. Paraguay was ruled off and on by dictators until 1989. Today, the country has an elected government.

The People About 95 percent of Paraguayans are mestizos. European descendants and Paraguayan Indians make up the rest of the population. Spanish is the official language. Almost all people speak both Spanish and Guaraní (gwah-ruh-NEE), an Indian language. As in Uruguay, most people are Roman Catholic.

Asunción (ah-soon-SYOHN) is Paraguay's capital and largest city. It is located along the Paraguay River near the border with Argentina.

Economy Much of Paraguay's wealth is controlled by a few rich families and companies. These families and companies have great influence over the country's government.

Agriculture is an important part of Paraguay's economy. Much of the economy is traditional—many people are subsistence farmers. They grow just enough to feed themselves and their families. In fact, nearly half of the country's workers are farmers. They grow corn, cotton, soybeans, and sugarcane, some for profit. Paraguay also has a market economy, with thousands of small businesses but not much industry. Many Paraguayans have moved to neighboring countries to find work.

Paraguay's future may be promising as the country learns how to use its resources effectively. For example, the country has built hydroelectric dams on the Paraná River. These dams provide Paraguay with much more power than it needs. Paraguay sells the surplus electricity to Brazil and Argentina.

▲ These Paraguayan cowboys are drinking yerba maté (yer-buh MAH-tay). The herbal tea is popular in the region. It is made from the leaves and shoots of a South American shrub called the maté.

✓ **READING CHECK:** (**Human Systems**) How is Paraguay's economy organized?

Section Review 4

go.hrw.com
Homework Practice Online
Keyword: SG5 HP9

Define and explain: landlocked

Working with Sketch Maps On the map you created in Section 3, label Uruguay, Paraguay, Montevideo, and Asunción. In a box in the margin, briefly explain the significance of Montevideo and Asunción.

Reading for the Main Idea

1. (**Human Systems**) When and from what country did Uruguay win independence? What about Paraguay?

2. (**Places and Regions**) Where is Paraguay's most productive agricultural land?

3. (**Environment and Society**) How has Paraguay used its natural resources for economic development?

Critical Thinking

4. **Comparing** What disadvantages do you think a landlocked country might have when compared with countries that are not landlocked?

Organizing What You Know

5. **Comparing/Contrasting** Copy the following graphic organizer. Use it to compare and contrast the populations of Uruguay and Paraguay.

Uruguay	Paraguay

Review and Practice

Define and Identify

Identify each of the following:

1. Pampas
2. estuary
3. soil exhaustion
4. favelas
5. *encomienda*
6. gauchos
7. Eva Perón
8. Mercosur
9. landlocked

Review the Main Ideas

10. Which mountains extend along the border between Argentina and Chile?
11. What major river systems drain much of northern and central Atlantic South America?
12. What are some features of the Amazon rain forest?
13. Which country in Atlantic South America was a Portuguese colony? What colonial power controlled the other countries before they gained independence?
14. What are the four main regions of Brazil? Of these four, which is the richest region?
15. What and where is the Río de la Plata?

16. What problems have Argentines faced throughout the 1900s and into the 2000s?
17. How does Argentina's agriculture influence what Argentines eat?
18. What is Uruguay's main city, and where is it located?
19. What is Paraguay's economy like?

Think Critically

20. **Analyzing Information** How are European influences reflected in the religions, languages, and other cultural characteristics of the countries of Atlantic South America?
21. **Finding the Main Idea** Why are large areas of Brazil's tropical rain forest being cleared?
22. **Comparing and Contrasting** How do the climates of northern Brazil and southern Argentina differ?
23. **Summarizing** How has the role of Argentina's gauchos changed?
24. **Comparing and Contrasting** How are the ethnic populations of Uruguay and Paraguay different?

Map Activity

25. On a separate sheet of paper, match the letters on the map with their correct labels.

Brazilian Highlands	Manaus
Patagonia	Brasília
Tierra del Fuego	Buenos Aires
Paraná River	Montevideo
São Paulo	Asunción

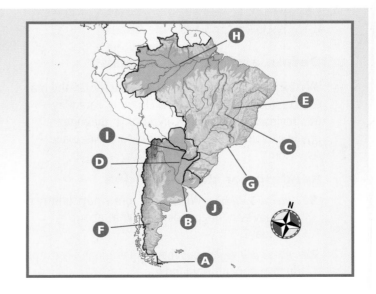

Writing Activity

Imagine that you are a gaucho working on an Argentine ranch in the 1800s. Write a short song or poem that describes your daily life as a gaucho. Also describe the physical geography of the ranch. What physical features do you see? What is the climate like? Be sure to use standard grammar, sentence structure, spelling, and punctuation.

▨ internet connect

Internet Activity: go.hrw.com
KEYWORD: SG5 GT9

Choose a topic to explore about Atlantic South America:
- Journey along the Amazon River.
- Compare Uruguayans and Paraguayans.
- Celebrate the Brazilian Carnival.

Social Studies Skills Practice

Interpreting Graphs

Study the graph below and answer the questions.

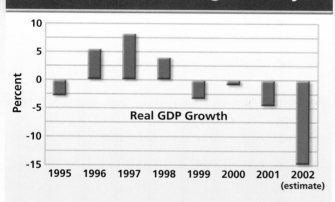

Argentina's Shrinking Economy

Real GDP Growth

Source: Business Week Online

1. What information does this graph show?
2. During what period did the economy show positive growth?
3. During which year did the economy grow most? Decline the most?
4. What conclusions regarding the Argentine economy can you draw from this graph?

Analyzing Primary Sources

Read the quotation by Siã Kaxiniawá, a member of the Huni Kui tribe in Brazil. Then answer the questions.

"Our lands remained in the hands of those who had taken them long ago. . . . We resolved to fight for our rights. To do this, we established a cooperative that allows us to buy and sell collectively. One problem that we had to confront at the outset of our cooperative's existence is that no one knew how to read or write . . . Today we have six Indian teachers on our land, and for the last nine years they have been offering classes and training for all members of our community. We have learned to read and write, not only in Portuguese but in our own language."

1. How would forming a cooperative benefit the Huni Kui economically?
2. What problem did the Huni Kui face when they formed the cooperative?
3. In what way has life changed for the Huni Kui since forming the cooperative?
4. Why would the Huni Kui learn to write in two languages?

CHAPTER 10

Pacific South America

To learn about Pacific South America, we first meet Mariana. She lives in Lima, the capital of Peru.

Hi! My name is Mariana Gonzales. I am 13 years old. I live in Lima, Peru, with my parents and my twin brother, Alejo. We speak Spanish. There is a Peruvian language called Quechua, but it is mostly spoken in the Andes. I understand only a few words of Quechua. I go to a French school, so I also speak French and some English. I am in the third grade of what we call secondary education. This is the same as your eighth or ninth grade. I love biology and art. I am not very good at other sports, but I really enjoy swimming and badminton. My favorite dish is *ají degallina*, a spicy chicken dish. We eat it with potatoes, hard-boiled eggs, black olives, and rice. There are lots of delicious exotic fruits in my country. Have you heard of cherimoya, papaya, *cocona*, or *maracuyá*? My favorite dessert is *lucuma* ice cream. It's made from a yellowish fruit and tastes like maple syrup. My favorite place to go in Lima is the Museo de Oro, or "gold museum". The incredible jewelry and other objects there really bring my country's ancient history to life.

As tumpa ta runasimita rimani.

◄

Translation: I speak a little Quechua.

Section 1 Physical Geography

Read to Discover

1. What are the major physical features of the region?
2. What climates and vegetation can be found in this region?
3. What are the region's major resources?

Vocabulary

strait
selvas
Peru Current
El Niño

Places

Andes
Strait of Magellan
Tierra del Fuego
Cape Horn
Amazon River

Iquitos
Altiplano
Lake Titicaca
Lake Poopó
Atacama Desert

Reading Strategy

VISUALIZING INFORMATION Look at the maps and photographs in this section. How do you think they will connect to the section's main ideas? Write down your answers.

Pacific South America: Physical-Political

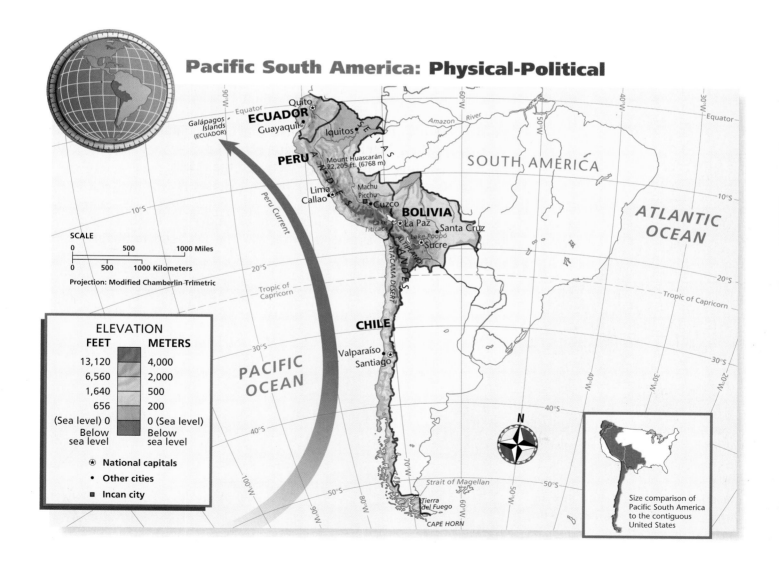

ELEVATION

FEET	METERS
13,120	4,000
6,560	2,000
1,640	500
656	200
(Sea level) 0	0 (Sea level)
Below sea level	Below sea level

⊛ National capitals
• Other cities
▪ Incan city

SCALE
0   500   1000 Miles
0   500   1000 Kilometers
Projection: Modified Chamberlin Trimetric

Size comparison of Pacific South America to the contiguous United States

Physical Features

Shaped like a shoestring, Chile (CHEE-lay) stretches about 2,650 miles (4,264 km) from north to south. However, at its broadest point Chile is just 221 miles (356 km) wide. As its name indicates, Ecuador (E-kwuh-dawr) lies on the equator. Peru (puh-ROO) forms a long curve along the Pacific Ocean. Bolivia (buh-LIV-ee-uh) is landlocked.

Mountains The snowcapped Andes run through all four of the region's countries. Some ridges and volcanic peaks rise more than 20,000 feet (6,096 m) above sea level. Because two tectonic plates meet at the region's edge, earthquakes and volcanoes are constant threats. Sometimes these earthquakes disturb Andean glaciers, sending ice and mud rushing down the mountain slopes.

In Chile's rugged south, the peaks are covered by an ice cap. This ice cap is about 220 miles (354 km) long. Mountains extend to the continent's southern tip. There, the Strait of Magellan links the Atlantic and Pacific Oceans. A **strait** is a narrow passageway that connects two large bodies of water. The large island south of the strait is Tierra del Fuego, or "land of fire." It is divided between Chile and Argentina. At the southernmost tip of the continent, storms swirl around Chile's Cape Horn. Many other islands lie along Chile's southern coast.

Tributaries of the Amazon River begin high in the Andes. In fact, ships can travel upriver about 2,300 miles (3,700 km) on the Amazon. This allows ships to sail from the Atlantic Ocean to Iquitos, Peru.

Altiplano In Ecuador, the Andes range splits into two ridges. The ridges separate further in southern Peru and Bolivia. A broad, high plateau called the Altiplano lies between the ridges.

Rivers on the Altiplano have no outlet to the sea. Water collects in two large lakes, Lake Titicaca and salty Lake Poopó (poh-oh-POH). Lake Titicaca lies at 12,500 feet (3,810 m) above sea level. Large ships carry freight and passengers across it. The lake covers about 3,200 square miles (8,288 sq km).

✓ **READING CHECK:** (*Places and Regions*) What are the major physical features of the region?

► Llamas are used to carry loads in the Altiplano region. Llamas are related to camels and can travel long distances without water.

Interpreting the Visual Record How do llamas appear to be well-suited to the Andes environment?

Canoes are an important form of transportation along the Napo River in eastern Ecuador.

Climate and Vegetation

Climate and vegetation vary widely in Pacific South America. Some areas, such as Chile's central valley, have a mild Mediterranean climate. Other areas have dry, wet, or cold weather conditions.

Grasslands and Forests Mountain environments change with elevation. The Altiplano region between the mountain ridges is a grassland with few trees. Eastern Ecuador, eastern Peru, and northern Bolivia are part of the Amazon River basin. These areas have a humid tropical climate. South Americans call the thick tropical rain forests in this region **selvas**. In Bolivia the rain forest changes to grasslands in the southeast. Far to the south, southern Chile is covered with dense temperate rain forests. Cool, rainy weather is typical of this area of rain forests.

Deserts Northern Chile contains the Atacama Desert. This desert is about 600 miles (965 km) long. Rain is extremely rare, but fog and low clouds are common. They form when the cold **Peru Current** chills warmer air above the ocean's surface. Cloud cover keeps air near the ground from being warmed by the Sun. The area receives almost no sunshine for about six months of the year. Yet it seldom rains. As a result, coastal Chile is one of the cloudiest—and driest— places on Earth.

In Peru, rivers cut through the dry coastal region. They bring snowmelt down from the Andes. About 50 rivers cross Peru. The rivers have made settlement possible in these dry areas.

Our Amazing Planet

The Atacama Desert is one of the driest places on Earth. Some spots in the desert have not received any rain for more than 400 years. Average rainfall is less than 0.004 inches (0.01 cm) per year.

El Niño About every two to seven years, an ocean and weather pattern affects the dry Pacific coast. This weather pattern is called **El Niño**. Cool ocean water near the coast warms. As a result, fish leave what is normally a rich fishing area. Areas along the coast often suffer flooding from heavy rains. El Niño is caused by the buildup of warm water in the Pacific Ocean. Ocean and weather events around the world can be affected. Some scientists think that greenhouse gases made a long El Niño during the 1990s even worse.

✓ **READING CHECK:** (*Physical Systems*) How does El Niño affect Earth?

Resources

The countries of Pacific South America have many important natural resources. The coastal waters of the Pacific Ocean are rich in fish. Forests in southern Chile and east of the Andes in Peru and Ecuador provide lumber. In addition, the region has oil, natural gas, silver, gold, and other valuable mineral resources. Bolivia has large deposits of tin. It also has resources such as copper, lead, and zinc. Chile has large copper deposits. In fact, Chile is the world's leading producer and exporter of copper.

✓ **READING CHECK:** (*Environment and Society*) How has Chile's copper supply affected its economy?

▲ A Bolivian miner uses a jackhammer to mine for tin.

 **Section Review 1**

Define: strait, *selvas*, Peru Current, El Niño

Working with Sketch Maps On a map of South America that you draw or that your teacher provides, label the following: Andes, Strait of Magellan, Tierra del Fuego, Cape Horn, Amazon River, Iquitos, Altiplano, Lake Titicaca, Lake Poopó, and Atacama Desert. Where is Lake Titicaca, and what is it like?

Reading for the Main Idea

1. (*Places and Regions*) What is the main landform region of Pacific South America?

2. (*Physical Systems*) What is El Niño? What effect does El Niño have on coastal flooding in Peru?

Homework Practice Online
Keyword: SG5 HP10

Critical Thinking

3. Finding the Main Idea What would you encounter on a journey from Iquitos, Peru, to Tierra del Fuego?

4. Making Generalizations and Predictions What problem would people living on the dry coast of Chile experience, and how could they solve it?

Organizing What You Know

5. Categorizing Copy the following graphic organizer. Use it to describe the landforms, climate, vegetation, and sources of water of Pacific South America.

	Western	Central	Eastern
Landforms			
Climate			
Vegetation			
Water sources			

Read to Discover

1. What were some achievements of the region's early cultures?
2. What was the Inca Empire like?
3. What role did Spain play in the region's history?
4. What governmental problems have the region's people faced?

Vocabulary

quinoa
quipus
viceroy
creoles
coup

Places

Cuzco
Machu Picchu

People

Atahualpa
Francisco Pizarro

Reading Strategy

TAKING NOTES As you read, use the headings in this section to create an outline. Write supporting details beneath each heading.

Early Cultures

Thousands of years ago, agriculture became the basis of the region's economy. To raise crops in the steep Andes, early farmers cut terraces into the mountainsides. Peoples of the region developed crops that would be important for centuries to come. They domesticated **quinoa** (KEEN-wah), a native Andean plant that yields nutritious seeds. They also grew many varieties of potatoes. Domesticated animals included the llama (LAH-muh) and alpaca (al-PA-kuh). Both have thick wool and are related to camels. Early inhabitants raised and ate guinea pigs, which are related to mice. The people wove many fabrics from cotton and wool. These fabrics had complicated, beautiful patterns.

Peru's first advanced civilization reached its height in about 900 B.C. The main town was located in an Andean valley. This town contained large stone structures decorated with carved jaguars and other designs. Later, people in coastal areas used sophisticated irrigation systems to store water and control flooding. They also built pyramids about 100 feet (30 m) high. Huge stone carvings remain near the Bolivian shores of Lake Titicaca. They were carved by the people of the Tiahuanaco (TEE-uh-wuh-NAH-koh) culture. Another people scratched outlines of animals and other shapes into the surface of the Peruvian desert. These designs are hundreds of feet long.

✓ **READING CHECK:** *Human Systems* What were some achievements of the region's early cultures?

This Peruvian woman is separating seeds from the quinoa plant.

▼

The ruins of Machu Picchu, an Inca city, were discovered in 1911.

Interpreting the Visual Record Why might the Inca have chosen this site for a settlement?

Quipus were used by the Inca to keep records.

The Inca

By the early 1500s, one people ruled most of the Andes region. This group, the Inca, conquered the other cultures around them. They controlled an area reaching from what is now southern Colombia to central Chile. The Inca Empire stretched from the Pacific Coast inland to the selvas of the Amazon rain forest. Perhaps as many as 12 million people from dozens of different ethnic groups were included. The Inca called their empire Tawantinsuyu (tah-WAHN-tin-SOO-yoo), which means "land of the four quarters." Four highways that began in the Inca capital, Cuzco (KOO-skoh), divided the kingdom into four sections.

The Inca Empire The Inca adopted many of the skills of the people they ruled. They built structures out of large stone blocks fitted tightly together without cement. Buildings in the Andean city of Machu Picchu have survived earthquakes and the passing of centuries. Inca metalworkers created gold and silver objects, some decorated with emeralds. Artists made a garden of gold plants with silver stems. They even made gold ears for the corn plants.

Perhaps the Inca's greatest achievement was the organization of their empire. Huge irrigation projects turned deserts into rich farmland that produced food for the large population. A network of thousands of miles of stone-paved roads connected the empire. Along the highways were rest houses, temples, and storerooms. The Inca used storerooms to keep supplies of food. For example, they stored potatoes that had been freeze-dried in the cold mountain air.

To cross the steep Andean valleys, the Inca built suspension bridges of rope. The Inca had no wheeled vehicles or horses. Instead, teams of runners carried messages throughout the land. An important message could be moved up to 150 miles (241 km) in one day.

The runners did not carry letters, however, because the Inca did not have a written language. Instead, they used **quipus** (KEE-pooz). Quipus were complicated systems of knots tied on strings of various colors. Numerical information about important events, populations, animals, and grain supplies was recorded on quipus. Inca officials were trained to read the knots' meaning.

Civil War Although it was rich and efficient, the Inca Empire did not last long. When the Inca emperor died in 1525, a struggle began. Two of his sons fought over who would take his place. About seven years later, his son Atahualpa (ah-tah-WAHL-pah) won the civil war.

✓ **READING CHECK:** (*Human Systems*) What was the Inca's greatest achievement?

CONNECTING TO *Technology*

Inca Roads

The road system was one of the greatest achievements of Inca civilization. The roads crossed high mountains, tropical rain forests, and deserts.

The main road, Capac-nan, or "royal road," connected the capitals of Cuzco and Quito. These cities were more than 1,500 miles (2,414 km) apart. This road crossed jungles, swamps, and mountains. It was straight for most of its length. Inca roads were built from precisely cut stones. One Spanish observer described how the builders worked.

❝ *The Indians who worked these stones used no mortar; they had no steel for cutting and working the stones, and no machines for transporting them; yet so skilled was their work that the joints between the stones were barely noticeable.* **❞**

Another longer highway paralleled the coast and joined Capac-nan, creating a highly

Inca roads had stairways to cross steep peaks.

efficient network. Along these roads were rest houses. The Inca also built suspension bridges to span deep ravines. They built floating bridges to cross wide rivers.

When the Spanish conquered the region in the 1530s, they destroyed the road system. Today, only fragments of the Inca roads still exist.

Understanding What You Read
1. How might the road system have allowed the Inca to control their territory?
2. What were the main features of the Inca road system?

Spain in Pacific South America

While on his way to Cuzco to be crowned, Atahualpa met Spanish explorer Francisco Pizarro. Pizarro's small group of men and horses had recently landed on the continent's shore. Pizarro wanted Inca gold and silver.

Conquest and Revolt Pizarro captured Atahualpa, who ordered his people to fill a room with gold and silver. These riches were supposed to be a ransom for his freedom. However, Pizarro ordered the Inca emperor killed. The Spaniards continued to conquer Inca lands.

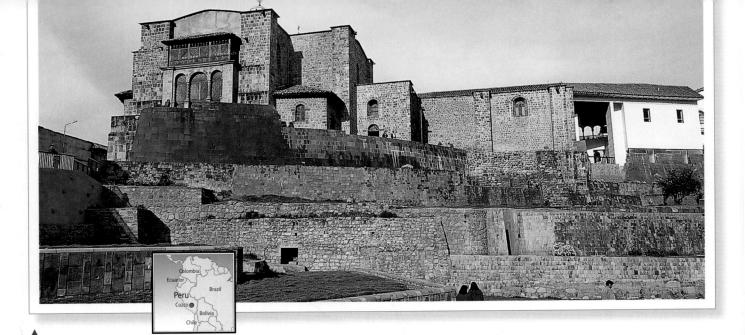

The stonework of an Inca temple in Cuzco now forms the foundation of this Catholic church.

Interpreting the Visual Record What does this photo suggest about how the Spanish viewed the religious practices of the Inca?

By 1535 the Inca Empire no longer existed. The last Inca rulers fled into the mountains. A tiny independent state in the foothills of the eastern Andes survived several decades more.

The new Spanish rulers often dealt harshly with the South American Indians. Many Indians had to work in gold and silver mines and on the Spaniards' plantations. Inca temples were replaced by Spanish-style Roman Catholic churches. A **viceroy**, or governor, appointed by the king of Spain enforced Spanish laws and customs.

From time to time, the people rebelled against their Spanish rulers. In 1780 and 1781 an Indian named Tupac Amarú II (too-PAHK ahm-AHR-oo) led a revolt. This revolt spread, but was put down quickly.

Independence By the early 1800s, the desire for independence had grown in South America. The people of Pacific South America began to break away from Spain. **Creoles**, American-born descendants of Europeans, were the main leaders of the revolts. Chile became an independent country in 1818. Ecuador achieved independence in 1822, and Peru became independent two years later. Bolivia became independent in 1825. In the 1880s Bolivia lost a war with Chile. As a result, Bolivia lost its strip of seacoast and became landlocked.

✓ **READING CHECK:** *Human Systems* What was Spain's role in the region's history?

Government

Since gaining their independence, the countries of Pacific South America have had periods during which their governments were unstable. Often military leaders have taken control and limited citizens' rights. However, in recent decades the region's countries have moved toward more democratic forms of government. These governments now face the challenge of widespread poverty.

Ecuador is a democracy. Ecuador's government is working to improve housing, medical care, and literacy. Bolivia has suffered from a series of violent revolutions and military governments. It is now also a democracy. Bolivia has had one of the most stable elected governments in the region in recent years.

Peru's recent history has been particularly troubled. A terrorist group called the Sendero Luminoso, or "shining path," was active in the 1980s. The group carried out deadly guerrilla attacks. With the arrest of the group's leader in 1992, hopes for calm returned. Peru has an elected president and congress.

Chile has also recently ended a long violent period. In 1970, Chileans elected a president who had been influenced by communist ideas. A few years later he was overthrown and killed during a military **coup** (KOO). A coup is a sudden overthrow of a government by a small group of people. In the years after the coup, the military rulers tried to crush their political enemies. The military government was harsh and often violent. Thousands of people were imprisoned or killed. In the late 1980s the power of the rulers began to weaken. After more than 15 years of military rule, Chileans rejected the military dictatorship. A new, democratic government was created. Chileans now enjoy many new freedoms.

▲
Although Peru now has a more stable government, unrest continues in some areas. In this 2003 photo, farmers protest a mining project by a Canadian company. Possible pollution from the mine was one of the demonstrators' concerns.

✓ **READING CHECK:** (*Human Systems*) How has unlimited government been a problem for some of the nations in the region?

Homework Practice Online
Keyword: SG5 HP10

Define or identify: quinoa, quipus, Atahualpa, Francisco Pizarro, viceroy, creoles, coup

Working with Sketch Maps On the map you created in Section 1, label Cuzco and Machu Picchu. Then shade in the area ruled by the Inca. What may have limited Inca expansion eastward?

Reading for the Main Idea

1. (*Human Systems*) How did the Inca communicate across great distances?

2. (*Environment and Society*) What attracted the Spanish conquerors to Pacific South America?

Critical Thinking

3. **Analyzing Information** What governmental problems have many of the region's nations experienced?

4. **Drawing Inferences and Conclusions** Why do you think many leaders of the independence movement were creoles rather than Spaniards?

Organizing What You Know

5. **Sequencing** Copy the following graphic organizer. Use it to show important events in the history of Pacific South America.

Read to Discover

1. What are the three regions of Ecuador?
2. How might Bolivia develop its economy?
3. What are the features of Peru's regions?
4. How is Chile different from its neighbors in Pacific South America?

Vocabulary

Quechua
junta

Places

Guayaquil
Quito
La Paz
Sucre
Santa Cruz

Callao
Lima
Santiago
Valparaíso

Reading Strategy

READING ORGANIZER Before you read, draw a large circle on a sheet of paper. Draw two intersecting lines to divide the circle into quarters. Label the quarters Ecuador, Bolivia, Peru, and Chile. As you read, fill in the quarters with information about the countries.

Ecuador Today

Many of Ecuador's people live in the coastal lowland. The country's largest city, Guayaquil (gwy-ah-KEEL), is located there. Guayaquil is Ecuador's major port and commercial center. The coastal lowland has valuable deposits of natural gas. It is also an important agricultural region. Rich fishing waters lie off the coast.

The Andean region in the heart of Ecuador is where Quito, the national capital, is located. Open-air markets and Spanish colonial buildings attract many tourists to Quito. Modern buildings surround the old city.

Large numbers of people are moving to the third region, the eastern lowlands. Here in the Amazon Basin are economically essential oil deposits.

Spanish is the official language of Ecuador. However, about 19 percent of the population speaks South American Indian languages such as **Quechua** (KE-chuh-wuh). Quechua was the language of the Inca. Ecuador's Indians are politically active and are represented in the parliament. However, many of them continue to live in terrible poverty.

Ecuador's Galápagos Islands are famous for animals, like these giant tortoises, found nowhere else in the world.

✔ **READING CHECK:** *Human Systems*
How do Ecuador's Indians participate in and influence the political process?

▲

La Paz lies in a valley. Because of recent population growth, the city has spread up the valley walls.

Interpreting the Visual Record

Human-Environment Interaction

How might the growth of La Paz affect the region's environment?

Bolivia Today

Bolivia has two capitals. La Paz is located in a valley of the Altiplano. At 12,001 feet (3,658 m), it is the highest capital in the world. It is also Bolivia's chief industrial city. Bolivia's congress meets in La Paz but the supreme court meets in Sucre (soo-kray), farther south. The country's fastest-growing region surrounds the city of Santa Cruz, east of the Andes.

In the plains of eastern Bolivia there are few roads and little money for investment. However, the region's fertile soil, adequate rainfall, and grazing land can help in its development. The country has other valuable resources, including natural gas and various metals, such as tin. However, coups and revolutions have slowed development. Bolivia remains a poor country.

Bolivia's population has the highest percentage of Indians of any South American country. Many Bolivian Indians follow customs and lifestyles that have existed for centuries. They often dress in traditional styles. Women wear full, sweeping skirts and derby hats. Men wear striped ponchos.

Bolivian music is bright and festive. Common instruments include flutes, drums, bronze gongs, and copper bells. The charango is a string instrument that resembles a small guitar. Its sound box is made from the shell of an armadillo.

▲

Shoppers buy food at a vegetable market in La Paz.

✓ **READING CHECK:** (*Human Systems*) What is Bolivia's music like?

Pacific South America

Country	Population/ Growth Rate	Life Expectancy	Literacy Rate	Per Capita GDP
Bolivia	8,586,443 1.6%	62, male 67, female	87%	$2,500
Chile	15,665,216 1.0%	73, male 79, female	96%	$10,000
Ecuador	13,710,234 2%	69, male 74, female	92%	$3,100
Peru	28,409,897 1.6%	68, male 73, female	90%	$4,800
United States	290,342,554 0.9%	74, male 80, female	97%	$37,600

Source: Central Intelligence Agency, *The World Factbook 2003*

Interpreting the Chart **Why may Bolivia's per capita GDP be lower than those of other countries in the region?**

Peru Today

Peru is making progress in its struggle against poverty and political violence. However, the government has been criticized for using harsh methods to solve political problems.

Peru, like Ecuador, has three major regions. The dense rain forests in eastern Peru provide lumber. Tropical fruit trees grow there. The Amazon River flows through this region.

The Andes highlands include the Altiplano and the heartland of what was the Inca Empire. Stone structures from the Inca period draw thousands of tourists to Machu Picchu and Cuzco. Potatoes and corn are among the crops grown in this region. Many of the people in the highlands are South American Indians. Millions of Peruvians speak Quechua.

Important mineral deposits are located near the Pacific coast. This is Peru's most modern and developed region. Hydroelectric projects on coastal rivers provide energy. The seaport city of Callao (kah-YAH-oh) serves Lima (LEE-mah), the capital, a few miles inland. Nearly one third of all Peruvians live in these two cities. Callao is Peru's leading fishing and trade center. Industry and government jobs draw many people from the countryside to Lima.

✓ **READING CHECK:** (*Human Systems*) What draws people to Callao and Lima?

Tourists explore icy landscapes in southern Chile.

Chile Today

In the late 1980s Chile ended the rule of a **junta** (HOOHN-tuh) and became a democracy. A junta is a small group of military officers who rule a country after seizing power. Chile is now also one of the most stable countries in South America. Its economy is also one of the most advanced. Chile's prospects for the future seem bright.

Chile's economy is based on mining, fishing, forestry, and farming. Copper mining is especially important. It accounts for more than one third of the country's exports. In fact, Chile has the world's largest open-pit copper mine. It is located in the Atacama Desert near the town of Chuquicamata.

About one third of all Chileans live in Central Chile. It includes the capital, Santiago, and its nearby seaport, Valparaíso (bahl-pah-rah-EE-soh). The mild Mediterranean climate allows farmers to grow a wide range of crops. Grapes grow well there, and wine is exported around the world. Cool, mountainous southern Chile has forests, oil, and farms. Few people live there, however. Northern Chile includes the Atacama Desert. Croplands along valleys there are irrigated by streams flowing down from the Andes.

Although poverty remains a problem, Chile's economy is becoming stronger. Small businesses and factories are growing quickly. More Chileans are finding work, and wages are rising. Chile hopes that the price of its main export, copper, remains high. Chile's economy would suffer if the world price of copper fell.

Chile wants to expand its trade links with the United States. Some people have suggested that Chile join the North American Free Trade Agreement (NAFTA). This free-trade group currently includes Canada, the United States, and Mexico.

✓ **READING CHECK:** *Environment and Society* How does copper affect Chile's economy?

go.hrw.com

Homework Practice Online

Keyword: SG5 HP10

Section Review 3

Define and explain: Quechua, junta

Working with Sketch Maps On the map you created in Section 2, label Guayaquil, Quito, La Paz, Sucre, Santa Cruz, Callao, Lima, Santiago, and Valparaíso. Why are there so few cities in the eastern part of the region?

Reading for the Main Idea

1. (*Places and Regions*) What features are drawing people to Ecuador's eastern lowlands?

2. (*Human Systems*) Why do many people move from the countryside to Lima, Peru?

Critical Thinking

3. Drawing Inferences and Conclusions What might be a disadvantage of Chile depending so heavily on its copper industry?

4. Analyzing Information Why have changes in Bolivia's government slowed development?

Organizing What You Know

5. Summarizing Copy the following graphic organizer. Use it to write phrases that describe each country.

Bolivia	
Chile	
Ecuador	
Peru	

Review and Practice

Define and Identify

Identify each of the following:

1. strait
2. *selvas*
3. El Niño
4. quinoa
5. quipus
6. Atahualpa
7. Francisco Pizarro
8. viceroy
9. creoles
10. coup
11. Quechua
12. junta

Review the Main Ideas

13. What is the Altiplano, and what kind of plants grow there?

14. How does El Niño affect the fish and weather of Pacific South America?

15. What are three types of construction projects that helped the Inca organize their empire?

16. What kinds of information did the Inca record on quipus?

17. What happened when the Spaniards arrived in Pacific South America?

18. What trend have the countries of this region experienced in their forms of government?

19. Which country's population has the highest percentage of Indians?

20. Why are many people moving to Lima, Peru from the countryside?

21. How are northern, central, and southern Chile different?

Think Critically

22. **Analyzing Information** Why is Spanish the most widely spoken language in Pacific South America?

23. **Drawing Inferences and Conclusions** Why do you think that the main leaders of revolts against Spain were creoles?

24. **Drawing Inferences and Conclusions** Why do you think the region's countries have had so many unstable governments since gaining their independence?

25. **Finding the Main Idea** How may Bolivia's landlocked position affect the country's economy?

26. **Analyzing Information** What role do Ecuador's Indians play in its political system?

Map Activity

27. On a separate sheet of paper, match the letters on the map with their correct labels.

Peru Current	Atacama Desert
Strait of Magellan	Quito
Tierra del Fuego	La Paz
Iquitos	Lima
Lake Poopó	Santiago

Writing Activity

Imagine that you are making a film about Ecuador, Bolivia, Peru, or Chile. Write a summary of the film you would like to make. List land features, industries, peoples, and customs that you want to cover. Explain why you think these topics would be interesting to audiences. Be sure to use standard grammar, spelling, sentence structure, and punctuation.

internet connect

Internet Activity: go.hrw.com
KEYWORD: SG5 GT10

Choose a topic to explore Pacific South America:
- Analyze Chile's climate.
- Hike the Inca Trail and visit Machu Picchu.
- Learn about Andean languages.

go.
hrw
.com

Social Studies Skills Practice

Interpreting Maps

Imagine that you are a runner for the Inca Empire carrying a message from Cuzco to Machu Picchu. Study the physical map of southern Peru. Then answer the questions.

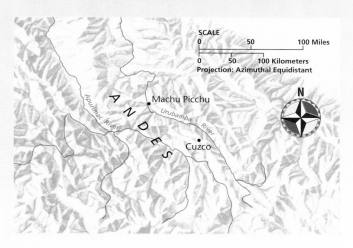

SCALE
0   50   100 Miles
0   50   100 Kilometers
Projection: Azimuthal Equidistant

ANDES
Apurímac River
Machu Picchu
Urubamba River
Cuzco
N

1. What kind of landforms lie along your route? In which direction do you travel?
2. At least how many miles do you have to run?
3. What physical feature may help you shorten your travel time? How?
4. Why might using this physical feature be dangerous? How can you tell from the map?

Analyzing Primary Sources

You have read about El Niño events. Read the following excerpts from the March 1999 issue of *National Geographic* in which Peruvian villagers tell about floods caused by a severe El Niño in 1998. Then answer the questions.

"'Suddenly we were surrounded from all directions,' Ipanaque Silva says. 'It took all the little animals. Then my house fell down completely.' . . . 'We thought that the water couldn't come here,' says Flora Ramirez, 'but we lost practically everything.' . . . 'They strung ropes from one house to another to rescue people,' recalls Manuel Guevara Sanchez. 'Some spent three days on the roof. Those who knew how to swim brought them food.'"

1. Did the flood happen quickly, or did the waters rise slowly?
2. What does the quote from Ipanaque Silva tell about how he made a living and what kind of house he may have had?
3. Do you think that Flora Ramirez had experienced El Niño floods before? Why or why not?
4. How did Manuel Guevara Sanchez's neighbors help each other?

COULD YOU SURVIVE THE AMAZON?

ONLINE EXPEDITIONS

GO TO: go.hrw.com
KEYWORD: SG5 CH10

A Land of Danger and Beauty

Welcome to the Amazon, the biggest rain forest in the world! The forest is very beautiful. Brightly colored orchids hang from the trees. Parrots and butterflies look like flying jewels. Watch out, though. The rain forest hides some dangerous residents. Just touching some of the frogs can kill a human. The bite of a fer-de-lance, one of the world's scariest snakes, causes death by internal bleeding. Really big anacondas can swallow a teenager whole. In the forest's many streams, electric eels and piranhas lurk. Caimans, which are related to alligators, can be 15 feet long. Their teeth are just as sharp as those of their relatives.

SURVIVAL CHALLENGE

Now place yourself in an airplane flying over the Amazon rain forest. You're exploring the area to investigate business opportunities. From the air, the trees look like a sea of green. Suddenly, you're *in* the trees because the plane has crashed! You're amazed to find that you are the only survivor and that you are unhurt. However, you are lost and surrounded by danger. How will you survive long enough to find your way back to a city?

Fortunately, you know some of the local language. When you ask someone for help, she draws a map in the dirt and colors it with natural dyes. Her mental map is shown on the next page. Can you read it? How does her map differ from your own mental map of the rain forest? Why do you think two people could have different mental maps of the same region?

A jaguar snarls to warn visitors away from his territory.

Seeing the Forest *and* the Trees

By carefully comparing the map to your surroundings, you unravel its secrets. What are they? You find food, avoid danger, and eventually return home. Then you see the other map below in a magazine. You also read that while many people worry about the loss of the rain forest, others see great benefits in developing it. Your experience and this new information give you plenty of food for thought. Will the way you think about the rain forest change?

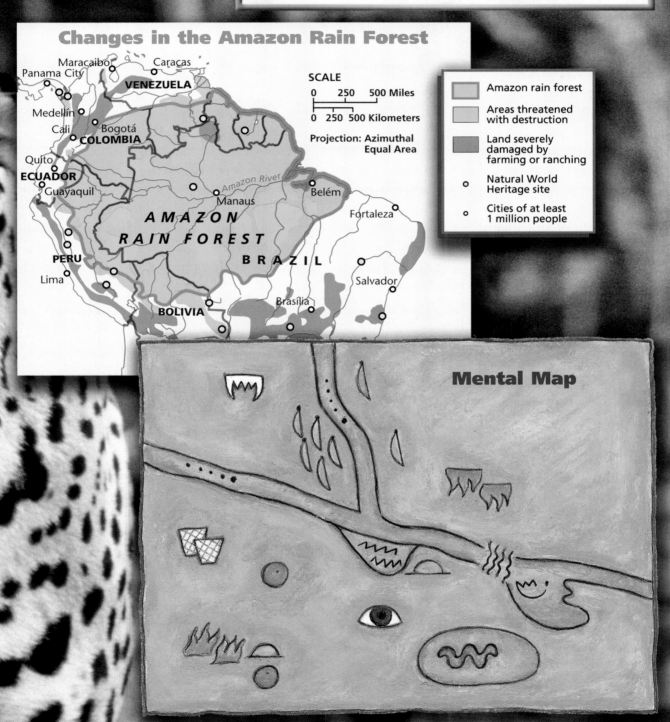

Changes in the Amazon Rain Forest

Panama City
Maracaibo
Caracas
VENEZUELA
Medellín
Cali
Bogotá
COLOMBIA
Quito
ECUADOR
Guayaquil
Amazon River
Manaus
Belém
AMAZON RAIN FOREST
Fortaleza
PERU
Lima
BRAZIL
Salvador
BOLIVIA
Brasília

SCALE

0   250   500 Miles

0   250   500 Kilometers

Projection: Azimuthal Equal Area

Amazon rain forest

Areas threatened with destruction

Land severely damaged by farming or ranching

o   Natural World Heritage site

o   Cities of at least 1 million people

Mental Map

Geo SKILLS

Building Skills for Life: Understanding Migration Patterns

People have always moved to different places. This movement is called migration. Understanding migration patterns is very important in geography. These patterns help explain why certain places are the way they are today. In South America, for example, there are people whose ancestors came from Africa, Asia, Europe, and North America. All of these people migrated to South America sometime in the past.

Why do people migrate? There are many different reasons. Sometimes, people do not want to move, but they are forced to. This is called forced migration. Other times, people migrate because they are looking for a better life. This is an example of voluntary migration.

Geographers who study migration patterns often use the words *push* and *pull*. They identify situations that push people out of places. For example, wars often push people away. They also identify situations that pull people to new places. A better job might pull someone to a

▲

Many people from Japan migrated to the area around São Paulo, Brazil in the 1900s.

new place. Usually, people migrate for a combination of reasons. They might be pushed from a place because there is not enough farmland. They might also be pulled to a new place by good farmland.

Geographers are also interested in barriers to migration. Barriers make it harder for people to migrate. There are cultural barriers, economic barriers, physical barriers, and political barriers. For example, deserts, mountains, and oceans can make it harder for people to migrate. Unfamiliar languages and ways of life can also block migration.

Migration changes people and places. Both the places that people leave and the places where they arrive are changed. Can you think of some ways that migration has changed the world?

PRACTICING THE SKILL

1. List some factors that can push people out of a place or pull them to a new place.

2. Research the migration of your ancestors or a friend's ancestors. Where did they come from? When did they migrate? Why?

3. Imagine you had to migrate to a new place. Where would you go? Why would you pick this place? Do you think you would be scared, excited, or both?

HANDS on
GEOGRAPHY

The following passage was written by a woman from Argentina who migrated to the United States. Read the passage and then answer the Lab Report questions.

" My nephew and I came from a faraway country called Argentina. When I mention this country to others, they say, "Oh, Argentina! It is so beautiful!" However, as beautiful as Argentina is, life there is very difficult now.

In Argentina, there are three social classes: rich, middle class, and poor. The middle class, of which I am a member, is the largest. We are the workers and the businesspeople. Because of bad economic decisions and corrupt government, the middle class has almost disappeared. Factories have closed, and people have no work. The big companies move to other countries. The small businesses depend on the big companies and often have to close. Argentina has a very high rate of unemployment. Many people are hungry.

My husband and I had some friends who worked in Argentina. They advised us to sell everything we owned and move to Houston.

They told us that life was better there and they had relatives who would help us find a house to rent. They told us a lawyer would help us put our papers in order so we could work. I had a small sewing shop with some sewing machines, which I sold so I could travel. "

▲
Poverty and unemployment are problems in some parts of Argentina.
Interpreting the Visual Record What evidence can you see of poor living conditions?

Lab Report

1. What pushed the author out of Argentina?

2. Why did she choose Houston as her destination?

3. According to the author, what do other people think Argentina is like? does she agree?

UNIT 4

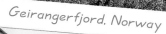
Geirangerfjord, Norway

Europe

A Professor in the Czech Republic

Meredith Walker teaches English at Clemson University. She also teaches English As a Second Language courses. Here she describes a visit to Prague, the capital of the Czech Republic. **WHAT DO YOU THINK?** *Does Prague sound like a city you would like to see?*

The castle in Prague sits on a hill high above the Vltava River. This river divides the city. A castle has stood on that hillside for 1,000 years. Rising from the inner courtyard of the castle is a huge medieval building, St. Vitus' Cathedral. Together, the castle and cathedral look almost magical, especially at night when spotlights shine on them. The castle is the most important symbol of the city. A great Czech writer, Franz Kafka, believed that the castle influenced everything and everyone in the city.

Another important landmark in Prague is Charles Bridge, one of eight bridges that cross the Vltava River. The bridge is part of the route that kings once traveled on their way to the castle to be crowned. Today, large crowds of tourists walk there. Many stop to photograph some of the 22 statues that line the bridge. No cars are allowed on the bridge today.

The first time I walked across the bridge, heading up toward the castle, it was at night. Fireworks were lighting the sky all around me. It was a colorful welcome.

Street scene in Prague, Czech Republic

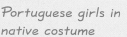

Portuguese girls in native costume

Understanding Primary Sources

1. How does the city's physical geography help make the castle a symbol of Prague?

2. How did the fireworks display affect Meredith Walker's feelings about Prague?

Whooper swan

Europe

Elevation Profile

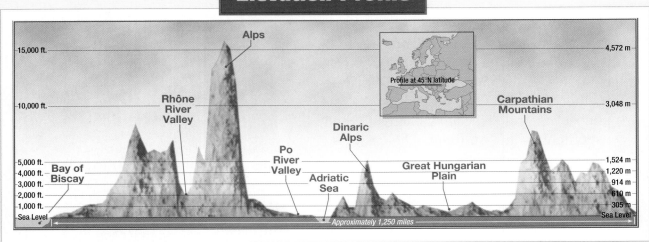

Alps

15,000 ft. — 4,572 m

Rhône
River
Valley

10,000 ft. — 3,048 m

Profile at 45°N latitude

Carpathian
Mountains

Dinaric
Alps

Po
River
Valley

Great Hungarian
Plain

5,000 ft.
4,000 ft. — Bay of
3,000 ft.   Biscay
2,000 ft.
1,000 ft.
Sea Level

Adriatic
Sea

1,524 m
1,220 m
914 m
610 m
305 m
Sea Level

Approximately 1,250 miles

The United States and Europe:
Comparing Sizes

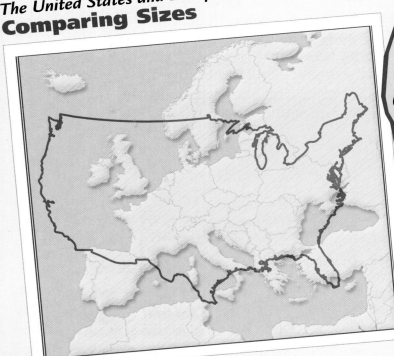

GEOSTATS:

World's largest island:
Greenland—839,999 sq. mi.
(2,175,597 sq km)

World's smallest independent
country: Vatican City—
0.17 sq. mi. (0.44 sq km)

World's northernmost town:
Longyearbyen, Spitsbergen
Island, Norway—about 77.5°N

Greenland (DENMARK)

ARCTIC OCEAN

NORWEGIAN SEA

ICELAND

Faeroe Islands (DENMARK)

North Atlantic Drift

Shetland Islands (U.K.)

KJØLEN MOUNTAINS

SCANDINAVIAN PENINSULA

NORWAY SWEDEN FINLAND

ESTONIA

LATVIA

BALTIC SEA

LITHUANIA

NORTH SEA

JUTLAND PENINSULA

DENMARK

NORTHERN EUROPEAN PLAIN

Vistula River

HIGHLANDS

IRELAND

Shannon

UNITED KINGDOM

Thames R.

NETHERLANDS

Elbe River

Oder River

Neisse River

POLAND

English Channel

BELGIUM

GERMANY

LUXEMBOURG

CZECH REPUBLIC

BOHEMIAN HIGHLANDS

CARPATHIAN MTS.

SLOVAKIA

NORTHWEST HIGHLANDS

Seine River

CENTRAL UPLANDS

Rhine River

Danube R.

BAVARIAN PLATEAU

Loire River

AUSTRIA

LIECHTENSTEIN

HUNGARY

GREAT HUNGARIAN PLAIN

ROMANIA

FRANCE

SWITZERLAND

Lake Geneva

A L P S

Drava R.

SLOVENIA

CROATIA

Danube River

Mont Blanc
15,781 ft. (4810m)

Po River

Rhône River

DINARIC ALPS

SAN MARINO

BOSNIA AND HERZEGOVINA

SERBIA AND MONTENEGRO

BULGARIA

PYRENEES

ANDORRA

MONACO

ITALY

A P E N N I N E S

ADRIATIC SEA

BALKAN PENINSULA

PORTUGAL

SPAIN

Ebro River

Corsica (FRANCE)

VATICAN CITY

MACEDONIA

ATLANTIC OCEAN

Tagus River

IBERIAN PENINSULA

Balearic Islands (SPAIN)

Sardinia (ITALY)

ALBANIA

GREECE

AEGEAN SEA

Strait of Gibraltar

MEDITERRANEAN

Sicily (ITALY)

SEA

Crete (GREECE)

MALTA

AFRICA

Greenland (DENMARK) inset

Greenland (DENMARK)

Nuuk (Godthab)

Arctic Circle

| 0 | 250 | 500 Miles |
SCALE
0 250 500 Kilometers
Projection: Polyconic

ELEVATION

FEET	METERS
13,120	4,000
6,560	2,000
1,640	500
656	200
(Sea level) 0	0 (Sea level)
Below sea level	Below sea level
	Ice caps

SCALE
0 250 500 Miles
0 250 500 Kilometers
Projection: Azimuthal Equal Area

---

1. (*Location*) What are two mountain ranges that occupy peninsulas?

2. (*Region*) What are the two major plains of Europe? Which is larger?

Critical Thinking

3. (*Movement*) In the days before air travel, which physical feature would have made it difficult to travel between Italy and the countries to its north?

4. (*Movement*) Which physical feature would have made travel between Greece, Italy, and Spain fairly easy?

Europe: Political

Legend:
- Boundaries
- ⊛ National capitals
- • Other cities

1. (*Place*) Which countries border both the Atlantic and the Mediterranean?

2. (*Region*) Compare this map to the **physical map** of the region. Which physical feature helps form the boundary between Spain and France?

Critical Thinking

3. (*Location*) Which countries have the shortest coastlines on the Adriatic Sea?

4. (*Location*) The United Kingdom has not been invaded successfully since A.D. 1066. Why do you think this is so?

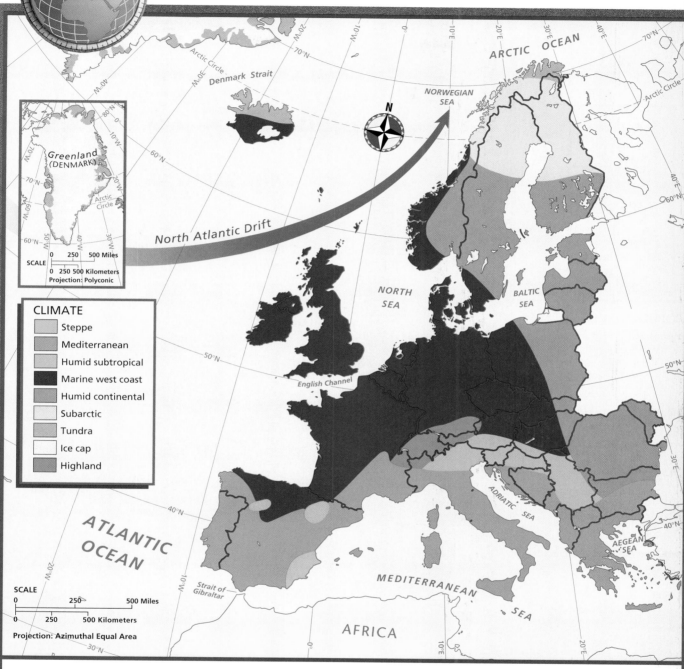

CLIMATE

- Steppe
- Mediterranean
- Humid subtropical
- Marine west coast
- Humid continental
- Subarctic
- Tundra
- Ice cap
- Highland

Greenland (DENMARK)

SCALE
0   250   500 Miles

0   250   500 Kilometers
Projection: Polyconic

North Atlantic Drift

ARCTIC OCEAN

NORWEGIAN SEA

Denmark Strait

NORTH SEA

BALTIC SEA

ENGLISH Channel

ATLANTIC OCEAN

ADRIATIC SEA

AEGEAN SEA

Strait of Gibraltar

MEDITERRANEAN SEA

AFRICA

SCALE
0   250   500 Miles

0   250   500 Kilometers

Projection: Azimuthal Equal Area

---

1. *Region* Which climate type takes its name from a sea in the region?

2. *Region* Which two independent countries have climate types that are not found in any other European country? Which climate types do these two countries have?

Critical Thinking

3. *Interaction* Compare this map to the **physical** and **population maps**. Which physical feature in central Europe has a highland climate and relatively few people? This physical feature is in which countries?

POPULATION DENSITY

Persons per sq. mile		Persons per sq. km
520		200
260		100
130		50
25		10
3		1
0		0

● Metropolitan areas with more than 2 million inhabitants

○ Metropolitan areas with 1 million to 2 million inhabitants

SCALE
0   250   500 Miles
0   250   500 Kilometers
Projection: Azimuthal Equal Area

Greenland (DENMARK)

SCALE
0   250   500 Miles
0   250 500 Kilometers
Projection: Polyconic

1. (*Region*) Examine the **climate map**. Why are northern Norway, Sweden, and Finland so thinly populated?

2. (*Place*) Compare this map to the **political map**. Which countries have between 25 and 130 persons per square mile in all areas?

Critical Thinking

3. (*Interaction*) Compare this map to the **land use and resources map** of the region. What type of power generation is common in central Europe but not in the far north? Why do you think this is so?

LAND USE

- Nomadic herding
- Livestock raising
- Commercial farming
- Forests
- Manufacturing
- Limited economic activity
- ● Major manufacturing and trade centers

RESOURCES

- 🛒 Coal
- 💧 Natural gas
- ⛏ Oil
- ✳ Nuclear power
- ⚡ Hydroelectric power
- ♨ Geothermal power
- Ⓤ Uranium
- ◆ Other minerals
- 🐟 Seafood

1. (Interaction) What is the only country in the region that uses geothermal power?

2. (Location) Which country in the region mines uranium?

3. (Interaction) In which body of water is oil and gas production concentrated?

Critical Thinking

4. (Interaction) Compare this map to the **physical map** of the region. In which mountain range is nomadic herding common?

5. (Interaction) What type of agriculture that you have read about is not common in Europe?

Fast FACTS
Europe

ALBANIA

CAPITAL: Tiranë

AREA:
11,100 sq. mi. (28,748 sq km)

POPULATION: 3,582,205

MONEY: lek

LANGUAGES:
Albanian, Greek

CARS: data not available

ANDORRA

CAPITAL:
Andorra la Vella

AREA:
181 sq. mi. (468 sq km)

POPULATION: 69,150

MONEY:
euro

LANGUAGES:
Catalan (official), French
Castilian

CARS: 35,358

AUSTRIA

CAPITAL: Vienna

AREA:
32,378 sq. mi.
(83,858 sq km)

POPULATION: 8,188,207

MONEY:
euro

LANGUAGES: German

CARS: 3,780,000

BELGIUM

CAPITAL:
Brussels

AREA:
11,780 sq. mi. (30,510 sq km)

POPULATION: 10,289,088

MONEY:
euro

LANGUAGES:
Dutch, French, German

CARS: 4,420,000

BOSNIA AND HERZEGOVINA

CAPITAL:
Sarajevo

AREA:
19,741 sq. mi. (51,129 sq km)

POPULATION: 3,989,018

MONEY:
marka

LANGUAGES:
Croatian, Serbian, Bosnian

CARS: data not available

BULGARIA

CAPITAL: Sofia

AREA:
42,822 sq. mi.
(110,910 sq km)

POPULATION: 7,537,929

MONEY:
lev

LANGUAGES:
Bulgarian

CARS: 1,650,000

CROATIA

CAPITAL:
Zagreb

AREA:
21,831 sq. mi.
(56,542 sq km)

POPULATION: 4,422,248

MONEY:
Croatian kuna

LANGUAGES:
Croatian

CARS: 698,000

CZECH REPUBLIC

CAPITAL: Prague

AREA:
30,450 sq. mi.
(78,866 sq km)

POPULATION: 10,249,216

MONEY:
Czech koruna

LANGUAGES:
Czech

CARS: 4,410,000

DENMARK

CAPITAL:
Copenhagen

AREA:
16,639 sq. mi.
(43,094 sq km)

POPULATION: 5,384,384

MONEY:
Danish krone

LANGUAGES:
Danish, Faroese, Greenlandic
(an Inuit dialect), German

CARS: 1,790,000

ESTONIA

CAPITAL:
Tallinn

AREA:
17,462 sq. mi.
(45,226 sq km)

POPULATION: 1,408,556

MONEY:
Estonian kroon

LANGUAGES:
Estonian (official), Russian,
Ukrainian, English, Finnish

CARS: 338,000

Countries not drawn to scale.

FINLAND

CAPITAL: Helsinki

AREA:
130,127 sq. mi.
(337,030 sq km)

POPULATION: 5,190,785

MONEY:
euro

LANGUAGES: Finnish, Swedish

CARS: 1,940,000

FRANCE

CAPITAL: Paris

AREA:
211,208 sq. mi.
(547,030 sq km)

POPULATION: 60,180,529

MONEY:
euro

LANGUAGES: French

CARS: 25,500,000

GERMANY

CAPITAL: Berlin

AREA:
137,846 sq. mi.
(357,021 sq km)

POPULATION: 82,398,326

MONEY:
euro

LANGUAGES: German

CARS: 41,330,000

GREECE

CAPITAL:
Athens

AREA:
50,942 sq. mi.
(131,940 sq km)

POPULATION: 10,665,989

MONEY:
euro

LANGUAGES:
Greek (official), English,
French

CARS: 2,340,000

HUNGARY

CAPITAL: Budapest

AREA:
35,919 sq. mi.
(93,030 sq km)

POPULATION: 10,045,407

MONEY:
forint

LANGUAGES:
Hungarian

CARS: 2,280,000

ICELAND

CAPITAL: Reykjavik

AREA:
39,768 sq. mi.
(103,000 sq km)

POPULATION: 280,798

MONEY:
Icelandic krona

LANGUAGES:
Icelandic

CARS: 132,468

IRELAND

CAPITAL:
Dublin

AREA:
27,135 sq. mi. (70,280 sq km)

POPULATION: 3,924,140

MONEY:
euro

LANGUAGES:
English, Irish (Gaelic)

CARS: 1,060,000

ITALY

CAPITAL:
Rome

AREA:
116,305 sq. mi.
(301,230 sq km)

POPULATION: 57,998,353

MONEY:
euro

LANGUAGES:
Italian, German, French,
Slovene

CARS: 31,000,000

LATVIA

CAPITAL: Riga

AREA:
24,938 sq. mi.
(64,589 sq km)

POPULATION: 2,348,784

MONEY: Latvian lat

LANGUAGES:
Lettish (official), Lithuanian,
Russian

CARS: 252,000

LIECHTENSTEIN

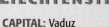

CAPITAL: Vaduz

AREA:
62 sq. mi. (160 sq km)

POPULATION:
33,145

MONEY:
Swiss franc

LANGUAGES: German

CARS: data not available

Sources: Central Intelligence Agency, *The World Factbook 2003; The World Almanac and Book of Facts 2003;* population figures are 2003 estimates.

LITHUANIA

CAPITAL: Vilnius

AREA:
25,174 sq. mi.
(65,200 sq km)

POPULATION:
3,592,561

MONEY:
litas

LANGUAGES:
Lithuanian (official), Polish, Russian

CARS: 653,000

LUXEMBOURG

CAPITAL:
Luxembourg

AREA:
998 sq. mi. (2,586 sq km)

POPULATION:
454,157

MONEY: euro

LANGUAGES:
Luxembourgish, German, French

CARS: 231,666

MACEDONIA

CAPITAL: Skopje

AREA:
9,781 sq. mi.
(25,333 sq km)

POPULATION: 2,063,122

MONEY:
Macedonian denar

LANGUAGES:
Macedonian, Albanian, Turkish, Serbo-Croatian

CARS: 263,000

MALTA

CAPITAL:
Valletta

AREA:
122 sq. mi. (316 sq km)

POPULATION:
400,420

MONEY:
Maltese lira

LANGUAGES:
Maltese (official), English (official)

CARS: 122,100

MOLDOVA

CAPITAL: Chișinău

AREA:
13,067 sq. mi.
(33,843 sq km)

POPULATION: 4,439,502

MONEY:
Moldovan leu

LANGUAGES:
Moldovan (official), Russian, Gagauz

CARS: 169,000

MONACO

CAPITAL:
Monaco

AREA:
0.75 sq. mi. (1.95 sq km)

POPULATION:
32,130

MONEY:
euro

LANGUAGES:
French (official), English, Italian, Monegasque

CARS: 17,000

NETHERLANDS

CAPITAL: Amsterdam

AREA:
16,033 sq. mi.
(41,526 sq km)

POPULATION: 16,150,511

MONEY:
euro

LANGUAGES: Dutch

CARS: 5,810,000

NORWAY

CAPITAL: Oslo

AREA:
125,181 sq. mi.
(324,220 sq km)

POPULATION: 4,546,123

MONEY:
Norwegian krone

LANGUAGES: Norwegian

CARS: 1,760,000

POLAND

CAPITAL: Warsaw

AREA:
120,728 sq. mi.
(312,685 sq km)

POPULATION: 38,622,660

MONEY:
zloty

LANGUAGES:
Polish

CARS: 7,520,000

PORTUGAL

CAPITAL: Lisbon

AREA:
35,672 sq. mi.
(92,391 sq km)

POPULATION: 10,102,022

MONEY:
euro

LANGUAGES: Portuguese

CARS: 2,950,000

Countries not drawn to scale.

ROMANIA

CAPITAL:
Bucharest

AREA:
91,699 sq. mi.
(237,500 sq km)

POPULATION: 22,271,839

MONEY:
leu

LANGUAGES:
Romanian, Hungarian,
German

CARS: 2,390,000

SAN MARINO

CAPITAL:
San Marino

AREA:
23.6 sq. mi. (61.2 sq km)

POPULATION: 28,119

MONEY:
euro

LANGUAGES:
Italian

CARS: 24,825

SERBIA AND MONTENEGRO

CAPITAL: Belgrade

AREA: 39,517 sq. mi.
(102,350 sq km)

POPULATION: 10,655,774

MONEY: New Yugoslav dinar

LANGUAGES:
Serbian, Albanian

CARS: 1,000,000

SLOVAKIA

CAPITAL:
Bratislava

AREA:
18,859 sq. mi.
(48,845 sq km)

POPULATION: 5,430,033

MONEY:
Slovak koruna

LANGUAGES:
Slovak (official), Hungarian

CARS: 994,000

SLOVENIA

CAPITAL:
Ljubljana

AREA:
7,820 sq. mi.
(20,253 sq km)

POPULATION: 1,935,677

MONEY:
tolar

LANGUAGES:
Slovenian, Serbo-Croatian

CARS: 657,000

SPAIN

CAPITAL: Madrid

AREA:
194,896 sq. mi.
(504,782 sq km)

POPULATION: 40,217,413

MONEY: euro

LANGUAGES:
Castilian Spanish, Catalan,
Galician

CARS: 15,300,000

SWEDEN

CAPITAL: Stockholm

AREA:
173,731 sq. mi.
(449,964 sq km)

POPULATION: 8,878,085

MONEY:
Swedish krona

LANGUAGES: Swedish

CARS: 3,700,000

SWITZERLAND

CAPITAL: Bern

AREA:
15,942 sq. mi.
(41,290 sq km)

POPULATION: 7,318,638

MONEY:
Swiss franc

LANGUAGES:
German, French, Italian

CARS: 3,320,000

UNITED KINGDOM

CAPITAL: London

AREA:
94,525 sq. mi.
(244,820 sq km)

POPULATION: 60,094,648

MONEY: British pound

LANGUAGES:
English, Welsh, Scottish form
of Gaelic

CARS: 25,590,000

VATICAN CITY

CAPITAL: Vatican City

AREA:
0.17 sq. mi. (0.44 sq km)

POPULATION: 911

MONEY: euro

LANGUAGES: Italian, Latin

CARS: data not available

📶 **internet** connect

COUNTRY STATISTICS
GO TO: go.hrw.com
KEYWORD: SG5 FactsU4
**FOR: more facts about
Europe**

Sources: Central Intelligence Agency, *The World Factbook 2003; The World Almanac and Book of Facts 2003;* population figures are 2003 estimates.

Southern Europe

Southern Europe's peninsulas, islands, mountains, and plateaus form a beautiful region. Tourists enjoy visiting this region to see its historical and cultural treasures.

Ciao. I am Paolo. I am 11 years old. I live in an apartment with my parents and my *nonna*, which is Italian for "grandma." Nonna is teaching me how to cook while she makes dinner for the family. I have no brothers or sisters, but on Sundays my aunts and uncles and three cousins all come for a big lunch. After lunch, the cousins play outside on the playground swings.

In the mornings, I walk to school with my mother before she goes to her job as a professor. My school is not too strict. We study English, Italian, and religion. After school I practice with my team at the swim club.

My favorite holiday is Christmas. On Christmas Eve we go to my other grandmother's house for a special dinner. We have smoked salmon, then grilled trout and spaghetti with mussels. Then there are special Christmas sweets: Pandoro—a cake sprinkled with sugar, and Torrone—a candy log with chocolate and nuts.

Abito a Roma, la capitale dell'Italia.

Translation: I live in Rome, the capital of Italy.

Read to Discover

1. What are the major landforms and rivers of southern Europe?
2. What are the major climate types and resources of this region?

Vocabulary

mainland
sirocco

Places

Mediterranean Sea
Strait of Gibraltar

Iberian Peninsula
Cantabrian Mountains
Pyrenees Mountains
Alps
Apennines
Aegean Sea
Peloponnesus

Ebro River
Douro River
Tagus River
Guadalquivir River
Po River
Tiber River

Reading Strategy

READING ORGANIZER Before you read, create a two-column chart. Title one column Advantages and the other column Challenges. As you read this section, list features of Southern Europe's physical geography that make life in the region easier for the people who live there. Under the other column, list those that create challenges for them.

Southern Europe: Physical-Political

Imports and Exports of Southern Europe

($ in billions)

| | 250 | 200 | 150 | 100 | 50 | 0 |

Greece   Italy   Spain and Portugal

■ Imports   ■ Exports

Source: Central Intelligence Agency, *The World Factbook, 2003*

Interpreting the Graph Which country has the fewest imports and exports?

Greece, a land of mountains and sea, is home to the ancient city of Lindos on the island of Rhodes.

Interpreting the Visual Record (Place)
Why do you think the people who founded Lindos chose this site?

Physical Features

Southern Europe is also known as Mediterranean Europe because most of its countries are on the sea's shores. The Mediterranean Sea stretches some 2,300 miles (3,700 km) from east to west. *Mediterranean* means "middle of the land" in Latin. In ancient times, the Mediterranean was considered the center of the Western world, since it is surrounded by Europe, Africa, and Asia. The narrow Strait of Gibraltar (juh-BRAWL-tuhr) links the Mediterranean to the Atlantic Ocean.

The Land Southern Europe is made up of three peninsulas. Portugal and Spain occupy one, Italy occupies another, and Greece is located on a third peninsula. Portugal and Spain are on the Iberian (eye-BRI-ee-uhn) Peninsula. Much of the peninsula is a high, rocky plateau. The Cantabrian (kan-TAY-bree-uhn) and the Pyrenees (PIR-uh-neez) Mountains form the plateau's northern edge. Italy's peninsula includes the southern Alps. A lower mountain range, the Apennines (A-puh-nynz), runs like a spine down the country's back. Islands in the central and western Mediterranean include Italy's Sicily and Sardinia (sahr-DI-nee-uh), as well as Spain's Balearic (ba-lee-AR-ik) Islands.

Greece's **mainland**, or the country's main landmass, extends into the Aegean (ee-JEE-uhn) Sea in many jagged little peninsulas. The largest one is the Peloponnesus (pe-luh-puh-NEE-suhs). Greece is mountainous and includes more than 2,000 islands. The largest island is Crete (KREET).

On all three peninsulas, coastal lowlands and river valleys provide excellent areas for growing crops and building cities. Soils on the region's uplands are thin and stony. They are also easily eroded. In this area of young mountains, earthquakes are common. They are particularly common in Greece and Italy.

The Rivers Several east-west rivers cut through the Iberian Peninsula. The Ebro River drains into the Mediterranean. The Douro, Tagus, and Guadalquivir (gwah-thahl-kee-VEER) Rivers, however, flow to the Atlantic Ocean. The Po (POH) is Italy's largest river. It creates a fertile agricultural region in northern Italy. Farther south, along the banks of the much smaller Tiber River, is the city of Rome.

✓ **READING CHECK:** (*Physical Systems*) What physical processes cause problems in parts of southern Europe?

Climate and Resources

Much of southern Europe enjoys a warm, sunny climate. Most of the rain falls during the mild winter. Rainfall sometimes causes floods and mudslides due to erosion from overgrazing and deforestation. A hot, dry wind from North Africa called a **sirocco** (suh-RAH-koh) picks up some moisture over the Mediterranean Sea. It blows over Italy during spring and summer. The Po Valley is humid. Northern Italy's Alps have a highland climate. In Spain, semiarid climates are found in pockets. Northern Spain is cool and humid.

Southern Europeans have often looked to the sea for trade. Important Mediterranean ports include Barcelona, Genoa, Naples, Piraeus (py-REE-uhs)—the port of Athens—and Valencia. Lisbon, the capital of Portugal, is an important Atlantic port. The Atlantic Ocean supports Portugal's fishing industry. Although the Mediterranean suffers from pollution, it has a wealth of seafood.

The region's resources vary. Northern Spain has iron ore mines. Greece mines bauxite, chromium, lead, and zinc. Italy and Greece quarry marble. Falling water generates hydroelectricity throughout the region's uplands. Otherwise, resources are scarce.

The region's sunny climate and natural beauty have long attracted visitors. Millions of people explore castles, museums, ruins, and other cultural sites each year. Spain's beaches help make that country one of Europe's top tourist destinations.

▲
Workers prepare to separate a giant block of marble from a wall in a quarry in Carrara, Italy.

✔ **READING CHECK:** ⟨ *Places and Regions* ⟩ What climate types and natural resources are found in the region?

Section Review 1

Define and explain: mainland, sirocco

Working with Sketch Maps On a map of southern Europe that you draw or that your teacher provides, label Greece, Italy, Spain, and Portugal. Also label the Mediterranean Sea and the Strait of Gibraltar.

Reading for the Main Idea

1. ⟨ *Places and Regions* ⟩ Why is southern Europe known as Mediterranean Europe?

2. ⟨ *Places and Regions* ⟩ What countries occupy the region's three main peninsulas?

3. ⟨ *Environment and Society* ⟩ Why might people settle in river valleys and in coastal Southern Europe?

go.hrw.com
Homework Practice Online
Keyword: SG5 HP11

Critical Thinking

4. **Drawing Inferences and Conclusions** In what ways could the region's physical geography aid the development of trade?

Organizing What You Know

5. **Summarizing** Copy the following graphic organizer. Use it to list the region's physical features, climate, and resources.

	Physical Features	Climate	Resources
Spain and Portugal			
Italy			
Greece ·			

Read to Discover

1. What were some of the achievements of the ancient Greeks?
2. What are two features of Greek culture?
3. What is Greece like today?

Vocabulary

city-states
mosaics

Places

Athens
Thessaloníki

People

Philip of Macedonia
Alexander the Great
Melina Mercouri

Reading Strategy

FOLDNOTES: THREE-PANEL FLIP CHART Create the FoldNote titled **Three-Panel Flip Chart** described in the Appendix. Title the flaps Greek History, Greek Culture, and Greece Today. As you read, write the information you learn about each topic beneath its flap.

History

The Greek islands took an early lead in the development of trade and shipping between Asia, Africa, and Europe. By about 2000 B.C. large towns and a complex civilization existed on Crete.

Ancient Greece About 800 B.C. Greek civilization arose on the mainland. The mountainous landscape there favored small, independent **city-states**. Each Greek city-state, or *polis*, was made up of a city and the land around it. Each had its own gods, laws, and form of government. The government of the city-state of Athens was the first known democracy. Democracy is the form of government in which all citizens take part. Greek philosophers, artists, architects, and writers made important contributions to Western civilization. For example, the Greeks are credited with inventing theater. Students still study ancient Greek literature and plays.

Eventually, Greece was conquered by King Philip. Philip ruled Macedonia, an area north of Greece. About 330 B.C. Philip's son, Alexander the Great, conquered Asia Minor, Egypt, Persia, and part of India. His empire combined Greek culture with influences from Asia and Africa. In the 140s B.C. Greece and Macedonia were conquered by the Roman Empire.

The Greeks believed that the Temple of Delphi—shown below—was the center of the world.

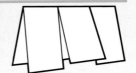

The Byzantine Empire About A.D. 400 the Roman Empire was divided into two parts. The western half was ruled from Rome. It soon fell to Germanic peoples the Romans called barbarians. Barbarian means both *illiterate* and *wanderer*. The eastern half of the Roman Empire was known as the Byzantine Empire. It was ruled from Constantinople. Constantinople was located on the shore of the Bosporus in what is now Turkey. This city—today known as Istanbul—served as a gathering place for people from Europe and Asia. The Byzantine Empire carried on the traditions of the Roman Empire for another 1,000 years. Gradually, an eastern form of Christianity developed. It was influenced by Greek language and culture. It became known as Eastern Orthodox Christianity. It is the leading form of Christianity in Greece, parts of eastern Europe, and Russia.

Turkish Rule In 1453 Constantinople was conquered by the Ottoman Turks, a people from Central Asia. Greece and most of the rest of the region came under the rule of the Ottoman Empire. It remained part of this empire for nearly 400 years. In 1821 the Greeks revolted against the Turks, and in the early 1830s Greece became independent.

Government In World War II Greece was occupied by Germany. After the war Greek communists and those who wanted a king and constitution fought a civil war. When the communists lost, the military took control. Finally, in the 1970s the Greek people voted to make their country a republic. They adopted a new constitution that created a government with a president and a prime minister.

✓ **READING CHECK:** (*Human Systems*) What were some of the achievements of ancient Greece?

The Acropolis in Athens was built in the 400s B.C. The word *acropolis* is Greek for "city at the top."

Interpreting the Visual Record

(*Human-Environment Interaction*) Why would it be important to build a city on a hill?

Culture

Turkish influences on Greek art, food, and music can still be seen. However, Turkey and Greece disagree over control of the islands and shipping lanes of the Aegean Sea.

Religion Some 98 percent of Greeks are Eastern Orthodox Christians, commonly known as Greek Orthodox. Easter is a major holiday and cause for much celebration. The traditional Easter meal is eaten on Sunday—roasted lamb, various vegetables, Easter bread, and many desserts. Because the Greek Orthodox Church has its own calendar, Christmas and Easter are usually celebrated one to two weeks later than in the West.

The people of Karpathos and their religious leaders are participating in an Easter celebration.

CONNECTING TO Math

Greek postage stamp of the Pythagorean Theorem

Greek Math and Science

Greek civilization made many contributions to world culture. We still admire Greek art and literature. Greek scholars also paved the way for modern mathematics and science.

More than 2,000 years ago Thales (THAY-leez), a philosopher, began the use of deduction in mathematical proofs. Pythagoras (puh-THAG-uh-ruhs) worked out an equation to calculate the dimensions of a right triangle. The equation became known as the Pythagorean Theorem. By 300 B.C. Euclid (YOO-kluhd) had stated the basic principles of geometry in his book *Elements*. Soon after, Archimedes (ahr-kuh-MEED-eez) calculated the value of *pi*. This value is used to measure circles and spheres. He also explained how and why the lever, a basic tool, works.

Aristarchus (ar-uh-STAHR-kuhs), an astronomer, worked out a model of the solar system. His model placed the Sun at the center of the universe. Eratosthenes (er-uh-TAHS-thuh-neez) estimated the circumference of Earth with great accuracy.

Two important figures in the life sciences were Hippocrates (hip-AHK-ruh-teez) and Aristotle (AR-uh-staht-uhl). Hippocrates was a doctor who treated medicine as a science. He understood that diseases have natural causes. Aristotle gathered information on a wide variety of plants and animals. He helped establish the importance of observation and classification in the study of nature. In many ways, the Greeks began the process of separating scientific fact from superstition.

Understanding What You Read
1. How did Greeks further the study of mathematics?
2. What were some of the Greeks' scientific achievements?

This Greek vase shows a warrior holding a shield. Kleophrades is thought to have made this vase, which dates to 500 B.C.

This mosaic of a dog bears the inscription "Good Hunting."

The Arts The ancient Greeks produced beautiful buildings, sculpture, poetry, plays, pottery, and gold jewelry. They also made **mosaics** (moh-ZAY-iks)—pictures created from tiny pieces of colored stone—that were copied throughout Europe. The folk music of Greece shares many features with the music of Turkey and Southwest Asia. In 1963 the Greek writer George Seferis won the Nobel Prize in literature.

✓ **READING CHECK:** (*Human Systems*) Why is there a Turkish influence in Greek culture?

Greece Today

When people think of Greece now, they often recall the past. For example, many have seen pictures of the Parthenon, a temple built in the 400s B.C. in Athens. It is one of the world's most photographed buildings.

Economy Greece today lags behind other European nations in economic growth. More people work in agriculture than in any other industry. However, only about 19 percent of the land can be farmed because of the mountains. For this reason old methods of farming are used rather than modern equipment. Farmers raise cotton, tobacco, vegetables, wheat, lemons, olives, and raisins.

Service and manufacturing industries are growing in Greece. However, the lack of natural resources limits industry. Tourism and shipping are key to the Greek economy.

Cities About 40 percent of Greeks live in rural areas. In the past few years, people have begun to move to the cities to find better jobs. More people now work in services than in agriculture.

Athens, in central Greece, is the capital and by far the largest city. About one third of Greece's population lives in the area in and around Athens. Athens and its seaport, Piraeus, have attracted both people and industries. Most of the country's economic growth is centered there. However, the city suffers from air pollution, which causes health problems. Air pollution also damages historical sites, such as the Parthenon. Greece's second-largest city is Thessaloníki. It is the major seaport for northern Greece.

✓ **READING CHECK:** (*Environment and Society*) How does scarcity of natural resources affect Greece's economy?

BIOGRAPHY

Melina Mercouri
(1925–1994)

Character Trait: Integrity

Melina Mercouri was among the Greek citizens who fought for personal rights. Mercouri was an international movie star. In the late 1960s, she entered politics to fight the army colonels who had taken over Greece's government. To punish her, the government took away Mercouri's citizenship. When the government later changed, Mercouri became Greece's minister of culture. Greece honored Mercouri in 1995 by putting her face on a postage stamp.

How did Melina Mercouri show her integrity?

Section Review 2

Define or identify: city-states, Philip of Macedonia, Alexander the Great, mosaics, Melina Mercouri

Working with Sketch Maps On the map you created in Section 1, label Athens and Thessaloníki. What physical features do these cities have in common? What economic activities might they share?

Reading for the Main Idea

1. (*Human Systems*) What groups influenced Greek culture?

2. (*Human Systems*) For what art forms is Greece famous?

Homework Practice Online
Keyword: SG5 HP11

Critical Thinking

3. Drawing Inferences and Conclusions How did the physical geography of this region influence the growth of major cities?

4. Finding the Main Idea On what does Greece rely to keep its economy strong?

Organizing What You Know

5. Sequencing Create a time line that documents the history of ancient Greece from 2000 B.C. to A.D. 1453.

2000 B.C. ———————————————— A.D. 1453

Read to Discover

1. What was the early history of Italy like?
2. How has Italy added to world culture?
3. What is Italy like today?

Vocabulary

pope
Renaissance
coalition
  governments

Places

Rome
Genoa
Naples
Milan
Turin
Florence

People

Leonardo da Vinci
Galileo Galilei

Reading Strategy

USING PRIOR KNOWLEDGE: ABC BRAINSTORM List the letters of the alphabet on a sheet of notebook paper. Try to think of a word or phrase about Italy for each of the letters. Then share your information with a partner. As you read this section, put a check beside the information you listed and add information for the letters that are still blank.

The Appian Way was a road from Rome to Brindisi. It was started in 312 B.C. by the emperor Claudius.

Interpreting the Visual Record

(Human-Environment Interaction) **How do you think this road has withstood more than 2,000 years of use?**

History

About 750 B.C. a tribe known as the Latins established the city of Rome on the Tiber River. Over time, these Romans conquered the rest of Italy. They then began to expand their rule to lands outside Italy.

Roman Empire At its height about A.D. 100, the Roman Empire stretched westward to what is now Spain and Portugal and northward to England and Germany. The Balkans, Turkey, parts of Southwest Asia, and coastal North Africa were all part of the empire. Roman laws, roads, engineering, and the Latin language could be found throughout this huge area. The Roman army kept order, and people could travel safely throughout the empire. Trade prospered.

The Romans made advances in engineering, including roads and aqueducts—canals that transported water. They also learned how to build domes and arches. Romans also produced great works of art and literature.

About A.D. 200, however, the Roman Empire began to weaken. The western part, with its capital in Rome, fell in A.D. 476. The eastern part, the Byzantine Empire, lasted until 1453.

Roman influences in the world can still be seen today. Latin developed into the modern languages of French, Italian, Portuguese, Romanian, and Spanish. Many English words have Latin origins as well. Roman laws and political ideas have influenced the governments and legal systems of many modern countries.

Christianity began in the Roman province of Judaea (modern Israel and the West Bank). It then spread through the Roman Empire. Some early Christians were persecuted for refusing to worship the traditional Roman gods. However, in the early A.D. 300s the Roman emperor, Constantine, adopted Christianity. It quickly became the main religion of the empire. The **pope**—the bishop of Rome—is the head of the Roman Catholic Church.

The Renaissance Beginning in the 1300s a new era of learning began in Italy. It was known as the **Renaissance** (re-nuh-SAHNS). In French this word means "rebirth." During the Renaissance, Italians rediscovered the work of ancient Roman and Greek writers. Scholars applied reason and experimented to advance the sciences. Artists pioneered new techniques. Leonardo da Vinci, painter of the *Mona Lisa*, was also a sculptor, engineer, architect, and scientist. Another Italian, Galileo Galilei, perfected the telescope and experimented with gravity.

Christopher Columbus opened up the Americas to European colonization. Although Spain paid for his voyages, Columbus was an Italian from the city of Genoa. The name *America* comes from another Italian explorer, Amerigo Vespucci.

Government Italy was divided into many small states until the late 1800s. Today Italy's central government is a democracy with an elected parliament. Italy has had many changes in leadership in recent years. This has happened because no political party has won a majority of votes in Italian elections. As a result, political parties must form **coalition governments**. A coalition government is one in which several parties join together to run the country. Unfortunately, these coalitions usually do not last long.

✓ **READING CHECK:** (*Human Systems*) How is the Italian government different from that of the United States?

Leonardo da Vinci painted the *Mona Lisa* about 1503–06.

Interpreting the Visual Record **Why do you think Leonardo's painting became famous?**

Culture

People from other places have influenced Italian culture. During the Renaissance, many Jews who had been expelled from Spain moved to Italian cities. Jews often had to live in segregated areas called ghettoes. Today immigrants have arrived from former Italian colonies in Africa. Others have come from the eastern Mediterranean and the Balkans.

Religion and Food Most Italians are Roman Catholics, but the number of practicing Catholics is declining. The leadership of the church is still based in the Vatican in Rome. Christmas and Easter are major holidays in Italy. Italians also celebrate All Souls' Day on November 2 by cleaning and decorating their relatives' graves.

Italians enjoy a range of regional foods. Recipes are influenced by the history and crops of each area. In the south, Italians eat a Mediterranean diet of olives, bread, and fish. Dishes are flavored with lemons from Greece and spices from Africa. Tomatoes, originally from the Americas, have become an important part of the diet. Some Italian foods, such as pizza, are popular in the United States. Modern pizza originated in Naples. Northern Italians eat more rice, butter, cheeses, and mushrooms than southern Italians.

The Arts The ancient Romans created beautiful glassware and jewelry as well as marble and bronze sculptures. During the Renaissance, Italy again became a center for art, particularly painting and sculpture. Italian artists discovered ways to make their paintings more lifelike. They did this by creating the illusion of three dimensions. Italian writers like Francesco Petrarch and Giovanni Boccaccio wrote some of the most important literature of the Renaissance. More recently, Italian composers have written great operas. Today, Italian designers, actors, and filmmakers are celebrated worldwide.

✓ **READING CHECK:** (*Human Systems*) What are some examples of Italian culture?

In Rome people attend mass in St. Peter's Square, Vatican City. Vatican City is an independent state within Rome.

Italy Today

Italy is slightly smaller than Florida and Georgia combined, with a population of about 58 million. A shared language, the Roman Catholic Church, and strong family ties continue to bind Italians together.

Economy After its defeat in World War II, Italy rebuilt its industries in the north. Rich soil and plenty of water make the north Italy's "breadbasket," or wheat growing area. Italy's most valuable crop is grapes. Although grapes are grown throughout the country, northern Italy produces the best crops. These grapes help make Italy the world's largest producer of wine. Tourists are also important to Italy's economy. They visit northern and central Italy to see ancient ruins and Renaissance art. Southern Italy remains poorer with lower crop yields. Industrialization there also lags behind the north. Tourist resorts, however, are growing in the south and promise to help the economy.

Cities The northern cities of Milan, Turin, and Genoa are important industrial centers. Their location near the center of Europe helps companies sell products to foreign customers. Also in the north are two popular tourist sites. One is Venice, which is famous for its romantic canals and beautiful buildings. The other is Florence, a center of art and culture. Rome, the capital, is located in central Italy. Naples, the largest city in southern Italy, is a major manufacturing center and port.

✔ **READING CHECK:** *Environment and Society* What geographic factors influence Italy's economy?

Italy

Country	Population/ Growth Rate	Life Expectancy	Literacy Rate	Per Capita GDP
Italy	57,998,353 .1%	76, male 83, female	98%	$25,000
United States	290,342,554 0.9%	74, male 80, female	97%	$37,600

Source: Central Intelligence Agency, *The World Factbook 2003*

Interpreting the Chart **What is the difference in the growth rate of Italy and the United States?**

Section Review 3

Define or identify: pope, Renaissance, Leonardo da Vinci, Galileo Galilei, coalition governments

Working with Sketch Maps On the map you created in Section 2, label Florence, Genoa, Milan, Naples, Rome, and Turin. Why are they important?

Reading for the Main Idea

1. *Human Systems* What were some of the important contributions of the Romans?

2. *Human Systems* What are some art forms for which Italy is well known?

Critical Thinking

3. Finding the Main Idea Which of Italy's physical features encourage trade? Which geographical features make trading difficult?

4. Analyzing Information Why is the northern part of Italy known as the country's "breadbasket"?

Organizing What You Know

5. Finding the Main Idea Copy the following graphic organizer. Use it to describe the movement of goods and ideas to and from Italy during the early days of trade and exploration.

	⇨	Italy	⇨	

Read to Discover

1. What were some major events in the history of Spain and Portugal?
2. What are the cultures of Spain and Portugal like?
3. What are Spain and Portugal like today?

Vocabulary

Moors
dialect
cork

Places

Lisbon
Madrid
Barcelona

People

Philip II
General Francisco Franco
Pablo Picasso

Reading Strategy

VENN DIAGRAM   Before you read, create a Venn diagram for Spain and Portugal. Draw two overlapping circles. Label one circle Spain and the other Portugal. As you read, fill in the circles with unique details about each country. Where the circles overlap, write down information about what the countries have in common.

These windmills in Consuegra, Spain, provided water for the people of the region.

Interpreting the Visual Record

Human-Environment Interaction **How do you think windmills pump water?**

History

Beautiful paintings of bison and other animals are found in caves in northern Spain. Some of the best known are at Altamira and were created as early as 16,000 B.C. Some cave paintings are much older. These paintings give us exciting clues about the early people who lived here.

Ancient Times Spain has been important to Mediterranean trade for several thousand years. First, the Greeks and then the Phoenicians, or Carthaginians, built towns on Spain's southern and eastern coasts. Then, about 200 B.C. Iberia became a part of the Roman Empire and adopted the Latin language.

The Muslim North Africans, or **Moors**, conquered most of the Iberian Peninsula in the A.D. 700s. Graceful Moorish buildings, with their lacy patterns and archways, are still found in Spanish and Portuguese cities. This is particularly true in the old Moorish city of Granada in southern Spain.

Great Empires From the early 900s to the 1400s Christian rulers fought to take back the peninsula. In 1492 King Ferdinand and Queen Isabella conquered the kingdom of Granada, the last Moorish outpost in Spain. That same year, they sponsored the voyage of Christopher Columbus to the Americas. Spain soon established a large empire in the Americas.

The Portuguese also sent out explorers. Some of them sailed around Africa to India. Others crossed the Atlantic and claimed Brazil. In the 1490s the Roman Catholic pope drew a line to divide the world between Spain and Portugal. Western lands, except for Brazil, were given to Spain, and eastern lands to Portugal.

With gold and agricultural products from their American colonies, and spices and silks from Asia, Spain and Portugal grew rich. In 1588 Philip II, king of Spain and Portugal, sent a huge armada, or fleet, to invade England. The Spanish were defeated, and Spain's power began to decline. However, most Spanish colonies in the Americas did not win independence until the early 1800s.

Government In the 1930s the king of Spain lost power. Spain became a workers' republic. The new government tried to reduce the role of the church and to give the nobles' lands to farmers. However, conservative military leaders under General Francisco Franco resisted. A civil war was fought from 1936 to 1939 between those who supported Franco and those who wanted a democratic form of government. Franco's forces won the war and ruled Spain until 1975. Today Spain is a democracy, with a national assembly and prime minister. The king also plays a modest role as head of state.

Portugal, like Spain, was long ruled by a monarch. In the early 1900s the monarchy was overthrown. Portugal became a democracy. However, the army later overthrew the government, and a dictator took control. A revolution in the 1970s overthrew the dictatorship. For a few years disagreements between the new political parties brought violence. Portugal is now a democracy with a president and prime minister.

✓ **READING CHECK:** (*Human Systems*) How did Spain and Portugal move from unlimited to limited governments?

The interior of the Great Mosque in Córdoba, Spain, shows the lasting beauty of Moorish architecture. A cathedral was built within the mosque after Christians took back the city.

Interpreting the Visual Record Why do you think arches are important in certain building designs?

Spain and Portugal

Country	Population/ Growth Rate	Life Expectancy	Literacy Rate	Per Capita GDP
Portugal	10,102,022 0.2%	73, male 80, female	93%	$18,000
Spain	40,217,413 0.2%	76, male 83, female	98%	$20,700
United States	290,342,554 0.9%	74, male 80, female	97%	$37,600

Source: Central Intelligence Agency, *The World Factbook 2003*

Interpreting the Chart How do the growth rates of these countries compare?

Culture

The most widely understood Spanish **dialect** (DY-uh-lekt), or variation of a language, is Castilian. This is the form spoken in central Spain. Spanish and Portuguese are not the only languages spoken on the Iberian Peninsula, however. Catalan is spoken in northeastern Spain (Catalonia). Basque is spoken by an ethnic group living in the Pyrenees.

Spain faces a problem of unrest among the Basque people. The government has given the Basque area limited self-rule. However, a small group of Basque separatists continue to use violence to protest Spanish control.

Food and Festivals Spanish and Portuguese foods are typical of the Mediterranean region. Many recipes use olives and olive oil, lemons, wheat, wine, and fish. Foods the explorers brought back from the Americas—such as tomatoes and peppers—are also important.

Both Spain and Portugal remain strongly Roman Catholic. The two countries celebrate major Christian holidays like Christmas and Easter. As in Italy, each village has a patron saint whose special day is the occasion for a fiesta, or festival. A bull fight, or *corrida*, may take place during the festival.

The Arts Spanish and Portuguese art reflects the many peoples who have lived in the region. The decoration of Spanish porcelain recalls Islamic art from North Africa. The sad melodies of the Portuguese fado singers and the intense beat of Spanish flamenco dancing also show African influences. In the 1900s the Spanish painter Pablo Picasso boldly experimented with shape and perspective. He became one of the most famous artists of modern times.

✔ **READING CHECK:** (**Human Systems**) How has the mixture of different ethnic groups created some conflict in Spanish society?

FOCUS ON CULTURE

Party Time!

One of Seville's major events, La Feria de Abril, or "The April Festival," features two of Spain's favorite things—horses and flamenco. Thousands of tents decorated with paper lanterns draw dancers and partygoers. Each day a parade of horses and horse-drawn carriages winds through the fairgrounds.

What role do dance or other arts play in your community's festivals?

Spain and Portugal Today

Both Spain and Portugal belong to the European Union (EU). The EU allows free trade, travel, and exchange of workers among its members. The economies of Spain and Portugal have been growing rapidly. However, they remain poorer than the leading EU countries.

Agricultural products of Spain and Portugal include wine, fruit, olives, olive oil, and **cork**. Cork is the bark stripped from a certain type of oak tree. Spain exports oranges from the east, beef from the north, and lamb from ranches on the Meseta, or central plateau. Portugal also makes and exports clothing and timber products. Spain makes cars and trucks, and most of its industry is located in the north. Tourism is also an important part of the Spanish economy. This is particularly true along Spain's coasts and on the Balearic Islands.

Portugal's capital and largest city is Lisbon. It is located on the Atlantic coast at the mouth of the Tagus River. Madrid, Spain's capital and largest city, is located inland on the Meseta. Spain's second-largest city is the Mediterranean port of Barcelona.

✓ **READING CHECK:** (*Places and Regions*) What are Spain and Portugal like today?

Homework Practice Online
Keyword: SG5 HP11

Section Review 4

Define or identify: Moors, Philip II, General Francisco Franco, dialect, Pablo Picasso, cork

Working with Sketch Maps On the map that you created in Section 3, label Lisbon, Madrid, and Barcelona. How are Lisbon and Barcelona different from Madrid?

Reading for the Main Idea

1. (*Human Systems*) How do the performing arts of this region reflect different cultures?

2. (*Human Systems*) How have Spain and Portugal worked to improve their economies?

Critical Thinking

3. **Analyzing Information** Which groups influenced the culture of Spain and Portugal?

4. **Summarizing** How was the government of Spain organized during the 1900s?

Organizing What You Know

5. **Sequencing** Copy the following graphic organizer. Use it to list important events in the history of Spain and Portugal from the 700s to the 1600s.

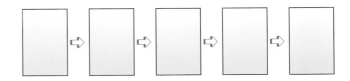

CHAPTER 11 · Review and Practice

Define and Identify
Identify each of the following:

1. mainland
2. sirocco
3. city-states
4. Alexander the Great
5. mosaics
6. pope
7. Renaissance
8. Leonardo da Vinci
9. coalition governments
10. Moors
11. dialect
12. Pablo Picasso
13. cork

Review the Main Ideas

14. What peninsulas do the countries of southern Europe occupy?
15. What features of southern Europe's physical geography have caused problems for the people who live there?
16. What are some of southern Europe's major port cities?
17. What are some of the accomplishments of the ancient Greeks?
18. What is the major religion of Greece?
19. How can Roman influence still be seen today?

20. What are the major economic differences between northern and southern Italy?
21. In what arts have many Italians excelled?
22. What was Spain's empire like? When did Spain's power begin to decline?
23. What languages are spoken in Spain and Portugal?
24. What ethnic group has used violence to protest Spanish control?

Think Critically

25. **Drawing Inferences and Conclusions** In what ways do you think the geography of southern Europe made trade and exploration possible?
26. **Summarizing** What parts of Greek culture have been most strongly influenced by Turkish customs? Why is this the case?
27. **Drawing Inferences and Conclusions** Recall what you have learned about the Roman Empire. What about the Italian peninsula made it a good location for a Mediterranean empire?
28. **Drawing Inferences and Conclusions** How are agricultural products of southern Europe used in food?
29. **Finding the Main Idea** Why do many tourists continue to visit historical cities in southern Europe?

Map Activity

30. On a separate sheet of paper, match the letters on the map with their correct labels.

Alps	Po River
Apennines	Tiber River
Aegean Sea	Naples
Peloponnesus	Sicily
Ebro River	Meseta

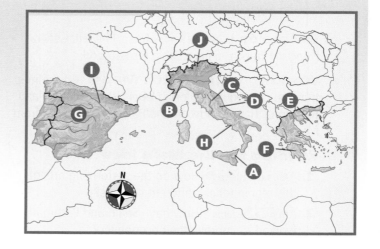

Writing Activity

Find a recording of Portuguese fado music. Then write a review that explains what the lyrics of the songs reveal about Portuguese culture. Be sure to use standard grammar, spelling, sentence structure, and punctuation in your review.

Social Studies Skills Practice

Interpreting Maps

You have read that starting in the 900s, Christian rulers began taking back the Iberian Peninsula from the Moors. Study the map of this re-conquest. Then answer the questions.

The Re-conquest of Spain

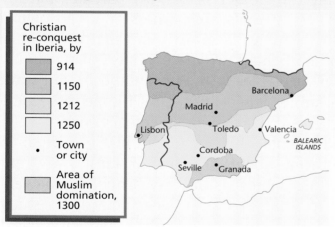

Christian re-conquest in Iberia, by

- 914
- 1150
- 1212
- 1250
- Town or city
- Area of Muslim domination, 1300

1. In what part of the Iberian Peninsula did the re-conquest begin? In what direction did it move?
2. By what year was Madrid again in Christian hands?
3. During what time period was the smallest amount of land taken from the Moors?

4. From the map, what can you assume about the political connections between Spain and Portugal during these centuries?

Analyzing Primary Sources

Read the following quote from a popular flamenco singer named Schwarma. Then answer the questions.

"For many years flamenco was seen as very bad in Spain. It came from the south, the poor region, and nobody was interested. It came from a sector of people who were poor, who lived outside the cities. Now it's just the opposite. Flamenco's very important. The Spanish people have recovered important cultural roots."

1. In what part of Spain did flamenco originate?
2. Why did many Spaniards ignore flamenco?
3. How may changes in Spain's settlement patterns affect flamenco's popularity?
4. Why does Schwarma think that flamenco is important?

CHAPTER 12

West-Central Europe

West-central Europe is an important agricultural, industrial, and manufacturing area. The countries of this region export many different products. They are some of the richest countries in the world.

Gruss dich (Hello). My name is Lizzi (LEE-zee). I live in southern Germany in the village of Deutenhausen. Lizzi is short for Felicitas—my grandmother's name—which means "happiness." I am in the eighth grade at the gymnasium, or high school. I live in a big house on a farm with my three older sisters, my parents, and my grandmother. My parents are farmers and also own a restaurant. In summer, I make sure the cows have enough water and I chase the geese home. I also help my parents chop vegetables in the restaurant. I don't want to be a farmer when I grow up! I hope to become a doctor and work in an emergency room.

At about 7:30, I take the bus to school in Weilheim, about 2 miles (3 km) away. My favorite subject is art. My school is not very strict, and we do not wear uniforms. I study German, geography, English, and Latin. Next year I will start classical Greek.

After school is over at 12:30, I go home to have lunch with my grandmother. Then, I play with my friends outdoors, even when it rains.

Willkommen in Deutschland. Wie geht es dir?

◄

Translation: Welcome to Germany! How are you?

Section 1 Physical Geography

Read to Discover

1. Where are the area's major landform regions?
2. What role do rivers, canals, and harbors play in the region?
3. What are west-central Europe's major resources?

Vocabulary

navigable
loess

Places

Northern European Plain
Pyrenees
Alps
Seine River
Rhine River
Danube River
North Sea
Mediterranean Sea
English Channel
Bay of Biscay

Reading Strategy

READING ORGANIZER Before you read, create a three-column chart. Title the columns Physical Features, Climate, and Resources. As you read this section, write down what you learn about those characteristics of West-Central Europe.

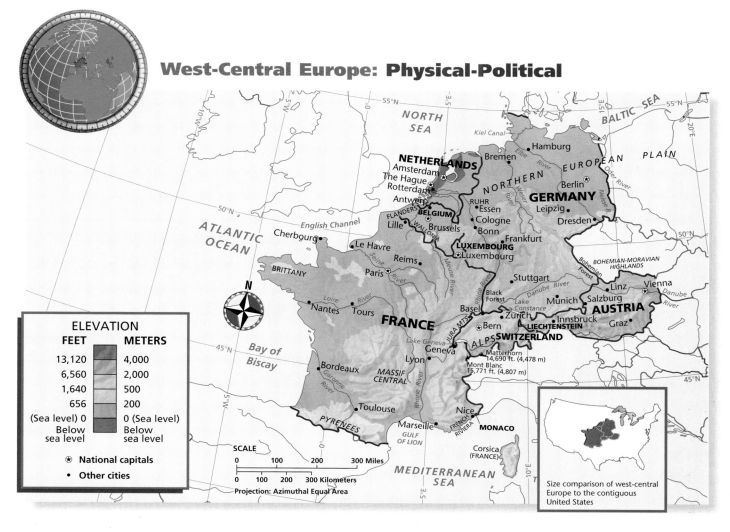

West-Central Europe: Physical-Political

ELEVATION

FEET	METERS
13,120	4,000
6,560	2,000
1,640	500
656	200
(Sea level) 0	0 (Sea level)
Below sea level	Below sea level

✸ National capitals
• Other cities

SCALE
0 100 200 300 Miles
0 100 200 300 Kilometers
Projection: Azimuthal Equal Area

Size comparison of west-central Europe to the contiguous United States

The Rhine River has been an important transportation route for many centuries.

Interpreting the Visual Record

(Movement) **How might the Rhine influence the location of German industry?**

The Alps have many large glaciers, lakes, and valleys.

Physical Features

West-central Europe includes France, Germany, Belgium, the Netherlands, Luxembourg, Switzerland, and Austria. Belgium, the Netherlands, and Luxembourg are called the Benelux countries. The word Benelux is a combination of the first letters of each country's name. They are also sometimes called the Low Countries. Large areas of Switzerland and Austria lie in the Alps mountain range. For this reason, they are called the Alpine countries.

Lowlands The main landform regions of west-central Europe are arranged like a fan. The outer edge of the fan is the Northern European Plain. Brittany, a peninsula jutting from northern France, rises slightly above the plain. In Belgium and the Netherlands, the Northern European Plain dips below sea level.

Uplands Toward the middle of the fan a wide band of uplands begins at the Pyrenees (PIR-uh-neez) Mountains. Another important uplands region is the Massif Central (ma-SEEF sahn-TRAHL) in France. Most of the southern two thirds of Germany is hilly. The Schwarzwald (SHFAHRTS-vahlt), or Black Forest, occupies the southwestern corner of Germany's uplands region.

Mountains At the center of the fan are the Alps, Europe's highest mountain range. Many peaks in the Alps reach heights of more than 14,000 feet (4,267 m). The highest peak, France's Mont Blanc (mawn BLAHN), reaches to 15,771 feet (4,807 m). Because of their high elevations, the Alps have large glaciers and frequent avalanches. During the Ice Age, glaciers scooped great chunks of rock out of the mountains, carving peaks such as the Matterhorn.

✔ **READING CHECK:** (*Places and Regions*) What are the area's major landforms?

Climate and Waterways

West-central Europe's marine west coast climate makes the region a pleasant place to live. Winters can be cold and rainy, but summers are mild. However, areas that lie farther from the warming influence of the North Atlantic are colder. For example, central Germany receives more snow than western France. The Alps have a highland climate.

Snowmelt from the Alps feeds west-central Europe's many **navigable** rivers. Navigable rivers are deep enough and wide enough to be used by ships. France has four major rivers: the Seine (SEN), the Loire

(LWAHR), the Garonne (gah-RAWN), and the Rhone (ROHN). Germany has five major rivers: the Rhine (RYN), the Danube (DAN-yoob), the Elbe (EL-buh), the Oder (OH-duhr), and the Weser (VAY-zuhr). These rivers and the region's many canals are important for trade and travel. Many large harbor cities are located where rivers flow into the North Sea, Mediterranean Sea, English Channel, or Bay of Biscay. The region's heavily indented coastline has hundreds of excellent harbors.

✓ **READING CHECK:** (*Environment and Society*) What economic role do rivers, canals, and harbors play in west-central Europe?

Resources

Most of the forests that once covered west-central Europe were cut down centuries ago. The fields that remained are now some of the most productive in the world. Germany's plains are rich in **loess** (LES)—fine, wind-blown soil deposits. Germany and France produce grapes for some of the world's finest wines. Switzerland's Alpine pastures support dairy cattle.

The distribution of west-central Europe's mineral resources is uneven. Germany and France have deposits of iron ore but must import oil. Energy resources are generally in short supply in the region. However, there are deposits of coal in Germany and natural gas in the Netherlands. Nuclear power helps fill the need for energy, particularly in France and Belgium. Alpine rivers provide hydroelectric power in Switzerland and Austria. Natural beauty is perhaps the Alpine countries' most valuable natural resource, attracting millions of tourists every year.

▲ The Grindelwald Valley in Switzerland has excellent pastures.

✓ **READING CHECK:** (*Places and Regions*) What geographic factors contribute to the economy of the region?

Section Review 1

Define and explain: navigable, loess

Working with Sketch Maps On a map of west-central Europe that you draw or that your teacher provides, label the following: the Northern European Plain, Alps, North Sea, Mediterranean Sea, English Channel, and Bay of Biscay.

Reading for the Main Idea

1. (*Places and Regions*) What are the landform regions of west-central Europe?

2. (*Places and Regions*) What type of climate dominates this region?

Critical Thinking

3. Making Generalizations and Predictions What might be the advantages of having many good harbors and navigable rivers?

4. Drawing Inferences and Conclusions How do you think an uneven distribution of resources has affected this region?

Organizing What You Know

5. Categorizing Copy the following graphic organizer. Use it to describe the major rivers of west-central Europe. Add rows as needed.

River	Country/Countries	Flows into. . .

go.hrw.com Homework Practice Online Keyword: SG5 HP12

Section 2 France

Read to Discover

1. Which foreign groups affected the historical development of France?
2. What are the main features of French culture?
3. What products does France export?

Vocabulary

medieval
NATO
impressionism

Places

Brittany
Normandy
Paris
Marseille
Nice

People

Franks
Charlemagne
Napoléon Bonaparte

Reading Strategy

READING ORGANIZER Before you read, create a spider map. Label the map France. Create a leg for each heading in the section. As you read the section, fill in the map with details about each heading.

In this illustration messengers inform Charlemagne of a recent military victory.

History

France has been occupied by people from many other parts of Europe. In ancient times, France was part of a region known as Gaul. Thousands of years ago, people moved from eastern Europe into Gaul. These people spoke Celtic languages related to modern Welsh and Gaelic. Breton is a Celtic language still spoken in the region of Brittany.

Early History About 600 B.C. the Greeks set up colonies on Gaul's southern coast. Several centuries later, the Romans conquered Gaul. They introduced Roman law and government to the area. The Romans also established a Latin-based language that developed into French.

Roman rule lasted until the A.D. 400s. A group of Germanic people known as the Franks then conquered much of Gaul. It is from these people that France takes its name. Charlemagne was the Franks' greatest ruler. He dreamed of building a Christian empire that would be as great as the old Roman Empire. In honor of this, the pope crowned Charlemagne Emperor of the Romans in

A.D. 800. During his rule, Charlemagne did much to strengthen government and improve education and the arts in Europe.

The Franks divided Charlemagne's empire after his death. Invading groups attacked from many directions. The Norsemen, or Normans, were one of these groups. They came from northern Europe. The area of western France where the Normans settled is known today as Normandy.

The period from the collapse of the Roman Empire to about 1500 is called the Middle Ages, or **medieval** period. The word medieval comes from the Latin words *medium*, meaning "middle," and *aevum*, meaning "age." During much of this period kings in Europe were not very powerful. They depended on cooperation from nobles, some of whom were almost as powerful as kings.

In 1066 a noble, the duke of Normandy, conquered England, becoming its king. As a result, the kings of England also ruled part of France. In the 1300s the king of England tried to claim the throne of France. This led to the Hundred Years' War, which lasted from 1337 to 1453. Eventually, French armies drove the English out of France. The French kings then slowly increased their power over the French nobles.

During the Middle Ages the Roman Catholic Church created a sense of unity among many Europeans. Many tall, impressive cathedrals were built during this time. Perhaps the most famous is the Cathedral of Notre Dame in Paris. It took almost 200 years to build.

Revolution and Napoléon's Empire From the 1500s to the 1700s France built a global empire. The French established colonies in the Americas, Asia, and Africa. During this period most French people lived in poverty and had few rights. In 1789 the French Revolution began. The French overthrew their king and established an elected government. About 10 years later a brilliant general named Napoléon Bonaparte took power. As he gained control, he took the title of emperor. Eventually, Napoléon conquered most of Europe. Napoléon built new roads throughout France, reformed the French educational system, and established the metric system of measurement. In 1815 an alliance including Austria, Great Britain, Prussia, and Russia finally defeated Napoléon. The French king regained the throne.

World Wars During World War I (1914–18) the German army controlled parts of northern and eastern France. In the early years of World War II, Germany defeated France and occupied the northern and western parts of the country. In 1944, Allied armies including U.S., British, and Canadian soldiers landed in Normandy and drove the Germans out. However, after two wars in 30 years France was devastated. Cities, factories, bridges, railroad lines, and train stations had been destroyed. The North Atlantic Treaty Organization, or **NATO**, was formed in 1949 with France as a founding member. This military alliance was created to defend Western Europe against future attacks.

French and English knights clash in this depiction of the Hundred Years' War.

Napoléon Bonaparte became the ruler of France and conquered most of Europe.

The euro replaced the currencies of most of the individual EU countries.

Interpreting the Visual Record *Region*
What are the advantages of a shared currency?

Government In the 1950s and 1960s most French colonies in Asia and Africa achieved independence. However, France still controls several small territories around the world. Today, France is a republic with a parliament and an elected president. France is also a founding member of the European Union (EU). France is gradually replacing its currency, the franc, with the EU currency, the euro.

✓ **READING CHECK:** (*Human Systems*) Which foreign groups have affected France's historical development?

Culture

About 85 percent of French people are Roman Catholic, and 5 to 10 percent are Muslims. Almost all French citizens speak French. However, small populations of Bretons in the northwest and Basques in the southwest speak other languages. In Provence-Alpes-Côte d'Azur and Languedoc-Roussillon in the south and on the island of Corsica, some people speak regional dialects along with French. Immigrants from former colonies in Africa, the Caribbean, and Southeast Asia also influence French culture through their own styles of food, clothing, music, and art.

Customs In southern France people eat Mediterranean foods like wheat, olives and olive oil, cheeses, and garlic. In the north food is more likely to be prepared with butter, herbs, and mushrooms. Wine is produced in many French regions, and France produces more than 400 different cheeses. French people celebrate many festivals, including Bastille Day on July 14. On this date in 1789 a mob stormed the Bastille, a royal prison in Paris. The French recognize this event as the beginning of the French Revolution.

Workers harvest grapes at a vineyard in the Rhone Valley near Lyon.

Interpreting the Visual Record

(*Human-Environment Interaction*) **Has modern technology changed the grape-growing process?**

The Arts and Literature France has a respected tradition of poetry, philosophy, music, and the visual arts. In the late 1800s and early 1900s France was the center of an artistic movement called **impressionism**. Impressionist artists tried to capture the rippling of light rather than an exact, realistic image. Famous impressionists include Monet, Renoir, and Degas. French painters, like Cézanne and Matisse, influenced styles of modern painting. Today, France is a world leader in the arts and film industry.

✓ **READING CHECK:** (*Human Systems*) How did French art affect the world?

France

Country	Population/ Growth Rate	Life Expectancy	Literacy Rate	Per Capita GDP
France	60,180,529 0.4%	75, male 83, female	99%	$26,000
United States	290,342,554 0.9%	74, male 80, female	97%	$37,600

Sources: Central Intelligence Agency, *The World Factbook 2003*

Interpreting the Chart **How do France's life expectancy and literacy rate compare to those of the United States?**

France Today

France is a major agricultural and industrial country. Its resources, labor force, and location in the heart of Europe have helped spur economic growth. France exports wheat, olives, wine, and cheeses as well as other dairy products. French factories produce cars, airplanes, shoes, clothing, machinery, and chemicals. France's largest city is Paris, which has nearly 10 million people in its metropolitan area. Other major cities include Marseille, Nice, Lyon, and Lille. France's major cities are linked by high-speed trains and excellent highways.

✓ **READING CHECK:** (*Human Systems*) What are some products that France exports?

go.hrw.com **Homework Practice Online** Keyword: SG5 HP12

Section Review 2

Define or identify: Franks, Charlemagne, medieval, Napoléon Bonaparte, NATO, impressionism

Working with Sketch Maps On the map you created in Section 1, label Brittany, Normandy, Paris, Marseille, and Nice.

Reading for the Main Idea

1. (*Human Systems*) What were the main periods of French history?

2. (*Human Systems*) What are the main features of French culture?

Critical Thinking

3. Finding the Main Idea What were some long-lasting achievements of Charlemagne and Napoléon?

4. Summarizing What is the French economy like?

Organizing What You Know

5. Identifying Cause and Effect Copy the following graphic organizer. Use it to list the causes and effects of the Hundred Years' War.

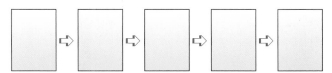

Read to Discover

1. What effects have wars had on Germany?
2. What are Germany's major contributions to world culture?
3. How did the division of Germany affect its economy?

Vocabulary

Reformation
Holocaust
chancellor

Places

Berlin
Bonn
Essen
Frankfurt
Munich
Hamburg
Cologne

People

Adolf Hitler
Johannes Gutenberg
Ludwig van Beethoven
Richard Wagner

Reading Strategy

FOLDNOTES: TRI-FOLD Create the FoldNote titled **Tri-Fold** as described in the Appendix. Label the columns Know, Want, and Learn. In the "Know" column, write down some facts that you already know about Germany. Then write down what you want to know. After you read the section, summarize what you have learned in the "Learn" column.

This medieval castle overlooks a German town.

Interpreting the Visual Record *Place*

What geographic features made this a good place to build a fortress?

▼

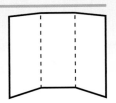

History

Many Germans are descendants of tribes that migrated from northern Europe in ancient times. The Romans conquered the western and southern fringes of the region. They called this land Germania, from the name of one of the tribes that lived there.

The Holy Roman Empire When the Roman Empire collapsed, the Franks became the most important tribe in Germany. The lands ruled by the Frankish king Charlemagne in the early 800s included most of what is now Germany. Charlemagne's empire was known as the Holy Roman Empire.

Reformation and Unification During the 1500s Germany was the center of the **Reformation**—a movement to reform Christianity. The reformers were called Protestants. Protestants rejected many practices of the Roman Catholic Church. At the time, Germany was made up of many small states. Each state was ruled by a prince who answered to the Holy Roman emperor. Many of the princes became Protestants. This angered the Holy Roman emperor, who was Catholic. He sent armies against the princes. Although the princes won the right to choose the religion of their states, conflict continued. This conflict eventually led to the Thirty Years' War (1618–48). This war was costly. Many towns were destroyed and nearly one third of the population died. Germany remained divided for more than 200 years. In the late 1800s Prussia, the strongest state, united Germany.

World Wars In 1914 national rivalries and a conflict in the Balkans led to World War I. Austria, Germany, and the Ottoman Empire, later joined by Bulgaria, fought against Britain, France, and Russia, later joined by Italy and the United States. By 1918 Germany and its allies were defeated.

During the 1920s Austrian war veteran Adolf Hitler led a new political party in Germany called the Nazis. The Nazis took power in 1933. In the late 1930s Germany invaded Austria, Czechoslovakia, and finally Poland, beginning World War II. By 1942 Germany and Italy had conquered most of Europe. The Nazis forced many people from the occupied countries into concentration camps to be enslaved or killed. About 6 million Jews and millions of other people were murdered in a mass killing called the **Holocaust**.

To defeat Germany, several countries formed an alliance. These Allies included Britain, the Soviet Union, the United States, and many others. The Allies defeated Germany in 1945. Germany and its capital, Berlin, were divided into Soviet, French, British, and U.S. occupation zones. Britain, France, and the United States later combined their zones to create a democratic West Germany with its capital at Bonn. In its zone, the Soviet Union set up the Communist country of East Germany with an unlimited totalitarian government. Its capital became East Berlin; however, West Berlin became part of West Germany. In 1961 the East German government built the Berlin Wall across the city to stop East Germans from escaping to the West.

Reunification and Modern Government West Germany's roads, cities, railroads, and industries were rebuilt after the war with U.S. financial aid. East Germany was also rebuilt, but it was not as prosperous as West Germany. Unlike the West German government, the East German government allowed people very little freedom. Also, its command economy—managed by the government—was less productive than the free enterprise, market system of West Germany. In the late 1980s East Germans and people throughout Eastern Europe demanded democratic reform. In 1989 the Berlin Wall was torn down. In 1990 East and West Germany reunited. Germany's capital again became Berlin. Today, all Germans enjoy democratic rights. A parliament elects the president and prime minister, or **chancellor**. Germany is a member of the EU and NATO.

✓ **READING CHECK:** (*Human Systems*) How were the economies of East and West Germany organized following World War II?

▲
German youth salute Adolf Hitler in Nürnberg in 1938.

▲
For nearly 30 years the Berlin Wall separated East and West Berlin. Many people in West Berlin protested by painting graffiti on the wall.

Interpreting the Visual Record Why would the government make the wall solid instead of a barrier that would allow people visual access?

Ludwig van Beethoven
(1770–1827)

Character Trait: Pursuit of Excellence

Perhaps the greatest composer who ever lived, Beethoven (BAYT-hoh-vuhn) didn't let a physical handicap keep him from writing glorious music. In his many songs and symphonies, Beethoven added powerful, intense emotion to established musical styles. Gradually Beethoven lost his hearing, but continued to compose. Beethoven's last works, which he could never hear performed, are often described as the most beautiful of his long career.

How did Beethoven pursue excellence?

Culture

About 34 percent of Germans are Roman Catholic, and 38 percent are Protestant. Most other Germans have no religious association. Many of these people are from eastern Germany, where the communist government suppressed religion from 1945 to 1990.

Diversity About 90 percent of Germany's inhabitants are ethnic Germans. However, significant numbers of Turks, Poles, and Italians have come to Germany to live and work. These "guest workers" do not have German citizenship. Germany has also taken in thousands of refugees from Eastern Europe during the last 50 years.

Customs Traditional German food emphasizes the products of the forests, farms, and seacoasts. Each region produces its own varieties of sausage, cheese, wine, and beer. German celebrations include Oktoberfest; *Sangerfast*, a singing festival; and *Fastnacht*, a religious celebration. The major German festival season is Christmas. The Germans began the custom of bringing an evergreen tree indoors at Christmas and decorating it with candles.

The Arts and Literature Germany has a great tradition of literature, music, and the arts. The first European to print books using movable metal type was a German, Johannes Gutenberg. In the 1700s and 1800s, Germany led Europe in the development of classical music. World-famous German composers include Johann Sebastian Bach and Ludwig van Beethoven. The operas of Richard Wagner revived the folktales of ancient Germany.

✓ **READING CHECK:** (*Human Systems*) What technology and other contributions have Germans made to world culture?

Crowds gather in a German town for a Christmas market. Christmas markets have been popular in Germany for more than 400 years. From the beginning of Advent until Christmas, booths are set up on the market place in most cities. Here people can buy trees, decorations, and gifts.

Germany Today

Germany has a population of 82 million, more people than any other European country. Germany also has Europe's largest economy. Nearly one fourth of all goods and services produced by the EU come from Germany.

Economy Ample resources, labor, and capital have made Germany one of the world's leading industrial countries. The nation exports a wide variety of products. You may be familiar with German automakers like Volkswagen, Mercedes-Benz, and BMW. The German government provides education, medical care, and pensions for its citizens, but Germans pay high taxes. Unemployment is high. Many immigrants work at low-wage jobs. These "guest workers" are not German citizens and cannot receive many government benefits. Since reunification, Germany has struggled to modernize the industries, housing, and other facilities of the former East Germany.

Cities Germany's capital city, Berlin, is a large city with wide boulevards and many parks. Berlin was isolated and economically restricted during the decades after World War II. However, Germans are now rebuilding their new capital to its former splendor.

Near the Rhine River and the coal fields of Western Germany is a huge cluster of cities, including Essen and Düsseldorf. They form Germany's largest industrial district, the Ruhr. Frankfurt is a city known for banking and finance. Munich is a manufacturing center. Other important cities include Hamburg, Bremen, Cologne, and Stuttgart.

✓ **READING CHECK:** (**Human Systems**) How did the division of Germany affect its economy?

Germany

COUNTRY	POPULATION/ GROWTH RATE	LIFE EXPECTANCY	LITERACY RATE	PER CAPITA GDP
Germany	82,398,326 0.04%	75, male 82, female	99%	$26,600
United States	290,342,554 0.9%	74, male 80, female	97%	$37,600

Source: Central Intelligence Agency, *The World Factbook 2003*

Interpreting the Chart **What might the literacy rate of Germany suggest about its culture?**

Section Review 3

Define or identify: Reformation, Adolf Hitler, Holocaust, chancellor, Ludwig van Beethoven, Johannes Gutenberg, Richard Wagner

Working with Sketch Maps On the map you created in Section 2, label Berlin, Bonn, Essen, Frankfurt, Munich, Hamburg, and Cologne.

Reading for the Main Idea

1. (**Human Systems**) How did wars affect the development of Germany in the 1900s?

2. (**Human Systems**) What are some notable features of the German economy?

Critical Thinking

3. Drawing Inferences and Conclusions How has Germany's history influenced the religious makeup of the population?

4. Summarizing What have been some results of the unification of Germany in 1990?

Organizing What You Know

5. Sequencing Create a time line listing key events in the history of Germany from 1000 B.C.. to 1990.

go.hrw.com **Homework Practice Online** Keyword: SG5 HP12

1000 B.C.   A.D. 1990

The Benelux Countries

Read to Discover

1. How were the Benelux countries influenced by larger countries?
2. What is this region's culture like?
3. What are the Benelux countries like today?

Vocabulary

cosmopolitan

Places

Flanders
Wallonia
Amsterdam
Antwerp
Brussels

People

Flemish
Walloons
Vincent van Gogh

Reading Strategy

TAKING NOTES Use the headings in this section to create an outline. As you read about the Benelux countries, write what you learn below each heading.

The Dutch city of Rotterdam is one of the world's busiest ports.

Interpreting the Visual Record

Movement Why might this city be an important transportation center?

History

Celtic and Germanic tribes once lived in this region, as in most of west-central Europe. They were conquered by the Romans. After the fall of the Roman Empire and the conquests of Charlemagne, the region was ruled alternately by French rulers and by the Holy Roman emperor.

In 1555 the Holy Roman emperor presented the Low Countries to his son, King Philip II of Spain. In the 1570s the Protestants of the Netherlands won their freedom from Spanish rule. Soon after, the Netherlands became a great naval and colonial power. Belgium had been ruled at times by France and the Netherlands. However, by 1830 Belgium had broken away to become an independent kingdom.

Both world wars scarred this region. Many of the major battles of World War I were fought in Belgium. Then in World War II Germany occupied the Low Countries. In 1949 Belgium, the Netherlands, and Luxembourg were founding members of NATO. Later they joined the EU. Today, each of the three countries is ruled by a parliament and a monarch. The monarchs' duties are mostly ceremonial. The Netherlands controls several Caribbean islands. However, its former colonies in Asia and South America are now independent.

✓ **READING CHECK:** *Human Systems* How are the governments of the Benelux countries organized?

CONNECTING TO Technology

Dutch Polders

A polder in the Netherlands

Much of the Netherlands lies below sea level and was once covered with water. For at least 2,000 years, the Dutch have been holding back the sea. First they lived on raised earthen mounds. Later they built walls or dikes to keep the water out. After building dikes, the Dutch installed windmills to pump the water out of reclaimed areas, called polders.

Using this system, the Dutch have reclaimed large amounts of land. Cities like Amsterdam and Rotterdam sit on reclaimed land. The dike and polder system has become highly sophisticated. Electric pumps have largely replaced windmills, and dikes now extend along much of the country's coastline. However, this system is difficult to maintain. It requires frequent and expensive repairs. Creating polders has also produced sinking lowlands and other environmental damage. As a result, the Dutch are considering changes to the system. These changes might include restoring some of the polders to wetlands and lakes.

Understanding What You Read
1. What are polders?
2. How did the Dutch use technology to live on land previously under water?

Culture

The people of Luxembourg and Belgium are mostly Roman Catholic. The Netherlands is more evenly divided among Catholic, Protestant, and those who have no religious ties.

Dutch is the language of the Netherlands. Flemish is a language related to Dutch that is spoken in Flanders, the northern part of Belgium. Belgium's coast and southern interior are called Wallonia. People in Wallonia speak mostly French and are called Walloons. In the past, cultural differences between Flemish and Walloons have produced conflict in Belgium. Today street signs and other notices are often printed in both Flemish and French. The Benelux countries are also home to immigrants from Asia and Africa.

Benelux Countries

Country	Population/ Growth Rate	Life Expectancy	Literacy Rate	Per Capita GDP
Belgium	10,289,088 0.1%	75, male 81, female	98%	$29,200
Luxembourg	454,157 1.2%	74, male 81, female	100%	$48,900
Netherlands	16,150,511 0.5%	76, male 82, female	99%	$27,200
United States	290,342,554 0.9%	74, male 80, female	97%	$37,600

Source: Central Intelligence Agency, *The World Factbook 2003*

Interpreting the Chart Which country's per capita GDP is closest to that of the United States?

The region's foods include dairy products, fish, and sausage. The Dutch spice trade led to dishes flavored with spices from Southeast Asia. The Belgians claim they invented french fries, which they eat with mayonnaise.

The Netherlands and Belgium have been world leaders in fine art. In the 1400s and 1500s, Flemish artists painted realistic portraits and landscapes. Dutch painters like Rembrandt and Jan Vermeer experimented with different qualities of light. In the 1800s Dutch painter Vincent van Gogh portrayed southern France with bold brush strokes and bright colors.

✓ **READING CHECK:** (*Human Systerms*) What is the relationship between cultures in Belgium?

The Benelux Countries Today

The Netherlands is famous for its flowers, particularly tulips. Belgium and the Netherlands export cheeses, chocolate, and cocoa. Amsterdam and Antwerp, Belgium, are major diamond-cutting centers. The Netherlands also imports and refines oil. Luxembourg earns much of its income from services such as banking. The region also produces steel, chemicals, and machines. Its **cosmopolitan** cities are centers of international business and government. A cosmopolitan city is one that has many foreign influences. Brussels, Belgium, is the headquarters for many international organizations such as the EU and NATO.

✓ **READING CHECK:** (*Places and Regions*) What are the Benelux countries like today?

go.hrw.com **Homework Practice Online**
Keyword: SG5 HP12

Section Review 4

Define or identify: Flemish, Walloons, Vincent van Gogh, cosmopolitan

Working with Sketch Maps On the map you created in Section 3, label Flanders, Wallonia, Amsterdam, Antwerp, and Brussels.

Reading for the Main Idea

1. (*Human Systems*) What are the main cultural features of the Benelux countries?

2. (*Human Systems*) In what ways do the people of the Benelux countries differ?

Critical Thinking

3. **Drawing Inferences and Conclusions** Why might the economies of the Benelux countries be dependent on international trade?

4. **Analyzing Information** Why have groups in Belgium been in conflict?

Organizing What You Know

5. **Comparing** Copy the following graphic organizer. Use it to compare the Benelux countries' industries.

Belgium	Luxembourg	Netherlands

Read to Discover

1. What are some of the major events in the history of the Alpine countries?
2. What are some cultural features of this region?
3. How are the economies of Switzerland and Austria similar?

Vocabulary

cantons
nationalism

Places

Geneva
Salzburg
Vienna
Zurich
Basel
Bern

People

Habsburgs
Wolfgang Amadeus Mozart

Reading Strategy

FOLDNOTES: TWO-PANEL FLIP CHART Create the FoldNote titled **Two-Panel Flip Chart** described in the Appendix. Write Switzerland on one of the flaps and Austria on the other. As you read, write what you learn about each country beneath its flap.

History

Austria and Switzerland share a history of Celtic occupation, Roman and Germanic invasions, and rule by the Holy Roman Empire.

Switzerland Swiss **cantons**, or districts, gradually broke away from the Holy Roman Empire, and in the 1600s Switzerland became independent. Today Switzerland is a confederation of 26 cantons. Each controls its own internal affairs, and the national government handles defense and international relations. Switzerland's location in the high Alps has allowed it to remain somewhat separate from the rest of Europe. It has remained neutral in the European wars of the last two centuries. Switzerland is not a member of the EU or NATO. In 2002, however, it joined the United Nations. Committed to its neutrality, Switzerland remains active in many international organizations.

Austria During the Middle Ages, Austria was a border region of Germany. This region was the home of the Habsburgs, a powerful family of German nobles. From the 1400s onward the Holy Roman emperor was always a Habsburg. At the height of their power the Habsburgs ruled Spain and the Netherlands, as well as large areas of Germany, eastern Europe, and Italy. This empire included different ethnic

The International Red Cross helps people around the world. This is the Red Cross headquarters in Geneva, Switzerland.

The Danube River passes through Vienna, the capital of Austria.

Interpreting the Visual Record

(*Movement*) **How does this river influence movement and trade?**

Austrians wearing carved wooden masks celebrate the return of spring and milder weather.

groups, each with its own language, government, and system of laws. The empire was united only in its allegiance to the emperor and in its defense of the Roman Catholic religion.

With the conquests of Napoléon after 1800, the Holy Roman Empire was formally eliminated. It was replaced with the Austrian Empire, which was also under Habsburg control. When Napoléon was defeated, the Austrian Empire became the dominant power in central Europe.

Through the 1800s the diverse peoples of the empire began to develop **nationalism**, or a demand for self-rule. In 1867 the Austrians agreed to share political power with the Hungarians. The Austrian Empire became the Austro-Hungarian Empire. After World War I the empire was dissolved. Austria and Hungary became separate countries. Shortly before World War II the Germans took over Austria and made it part of Germany. After the war, the Allies occupied Austria. Today Austria is an independent member of the EU.

✓ **READING CHECK:** (*Human Systems*) What were the major events in the history of the Alpine countries?

Culture

About 46 percent of the population in Switzerland is Roman Catholic, and 40 percent is Protestant. Austria's population is mainly Roman Catholic. Only about 5 percent of its people are Protestant, while 17 percent follow Islam or other religions.

Languages and Diversity About 64 percent of Swiss speak German, 18 percent speak French, and 10 percent speak Italian. Small groups in the southeast speak a language called Romansh. Other European languages are also spoken in Switzerland. Austria is almost entirely German-speaking, but contains small minorities of Slovenes and Croatians.

Customs Christmas is a major festival in both countries. People make special cakes and cookies at this time. In rural parts of Switzerland people take cattle up to the high mountains in late spring and return in the fall. Their return is celebrated by decorating homes and cows' horns with flowers. A special feast is also prepared.

The Alpine region is well known for its music. In the 1700s Wolfgang Amadeus Mozart wrote symphonies and operas in the Austrian city of Salzburg. Every year a music festival is held there in his honor. Austria's capital, Vienna, is also a center for music and fine art.

✓ **READING CHECK:** (*Human Systems*) What role have the arts played in this region?

The Alpine Countries

COUNTRY	POPULATION/ GROWTH RATE	LIFE EXPECTANCY	LITERACY RATE	PER CAPITA GDP
Austria	8,188,207 0.2%	75, male 81, female	98%	$27,700
Switzerland	7,318,638 0.3%	77, male 83, female	99%	$31,700
United States	290,342,554 0.9%	74, male 80, female	97%	$37,600

Source: Central Intelligence Agency, *The World Factbook 2003*

Interpreting the Chart How do the populations of the Alpine countries compare with that of the United States?

The Alpine Countries Today

Switzerland and Austria both produce dairy products, including many kinds of cheese. Switzerland is also famous for the manufacturing of watches, optical instruments, and other machinery. Swiss chemists discovered how to make chocolate bars. Switzerland is a major producer of chocolate, although it must import the cocoa beans.

Switzerland and Austria are linked to the rest of Europe by excellent highways, trains, and airports. Several long tunnels allow trains and cars to pass through mountains in the Swiss Alps. Both countries attract many tourists with their mountain scenery, lakes, and ski slopes.

Located on the Danube, Vienna is Austria's commercial and industrial center. Switzerland's two largest cities are both in the German-speaking north. Zurich is a banking center, while Basel is the starting point for travel down the Rhine to the North Sea. Switzerland's capital is Bern, and Geneva is located in the west.

✓ **READING CHECK:** (*Places and Regions*) How are the economies of Switzerland and Austria similar?

Section Review 5

Define or identify: cantons, Habsburgs, nationalism, Wolfgang Amadeus Mozart

Working with Sketch Maps On the map you created in Section 4, label Geneva, Salzburg, Vienna, Zurich, Basel, and Bern.

Reading for the Main Idea

1. (*Human Systems*) What were the main events in the history of the Alpine countries?

2. (*Human Systems*) What are some notable aspects of Swiss and Austrian culture?

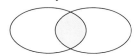
Homework Practice Online
Keyword: SG5 HP12

Critical Thinking

3. **Drawing Inferences and Conclusions** How might geography have been a factor in Switzerland's historical neutrality?

4. **Drawing Inferences and Conclusions** How have foreign invasions of Austria shaped its history?

Organizing What You Know

5. **Comparing/Contrasting** Use this graphic organizer to compare and contrast the culture, language, economies, and history of Switzerland and Austria.

Review and Practice

Define and Identify

Identify each of the following:

1. navigable
2. loess
3. Charlemagne
4. medieval
5. impressionism
6. Reformation
7. Holocaust
8. Ludwig van Beethoven
9. cosmopolitan
10. cantons
11. nationalism

Review the Main Ideas

12. What are the three main landform regions of west-central Europe?
13. How have the region's rivers affected the location of harbor cities?
14. How did Roman rule affect the history of France?
15. How did the world wars affect France?
16. How did the economies of East Germany and West Germany differ?
17. What are some of Germany's holidays?
18. What country controlled the Low Countries after 1555? What happened to the Netherlands soon after?

19. For what products are the Benelux countries famous?
20. What happened to the Austro-Hungarian Empire after World War I? What happened to Austria during World War II?
21. How is Switzerland's position in world affairs unique?

Think Critically

22. **Drawing Inferences and Conclusions** What geographic features have encouraged travel and trade in west-central Europe? What geographic features have hindered travel and trade?
23. **Finding the Main Idea** How have the people of Switzerland altered their environment?
24. **Analyzing Information** What landform regions give France natural borders? Which French borders do not coincide with physical features?
25. **Drawing Inferences and Conclusions** Why might Brussels, Belgium, be called the capital of Europe?
26. **Comparing** What demographic factors are shared by all countries of west-central Europe today? How do they reflect levels of economic development?

Map Activity

27. On a separate sheet of paper, match the letters on the map with their correct labels.

Northern European Plain
Pyrenees
Alps
Seine River
Rhine River
Danube River
North Sea
Mediterranean Sea
Paris
Berlin

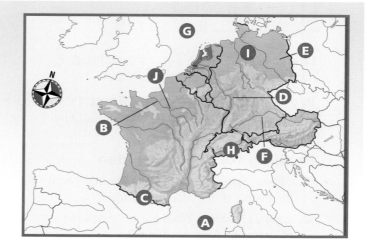

Writing Activity

Imagine you are taking a boat tour down the Rhine River. You will travel from Basel, Switzerland, to Rotterdam, the Netherlands. Keep a journal describing the places you see and the stops you make. Be sure to use standard grammar, spelling, sentence structure, and punctuation.

internet connect

Internet Activity: **go.hrw.com**
KEYWORD: SG5 GT12

Choose a topic to explore about west-central Europe:

- Tour the land and rivers of Europe.
- Travel back in time to the Middle Ages.
- Visit Belgian and Dutch schools.

Social Studies Skills Practice

Interpreting Maps

Study this map of Germany after World War II. Then answer the questions.

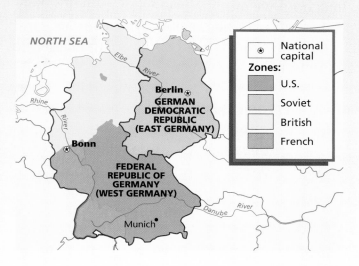

1. Which countries occupied zones of West Germany?
2. Which country occupied East Germany?
3. Which country may have had the most difficulty re-supplying its troops? Why?
4. How did Berlin's location increase the difficulty of re-supplying troops and civilians in West Berlin?

Analyzing Primary Sources

France is a leader in the fashion industry. Read the following quote from TIME Magazine about Coco Chanel, a French designer. Then answer the questions.

"Coco Chanel wasn't just ahead of her time. She was ahead of herself. If one looks at the work of contemporary [today's] fashion designers . . . one sees that many of their strategies echo what Chanel once did. The way, 75 years ago, she mixed up the vocabulary of male and female clothes and created fashion that offered the wearer a feeling of hidden luxury rather than ostentation [fancy show] are just two examples of how her taste and sense of style overlap with today's fashion."

1. What impact has Coco Chanel's work had on other designers?
2. In the first sentence, what does it mean that Chanel was "ahead of her time?"
3. In the fourth sentence, what does the word vocabulary mean?
4. What about Chanel's designs was highly unusual for the time?

CHAPTER 13

Northern Europe

Now we will study the countries of northern Europe. First we meet Lars, a student in Norway. He lives in a place where the Sun does not rise during much of the winter.

Hi! My name is Lars. I am 13, and I live in Tromsø, one of the northernmost cities in Europe. I am in my seventh year at school. In school we study Norwegian, plus English, French or German, social studies, science, music, art, and cooking. If I do well in junior high, I will go to an academic high school and prepare for a university.

Usually I walk to school, which is about 3 km (1.9 miles) away. In the winter, everyone skis to school. The Sun never shines on many winter days because we live north of the Arctic Circle. On January 20, when the Sun appears again for just a few minutes, we celebrate Sun Day.

In the summer the Sun never sets. This is my favorite time of the year. It still can be cold then. Last summer the temperature was mostly around 6° or 7°C (about 43° or 44°F).

Jeg bor i midnattssolens land.

Translation: I live in the Land of the Midnight Sun.

Section 1 Physical Geography

Read to Discover

1. What are the region's major physical features?
2. What are the region's most important natural resources?
3. What climates are found in northern Europe?

Vocabulary

fjords
lochs
North Atlantic Drift

Places

British Isles
English Channel
North Sea
Great Britain
Ireland
Iceland
Greenland

Scandinavian
  Peninsula
Jutland Peninsula
Kjølen Mountains
Northwest Highlands
Shannon River
Baltic Sea

Reading Strategy

USING PRIOR KNOWLEDGE Look at the Physical-Political map of Northern Europe. Where are the cities located? Why do you think people settled there? Write down your answers. As you read this section, compare your answers to what you learn.

Northern Europe: Physical-Political

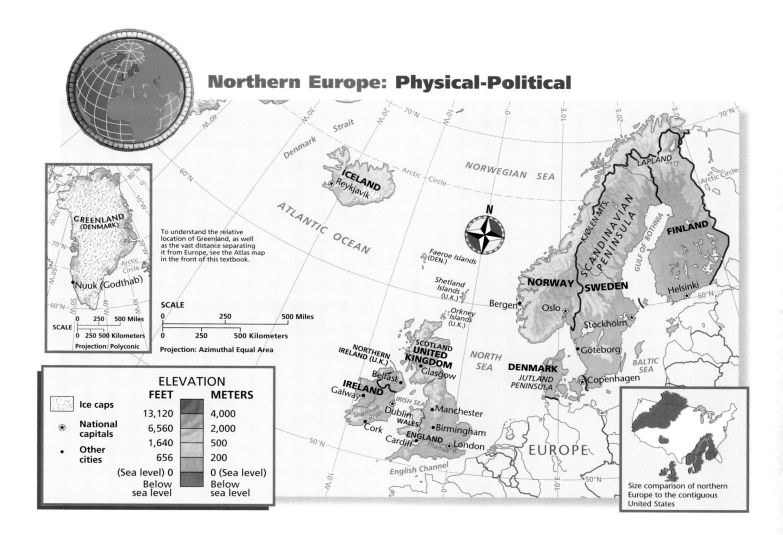

To understand the relative location of Greenland, as well as the vast distance separating it from Europe, see the Atlas map in the front of this textbook.

GREENLAND (DENMARK)
Nuuk (Godhab)

SCALE
0   250   500 Miles
0 250 500 Kilometers
Projection: Polyconic

SCALE
0   250   500 Miles
0   250   500 Kilometers
Projection: Azimuthal Equal Area

ELEVATION

	FEET	METERS
Ice caps		
National capitals	13,120	4,000
	6,560	2,000
Other cities	1,640	500
	656	200
	(Sea level) 0	0 (Sea level)
	Below sea level	Below sea level

Size comparison of northern Europe to the contiguous United States

Physical Features

Northern Europe includes several large islands and peninsulas. The British Isles lie across the English Channel and North Sea from the rest of Europe. They include the islands of Great Britain and Ireland and are divided between the United Kingdom and the Republic of Ireland. This region also includes the islands of Iceland and Greenland. Greenland is the world's largest island.

To the east are the Scandinavian and Jutland Peninsulas. Denmark occupies the Jutland Peninsula and nearby islands. The Scandinavian Peninsula is divided between Norway and Sweden. Finland lies farther east. These countries plus Iceland make up Scandinavia.

Landforms The rolling hills of Ireland, the highlands of Great Britain, and the Kjølen (CHUH-luhn) Mountains of Scandinavia are part of Europe's Northwest Highlands region. This is a region of very old, eroded hills and low mountains.

Southeastern Great Britain and southern Scandinavia are lowland regions. Much of Iceland is mountainous and volcanic. More than 10 percent of it is covered by glaciers. Greenland is mostly covered by a thick ice cap.

Coasts Northern Europe has long, jagged coastlines. The coastline of Norway includes many **fjords** (fee-AWRDS). Fjords are narrow, deep inlets of the sea set between high, rocky cliffs. Ice-age glaciers carved the fjords out of coastal mountains.

Lakes and Rivers Melting ice-age glaciers left behind thousands of lakes in the region. In Scotland, the lakes are called **lochs**. Lochs are found in valleys carved by glaciers long ago.

Northern Europe does not have long rivers like the Mississippi River in the United States. The longest river in the British Isles is the Shannon River in Ireland. It is just 240 miles (390 km) long.

✔ **READING CHECK:** (*Places and Regions*) What are the physical features of the region?

Natural Resources

Northern Europe has many resources. They include water, forests, and energy sources.

Water The ice-free North Sea is especially important for trade and fishing. Parts of the Baltic Sea freeze over during the winter months. Special ships break up the ice to keep sea lanes open to Sweden and Finland.

Forests and Soil Most of Europe's original forests were cleared centuries ago. However,

Fjords like this one shelter many harbors in Norway.

Interpreting the Visual Record

How are fjords created?

Norway
Sweden Finland

Sweden and Finland still have large, coniferous forests that produce timber. The region's farmers grow many kinds of cool-climate crops.

Energy Beneath the North Sea are rich oil and natural gas reserves. Nearly all of the oil reserves are controlled by the nearby United Kingdom and Norway. However, these reserves cannot satisfy all of the region's needs. Most countries import oil and natural gas from southwest Asia, Africa, and Russia. Some, such as Iceland, use geothermal and hydroelectric power.

✓ **READING CHECK:** (*Environment and Society*) In what way has technology allowed people in the region to keep the North Sea open during the winter?

Climate

Despite its northern location, much of the region has a marine west coast climate. Westerly winds blow over a warm ocean current called the **North Atlantic Drift**. These winds bring mild temperatures and rain to the British Isles and coastal areas. Atlantic storms often bring even more rain. Snow and frosts may occur in winter.

Central Sweden and southern Finland have a humid continental climate. This area has four true seasons. Far to the north are subarctic and tundra climates. In the forested subarctic regions, winters are long and cold with short days. Long days fill the short summers. In the tundra region it is cold all year. Only small plants such as grass and moss grow there.

✓ **READING CHECK:** (*Places and Regions*) What are the region's climates?

Homework Practice Online
Keyword: SG5 HP13

Define and explain: fjords, lochs, North Atlantic Drift

Working with Sketch Maps On an outline map that you draw or that your teacher provides, label the following: British Isles, English Channel, North Sea, Great Britain, Ireland, Iceland, Greenland, Scandinavian Peninsula, Jutland Peninsula, Kjølen Mountains, Northwest Highlands, Shannon River, and Baltic Sea. In the margin, write a short caption explaining how the North Atlantic Drift affects the region's climates.

Reading for the Main Idea

1. (*Places and Regions*) Which parts of northern Europe are highland regions? Which parts are lowland regions?

2. (*Places and Regions*) What major climate types are found in northern Europe?

Critical Thinking

3. Finding the Main Idea How has ice shaped the region's physical geography?

4. Making Generalizations and Predictions Think about what you have learned about global warming. How might warmer temperatures affect the climates and people of northern Europe?

Organizing What You Know

5. Summarizing Copy the following graphic organizer. Use it to describe the region's important natural resources.

Water	Forests and soil	Energy

COULD YOU SURVIVE IN ICELAND?

A Land of Fire and Ice

Iceland doesn't seem like a country where anyone could live in peace. It lies where two tectonic plates meet, so volcanoes are everywhere. Hot rock, ash, and lava gush from the Earth. Floods crash downstream when volcanoes erupt beneath ice caps. Geysers shoot hot water into the sky. Summers are short, and winters are dark. In addition, Iceland can't grow much food, so it has to import basic supplies.

SURVIVAL CHALLENGE

Now imagine that you want to build a fine country house in Iceland. Use the chart and the map to locate some of Iceland's dangers. Be sure to notice which volcanoes lie under ice and in which direction floodwaters would flow. Notice also the long fissures, or cracks in Earth's surface. Lava may bubble out anywhere along these cracks. Finally, find transportation links that would connect you to food sources and other necessities. Then decide where you might build your house.

Some of Iceland's Major Volcanoes

Name of Volcano	Eruption Details
Bardarbunga	has erupted 19 times since the Norse settled Iceland
Eldfell	in 1973, dumped more than 250 million tons of rock, ash, and lava on the town of Vestmannaeyjar
Grimsvotn	almost covered by Vatnajokull ice cap; has erupted about 49 times since settlement; flood caused by 1996 eruption flowed at more than 55,000 cubic yards per second
Hekla	may have erupted 167 times since A.D. 1104; most recent eruption in 2000
Katla	hidden beneath an ice cap; has caused many floods; eruption in A.D. 935 lasted about 8 years
Krafla	has erupted 29 times; lava from 1724 eruption flowed more than 12 miles in one year
Laki	lava from 1783–84 eruption covered 135 cubic miles—the largest lava flow of historic time; poison gases killed live stock; one fourth of population starved to death; ash fell on mainland Europe
Surtsey	from 1963 to 1967 grew from ocean floor to form volcanic island a square mile in area

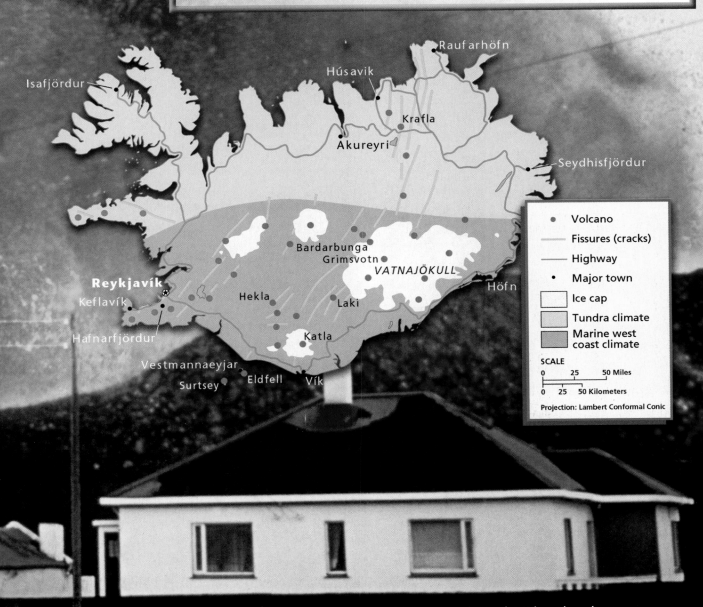

Living with the Lava

With so much danger nearby, you may be surprised to know that some of Iceland's towns were first settled more than a thousand years ago. How have they endured for so long? Look at the map again for clues to how the towns marked on it survived. For example, find Akureyri (AH-koor-AYE-ree) on the north coast. It lies in the tundra climate region. Yet local gardeners grow plants that came from Africa, and Akureyri is Iceland's second-largest city. It even has a booming tourist industry. How may Akureyri's location have affected its economy, climate, and safety? What advantages may Akureyri share with some of the other towns? Should you build your new house near one of these towns?

Ísafjördur

Raufarhöfn

Húsavík

Krafla

Akureyri

Seydhisfjördur

Bardarbunga
Grimsvotn

VATNAJÖKULL

Höfn

Reykjavík

Keflavík

Hekla

Laki

Hafnarfjördur

Katla

Vestmannaeyjar

Surtsey Eldfell Vík

Legend

- Volcano
- Fissures (cracks)
- Highway
- Major town
- Ice cap
- Tundra climate
- Marine west coast climate

SCALE

0   25   50 Miles

0   25   50 Kilometers

Projection: Lambert Conformal Conic

In the photo, lava buries the town of Vestmannaeyjar (VEST-mahn-nah-AY-yahr). When the volcano Eldfell began erupting at 2:00 AM, January 23, 1973, workers started evacuating the townspeople. All were safe within a few hours. The flowing lava threatened to close off the harbor, however, which would have ruined the town's fishing industry. For weeks, workers sprayed seawater on the lava to harden it and stop its spread. They were successful. The town, the harbor, and the fishing industry all survived.

The United Kingdom

Read to Discover

1. What are some important events in the history of the United Kingdom?
2. What are the people and culture of the country like?
3. What is the United Kingdom like today?

Vocabulary

textiles
constitutional monarchy
glen

Places

England
Scotland
Wales
London
Birmingham
Manchester
Northern Ireland
Glasgow
Cardiff
Belfast

People

Normans
William Shakespeare

Reading Strategy

TAKING NOTES Use the headings in this section to create an outline. As you read about the United Kingdom, write details you learn beneath each heading.

Early peoples of the British Isles built Stonehenge in stages from about 3100 B.C. to about 1800 B.C.

This beautiful Anglo-Saxon shoulder clasp from about A.D. 630 held together pieces of clothing.

History

Most of the British are descended from people who came to the British Isles long ago. The Celts (KELTS) are thought by some scholars to have come to the islands around 450 B.C. Mountain areas of Wales, Scotland, and Ireland have remained mostly Celtic.

Later, from the A.D. 400s to 1000s, new groups of people came. The Angles and Saxons came from northern Germany and Denmark. The Vikings came from Scandinavia. Last to arrive in Britain were the Normans from northern France. They conquered England in 1066. English as spoken today reflects these migrations. It combines elements from the Anglo-Saxon and Norman French languages.

A Global Power England became a world power in the late 1500s. Surrounded by water, the country developed a powerful navy that protected trade routes. In the 1600s the English began establishing colonies around the world. By the early 1800s they had also united England, Scotland, Wales, and Ireland into one kingdom. From London the United Kingdom built a vast British Empire. By 1900 the empire covered nearly one fourth of the world's land area.

The United Kingdom also became an economic power in the 1700s and 1800s. It was the cradle of the Industrial Revolution, which began in the last half of the 1700s. Large supplies of coal and iron and a large labor force helped industries grow. The country also developed a good transportation network of rivers, canals, and railroads. Three of the early industries were **textiles**, or cloth products, shipbuilding, iron, and later steel. Coal powered these industries. Birmingham, Manchester, and other cities grew up near Britain's coal fields.

Decline of Empire World wars and economic competition from other countries weakened the United Kingdom in the 1900s. All but parts of northern Ireland became independent in 1921. By the 1970s most British colonies also had gained independence. Most now make up the British Commonwealth of Nations. Members of the Commonwealth meet to discuss economic, scientific, and business matters.

The United Kingdom still plays an important role in world affairs. It is a leading member of the United Nations (UN), the European Union (EU), and the North Atlantic Treaty Organization (NATO).

The Government The United Kingdom's form of government is called a **constitutional monarchy**. That is, it has a monarch—a king or queen—but a parliament makes the country's laws. The monarch is the head of state but has largely ceremonial duties. Parliament chooses a prime minister to lead the national government.

In recent years the national government has given people in Scotland and Wales more control over local affairs. Some people think Scotland might one day seek independence.

✓ **READING CHECK:** (*Human Systems*) How are former British colonies linked today?

▲
Queen Elizabeth I (1533–1603) ruled England as it became a world power in the late 1500s.

The British government is seated in London, the capital. The Tower Bridge over the River Thames [TEMZ] is one of the city's many famous historical sites.

Interpreting the Visual Record
Why do you think London became a large city?

▼

Millions of Americans watched the Beatles, a British rock band, perform on television in 1964. The Beatles and other British bands became popular around the world.

Interpreting the Visual Record

(Movement) **How do you think television helps shape world cultures today?**

Culture

More than 60 million people live in the United Kingdom today. English is the official language. Some people in Wales and Scotland also speak the Celtic languages of Welsh and Gaelic [GAY-lik]. The Church of England is the country's official church. However, many Britons belong to other Protestant churches or are Roman Catholic.

Food and Festivals Living close to the sea, the British often eat fish. One popular meal is fish and chips—fried fish and potatoes. However, British food also includes different meats, oat porridge and cakes, and potatoes in many forms.

The British celebrate many religious holidays, such as Christmas. Other holidays include the Queen's official birthday celebration in June. In July many Protestants in Northern Ireland celebrate a battle in 1690 in which Protestants defeated Catholic forces. In recent years the day's parades have sometimes sparked protests and violence between Protestants and Catholics.

Art and Literature British literature, art, and music have been popular around the world. Perhaps the most famous British writer is William Shakespeare. He died in 1616, but his poetry and plays, such as *Romeo and Juliet*, remain popular. In the 1960s the Beatles helped make Britain a major center for modern popular music. Ever since then, British performers have attracted fans around the world.

✓ **READING CHECK:** (*Human Systems*) What aspects of British culture have spread around the world?

The United Kingdom

COUNTRY	POPULATION/ GROWTH RATE	LIFE EXPECTANCY	LITERACY RATE	PER CAPITA GDP
United Kingdom	60,094,648 0.3%	76, male 81, female	99%	$25,300
United States	290,342,554 0.9%	74, male 80, female	97%	$37,600

Source: Central Intelligence Agency, *The World Factbook 2003*

Interpreting the Chart How does the literacy rate in the United Kingdom compare with that of the United States?

The United Kingdom Today

Nearly 90 percent of Britons today live in urban areas. London, the capital of England, is the largest city. It is located in southeastern England. London is also the capital of the whole United Kingdom.

More than 7 million people live in London. The city is a world center for trade, industry, and services, particularly banking and insurance. London also has one of the world's busiest airports. Many tourists visit London to see its famous historical sites, theaters, and shops. Other important cities include Glasgow, Scotland; Cardiff, Wales; and Belfast, Northern Ireland.

The Economy Old British industries like mining and manufacturing declined after World War II. Today, however, the economy is stronger. North Sea reserves have made the country a major producer of oil and natural gas. Birmingham, Glasgow, and other cities are attracting new industries. One area of Scotland is called Silicon Glen. This is because it has many computer and electronics businesses. **Glen** is a Scottish term for a valley. Today many British work in service industries, including banking, insurance, education, and tourism.

Agriculture Britain's modern farms produce about 60 percent of the country's food. Still, only about 1 percent of the labor force works in agriculture. Important products include grains, potatoes, vegetables, and meat.

Northern Ireland One of the toughest problems facing the country has been violence in Northern Ireland. Sometimes Northern Ireland is called Ulster. The Protestant majority and the Roman Catholic minority there have bitterly fought each other. Violence on both sides has resulted in many deaths.

Many Catholics in Northern Ireland believe they have not been treated fairly by the Protestant majority. Therefore, many want Northern Ireland to join the mostly Roman Catholic Republic of Ireland. Protestants fear becoming a minority on the island. They want to remain part of the United Kingdom. Many people hoped that agreements made in 1999 by Protestant and Roman Catholic political leaders would lead to lasting peace. However, the new government's assembly stopped meeting in 2002. Today, peace talks continue between the two sides.

✓ **READING CHECK:** (*Human Systems*) What has been the cause of conflict in Northern Ireland?

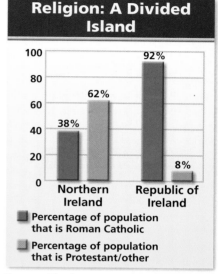

Religion: A Divided Island

- Percentage of population that is Roman Catholic
- Percentage of population that is Protestant/other

Source: *The Statesman's Year Book,* 1998–99.

Interpreting the Graph (*Place*) **How does the number of Roman Catholics in the Republic of Ireland differ from that of Northern Ireland?**

Define or identify: Normans, textiles, constitutional monarchy, William Shakespeare, glen

Working with Sketch Maps On the map you created in Section 1, label the United Kingdom, England, Scotland, Wales, London, Birmingham, Manchester, Northern Ireland, Glasgow, Cardiff, and Belfast.

Reading for the Main Idea

1. (*Human Systems*) What peoples came to the British Isles after the Celts? When did they come?

2. (*Places and Regions*) What was the British Empire?

Homework Practice Online Keyword: SG5 HP13

Critical Thinking

3. **Contrasting** How is the British government different from the U.S. government?

4. **Drawing Inferences and Conclusions** Why do you think Protestants in Northern Ireland want to remain part of the United Kingdom?

Organizing What You Know

5. **Sequencing** Create a timeline that lists important events in the period.

800 B.C.   A.D. 2003

Read to Discover

1. What are the key events in Ireland's history?
2. What are the people and culture of Ireland like?
3. What kinds of economic changes has Ireland experienced in recent years?

Vocabulary

famine
bog
peat

Places

Dublin
Cork
Galway

People

Celts
Mary Robinson

Reading Strategy

READING ORGANIZER Before you read, draw a line down the center of a sheet of notebook paper. Write A.D. 400 at the bottom and A.D. 2000 near the top. As you read, fill in your time line with information about events in Irish history.

History

The Irish are descendants of the Celts. Irish Gaelic, a Celtic language, and English are the official languages. Most people in Ireland speak English. Gaelic is spoken mostly in rural western areas.

English Conquest England conquered Ireland in the A.D. 1100s. By the late 1600s most of the Irish had become farmers on land owned by the British. This created problems between the two peoples. Religious differences added to these problems. Most British were Protestant, while most Irish were Roman Catholic. Then, in the 1840s, millions of Irish left for the United States and other countries because of a poor economy and a potato famine. A **famine** is a severe shortage of food.

Independence The Irish rebelled against British rule. In 1916, for example, Irish rebels attacked British troops in the Easter Rising.

Stone fences divide the green fields of western Ireland, the Emerald Isle.

Interpreting the Visual Record *Place*

What kind of climate would you expect to find in a country with rich, green fields such as these?

At the end of 1921, most of Ireland gained independence. Some counties in northern Ireland remained part of the United Kingdom. Ties between the Republic of Ireland and the British Empire were cut in 1949.

Government Ireland has an elected president and parliament. The president has mostly ceremonial duties. In 1990, Irish voters elected Mary Robinson as Ireland's first woman president. Mary McAleese succeeded Robinson as president in 1997.

The parliament makes the country's laws. The Irish parliament chooses a prime minister to lead the government.

✓ **READING CHECK:** (*Human Systems*) What are some important events in Ireland's history?

Culture

Centuries of English rule have left their mark on Irish culture. For example, today nearly everyone in Ireland speaks English. Irish writers, such as George Bernard Shaw and James Joyce, have been among the world's great English-language writers.

A number of groups promote traditional Irish culture in the country today. The Gaelic League, for example, encourages the use of Irish Gaelic. Gaelic and English are taught in schools and used in official documents. Another group promotes Irish sports, such as hurling. Hurling is an outdoor game similar to field hockey and lacrosse.

Elements of Irish culture have also become popular outside the country. For example, traditional Irish folk dancing and music have attracted many fans. Music has long been important in Ireland. In fact, the Irish harp is a national symbol. Many musicians popular today are from Ireland, including members of the rock band U2.

More than 90 percent of the Irish today are Roman Catholic. St. Patrick's Day on March 17 is a national holiday. St. Patrick is believed to have brought Christianity to Ireland in the 400s.

✓ **READING CHECK:** (*Human Systems*) What is Irish culture like today?

Ireland Today

Ireland used to be one of Europe's poorest countries. Today it is a modern, thriving country with a strong economy and growing cities.

Ireland

Country	Population/ Growth Rate	Life Expectancy	Literacy Rate	Per Capita GDP
Ireland	3,924,140 1.0%	75, male 80, female	98%	$30,500
United States	290,342,554 0.9%	74, male 80, female	97%	$37,600

Source: Central Intelligence Agency, *The World Factbook 2003*

Interpreting the Chart How does life expectancy in Ireland compare with that of the United States?

Economy Until recently, Ireland was mostly an agricultural country. This was true even though much of the country is either rocky or boggy. A **bog** is soft ground that is soaked with water. For centuries, **peat** dug from bogs has been used for fuel. Peat is made up of dead plants, usually mosses.

Today Ireland is an industrial country. Irish workers produce processed foods, textiles, chemicals, machinery, crystal, and computers. Finance, tourism, and other service industries are also important.

How did this change come about? Ireland's low taxes, well-educated workers, and membership in the European Union have attracted many foreign companies. Those foreign companies include many from the United States. These companies see Ireland as a door to millions of customers throughout the EU. In fact, goods from their Irish factories are exported to markets in the rest of Europe and countries in other regions.

Cities Many factories have been built around Dublin. Dublin is Ireland's capital and largest city. It is a center for education, banking, and shipping. Nearly 1 million people live there. Housing prices rapidly increased in the 1990s as people moved there for work.

Other cities lie mainly along the coast. These cities include the seaports of Cork and Galway. They have old castles, churches, and other historical sites that are popular among tourists.

✓ **READING CHECK:** (*Human Systems*) What important economic changes have occurred in Ireland and why?

Homework Practice Online
Keyword: SG5 HP13

Section Review 3

Define or identify: Celts, famine, Mary Robinson, bog, peat

Working with Sketch Maps On the map you created in Section 2, label Ireland, Dublin, Cork, and Galway. In the margin explain the importance of Dublin to the Republic of Ireland.

Reading for the Main Idea

1. (*Human Systems*) What were two of the reasons many Irish moved to the United States and other countries in the 1800s?

2. (*Human Systems*) What are some important reasons why the economy in Ireland has grown so much in recent years?

Critical Thinking

3. **Drawing Inferences and Conclusions** Why do you think the Irish fought against British rule?

4. **Drawing Inferences and Conclusions** Why do you suppose housing prices rapidly increased in Dublin in the 1990s?

Organizing What You Know

5. **Comparing/Contrasting** Copy the following graphic organizer. Use it to compare and contrast the history, culture, and governments of the Republic of Ireland and the United Kingdom.

Ireland	United Kingdom
Conquered by England in the 1100s	Created vast world empire

Read to Discover

1. What are the people and culture of Scandinavia like?
2. What are some important features of each of the region's countries, plus Greenland, and Lapland?

Vocabulary

neutral
uninhabitable
geysers

Places

Oslo
Bergen
Stockholm
Göteborg
Copenhagen
Nuuk (Godthab)
Reykjavik

Gulf of Bothnia
Gulf of Finland
Helsinki
Lapland

People

Vikings

Reading Strategy

READING ORGANIZER Before you read, create a spider map. Label the center Scandinavia. Create a leg for each Scandinavian country. As you read the section, fill in the map with details about each country.

People and Culture

Scandinavia once was home to fierce, warlike Vikings. Today the countries of Norway, Sweden, Denmark, Iceland, and Finland are peaceful and prosperous.

The people of the region enjoy high standards of living. They have good health care and long life spans. Each government provides expensive social programs and services. These programs are paid for by high taxes.

The people and cultures in the countries of Scandinavia are similar in many ways. For example, the region's national languages, except for Finnish, are closely related. In addition, most people in Scandinavia are Lutheran Protestant. All of the Scandinavian countries have democratic governments.

✔ **READING CHECK:**

Human Systems How are the people and cultures of Scandinavia similar?

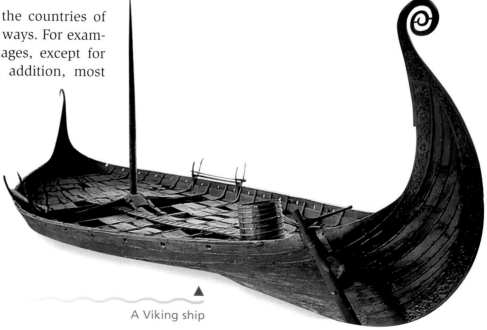

▲ A Viking ship

Scandinavia

Country	Population/ Growth Rate	Life Expectancy	Literacy Rate	Per Capita GDP
Denmark	5,384,384 0.3%	74, male 80, female	100%	$28,900
Finland	5,190,785 0.2%	74, male 81, female	100%	$25,800
Iceland	280,798 0.5%	77, male 82, female	100%	$30,200
Norway	4,546,123 0.5%	76, male 82, female	100%	$33,000
Sweden	8,878,085 .02%	77, male 83, female	99%	$26,000
United States	290,342,554 0.9%	74, male 80, female	97%	$37,600

Source: Central Intelligence Agency, *The World Factbook 2003*

Interpreting the Chart What is noteworthy about life expectancy in Iceland, Norway, and Sweden?

Norway

Norway is a long, narrow, and rugged country along the western coast of the Scandinavian Peninsula. Norway once was united with Denmark and then Sweden. In 1905 Norway became independent. Today Norway is a constitutional monarchy with an elected parliament.

About 75 percent of the people live in urban areas. The largest cities are the capital, Oslo, and Bergen on the Atlantic coast. Oslo is a modern city. It lies at the end of a wide fjord on the southern coast. The city is Norway's leading seaport, as well as its industrial and cultural center.

Norway has valuable resources, especially oil and natural gas. However, Norway's North Sea oil fields are expected to run dry over the next century. A long coastline and location on the North Sea have helped make Norway a major fishing and shipping country. Fjords shelter Norway's harbors and its fishing and shipping fleets.

Sweden

Sweden is Scandinavia's largest and most populous country. It is located between Norway and Finland. Most Swedes live in cities and towns. The largest cities are Stockholm, which is Sweden's capital, and Göteborg. Stockholm is located on the Baltic Sea coast. It is a beautiful city of islands and forests. Göteborg is a major seaport.

Like Norway, Sweden is a constitutional monarchy. The country has been at peace since the early 1800s. Sweden remained **neutral** during World Wars I and II. A neutral country is one that chooses not to take sides in an international conflict.

Sweden's main sources of wealth are forestry, farming, mining, and manufacturing. Wood, iron ore, automobiles, and wireless telephones are exports. Hydroelectricity is important.

Riddarholmen—Knight's Island—is one of several islands on which the original city of Stockholm was built.
Interpreting the Visual Record
(*Human-Environment Interaction*) Why might a group of islands be a good place to build a city?

A stave church in Norway

Stave Churches

In Norway you will find some beautiful wooden churches built during the Middle Ages. They are known as stave churches because of their corner posts, or staves. The staves provide the building's basic structure. Today stave churches are a reminder of the days when Viking and Christian beliefs began to merge in Norway.

As many as 800 stave churches were built in Norway during the 1000s and 1100s. Christianity was then beginning to spread throughout the country. It was replacing the old religious beliefs of the Viking people. Still, Viking culture is clearly seen in stave buildings.

Except for a thick stone foundation, stave churches are made entirely of wood. Workers used methods that had been developed by Viking boat builders. For example, wood on Viking boats was coated with tar to keep it from rotting. Church builders did the same with the wood for their churches. They also decorated the churches with carvings of dragons and other fanciful creatures. The stave church at Urnes even has a small Viking ship decorated with nine candles.

When the plague, or Black Death, arrived in Norway about 1350, many communities were abandoned. Many stave churches fell apart. Others were replaced by larger stone buildings. Today only 28 of the original buildings remain. They have been preserved for their beauty and as reminders of an earlier culture.

Understanding What You Read

1. What are staves?
2. How did stave churches reflect new belief systems in Norway?

Denmark

Denmark is the smallest and most densely populated of the region's countries. Most of Denmark lies on the Jutland Peninsula. About 500 islands make up the rest of the country.

Denmark is also a constitutional monarchy. The capital and largest city is Copenhagen. It lies on an island between the Jutland Peninsula and Sweden. Some 1.4 million people—about 25 percent of Denmark's population—live there.

About 60 percent of Denmark's land is used for farming. Farm products, especially meat and dairy products, are important exports. Denmark also has a modern industrial economy. Industries include food processing, machinery, furniture, and electronics.

Greenland's capital lies on the island's southwestern shore.

Interpreting the Visual Record

(Place) Why do most people in Greenland live along the coast?

Greenland

The huge island of Greenland is part of North America, but it is a territory of Denmark. Greenland's 56,000 people have their own government. They call their island Kalaallit Nunaat. The capital is Nuuk, also called Godthab. Most of the island's people are Inuit (Eskimo). Fishing is the main economic activity. Some Inuit still hunt seals and small whales.

The island's icy interior is **uninhabitable**. An uninhabitable area is one that cannot support human settlement. Greenland's people live mostly along the southwestern coast in the tundra climate regions.

The Great Geysir in southwestern Iceland can spout water nearly 200 feet (61 m) into the air. Some geysers shoot steam and boiling water to a height of more than 1,600 feet (nearly 500 m)!

Iceland

Between Greenland and Scandinavia is the country of Iceland. This Atlantic island belonged to Denmark until 1944. Today it is an independent country. It has an elected president and parliament.

Unlike Greenland, Iceland is populated mostly by northern Europeans. The capital and largest city is Reykjavik (RAYK-yuh-veek). More than 60 percent of the country's people live there.

Icelanders make good use of their country's natural resources. For example, about 70 percent of the country's exports are fish. These fish come from the rich waters around the island. In addition, hot water from Iceland's **geysers** heats homes and greenhouses. The word geyser is an Icelandic term for hot springs that shoot hot water and steam into the air. Volcanic activity forces heated underground water to rise from the geyser.

Finland

Finland is the easternmost of the region's countries. It lies mostly between two arms of the Baltic Sea: the Gulf of Bothnia and the Gulf of Finland. The capital and largest city is Helsinki, which is located on the southern coast.

The original Finnish settlers probably came from northern Asia. Finnish belongs to a language family that includes Estonian and Hungarian. About 6 percent of Finns speak Swedish. Finland was part of Sweden from the 1100s to 1809. It then became part of Russia. Finland gained independence at the end of World War I.

As in the other countries of the region, trade is important to Finland. The country is a major producer of paper and other forest products as well as wireless telephones. Metal products, shipbuilding, and electronics are also important industries. Finland imports energy and many of the raw materials needed in manufacturing.

Lapland

Across northern Finland, Sweden, and Norway is a culture region known as Lapland. This region is populated by the Lapps, or Sami, as they call themselves.

The Sami are probably descended from hunters who moved to the region from northern Asia. The languages they speak are related to Finnish. The Sami have tried to keep their culture and traditions, such as reindeer herding. Many now earn a living from tourism.

Young Sami couples here are dressed in traditional clothes for an Easter celebration in northern Norway.

✓ **READING CHECK:** (**Human Systems**) Around what activities are the economies of the countries and territories discussed in this section organized?

Define or identify: Vikings, neutral, uninhabitable, geysers

Working with Sketch Maps On the map you created in Section 3, label Scandinavia, Oslo, Bergen, Stockholm, Göteborg, Copenhagen, Nuuk (Godthab), Reykjavik, Gulf of Bothnia, Gulf of Finland, Helsinki, and Lapland. In the margin describe the people of the Lapland region.

Reading for the Main Idea

1. (**Human Systems**) What are two of the cultural similarities among the peoples of Scandinavia?

2. (**Environment and Society**) In what ways have Icelanders adapted to their natural environment?

3. (**Human Systems**) How have the history and culture of Finland been different from that of other countries in Scandinavia?

go.hrw.com **Homework Practice Online** Keyword: SG5 HP13

Critical Thinking

4. Making Generalizations and Predictions How do you think the location of Greenland and the culture of its people will affect the island's future relationship with Denmark?

Organizing What You Know

5. Summarizing Copy the following graphic organizer. Label the center of the organizer "Scandinavia." In the ovals, write one characteristic of each country and region discussed in this section. Then do the same for the other countries, as well as for Greenland and Lapland.

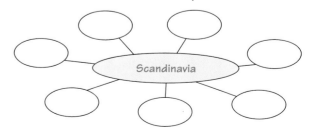

Scandinavia

Review and Practice

Define and Identify

Identify each of the following:

1. fjords
2. North Atlantic Drift
3. Normans
4. constitutional monarchy
5. famine
6. peat
7. Celts
8. neutral
9. uninhabitable
10. geysers
11. Vikings

Review the Main Ideas

12. Which countries in Northern Europe still have large forests?
13. How does the North Atlantic Drift affect the climate of Northern Europe?
14. Why did the British Empire go into decline?
15. What service industries employ many British workers?
16. What problems still trouble Northern Ireland?
17. How did the potato famine affect Ireland?
18. What are the official languages of Ireland?
19. Which Scandinavian country benefits from North Sea oil?
20. How does Iceland use the island's geysers?
21. What do the Lapps call themselves?

Think Critically

22. **Drawing Inferences and Conclusions** Why do you think British literature, art, and music have been popular around the world?
23. **Drawing Inferences and Conclusions** Why do you think industrial cities like Birmingham and Manchester in Great Britain grew up near coal deposits?
24. **Drawing Inferences and Conclusions** Why do you think most Irish speak English rather than Gaelic?
25. **Making Generalizations and Predictions** How do you think Scandinavians have adapted to life in these very cold environments?
26. **Comparing and Contrasting** What are some ways in which Finland is different from its Scandinavian neighbors?

Map Activity

27. On a separate sheet of paper, match the letters on the map with their correct labels.

London	Oslo
Manchester	Stockholm
Belfast	Copenhagen
Dublin	Reykjavik
Cork	Helsinki

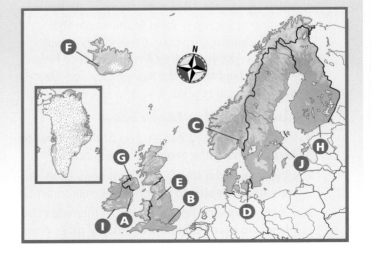

Writing Activity

Use print resources to find out more about the Vikings and how they lived in their cold climate. Write a short story set in a Viking village or on a Viking voyage. Describe daily life in the village or on the voyage. Include a bibliography showing references you used. Be sure to use standard grammar, spelling, sentence structure, and punctuation.

internet connect

Internet Activity: go.hrw.com
KEYWORD: SG5 GT13

Choose a topic to explore northern Europe:
- Explore the islands and fjords on the Scandinavian coast.
- Visit historic palaces in the United Kingdom.
- Investigate the history of skiing.

Social Studies Skills Practice

Interpreting Charts

Study the chart below and answer the questions.

Health Spending Per Person in Scandinavia

Country	Health spending per person (in U.S. dollars)	Ranking among world countries
Denmark	1,588	11
Finland	2,046	4
Iceland	1,884	6
Norway	1,835	8
Sweden	2,343	3

Source: *The Illustrated Book of World Rankings,* Fifth Edition

1. Which Scandinavian country spends the most per person on health? the least?

2. Which two countries spend roughly the same amount per capita on health?

3. What conclusions can you draw about Scandinavian spending on health when compared to the rest of the world?

4. What can you learn from the chart about the actual health of Scandinavians?

Analyzing Primary Sources

Read the following passage from a newspaper editorial in the *Irish Independent.* Then answer the questions.

"If the Irish people, or a big majority of them, do not love their language, do not treasure it, do not care two hoots if it is allowed to die, there must be good reasons for their attitude. . . . In spite of all the blather, Irish is rarely spoken in the Irish Parliament. . . . Boys and girls exclaim: 'I hate having to waste time doing the old Irish language.' We hold that those boys and girls . . . are basically wrong in their outlook towards their native language. But they have . . . lost respect for it; even worse, they often despise it."

1. What issue does the newspaper article address?

2. According to the writer, how do most young people regard this issue?

3. Why does the writer criticize government officials in Parliament?

4. In the second sentence, what do you think the word *blather* means?

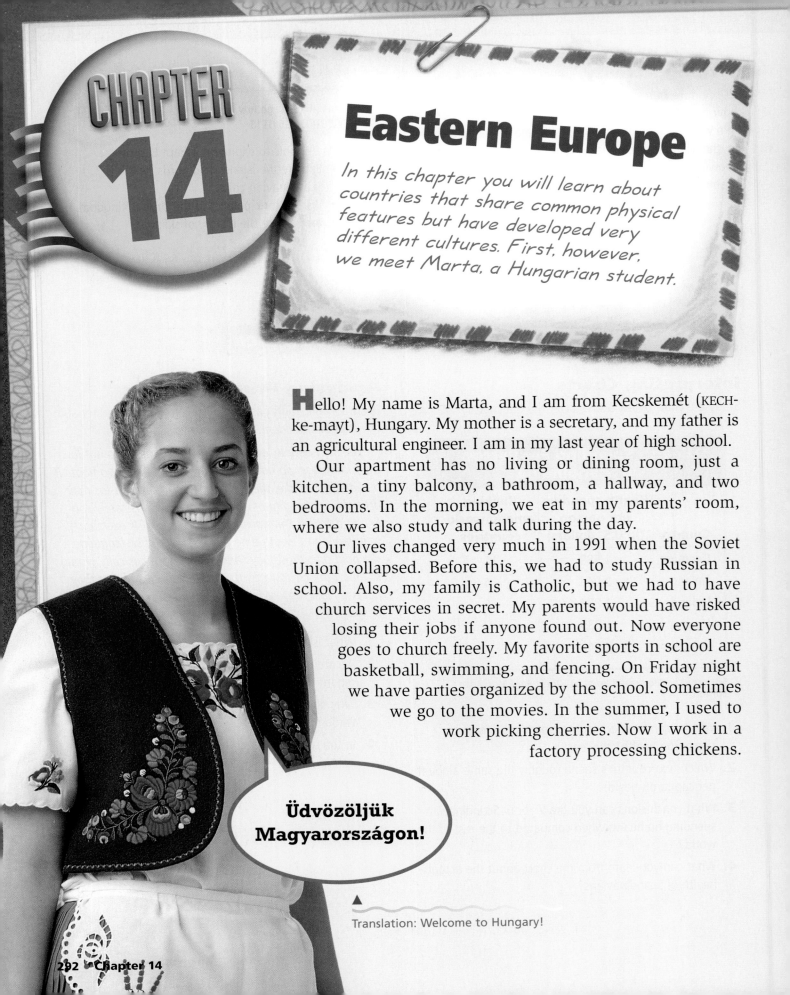

CHAPTER 14

Eastern Europe

In this chapter you will learn about countries that share common physical features but have developed very different cultures. First, however, we meet Marta, a Hungarian student.

Hello! My name is Marta, and I am from Kecskemét (KECH-ke-mayt), Hungary. My mother is a secretary, and my father is an agricultural engineer. I am in my last year of high school.

Our apartment has no living or dining room, just a kitchen, a tiny balcony, a bathroom, a hallway, and two bedrooms. In the morning, we eat in my parents' room, where we also study and talk during the day.

Our lives changed very much in 1991 when the Soviet Union collapsed. Before this, we had to study Russian in school. Also, my family is Catholic, but we had to have church services in secret. My parents would have risked losing their jobs if anyone found out. Now everyone goes to church freely. My favorite sports in school are basketball, swimming, and fencing. On Friday night we have parties organized by the school. Sometimes we go to the movies. In the summer, I used to work picking cherries. Now I work in a factory processing chickens.

Üdvözöljük Magyarországon!

▲
Translation: Welcome to Hungary!

Read to Discover

1. What are the major physical features of Eastern Europe?
2. What climates and natural resources does this region have?

Vocabulary

oil shale
lignite
amber

Places

Baltic Sea
Adriatic Sea
Black Sea
Danube River
Dinaric Alps
Balkan Mountains
Carpathian
   Mountains

Reading Strategy

FOLDNOTES: LAYERED BOOK Create the FoldNote titled **Layered Book** described in the Appendix. Label the pages Location and Place, Human-Environment Interaction, Movement, and Region. As you read, write details that support these Five Themes of Geography. Illustrate your layered book if time permits.

Eastern Europe: Physical-Political

ELEVATION

FEET		METERS
13,120		4,000
6,560		2,000
1,640		500
656		200
(Sea level) 0		0 (Sea level)
Below sea level		Below sea level

⊛ National capitals
• Other cities

Size comparison of Eastern Europe to the contiguous United States

SCALE
0   200   400 Miles
0   200   400 Kilometers
Projection: Azimuthal Equal Area

Physical Features

Eastern Europe stretches southward from the often cold, stormy shores of the Baltic Sea. In the south are the warmer and sunnier beaches along the Adriatic and Black Seas. We can divide the countries of this region into three groups. Poland, the Czech Republic, Slovakia, and Hungary are in the geographical heart of Europe. The Baltic countries are Estonia, Latvia, and Lithuania. Serbia and Montenegro, Bosnia and Herzegovina, Croatia, Slovenia, Macedonia, Romania, Moldova, Bulgaria, and Albania are the Balkan countries.

Landforms Eastern Europe is a region of mountains and plains. The plains of Poland and the Baltic countries are part of the huge Northern European Plain. The Danube River flows through the Great Hungarian Plain, also called the Great Alföld.

The Alps extend from central Europe southeastward into the Balkan Peninsula. Where they run parallel to the Adriatic coast, the mountains are called the Dinaric (duh-NAR-ik) Alps. As the range continues eastward across the peninsula its name changes to the Balkan Mountains. The Carpathian (kahr-PAY-thee-uhn) Mountains stretch from the Czech Republic across southern Poland and Slovakia and into Ukraine. There they curve south and west into Romania. In Romania they are known as the Transylvanian Alps.

Rivers Eastern Europe's most important river for trade and transportation is the Danube. The Danube stretches for 1,771 miles (2,850 km) across nine countries. It begins in Germany's Alps and flows eastward to the Black Sea. Some 300 tributaries flow into the Danube. The river carries and then drops so much silt that its Black Sea delta grows by 80 to 100 feet (24 to 30 m) every year. The river also carries a heavy load of industrial pollution.

✓ **READING CHECK:** (*Places and Regions*) What are the main physical features in Eastern Europe?

Our Amazing Planet

Amber is golden, fossilized tree sap. The beaches along the eastern coast of the Baltic Sea are the world's largest and most famous source of amber. Baltic amber is approximately 40 million years old.

This aerial view of the Danube Delta shows Romania's rich farmland.

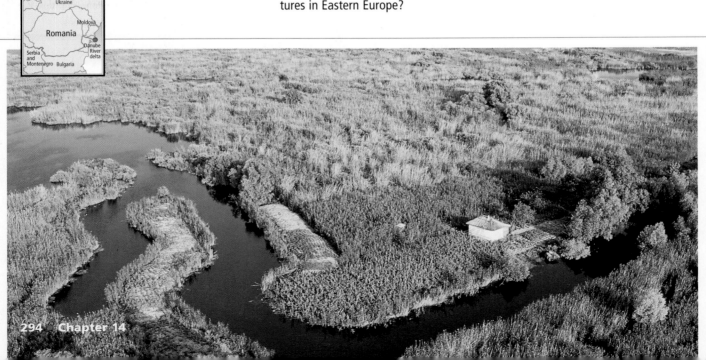

Climate and Resources

The eastern half of the region has long, snowy winters and short, rainy summers. Farther south and west, winters are milder and summers become drier. A warm, sunny climate has drawn visitors to the Adriatic coast for centuries.

Eastern Europe's mineral and energy resources include coal, natural gas, oil, iron, lead, silver, sulfur, and zinc. The region's varied resources support many industries. Some areas of the Balkan region and Hungary are major producers of bauxite. Romania has oil. Estonia has deposits of **oil shale**, or layered rock that yields oil when heated. Estonia uses this oil to generate electricity, which is exported to other Baltic countries and Russia. Slovakia and Slovenia mine a soft form of coal called **lignite**. Nevertheless, many countries must import their energy because demand is greater than supply.

For thousands of years, people have traded **amber**, or fossilized tree sap. Amber is found along the Baltic seacoast. Salt mining, which began in Poland in the 1200s, continues in central Poland today.

During the years of Communist rule industrial production was considered more important than the environment. The region suffered serious environmental damage. Air, soil, and water pollution, deforestation, and the destruction of natural resources were widespread. Many Eastern European countries have begun the long and expensive task of cleaning up their environment.

✓ **READING CHECK:** *Environment and Society* What factors affect the location of economic activities in the region?

Homework Practice Online
Keyword: SG5 HP14

Define and explain: oil shale, lignite, amber

Working with Sketch Maps On a map of Eastern Europe that you draw or that your teacher provides, label the following: Baltic Sea, Adriatic Sea, Black Sea, Danube River, Dinaric Alps, Balkan Mountains, and Carpathian Mountains.

Reading for the Main Idea

1. (*Places and Regions*) On which three major seas do the countries of Eastern Europe have coasts?

2. (*Environment and Society*) What types of mineral and energy resources are available in this region? How does this influence individual economies?

Critical Thinking

3. Making Generalizations and Predictions Would this region be suitable for agriculture? Why?

4. Identifying Cause and Effect How did Communist rule contribute to the pollution problems of this region?

Organizing What You Know

5. Summarizing Copy the following graphic organizer. Use it to summarize the physical features, climate, and resources of the heartland, the Baltics, and the Balkans. Then write and answer one question about the region's geography based on the chart.

Region	Physical features	Climate	Resources

The Countries of Northeastern Europe

Read to Discover

1. What peoples contributed to the early history of northeastern Europe?
2. How was northeastern Europe's culture influenced by other cultures?
3. How has the political organization of this region changed since World War II?

Vocabulary

Indo-European

Places

Estonia
Poland
Czech Republic
Slovakia

Hungary
Lithuania
Latvia
Prague
Tallinn
Riga
Warsaw

Vistula River
Bratislava
Budapest

People

Vaclav Havel

Reading Strategy

READING ORGANIZER Before you read, draw a circle in the center of a sheet of paper. Draw seven surrounding circles connected by lines to the center circle. Label the center circle Northeastern Europe. As you read, write information about each of the seven countries in the outer circles.

The Teutonic knights, a German order of soldier monks, brought Christianity and feudalism to northeastern Europe. They built this castle at Malbork, Poland, in the 1200s.

History

Migrants and warring armies have swept across Eastern Europe over the centuries. Each group of people brought its own language, religion, and customs. Together these groups contributed to the mosaic of cultures we see in Eastern Europe today.

Early History Among the region's early peoples were the Balts. The Balts lived on the eastern coast of the Baltic Sea. They spoke **Indo-European** languages. The Indo-European language family includes many languages spoken in Europe. These include Germanic, Baltic, and Slavic languages. More than 3,500 years ago, hunters from the Ural Mountains moved into what is now Estonia. They spoke a very different, non-Indo-European language. The language they spoke provided the early roots of today's Estonian and Finnish languages. Beginning around A.D. 400, a warrior people called the Huns invaded the region from Asia. Later, the Slavs came to the region from the plains north of the Black Sea.

In the 800s the Magyars moved into the Great Hungarian Plain. They spoke a language related to Turkish. In the 1200s the Mongols rode out of Central Asia into Hungary. At the same time German settlers pushed eastward, colonizing Poland and Bohemia—the western region of the present-day Czech Republic.

Emerging Nations Since the Middle Ages, Austria, Russia, Sweden, and the German state of Prussia have all ruled parts of Eastern Europe. After World War I ended in 1918, a new map of Eastern Europe was drawn. The peace treaty created two new countries: Yugoslavia and Czechoslovakia. Czechoslovakia included the old regions of Bohemia, Moravia, and Slovakia. At about the same time, Poland, Lithuania, Latvia, and Estonia also became independent countries.

✓ **READING CHECK:** (*Places and Regions*) What peoples contributed to the region's early history?

Culture

The culture and festivals of this region show the influence of the many peoples who contributed to its history. As in Scandinavia, Latvians celebrate a midsummer festival. The festival marks the summer solstice, the year's longest day. Poles celebrate major Roman Catholic festivals. Many of these have become symbols of the Polish nation. The annual pilgrimage, or journey, to the shrine of the Black Madonna of Częstochowa (chen-stuh-KOH-vuh) is an example.

Traditional Foods The food of the region reflects German, Russian, and Scandinavian influences. As in northern Europe, potatoes and sausages are important in the diets of Poland and the Baltic countries. Although the region has only limited access to the sea, the fish of lakes and rivers are often the center of a meal. These fish often include trout and carp. Many foods are preserved to last through the long winter. These include pickles, fruits in syrup, dried or smoked hams and sausages, and cured fish.

The Arts, Literature, and Science Northeastern Europe has made major contributions to the arts, literature, and sciences. For example, Frédéric Chopin (1810–1849) was a famous Polish pianist and composer. Marie Curie (1867–1934), one of the first female physicists, was also born in Poland. The writer Franz Kafka (1883–1924) was born to Jewish parents in Prague (PRAHG), the

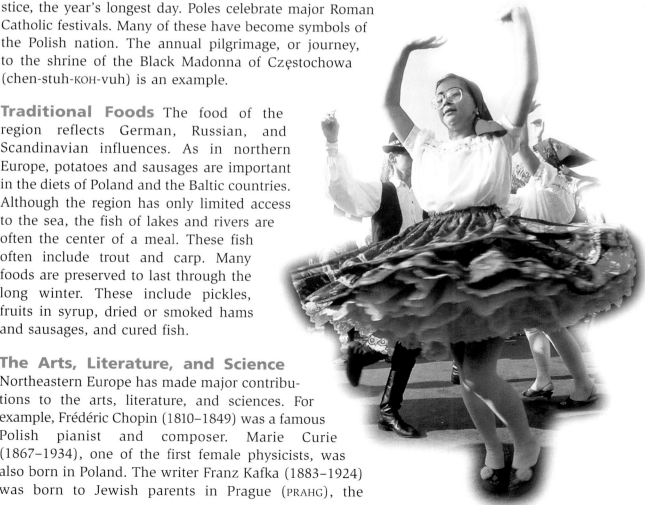

Hungarian dancers perform in traditional dress.

Interpreting the Visual Record

(Region) **How does this Hungarian costume compare to those you have seen from other countries?**

Northeastern Europe

COUNTRY	POPULATION/ GROWTH RATE	LIFE EXPECTANCY	LITERACY RATE	PER CAPITA GDP
Czech Republic	10,249,216 −0.1%	72, male 79, female	100%	$15,300
Estonia	1,408,566 −0.5%	64, male 77, female	100%	$10,900
Hungary	10,045,407 −0.3%	68, male 77, female	99%	$13,300
Latvia	2,348,784 −0.7%	63, male 75, female	100%	$8,300
Lithuania	3,592,561 −0.2%	64, male 76, female	100%	$8,400
Poland	38,622,660 0%	70, male 78, female	99%	$9,500
Slovakia	5,430,033 0.1%	70, male 79, female	not available	$10,200
United States	290,342,554 0.9%	74, male 80, female	97%	$37,600

Source: Central Intelligence Agency, *The World Factbook 2003*

Interpreting the Chart (*Place*) **Which two countries have the lowest levels of economic development?**

This suspension bridge spans the Western Dvina River in Riga, the capital of Latvia.

present-day capital of the Czech Republic. Astronomer Nicolaus Copernicus (1473–1543) was born in Toruń (TAWR-oon), a city in north-central Poland. He set forth the theory that the Sun—not Earth—is the center of the universe.

✓ **READING CHECK:** (*Human Systems*) How is the region's culture a reflection of its past and location?

Northeastern Europe Today

Estonia, Latvia, and Lithuania lie on the flat plain by the eastern Baltic Sea. Once part of the Russian Empire, the Baltic countries gained their independence after World War I ended in 1918. However, they were taken over by the Soviet Union in 1940 and placed under Communist rule. The Soviet Union collapsed in 1991. Since then, the countries of northeastern Europe have been moving from communism to capitalism and democracy.

Estonia A long history of Russian control is reflected in Estonia today. Nearly 30 percent of Estonia's population is ethnic Russian. Russia remains one of Estonia's most important trading partners. However, Estonia is also building economic ties to other countries, particularly Finland. Ethnic Estonians have close cultural ties to Finland. In fact, the Estonian language is related to Finnish. Also, most people in both countries are Lutherans. Ferries link the Estonian capital of Tallinn (TA-luhn) with Helsinki, Finland's capital.

CONNECTING TO *Literature*

Toy robot

While he wrote many books, Czech writer Karel Capek is probably best known for his play R.U.R. *This play added the word* robot *to the English language. The Czech word* robota *means "drudgery" or forced labor. The term is given to the artificial workers that Rossum's Universal Robots factory make to free humans from drudgery. Eventually, the Robots develop feelings and revolt. The play is* science fiction. *Here, Harry Domin, the factory's manager, explains the origin of the Robots to visitor Helena Glory.*

ROBOT ROBOTA

Domin: "Well, any one who has looked into human anatomy will have seen at once that man is too complicated, and that a good engineer could make him more simply. So young Rossum began to overhaul anatomy and tried to see what could be left out or simplified. . . . [He] said to himself: 'A man is something that feels happy, plays the piano, likes going for a walk, and in fact, wants to do a whole lot of things that are really unnecessary. . . .

But a working machine must not play the piano, must not feel happy, must not do a whole lot of other things. A gasoline motor must not have tassels or ornaments, Miss Glory. And to manufacture artificial workers is the same thing as to manufacture gasoline motors. The process must be of the simplest, and the product of the best from a practical point of view. . . .

Young Rossum . . . rejected everything that did not contribute directly to the progress of work—everything that makes man more expensive. In fact, he rejected man and made the Robot. My dear Miss Glory, the Robots are not people. Mechanically they are more perfect than we are, they have an enormously developed intelligence, but they have no soul."

Analyzing Primary Sources

1. Why does Rossum design the Robots without human qualities?
2. How has Karel Capel's play influenced other cultures?

Latvia Latvia is the second largest of the Baltic countries. Its population has the highest percentage of ethnic minorities. Some 57 percent of the population is Latvian. About 30 percent of the people are Russian. The capital, Riga (REE-guh), has more than 1 million people. It is the largest urban area in the three Baltic countries. Like Estonia, Latvia also has experienced strong Scandinavian and Russian influences. As well as having been part of the Russian Empire, part of the country once was ruled by Sweden. Another tie between Latvia, Estonia, and the Scandinavian countries is religion. Traditionally most people in these countries are Lutheran. In addition, Sweden and Finland are important trading partners of Latvia today.

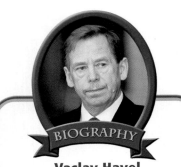
Lithuania Lithuania is the largest and southernmost Baltic country. Its capital is Vilnius (VIL-nee-uhs). Lithuania's population has the smallest percentage of ethnic minorities. More than 80 percent of the population is Lithuanian. Nearly 9 percent is Russian, while 7 percent is Polish. Lithuania has ancient ties to Poland. For more than 200 years, until 1795, they were one country. Roman Catholicism is the main religion in both Lithuania and Poland today. As in the other Baltic countries, agriculture and production of basic consumer goods are important parts of Lithuania's economy.

Poland Poland is northeastern Europe's largest and most populous country. The total population of Poland is about the same as that of Spain. The country was divided among its neighbors in the 1700s. Poland regained its independence shortly after World War I. After World War II the Soviet Union established a Communist government to rule the country.

In 1989 the Communists finally allowed free elections. Many businesses now are owned by people in the private sector rather than by the government. The country has also strengthened its ties with Western countries. In 1999 Poland, the Czech Republic, and Hungary joined the North Atlantic Treaty Organization (NATO).

Warsaw, the capital, has long been the cultural, political, and historical center of Polish life. More than 2 million people live in the urban area. The city lies on the Vistula River in central Poland. This location has made Warsaw the center of the national transportation and communications networks as well.

The Former Czechoslovakia Czechoslovakia became an independent country after World War I. Until that time, its lands had been part of the Austro-Hungarian Empire. Then shortly before World War II, it fell under German rule. After the war the Communists, with the support of the Soviet Union, gained control of the government. As in Poland, the Communists lost power in 1989. In 1993 Czechoslovakia peacefully split into two countries. The western part became the Czech Republic. The eastern part became Slovakia. This peaceful split helped the Czechs and Slovaks avoid the ethnic problems that have troubled other countries in the region.

The Czech Republic The Czech Republic's economy is growing and attracting foreign investment. Most of the country's businesses are completely or in part privately owned. However, some Czechs worry that the government remains too involved in the economy. As in Poland, a variety of political parties compete in free elections. Czech lands have coal and other

Prague's Charles Bridge is lined with historical statues.

▼

important mineral resources that are used in industry. Much of the country's industry is located in and around Prague, the capital. The city is located on the Vltava River. More than 1.2 million people live there. Prague has beautiful medieval buildings. It also has one of Europe's oldest universities.

Slovakia Slovakia is more rugged and rural, with incomes lower than in the Czech Republic. The move toward a freer political system has been slow. However, progress has been made. Bratislava (BRAH-tyee-slah-vah), the capital, is located on the Danube River. The city is the country's most important industrial area and cultural center. Many rural Slovaks move to Bratislava looking for better-paying jobs. Most of the country's population is Slovak. However, ethnic Hungarians account for more than 10 percent of Slovakia's population.

Hungary Hungary separated from the Austro-Hungarian Empire at the end of World War I. Following World War II, a Communist government came to power. A revolt against the government was put down by the Soviet Union in 1956. The Communists ruled until 1989.

Today the country has close ties with the rest of Europe. In fact, most of Hungary's trade is with members of the European Union. During the Communist era, the government experimented with giving some businesses the freedom to act on their own. For example, it allowed local farm managers to make key business decisions. These managers kept farming methods modern, chose their crops, and marketed their products. Today, farm products from Hungary's fertile plains are important exports. Much of the country's manufacturing is located in and around the capital, Budapest (BOO-duh-pest). Budapest is Hungary's largest city. Nearly 20 percent of the population lives there.

▲
The Danube River flows through Budapest, Hungary.

Interpreting the Visual Record

(*Human-Environment Interaction*)

Why might Hungary's capital have grown up along a river?

✔ **READING CHECK:** (*Human Systems*) How have the governments and economies of the region been affected by recent history?

go.hrw.com
Homework Practice Online
Keyword: SG5 HP14

Define or identify: Indo-European, Vaclav Havel

Working with Sketch Maps On the map you drew in Section 1, label the countries of the region, Prague, Tallinn, Riga, Warsaw, Vistula River, Bratislava, and Budapest.

Reading for the Main Idea

1. (*Human Systems*) How did invasions and migrations help shape the region?

2. (*Places and Regions*) What has the region contributed to the arts?

Critical Thinking

3. **Drawing Inferences and Conclusions** How did the Soviet Union influence the region?

4. **Summarizing** What social changes have taken place here since the early 1990s?

Organizing What You Know

5. **Sequencing** Copy the following graphic organizer. Use it to show the history of the Baltics since 1900.

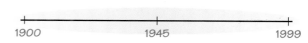

1900   1945   1999

The Countries of Southeastern Europe

Read to Discover

1. How did Southeastern Europe's early history help shape its modern societies?
2. How does culture both link and divide the region?
3. How has the region's past contributed to current conflicts?

Vocabulary

Roma

Places

Bulgaria
Romania
Croatia
Slovenia
Serbia

Bosnia and
    Herzegovina
Albania
Kosovo
Serbia and
    Montenegro
Macedonia
Belgrade
Podgorica

Sarajevo
Zagreb
Ljubljana
Skopje
Bucharest
Moldova
Chişinău
Sofia
Tiranë

Reading Strategy

ANTICIPATING INFORMATION This region is sometimes called the Powder Keg of Europe. What do you think that means? Write down your answer. As you read this section, write down information that explains why the Balkan countries were given this nickname.

▲
These ancient ruins in southern Albania date to the 500s B.C.

Interpreting the Visual Record
(Place) What cultural influence does this building show?

History

Along with neighboring Greece, this was the first region of Europe to adopt agriculture. From here farming moved up the Danube River valley into central and western Europe. Early farmers and metalworkers in the south may have spoken languages related to Albanian. Albanian is an Indo-European language.

Early History Around 750–600 B.C. the ancient Greeks founded colonies on the Black Sea coast. The area they settled is now Bulgaria and Romania. Later, the Romans conquered most of the area from the Adriatic Sea to the Danube River and across into Romania. When the Roman Empire divided into west and east, much of the Balkans and Greece became part of the Eastern Roman Empire. This eastern region eventually became known as the Byzantine Empire. Under Byzantine rule, many people of the Balkans became Orthodox Christians.

Kingdoms and Empires Many of today's southeastern European countries first appear as kingdoms between A.D. 800 and 1400. The Ottoman Turks conquered the region and ruled until the 1800s. The Ottomans, who were Muslims, tolerated other religious faiths. However, many peoples, such as the Bosnians and Albanians, converted to Islam. As the Ottoman Empire began to weaken in the late 1800s, the Austro-Hungarians took control of Croatia and Slovenia. They imposed Roman Catholicism.

Slav Nationalism The Russians, meanwhile, were fighting the Turks for control of the Black Sea. The Russians encouraged Slavs in the Balkans to revolt against the Turks. The Russians appealed to Slavic nationalism— to the Slav's sense of loyalty to their country. The Serbs did revolt in 1815 and became self-governing in 1817. By 1878 Bulgaria and Romania were also self-governing.

The Austro-Hungarians responded to Slavic nationalism by occupying additional territories. Those territories included the regions of Bosnia and Herzegovina. To stop the Serbs from expanding to the Adriatic coast, European powers made Albania an independent kingdom.

In August 1914 a Serb nationalist shot and killed the heir to the Austro-Hungarian throne. Austria declared war on Serbia. Russia came to Serbia's defense. These actions sparked World War I. All of Europe's great powers became involved. The United States entered the war in 1917.

Creation of Yugoslavia At the end of World War I Austria-Hungary was broken apart. Austria was reduced to a small territory. Hungary became a separate country but lost its eastern province to Romania. Romania also gained additional lands from Russia. Albania remained independent. The peace settlement created Yugoslavia. Yugoslavia means "land of the southern Slavs." Yugoslavia brought the region's Serbs, Bosnians, Croatians, Macedonians, Montenegrins, and Slovenes together into one country. Each ethnic group had its own republic within Yugoslavia. Some Bosnians and other people in Serbia were Muslims. Most Serbs were Orthodox Christians, and the Slovenes and Croats were Roman Catholics. These ethnic and religious differences created problems that eventually led to civil war in the 1990s.

✓ **READING CHECK:** (*Human Systems*) How is southeastern Europe's religious and ethnic makeup a reflection of its past?

This bridge at Mostar, Bosnia, was built during the 1600s. This photograph was taken in 1982.

This photograph shows Mostar after civil war in the 1990s.
Interpreting the Visual Record (*Place*)
What differences can you find in the two photos?

Ethnic Albanians worship at a mosque in Pristina, Serbia.

Culture

The Balkans are the most diverse region of Europe in terms of language, ethnicity, and religion. It is the largest European region to have once been ruled by a Muslim power. It has also been a zone of conflict between eastern and western Christianity. The three main Indo-European language branches—Romance (from Latin), Germanic, and Slavic—are all found here, as well as other branches such as Albanian. Non-Indo-European languages like Hungarian and Turkish are also spoken here.

Balkan diets combine the foods of the Hungarians and the Slavs with those of the Mediterranean Greeks, Turks, and Italians. In Greek and Turkish cuisines, yogurt and soft cheeses are an important part of most meals, as are fresh fruits, nuts, and vegetables. Roast goat or lamb are the favorite meats for a celebration.

In the Balkans Bosnian and ethnic Albanian Muslims celebrate the feasts of Islam. Christian holidays—Christmas and Easter—are celebrated on one day by Catholics and on another by Orthodox Christians. Holidays in memory of ancient battles and modern liberation days are sources of conflict between ethnic groups.

✔ **READING CHECK:** (**Places and Regions**) Why is religion an important issue in southeastern Europe?

Our Amazing Planet

The Danube Delta, on the Romanian coast of the Black Sea, is part of a unique ecosystem. Most of the Romanian caviar-producing sturgeon are caught in these waters. Caviar is made from the salted eggs from three types of sturgeon fish. Caviar is considered a delicacy and can cost as much as $50 per ounce.

Southeastern Europe Today

Like other southeastern European countries, Yugoslavia was occupied by Germany in World War II. A Communist government under Josip Broz Tito took over after the war. Tito's strong central government prevented ethnic conflict. After Tito died in 1980, Yugoslavia's Communist government held the republics together. Then in 1991 the republics of Slovenia, Croatia, Bosnia and Herzegovina, and Macedonia began to break away. Years of bloody civil war followed. Today the region struggles with the violence and with rebuilding economies left weak by years of Communist-government control.

The Former Yugoslavia Located on the Danube River, Belgrade is the capital of Serbia and Montenegro. The Serbian government supported ethnic Serbs fighting in civil wars in Croatia and in Bosnia and Herzegovina in the early 1990s. Tensions between ethnic groups also have been a problem within Serbia. About 65 percent of the people in Serbia and Montenegro are Orthodox Christians. In the southern Serbian province of Kosovo, the majority of people are ethnic Albanian and Muslim. Many of the Albanians want independence. Conflict between Serbs and Albanians led to civil war in the late 1990s. In 1999 the United States, other Western countries, and Russia sent troops to keep the peace. In Feburary, 2003, Serbia and Montenegro unified as one country. Today, 2,500 troops remain in the region.

Bosnia and Herzegovina Bosnia and Herzegovina generally are referred to as Bosnia. Some 40 percent of Bosnians are Muslims, but large numbers of Roman Catholic Croats and Orthodox Christian Serbs also live there. Following independence, a bloody civil war broke out between these groups as they struggled for control of territory. During the fighting the once beautiful capital of Sarajevo (sar-uh-YAY-voh) was heavily damaged.

Croatia Croatia's capital is Zagreb (ZAH-greb). Most of the people of Croatia are Roman Catholic. In the early 1990s, Serbs made up about 12 percent of the population. In 1991 the ethnic Serbs living in Croatia claimed part of the country for Serbia. This resulted in heavy fighting. By the end of 1995 an agreement was reached and a sense of stability returned to the country. Many Serbs left the country.

These Muslim refugees are walking to Travnik, Bosnia, with the assistance of UN troops.

Interpreting the Visual Record

Movement **What effect might the movement of refugees have on a region?**

▼

Slovenia Slovenia is a former Austrian territory. It looks to Western European countries for much of its trade. Most people in Slovenia are Roman Catholic, and few ethnic minorities live there. Partly because of the small number of ethnic minorities, little fighting occurred after Slovenia declared independence from Yugoslavia. The major center of industry is Ljubljana (lee-oo-blee-AH-nuh), the country's capital.

Slovenia's capital, Ljubljana, lies on the Sava River.

▼

Macedonia When Macedonia declared its independence from Yugoslavia, Greece immediately objected to the country's new name. Macedonia is also the name of a province in northern Greece that has historical ties to the republic. Greece feared that Macedonia might try to take over the province.

Greece responded by refusing to trade with Macedonia until the mid-1990s. This slowed Macedonia's movement from the command— or government-controlled—economy it had under Communist rule to a market economy in which consumers help to determine what is to be produced by buying or not buying certain goods and services. Despite its rocky start, in recent years Macedonia has made progress in establishing free markets.

Romania A Communist government took power in Romania at the end of World War II. Then in 1989 the Communist government was overthrown during bloody fighting. Change, however, has been slow. Bucharest, the capital, is the biggest industrial center. Today more people work in agriculture than in any other part of the economy. Nearly 90 percent of the country's population is ethnic Romanian. **Roma**, or Gypsies as they were once known, make up more than 2 percent of the population. They are descended from people who may have lived in northern India and began migrating centuries ago. Most of the rest of Romania's population are ethnic Hungarian.

Moldova Throughout history control of Moldova has shifted many times. It has been dominated by Turks, Polish princes, Austria, Hungary, Russia, and Romania. Not surprisingly, the country's popu-

FOCUS ON CULTURE

Roma Women in a Changing World

The Roma nomadic way of life has changed. Now some Roma live in cities, go to school, and enter professions. Many Roma, however, are poor and have no jobs. They also experience discrimination. Part of the problem is that some Roma customs conflict with non-Roma customs. Some of these customs relate to women.

In traditional Roma communities, girls quit school early and marry when very young. Parents arrange many marriages. A ceremony seals the arrangement. The groom's father places a necklace of gold coins around the bride's neck to show that she is promised to his son. During their marriage, the young couple will

probably have many children. Families celebrate the birth of a boy more than the birth of a girl.

Now, some Roma women are organizing for better social services and more respect in their communities.

What are some opportunities that Roma girls lose if they marry when very young?

lation reflects this diverse past. Moldova declared its independence in 1991 from the Soviet Union. However, the country suffers from difficult economic and political problems. About 40 percent of the country's labor force works in agriculture. Chişinău (kee-shee-NOW), the major industrial center of the country, is also Moldova's capital.

Bulgaria Mountainous Bulgaria has progressed slowly since the fall of communism. However, a market economy is growing gradually, and the people have more freedoms. Most industries are located near Sofia (SOH-fee-uh), the capital and largest city. About 9 percent of Bulgaria's people are ethnic Turks.

Albania Albania is one of Europe's poorest countries. The capital, Tiranë (ti-RAH-nuh), has a population of about 270,000. About 70 percent of Albanians are Muslim. Albania's Communist government feuded with the Communist governments in the Soviet Union and, later, in China. As a result, Albania became isolated. Since the fall of its harsh Communist government in the 1990s, the country has tried to move toward both democracy and a free market system.

✔ **READING CHECK:** (*Human Systems*) What problems does the region face, and how are they reflections of its Communist past?

Southeastern Europe

COUNTRY	POPULATION/ GROWTH RATE	LIFE EXPECTANCY	LITERACY RATE	PER CAPITA GDP
Albania	3,582,205 1.0%	70, male 75, female	87%	$4,500
Bosnia and Herzegovina	3,989,018 0.5%	70, male 75, female	not available	$1,900
Bulgaria	7,537,929 −1.1%	68, male 76, female	99%	$6,600
Croatia	4,422,248 .3%	71, male 78, female	99%	$8,800
Macedonia	2,063,122 0.4%	72, male 77, female	not available	$5,000
Moldova	4,439,502 0.1%	61, male 69, female	99%	$2,500
Romania	22,271,839 −0.2%	67, male 75, female	98%	$7,400
Serbia and Montenegro	10,655,774 −0.1%	71, male 77, female	93%	$2,370
United States	290,342,554 0.9%	74, male 80, female	97%	$37,600

Source: Central Intelligence Agency, *The World Factbook 2003*

Interpreting the Chart (*Place*) **Which southeastern European country has the highest level of economic development?**

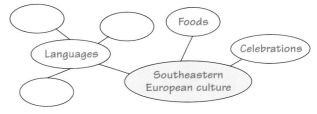

Homework Practice Online
go.hrw.com
Keyword: SG5 HP14

Section Review 3

Define and explain: Roma

Working with Sketch Maps On the map you drew in Section 2, label the region's countries and their capitals. They are listed at the beginning of the section. In a box in the margin, identify the countries that once made up Yugoslavia.

Reading for the Main Idea

1. (*Human Systems*) How has the region's history influenced its religious and ethnic makeup?

2. (*Human Systems*) What events and factors have contributed to problems in Bosnia and other countries in the region since independence?

Critical Thinking

3. **Summarizing** How was Yugoslavia created?

4. **Analyzing Information** How are the region's governments and economies changing?

Organizing What You Know

5. **Categorizing** Copy the following graphic organizer. Use it to identify languages, foods, and celebrations in the region.

Languages — Foods — Celebrations — Southeastern European culture

Review and Practice

Define and Identify

Identify each of the following:

1. oil shale
2. lignite
3. amber
4. Indo-European
5. Vaclav Havel
6. Roma

Review the Main Ideas

7. What are the major landforms of Eastern Europe?
8. What is Eastern Europe's major river?
9. What are some of Eastern Europe's resources?
10. What groups influenced the culture of Eastern Europe? How can these influences be seen today?
11. How did the close of World War I change the countries of Eastern Europe?
12. Who are some important contributors to art, literature, and sciences that came from Northeastern Europe?
13. How did changes of the 1990s affect the politics and economics of Eastern Europe?
14. What are the main cities of Northeastern Europe? of Southeastern Europe?

15. What makes the Balkans the most diverse region in Europe?
16. What countries broke away from Yugoslavia in the early 1990s? What happened in the region in 2003?

Think Critically

17. **Drawing Inferences and Conclusions** How has Eastern Europe's location influenced the diets of the region's people?
18. **Analyzing Information** How did Communist economic policies affect the region's environment? its major river?
19. **Identifying Cause and Effect** What geographic factors help make Warsaw the transportation and communication center of Poland? If Warsaw were located along the Baltic coast of Poland or near the German border instead, how may the city have developed differently?
20. **Comparing and Contrasting** Compare and contrast the breakups of Yugoslavia and Czechoslovakia.
21. **Summarizing** How has political change affected the economies of Eastern European countries?

Map Activity

22. On a separate sheet of paper, match the letters on the map with their correct labels.

    Baltic Sea
    Adriatic Sea
    Black Sea
    Danube River
    Dinaric Alps
    Balkan Mountains
    Carpathian Mountains

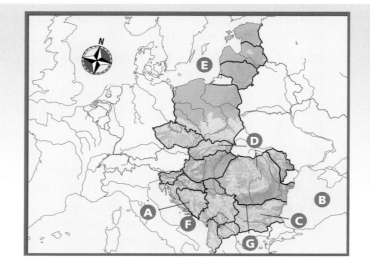

Writing Activity

Imagine that you are a teenager living in Romania and want to write a family memoir of life in Romania. Include accounts of life for your grandparents under strict Soviet rule and life for your parents during the Soviet Union's breakup. Also describe your life in free Romania. Be sure to use standard grammar, sentence structure, and punctuation.

internet connect

Internet Activity: **go.hrw.com**
KEYWORD: **SG5 GT14**

Choose a topic to explore Eastern Europe:
- Investigate the conflicts in the Balkans.
- Take a virtual tour of Eastern Europe.
- Learn about Baltic amber.

Social Studies Skills Practice

Interpreting Graphs

You have learned about the cultural diversity of the Balkan region. Study the following graph about Bosnia and Herzegovina. Then answer the questions below.

Religious Practice in Bosnia and Herzegovina

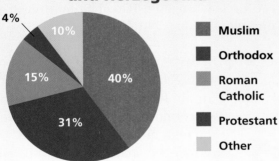

- Muslim
- Orthodox
- Roman Catholic
- Protestant
- Other

4%
10%
15%
40%
31%

Source: Central Intelligence Agency, *The World Factbook,* 2003

1. Which religion claims the largest percentage of followers? the smallest?

2. Which two religions, when combined, total almost three-fourths of the country's people?

3. Based on this information, what is one thing that you may conclude about the country's history?

4. What can you assume about how many people follow any one of the "other" religions? Why?

Analyzing Primary Sources

Attila the Hun was a fierce warrior who invaded Eastern Europe in the A.D. 400s. Attila spread terror among the peoples he conquered. In this passage, a Roman historian named Priscus reports on having dinner in Attila's tent and on the entertainment that followed the meal. Read the passage. Then answer the questions.

"After the songs a Scythian entered, a crazy fellow who told a lot of strange and completely false stories, not a word of truth in them, which made everyone laugh. Following him came the Moor, Zerkon, totally disorganized in appearance, clothes, voice and words. By mixing up the languages of the Italians with those of the Huns and Goths, he fascinated everyone and made them break out into uncontrollable laughter, all that is except Attila. He remained impassive, without any change of expression . . ."

1. How do the guests react to the entertainment? How does Attila react?

2. What indicates that Attila had contacts with many different peoples?

3. If the Scythian and Zerkon were living and entertaining today, what would we call their profession?

4. How does the image of Attila's court in this report compare to Attila's reputation among the peoples he conquered?

The European Union

What if . . . ? Imagine you are traveling from Florida to Pennsylvania. You have to go through a border checkpoint in Georgia to prove your Florida identity. The guard charges a tax on the cookies you are bringing to a friend in Pennsylvania. Buying gas presents more problems. You try to pay with Florida dollars, but the attendant just looks at you. You discover that they speak "Virginian" in Virginia and use Virginia coins. All this would make traveling from one place to another much more difficult.

The European Union Fortunately, that was just an imaginary situation. However, it is similar

The Eurostar train carries passengers from London to Paris. These two cities are only about 200 miles (322 km) apart. However, they have different cultures and ways of life.

to what might happen while traveling across Europe. European countries have different languages, currencies, laws, and cultures. For example, someone from France has different customs than someone from Ireland.

However, many Europeans also share common interests. For example, they are interested in peace in the region. They also have a common interest in Europe's economic success.

A shared belief in economic and political cooperation has resulted in the creation of the European Union (EU). The EU has eliminated boundaries to job opportunities. For example, it is estimated that as many as 40,000 people from member countries in Eastern Europe may migrate to the United Kingdom (Great Britain) each year to find work.

The Beginnings of a Unified Europe

Proposals for an economically integrated Europe first came about in the 1950s. After World War II, the countries of Europe had many economic problems. A plan was made to unify the coal and steel production of some countries. In 1957 France, West Germany, Italy, Belgium, the Netherlands, and Luxembourg formed the European Economic Community (EEC). The name was shortened in 1992 to simply the European Community (EC). The goal of the EC was to combine each country's economy into a single market. Having one market would make trading among them easier. Eventually, more countries became interested in joining the EC. In 1973 the United Kingdom, Denmark, and

ATLANTIC OCEAN

FINLAND

SWEDEN

ESTONIA

LATVIA

LITHUANIA

UNITED KINGDOM

IRELAND

DENMARK

NETHERLANDS

BELGIUM

GERMANY

POLAND

LUXEMBOURG

CZECH REPUBLIC

SLOVAKIA

FRANCE

AUSTRIA

HUNGARY

SLOVENIA

PORTUGAL

SPAIN

ITALY

GREECE

MALTA

CYPRUS

MEDITERRANEAN SEA

The European Union (EU)

Countries that joined the EU in 2004

The 25 EU countries produce a wide range of exports and are one of the world's richest markets.

The flag of the EU features 12 gold stars on a blue background. The EU's currency, the euro, replaced the currencies of most EU countries.

Ireland joined. In the 1980s Greece, Portugal, and Spain joined. Austria, Finland, and Sweden were added in the 1990s.

In 2004 countries from Eastern Europe and the Mediterranean joined the EU. (See the map to locate these countries.) Bulgaria, Romania, and Turkey are candidates to join in the next several years.

The Future Some people believe the EU is laying the foundation for a greater sense of European identity. A European Court of Justice has been set up to enforce EU rules. According to some experts, this is helping to build common European beliefs, responsibilities, and rights.

On January 1, 2002, the euro became the common currency for most EU countries. The symbol of the euro is €. With the exception of Denmark, Sweden, and the United Kingdom, the euro replaced the currencies of all other member coun-

tries. The 12 countries that currently use the euro are commonly referred to as the "euro zone."

The EU has resulted in many important changes in Europe. Cooperation between member countries has increased. Trade has also increased. EU members have adopted a common currency and common economic laws. The EU is creating a more unified Europe. Some people even believe that the EU might someday lead to a "United States of Europe."

Understanding What You Read

1. What was the first step toward European economic unity?

2. What is the euro? How do you think the euro helps unify Europe?

Building Skills for Life: Analyzing Settlement Patterns

This illustration shows a German medieval city in the 1400s.

There are many different kinds of human settlements. Some people live in villages where they farm and raise animals. Others live in small towns or cities and work in factories or offices. Geographers analyze these settlement patterns. They are interested in how settlements affect people's lives.

All settlements are unique. Even neighboring villages are different. One village might have better soil than its neighbors. Another village might be closer to a main road or highway. Geographers are interested in the unique qualities of human settlements.

Geographers also study different types of settlements. For example, many European settlements could be considered medieval cities. Medieval cities are about 500–1,500 years old. They usually have walls around them and buildings made of stone and wood. Medieval cities also have tall churches and narrow, winding streets.

Analyzing settlement patterns is important. It helps us learn about people and environments. For example, the architecture of a city might give us clues about the culture, history, and technology of the people who live there. You can ask questions about individual villages, towns, and cities to learn about settlement patterns. What kinds of activities are going on? How are the streets arranged? What kinds of transportation do people use? You can also ask questions about groups of settlements. How are they connected? Do they trade with each other? Are some settlements bigger or older than others? Why is this so?

THE SKILL

1. How do you think a city, a town, and a village are different from each other? Write down your own definition of each word on a piece of paper. Then look them up in a dictionary and write down the dictionary's definition. Were your definitions different?

2. Analyze the settlement where you live. How old is it? How many people live there? What kinds of jobs do people have? How is it connected to other settlements? How is it unique?

3. Besides medieval cities, what other types of cities can you think of? Make a list of three other possible types.

HANDS on GEOGRAPHY

One type of settlement is called a planned city. A planned city is carefully designed before it is built. Each part fits into an overall plan. For example, the size and arrangement of streets and buildings might be planned.

There are many planned cities in the world. Some examples are Brasília, Brazil; Chandigarh, India; and Washington, D.C. Many other cities have certain parts that are planned, such as individual neighborhoods. These neighborhoods are sometimes called planned communities.

Suppose you were asked to plan a city. How would you do it? On a separate sheet of paper, create your own planned city. These guidelines will help you get started.

1. First, decide what the physical environment will be like. Is the city on the coast, on a river, or somewhere else? Are there hills, lakes, or other physical features in the area?

2. Decide what to include in your city. Most cities have a downtown, different neighborhoods, and roads or highways that connect areas together. Many cities also have parks, museums, and an airport.

3. Plan the arrangement of your city. Where will the roads and highways go? Will the airport be close to downtown? Try to arrange the different parts of your city so that they fit together logically.

4. Draw a map of your planned city. Be sure to include a title, scale, and orientation.

Some people think the city plan for Brasília looks like a bird, a bow and arrow, or an airplane.
Interpreting the Visual Record What do you notice about the arrangement of Brasília's streets?

Lab Report

1. How was your plan influenced by the physical environment you chose?

2. How do you think planned cities are different from cities that are not planned?

3. What problems might people have when they try to plan an entire city?

UNIT 5

Russia and Its Western Neighbors

CHAPTER 15
Russia

CHAPTER 16
Ukraine, Belarus, and the Caucasus

Dancers in Russian national dress

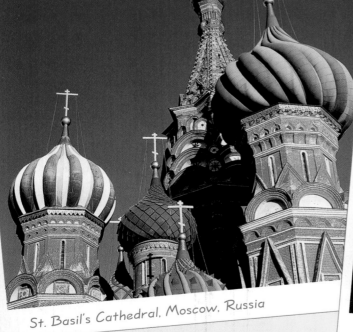

St. Basil's Cathedral, Moscow, Russia

Church overlooking the Black Sea, Ukraine

Journalists in Russia

Journalists Gary Matoso and Lisa Dickey traveled more than 5,000 miles across Russia. They wrote this account of their visit with Buyanto Tsydypov. He is a Buryat farmer who lives in the Lake Baikal area. The Buryats are one of Russia's many minority ethnic groups. **WHAT DO YOU THINK?** *If you visited a Buryat family, what would you like to see or ask?*

"You came to us like thunder out of the clear blue sky," said our host. The surprise of our visit did not, however, keep him from greeting us warmly.

Buyanto brought us to a special place of prayer. High on a hillside, a yellow wooden frame holds a row of tall, narrow sticks. On the end of each stick, Buddhist prayer cloths flutter in the biting autumn wind.

In times of trouble and thanks, Buryats come to tie their prayer cloths—called *khimorin*—to the sticks and make their offerings to the gods. Buyanto builds a small fire. He unfolds an aqua-blue *khimorin* to show the drawings.

"All around are the Buddhist gods," he says, "and at the bottom we have written our names and the names of others we are praying for."

He fans the flames slowly with the cloth, purifying it with sacred smoke. After a time he moves to the top of the hill where he ties the *khimorin* to one of the sticks.

Buryat people, Lake Baikal area, Russia

Understanding Primary Sources

1. How do you know that Buyanto Tsydypov was surprised to meet the two American journalists?

2. What is a *khimorin*?

Brown bear

Russia and Its Western Neighbors

Elevation Profile

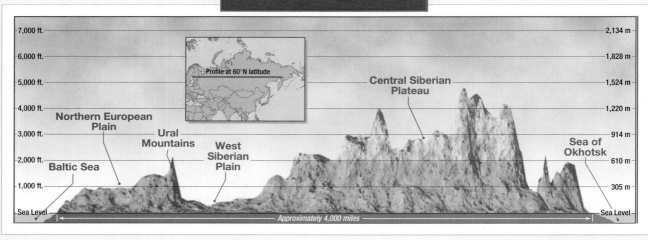

7,000 ft. — 2,134 m
6,000 ft. — 1,828 m
5,000 ft. — 1,524 m
4,000 ft. — 1,220 m
3,000 ft. — 914 m
2,000 ft. — 610 m
1,000 ft. — 305 m
Sea Level — Sea Level

Profile at 60° N latitude

Central Siberian Plateau

Northern European Plain

Ural Mountains

West Siberian Plain

Baltic Sea

Sea of Okhotsk

Approximately 4,000 miles

The United States and Russia and Its Western Neighbors
Comparing Sizes

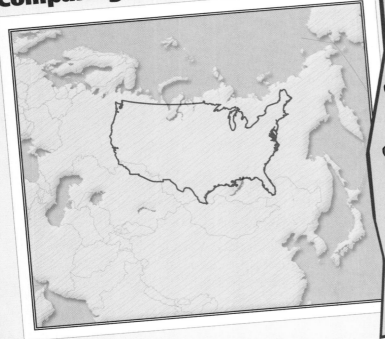

GEOSTATS:

Russia

- World's largest country in area: 6,659,328 sq. mi. (17,075,200 sq km)

- World's seventh-largest population: 144,526,278 (July 2003 estimate)

- World's largest lake: Caspian Sea—143,244 sq. mi. (371,002 sq km)

- World's deepest lake: Lake Baikal—5,715 ft. (1,742 m)

- Largest number of time zones: 11

- Highest mountain in Europe: Mount Elbrus—18,510 ft. (5,642 m)

Physical

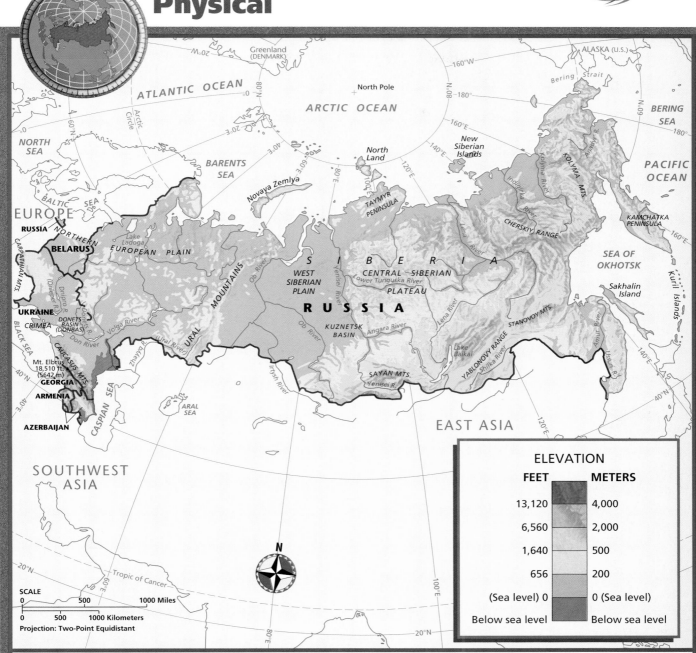

ELEVATION

FEET		METERS
13,120		4,000
6,560		2,000
1,640		500
656		200
(Sea level) 0		0 (Sea level)
Below sea level		Below sea level

SCALE
0   500   1000 Miles
0   500   1000 Kilometers
Projection: Two-Point Equidistant

1. (*Region*) In what general direction do the great rivers of Siberia flow?

2. (*Region*) Which countries have areas that are below sea level?

Critical Thinking

3. (*Movement*) Russia has often been invaded by other countries. Which part of Russia might be easy to invade? Why do you think this area would be a good invasion route?

4. (*Interaction*) Northern Russia appears to have many good harbors. Compare this map to the **climate map** of the region. Why have few harbors been developed on Russia's north coast?

1. *Region* Compare this map to the **physical map** of the region. What physical feature seems to define a border between Russia and the countries of Europe?

2. *Location* What is the southernmost Russian city shown on the map?

Critical Thinking

3. *Location* About how far apart are Russia and the Alaskan mainland? the Russian mainland and the North Pole?

4. *Region* Do Russia's western and southern borders appear to follow natural boundaries? Why or why not?

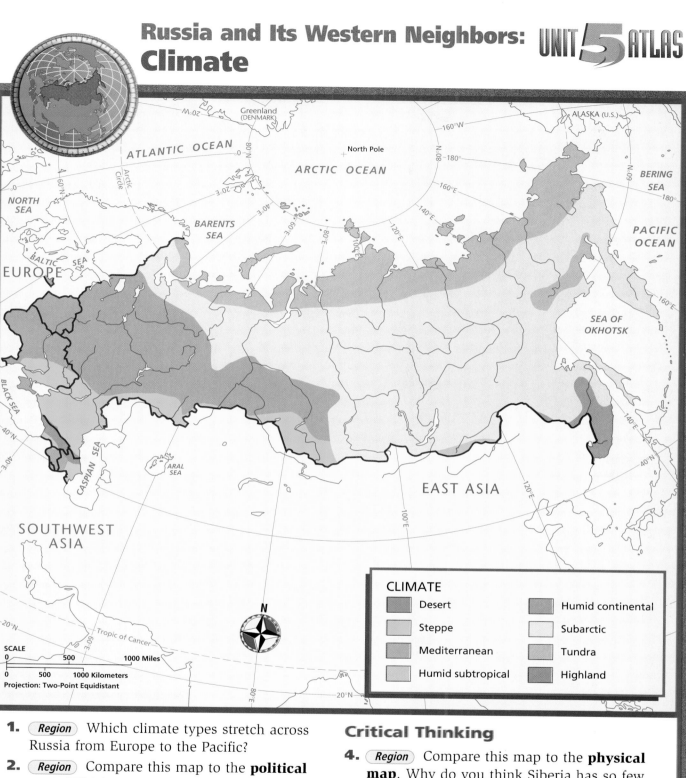

CLIMATE

- Desert
- Steppe
- Mediterranean
- Humid subtropical
- Humid continental
- Subarctic
- Tundra
- Highland

SCALE
0   500   1000 Miles
0   500   1000 Kilometers
Projection: Two-Point Equidistant

1. *Region* Which climate types stretch across Russia from Europe to the Pacific?

2. *Region* Compare this map to the **political map**. Which country has only a humid continental climate?

3. *Region* Which climate region in Russia is the smallest?

Critical Thinking

4. *Region* Compare this map to the **physical map**. Why do you think Siberia has so few climate types?

5. *Interaction* Compare this map to the **land use and resources map**. What is one reason why most commercial farming is in Russia's western region?

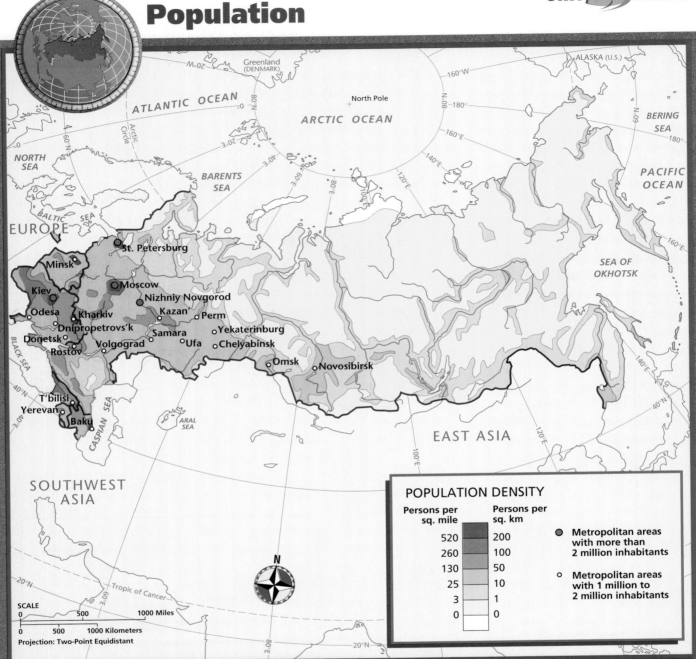

POPULATION DENSITY

Persons per sq. mile	Persons per sq. km
520	200
260	100
130	50
25	10
3	1
0	0

● Metropolitan areas with more than 2 million inhabitants

○ Metropolitan areas with 1 million to 2 million inhabitants

SCALE
0   500   1000 Miles
0   500   1000 Kilometers
Projection: Two-Point Equidistant

1. (*Region*) Which countries have a large area with more than 260 people per square mile and cities of more than 2 million people?

2. (*Region*) Which country has areas in the north where no one lives?

Critical Thinking

3. (*Interaction*) What can you assume about landforms and farming in western Russia, Ukraine, and Belarus just by looking at the **population map**? Check the **physical** and **land use and resources maps** to be sure.

4. (*Interaction*) Compare this map to the **physical map**. What is one reason why the area between the Black Sea and Caspian Sea has few big cities?

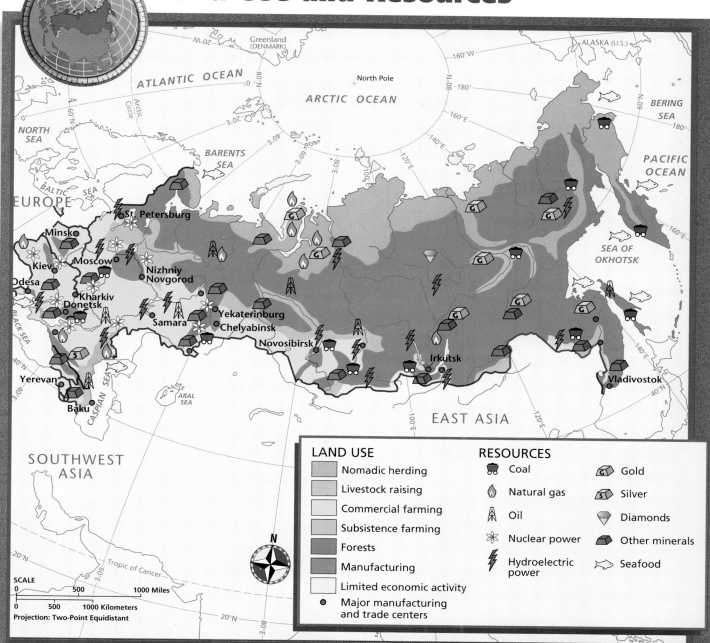

LAND USE
- Nomadic herding
- Livestock raising
- Commercial farming
- Subsistence farming
- Forests
- Manufacturing
- Limited economic activity
- ● Major manufacturing and trade centers

RESOURCES
- Coal
- Natural gas
- Oil
- Nuclear power
- Hydroelectric power
- G Gold
- S Silver
- Diamonds
- Other minerals
- Seafood

SCALE
0   500   1000 Miles
0   500   1000 Kilometers
Projection: Two-Point Equidistant

1. *Interaction* Where are most oil reserves in the region located?

2. *Interaction* Where are most gold mines in the region located?

3. *Interaction* Which country has diamonds? Which countries in the region have natural gas deposits?

Critical Thinking

4. *Interaction* Compare this to the **physical map**. Which waterways might be used to transport mineral resources mined near Irkutsk to manufacturing and trade centers?

5. *Region* Why do you think there are more nuclear power plants in the western part of the region?

Fast FACTS

Russia and Its Western Neighbors

ARMENIA

CAPITAL:
Yerevan

AREA:
11,506 sq. mi. (29,800 sq km)

POPULATION:
3,326,448

MONEY:
dram

LANGUAGES:
Armenian, Russian

UNEMPLOYMENT:
20 percent

BELARUS

CAPITAL:
Minsk

AREA:
80,154 sq. mi.
(207,600 sq km)

POPULATION:
10,322,151

MONEY:
Belarusian rubel

LANGUAGES:
Byelorussian, Russian

UNEMPLOYMENT:
2.1 percent (and many underemployed workers)

AZERBAIJAN

CAPITAL:
Baku

AREA:
33,436 sq. mi.
(86,600 sq km)

POPULATION:
7,830,764

MONEY:
manat

LANGUAGES:
Azeri, Russian, Armenian

UNEMPLOYMENT:
16 percent

GEORGIA

CAPITAL:
T'bilisi

AREA:
26,911 sq. mi.
(69,700 sq km)

POPULATION:
4,934,413

MONEY:
lari

LANGUAGES:
Georgian (official), Russian, Armenian, Azeri

UNEMPLOYMENT:
17 percent

Family eating breakfast in Georgia

Geese flock to this pasture in Ukraine

Countries not drawn to scale.

RUSSIA

CAPITAL: Moscow

AREA:
6,592,735 sq. mi.
(17,075,200 sq km)

POPULATION:
144,526,278

MONEY: Russian ruble

LANGUAGES:
Russian

UNEMPLOYMENT:
7.9 percent (and many
underemployed workers)

UKRAINE

CAPITAL: Kiev

AREA: 233,089 sq. mi.
(603,700 sq km)

POPULATION:
48,055,439

MONEY:
hryvna

LANGUAGES:
Ukranian, Russian, Romanian,
Polish, Hungarian

UNEMPLOYMENT:
3.8 percent officially regis-
tered (and many unregis-
tered or underemployed)

Church of the Transfiguration, Kizhi Island, Russia

Russian ballet dancers

internet connect

COUNTRY STATISTICS
GO TO: go.hrw.com
KEYWORD: SG5 FactsU5
FOR: more facts about Russia
and its western neighbors

Sources: Central Intelligence Agency, *The World Factbook 2003;*
The World Almanac and Book of Facts 2003; pop. figures are 2003 estimates.

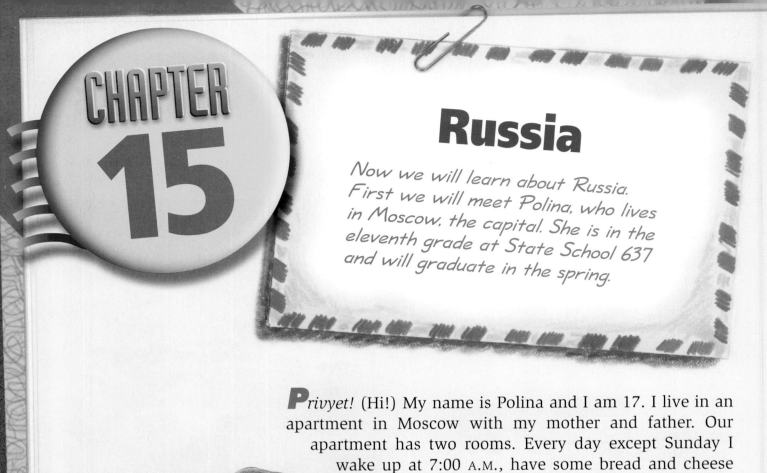

CHAPTER 15

Russia

Now we will learn about Russia. First we will meet Polina, who lives in Moscow, the capital. She is in the eleventh grade at State School 637 and will graduate in the spring.

Privyet! (Hi!) My name is Polina and I am 17. I live in an apartment in Moscow with my mother and father. Our apartment has two rooms. Every day except Sunday I wake up at 7:00 A.M., have some bread and cheese with tea, and take the subway to school. At the end of eighth grade, we had to choose whether to study science or humanities. I chose humanities. My favorite subjects are history, literature, and English—my history teacher is great!

We have about five or six classes with a 15-minute break between each one. During the breaks, I often eat a snack like *pirozhki*, a small meat pie, at the school snack bar. I go home at 2:00 P.M. for lunch (meat, potatoes, and a salad of cooked vegetables and mayonnaise) and a nap. When I wake up, I go out with my friends to a park. Sometimes my parents and I join my uncle, aunt, and grandmother for Sunday dinner. My uncle makes my favorite dishes, like meat salad with mayonnaise. I love ice cream, too!

Привет! Я живу в Москве.

▲

Translation: Hi! I live in Moscow.

Section 1 Physical Geography

Read to Discover

1. What are the physical features of Russia?
2. What climates and vegetation are found in Russia?
3. What natural resources does Russia have?

Vocabulary

taiga
steppe

Places

Arctic Ocean
Caucasus Mountains
Caspian Sea
Ural Mountains
West Siberian Plain
Central Siberian Plateau

Kamchatka Peninsula
Kuril Islands
Volga River
Baltic Sea

Reading Strategy

USING VISUAL INFORMATION Look at the map below. Why do you think the Trans-Siberian Railroad is shown on the map? Why do you think it was built? Would it have been difficult to build? Write down your answers. As you read, write down facts that support or disprove your statements.

Russia: Physical-Political

ELEVATION

	FEET		METERS
★ National capital	13,120		4,000
• Other cities	6,560		2,000
	1,640		500
	656		200
	(Sea level) 0		0 (Sea level)
	Below sea level		Below sea level

Size comparison of Russia to the contiguous United States

SCALE
0   500   1000 Miles
0   500   1000 Kilometers
Projection: Two-Point Equidistant

Physical Features

Russia was by far the largest republic of what was called the Union of Soviet Socialist Republics, or the Soviet Union. Russia is the largest country in the world. It stretches 6,000 miles (9,654 km), from Eastern Europe to the Bering Sea and Pacific Ocean.

A train chugs through the cold Siberian countryside.

Interpreting the Visual Record *Place*
What does this photograph tell you about the physical features and climate of Siberia?

The Land Much of western, or European, Russia is part of the Northern European Plain. This is the country's heartland, where most Russians live. To the north are the Barents Sea and the Arctic Ocean. Far to the south are the Caucasus (KAW-kuh-suhs) Mountains. There Europe's highest peak, Mount Elbrus, rises to 18,510 feet (5,642 m). The Caucasus Mountains stretch from the Black Sea to the Caspian (KAS-pee-uhn) Sea. The Caspian is the largest inland body of water in the world.

East of the Northern European Plain is a long range of eroded low mountains and hills. These are called the Ural (YOOHR-uhl) Mountains. The Urals divide Europe from Asia. They stretch from the Arctic coast in the north to Kazakhstan in the south. The highest peak in the Urals rises to just 6,214 feet (1,894 m).

East of the Urals lies a vast region known as Siberia. Much of Siberia is divided between the West Siberian Plain and the Central Siberian Plateau. The West Siberian Plain is a large, flat area with many marshes. The Central Siberian Plateau lies to the east. It is a land of elevated plains and valleys.

A series of high mountain ranges runs through southern and eastern Siberia. The Kamchatka (kuhm-CHAHT-kuh) Peninsula, Sakhalin (sah-kah-LEEN) Island, and the Kuril (KYOOHR-eel) Islands surround the Sea of Okhotsk (uh-KAWTSK). These are in the Russian Far East. The rugged Kamchatka Peninsula and the Kurils have active volcanoes. Earthquakes and volcanic eruptions are common. The Kurils separate the Sea of Okhotsk from the Pacific Ocean.

Rivers Some of the world's longest rivers flow through Russia. These include the Volga (VAHL-guh) and Don Rivers in European Russia. The Ob (AWB), Yenisey (yi-ni-SAY), Lena (LEE-nuh), and Amur (ah-MOOHR) Rivers are located in Siberia and the Russian Far East. The Amur forms part of Russia's border with China.

The Volga is Europe's longest river. Its course and length make it an important transportation route. It flows southward for 2,293 miles (3,689 km) across the Northern European Plain to the Caspian Sea. Barges can travel by canal from the Volga to the Don River. The Don empties into the Black Sea. Canals also connect the Volga to rivers that drain into the Baltic Sea far to the northwest.

In Siberia, the Ob, Yenisey, and Lena Rivers all flow thousands of miles northward. Eventually, they reach Russia's Arctic coast. These and other Siberian rivers that drain into the Arctic Ocean freeze in winter. In spring, these rivers thaw first in the south. Downstream in

The coldest temperature ever recorded outside of Antarctica in the last 100 years was noted on February 6, 1933, in eastern Siberia: −90° F (−68°C).

the north, however, the rivers remain frozen much longer. As a result, ice jams there block water from the melting ice and snow. This causes annual floods in areas along the rivers.

✔ **READING CHECK:** (*Places and Regions*) What are the major physical features of Russia?

Climate and Vegetation

Nearly all of Russia is located at high northern latitudes. The country has tundra, subarctic, humid continental, and steppe climates. Because there are no high mountain barriers, cold Arctic winds sweep across much of the country in winter. Winters are long and cold. Ice blocks most seaports until spring. However, the winters are surprisingly dry in much of Russia. This is because the interior is far from ocean moisture.

Winters are particularly severe throughout Siberia. Temperatures often drop below −40°F (−40°C). Although they are short, Siberian summers can be hot. Temperatures can rise to 100°F (38°C).

Vegetation varies with climates from north to south. Very cold temperatures and permafrost in the far north keep trees from taking root. Mosses, wildflowers, and other tundra vegetation grow there.

The vast **taiga** (TY-guh), a forest of mostly evergreen trees, grows south of the tundra. The trees there include spruce, fir, and pine. In European Russia and in the Far East are deciduous forests. Many temperate forests in European Russia have been cleared for farms and cities.

Wide grasslands known as the **steppe** (STEP) stretch from Ukraine across southern Russia to Kazakhstan. Much of the steppe is used for growing crops and grazing livestock.

✔ **READING CHECK:** (*Physical Systems*) How does Russia's location affect its climate?

FOCUS ON CULTURE

A Wooden World

One of Russia's main resources, its huge forests, have affected many aspects of daily life. For centuries, the people of northern Russia have made things they needed from wood—from roads to houses to toys.

Snow and mud make travel difficult. Long ago, Russians learned to "pave" roads by laying logs side by side on the ground. These are called corduroy roads, after the ribbed fabric.

Most early houses of Siberia were made of whole logs fitted together without nails. They were similar to the log cabins of the American frontier. Finely cut carvings decorated the houses' windows. Inside, the furni-

ture, shelves, kitchen utensils, and toys were all handmade from wood. Today, several outdoor museums preserve Russia's heritage of wooden architecture.

(*Human-Environment Interaction*) **How have local resources shaped your community's architecture?**

A blast furnace is used to process nickel in Siberia. Nickel is just one of Russia's many natural resources.

Resources

Russia has enormous energy, mineral, and forest resources. However, those resources have been poorly managed. For example, much of the forest west of the Urals has been cut down. Now wood products must be brought long distances from Siberia. Still, the taiga provides a vast supply of trees for wood and paper pulp.

Russia has long been a major oil producer. However, many of its oil deposits are far from cities, markets, and ports. Coal is also plentiful. More than a dozen metals are available in large quantities. Russia also is a major diamond producer. Many valuable mineral deposits in remote Siberia have not yet been mined.

✓ **READING CHECK:** (*Places and Regions*) How might the location of its oil deposits prevent Russia from taking full advantage of this resource?

Homework Practice Online

Keyword: SG5 HP15

Define and explain: taiga, steppe

Working with Sketch Maps On a map of Russia that you sketch or that your teacher provides, label the following: Arctic Ocean, Caucasus Mountains, Caspian Sea, Ural Mountains, West Siberian Plain, Central Siberian Plateau, Kamchatka Peninsula, Kuril Islands, Volga River, and Baltic Sea.

Reading for the Main Idea

1. (*Places and Regions*) What low mountain range in central Russia divides Europe from Asia?

2. (*Places and Regions*) How is the Volga River linked to the Baltic and Black Seas?

3. (*Environment and Society*) What are winters like in much of Russia? How might they affect people?

Critical Thinking

4. **Making Generalizations and Predictions** How might Russia's natural resources make the country more prosperous?

Organizing What You Know

5. **Categorizing** Copy the following graphic organizer. Use it to list the climates, vegetation, and resources of Russia.

Climates	Vegetation	Resources

Read to Discover

1. What was Russia's early history like?
2. How did the Russian Empire grow and then fall?
3. What was the Soviet Union?
4. What is Russia like today?

Vocabulary

czar
abdicated
allies
superpowers
Cold War
consumer goods

Places

Moscow

People

Ivan the Terrible
Peter the Great
Vladimir Lenin
Joseph Stalin
Mikhail Gorbachev

Reading Strategy

READING ORGANIZER As you read this section, create a time line that begins in A.D. 800 and goes to 2000. Write down important events in the history of Russia on your time line.

Early Russia

The roots of the Russian nation lie deep in the grassy plains of the steppe. For thousands of years, people moved across the steppe bringing new languages, religions, and ways of life.

Early Migrations Slavic peoples have lived in Russia for thousands of years. In the A.D. 800s, Viking traders from Scandinavia helped shape the first Russian state among the Slavs. These Vikings called themselves Rus (ROOS). The word *Russia* comes from their name. The state they created was centered on Kiev. Today Kiev is the capital of Ukraine.

In the following centuries, missionaries from southeastern Europe brought Orthodox Christianity and a form of the Greek alphabet to Russia. Today the Russian language is written in this Cyrillic alphabet.

Mongols After about 200 years, Kiev's power began to decline. In the 1200s, Mongol invaders called Tatars swept out of Central Asia across the steppe. The Mongols conquered Kiev and added much of the region to their vast empire.

The Mongols demanded taxes but ruled the region through local leaders. Over time, these local leaders established various states. The strongest of these was Muscovy, north of Kiev. Its chief city was Moscow.

✓ **READING CHECK:** (*Human Systems*) What was the effect of Viking traders on Russia?

▲
This painting from the mid-1400s shows a battle between soldiers of two early Russian states.

History of Russian Expansion

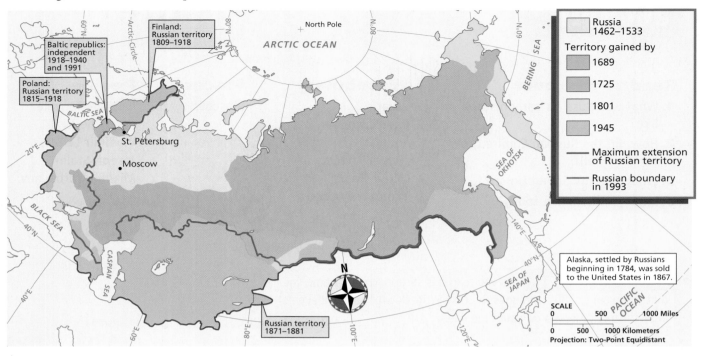

The colors in this map show land taken by the Russian Empire and the Soviet Union over time.

Interpreting the Map **When was the period of Russia's greatest expansion?**

Ivan the Terrible became grand prince of Moscow in 1533. He was just three years old. He ruled Russia from 1547 to his death in 1584.

The Russian Empire

In the 1400s Muscovy won control over parts of Russia from the Mongols. In 1547 Muscovy's ruler, Ivan IV—known as Ivan the Terrible—crowned himself **czar** (ZAHR) of all Russia. The word *czar* comes from the Latin word *Caesar* and means "emperor."

Expansion Over more than 300 years, czars like Peter the Great (1672–1725) expanded the Russian empire. By the early 1700s the empire stretched from the Baltic to the Pacific.

Russian fur traders crossed the Bering Strait in the 1700s and 1800s. They established colonies along the North American west coast. Those colonies stretched from coastal Alaska to California. Russia sold Alaska to the United States in 1867. Around the same time, Russia expanded into Central Asia.

Decline The Russian Empire's power began to decline in the late 1800s. Industry grew slowly, so Russia remained largely agricultural. Most people were poor farmers. Far fewer were the rich, factory workers, or craftspeople. Food shortages, economic problems, and defeat in war further weakened the empire in the early 1900s.

In 1917, during World War I, the czar **abdicated**, or gave up his throne. Later in 1917 the Bolshevik Party, led by Vladimir Lenin, overthrew the government. This event is known as the Russian Revolution.

✓ **READING CHECK:** (**Human Systems**) What conflict brought a change of government to Russia?

The Soviet Union

The Bolsheviks, or Communists, established the Soviet Union in 1922. Most of the various territories of the Russian Empire became republics within the Soviet Union.

Under Lenin and his successor, Joseph Stalin, the Communists took over all industries and farms. Religious practices were discouraged. The Communists outlawed all other political parties. Many opponents were imprisoned, forced to leave the country, or even killed.

The Soviet leaders established a command economy, in which industries were controlled by the government. At first these industries grew dramatically. However, over time the lack of competition made them inefficient and wasteful. The quality of many products was poor. Government-run farms failed to produce enough food to feed the population. By the late 1950s the Soviet Union had to import large amounts of grain.

Cold War The Soviet Union in the 1950s was still recovering from World War II. The country had been a major battleground in the war. The United States and the Soviet Union had been **allies**, or friends, in the fight against Germany. After the war the two **superpowers**, or powerful countries, became rivals. This bitter rivalry became known as the **Cold War**. The Cold War lasted from the 1940s to the early 1990s. The Soviet Union and the United States built huge military forces, including nuclear weapons. The two countries never formally went to war with each other. However, they supported allies in small wars around the world.

Collapse of the Soviet Union The costs of the Cold War eventually became too much for the Soviet Union. The Soviet government spent more and more money on military goods. **Consumer goods** became expensive and in short supply. Consumer goods are products used at home and in everyday life. The last Soviet leader, Mikhail Gorbachev, tried to bring about changes to help the economy. He also promoted a policy allowing more open discussion of the country's problems. However, the various Soviet republics pushed for independence. Finally, in 1991 the Soviet Union collapsed. The huge country split into 15 republics.

In late 1991 Russia and most of the other former Soviet republics formed the Commonwealth of Independent States, or CIS. Minsk, Belarus, serves as the CIS administrative capital. The CIS does not have a strong central government. Instead, it provides a way for the former Soviet republics to address shared problems. For example, CIS representatives meet to discuss foreign relations, defense, economics, law enforcement, immigration policies, and environmental issues.

✓ **READING CHECK:** (*Human Systems*) What was the Cold War, and how did it eventually cause the Soviet Union's collapse?

▲ Tourists can visit the czar's Summer Palace in St. Petersburg.

BIOGRAPHY

Mikhail Gorbachev
(1931–)

Character Trait: Citizenship

Mikhail Gorbachev saw problems in his country and set out to solve them. Although he was a member of the Communist party, Gorbachev supported two new ideas that led to the party's decline. One was *glasnost*, or "openness" in Russian. It meant that Russians could finally talk openly about their country's problems. The other was *perestroika*, or "restructuring" of the Soviet Union's crumbling economy. These policies helped end communist rule of the Soviet Union.

How did Gorbachev's actions show good citizenship?

CONNECTING TO *Literature*

The former Soviet Union was composed of many republics, which are now independent countries. Nina Gabrielyan's The Lilac Dressing Gown *is told from the point of view of an Armenian girl living in Moscow before the Soviet breakup.*

AUNT RIMMA'S TREAT

Aunt Rimma. . . came to visit and gave me a pink caramel which I, naturally, popped straight in my mouth. "Don't swallow it," Aunt Rimma says in an odd sort of voice. "You're not supposed to swallow it, only chew it." "Why," I ask, puzzled by her solemn tone. "It's chewing gum," she says with pride in her eyes. "Chewing gum?" I don't know what she means. "American chewing gum," Aunt Rimma explains. "Mentor's sister sent it to us from America." "Oh, from America? Is that where the capitalists are? What is she doing there?" "She's living there," says Aunt Rimma, condescending to my foolishness.

But I am not as foolish as I used to be. I know that Armenians live in Armenia. Our country is very big and includes many republics: Armenia, Georgia, Azerbaijan, Tajikistan, Uzbekistan, Ukraine, Belorussia [Belarus], the Caucasus and Transcaucasia. All this together is the Soviet Union. Americans . . . live in America. Clearly, Mentor's sister cannot possibly be American. . . . Rimma goes on boasting: "Oh! the underwear they have there! . . . And the children's clothes!" I begin to feel a bit envious. . . . Nobody in our house has anyone living in America, but Aunt Rimma does. My envy becomes unbearable. So I decide to slay our boastful neighbor on the spot: "Well we have cockroaches! This big! Lots and lots of them!"

Analyzing Primary Sources

1. How does the Armenian girl's frame of reference affect her view of the United States?
2. What does Aunt Rimma seem to think the United States is like?

Russia Today

Russia has been making a transition from communism to democracy and a free market economy since 1991. Change has been slow, and the country faces difficult challenges.

People and Religion More than 144 million people live in Russia today. More than 80 percent are ethnic Russians. The largest of Russia's many minority groups are Ukrainians and Tatars. These Tatars are the descendants of the early Mongol invaders of Russia.

In the past, the government encouraged ethnic Russians to settle in areas of Russia far from Moscow. They were encouraged to move to places where other ethnic groups were in the majority. Today, many non-Russian peoples in those areas resent the domination of ethnic Russians. Some non-Russians want independence from Moscow. At times this has led to violence and even war, as in Chechnya in southern Russia.

Since 1991 a greater degree of religious expression has been allowed in Russia. Russian Orthodox Christianity is becoming popular again. Cathedrals have been repaired, and their onion-shaped domes have been covered in gold leaf and brilliant colors. Muslims around the Caspian Sea and the southern Urals have revived Islamic practices.

Food and Festivals Bread is an important part of the Russian diet. It is eaten with every meal. It may be a rich, dark bread made from rye and wheat flour or a firm white bread. As in other northern countries, the growing season is short and winter is long. Therefore, the diet includes many canned and preserved foods, such as sausages, smoked fish, cheese, and vegetable and fruit preserves.

Black caviar, one of the world's most expensive delicacies, comes from Russia. The fish eggs that make up black caviar come from sturgeon. Sturgeon are fish found in the Caspian Sea.

The anniversary of the 1917 Russian Revolution was an important holiday during the Soviet era. Today the Orthodox Christian holidays of Christmas and Easter are again becoming popular in Russia. Special holiday foods include milk puddings and cheesecakes.

The Arts and Sciences Russia has given the world great works of art, literature, and music. For example, you might know *The Nutcracker,* a ballet danced to music composed by Peter Tchaikovsky (1840–93). It is a popular production in many countries.

Russia

Country	Population/ Growth Rate	Life Expectancy	Literacy Rate	Per Capita GDP
Russia	144,526,278 −0.3%	62, male 73, female	99%	$9,300
United States	290,342,554 0.9%	74, male 80, female	97%	$37,600

Source: Central Intelligence Agency, *The World Factbook 2003*

Interpreting the Chart **How many times greater is the U.S. population than the Russian population?**

Ballet dancers perform Peter Tchaikovsky's *Swan Lake* at the Mariinsky Theater in St. Petersburg.

◄

Many Russian writers are known for how they capture the emotions of characters in their works. Some writers, such as Aleksandr Solzhenitsyn (1918–), have written about Russia under communism.

Russian scientists also have made important contributions to their professions. For example, in 1957 the Soviet Union launched *Sputnik*. It was the first artificial satellite in space. Today U.S. and Russian engineers are working together on space projects. These include building a large space station and planning for a mission to Mars.

Government Like the U.S. government, the Russian Federation is governed by an elected president and a legislature called the Federal Assembly. The Federal Assembly includes representatives of regions and republics within the Federation. Non-Russians are numerous or in the majority in many of those regions and republics.

The government faces tough challenges. One is improving the country's struggling economy. Many government-owned companies have been sold to the private sector. However, financial problems have limited investment. In addition, many Russians criticized the government in the 2000s for limiting freedom of the press.

Corruption is a serious problem. A few people have used their connections with government officials to get rich. Also, many Russians avoid paying taxes. This means the government has less money for salaries and services. Agreement on solutions to these problems has been hard.

Republics of the Russian Federation

Adygea	Karachay-Cherkessia
Alania	Karelia
Bashkortostan	Khakassia
Buryatia	Komi
Chechnya	Mari El
Chuvashia	Mordvinia
Dagestan	Sakha
Gorno-Altay	Tatarstan
Ingushetia	Tuva
Kabardino-Balkaria	Udmurtia
Kalmykia	

✔ **READING CHECK:** (*Human Systems*)
What are the people and culture of Russia like today?

go.hrw.com **Homework Practice Online**
Keyword: SG5 HP15

Section Review 2

Define or identify: Ivan the Terrible, czar, Peter the Great, abdicated, Vladimir Lenin, Joseph Stalin, allies, superpowers, Cold War, consumer goods, Mikhail Gorbachev

Working with Sketch Maps On the map you created in Section 1, label Moscow. In the margin, explain the role Kiev played in Russia's early history.

Reading for the Main Idea

1. (*Places and Regions*) How did Russia get its name?

2. (*Human Systems*) What was the Bolshevik Party?

3. (*Places and Regions*) What are some of the challenges that Russia faces today?

Critical Thinking

4. Comparing Compare the factors that led to the decline of the Russian Empire and the Soviet Union. List the factors for each.

Organizing What You Know

5. Summarizing Copy the following graphic organizer. Use it to identify important features of Russia's ethnic population, religion, food, and arts and sciences.

Russian people and culture

Read to Discover

1. Why is European Russia considered the country's heartland?
2. What are the characteristics of the four regions of European Russia?

Vocabulary

light industry
heavy industry
smelters

Places

St. Petersburg
Nizhniy Novgorod
Astrakhan

Yekaterinburg
Chelyabinsk
Magnitogorsk

Reading Strategy

READING ORGANIZER Draw a circle on a sheet of paper and label it Russian Heartland. Add four circles around the central one and connect them to it by spokes. Label the outer circles as the four regions discussed in the section and write down what you learn in each circle.

The Heartland

The European section of Russia is the country's heartland. The Russian nation expanded outward from there. It is home to the bulk of the Russian population. The national capital and large industrial cities are also located there.

The plains of European Russia make up the country's most productive farming region. Farmers focus mainly on growing grains and raising livestock. Small gardens near cities provide fresh fruits and vegetables for summer markets.

The Russian heartland can be divided into four major regions. These four are the Moscow region, the St. Petersburg region, the Volga region, and the Urals region.

✓ **READING CHECK:** (*Places and Regions*) Why is European Russia the country's heartland?

Twenty towers, like the one in the lower left, are spaced along the Kremlin's walls.

Interpreting the Visual Record Why would leaders place government buildings and palaces within the walls of one central location?

▼

The Moscow Region

Moscow is Russia's capital and largest city. More than 9 million people live there. In addition to being Russia's political center, Moscow is the country's center for transportation and communication. Roads, railroads, and air routes link the capital to all points in Russia.

At Moscow's heart is the Kremlin. The Kremlin's red brick walls and towers were built in the late 1400s. The government offices, beautiful palaces, and gold-domed churches within its walls are popular tourist attractions.

Vendors sell religious art and other crafts at a sidewalk market in Moscow.

Interpreting the Visual Record What do the items in this market suggest about the status of religion in Russia since the communist era?

▶

Moscow is part of a huge industrial area. This area also includes the city of Nizhniy Novgorod, called Gorky during the communist era. About one third of Russia's population lives in this region.

The Soviet government encouraged the development of **light industry**, rather than **heavy industry**, around Moscow. Light industry focuses on the production of lightweight goods, such as clothing. Heavy industry usually involves manufacturing based on metals. It causes more pollution than light industry. The region also has advanced-technology and electronics industries.

The St. Petersburg Region

Northwest of Moscow is St. Petersburg, Russia's second-largest city and a major Baltic seaport. More than 5 million people live there. St. Petersburg was Russia's capital and home to the czars for more than 200 years. This changed in 1918. Palaces and other grand buildings constructed under the czars are tourist attractions today. St. Petersburg was known as Leningrad during the communist era.

Much of the city was heavily damaged during World War II.

The surrounding area has few natural resources. Still, St. Petersburg's harbor, canals, and rail connections make the city a major center for trade. Important universities and research institutions are located there. The region also has important industries.

✓ **READING CHECK:** (**Human Systems**)
Why are Moscow and St. Petersburg such large cities?

The Mariinsky Theater of Opera and Ballet is one of St. Petersburg's most beautiful buildings. It was called the Kirov during the communist era.

▼

The Volga Region

The Volga region stretches along the middle part of the Volga River. The Volga is often more like a chain of lakes. It is a major shipping route for goods produced in the region. Hydroelectric power plants and nearby deposits of coal and oil are important sources of energy.

During World War II, many factories were moved to the Volga region. This was done to keep them safe from German invaders. Today the region is famous for its factories that produce goods such as motor vehicles, chemicals, and food products. Russian caviar comes from a fishery based at the old city of Astrakhan on the Caspian Sea.

The Urals Region

Mining has long been important in the Ural Mountains region. Nearly every important mineral except oil has been discovered there. Copper and iron **smelters** are still important. Smelters are factories that process copper, iron, and other metal ores.

Many large cities in the Urals started as commercial centers for mining districts. The Soviet government also moved factories to the region during World War II. Important cities include Yekaterinburg (yi-kah-ti-reem-BOOHRK) (formerly Sverdlovsk), Chelyabinsk (chel-YAH-buhnsk), and Magnitogorsk (muhg-nee-tuh-GAWRSKY). Now these cities manufacture machinery and metal goods.

✓ **READING CHECK:** (*Places and Regions*) What industries are important in the Volga and Urals regions?

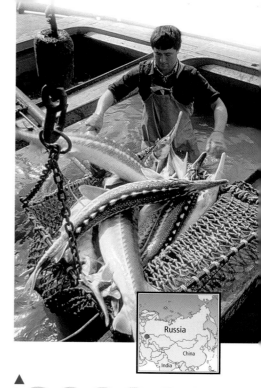

▲ A fisher gathers sturgeon in a small shipboard pool in the Volga region.

Section Review 3

Define and explain: light industry, heavy industry, smelters

Working with Sketch Maps On the map you created in Section 2, label St. Petersburg, Nizhniy Novgorod, Astrakhan, Yekaterinburg, Chelyabinsk, and Magnitogorsk. In the margin of your map, write a short caption explaining the significance of Moscow and St. Petersburg.

Reading for the Main Idea

1. (*Places and Regions*) Why might so many people settle in Russia's heartland?

2. (*Places and Regions*) Where did the Soviet government move factories during World War II?

go.hrw.com **Homework Practice Online** Keyword: SG5 HP15

Critical Thinking

3. **Drawing Inferences and Conclusions** Why do you think the Soviet government encouraged the development of light industry around Moscow?

4. **Finding the Main Idea** What role has the region's physical geography played in the development of European Russia's economy?

Organizing What You Know

5. **Contrasting** Use this graphic organizer to identify European Russia's four regions. Write one feature that makes each region different from the other three.

European Russia

Read to Discover

1. What is the human geography of Siberia like?
2. What are the economic features of the region?
3. How has Lake Baikal been threatened by pollution?

Vocabulary

habitation fog

Places

Siberia
Trans-Siberian Railroad
Baikal-Amur Mainline

Kuznetsk Basin
Ob River
Yenisey River
Novosibirsk
Lake Baikal

Reading Strategy

READING ORGANIZER Draw a line down the center of a sheet of paper. Title one column "What I know about Siberia." Title the other column "What I learned about Siberia." Write down what you already know about Siberia in the first column. As you read, add what you learn in the other column.

A Sleeping Land

East of European Russia, across the Ural Mountains, is Siberia. Siberia is enormous. It covers more than 5 million square miles (12.95 million sq. km) of northern Asia. It extends all the way to the Pacific Ocean. That is nearly 1.5 times the area of the United States! To the north of Siberia is the Arctic Ocean. To the south are the Central Asian countries, Mongolia, and China.

Many people think of Siberia as simply a vast, frozen wasteland. In fact, in the Tatar language, *Siberia* means "Sleeping Land." In many ways, this image is accurate. Siberian winters are long, dark, and severe. Often there is little snow, but the land is frozen for months. During winter, **habitation fog** hangs over cities. A habitation fog is a fog caused by fumes and smoke from cities. During the cold Siberian winter, this fog is trapped over cities.

Siberia has lured Russian adventurers for more than 400 years. It continues to do so today. This vast region has a great wealth of natural resources. Developing those resources may be a key to transforming Russia into an economic success.

Reindeer graze around a winter camp in northern Siberia.

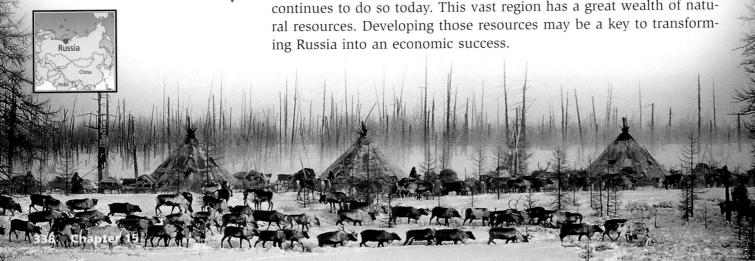

People Siberia is sparsely populated. In fact, large areas have no human population at all. Most of the people live in cities in western and southern parts of the region.

Ethnic Russians make up most of the population. However, minority groups have lived there since long before Russians began to expand into Siberia.

Settlements Russian settlement in Siberia generally follows the route of the Trans-Siberian Railroad. Construction of this railway started in 1891. When it was completed, it linked Moscow and Vladivostok, a port on the Sea of Japan.

Russia's Trans-Siberian Railroad is the longest single rail line in the world. It is more than 5,700 miles (9,171 km) long. For many Siberian towns, the railroad provides the only transportation link to the outside world. Another important railway is the Baikal-Amur Mainline (BAM), which crosses many mountain ranges and rivers in eastern Siberia.

▲

The Omsk (AWMSK) Cathedral in Omsk, Siberia, provides an example of Russian architecture. Omsk was founded in the early 1700s.

✔ **READING CHECK:** (*Places and Regions*) Where is Russian settlement located in Siberia, and why do you think this is the case?

Siberia's Economy

The Soviet government built the Baikal-Amur Mainline so that raw materials from Siberia could be easily transported to other places. Abundant natural resources form the foundation of Siberia's economy. They are also important to the development of Russia's struggling economy. Siberia's natural resources include timber, mineral ores, diamonds, and coal, oil, and natural gas deposits.

Although Siberia has rich natural resources, it contains a small percentage of Russia's industry. The harsh climate and difficult terrain have discouraged settlement. Many people would rather live in European Russia, even though wages may be higher in Siberia.

Lumbering and mining are the most important Siberian industries. Large coal deposits are mined in the Kuznetsk Basin, or the Kuzbas. The Kuzbas is located in southwestern Siberia between the Ob and Yenisey Rivers. It is one of Siberia's most important industrial regions.

Siberia's largest city, Novosibirsk, is located near the Kuznetsk Basin. The city's name means "New Siberia." Almost 1.5 million people live there. It is located about halfway between Moscow and Vladivostok on the Trans-Siberian Railroad. Novosibirsk is Siberia's manufacturing and transportation center.

✔ **READING CHECK:** (*Environment and Society*) How do Siberia's natural resources influence the economies of Siberia and Russia?

Lake Baikal is seven times as deep as the Grand Canyon.

Interpreting the Visual Record

(*Human-Environment Interaction*) **How would pollution affect this lake and the plants and animals that live there?**

Lake Baikal covers less area than do three of the Great Lakes: Superior, Huron, and Michigan. Still, Baikal is so deep that it contains about one fifth of all the world's freshwater!

Lake Baikal

Some people have worried that economic development in Siberia threatens the region's natural environment. One focus of concern has been Lake Baikal (by-KAHL), the "Jewel of Siberia."

Baikal is located north of Mongolia. It is the world's deepest lake. In fact, it holds as much water as all of North America's Great Lakes. The scenic lake and its surrounding area are home to many kinds of plants and animals. Some, such as the world's only freshwater seal, are endangered.

For decades people have worried about pollution from a nearby paper factory and other development. They feared that pollution threatened the species that live in and around the lake. In recent years scientists and others have proposed plans that allow some economic development while protecting the environment.

✓ **READING CHECK:** (*Environment and Society*) How has human activity affected Lake Baikal?

go.hrw.com **Homework Practice Online**
Keyword: SG5 HP15

Section Review 4

Define and explain: habitation fog

Working with Sketch Maps On the map you created in Section 3, label Siberia, Trans-Siberian Railroad, Baikal-Amur Mainline, Kuznetsk Basin, Ob River, Yenisey River, Novosibirsk, and Lake Baikal.

Reading for the Main Idea

1. (*Places and Regions*) What are the boundaries of Siberia?

2. (*Human Systems*) Where do most people in Siberia live? Why?

3. (*Places and Regions*) Why does this huge region with many natural resources have little industry?

Critical Thinking

4. Making Generalizations and Predictions Do you think Russians should be more concerned about rapid economic development or protecting the environment? Why?

Organizing What You Know

5. Categorizing Use this organizer to list the region's resources and industries that use them.

| Natural Resources | ⇨ | Major Industries |

Section 5 The Russian Far East

Read to Discover

1. How does the Russian Far East's climate affect land use in the region?
2. What are the major resources and cities of the region?
3. What island regions are part of the Russian Far East?

Vocabulary

icebreakers

Places

Sea of Okhotsk
Sea of Japan
Khabarovsk

Vladivostok
Amur River
Sakhalin Island

Reading Strategy

TAKING NOTES Use the headings in this section to create an outline. As you read, write down what you learn under each heading.

Land Use

Off the eastern coast of Siberia are the Sea of Okhotsk and the Sea of Japan. Their coastal areas and islands make up a region known as the Russian Far East.

The Russian Far East has a less severe climate than the rest of Siberia. Summer weather is mild enough for some successful farming. Farms produce many goods, including wheat, sugar beets, sunflowers, meat, and dairy products. However, the region cannot produce enough food for itself. As a result, food must also be imported.

Fishing and hunting are important in the region. There are many kinds of animals, including deer, seals, rare Siberian tigers, and sables. Sable fur is used to make expensive clothing.

✓ **READING CHECK:** (*Environment and Society*) How does scarcity of food affect the Russian Far East?

◀

The Siberian tiger is endangered. The few remaining of these large cats roam parts of the Russian Far East. They are also found in northern China and on the Korean Peninsula.

Economy

Like the rest of Siberia, the Russian Far East has a wealth of natural resources. These resources have supported the growth of industrial cities and ports in the region.

Resources Much of the Russian Far East remains forested. The region's minerals are only beginning to be developed. Lumbering, machine manufacturing, woodworking, and metalworking are the major industries there.

The region also has important energy resources, including coal and oil. Another resource is geothermal energy. This resource is available because of the region's tectonic activity. Two active volcanic mountain ranges run the length of the Kamchatka Peninsula. Russia's first geothermal electric-power station was built on this peninsula.

Cities Industry and the Trans-Siberian Railroad aided the growth of cities in the Russian Far East. Two of those cities are Khabarovsk (kuh-BAHR-uhfsk) and Vladivostok (vla-duh-vuh-STAHK).

Some 700,000 people live in Khabarovsk, which was founded in 1858. It is located where the Trans-Siberian Railroad crosses the Amur River. This location makes Khabarovsk ideal for processing forest and mineral resources from the region.

Vladivostok is slightly larger than Khabarovsk. *Vladivostok* means "Lord of the East" in Russian. The city was established in 1860 on the coast of the Sea of Japan. Today it lies at the eastern end of the Trans-Siberian Railroad.

Vladivostok is a major naval base and the home port for a large fishing fleet. **Icebreakers** must keep the city's harbor open in winter. An icebreaker is a ship that can break up the ice of frozen waterways. This allows other ships to pass through them.

Historical monuments and old architecture compete for attention in Vladivostok.

The Soviet Union considered Vladivostok very important for defense. The city was therefore closed to foreign contacts until the early 1990s. Today it is an important link with China, Japan, the United States, and the rest of the Pacific region.

READING CHECK: (*Environment and Society*) How do the resources of the Russian Far East affect its economy?

Islands

The Russian Far East includes two island areas. Sakhalin is a large island that lies off the eastern coast of Siberia. The Kuril Islands are much smaller. They stretch in an arc from Hokkaido to the Kamchatka Peninsula.

Sakhalin has oil and mineral resources. The waters around the Kurils are important for commercial fishing. Russia and Japan have argued over who owns these islands since the 1850s. At times they have been divided between Japan and Russia or the Soviet Union. The Soviet Union took control of the islands after World War II. Japan still claims rights to the southernmost islands. By the 2000s, however, increased tourism had helped ease tensions.

Like other Pacific regions, Sakhalin and the Kurils sometimes experience earthquakes and volcanic eruptions. An earthquake in 1995 caused severe damage on Sakhalin Island, killing nearly 2,000 people.

READING CHECK: (*Environment and Society*) How does the environment of the Kuril Islands and Sakhalin affect people?

▲

An old volcano created Crater Bay in the Kuril Islands. The islands' beauty is matched by the terrible power of earthquakes and volcanic eruptions in the area.

Interpreting the Visual Record What do you think happened to the volcano that formed Crater Bay?

Section Review 5

Homework Practice Online
Keyword: SG5 HP15

Define and explain: icebreakers

Working with Sketch Maps On the map you created in Section 4, label the Sea of Okhotsk, the Sea of Japan, Khabarovsk, Vladivostok, the Amur River, and Sakhalin Island. In the margin, explain which countries dispute possession of Sakhalin Island and the Kuril Islands.

Reading for the Main Idea

1. (*Places and Regions*) How does the climate of the Russian Far East compare to the climate throughout the rest of Siberia?

2. (*Places and Regions*) What are the region's major crops and energy resources?

Critical Thinking

3. Drawing Inferences and Conclusions In what ways do you think Vladivostok is "Lord of the East" in Russia today?

4. Drawing Inferences and Conclusions Why do you think Sakhalin and the Kuril Islands have been the subject of dispute between Russia and Japan?

Organizing What You Know

5. Finding the Main Idea Copy the following graphic organizer. Use it to explain how the location of each city has played a role in its development.

Khabarovsk	Vladivostok

Define and Identify

Identify each of the following:

1. taiga
2. steppe
3. czar
4. Peter the Great
5. Vladimir Lenin
6. Joseph Stalin
7. superpowers
8. Cold War
9. consumer goods
10. Mikhail Gorbachev
11. heavy industry
12. smelters
13. habitation fog

Review the Main Ideas

14. What are Russia's major mountain ranges? Which range separates Europe from Asia?
15. What are Russia's major rivers?
16. How did Russia's government change in 1917?
17. Why did the Soviet Union collapse?
18. How has Russia contributed to world culture?
19. What four major regions make up the Russian Heartland, and what are their main features?
20. What are Siberia's climate and vegetation like?
21. What resources can be found in Siberia?

22. How has Vladivostok changed? Why is it still an important city?
23. What natural hazards threaten Sakhalin and the Kuril Islands?

Think Critically

24. **Finding the Main Idea** How might Siberia help make Russia an economic success?
25. **Contrasting** What kind of economic system did the Soviet Union have, and how did it differ from that of the United States?
26. **Drawing Inferences and Conclusions** Why is transportation an issue for Russia? What have Russians done to ease transportation between European Russia and the Russian Far East?
27. **Summarizing** What issues trouble some of Russia's ethnic groups?
28. **Identifying Cause and Effect** What problems existed in the Russian Empire and the Soviet Union in the 1900s, and what was their effect?

Map Activity

29. On a separate sheet of paper, match the letters on the map with their correct labels.

Arctic Ocean
Caucasus Mountains
Caspian Sea
West Siberian Plain
Central Siberian Plateau
Kamchatka Peninsula
Volga River
Moscow
St. Petersburg
Vladivostok

Writing Activity

Imagine that you are a tour guide on a trip by train from St. Petersburg to Vladivostok. Use the chapter map or a classroom globe to write a one-page description of some of the places people would see along the train's route. How far would you travel? Be sure to use standard grammar, spelling, sentence structure, and punctuation.

internet connect

Internet Activity: go.hrw.com
KEYWORD: SG5 GT15

Choose a topic to explore about Russia:
- Take a trip on the Trans-Siberian Railroad.
- Examine the breakup of the Soviet Union.
- View the cultural treasures of Russia.

Social Studies Skills Practice

Interpreting Political Cartoons

Study the political cartoon below. Then answer the questions.

Harvell/The Greenville Piedmont, S.C. Reprinted with permission.

1. To what period in Russian history do you think this cartoon refers?
2. How does the cartoonist show that it is about Russia?
3. What economic problem does the cartoonist show?
4. How might the situation shown in the cartoon affect the Russian people?

Analyzing Primary Sources

Read the following passage by B. Frederick Kempe, who visited the Siberian city of Novokuznetsk. Then answer the questions.

"*The doctors at Novokuznetsk's Hospital Number 7 know by the way the wind is blowing whether they will have a busy day. If the air is calm and humid, the poisons from the two of the largest steel smelters in the world hang in the air. The hospital's waiting room will then fill . . . parents will rush in with children who can't breathe. Hospital emergency rooms across town will register more heart attacks than usual. . . . My eyes watered as we drove through Novokuznetsk . . . The city produced more steel than any other place in the Soviet Union. And it smelled it. The moist air reeked of rotten egg . . .*"

1. What kind of economic activity takes place in Novokuznetsk?
2. What health problems has pollution caused the city's residents?
3. How do weather patterns affect the pollution levels in the city?
4. What problems did Kempe experience when he visited Novokuznetsk?

Ukraine, Belarus, and the Caucasus

This region consists of plains in the north and mountains in the south. Both of these physical features made this area important to ancient invaders. Before you learn the history of this region, you should meet Ana.

Hi! I am a senior in high school in the city of T'bilisi, Georgia. I live with my parents and my younger sister. I go to school from 9:00 A.M. to 2:00 P.M. and study foreign languages—English and Spanish. I hope to be a journalist. In school the teachers decide which classes everyone must take.

After school I do my homework as fast as possible and then get together with my friends. I come home in the early evening and listen to music, read, or watch television.

We also have great food. My favorite dish is baked chicken with nuts. If you came to Georgia, I would take you to the mountains, to the seaside, and to some hot springs. We might also go to a festival where you could see Georgians in the country's national dress. Women wear a long red or purple robe with a white head scarf. Men wear a black suit or robe with gold embroidery.

Привіт! Я Анна.

Translation: Hi! I am Ana.

Section 1 Physical Geography

Read to Discover

1. What are the region's major physical features?
2. What climate types and natural resources are found in the region?

Vocabulary

nature reserves

Places

Black Sea
Caucasus Mountains
Caspian Sea
Pripyat Marshes
Carpathian Mountains
Crimean Peninsula
Sea of Azov
Mount Elbrus
Dnieper River
Donets Basin

Reading Strategy

USING VISUAL INFORMATION Draw a line down the center of a sheet of paper. Title one column Similarities. Title the other column Differences. Look at the two colored regions on the Physical-Political map. What geographical characteristics do they share? How may they be different? Write your answers in the proper column. As you read, add more details.

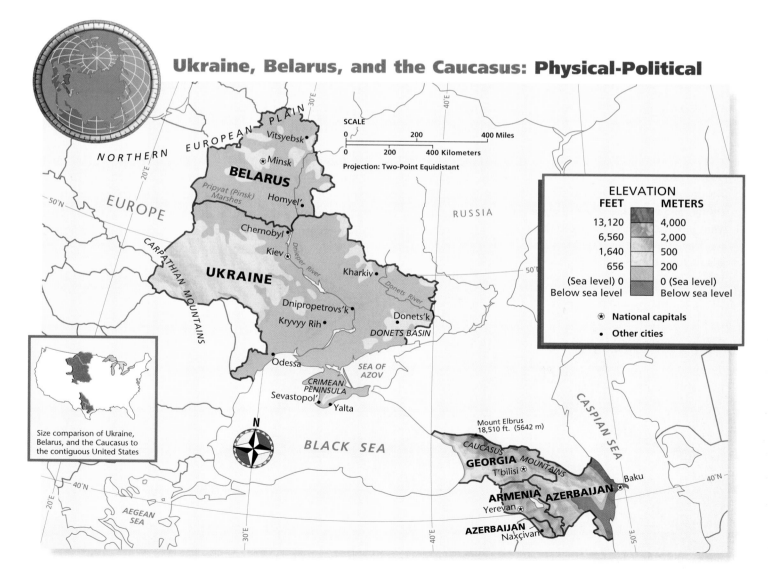

Ukraine, Belarus, and the Caucasus: Physical-Political

SCALE
0   200   400 Miles
0   200   400 Kilometers
Projection: Two-Point Equidistant

ELEVATION

FEET	METERS
13,120	4,000
6,560	2,000
1,640	500
656	200
(Sea level) 0	0 (Sea level)
Below sea level	Below sea level

⊛ National capitals
• Other cities

Size comparison of Ukraine, Belarus, and the Caucasus to the contiguous United States

NORTHERN EUROPEAN PLAIN
EUROPE
CARPATHIAN MOUNTAINS
BELARUS
Vitsyebsk
⊛ Minsk
Pripyat (Pinsk) Marshes
Homyel'
Chernobyl
Kiev
Dnieper River
UKRAINE
Kharkiv
Donets River
Dnipropetrovs'k
Kryvyy Rih
Donets'k
DONETS BASIN
Odessa
SEA OF AZOV
CRIMEAN PENINSULA
Sevastopol'
Yalta
RUSSIA
BLACK SEA
AEGEAN SEA
Mount Elbrus 18,510 ft. (5642 m)
CAUCASUS MOUNTAINS
CASPIAN SEA
GEORGIA
T'bilisi ⊛
Baku
ARMENIA   AZERBAIJAN
Yerevan ⊛
AZERBAIJAN
Naxçivan

Physical Features

The countries of Ukraine (yoo-KRAYN) and Belarus (byay-luh-ROOS) border western Russia. Belarus is landlocked. Ukraine lies on the Black Sea. Georgia, Armenia (ahr-MEE-nee-uh), and Azerbaijan (a-zuhr-by-JAHN) lie in a rugged region called the Caucasus (KAW-kuh-suhs). It is named for the area's Caucasus Mountains. The Caucasus region is located between the Black Sea and the Caspian Sea.

Landforms Most of Ukraine and Belarus lie in a region of plains. The Northern European Plain sweeps across northern Belarus. The Pripyat (PRI-pyuht) Marshes, also called the Pinsk Marshes, are found in the south. The Carpathian Mountains run through part of western Ukraine. The Crimean (kry-MEE-uhn) Peninsula lies in southern Ukraine. The southern Crimean is very rugged and has high mountains. It separates the Black Sea from the Sea of Azov (uh-ZAWF).

In the north along the Caucasus's border with Russia is a wide mountain range. The region's and Europe's highest peak, Mount Elbrus (el-BROOS), is located here. As you can see on the chapter map, the land drops below sea level along the shore of the Caspian Sea. South of the Caucasus is a rugged, mountainous plateau. Earthquakes often occur in this region.

Rivers One of Europe's major rivers, the Dnieper (NEE-puhr), flows south through Belarus and Ukraine. Ships can travel much of its length. Dams and reservoirs on the Dnieper River provide hydroelectric power and water for irrigation.

Vegetation Mixed forests were once widespread in the central part of the region. Farther south, the forests opened onto the grasslands of the steppe. Today, farmland has replaced much of the original vegetation.

Ukraine is trying to preserve its natural environments and has created several **nature reserves**. These are areas the government has set aside to protect animals, plants, soil, and water.

✓ **READING CHECK:** (*Places and Regions*) What are the region's major physical features?

Snow-capped Mount Elbrus is located along the border between Georgia and Russia.

Interpreting the Visual Record (*Place*)
What physical processes do you think may have formed the mountains in this region of earthquakes?

Russia

● Mt. Elbrus

Georgia

Turkey

Climate

Like much of western Russia, the northern two thirds of Ukraine and Belarus have a humid continental climate. Winters are cold. Summers are warm but short. Southern Ukraine has a steppe climate. Unlike the rest of the country, the Crimean Peninsula has a Mediterranean climate. There are several different climates in the Caucasus. Georgia's coast has a mild climate similar to the Carolinas in the United States. Azerbaijan contains mainly a steppe climate. Because it is so mountainous, Armenia's climate changes with elevation.

✔ **READING CHECK:** *Places and Regions* What climate types are found in this area?

Resources

Rich farmlands are Ukraine's greatest natural resource. Farming is also important in Belarus. Lowland areas of the Caucasus have rich soil and good conditions for farming.

The Donets (duh-NYETS) Basin in southeastern Ukraine is a rich coal-mining area. Kryvyy Rih (kri-VI RIK) is the site of a huge open-pit iron-ore mine. The region's most important mineral resources are Azerbaijan's large and valuable oil and gas deposits. These are found under the shallow Caspian Sea. Copper, manganese, iron, and other metals are also present in the Caucasus.

✔ **READING CHECK:** *Environment and Society* How have this region's natural resources affected economic development?

Define and explain: nature reserves

Working with Sketch Maps   On a map of Europe that you draw or that your teacher provides, label the following: Black Sea, Caucasus Mountains, Caspian Sea, Pripyat Marshes, Carpathian Mountains, Crimean Peninsula, Sea of Azov, Mount Elbrus, Dnieper River, and Donets Basin. Where in the region is a major coal-mining area?

Reading for the Main Idea

1. *Places and Regions* What three seas are found in this region?

2. *Places and Regions* What creates variation in Armenia's climate?

Critical Thinking

3. Drawing Inferences and Conclusions Why has so much farming developed in Ukraine, Belarus, and the Caucasus?

4. Drawing Inferences and Conclusions How do you think heavy mining in this region could create pollution?

Organizing What You Know

5. Categorizing Copy the following graphic organizer. Use it to describe the region's physical features, climates, and resources.

	Physical features	Climate	Resources
Belarus			
Caucasus			
Ukraine			

Section 2 Ukraine and Belarus

Read to Discover

1. Which groups have influenced the history of Ukraine and Belarus?
2. What are some important economic features and environmental concerns of Ukraine?
3. How has the economy of Belarus developed?

Vocabulary

serfs
soviet

Places

Ukraine
Belarus
Kiev
Chernobyl
Minsk

People

Mongols
Cossacks

Reading Strategy

TAKING NOTES Use the headings in this section to create an outline. As you read, write down details about Ukraine and Belarus beneath each heading.

гео·
гра·
фия

▲
These are the syllables for the Russian word for geography, written in the Cyrillic alphabet.

History and Government

About 600 B.C. the Greeks established trading colonies along the coast of the Black Sea. Much later—during the A.D. 400s—the Slavs began to move into what is now Ukraine and Belarus. Today, most people in this region speak closely related Slavic languages.

Vikings and Christians In the 800s Vikings took the city of Kiev. Located on the Dnieper River, it became the capital of the Vikings' trading empire. Today, this old city is Ukraine's capital. In the 900s the Byzantine, or Greek Orthodox, Church sent missionaries to teach the Ukrainians and Belorussians about Christianity. These missionaries introduced the Cyrillic alphabet.

St. Sophia Cathedral in Kiev was built in the 1000s. It was one of the earliest Orthodox cathedrals in this area. Religious images decorate the dome's interior.

◀

Mongols and Cossacks A grandson of Genghis Khan led the Mongol horsemen who conquered Ukraine in the 1200s. They destroyed most of the towns and cities there, including Kiev.

Later, northern Ukraine and Belarus came under the control of Lithuanians and Poles. Under foreign rule, Ukrainian and Belorussian **serfs** suffered. Serfs were people who were bound to the land and worked for a lord. In return, the lords provided the serfs with military protection and other services. Some Russian and Ukrainian serfs left the farms and formed bands of nomadic horsemen. Known as Cossacks, they lived on the Ukrainian frontier.

The Russian Empire North and east of Belarus, a new state arose around Moscow. This Russian kingdom of Muscovy won independence from the Mongols in the late 1400s. The new state set out to expand its borders. By the 1800s all of modern Belarus and Ukraine were under Moscow's rule. Now the Cossacks served the armies of the Russian czar. However, conditions did not improve for the Ukrainian and Belorussian serfs and peasants.

Soviet Republics The Russian Revolution ended the rule of the czars in 1917. Ukraine and Belarus became republics of the Soviet Union in 1922. Although each had its own governing **soviet**, or council, Communist leaders in Moscow made all major decisions.

Ukraine was especially important as the Soviet Union's richest farming region. On the other hand, Belarus became a major industrial center. It produced heavy machinery for the Soviet Union. While Ukraine and Belarus were part of the Soviet Union, the Ukrainian and Belorussian languages were discouraged. Practicing a religion was also discouraged.

After World War II economic development continued in Ukraine and Belarus. Factories and power plants were built with little concern for the safety of nearby residents.

This watercolor on rice paper depicts Kublai Khan. He was the founder of the vast Mongol empire in the 1200s. The Mongols conquered large areas of Asia and Europe, including Ukraine.

Kiev remained an important cultural and industrial center during the Soviet era. Parts of the city were destroyed during World War II and had to be rebuilt. Today tree-lined streets greet shoppers in the central city.

Near the end of World War II, Soviet, American, and British leaders met at Livadia Palace in Yalta, Ukraine. There they planned the defeat and occupation of Germany.

End of Soviet Rule When the Soviet Union collapsed in 1991, Belarus and Ukraine declared independence. Each now has a president and a prime minister. Both countries still have economic problems. Ukraine has also had disagreements with Russia over control of the Crimean Peninsula and the Black Sea naval fleet.

✓ **READING CHECK:** (**Human Systems**) Which groups have influenced the history of Ukraine and Belarus?

Ukraine

Ethnic Ukrainians make up almost 78 percent of Ukraine's population. The largest minority group in the country is Russian. There are other ties between Ukraine and Russia. For example, the Ukrainian and Russian languages are closely related. In addition, both countries use the Cyrillic alphabet.

Economy Ukraine has a good climate for growing crops and some of the world's richest soil. As a result, agriculture is important to its economy. Ukraine is the world's largest producer of sugar beets. Ukraine's food-processing industry makes sugar from the sugar beets. Farmers also grow fruits, potatoes, vegetables, and wheat. Grain is made into flour for baked goods and pasta. Livestock is also raised. Ukraine is one of the world's top steel producers. Ukrainian factories make automobiles, railroad cars, ships, and trucks.

CONNECTING TO Science

A combine used during July harvest

Wheat: From Field to Consumer

Wheat is one of Ukraine's most important farm products. The illustration below shows how wheat is processed for use by consumers.

- The head of the wheat plant contains the wheat kernels, wrapped in husks. The kernel includes the bran or seed coat, the endosperm, and the germ from which new wheat plants grow.

- Whole wheat flour contains all the parts of the kernel. White flour is produced by grinding only the endosperm. Vitamins are added to some white flour to replace vitamins found in the bran and germ.

- People use wheat to make breads, pastas, and breakfast foods. Wheat by-products are used in many other foods.

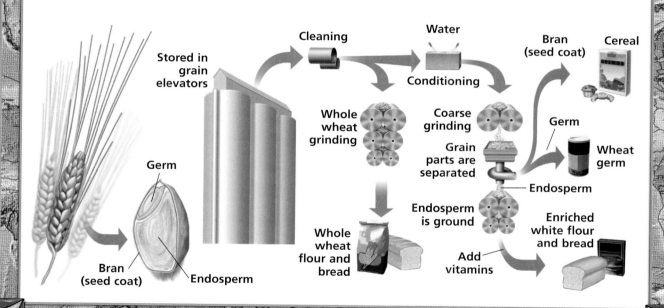

Environment During the Soviet period, Ukraine experienced rapid industrial growth. There were few pollution controls, however. In 1986 at the town of Chernobyl, the world's worst nuclear-reactor disaster occurred. Radiation spread across Ukraine and parts of northern Europe. People near the accident died. Others are still suffering from cancer. Many Ukrainians now want to reduce their country's dependence on nuclear power. This has been hard because the country has not developed enough alternative sources of power.

✓ **READING CHECK:** (*Environment and Society*) How has the scarcity of alternative sources of power affected Ukraine?

Ukraine, Belarus, and the Caucasus • 353

Belarus and Ukraine

Country	Population/ Growth Rate	Life Expectancy	Literacy Rate	Per Capita GDP
Belarus	10,322,151 −0.1%	63, male 75, female	99%	$8,200
Ukraine	48,055,439 −0.7%	61, male 72, female	99%	$4,500
United States	290,342,554 0.9%	74, male 80, female	97%	$37,600

Source: Central Intelligence Agency, *The World Factbook 2003*

Interpreting the Chart (*Place*) **How does life expectancy in the region compare to that of the United States? Why do you think this is the case?**

Belarus

The people of Belarus are known as Belorussians, which means "white Russians." Ethnically they are closely related to Russians. Their language is also very similar to Russian.

Culture Ethnic Belorussians make up about 80 percent of the country's population. Russians are the second-largest ethnic group. Both Belorussian and Russian are official languages. Belorussian also uses the Cyrillic alphabet. Minsk, the capital of Belarus, is the administrative center of the Commonwealth of Independent States.

Economy Belarus has faced many difficulties. Fighting in World War II destroyed most of the agriculture and industry in the country. Belarus also received the worst of the radiation fallout from the Chernobyl nuclear disaster, which contaminated the country's farm products and water. Many people developed health problems as a result. Another problem has been slow economic progress since the collapse of the Soviet Union. Belarus has resisted economic changes made by other former Soviet republics.

There are various resources in Belarus, however. The country has a large reserve of potash, which is used for fertilizer. Belarus leads the world in the production of peat, a source of fuel found in the damp marshes. Mining and manufacturing are important to the economy. Flax, one of the country's main crops, is grown for fiber and seed. Cattle and pigs are also raised. Nearly one third of Belarus is covered by forests that produce wood and paper products.

✔ **READING CHECK:** (*Human Systems*) How has the economy of Belarus developed?

Homework Practice Online
Keyword: SG5 HP16

Section Review 2

Define or identify: Mongols, serfs, Cossacks, soviet

Working with Sketch Maps On your map from Section 1, label Ukraine, Belarus, Kiev, Chernobyl, and Minsk.

Reading for the Main Idea

1. (*Human Systems*) What contributions were made by early groups that settled in this region?

2. (*Human Systems*) What ethnic groups and languages are found in this region today?

Critical Thinking

3. **Finding the Main Idea** How did the end of Soviet rule affect Ukraine and Belarus?

4. **Summarizing** How has the nuclear disaster at Chernobyl affected the region?

Organizing What You Know

5. **Sequencing** Copy the time line below. Use it to trace the region's history from the A.D. 900s to today.

A.D. 900   Today

Read to Discover
1. What groups influenced the early history and culture of the Caucasus?
2. What is the economy of Georgia like?
3. What is Armenia like today?
4. What is Azerbaijan like today?

Vocabulary
homogeneous
agrarian

Places
Georgia
Armenia
Azerbaijan

Reading Strategy

READING ORGANIZER Before you read, create a spider map. Label the center of the map The Caucasus. Create a leg for Georgia, Armenia, and Azerbaijan. As you read the section, fill in the map with details about each country.

History

In the 500s B.C. the Caucasus region was controlled by the Persian Empire. Later it was brought under the influence of the Byzantine Empire and was introduced to Christianity. About A.D. 650, Muslim invaders cut the region off from Christian Europe. By the late 1400s other Muslims, the Ottoman Turks, ruled a vast empire to the south and west. Much of Armenia eventually came under the rule of that empire.

Modern Era During the 1800s Russia took over eastern Armenia, much of Azerbaijan, and Georgia. The Ottoman Turks continued to rule western Armenia. Many Armenians spread throughout the Ottoman Empire. However, they were not treated well. Their desire for more independence led to the massacre of thousands of Armenians. Hundreds of thousands died while being forced to leave Turkey during World War I. Some fled to Russian Armenia.

After the war Armenia, Azerbaijan, and Georgia were briefly independent. By 1922 they had become part of the Soviet Union. They again became independent when the Soviet Union collapsed in 1991.

This wall painting is one of many at the ancient Erebuni Citadel in Yerevan, Armenia's capital. The fortress was probably built in the 800s B.C. by one of Armenia's earliest peoples, the Urartians.

This Georgian family's breakfast includes local specialties such as *khachapuri*—bread made with goat cheese.

Interpreting the Visual Record

What other agricultural products do you see on the table?

Government Each country has an elected parliament, president, and prime minister. In the early 1990s there was civil war in Georgia. Armenia and Azerbaijan were also involved in a war during this time. Ethnic minorities in each country want independence. Disagreements about oil and gas rights may cause more regional conflicts in the future.

✓ **READING CHECK:** (*Human Systems*) How has conflict among cultures been a problem in this region?

Georgia

Georgia is a small country located between the high Caucasus Mountains and the Black Sea. About 70 percent of the people are ethnic Georgians. The official language, Georgian, has its own alphabet. This alphabet was used as early as A.D. 400.

When the Soviet Union fell, Georgia lost a valuable trading partner and a source of cheap fuel. Since then, poverty, corruption, and civil war have troubled the country. In 2003, the Georgians forced the government to resign in a bloodless revolution.

Georgia has little good farmland. Tea and citrus fruits are the major crops. Vineyards are an important part of Georgian agriculture. Fish, livestock, and poultry contribute to the economy. Tourism on the Black Sea has also helped the economy. Because its only energy resource is hydropower, Georgia imports most of its energy supplies.

✓ **READING CHECK:** (*Human Systems*) In what way has scarcity of energy resources affected Georgia's economy?

Armenia

Armenia is a little smaller than Maryland. It lies just east of Turkey. It has fewer than 4 million people and is not as diverse as other countries

The Orthodox Christian Haghartsin Monastery was built in Armenia in the 1100s.

in the Caucasus. Almost all the people are Armenian, belong to the Armenian Orthodox Church, and speak Armenian.

Armenia's progress toward economic reform has not been easy. In 1988 a massive earthquake destroyed nearly one third of its industry. Armenia's industry today is varied. It includes mining and the production of carpets, clothing, and footwear.

Agriculture accounts for about 40 percent of Armenia's gross domestic product. High-quality grapes and fruits are important. Beef and dairy cattle and sheep are raised on mountain pastures.

✔ **READING CHECK:** (*Environment and Society*) How did the 1998 earthquake affect the people of Armenia?

A troupe performs traditional folk dances of Azerbaijan.

Azerbaijan

Azerbaijan has nearly 8 million people. Its population is becoming ethnically more **homogeneous**, or the same. The Azeri, who speak a Turkic language, make up about 90 percent of the population.

Azerbaijan has few industries except for oil production. It is mostly an **agrarian** society. An agrarian society is organized around farming. The country's main resources are cotton, natural gas, and oil. Baku, the national capital, is the center of a large oil-refining industry. Oil is the most important part of Azerbaijan's economy. Fishing is also important because of the sturgeon of the Caspian Sea.

✔ **READING CHECK:** (*Human Systems*) What are some cultural traits of the people of Azerbaijan?

Homework Practice Online

Keyword: SG5 HP16

Section Review 3

Define and explain: homogeneous, agrarian

Working with Sketch Maps On the map you created for Section 2, label Georgia, Armenia, and Azerbaijan. How has the location of this region helped and hindered its growth?

Reading for the Main Idea

1. (*Human Systems*) Which groups influenced the early history of the Caucasus?

2. (*Human Systems*) Which country controlled the Caucasus during most of the 1900s?

Critical Thinking

3. **Analyzing Information** Why has economic reform been difficult in Armenia?

4. **Finding the Main Idea** How is Azerbaijan's economy organized?

Organizing What You Know

5. **Comparing/Contrasting** Copy the following graphic organizer. Use it to show the similarities and differences among the countries of the Caucasus region.

CHAPTER 16 Review and Practice

Define and Identify

Identify each of the following:

1. nature reserves
2. Mongols
3. serfs
4. Cossacks
5. soviet
6. homogeneous
7. agrarian

Review the Main Ideas

8. Where are this region's highest and lowest points?
9. What part of Ukraine has a Mediterranean climate?
10. What is Ukraine's greatest natural resource?
11. How did Vikings and Byzantine missionaries affect Ukraine?
12. Why were Ukraine and Belarus so valuable to the Soviet Union?
13. How did Soviet rule affect Ukraine and Belarus?
14. What happened at Chernobyl in 1986? How did this event affect Belarus?
15. What groups of people have ruled the Caucasus region?
16. What happened to the Armenians during World War I?

17. What happened in Georgia in 2003?
18. What natural disaster occured in Armenia in 1988?
19. What kind of society does Azerbaijan have?
20. What is Azerbaijan's main industry?

Think Critically

21. **Drawing Inferences and Conclusions** How might ethnic diversity affect relations among the countries in this chapter?
22. **Summarizing** What is the history of the serfs in Ukraine and Belarus?
23. **Analyzing Information** Of the countries covered in this chapter, which do you think was the most important to the former Soviet Union? Why do you think this was so?
24. **Summarizing** Why did the countries of the Caucasus develop so differently from Russia, Ukraine, and Belarus?
25. **Finding the Main Idea** Why are the economies of each of the Caucasus countries so different from one another?

Map Activity

26. On a separate sheet of paper, match the letters on the map with their correct labels.

Caucasus Mountains
Pripyat Marshes
Carpathian Mountains
Crimean Peninsula
Mount Elbrus
Donets Basin
Chernobyl

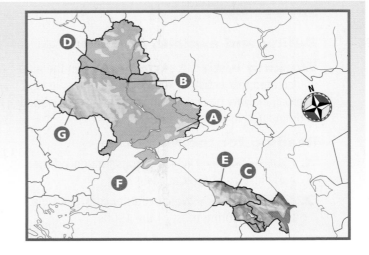

Writing Activity

Choose one of the countries covered in this chapter to research. Write a report about your chosen country's struggle to establish stability since 1991. Include information about the country's government and economic reforms. Describe the social, political, and economic problems the country has faced. Be sure to use standard grammar, sentence structure, spelling, and punctuation.

☑ internet connect ▭▭▭▭

Internet Activity: **go.hrw.com**
KEYWORD: SG5 G16

Choose a topic to explore about Ukraine, Belarus, and the Caucasus.
- Trek through the Caucasus Mountains.
- Design Ukrainian Easter eggs.
- Investigate the Chernobyl disaster.

Social Studies Skills Practice

Interpreting Maps

Study the following map of Azerbaijan. Then answer the questions.

Source: Central Intelligence Agency, *The World Factbook 2003*

1. How may Baku's location have affected the city's economic development?

2. Note the part of Azerbaijan named Naxçivan. How is its connection to the rest of the country indicated?

3. How may the location of Naxçivan lead to political problems?

4. Compare this map to the physical-political map at the beginning of the chapter. What is unusual about the area labeled Kur-Araz Ovaligi?

Analyzing Primary Sources

Read the following passage from *Chernobyl Legacy,* by Paul Fusco. Then answer the questions.

"The Chernobyl disaster revealed that the world community was not ready to face global disasters. Today, due to the grievous [painful] experience gained from Chernobyl, people are better prepared to combat possible catastrophes protecting life and health of themselves and those of their children. Chernobyl resulted in a worldwide realization of the fact that the Earth is our common home . . . having become so fragile in the hands of man who harnessed atomic power."

1. According to the passage, what truth did the disaster reveal?

2. What does the author think has been gained from the Chernobyl disaster?

3. Do you think the author is hopeful about the future? Why or why not?

4. In the last sentence, what does the word *fragile* mean?

FOCUS ON CULTURE

Changing Perceptions of Russia's Southern Neighbors

Connections between countries can change quickly. For example, trade relationships change as new industries or new sources for products develop. Changes in government also affect relationships between countries. A country that becomes more democratic may gain allies among other democratic countries. Shifts in government have had a big effect on one area in particular. That area is Central Asia. The countries that make up the region are Kazakhstan, Kyrgyzstan, Tajikistan, Turkmenistan, and Uzbekistan. These are Russia's southern neighbors.

Central Asia Since the breakup of the Soviet Union, many changes have taken place in Central Asia. In the past, Central Asia had strong ties to the Soviet Union. For example, the economies of the two regions were linked. Central Asia exported cotton and oil to Russia and to countries in Eastern Europe. In exchange, Central Asia received manufactured goods. The Soviet Union also influenced Central Asian culture. Many Central Asians learned to speak Russian.

Looking South Today, Central Asia's links to the former Soviet Union have weakened. At the same time, it has strengthened ancient ties to Southwest Asia—sometimes called the Middle East. The Silk Road once linked Central Asian cities to Southwest Asian ports on the Mediterranean. Now the peoples of Central Asia are again looking southward. New links are forming between Central Asia and Turkey. Many people in Central Asia are traditionally Turkic in culture and language. Turkey's business leaders are expanding their industries in Central Asia. Also, regular air travel from Turkey to cities in Central Asia is now possible.

Religion also links Central and Southwest Asia. Islam was introduced into Central Asia in the A.D. 700s and became the region's main religion. However, Islam declined during the Soviet era. Missionaries from Arab countries and Iran are now strengthening this connection. Iran is also building roads and rail lines to Central Asia.

◄

Region These children are learning about Islam in Dushanbe, Tajikistan. Although the former Communist government discouraged the practice of religion, today Islam flourishes in the independent Central Asian republics.

Language Groups of Southwest and Central Asia

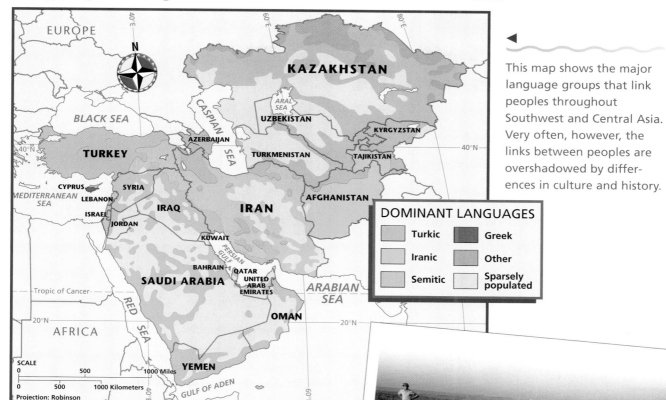

This map shows the major language groups that link peoples throughout Southwest and Central Asia. Very often, however, the links between peoples are overshadowed by differences in culture and history.

DOMINANT LANGUAGES

- Turkic
- Iranic
- Semitic
- Greek
- Other
- Sparsely populated

Place Many people in Central and Southwest Asia grow cotton, such as here in Uzbekistan.

Central Asia and Southwest Asia share a similar climate, environment, and way of life. Both regions are dry, and water conservation and irrigation are important. Many people in both regions grow cotton and herd animals. In addition, both Central Asia and Southwest Asia are dealing with changes caused by the growing influence of Western culture. Some people are worried that compact discs, videotapes, and satellite television from the West threaten traditional beliefs and ways of life. Shared fears of cultural loss may bring Central Asia and Southwest Asia closer together.

Defining the Region As the world changes, geographers must reexamine this and other regions of the world. Will geographers decide to include the countries of Central Asia in the region of Southwest Asia? Will Russia regain control of Central Asia? The geographers are watching and waiting.

Understanding What You Read

1. What ties did Central Asia have to the Soviet Union in the past?

2. Why are ties between Central Asia and Southwest Asia growing today?

Building Skills for Life: Addressing Environmental Problems

The natural environment is the world around us. It includes the air, animals, land, plants, and water. Many people today are concerned about the environment. They are called environmentalists. Environmentalists are worried that human activities are damaging the environment. Environmental problems include air, land, and water pollution, global warming, deforestation, plant and animal extinction, and soil erosion.

People all over the world are working to solve these environmental problems. The governments of many countries are trying to work together to protect the environment. International organizations like the United Nations are also addressing environmental issues.

▲

An oil spill in northwestern Russia caused serious environmental damage in 1995.

Interpreting the Visual Record

Can you see how these people are cleaning up the oil spill?

THE SKILL

1. **Gather Information.** Create a plan to present to the city council for solving a local environmental problem. Select a problem and research it using databases or other reference materials. How does it affect people's lives and your community's culture or economy?

2. **List and Consider Options.** After reviewing the information, list and consider options for solving this environmental problem.

3. **Consider Advantages and Disadvantages.** Now consider the advantages and disadvantages of taking each option. Ask yourself questions like, "How will solving this environmental problem affect business in the area?" Record your answers.

4. **Choose, Implement, and Evaluate a Solution.** After considering the advantages and disadvantages, you should create your plan. Be sure to make your proposal clear. You will need to explain the reasoning behind the choices you made in your plan.

HANDS on GEOGRAPHY

The countries of the former Soviet Union face some of the worst environmental problems in the world. For more than 50 years, the region's environment was polluted with nuclear waste and toxic chemicals. Today, environmental problems in this region include air, land, and water pollution.

One place that was seriously polluted was the Russian city of Chelyabinsk. Some people have called Chelyabinsk the most polluted place on Earth. The passage below describes some of the environmental problems in Chelyabinsk. Read the passage and then answer the Lab Report questions.

Chelyabinsk was one of the former Soviet Union's main military production centers. A factory near Chelyabinsk produced nuclear weapons. Over the years, nuclear waste from this factory polluted a very large area. A huge amount of nuclear waste was dumped into the Techa River. Many people in the region used this river as their main source of water. They also ate fish from the river.

In the 1950s many deaths and health problems resulted from pollution in the Techa River. Because it was so polluted, the Soviet government evacuated 22 villages along the river. In 1957 a nuclear accident in the region released twice as much radiation as the Chernobyl accident in 1986. However, the accident near Chelyabinsk was kept secret. About 10,000 people were evacuated. The severe environmental problems in the Chelyabinsk region led to dramatic increases in birth defects and cancer rates.

▲ The village of Mitlino was evacuated after a nuclear accident in 1957.

Lab Report

1. How did environmental problems near Chelyabinsk affect people who lived in the region?

2. What might be done to address environmental problems in the Chelyabinsk region?

3. How can a geographical perspective help to solve these problems?

Southwest and Central Asia

Bottle trees, Yemen

An Exchange Student in Turkey

Sara Lewis was an American exchange student in Turkey. Here she describes how teenagers live in Istanbul, Turkey's largest city, and the month-long fast of Ramadan. **WHAT DO YOU THINK?** *What would it be like to live in a place where you can see the remains of thousands of years of history?*

The people of Istanbul are very traditional and family-oriented, but today's Turk also has European-style tastes. Turkish teens go dancing and hang out in coffeehouses. All around them, though, are reminders of the past. There are many monuments left over from Greek, Roman, Byzantine, and Ottoman times.

Islam plays a big part in daily life. Five times every day I can hear the people being called to prayer. For more than a month, my host parents fasted during Ramadan. They didn't eat or drink anything while the sun was up. My host sister and I fasted for one day. By the time the sun went down we were starving! I'm glad we weren't expected to continue the fast. Then we shopped for new clothes. It is the custom to wear new clothes to the feast at the end of Ramadan. The fresh clothes seem to stand for the cleanliness one achieves during the month of fasting.

Family preparing food for the end of Ramadan

Jewish girls, Zefat, Israel

Understanding Primary Sources

1. What do modern Turkish teenagers do for fun?

2. How is Ramadan observed in Turkey?

Sooty falcon

Southwest and Central Asia

Elevation Profile

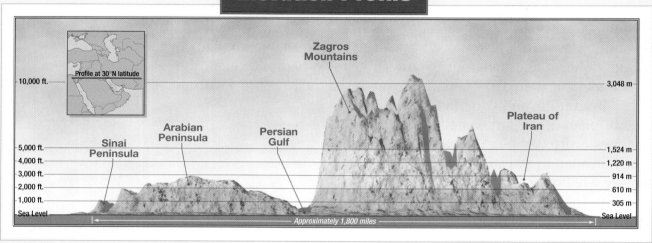

Profile at 30°N latitude

Zagros Mountains

Plateau of Iran

Arabian Peninsula

Sinai Peninsula

Persian Gulf

10,000 ft.	3,048 m
5,000 ft.	1,524 m
4,000 ft.	1,220 m
3,000 ft.	914 m
2,000 ft.	610 m
1,000 ft.	305 m
Sea Level	Sea Level

Approximately 1,800 miles

The United States and Southwest and Central Asia:
Comparing Sizes

GEOSTATS:

World's lowest point on land: the Dead Sea, in Israel and Jordan—1,312 feet (400 m) below sea level

World's leading exporter of oil: Saudi Arabia

Approximate amount of proven oil reserves in Saudi Arabia: 261 billion barrels

Estimated number of barrels of oil that pass through the Strait of Hormuz every day: 15.4 million

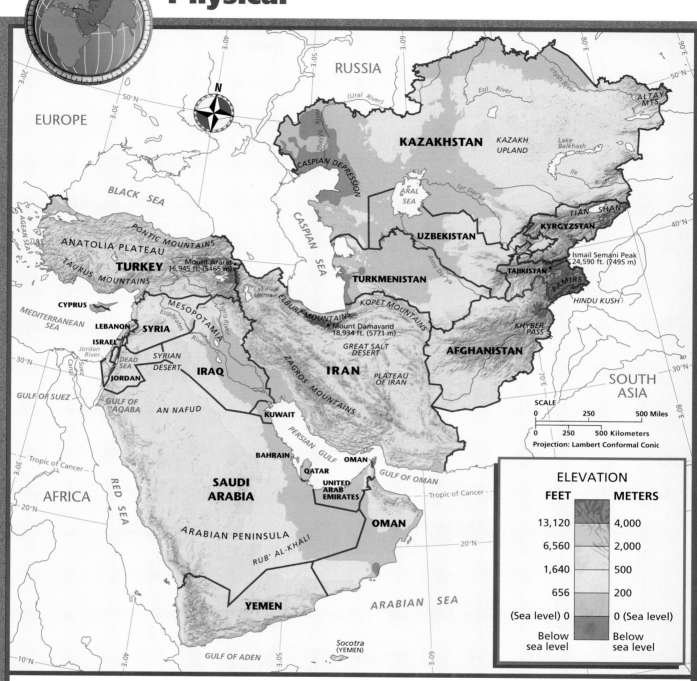

RUSSIA

KAZAKHSTAN

KAZAKH UPLAND

Lake Balkhash

Esil River

Irtysh River

ALTAY MTS

EUROPE

N

CASPIAN DEPRESSION

ARAL SEA

Syr Dar'ya

UZBEKISTAN

TIAN SHAN

KYRGYZSTAN

Ismail Semani Peak 24,590 ft. (7495 m)

BLACK SEA

PONTIC MOUNTAINS

ANATOLIA PLATEAU

TURKEY

TAURUS MOUNTAINS

Mount Ararat 16,945 ft. (5165 m)

AEGAN SEA

CYPRUS

MEDITERRANEAN SEA

LEBANON

SYRIA

ISRAEL

Jordan River

DEAD SEA

JORDAN

SYRIAN DESERT

MESOPOTAMIA

Euphrates River

Lake Urmia

Tigris River

ELBURZ MOUNTAINS

Amu Dar'ya

KOPET MOUNTAINS

Mount Damavand 18,934 ft. (5771 m)

GREAT SALT DESERT

IRAQ

ZAGROS MOUNTAINS

IRAN

PLATEAU OF IRAN

TAJIKISTAN

PAMIRS

HINDU KUSH

KHYBER PASS

AFGHANISTAN

TURKMENISTAN

SOUTH ASIA

GULF OF SUEZ

Suez Canal

GULF OF AQABA

AN NAFUD

KUWAIT

BAHRAIN

QATAR

UNITED ARAB EMIRATES

OMAN

GULF OF OMAN

PERSIAN GULF

SCALE

0   250   500 Miles

0   250   500 Kilometers

Projection: Lambert Conformal Conic

Tropic of Cancer

AFRICA

RED SEA

SAUDI ARABIA

ARABIAN PENINSULA

RUB' AL-KHALI

OMAN

Tropic of Cancer

ELEVATION

FEET		METERS
13,120		4,000
6,560		2,000
1,640		500
656		200
(Sea level) 0		0 (Sea level)
Below sea level		Below sea level

YEMEN

Socotra (YEMEN)

ARABIAN SEA

GULF OF ADEN

1. (Place) Which rivers flow into the Aral Sea?

2. (Region) Where are the region's highest mountains? What are these mountains called?

3. (Place) Which country is partly in Europe and partly in Asia?

Critical Thinking

4. (Movement) How might one travel overland from Syria to Oman? Why?

5. (Interaction) Compare this map to the **population map**. What physical features contribute to Iraq's relatively high population density?

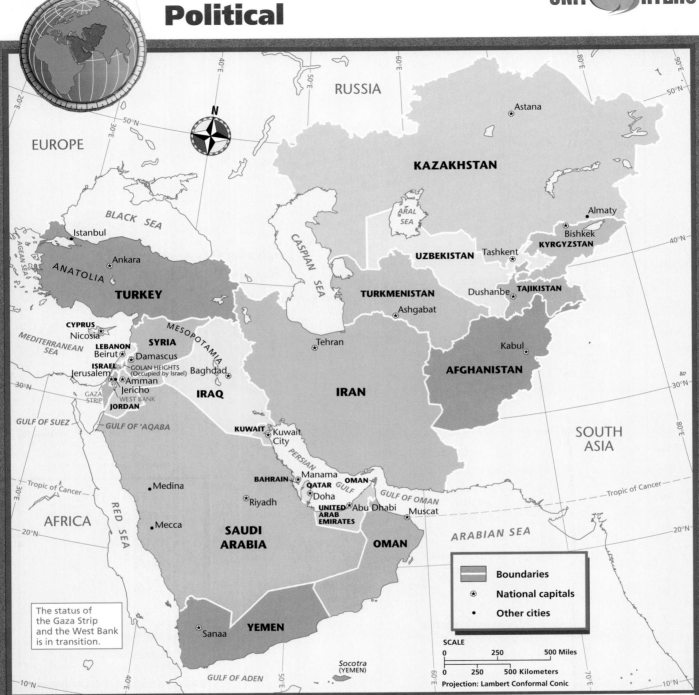

The status of the Gaza Strip and the West Bank is in transition.

Boundaries

⊛ **National capitals**

• **Other cities**

SCALE

0 — 250 — 500 Miles

0 — 250 — 500 Kilometers

Projection: Lambert Conformal Conic

---

1. **Place** What is the region's largest country? the region's smallest?

2. **Location** Which capital lies near latitude 30°N and longitude 50°E?

Critical Thinking

3. **Region** Examine the **climate map**. Why do you think so many of the boundaries in this region are straight lines?

4. **Movement** Which countries lie along the Persian Gulf and the Gulf of Oman? Why might conflicts occur among these countries?

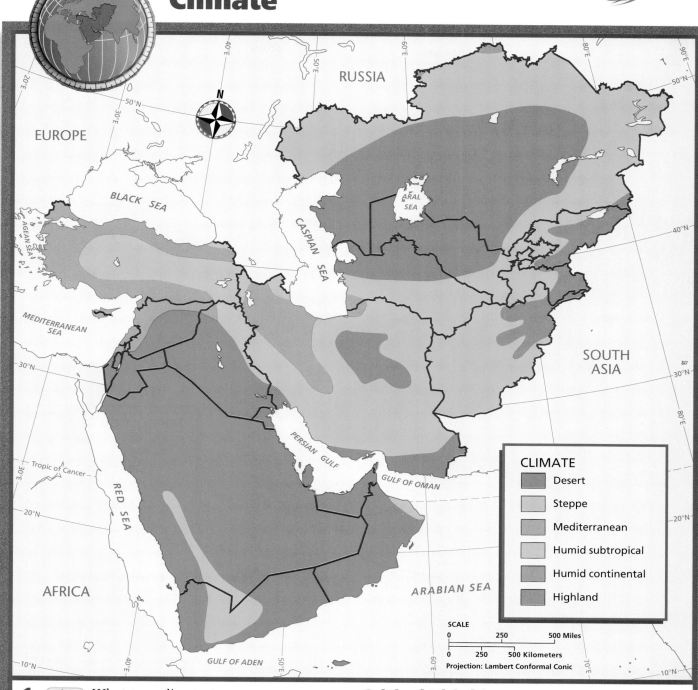

RUSSIA

EUROPE

BLACK SEA

AEGEAN SEA

CASPIAN SEA

ARAL SEA

MEDITERRANEAN SEA

SOUTH ASIA

Tropic of Cancer

RED SEA

PERSIAN GULF

GULF OF OMAN

AFRICA

ARABIAN SEA

GULF OF ADEN

50°N
40°N
30°N
20°N
10°N

20°E 30°E 40°E 50°E 60°E 70°E 80°E 90°E

CLIMATE
- Desert
- Steppe
- Mediterranean
- Humid subtropical
- Humid continental
- Highland

SCALE
0   250   500 Miles
0   250   500 Kilometers
Projection: Lambert Conformal Conic

1. *(Place)* What two climate types are most common in this region?

2. *(Place)* Compare this map to the **physical map**. What mountain ranges do not have a highland climate?

Critical Thinking

3. *(Interaction)* Compare this map to the **land use and resources map**. In which climate regions are nomadic herding most common?

4. *(Interaction)* Compare this map to the **population map**. How may climate influence the region's population patterns?

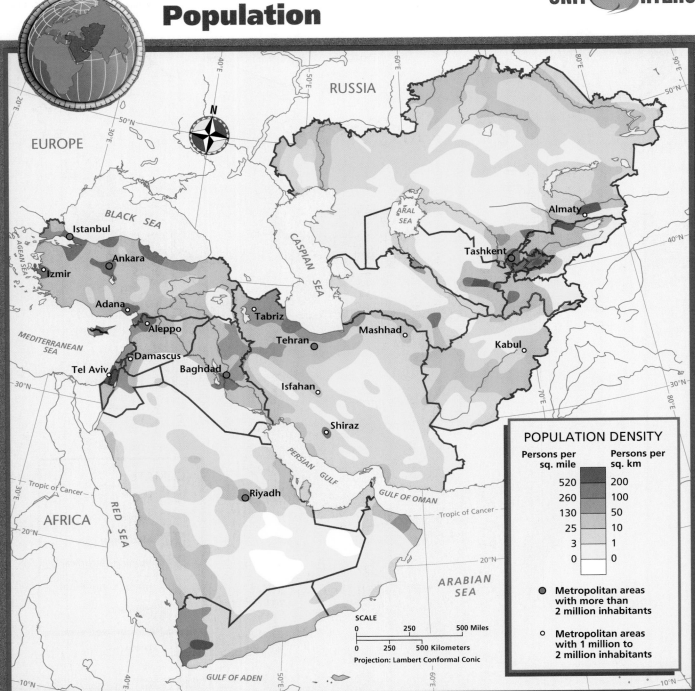

RUSSIA

EUROPE

BLACK SEA

Istanbul

Ankara

Izmir

Adana

Aleppo

MEDITERRANEAN SEA

Damascus

Tel Aviv

Baghdad

AFRICA

RED SEA

Riyadh

Tropic of Cancer

CASPIAN SEA

ARAL SEA

Tabriz

Tehran

Mashhad

Isfahan

Shiraz

PERSIAN GULF

GULF OF OMAN

Tropic of Cancer

ARABIAN SEA

Almaty

Tashkent

Kabul

GULF OF ADEN

SCALE

0   250   500 Miles

0   250   500 Kilometers

Projection: Lambert Conformal Conic

POPULATION DENSITY

Persons per sq. mile	Persons per sq. km
520	200
260	100
130	50
25	10
3	1
0	0

● Metropolitan areas with more than 2 million inhabitants

○ Metropolitan areas with 1 million to 2 million inhabitants

1. (Region) Which country has an area of high population density but no large cities?

2. (Region) What is the largest city in the easternmost part of the region?

Critical Thinking

3. (Location) Look at Istanbul's location. Why is it good for a large city?

4. (Region) Compare this map to the **land use and resources map**. Why do you think the southwestern tip of the Arabian Pennisula has a high population density?

Southwest and Central Asia: Land Use and Resources

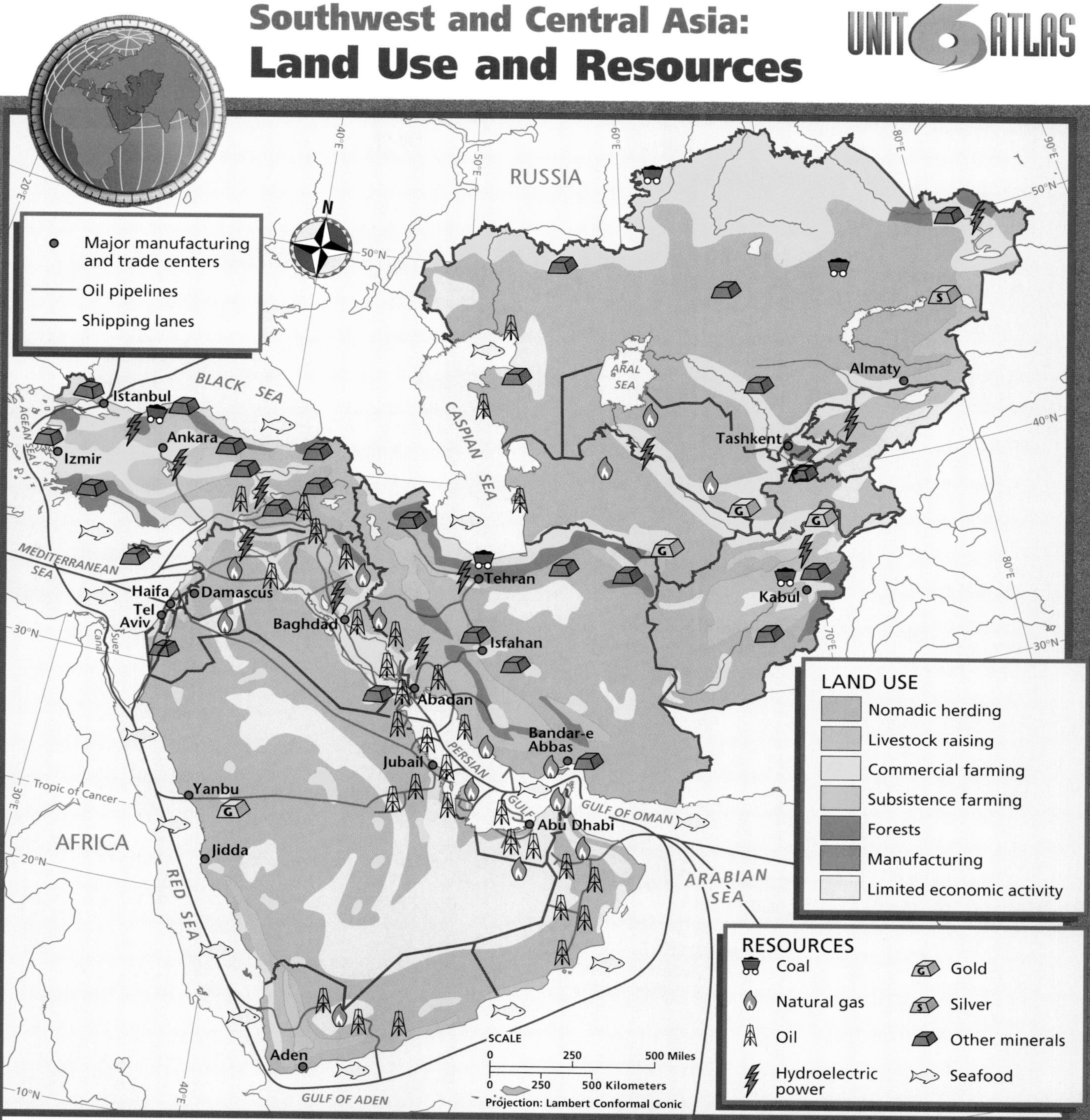
RUSSIA
Major manufacturing and trade centers
Oil pipelines
Shipping lanes
N
50°N
40°E
50°E
60°E
80°E
90°E
20°E
70°E
30°N
40°N
20°N
10°N
30°E
Tropic of Cancer
BLACK SEA
CASPIAN SEA
ARAL SEA
AEGEAN SEA
MEDITERRANEAN SEA
Suez Canal
RED SEA
PERSIAN GULF
GULF OF OMAN
ARABIAN SEA
GULF OF ADEN
AFRICA
Istanbul
Ankara
Izmir
Haifa
Tel Aviv
Damascus
Baghdad
Tehran
Isfahan
Abadan
Bandar-e Abbas
Jubail
Abu Dhabi
Yanbu
Jidda
Aden
Almaty
Tashkent
Kabul
LAND USE
Nomadic herding
Livestock raising
Commercial farming
Subsistence farming
Forests
Manufacturing
Limited economic activity
RESOURCES
Coal
Natural gas
Oil
Hydroelectric power
Gold
Silver
Other minerals
Seafood
SCALE
0 250 500 Miles
0 250 500 Kilometers
Projection: Lambert Conformal Conic

1. *Interaction* Where are the region's gold mines located?
2. *Interaction* What two energy resources are often found together in the region?
3. *Movement* By what route would an oil tanker travel from Abadan to Mediterranean ports?

Critical Thinking

4. *Place* Why might fresh vegetables be costly in Kuwait?
5. *Interaction* Compare this map to the physical map. Which waterway might be used to transport minerals to Tashkent?

Southwest and Central Asia

AFGHANISTAN

CAPITAL:
Kabul

AREA:
250,000 sq. mi.
(647,500 sq km)

POPULATION:
28,717,213

LANGUAGES:
Pashtu,
Afghan Persian (Dari), Turkic
languages

UNEMPLOYMENT:
data not available

IRAQ

CAPITAL:
Baghdad

AREA:
168,753 sq. mi.
(437,072 sq km)

POPULATION: 24,683,313

LANGUAGES:
Arabic, Kurdish

UNEMPLOYMENT:
70 percent

BAHRAIN

CAPITAL:
Manama

AREA:
239 sq. mi.
(620 sq km)

POPULATION:
667,238

LANGUAGES:
Arabic, English, Farsi, Urdu

UNEMPLOYMENT:
15 percent

ISRAEL

CAPITAL:
Jerusalem

AREA:
8,019 sq. mi.
(20,770 sq km)

POPULATION:
6,116,533

LANGUAGES:
Hebrew (official), Arabic,
English

UNEMPLOYMENT:
10.4 percent

CYPRUS

CAPITAL:
Nicosia

AREA:
3,571 sq. mi. (9,250 sq km)

POPULATION:
771,657

LANGUAGES:
Greek, Turkish, English

UNEMPLOYMENT:
Greek Cypriot area: 3.3 percent; Turkish Cypriot area:
5.6 percent

Western Wall and Dome of the Rock, Jerusalem, Israel

IRAN

CAPITAL:
Tehran

AREA:
636,293 sq. mi.
(1,648,000 sq km)

POPULATION:
68,278,826

LANGUAGES:
Persian, Turkic,
Kurdish

UNEMPLOYMENT:
16.3 percent

Jordanian boys with camel

KYRGYZSTAN

CAPITAL:
Bishkek

AREA:
76,641 sq. mi.
(198,500 sq km)

POPULATION:
4,892,808

LANGUAGES:
Kirghiz, Russian

UNEMPLOYMENT:
7.2 percent

KUWAIT

CAPITAL:
Kuwait City

AREA:
6,880 sq. mi.
(17,820 sq km)

POPULATION:
2,183,161

LANGUAGES:
Arabic, English

UNEMPLOYMENT:
7 percent

JORDAN

CAPITAL:
Amman

AREA:
35,637 sq. mi.
(92,300 sq km)

POPULATION:
5,460,265

LANGUAGES:
Arabic, English

UNEMPLOYMENT:
30 percent

LEBANON

CAPITAL:
Beirut

AREA:
4,015 sq. mi.
(10,400 sq km)

POPULATION: 3,727,703

LANGUAGES:
Arabic (official), French

UNEMPLOYMENT:
18 percent

KAZAKHSTAN

CAPITAL:
Astana

AREA:
1,049,150 sq. mi.
(2,717,300 sq km)

POPULATION:
16,763,795

LANGUAGES:
Kazakh, Russian

UNEMPLOYMENT:
8.8 percent

A warrior's armor from Kazakhstan.

Sources: Central Intelligence Agency, *The World Factbook 2003*, CPA and Labor Secretary, Iraqi Interim Government; population figures are 2003 estimates.

OMAN

CAPITAL:
Muscat

AREA:
82,031 sq. mi.
(212,460 sq km)

POPULATION: 2,807,125

LANGUAGES:
Arabic (official), English

UNEMPLOYMENT:
data not available

SYRIA

CAPITAL:
Damascus

AREA:
71,498 sq. mi.
(185,180 sq km)

POPULATION: 17,585,540

LANGUAGES:
Arabic (official), Kurdish

UNEMPLOYMENT:
20 percent

QATAR

CAPITAL:
Doha

AREA:
4,416 sq. mi.
(11,437 sq km)

POPULATION:
817,052

LANGUAGES:
Arabic (official),
English

UNEMPLOYMENT:
2.7 percent

TAJIKISTAN

CAPITAL:
Dushanbe

AREA:
55,251 sq. mi.
(143,100 sq km)

POPULATION:
6,863,752

LANGUAGES:
Tajik (official), Russian

UNEMPLOYMENT:
40 percent (and many underemployed)

SAUDI ARABIA

CAPITAL:
Riyadh

AREA:
756,981 sq. mi.
(1,960,582 sq km)

POPULATION:
24,293,844

LANGUAGES:
Arabic

UNEMPLOYMENT:
25 percent

Children learning Islam in Tajikistan

Mosque in Uzbekistan

UNITED ARAB EMIRATES

CAPITAL: Abu Dhabi
AREA:
32,000 sq. mi.
(82,880 sq km)
POPULATION: 2,484,818

LANGUAGES:
Arabic (official), Persian
UNEMPLOYMENT:
data not available

UZBEKISTAN

CAPITAL:
Tashkent
AREA:
172,741 sq. mi.
(447,400 sq km)
POPULATION:
25,981,647

LANGUAGES:
Uzbek, Russian, Tajik
UNEMPLOYMENT:
10 percent (and many underemployed)

TURKEY

CAPITAL: Ankara
AREA:
301,382 sq. mi.
(780,580 sq km)
POPULATION:
68,109,469

LANGUAGES:
Turkish (official), Kurdish
UNEMPLOYMENT:
10.8 percent (6.1 percent underemployed)

YEMEN

CAPITAL:
Sanaa
AREA:
203,849 sq. mi.
(527,970 sq km)
POPULATION:
19,349,881

LANGUAGES:
Arabic
UNEMPLOYMENT:
30 percent

TURKMENISTAN

CAPITAL:
Ashgabat
AREA:
188,455 sq. mi.
(488,100 sq km)
POPULATION: 4,775,544

LANGUAGES:
Turkmen, Uzbek, Russian
UNEMPLOYMENT:
data not available

internet connect
go.hrw.com
COUNTRY STATISTICS
GO TO: go.hrw.com
KEYWORD: SG5 FactsU6
FOR: more facts about
Southwest and Central Asia

Sources: Central Intelligence Agency, *The World Factbook 2003*, CPA and Labor Secretary, Iraqi Interim Government; population figures are 2003 estimates.

CHAPTER 17

The Eastern Mediterranean

The next student we will meet lives in Turkey, a country that lies partly in Europe, partly in Asia.

My name is Adalet, and I am in the tenth grade at Ted College, a private school in Ankara, the capital of Turkey. I live in an apartment a little outside the city with my mom and dad. We live on the twelfth floor, and have a view of the city, the distant mountains, and of course the parking lot. In the summers, my favorite time is when I can go to stay with my grandma and my grandpa in their summer house on the Aegean Sea, in Kusadasi near the ancient Greek city of Ephesus. I sleep until 11:00 A.M. or noon, then spend the day at the beach with my friends until the sun goes down.

On school days, from September to June, I get up at 8:00 A.M., put on my school uniform, and have breakfast of corn flakes or bread and cheese with milk or tea. At school we go directly to our classes. I am studying biology, physics, algebra, geometry, history, Turkish, and English. The English, science, and math classes are taught in English, the others in Turkish.

Türkiye´den selamlar!

Translation: Greetings from Turkey!

Section 1 · Physical Geography

Read to Discover

1. What are the main physical features of the eastern Mediterranean?
2. What are the climate types of the region?
3. What natural resources are found in this area?

Vocabulary

phosphates
asphalt

Places

Dardanelles
Bosporus
Sea of Marmara
Jordan River
Dead Sea

Syrian Desert
Negev

Reading Strategy

BRAINSTORMING Write the letters of the alphabet down a sheet of paper. With a partner, brainstorm what you already know about the eastern Mediterranean region. List your ideas next to as many letters as possible.

The Eastern Mediterranean: Physical-Political

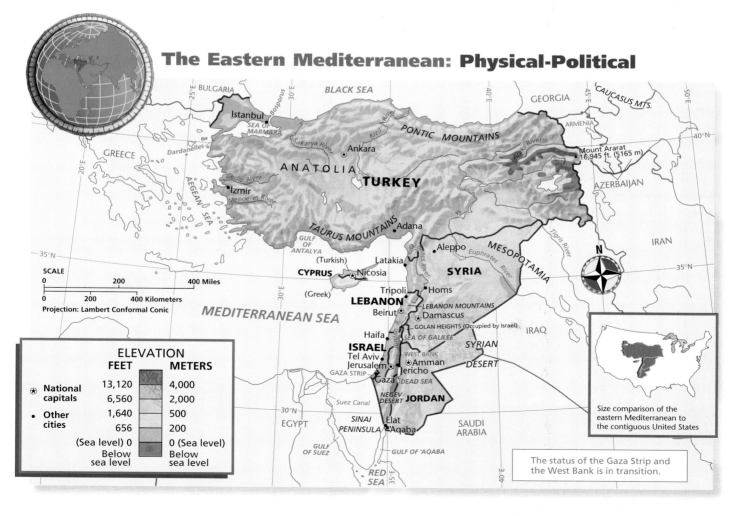

SCALE
0   200   400 Miles
0   200   400 Kilometers
Projection: Lambert Conformal Conic

ELEVATION

	FEET	METERS
⊛ National capitals	13,120	4,000
• Other cities	6,560	2,000
	1,640	500
	656	200
	(Sea level) 0	0 (Sea level)
	Below sea level	Below sea level

Size comparison of the eastern Mediterranean to the contiguous United States

The status of the Gaza Strip and the West Bank is in transition.

Our Amazing Planet

The Dead Sea, which covers an area of just 394 square miles (1,020 sq km), contains approximately 12.7 billion tons of salt. Each year the Jordan River deposits 850,000 additional tons.

Istanbul lies on both sides of the waterway known as the Bosporus. This waterway divides Europe from Asia.

Interpreting the Visual Record

(*Movement*) **Why do you think the Bosporus would be an important crossroads of trade?**

Physical Features

The countries of the eastern Mediterranean are Turkey, Lebanon, Syria, Jordan, and Israel. In addition to its own territory, Israel controls areas known as the Occupied Territories. These include the West Bank, the Gaza Strip, and the Golan Heights.

On Two Continents The eastern Mediterranean region straddles two continents. A small part of Turkey lies on Europe's Balkan Peninsula. This area consists of rolling plains and hills. A narrow waterway, made up of the Dardanelles (dahrd-uhn-ELZ), the Bosporus (BAHS-puh-ruhs), and the Sea of Marmara (MAHR-muh-ruh), separates Europe from Asia. The larger, Asian part of Turkey is mostly plateaus and highlands.

Hills, Valleys, and Plains Heading south from Turkey and into Syria, we cross a narrow plain. The Euphrates River, fed by precipitation in Turkey's eastern mountains, flows southeast through this plain. Farther south are more hills and plateaus. Two main ridges run north-south. One runs from southwestern Syria through western Jordan. The other, closer to the coast, runs through Lebanon, Israel, and the West Bank. The Jordan River valley separates these two ridges. A narrow coastal plain rims the region along its seacoasts. In western Turkey the coastal plain is wider.

River and Sea The Jordan River begins in Syria and flows south. Israel and the West Bank lie on the west side of the river. The country of Jordan lies on the east side. The Jordan River flows into the Dead Sea. This unusual body of water is the lowest point on any continent—1,312 feet (400 m) below sea level. It is so salty that swimmers cannot sink in it.

✓ **READING CHECK:**   (*Places and Regions*) What are the region's main physical features?

Climate

Dry climates are the rule in most of this region. However, there are important variations. Turkey's Black Sea coast and the Mediterranean coast all the way to Israel have a Mediterranean climate. Central Syria

and lands farther south have a desert climate. A small area of north-eastern Turkey has a humid subtropical climate.

The Syrian Desert covers much of Syria and Jordan. It usually receives less than five inches (12.7 cm) of rainfall a year. Another desert, the Negev (NE-gev), lies in southern Israel.

✓ **READING CHECK:** (*Places and Regions*) What are the climates of the eastern Mediterranean?

Resources

Unlike nearby countries in Southwest Asia, the countries of the eastern Mediterranean do not have large oil reserves. The people of this region make their living from the land in other ways.

Limited Farming Commercial farming is possible only where rain or irrigation provides enough water. Subsistence farming and livestock herding are common in drier areas. Desert areas support a few nomadic herders.

Mineral Resources Many minerals, including sulfur, mercury, and copper, are found in the region. **Phosphates**—mineral salts containing the element phosphorus—are produced in Syria, Jordan, and Israel. Phosphates are used to make fertilizers. The area also exports **asphalt**—the dark tar-like material used to pave streets. The Dead Sea is a source of mineral salts.

✓ **READING CHECK:** (*Places and Regions*) What natural resources are found in this area?

A shepherd in eastern Turkey watches his sheep.
Interpreting the Visual Record
(*Human-Environment Interaction*) **Why is livestock herding common in many parts of the eastern Mediterranean region?**

▼

Section Review 1

Define and explain: phosphates, asphalt

Working with Sketch Maps On a map of the eastern Mediterranean that you draw or that your teacher provides, label the following: Dardanelles, Bosporus, Sea of Marmara, Jordan River, Dead Sea, Syrian Desert, and the Negev.

Reading for the Main Idea

1. (*Places and Regions*) What country lies on two continents?

2. (*Places and Regions*) What are the most common climates of the region?

3. (*Places and Regions*) How do geographic factors affect the economic activities of the region?

go.hrw.com **Homework Practice Online**
Keyword: SG5 HP17

Critical Thinking

4. Drawing Inferences and Conclusions How do you think the Dead Sea got its name?

Organizing What You Know

5. Categorizing Copy the following graphic organizer. Use it to list the major landforms and bodies of water of each region.

Country/ territory	Landforms and bodies of water

Read to Discover

1. What is the history of the area that is now Turkey?

2. What kind of government and economy does Turkey have?

3. How is Turkish society divided?

Vocabulary

secular

Places

Ankara
Istanbul

People

Kemal Atatürk

Reading Strategy

FOLDNOTES: LAYERED BOOK Create the FoldNote titled **Layered Book** described in the Appendix. Label the book Turkey. Label the pages with these geography themes: Location and Place, Human-Environment Interaction, Movement, and Region. As you read, write what you learn about Turkey that supports the themes.

▲ *Place* Ottoman monarchs lived in the Topkapi Palace built in 1462.

History

Turkey, except for the small part that lies in Europe, makes up a region called Asia Minor. In ancient times this area was part of the Hittite and Persian Empires. In the 330s B.C. Alexander the Great conquered Asia Minor. Later it became part of the Roman Empire. Byzantium, renamed Constantinople, was one of the most important cities of the empire. After the fall of Rome, Constantinople became the capital of the Byzantine Empire.

In the A.D. 1000s the Seljuk Turks invaded Asia Minor. The Seljuks were a nomadic people from Central Asia who had converted to Islam. In 1453 another Turkish people, the Ottoman Turks, captured the city of Constantinople. They made it the capital of their Islamic empire.

Ottoman Empire During the 1500s and 1600s the Ottoman Empire was very powerful. It controlled territory in North Africa, Southwest Asia, and southeastern Europe. In the 1700s and 1800s the empire gradually weakened.

In World War I the Ottoman Empire fought on the losing side. When the war ended, the Ottomans lost all their territory outside of what is now Turkey. Greece even invaded western Asia Minor in an attempt to take more land. However, the Turkish army pushed out the invaders. Military officers

A boy holds a Turkish national flag during celebrations on Republic Day. A banner behind him shows Atatürk, the founder of modern Turkey.

then took over the government. Their leader was a war hero, Mustafa Kemal. He later adopted the name Kemal Atatürk, which means "father of the Turks." He formally dissolved the Ottoman Empire and created the nation of Turkey. He made the new country a democracy and moved the capital to Ankara. Constantinople was renamed Istanbul in 1930.

Modern Turkey Atatürk wanted to modernize Turkey. He believed that to be strong Turkey had to westernize. He banned the fez, the traditional hat of Turkish men, and required that they wear European-style hats. The Latin alphabet replaced the Arabic one. The European calendar and metric system replaced Islamic ones. Women were encouraged to vote, work, and hold office. New laws made it illegal for women to wear veils.

✓ **READING CHECK:** (*Human Systems*) What is the history of what is now Turkey?

Government and Economy

Today, Turkey has a legislature called the National Assembly. A president and a prime minister share executive power. The Turkish military has taken over the government three times. However, each time it has returned power to civilian hands.

Although most of its people are Muslim, Turkey is a **secular** state. This means that religion is kept separate from government. For example, the religion of Islam allows a man to have up to four wives. However, by Turkish law a man is permitted to have just one wife. In recent years Islamic political parties have attempted to increase Islam's role in Turkish society.

Turkish women harvest grapes.
Interpreting the Visual Record (*Place*)
What kind of climate do Turkey's coastal plains have?

CONNECTING TO *Literature*

Statue of Gilgamesh

Epic of Gilgamesh

Gilgamesh is the hero of this ancient story that was popular all over Southwest Asia. In this passage Utnapishtim (oot-nuh-peesh-tuhm), whom the gods have given everlasting life, tells Gilgamesh about surviving a great flood.

"In those days . . . the people multiplied, the world bellowed like a wild bull, and the great god was aroused by the clamor[1]. Enlil (en-LIL) heard the clamor and he said to the gods in council, 'The uproar of mankind is intolerable[2] and sleep is no longer possible by reason of the babel[3].' So the gods agreed to exterminate[4] mankind. Enlil did this, but Ea (AY-uh) because of his oath warned me in a dream. . . . 'Tear down your house, I say, and build a boat. . . . then take up into the boat the seed of all living creatures.'

Utnapishtim does as he is told. He builds a boat and fills it with supplies, his family, and animals. Then terrible rains come and flood Earth.

"When the seventh day dawned the storm from the south subsided, the sea grew calm, the flood was stilled; I looked at the face of the world and there was silence, all mankind was turned to clay. . . . I opened a hatch and the light fell on my face. Then I bowed low, I sat down and I wept, . . . for on every side was the waste of water."

Analyzing Primary Sources
1. Why did the god bring the flood?
2. Why does Utnapishtim cry?

Vocabulary   [1]clamor: noise   [2]intolerable: not bearable   [3]babel: confusing noise   [4]exterminate: kill off

---

Turkey's economy includes modern factories as well as village farming and craft making. The most important industries are clothing, chemicals, and oil processing. About 40 percent of Turkey's labor force works in agriculture. Grains, cotton, sugar beets, and hazelnuts are major crops. The Turkish economy has grown rapidly in recent years, but inflation is a problem. Large numbers of Turks have left Turkey in search of better jobs. By 2001, an estimated 1.2 million Turks were working abroad to earn higher wages.

In the 1990s Turkey began building dams on the Tigris and Euphrates Rivers. These will provide electricity and irrigation water. However, the dams have caused concern for Syria and Iraq. They are disturbed that another country controls the sources of their water.

✔ **READING CHECK:**   (*Human Systems*)   What kind of government and economy does Turkey have?

People and Culture

Turkey has more than 68 million people. Ethnic Turks make up 80 percent of the population. Kurds are the largest minority. They are about 20 percent of the population. Since ancient times the Kurds have lived in what is today southeastern Turkey. Kurds also live in nearby parts of Iran, Iraq, and Syria. In the 1980s and 1990s some Kurds fought for independence from Turkey. The Turkish government has used military force against this rebellion.

Kemal Atatürk's changes created a cultural split between Turkey's urban middle class and rural villagers. The lifestyle and attitudes of middle-class Turks have much in common with those of middle-class Europeans. Most Turks, though, are more traditional. Islam influences their attitudes on matters such as the role of women. This cultural division is a factor in Turkish politics.

Turkish cooking is much like that of the rest of the Mediterranean region. It features olives, vegetables, cheese, yogurt, and bread. Shish kebab—grilled meat on a skewer—is a favorite Turkish dish.

✓ **READING CHECK:** (*Human Systems*) What are the divisions in Turkish society?

(Place) Crowds pass through a square near the University of Istanbul. Different styles of dress reflect the diverse attitudes that exist in Turkey today.

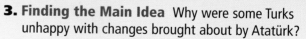

Section Review 2

Define or identify: Kemal Atatürk, secular

Working with Sketch Maps On the map you created in Section 1, label Ankara and Istanbul. What are the advantages of Istanbul's location?

Reading for the Main Idea

1. (*Human Systems*) How did Atatürk try to modernize Turkey?

2. (*Human Systems*) What foods are popular in Turkish cooking?

Homework Practice Online
Keyword: SG5 HP17

Critical Thinking

3. **Finding the Main Idea** Why were some Turks unhappy with changes brought about by Atatürk?

4. **Analyzing Information** Why is the Turkish government building dams on the Tigris and Euphrates Rivers? How will this affect countries downriver?

Organizing What You Know

5. **Sequencing** Create a time line listing major events in Turkey's history. List major people, groups, invasions, empires, and changes in government.

400 B.C.   A.D. 2000

Israel and the Occupied Territories

Read to Discover

1. What was the early history of Israel like?
2. What is modern Israel like?
3. What is the conflict over the Occupied Territories?

Vocabulary

Diaspora
Zionism

Places

Jerusalem
Gaza Strip
Golan Heights
West Bank
Tel Aviv

Reading Strategy

TAKING NOTES Before you read, write the main ideas down the left side of a sheet of paper. As you read this section, write what you learn about Israel next to the main ideas.

Place The ancient port of Caesarea lies on the coast of Israel. It was the regional capital during the time of Roman control. Today the harbor structure is partly underwater.

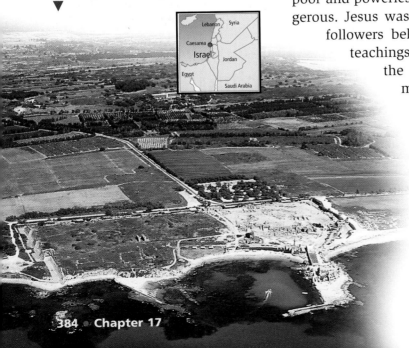

Ancient Israel

The Hebrews, the ancestors of the Jews, first established the kingdom of Israel about 3,000 years ago. It covered roughly the same area as the modern State of Israel. In the 60s B.C. the Roman Empire conquered the region, which they called Palestine. After a series of Jewish revolts, the Romans forced most Jews to leave the region. This scattering of the Jewish population is known as the **Diaspora**.

During the era of Roman control, a Jewish man named Jesus began preaching. Jesus taught that faith and love were more important than Judaism's many laws. His teachings particularly appealed to the poor and powerless. Both Roman and Jewish rulers saw Jesus as dangerous. Jesus was tried and executed by the Roman authorities. His followers believe he rose from the dead. Christianity—Jesus's teachings and the belief in his resurrection—spread through the Roman Empire. In time, Christianity became the most common religion of the Mediterranean region.

Arabs conquered Palestine in the mid-600s. From the 1000s to the 1200s, European armies launched a series of invasions called the Crusades. Crusaders captured Jerusalem in 1099. In time the Crusaders were pushed out of the area altogether. From the 1500s to World War I, Palestine was part of the Ottoman Empire. At the end of the war, it came under British control.

✓ **READING CHECK:** *Human Systems* What significant events occurred in the early history of the area of Israel?

FOCUS ON CULTURE

Dialing for Peace

"Hello Peace!" is the name of a popular phone service in Israel, the West Bank, and Gaza. This free service gives Israelis and Palestinians the rare chance to talk directly to each other. The service's organizers hope it will lead to a better understanding between the two cultures. For example, a 20-year-old Palestinian man named Sammy used the service to chat with an Israeli soldier. After the soldier explained to Sammy that he felt bad about guarding Palestinian neighborhoods, Sammy said, "Now I know they do care. And now I have hope that there can be peace." By keeping the lines of communication open, the "Hello Peace" organizers are bringing new hope to the region.

In what other ways could groups in conflict ease tensions?

Modern Israel

In the late 1800s a movement called **Zionism** began among European Jews. Zionism called for Jews to establish a country or community in Palestine. Tens of thousands of Jews moved to the area.

After World War II, the United Nations recommended dividing Palestine into Arab and Jewish states. Jewish leaders declared the independent state of Israel. Armies from surrounding Arab countries invaded Israel. The Israelis defeated the Arabs.

Many Palestinians fled to other Arab states, particularly to Jordan and Lebanon. Some used terrorist attacks to strike at Israel. Israel and its Arab neighbors also fought wars in 1956, 1967, and 1973.

Government and Economy Israel has a prime minister and a parliament, called the Knesset. There are two major political parties and many smaller parties.

Israel has built a strong military for protection from the Arab countries around it. Terrorist attacks have also occurred. At age 18 most Israeli men and women must serve in the military.

▲
Thousands of devout Jews gather for prayer during Passover at the Western Wall. This wall is all that survives from an ancient temple complex.

The West Bank in Transition

SCALE
0   5   10 Miles
0   5   10 Kilometers
Projection:
Transverse Cylindrical

Qabatiya

Tulkarm

Nablus

Qalqilyah

N

West Bank

Jordan R.

Ramallah

Jericho

Jerusalem

ISRAEL

Bethlehem

Dead Sea

Hebron

Control of West Bank:

- Israeli
- Palestinian civil, Israeli security
- Palestinian before 2003
- Palestinian, 2003
- City of Jerusalem

The Gaza Strip is densely populated and has few natural resources. Israel captured this territory from Egypt in 1967.

▼

Israel has a modern, diverse economy. Items like high-technology equipment and cut diamonds are important exports. Tourism is a major industry. Israel's lack of water limits farming. However, using highly efficient irrigation, Israel has successfully increased food production. It imports grain but exports citrus fruit and eggs.

Languages and Diversity Israel's population includes Jews from all parts of the world. Both Hebrew and Arabic are official languages. When they arrive in Israel, many Jews speak English, Russian, German, Hungarian, Yiddish, or Arabic. The government provides classes to help them learn Hebrew.

About 82 percent of Israel's population is Jewish. The rest of it is mostly Arab. About three fourths of these are Muslim. The rest are Christian.

Food and Festivals Israeli food is influenced by Jewish religious laws. Jews are forbidden to eat pork and shellfish. They also cannot eat meat and milk products at the same meal. The country's food is as diverse as the population. Eastern European dishes are popular, as are Southwest Asian foods.

For Jews, Saturday is a holy day. Yom Kippur, the most important Jewish holiday, is celebrated in October. Passover, in the spring, celebrates the Hebrews' escape from captivity in Egypt. During Passover, people eat matzo (MAHT-suh), a special bread without yeast.

✓ **READING CHECK:** (*Human Systems*) What are modern Israel's government, economy, and culture like?

The Occupied Territories

In 1967 Israel captured the Gaza Strip, the Golan Heights, and the West Bank. These are sometimes called the Occupied Territories.

Disputed Land The Gaza Strip is a small, crowded piece of coastal land. More than a million Palestinians live there. The area has almost no resources. The Golan Heights is a hilly area on the Syrian

border. In 1981 Israel formally declared the Golan Heights part of Israel. Syria still claims this territory.

The West Bank is the largest of the occupied areas, with a population of about 2.2 million. Since Israel took control of the West Bank, more than 187,000 Jews have moved into settlements there. The Palestinians consider this an invasion of their land. This has caused tension and violence between Arabs and Israelis.

Israel annexed East Jerusalem in 1980. Even before this, the Israeli government had moved the capital from Tel Aviv to Jerusalem. Most foreign countries have chosen not to recognize this transfer. The Palestinians still claim East Jerusalem as their rightful capital.

Control of Jerusalem is a difficult and often emotional question for Jews, Muslims, and Christians. The city contains sites that are holy to all three religions.

The Future of the Territories In the 1990s Israel agreed to turn over parts of the Occupied Territories to the Palestinians. In return, the Palestinian leadership—the Palestinian Authority—agreed to work for peace. Parts of the Gaza Strip and West Bank have been transferred to the Palestinian Authority. More areas of the West Bank are expected to be handed over in the future.

The future of the peace process is uncertain. Some Palestinian groups have continued to commit acts of terrorism. Some Jewish groups believe for religious reasons that Israel must not give up the West Bank. Other Israelis fear they would be open to attack if they withdrew from the territories.

✓ **READING CHECK:** (*Human Systems*) Why have the Occupied Territories been a source of conflict?

Muslim women gather to pray at the Dome of the Rock in Jerusalem.

Section Review 3

Define and explain: Diaspora, Zionism

Working with Sketch Maps On the map you created in Section 2, label Jerusalem, Gaza Strip, Golan Heights, West Bank, and Tel Aviv.

Reading for the Main Idea

1. (*Environment and Society*) How has technology allowed Israel to increase its food production?

2. (*Human Systems*) What historical factors helped create a culturally diverse region in Israel?

Critical Thinking

3. **Finding the Main Idea** How do political boundaries in Israel create conflicts?

4. **Summarizing** What are some difficult issues involved in the Israeli-Palestinian peace process?

Organizing What You Know

5. **Sequencing** Copy the following graphic organizer. Use it to list the sequence of events that led to the formation of modern Israel.

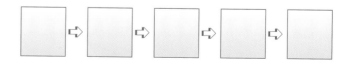

The Eastern Mediterranean • 387

Syria, Lebanon, and Jordan

Read to Discover

1. What kind of government and economy does Syria have?
2. How is Lebanese society divided?
3. What events have shaped the history of Jordan?

Vocabulary

mandate

Places

Damascus
Beirut
Amman

People

Hafiz al-Hassad
King Hussein

Reading Strategy

FOLDNOTES: DOUBLE-DOOR Create a FoldNote titled **Double-Door** described in the Appendix. Write Syria, Lebanon, and Jordan on the upper flap. Label the three sections Syria, Lebanon, and Jordan. As you read, write what you learn about each country.

Syria

The capital of Syria, Damascus, is believed to be the oldest continuously inhabited city in the world. For centuries it was a leading regional trade center. Syria became part of the Ottoman Empire in the 1500s. After World War I, France controlled Syria as a **mandate**. Mandates were former territories of the defeated nations of World War I. They were placed under the control of the winning countries after the war. Syria finally became independent in the 1940s.

Politics and Economy From 1971 to 2000, the Syrian government was led by Hafiz al-Assad. Assad increased the size of Syria's military. He wanted to match Israel's military strength and protect his rule from his enemies within Syria. Assad's son, Bashar, was elected president after his father's death in 2000.

Syria's government owns the country's oil refineries, larger electrical plants, railroads, and some factories. Syria's key manufactured goods are textiles, food products, and chemicals. Agriculture remains important.

Place Roman columns still stand in the ancient city of Apamea, Syria.

Syria has only small deposits of oil and natural gas. It is rich in limestone, basalt, and phosphates.

People Syria's population of more than 17 million is about 90 percent Arab. The other 10 percent includes Kurds and Armenians. About 74 percent of Syrians are Sunni Muslim. Another 16 percent are Alawites and Druze, members of small branches of Islam. About 10 percent of Syrians are Christian. There are also small Jewish communities in some cities.

✔ **READING CHECK:** (*Places and Regions*) How is Syria's economy organized?

Lebanon

Lebanon is a small, mountainous country on the Mediterranean coast. It is home to several different groups of people. At times these different groups have fought each other.

History and People During the Ottoman period many religious and ethnic minority groups settled in Lebanon. After World War I Lebanon, along with Syria, became a French mandate. Lebanon finally gained independence in the 1940s.

The Lebanese are overwhelmingly Arab, but they are divided by religion. Most Lebanese are either Muslim or Christian. Each of those groups is divided into several smaller groups. Muslims are divided into Sunni, Shia, and Druze. The Maronites are the largest of the Christian groups in Lebanon. At the time of independence, there were slightly more Christians than Muslims. Over time, however, Muslims became the majority.

▲
People must drill for water in dry areas of Syria.

Interpreting the Visual Record
(*Human-Environment Interaction*)
Judging from this photo, how has technology affected the lifestyle of people in desert areas?

▲
This photograph from the early 1900s shows a tall cedar tree in the mountains of northern Lebanon. Lebanon's cedars have long been a symbol of the country.

A vendor in Beirut sells postcards of what the city looked like before it was scarred by war.

Interpreting the Visual Record What were the effects of the civil war in Lebanon?

Civil War For some decades after independence, Christian and Muslim politicians managed to share power. A complex system assigned certain government positions to different religious groups. For example, the president was always a Maronite. However, over time this cooperation broke down. The poorest group, the Shia, grew rapidly but were not given additional power. Tensions mounted. Adding to the divisions between Lebanese was the presence of hundreds of thousands of Palestinian refugees living in Lebanon. Ethnic and religious groups armed themselves, and in the 1970s fighting broke out. Warfare between Lebanese groups lasted until 1990. Tens of thousands of people died, and the capital, Beirut, was badly damaged.

During the 1990s Lebanon's economy slowly recovered from the civil war. The refining of crude oil brought in by pipeline is a leading industry. Other industries include food processing, textiles, cement, chemicals, and jewelry making. Lebanese farmers produce tobacco, fruit, grains, and vegetables.

✓ **READING CHECK:** (*Human Systems*) What is causing divisions in Lebanese society?

Jordan

Jordan's short history has been full of conflict. Great Britain drew its borders, and Jordan's royal family is actually from Arabia. The country has few resources and several powerful neighbors. In addition, most of its people think of another country as their homeland. Yet Jordan has survived.

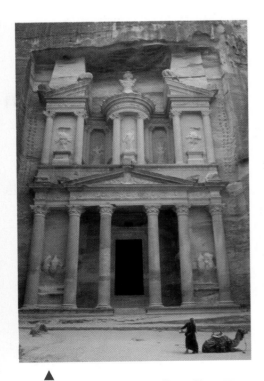

The city of Petra in Jordan dates back more than 2,000 years. This building was carved out of the sandstone cliff.

History and Government The country of Jordan (called Transjordan until 1949) was created from Ottoman territory following World War I. The British controlled the area as a mandate. They established an Arabian prince named Abdullah as the monarch of the new country. Abdullah had helped the British in World War I, but he had been driven out of Saudi Arabia. In the 1940s the country became fully independent. After the creation of Israel and the war of 1948, Jordan annexed the Arab lands of the West Bank.

At the time of its independence, Jordan's population was small. Most Jordanians lived a nomadic or seminomadic life. After each of the Arab-Israeli wars of 1948 and 1967, hundreds of thousands of Palestinian Arab refugees came to live in Jordan. These immigrants strained Jordan's resources. In addition, a cultural division arose between the Palestinians and the "original" Jordanian Arabs. After 1967 Palestinians actually made up a majority of Jordan's people.

From 1952 to 1999 Jordan was ruled by King Hussein. Most observers, both inside and outside Jordan, considered him one of the

King Hussein (1935–1999) Character Trait: Kindness

On his 18th birthday, Hussein ibn Talal was crowned king of Jordan. King Hussein is known to Jordanians as "The Humane King" for the ways he improved living conditions in Jordan. He also developed economic opportunities for Jordanians and built new highways across the country. Throughout his reign, Hussein also made many attempts to bring about peace in the Middle East. In 1994, he signed a peace treaty with Israel.

Why is Hussein known as "The Humane King"?

best rulers in the region. Hussein's popularity allowed him to begin some democratic reforms in the 1980s and 1990s. Today, the division between Palestinian and Jordanian Arabs causes less conflict.

Economy and Resources Jordan is a poor country with limited resources. The country does produce phosphates, cement, and potash. Tourism and banking are becoming important industries. Jordan depends on economic aid from the oil-rich Arab nations and the United States. Amman, the capital, is Jordan's only large city.

Jordanian farmers raise fruits and vegetables in the Jordan River valley, using irrigation. Some highland areas receive enough winter rainfall to grow grains. Raising sheep and goats is an important source of income. However, overgrazing has caused soil erosion. A crucial resource issue for Jordan is its shortage of water.

✓ **READING CHECK:** (**Human Systems**) How did King Hussein affect Jordan's history?

Section Review 4

Define or identify: mandate, Hafiz al-Hassad, King Hussein

Working with Sketch Maps On the map you created in Section 3, label Damascus, Beirut, and Amman.

Reading for the Main Idea

1. (**Human Systems**) How did Hafiz al-Assad affect Syria?

2. (**Human Systems**) What divisions led to conflict in Lebanon?

3. (**Places and Regions**) Which of the countries discussed in this section does not border the Mediterranean Sea?

go.hrw.com **Homework Practice Online** Keyword: SG5 HP17

Critical Thinking

4. Finding the Main Idea How have foreign countries influenced Jordan?

Organizing What You Know

5. Categorizing Use the graphic organizer to gather information about Syria, Lebanon, and Jordan.

	Syria	Lebanon	Jordan
Major religion(s)			
Type of government			
Major problem(s)			
Greatest strength(s)			

CHAPTER 17 Review and Practice

Define and Identify

Identify each of the following:

1. phosphates
2. asphalt
3. Kemal Atatürk
4. secular
5. Diaspora
6. Zionism
7. mandate
8. Hafiz al-Hassad
9. King Hussein

Review the Main Ideas

10. What are the region's main rivers? Where do they flow?
11. What makes the Dead Sea an unusual body of water? What are its commercial uses?
12. What mineral resources are located in the eastern Mediterranean?
13. People and customs from what three continents have influenced the eastern Mediterranean region?
14. How did the Ottoman Empire come to an end?
15. How has westernization changed Turkey's government, economy, and culture?
16. What three major religions have holy sites in Jerusalem?

17. What cultures have ruled the lands now called Israel and the Occupied Territories?
18. What is the conflict over the Occupied Territories?
19. What issue divides the Arabs of Lebanon?

Think Critically

20. **Drawing Inferences and Conclusions** Why do you think Atatürk moved Turkey's capital from Istanbul to Ankara?
21. **Finding the Main Idea** How has human migration to Israel affected its population?
22. **Analyzing Information** Why is conflict over dams in this region so important?
23. **Analyzing Information** How did refugees from Palestine affect Jordan?
24. **Drawing Inferences and Conclusions** Why did attempts to balance religious groups' participation in Lebanon's government fail?

Map Activity

25. On a separate sheet of paper, match the letters on the map with their correct labels.

Dardanelles	Negev
Bosporus	Istanbul
Sea of Marmara	Tel Aviv
Jordan River	Jerusalem
Dead Sea	Damascus

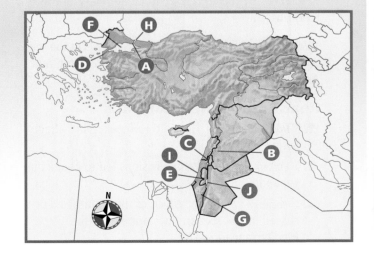

Writing Activity

Imagine that your family is about to travel to the eastern Mediterranean for a vacation. Your parents have asked you to help plan the trip. Write about the places you would like to visit and the reasons you would find them interesting. Be sure to use standard grammar, spelling, sentence structure, and punctuation.

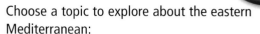

internet connect

Internet Activity: go.hrw.com
KEYWORD: SG5 GT17

Choose a topic to explore about the eastern Mediterranean:

• Visit the Dead Sea.
• Compare Israeli and Arab foods.
• Travel to historic Jerusalem.

Social Studies Skills Practice

Interpreting Charts

Study the following chart and answer the questions.

	Projected Growth of Turkey's Kurdish Population		
Year	Total Population of Turkey (in millions)	Kurdish Population in Turkey (in millions)	Percentage of Turkish Population that is Kurdish
1990	56.7	13.7	24.1
2000	65.9	18.7	28.4
2020	87.5	32.3	36.9
2050	105.8	47.0	44.4

Source: Mehrdad R. Izady, *The Kurds: A Concise Handbook,* 1992

1. In what year will the Kurds make up the greatest percentage of the Turkish population?
2. What prediction can you make about Kurdish population growth?
3. Which group appears to have a higher birthrate? the Kurds or the overall Turkish population?
4. Based on this chart and your knowledge of the region, what might result from the continued growth of the Kurdish population?

Analyzing Primary Sources

Read the following passage from a 2003 newspaper article about the Dead Sea. Then answer the questions.

"In less than 50 years, the lowest point on earth has dropped even lower—from 1,294 feet below sea level to 1,360 feet. . . . The Dead Sea's only sources of water are sparse rainfall—less than 3 inches a year—and the Jordan River. But Israel and Jordan have diverted so much of the river's flow for agricultural use that the Dead Sea gets just 10 percent of the water it once did. At the same time, the sea's own waters are being sucked out by Israeli and Arab companies that extract the potassium and other minerals . . . The result? The level of the Dead Sea is dropping by more than 3 feet per year."

1. By how many feet has the Dead Sea dropped in the past 50 years?
2. What is the Dead Sea's only source for water?
3. What two factors are causing the level of the Dead Sea to drop?
4. At the current rate, how much lower will the Dead Sea be in 10 years?

CHAPTER 18

The Arabian Peninsula, Iraq, Iran, and Afghanistan

Let's meet Mitra, a girl who lives in Tehran, the capital of Iran.

I am Mitra and I am 13 years old. I live with my sister and my parents on the top floor of a house in Tehran, the capital of Iran. On the ground floor, my father has a business printing pictures on metal, and the lower two floors are rented to tenants. My dad is also the president of an architectural firm in Tehran, but he is always working at home when we are home from school. Our house has a wall all around, touching the wall of the houses on both sides. Behind the house is a huge garden with roses and fruit trees. My sister is seven years older and works with my dad making architectural drawings. She raises chickens in the garden and collects their eggs. Food is sometimes hard to get, so we are very glad to have the chickens. My dad built them a very nice house, and it is exciting to watch the baby chicks hatch. The roof of our house is flat, and in nice weather we sit up there and look out to the mountains around the city. In the summer we sleep there too.

سلام بر شما!

Translation: Greetings to you.

Section 1 Physical Geography

Read to Discover

1. What are the major physical features of the region?
2. What climates are found in this region?
3. What are the region's important resources?

Vocabulary

exotic rivers
wadis
fossil water

Places

Persian Gulf
Arabian Peninsula
Red Sea
Arabian Sea
Tigris River

Euphrates River
Elburz Mountains
Zagros Mountains
Hindu Kush
Rub' al-Khali

Reading Strategy

READING ORGANIZER Create a three-column chart. Title the first column Arabian Peninsula, the second column Tigris-Euphrates plain, and the third column Mountains and Plateaus. As you read this section, list the countries and characteristics found in each region.

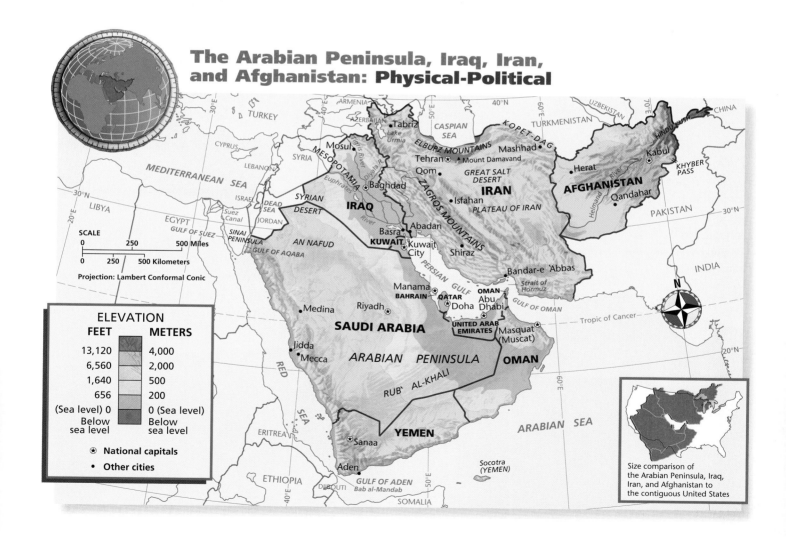

The Arabian Peninsula, Iraq, Iran, and Afghanistan: Physical-Political

ELEVATION

FEET	METERS
13,120	4,000
6,560	2,000
1,640	500
656	200
(Sea level) 0	0 (Sea level)
Below sea level	Below sea level

⊛ National capitals
• Other cities

SCALE
0   250   500 Miles
0   250   500 Kilometers
Projection: Lambert Conformal Conic

Size comparison of the Arabian Peninsula, Iraq, Iran, and Afghanistan to the contiguous United States

internet connect

GO TO: go.hrw.com
KEYWORD: SG5 CH18
FOR: Web sites about the
Arabian Peninsula, Iraq,
Iran, and Afghanistan

Physical Features

The 10 countries of this region are laid out like a semicircle, with the Persian Gulf in the center. They are Saudi Arabia, Kuwait (koo-WAYT), Bahrain (bah-RAYN), Qatar (KAH-tuhr), the United Arab Emirates (E-muh-ruhts), Oman (oh-MAHN), Yemen (YE-muhn), Iraq (i-RAHK), Iran (i-RAN), and Afghanistan (af-GA-nuh-stan).

This area can be divided into three landform regions. The Arabian Peninsula is a large rectangular area. The Red Sea, Gulf of Aden, Arabian Sea, and Persian Gulf border the peninsula. North of the Arabian Peninsula is the plain of the Tigris (TY-gruhs) and Euphrates (yooh-FRAY-teez) Rivers. In ancient times, this area was called Mesopotamia (me-suh-puh-TAY-mee-uh), or the "land between the rivers." East of this plain is a region of mountains and plateaus. It stretches through Iran and Afghanistan.

The surface of the Arabian Peninsula rises gradually as one moves westward from the Persian Gulf. The highest point is in the southwest, in the mountains of Yemen.

North of the Arabian Peninsula is a low, flat plain. It runs from the Persian Gulf into northern Iraq. The Tigris and Euphrates Rivers flow across this plain. They are what are known as **exotic rivers**. Exotic rivers begin in humid regions and then flow through dry areas.

East of this low plain the land climbs sharply. Most of Iran is a plateau bordered by mountains. The Elburz (el-BOOHRZ) Mountains and Kopet-Dag range lie in the north. The Zagros (ZA-gruhs) Mountains lie in the southwest. Afghanistan includes many mountain ranges, such as the towering Hindu Kush range.

✓ **READING CHECK:** (*Places and Regions*) What are the major physical features of this area?

Climate

Most of Southwest Asia has a desert climate. A nearly constant high-pressure system in the atmosphere causes this climate. Some areas—mostly high plateaus and the region's edges—do get winter rains or snow. These areas generally have steppe climates. Some mountain peaks receive more than 50 inches (130 cm) of rain per year.

Cold nighttime temperatures and extremely hot days help break rock into sand in Saudi Arabia's Rub' al-Khali, or "empty quarter."

Interpreting the Visual Record How do you think wind affects these sand dunes?

The desert can be both very hot and very cold. In summer, afternoon temperatures can reach 129°F (54°C). During the night, however, the temperature may drop quickly. Temperatures sometimes dip below freezing during winter nights.

The Rub' al-Khali (ROOB ahl-KAH-lee), or "empty quarter," of southern Saudi Arabia is the largest sand desert in the world. In northern Saudi Arabia is the An Nafud (ahn nah-FOOD), another desert.

✔ **READING CHECK:** (*Places and Regions*) What are the climates of this region?

Resources

Water is an important resource everywhere, but in this region it is crucial. Many desert regions are visited only by nomads and their animal herds. In many places, springs or wells provide water. Nomads sometimes get water by digging shallow wells into dry streambeds called **wadis**. Wells built with modern technology can reach water deep underground. The groundwater in these wells is often **fossil water**. Fossil water is water that is not being replaced by rainfall. Wells that pump fossil water will eventually run dry.

Other than water, oil is the region's most important mineral resource. Most of the oilfields are located near the shores of the Persian Gulf. The countries of the region are not rich in resources other than oil. Iran is an exception, with deposits of many metals.

✔ **READING CHECK:** (*Places and Regions*) What are the region's important resources?

Section Review 1

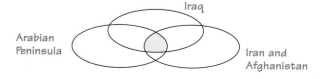

Homework Practice Online
Keyword: SG5 HP18

Define and explain: exotic rivers, wadis, fossil water

Working with Sketch Maps On a map of the Arabian Peninsula, Iraq, Iran, and Afghanistan that you draw or that your teacher provides, label the following: Persian Gulf, Arabian Peninsula, Red Sea, Arabian Sea, Tigris River, Euphrates River, Elburz Mountains, Zagros Mountains, Hindu Kush, and Rub' al-Khali.

Reading for the Main Idea

1. (*Places and Regions*) Why do you think Mesopotamia was important in ancient times?

2. (*Places and Regions*) What is the region's climate?

Critical Thinking

3. Drawing Inferences and Conclusions Why do you think the Persian Gulf is important to international trade?

4. Drawing Inferences and Conclusions What settlement pattern might you find in this region?

Organizing What You Know

5. Summarizing Copy the following graphic organizer. Use it to list as many details of landforms, resources, and climate as you can. Place them in the correct part of the diagram.

Iraq

Arabian Peninsula

Iran and Afghanistan

Section 2 The Arabian Peninsula

Read to Discover

1. What are Saudi Arabia's history, government, and people like?
2. What kinds of government and economy do the other countries of the Arabian Peninsula have?

Vocabulary

Muslims
caliph
Sunni
Shia
Qur'an
OPEC

Places

Mecca
Riyadh

People

Muhammad

Reading Strategy

FOLDNOTE: TRI-FOLD Create the FoldNote titled **Tri-Fold** described in the Appendix. Write what you know about the Arabian Peninsula in the column labeled "Know." Then write what you want to know in the column labeled "Want." As you read the section, write what you learn in the column labeled "Learn."

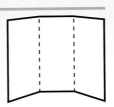

Saudi Arabia

Saudi Arabia is by far the largest country of the Arabian Peninsula. Although the kingdom of Saudi Arabia was not created until the 1930s, the region has long been an important cultural center.

Islam The history of the Arabian Peninsula is closely linked to Islam. This religion was founded by Muhammad, a merchant from the Arabian town of Mecca. Around A.D. 610 he had a vision that he had been named a prophet by Allah, or God. Arab armies and merchants carried Muhammad's teachings to new areas. Islam spread quickly across North Africa, much of Asia, and parts of Europe. Followers of Islam are called **Muslims**. Islam provides a set of rules to guide human behavior.

The Islamic world was originally ruled by a religious and political leader called a **caliph**. Gradually this area broke up into several empires. There are also religious divisions within Islam. Followers of the largest branch of Islam are called **Sunni**. Followers of the second-largest branch of Islam are called **Shia**. In the late 600s

Place Non-Muslims are not allowed to enter Mecca, Islam's holiest city.

these two groups disagreed over who should lead the Islamic world. There are many smaller groups within Islam as well.

Islamic culture helps to unite Muslims around the world. For example, all Muslims learn Arabic to read the **Qur'an**, the holy book of Islam. Muslims are also expected to visit Mecca at least once. These practices and many others help make Muslims part of a global community.

Government and Economy In the 1920s a local ruler from the Saud family of central Arabia conquered his neighbors and in 1932 created the kingdom of Saudi Arabia. Members of the Saud family have ruled the country ever since. Riyadh, a city near the center of the country, became the capital.

Saudi Arabia is a monarchy with no written constitution or elected legislature. Most government officials are relatives of the king. The king may ask members of his family, Islamic scholars, and tribal leaders for advice on important decisions.

For some time, Saudi Arabia and the United States have had a close relationship. Both countries have strategic military and economic interests in the region. Saudi Arabia purchases U.S. weapons, such as fighter planes. In 1990, when Iraq invaded Kuwait, the Saudi government allowed U.S. military forces to operate from Saudi Arabia. However, the September 11 terrorist attacks strained the relationship because most of the hijackers were from Saudi Arabia.

Oil and related industries are the most important part of the Saudi economy. Saudi Arabia has the world's largest reserves of oil. It is also the world's leading exporter of oil. Saudi Arabia is a leader of the Organization of Petroleum Exporting Countries, or **OPEC**. The members of OPEC try to influence the price of oil on world markets.

Opened in 1986, this causeway links Saudi Arabia to Bahrain.
Interpreting the Visual Record Why are modern transportation systems important to a country's economy?

This aerial view shows how fossil water has converted desert land near Riyadh into farmers' fields. Each circular plot has a water source at its center.

Oil was discovered in Saudi Arabia in the 1930s. Before then farming and herding had been the main economic activities. Crops included barley, dates, fruits, millet, vegetables, and wheat. Nomads kept herds of sheep, goats, horses, and camels.

Like other oil-rich states in the region, Saudi Arabia has tried to increase its food production. Because freshwater is scarce, desalination plants remove the salt from seawater. This water is then used in farming. Income from oil allows the Saudi government to pay for this expensive process. Even so, Saudi Arabia imports much of its food.

People and Customs Nearly all Saudis are ethnic Arabs and speak Arabic. About 85 percent are Sunni. The rest are Shia. Most Saudis now live in cities, and a sizable middle class has developed. The Saudi government provides free health care and education to its citizens.

Some 65 percent of Saudi Arabia's workers are from other countries, including Yemen and Pakistan. Unemployment is very high among young Saudis. One reason is the very high population growth rate. More than 40 percent of Saudis are younger than 15. Another reason is that many young Saudis study religion instead of the technical subjects their economy requires.

Saudi laws and customs limit women's activities. For example, a woman rarely appears in public without her husband or a male relative. Women may not drive cars. However, women may make up two thirds of the country's Internet users.

Islam is an important part of Saudi Arabia's culture. Muslims pray five times each day. Friday is their holy day. Because Islam encourages modesty, Saudi clothing keeps arms and legs covered. Men traditionally wear a loose, ankle-length shirt. They often wear a cotton headdress held in place with a cord. These styles are practical in the desert, giving protection from sun, wind, and dust. Saudi women usually wear a black cloak and veil in public.

Saudi Arabia has several Islamic holidays. One of the most important is 'Id al-Fitr, a feast ending the month of Ramadan. During Ramadan, Muslims do not eat or drink anything between dawn and sunset. Saudis may attend huge dinner parties after sundown, however.

✓ **READING CHECK:** (**Human Systems**) What is significant about Saudi Arabia's history, government, and people?

Our Amazing Planet

A sabchat is a thick, slushy deposit of sand, silt, mud, and salt found in coastal Saudi Arabia. A sabchat can trap people and animals who do not see it in time.

Other Countries of the Arabian Peninsula

Six small coastal countries share the Arabian Peninsula with Saudi Arabia. All are heavily dependent on oil. All but Yemen are monarchies, and each is overwhelmingly Islamic. Oil is a major part of each country's economy. However, possession of differing amounts of oil has made some countries much richer than others.

CONNECTING TO Math

Muslim Contributions to Mathematics

During the early centuries of the Middle Ages, European art, literature, and science declined. However, during this same period Islamic civilization, stretching from Spain to the borders of China, was flowering. Muslim scholars made important advances in art, literature, medicine, and mathematics.

The system of numerals we call Arabic, including the use of the zero, was first created in India. However, it was Muslim thinkers who introduced that system to Europe. They also developed algebra, geometry, and trigonometry. In fact, words like *algebra* and *algorithm* come from Arabic words.

Other Muslims advanced the study of astronomy and physics. Arab geographers calculated

Muslim astronomers in the 1500s

distances between cities, longitudes and latitudes, and the direction from one city to another. Muslims developed the first solution for cubic equations. They also defined ratios and used mathematics to explain the rainbow.

Understanding What You Read
1. Where did the Arabic system of numerals originate, and how did it get to Europe?
2. How did Muslim scholars contribute to our knowledge of geography?

Kuwait The country of Kuwait was established in the mid-1700s. Trade and fishing were once the main economic activities there. Oil, which was discovered in the 1930s, has made Kuwait very rich. The Iraqi invasion of 1990 caused massive destruction.

As in Saudi Arabia, a royal family dominates politics in Kuwait. In 1992, however, Kuwait held elections for a legislature. Less than 15 percent of Kuwait's population were given the right to vote. These people were all men from well-established families.

Bahrain and Qatar Bahrain is a group of small islands in the western Persian Gulf. It is a constitutional monarchy headed by a ruling royal family and a legislature. These islands have been a center for trade since ancient times. In 1986 a 15.5 mile (25 km) bridge was completed that connects Bahrain to Saudi Arabia, making movement between the two countries easier.

The Arabian Peninsula

Country	Population/ Growth Rate	Life Expectancy	Literacy Rate	Per Capita GDP
Bahrain	667,238 1.6%	71, male 76, female	89%	$14,000
Kuwait	2,183,161 3.3%	76, male 78, female	85%	$15,000
Oman	2,807,125 3.4%	70, male 74, female	76%	$8,300
Qatar	817,052 2.9%	71, male 76, female	83%	$21,500
Saudi Arabia	24,293,844 3.3%	67, male 71, female	79%	$10,500
United Arab Emirates	2,484,818 1.6%	72, male 77, female	78%	$22,000
Yemen	19,349,881 3.4%	59, male 63, female	50%	$840
United States	290,342,554 0.9%	74, male 80, female	97%	$37,600

Source: Central Intelligence Agency, *The World Factbook 2003*

Interpreting the Chart **Which country has the lowest standard of living?**

Oil was discovered in Bahrain in the 1930s, creating wealth for the country. However, by the 1990s this oil was starting to run out, and banking and tourism are now becoming important to the economy. Bahrain also refines crude oil imported from nearby Saudi Arabia.

Qatar occupies a small peninsula in the Persian Gulf. Like Bahrain, Qatar is ruled by a powerful monarch. In the 1990s, Qatar's ruler announced a plan to make the country more democratic. He also ended censorship of Qatari newspapers and television.

Qatar's economy used to be based on pearl fishing. Today Qatar relies on oil and huge natural gas reserves for its income.

The United Arab Emirates
The United Arab Emirates, or UAE, consists of seven tiny kingdoms. They are ruled by emirs. This country also has great reserves of oil and natural gas. Profits from these resources have created a modern, comfortable lifestyle for the people of the UAE. The government has also worked to build up other industries.

Like Saudi Arabia and many of the small Persian Gulf countries, the UAE depends on foreign workers. In the UAE, foreign workers outnumber citizens.

Oman
Oman is located just outside the mouth of the Persian Gulf. The country is slightly smaller than Kansas. In ancient times, Oman was a major trade center for merchants traveling the Indian Ocean. Today, Oman's economy is heavily dependent on oil. However, Oman does not have the oil wealth of Kuwait or the UAE. Therefore, the government, ruled by the Al Bu Sa'id family, is attempting to create new industries.

◄

Kindergarten students in the United Arab Emirates kneel to pray.
Interpreting the Visual Record *Place* **For what cultural reason do you think these girls and boys are seated in separate rows?**

Yemen Yemen is located on the southern corner of the Arabian Peninsula. It borders the Red Sea and the Gulf of Aden. Yemen was formed in 1990 by the joining of North Yemen and South Yemen. The country has an elected government and several political parties. However, political corruption and internal conflicts have threatened this young democracy.

In ancient times, farmers in this area used very advanced methods of irrigation and farming. Yemen was famous for its coffee. Today, Yemen is the poorest country on the Arabian Peninsula. Oil was not discovered there until the 1980s. It now generates a major part of the national income.

✔ **READING CHECK:** (*Human Systems*) How are the governments and economies of the countries of the Arabian Peninsula organized?

(*Place*) An important part of Yemen's culture is its distinctive architecture, which features tall buildings and carved wooden windows.

Homework Practice Online
Keyword: SG5 HP18

Section Review 2

Define and explain: Muhammad, Muslims, caliph, Sunni, Shia, Qur'an, OPEC

Working with Sketch Maps On the map you created in Section 1, label Mecca and Riyadh. Why is Riyadh's location more suitable than Mecca's to be the capital city of Saudi Arabia?

Reading for the Main Idea

1. (*Places and Regions*) What kind of government does Saudi Arabia have?

2. (*Environment and Society*) What role does oil play in the economies of small countries on the Arabian Peninsula?

Critical Thinking

3. Drawing Inferences and Conclusions How might trips to Mecca help create a sense of community among Muslims?

4. Drawing Inferences and Conclusions Why would a country like Saudi Arabia or the United Arab Emirates bring in large numbers of foreign workers?

Organizing What You Know

5. Comparing Copy the following graphic organizer. Use it to list these countries' locations, governments, and economies. Place them in the appropriate part of the chart.

	Location	Government	Economy
Saudi Arabia			
Kuwait			
Bahrain			
Qatar			
UAE			
Oman			
Yemen			

The Arabian Peninsula, Iraq, Iran, and Afghanistan • 403

CASE STUDY

SAUDI ARABIA: HOW OIL HAS CHANGED A COUNTRY

At the beginning of the 1900s, Saudi Arabia was a poor country. Most people followed traditional ways of life and lived by herding animals, farming, or fishing. There were few good roads or transportation systems, and health care was poor.

Major Oil Fields in Saudi Arabia

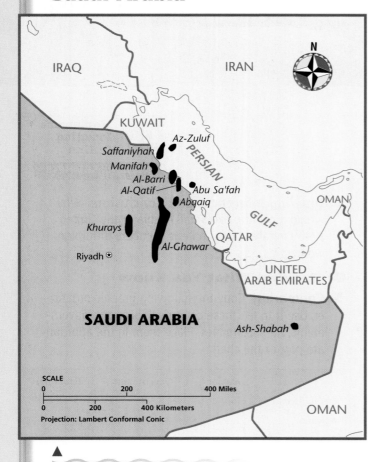

▲

Place Saudi Arabia's huge oil fields contain about one quarter of the world's known oil reserves.

Then, in the mid-1930s, oil was discovered in Saudi Arabia. Soon, even larger oil reserves were found. Eventually it was learned that Saudi Arabia had the largest oil reserves in the world. Most of the country's oil reserves are located in eastern Saudi Arabia along the Persian Gulf coast. The Al-Ghawar oil field, discovered in 1948, is the largest in the world. In addition to this field, Saudi Arabia has at least nine other major oil fields. The discovery of these huge oil reserves changed Saudi Arabia's economy and society.

Rising income from oil exports gave Saudi Arabia's government more and more money to invest. New airports, apartments, communications systems, oil pipelines, and roads were built. In 1960 Saudi Arabia had about 1,000 miles (1,600 km) of roads. By 1997 it had about 91,000 miles (145,600 km). Saudi Arabia's cities grew as people left small villages. These changes helped modernize Saudi Arabia's economy.

Saudi society was also affected. The standard of living rose, and people had more money to spend on goods. Foreign companies began to open stores and restaurants in Saudi Arabia. New schools were built throughout the country, and education became available to all citizens. The literacy rate increased from about 3 percent to about 63 percent. Thousands of Saudis traveled to other countries, and many new universities were opened. Health care also improved.

As Saudi Arabia's economy grew, many foreign workers came to the country to work. In the early 2000s foreign workers made up about 25 percent of Saudi Arabia's population. These workers included people from Yemen, Egypt, Palestine, Syria, Iraq, South Korea, and the Philippines. Americans and Europeans also went to Saudi Arabia to work in the oil industry.

The development of the oil industry greatly increased Saudi Arabia's importance in the world. In 1960 Saudi Arabia was a founding member of

◀

Movement Oil is refined in eastern Saudi Arabia. Then it is pumped into ships and exported to countries around the world.

the Organization of Petroleum Exporting Countries (OPEC). Members of OPEC try to influence the price of oil on the world market. Saudi Arabia's huge oil reserves make it one of OPEC's most powerful member countries.

The Saudi government has also bought military equipment from the United States and other countries. This military strength has increased Saudi Arabia's importance in the Persian Gulf region. Since 1991, Saudi Arabia has given large sums to countries that sided with it against Iraq in the Persian Gulf War. Egypt, Turkey, and Syria have especially benefited from this aid.

Today, Saudi Arabia is a wealthy country. This wealth has come almost entirely from the sale of oil. Saudi Arabia is currently the world's leading oil exporter. Oil provides about 90 percent of the government's export earnings. Saudi Arabia exports oil to Japan, the United States, South Korea, and many other countries.

◀

Movement Since the mid-1960s Saudi Arabia has expanded its transportation network. A modern road system now connects many parts of the country.

Understanding What You Read

1. What was Saudi Arabia like before oil was discovered there?

2. How has oil changed Saudi Arabia's economy and society?

Read to Discover

1. What were the key events in Iraq's history?
2. What are Iraq's government and economy like?
3. What is the makeup of Iraq's population?

Vocabulary

embargo

Places

Baghdad

Reading Strategy

TAKING NOTES Draw a large triangle on a sheet of paper. Draw two lines across the triangle to create three sections. As you read, write details about Iraq's history in the lower part of the triangle. Write details about its government and economy in the middle of the triangle. Finally, write the details about its people in the top part of the triangle.

▲

Before March 2003, murals and posters of Saddam Hussein were found throughout Baghdad, Iraq's capital.

History

The history of Mesopotamia, an ancient region in Iraq, stretches back to some of the world's first civilizations. The Sumerian, Babylonian, and Assyrian cultures arose there. The Persians conquered Mesopotamia in the 500s B.C. Alexander the Great made it part of his empire in 331 B.C. In the A.D. 600s Arabs conquered Mesopotamia, and the people gradually converted to Islam.

Mesopotamia became part of the Ottoman Empire in the 1500s. During World War I Great Britain took over the region. The British set up a kingdom of Iraq in 1932 and placed a pro-British ruler in power. In the 1950s a group of Iraqi army officers overthrew this government.

After several more changes in government, the Ba'ath (BAH-ahth) Party took power in 1968. A Ba'ath leader named Saddam Hussein became the president and leader of the armed forces. He was a harsh ruler. Saddam controlled the press, restricted personal freedoms, and killed an unknown number of political enemies.

In 1980 Iraq invaded Iran. Saddam Hussein hoped to take advantage of the confusion following the Iranian Revolution. The Iranians fought back, however, and the Iran-Iraq War dragged on until 1988. Casualties were high on both sides. Both countries' economies were damaged.

In 1990, Iraq invaded Kuwait, a small oil-rich country. This event shocked Western leaders. They were also concerned that Iraq would control such a large share of the world's oil. In addition, Iraq had weapons of mass destruction (WMDs), including chemical and biological weapons. An alliance of countries, led by the United States and Great Britain, soon forced the Iraqis out of Kuwait. This 1991 event was called the Persian Gulf War. Saddam remained in power, however.

Because he would not accept all the UN's terms for peace, the UN placed an **embargo**, or limit on trade, on Iraq. As a result, Iraq's economy suffered.

✔ **READING CHECK:** (*Human Systems*) What are some key events in Iraq's history?

Iraq Today

Shortly after the fighting stopped, Saddam faced two rebellions. He brutally put down uprisings of Shia Muslims in the south and of Kurds in the north. The UN forced Saddam to end all military activity in the Kurdish area of northern Iraq. The UN also required that Iraq allow inspectors into the country to make sure he had destroyed the WMDs. Iraq failed to cooperate completely with the UN and armed conflict continued off and on.

In the meantime, the events of September 11, 2001 had created new tensions. The U.S. government believed Iraq aided terrorists. In March 2003, U.S. forces began attacking Iraqi targets. Within a few weeks Saddam's government fell. The United States then began the long, difficult process of rebuilding the country.

One of the main goals of U.S. officials was creating a stable, democratic country. Another was repairing Iraq's oil industry. Before the war with Iran, Iraq was the world's second-largest oil exporter. Time will tell if Iraq can again be a major oil producer.

Oil isn't Iraq's only resource. From earliest times its wide plains have produced many food crops. Irrigation from the Tigris and Euphrates Rivers allows farmers to grow barley, cotton, rice, vegetables, wheat, dates, and other fruits.

✔ **READING CHECK:** (*Environment and Society*) What happened to Iraq's oil industry?

Our Amazing Planet

Dust storms occur throughout Iraq and can rise to several thousand feet above the ground. These storms often happen during the summer. Five or six usually strike central Iraq in July, the worst month.

In March 2003, war left much of Baghdad without electricity and water. Some restaurants, however, stayed open by cooking with propane gas on the city's sidewalks.

(Place) The Ma'dan are a minority people who live in Iraq's southern marshes. Saddam's government drained part of the marshes, putting the Ma'dan way of life in danger.

People

More than 75 percent of the population are Arabs. Some 15 to 20 percent are Kurds, and the rest belong to small minority groups. Nearly all Iraqis are Muslim. About two thirds of Iraqis are Shia. Saddam and his supporters, however, were Sunnis. Under Saddam, the government often conflicted with Shia leaders.

After decades of harsh government and warfare Iraq's future remains uncertain. Rebuilding schools, hospitals, roads, and other basic structures may take years. Creating a free and prosperous society may be an even bigger challenge.

✓ **READING CHECK:** (**Human Systems**) What challenges face Iraqis?

Section Review 3

Define and explain: embargo

Working with Sketch Maps On the map you created in Section 2, label Baghdad. Where would you expect most of Iraq's population to be concentrated? Why?

Reading for the Main Idea

1. (**Human Systems**) What are some different groups that have controlled Mesopotamia?

2. (**Human Systems**) What was Iraq's government like under Saddam Hussein?

go.hrw.com **Homework Practice Online**
Keyword: SG5 HP18

Critical Thinking

3. **Finding the Main Idea** Why did several countries force Iraqi troops out of Kuwait?

4. **Analyzing Information** How have recent wars affected Iraq's economy?

Organizing What You Know

5. **Sequencing** Create a time line tracing the history of the area now known as Iraq. List events from the Arab conquest to 2003.

A.D. 600s   2003

Section 4 — Iran and Afghanistan

Read to Discover

1. What were some important events in Iran's history?
2. What are Iran's government and people like?
3. What problems does Afghanistan face today?

Vocabulary

shah
theocracy

Places

Tehran
Khyber Pass
Kabul

People

Shirin Ebadi

Reading Strategy

READING ORGANIZER Before you read, draw two large overlapping circles on a sheet of paper. As you read, write what you learn about Iran in one circle. Then write what you learn about Afghanistan in the other circle. Where the circles overlap, write the characteristics that the countries share.

Iran

Iran is a large country with a large population, rich history, and valuable natural resources. A revolution in 1979 made Islam the guiding force in Iran's government.

History The Persian Empire, established in the 500s B.C., was centered in what is now Iran. It was the greatest empire of its time and was an important center of learning. In the 300s B.C. Alexander the Great conquered the Persian Empire. In the A.D. 600s Arabs invaded the region and established Islam. Persian cultural and scientific contributions became elements of Islamic civilization. Later, different peoples ruled the region, including the Mongols and the Safavids.

Human-Environment Interaction In the dry climates of Iran and Afghanistan, some farmers use an ancient irrigation method. Runoff from mountains moves through tunnels, called *qanats* (kuh-NAHTS), to fields. The Taliban destroyed some *qanats* in Afganistan.

▼

Qanat Irrigation System

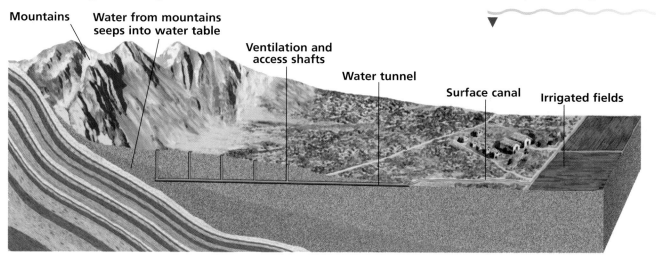

Mountains

Water from mountains seeps into water table

Ventilation and access shafts

Water tunnel

Surface canal

Irrigated fields

Shirin Ebadi
(1947–)

Character Trait: Respect

Iranians hoping for more democratic reforms were encouraged in 2003 by Shirin Ebadi's receiving the Nobel Peace Prize. Ebadi is a lawyer, judge, and author. However, her work improving human rights in Iran has at times made her unpopular with the country's authorities. Ebadi's special interests include better conditions for women, children, and refugees.

How does Shirin Ebadi show respect towards others?

During New Year celebrations, Iranians grow or buy fresh grass to symbolize spring and life.

▼

In 1921 an Iranian military officer took power and encouraged reform. He claimed the old Persian title of **shah**, or king. In 1941 the Shah's son took control. He was an ally of the United States and Britain and tried to modernize Iran. His programs were unpopular, however, and in 1979 he was overthrown.

Iran's new government set up an Islamic republic. Soon afterward, relations with the United States broke down. A mob of students attacked the U.S. Embassy in Iran's capital, Tehran, in November 1979. They took Americans hostage with the approval of Iran's government. More than 50 Americans were held by force for a year. The Iranian Revolution itself was soon followed by a long, destructive war with Iraq beginning in 1980.

Government and Economy Iran is a **theocracy**—a government ruled by religious leaders. The country has an elected president and legislature. An expert on Islamic law is the supreme leader, however.

Iran's government has supported many hard-line policies. For example, the country's government has called for the destruction of the state of Israel. Iran has also supported terrorist groups in other countries. However, in the 2000s some signs indicated that Iran was trying to make democratic reforms.

Iran has the fifth-largest oil reserves in the world. Oil is its main industry. Iran is a member of OPEC. Iran's other industries include construction, food processing, and the production of beautiful woven carpets. About one third of Iran's workforce is employed in agriculture.

People and Customs Iran has a population of about 68 million—one of the largest in Southwest Asia. It is also quite diverse. Ethnic Persians make up a slight majority. Other groups include ethnic Azerbaijanis, Kurds, Arabs, and Turkomans. Persian is the official language. Almost all Iranians speak Persian, although some speak it as a second language. The region's other languages include several Kurdish dialects, some Turkic languages, and Arabic.

The Shia branch of Islam is Iran's official religion. About 90 percent of Iranians are Shia. About 10 percent of Iran's residents are Sunni Muslim. The rest are Christian, Jewish, or practice other religions.

In addition to the Islamic holy days, Iranians celebrate Nauruz—the Persian New Year. They also recognize the anniversary of the Iranian Revolution on February 11. Iranian food features rice, bread, vegetables, fruits, and lamb. Strong tea is a popular drink among many Iranians.

✓ **READING CHECK:** (*Human Systems*) What are Iraq's government and people like?

Afghanistan

Afghanistan is a landlocked country of high mountains and fertile valleys. Merchants, warriors, and missionaries have long used the Khyber (KY-buhr) Pass to reach India. This narrow passage through the Hindu Kush lies between Afghanistan and Pakistan.

History and People In 1979 the Soviet Union sent troops into Afghanistan to help the communist government there in a civil war. This led to a long war between Soviet troops and Afghan rebels. The Soviets left in 1989, and an alliance of Afghan groups took power. Turmoil continued, and in the mid-1990s a radical Muslim group known as the Taliban arose. Its leaders took over most of the country, including the capital, Kabul. The Taliban ruled Afghanistan strictly. For example, they forced women to wear veils and to stop working outside the home.

In 2001 Taliban officials came into conflict with the United States. Investigation of terrorist attacks on September 11 on Washington, D.C., and New York City led to terrorist Osama bin Laden and his al Qaeda network, based in Afghanistan. U.S. and British forces then attacked Taliban and al Qaeda targets and toppled the Taliban government.

The long period of war has damaged Afghanistan's industry, trade, and transportation systems. Farming and herding are the most important economic activities now.

Afghans belong to many different ethnic groups. The most numerous are the Pashtun, Tajik, Hazara, and Uzbek. Almost all Afghans are Muslims, and about 84 percent are Sunni.

Iran and Afghanistan

Country	Population/ Growth Rate	Life Expectancy	Literacy Rate	Per Capita GDP
Afghanistan	28,717,213 3.4%	47, male 46, female	36%	$700
Iran	68,278,826 1.1%	69, male 71, female	79%	$6,800
United States	290,342,554 0.9%	74, male 80, female	97%	$37,600

Source: Central Intelligence Agency, *The World Factbook 2003*

Interpreting the Chart How many times greater is the U.S. per capita GDP than Afghanistan's?

✓ **READING CHECK:** (*Human Systems*) What are some of the challenges Afghanistan faces today?

Section Review 4

Define or identify: Shirin Ebadi, shah, theocracy

Working with Sketch Maps On the map you created in Section 3, label Tehran, Khyber Pass, and Kabul. What physical features do Tehran and Kabul have in common?

Reading for the Main Idea

1. (*Places and Regions*) What ethnic and religious groups live in Iran?

2. (*Human Systems*) How have Afghanistan's recent wars affected the country?

Homework Practice Online
Keyword: SG5 HP18

Critical Thinking

3. Making Generalizations and Predictions What challenges might the Iranian government face in the future?

4. Drawing Inferences and Conclusions How might Afghanistan's political problems be affected by its rugged physical geography?

Organizing What You Know

5. Sequencing Copy the following graphic organizer. Use it to show the main events in Iran in recent decades.

Define and Identify

Identify each of the following:

1. exotic rivers
2. wadis
3. fossil water
4. Muslims
5. Muhammad
6. Sunni
7. Shia
8. Qur'an
9. OPEC
10. embargo
11. theocracy
12. Shirin Ebadi

Review the Main Ideas

13. What are the three landform regions that make up this part of Southwest Asia?
14. What is the climate in Southwest Asia like?
15. What is the most important resource of this region?
16. Which countries in this area have large reserves of oil?
17. Which small country has some of the largest natural gas reserves in the world?
18. What language is widely spoken in Iran?
19. Why were Western leaders concerned when Iraq invaded Kuwait?

20. What two groups in Iraq rebelled against Saddam Hussein's regime?
21. What ethnic group do most Iraqis belong to?
22. How have wars affected politics in this region?
23. What group ruled Afghanistan after the Soviets left the country?

Think Critically

24. **Drawing Inferences and Conclusions** Why might it be dangerous for these countries' economies to be almost entirely dependent on the sale of oil?
25. **Summarizing** Some of the countries of Southwest Asia are trying to increase crop production. What environmental factors might make this difficult?
26. **Drawing Inferences and Conclusions** How might Iran's recent history have been different if the 1979 revolution had not taken place?
27. **Finding the Main Idea** Why has the United States become involved in the politics of this region?
28. **Summarizing** What are the main goals to rebuilding Iraq?

Map Activity

29. On a separate sheet of paper, match the letters on the map with their correct labels.

Persian Gulf	Riyadh
Tigris River	Baghdad
Euphrates River	Tehran
Hindu Kush	Khyber Pass
Mecca	Kabul

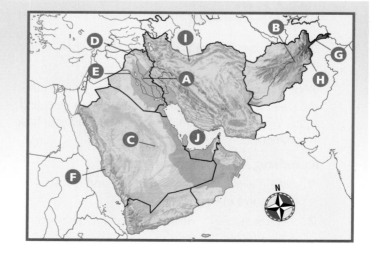

Writing Activity

Imagine that you have been asked to write a description of travel conditions in one of the following countries: Afghanistan, Iran, Iraq, or Saudi Arabia. Use your textbook, the library, and the Internet to research your country. Then write a few paragraphs about its climate, attractions, and cultural events.

internet connect

Internet Activity: **go.hrw.com**
KEYWORD: **SG5 GT18**

Choose a topic to explore about the Arabian Peninsula, Iraq, Iran, and Afghanistan:
- Visit Mesopotamia.
- Discover the importance of camels.
- See Arabian arts and crafts.

Social Studies Skills Practice

Interpreting Graphs

In the countries you learned about in this chapter, education for women is often limited. Study the following graph and answer the questions.

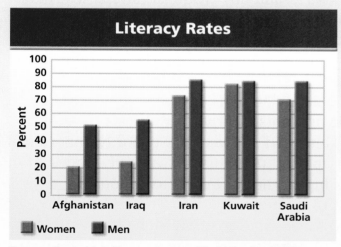

Literacy Rates

Women ■ Men

Source: Central Intelligence Agency, *World Factbook 2003*

1. Which countries have the highest literacy rates for women?

2. What can you tell about the education of women in Afghanistan and Iraq?

3. Which country has nearly the same number of literate men and women?

Analyzing Primary Sources

In this chapter, you have learned that Iran is a theocracy. However, Iran's president Mohammad Khatami hopes to move the country towards democracy. Read the following quote from Khatami and answer the questions.

"Our constitution explicitly states that absolute power belongs to God and it is God that has made man the ruler of his fate. Nothing and no one can take this right away from humans. This is a view of Islam which results in a system based on the rule of the people, a free system, a democratic one, and a system based on the rule of laws which themselves have been accepted and approved by the people.

We believe our country has suffered . . . from dependence on foreigners. Therefore, the kind of Islam that we offer is the kind . . . that leads us to independence."

Source: *New York Times*, November 10, 2001

1. According to Iran's constitution, who has absolute power?

2. What does Khatami claim Iran has suffered from?

3. According to Khatami, what will lead Iran towards independence?

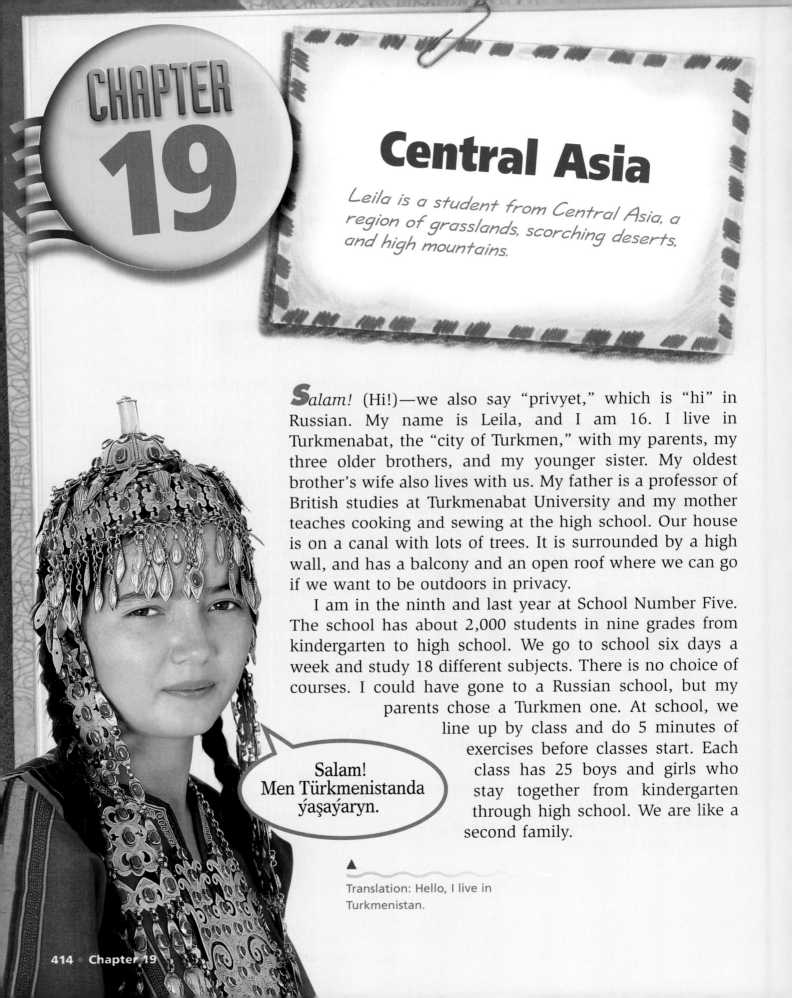

CHAPTER 19

Central Asia

Leila is a student from Central Asia, a region of grasslands, scorching deserts, and high mountains.

Salam! (Hi!)—we also say "privyet," which is "hi" in Russian. My name is Leila, and I am 16. I live in Turkmenabat, the "city of Turkmen," with my parents, my three older brothers, and my younger sister. My oldest brother's wife also lives with us. My father is a professor of British studies at Turkmenabat University and my mother teaches cooking and sewing at the high school. Our house is on a canal with lots of trees. It is surrounded by a high wall, and has a balcony and an open roof where we can go if we want to be outdoors in privacy.

I am in the ninth and last year at School Number Five. The school has about 2,000 students in nine grades from kindergarten to high school. We go to school six days a week and study 18 different subjects. There is no choice of courses. I could have gone to a Russian school, but my parents chose a Turkmen one. At school, we line up by class and do 5 minutes of exercises before classes start. Each class has 25 boys and girls who stay together from kindergarten through high school. We are like a second family.

Salam!
Men Türkmenistanda
ýaşaýaryn.

▲
Translation: Hello, I live in Turkmenistan.

Section 1 Physical Geography

Read to Discover

1. What are the main landforms and climates of Central Asia?
2. What resources are important to Central Asia?

Vocabulary

landlocked
oasis

Places

Pamirs
Tian Shan
Aral Sea
Kara-Kum
Kyzyl Kum
Syr Dar'ya
Amu Dar'ya
Fergana Valley

Reading Strategy

FOLDNOTES: TWO-PANEL FLIP CHART Create the FoldNote titled
Two-Panel Flip Chart described in the Appendix. Label one panel
Landforms and Climates. Label the other panel Resources. As you read
this section, write what you learn beneath each panel.

Central Asia: Physical-Political

Size comparison of Central Asia to the contiguous United States

ELEVATION

	FEET	METERS
⊛ National capitals	13,120	4,000
	6,560	2,000
• Other cities	1,640	500
	656	200
	(Sea level) 0	0 (Sea level)
	Below sea level	Below sea level

SCALE
0   250   500 Miles
0   250   500 Kilometers
Projection: Two-Point Equidistant

Ismail Semani Peak 24,590 ft. (7495 m)

Mountain climbers make camp before attempting to scale a peak in the Pamirs.

With temperatures above 122°F (50°C), it is not surprising that the creatures that live in the Kara-Kum are a tough group. Over a thousand species live there, including cobras, scorpions, tarantulas, and monitor lizards. These lizards can grow to more than 5 feet (1.5 m) long.

Lynxes can still be found in the mountains of Central Asia.

Interpreting the Visual Record How are these lynxes well suited to the environment in which they live?

Landforms and Climate

This huge, **landlocked** region is to the east of the Caspian Sea. Landlocked means the region does not border an ocean. The region lies north of the Pamirs (puh-MIRZ) and Tian Shan (TYEN SHAHN) mountain ranges.

Diverse Landforms As the name suggests, Central Asia lies in the middle of the largest continent. Plains and low plateaus cover much of this area. Around the Caspian Sea the land is as low as 95 feet (29 m) below sea level. However, the region includes high mountain ranges along the borders with China and Afghanistan.

Arid Lands Central Asia is a region of mainly steppe, desert, and highland climates. Summers are hot, with a short growing season. Winters are cold. Rainfall is sparse. However, north of the Aral (AR-uhl) Sea rainfall is heavy enough for steppe vegetation. Here farmers can grow crops using rain, rather than irrigation, as their water source. South and east of the Aral Sea lie two deserts. One is the Kara-Kum (kahr-uh-KOOM) in Turkmenistan. The other is the Kyzyl Kum (ki-ZIL KOOM) in Uzbekistan and Kazakhstan. Both deserts contain several **oasis** settlements where a spring or well provides water.

✔ **READING CHECK:** (**Places and Regions**) What are the landforms and climates of Central Asia?

Resources

The main water sources in southern Central Asia are the Syr Dar'ya (sir duhr-YAH) and Amu Dar'ya (uh-MOO duhr-YAH) rivers. These rivers flow down from the Pamirs and then across dry plains. Farmers have used them for irrigation for thousands of years. When it first flows down from the mountains, the Syr Dar'ya passes through the

Fergana Valley. This large valley is divided among Uzbekistan, Kyrgyzstan, and Tajikistan. As the river flows toward the Aral Sea, irrigated fields line its banks.

During the Soviet period, the region's population grew rapidly. Also, the Soviets encouraged farmers to grow cotton. This crop grows well in Central Asia's sunny climate. However, growing cotton uses a lot of water. Increased use of water has caused the Aral Sea to shrink.

A Dying Sea Today, almost no water from the Syr Dar'ya or Amu Dar'ya reaches the Aral Sea. The rivers' waters are used up by human activity. The effect on the Aral Sea has been devastating. It has lost more than 75 percent of its water since 1960. By 2003 it had shrunk to two smaller seas divided by a desert. Towns that were once fishing ports are now dozens of miles from the shore. Winds sweep the dry seafloor, blowing dust, salt, and pesticides hundreds of miles.

Mineral Resources The Central Asian countries' best economic opportunity is in their fossil fuels. Uzbekistan, Kazakhstan, and Turkmenistan all have huge oil and natural gas reserves. However, transporting the oil and gas to other countries is a problem. Economic and political turmoil in some surrounding countries has made it difficult to build pipelines.

Several Central Asian countries are also rich in other minerals. They have deposits of gold, copper, uranium, zinc, and lead. Kazakhstan has vast amounts of coal. Rivers in Kyrgyzstan and Tajikistan could be used to create hydroelectric power.

✓ **READING CHECK:** *Environment and Society* How has human activity affected the Aral Sea?

This boat sits rusting on what was once part of the Aral Sea. The sea's once thriving fishing industry has been destroyed.

go.hrw.com **Homework Practice Online** Keyword: SG5 HP19

Section Review 1

Define and explain: landlocked, oasis

Working with Sketch Maps On a map of Central Asia that you draw or that your teacher provides, label the following: Pamirs, Tian Shan, Aral Sea, Kara-Kum, Kyzyl Kum, Syr Dar'ya, Amu Dar'ya, and Fergana Valley.

Reading for the Main Idea

1. *Environment and Society* What has caused the drying up of the Aral Sea?

2. *Places and Regions* What mineral resources does Central Asia have?

Critical Thinking

3. **Analyzing Information** Why did the Soviets encourage Central Asian farmers to grow cotton?

4. **Finding the Main Idea** What factors make it hard for the Central Asian countries to export oil and gas?

Organizing What You Know

5. **Sequencing** Copy the following graphic organizer. Use it to describe the courses of the Syr Dar'ya and Amu Dar'ya, including human activities that use water.

| Melting snows in the Pamirs | ⇨ | | ⇨ | Aral Sea |

Central Asia • 417

Read to Discover

1. How did trade and invasions affect the history of Central Asia?
2. What are political and economic conditions like in Central Asia today?

Vocabulary

nomads
caravans

Reading Strategy

READING ORGANIZER Before you read, draw three large boxes on a sheet of paper. Label the first box Trade. Label the second box Invasions and the Soviet Era. Finally, label the third box Today. As you read this section, write what you learn about the history and culture of Central Asia in the boxes.

History

Bukhara, in Uzbekistan, was once a powerful and wealthy trading center of Central Asia.

Interpreting the Visual Record *Place*
What architectural features can you see that distinguish Bukhara as an Islamic city?

For centuries, Central Asians have made a living by raising horses, cattle, sheep, and goats. Many of these herders lived as **nomads**, people who often move from place to place. Other people became farmers around rivers and oases.

Trade At one time, the best land route between China and the eastern Mediterranean ran through Central Asia. Merchants traveled in large groups, called **caravans**, for protection. The goods they carried included silk and spices. As a result, this route came to be called the Silk Road. Cities along the road became centers of wealth and culture.

Central Asia's situation changed after Europeans discovered they could sail to East Asia through the Indian Ocean. As a result, trade through Central Asia declined. The region became isolated and poor.

Silk processing in modern Uzbekistan

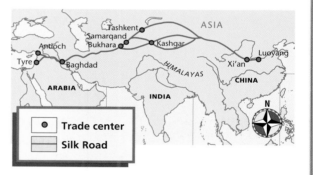

The Silk Road

The Silk Road stretched 5,000 miles (8,000 km) across Central Asia from China to the Mediterranean Sea. Along this route passed merchants, armies, and diplomats. These people forged links between East and West.

The facts of the Silk Road are still wrapped in mystery. Chinese trade and military expeditions probably began moving into Central Asia in the 100s B.C. Chinese trade goods soon were making their way to eastern Mediterranean ports.

Over the next several centuries, trade in silk, spices, jewels, and other luxury goods increased. Great caravans of camels and oxcarts traveled the Silk Road in both directions. They crossed the harsh deserts and mountains of Central Asia. Cities like Samarqand and Bukhara grew rich from the trade. In the process, ideas and technology also moved between Europe and Asia.

Travel along the Silk Road was hazardous. Bandits often robbed the caravans. Some travelers lost their way in the desert and died. In addition, religious and political turmoil occasionally disrupted travel.

Understanding What You Read
1. What was the Silk Road?
2. Why was the Silk Road important?

Invasions and the Soviet Era About A.D. 500, Turkic-speaking nomads from northern Asia spread through Central Asia. In the 700s Arab armies took over much of the region, bringing Islam. In the 1200s the armies of Mongol leaders conquered Central Asia. Later, another Turkic people, the Uzbeks, took over parts of the region. In the 1800s the Russian Empire conquered Central Asia.

After the Russian Revolution, the Soviet government set up five republics in Central Asia. The Soviets encouraged ethnic Russians to move to this area and made the nomads settle on collective ranches or farms. Religion was discouraged. Russian became the language of government and business. The government set up schools and hospitals. Women were allowed to work outside the home.

✓ **READING CHECK:** (*Human Systems*) What type of government system did the five republics set up by the Soviet Union have?

A Kyrgyz teacher conducts class.

Interpreting the Visual Record How is this class similar to yours?

Central Asia Today

The five republics became independent countries when the Soviet Union broke up in 1991. All have strong economic ties to Russia. Ethnic Russians still live in every country in the region. However, all five countries are switching from the Cyrillic alphabet to the Latin alphabet. The Cyrillic alphabet had been imposed on them by the Soviet Union. The Latin alphabet is used in most Western European languages, including English, and in Turkey.

Government All of these new countries have declared themselves to be democracies. However, they are not very free or democratic. Each is ruled by a strong central government that limits opposition and criticism.

Economy Some of the Central Asian countries have oil and gas reserves that may someday make them rich. For now, though, all are suffering economic hardship. Causes of the hardships include outdated equipment, lack of funds, and poor transportation links.

Farming is important in the Central Asian economies. Crops include cotton, wheat, barley, fruits, vegetables, almonds, tobacco, and rice. Central Asians raise cattle, sheep, horses, goats, and camels. They also raise silkworms to make silk thread.

Industry in Central Asia includes food processing, wool textiles, mining, and oil drilling. Oil-rich Turkmenistan and Kazakhstan also process oil into other products. Kazakhstan and Uzbekistan make heavy equipment such as tractors.

✓ **READING CHECK:** (*Human Systems*) How do political freedoms in the region compare to those of the United States?

Section Review 2

Define and explain: nomads, caravans

Working with Sketch Maps On the map you created in Section 1, draw and label the five Central Asian countries.

Reading for the Main Idea

1. (*Environment and Society*) How have the people of Central Asia made a living over the centuries?

2. (*Human Systems*) What are four groups that invaded Central Asia?

3. (*Human Systems*) How did Soviet rule change Central Asia?

go.hrw.com
Homework Practice Online
Keyword: SG5 HP19

Critical Thinking

4. Drawing Inferences and Conclusions What does the switch to the Latin alphabet suggest about the Central Asian countries?

Organizing What You Know

5. Categorizing Copy the following graphic organizer. Use it to categorize economic activities in Central Asia. Place the following items in the chart: making cloth, growing crops, mining metals, making food products, raising livestock, making chemicals from oil, drilling for oil, and manufacturing tractors.

Primary industries	Secondary industries

The Countries of Central Asia

Read to Discover

1. What are some important aspects of culture in Kazakhstan?
2. How does Kyrgyz culture reflect nomadic traditions?
3. Why have politics in Tajikistan in recent years been marked by violence?
4. What are two important art forms in Turkmenistan?
5. How is Uzbekistan's population significant?

Vocabulary

yurt
mosques

Places

Tashkent
Samarqand

Reading Strategy

READING ORGANIZER Draw a circle in the center of a sheet of paper. Label the circle Central Asian Countries. Draw five lines from the circle. Then, draw a small circle at the end of each line. Label the five circles Kazakhstan, Kyrgyzstan, Tajikistan, Turkmenistan, and Uzbekistan. As you read this section, write what you learn about each country next to each circle.

Kazakhstan

Of the Central Asian nations, Kazakhstan was the first to be conquered by Russia. Russian influence remains strong there. About one third of Kazakhstan's people are ethnic Russians. Kazakh and Russian are both official languages. Many ethnic Kazakhs grow up speaking Russian at home and have to learn Kazakh in school.

Kazakhstanis celebrate the New Year twice—on January 1 and again on Nauruz, the start of the Persian calendar's year. Nauruz falls on the spring equinox.

Food in Central Asia combines influences from Southwest Asia and China. Rice, yogurt, and grilled meat are common ingredients. One Kazakh specialty is smoked horsemeat sausage with cold noodles.

✓ **READING CHECK:** *Human Systems* How has Kazakhstan been influenced by Russia?

A woman in Uzbekistan grills meat on skewers.
▼

Kyrgyzstan

Kyrgyzstan has many mountains, and the people live mostly in valleys. People in the southern part of the country generally share cultural ties with Uzbekistan. People in northern areas are more linked to nomadic cultures and to Kazakhstan.

The word *kyrgyz* means "forty clans." Clan membership is still important in Krygyz social, political, and economic life. Many Kyrgyz men wear black and white felt hats that show their clan status.

Nomadic traditions are still important to many Kyrgyz. The **yurt** is a movable round house of wool felt mats over a wood frame. Today the yurt is a symbol of the nomadic heritage. Even people who live in cities may put up yurts for weddings and funerals.

✔ **READING CHECK:** (*Human Systems*) In what ways do the Kyrgyz continue traditions of their past?

Tajikistan

In the mid-1990s Tajikistan experienced a civil war. The Soviet-style government fought against a mixed group of reformers, some of whom demanded democracy. Others called for government by Islamic law. A peace agreement was signed in 1996, but tensions remain high.

The other major Central Asian languages are related to Turkish. However, the Tajik language is related to Persian. Tajiks consider the great literature written in Persian to be part of their cultural heritage.

✔ **READING CHECK:** (*Human Systems*) What has happened in politics in recent years in Tajikistan?

Turkmenistan

The major first language of Turkmenistan is Turkmen. In 1993 Turkmenistan adopted English, rather than Russian, as its second official language. However, some schools teach in Russian, Uzbek, or Kazakh.

Islam has experienced a revival in Central Asia since the breakup of the Soviet Union. Many new **mosques**, or Islamic houses of worship, are being built and old ones are being restored. Donations from other Islamic countries, such as Saudi Arabia and Iran, have helped

Turkoman women display carpets. Central Asian carpets are famous for their imaginative patterns, bright colors, and expert artistry.

Interpreting the Visual Record

(*Movement*) **Why were carpets suited to the nomadic way of life?**

▶

these efforts. The government of Turkmenistan supports this revival and has ordered schools to teach Islamic principles. However, like the other states in the region, Turkmenistan's government views Islam with some caution. It does not want Islam to become a political movement.

Historically, the nomadic life required that all possessions be portable. Decorative carpets were the essential furniture of a nomad's home. They are still perhaps the most famous artistic craft of Turkmenistan. Like others in Central Asia, the people of Turkmenistan also have an ancient tradition of poetry.

✓ **READING CHECK:** (*Human Systems*) What are two forms of art in Turkmenistan, and how do they reflect its cultural traditions?

Central Asia

COUNTRY	POPULATION/ GROWTH RATE	LIFE EXPECTANCY	LITERACY RATE	PER CAPITA GDP
Kazakhstan	16,763,795 .02%	58, male 69, female	98%	$7,200
Kyrgyzstan	4,892,808 1.5%	59, male 68, female	97%	$2,900
Tajikistan	6,863,752 2.1%	61, male 67, female	99%	$1,300
Turkmenistan	4,775,544 1.8%	57, male 65, female	98%	$6,700
Uzbekistan	25,981,647 1.6%	60, male 68, female	99%	$2,600
United States	290,342,554 0.9%	74, male 80, female	97%	$37,600

Source: Central Intelligence Agency, *The World Factbook 2003*

Interpreting the Chart **Which country has the lowest per capita GDP in the region?**

Uzbekistan

Uzbekistan has the largest population of the Central Asian countries—about 24 million people. Uzbek is the official language. People are required to study Uzbek to be eligible for citizenship.

Tashkent and Samarqand are ancient Silk Road cities in Uzbekistan. They are famous for their mosques and Islamic monuments. Uzbeks are also known for their art of embroidering fabric with gold.

✓ **READING CHECK:** (*Human Systems*) What is one of an Uzbekistan citizen's responsibilities?

go.hrw.com **Homework Practice Online**
Keyword: SG5 HP19

Section Review 3

Define and explain: yurt, mosques

Working with Sketch Maps On the map you created in Section 2, label Tashkent and Samarqand.

Reading for the Main Idea

1. (*Places and Regions*) In which Central Asian nation is the influence of Russia strongest? Why is this true?

2. (*Human Systems*) What were the two sides in Tajikistan's civil war fighting for?

3. (*Human Systems*) What is the role of Islam in the region today?

Critical Thinking

4. **Finding the Main Idea** What are two customs or artistic crafts of modern Central Asia that are connected to the nomadic lifestyle?

Organizing What You Know

5. **Contrasting** Copy the following graphic organizer. Use it to describe the conditions in Central Asia during the Soviet era and today.

	Soviet era	Today
Type of government		
Official language		
Alphabet		
Government attitude toward Islam		

CASE STUDY

KAZAKHS: PASTORAL NOMADS OF CENTRAL ASIA

Nomads are people who move around from place to place during the year. Nomads usually move when the seasons change so that they will have enough food to eat. Herding, hunting, gathering, and fishing are all ways that different nomadic groups get their food.

Nomads that herd animals are called pastoral nomads. Their way of life depends on the seasonal movement of their herds. Pastoral nomads may herd cattle, horses, sheep, goats, yaks, reindeer, camels, or other animals. Instead of keeping their animals inside fenced pastures, pastoral nomads let them graze on open fields. However, they must make sure the animals do not overgraze and damage the pastureland. To do this, they keep their animals moving throughout the year. Some pastoral nomads live in steppe or desert environments. These nomads often have to move their animals very long distances between winter and summer pastures.

The Kazakhs of Central Asia are an example of a pastoral nomadic group. They have herded horses, sheep, goats, and cattle for hundreds of years. Because they move so much, the Kazakhs do not have permanent homes. They bring their homes with them when they travel to new places.

A Kazakh nomad keeps a watchful eye over a herd of horses.

Movement Yurts are carefully stitched together by hand. When it is time to move to new pastures, they are carried from place to place on horseback or on small wagons.

The Kazakhs live in tent-like structures called yurts. Yurts are circular structures made of bent poles covered with thick felt. Yurts can be easily taken apart and moved. They are perfect homes for the Kazakhs' nomadic lifestyle.

During the year, a Kazakh family may move its herds of sheep, horses, and cattle as far as 500 miles (805 km). For one Kazakh family, each year is divided into four different parts. The family spends the first part of the year in winter grazing areas. Then, in early spring, they move to areas with fresh grass shoots. When these spring grasses are gone, the family moves their animals to summer pastures. In the fall, the animals are kept for six weeks in autumn pastures. Finally, the herds are taken back to their winter pastures. Each year, the cycle is repeated.

The nomadic lifestyle of the Kazakhs has changed, however. In the early 1800s people from Russia and eastern Europe began to move into the region. These people were farmers. They started planting crops in areas that the Kazakhs used for pasture. This made it more difficult for the Kazakhs to move their animals during the year. Later, when Kazakhstan was part of the Soviet Union, government officials encouraged the Kazakhs to settle in villages and cities. Many Kazakhs still move their animals during the year. However, tending crops has also become an important way to get food.

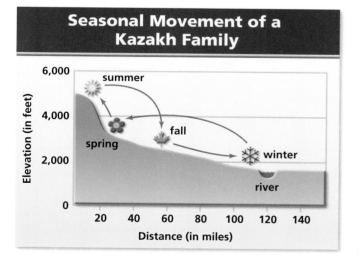

During the year, a Kazakh family may move its herds to several different pasture areas as the seasons change.

Interpreting the Graph Why do you think animals are moved to higher elevations during the summer and to lower elevations during the winter?

Understanding What You Read

1. Why do some pastoral nomads have to travel such great distances?

2. How has the nomadic lifestyle of the Kazakhs changed during the last 100 years?

Define and Identify

Identify each of the following:

1. landlocked
2. oasis
3. nomads
4. caravans
5. yurt
6. mosques

Review the Main Ideas

7. What types of climates are most common in Central Asia?
8. What problems have resulted from the shrinking of the Aral Sea?
9. What was the Silk Road?
10. Why did trade through Central Asia decline?
11. How did Soviet rule change Central Asians' way of life?
12. What are the Central Asian governments like?
13. What are some of Central Asia's main crops and products?
14. Which of the Central Asian countries still has a strong Russian presence?
15. What happened in the mid-1990s in Tajikistan?

16. How has the government of Turkmenistan responded to the revival of Islam?
17. What are some of the languages spoken in Central Asia?
18. Which of the region's countries has the largest population?

Think Critically

19. **Summarizing** How have politics influenced language and the alphabet used in Central Asia?
20. **Finding the Main Idea** How do the artistic crafts of Central Asia reflect the nomadic lifestyle?
21. **Analyzing Information** Why did the Soviets encourage cotton farming in the region? What were the environmental consequences?
22. **Finding the Main Idea** What obstacles are making it hard for the Central Asian countries to export their oil?
23. **Summarizing** What are some reasons the Central Asian countries have experienced slow economic growth since independence? How are they trying to improve the situation?

Map Activity

24. On a separate sheet of paper, match the letters on the map with their correct labels.

    Caspian Sea   Kara-Kum
    Pamirs   Kyzyl Kum
    Tian Shan   Tashkent
    Aral Sea   Samarqand

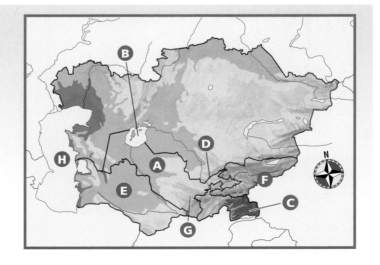

Writing Activity

Imagine that you are a caravan trader traveling along the Silk Road during the 1200s. Write a journal entry describing your journey from the Mediterranean Sea through Central Asia. You may want to describe the landscape, other people that you meet, or dangers that you face. Be sure to use standard grammar, spelling, sentence structure, and punctuation.

internet connect

Internet Activity: **go.hrw.com**
KEYWORD: SG5 GT19

Choose a topic to explore about Central Asia:
- Study the climate of Central Asia.
- Travel along the historic Silk Road.
- Learn about nomads and caravans.

Social Studies Skills Practice

Interpreting Charts

Study the following chart and then answer the questions.

Rural and Urban Population in Central Asia, 1989–1992

Country	Urban Population	Rural Population
Kazakhstan	9,610,000	7,120,000
Kyrgyzstan	1,680,000	2,770,000
Tajikistan	1,660,000	3,440,000
Turkmenistan	1,590,000	1,930,000
Uzbekistan	8,040,000	11,770,000

Source: Federal Research Division, Library of Congress

1. Which country had the largest urban population? The smallest?

2. Which country had the largest rural population? The smallest?

3. Which country's urban population was larger than its rural population?

4. Which country had urban and rural populations that were roughly the same size?

Analyzing Primary Sources

Read the following quote from Mrs. B. Ospanova, a citizen of Kazakhstan. Then answer the questions.

"I am glad that the republic is independent. My husband and I feel more liberated. Earlier we lived from salary to salary, the flat [apartment] was small, we stood in turn for a car during 20 years. But another times came and my husband organized his own small-scale business. We bought a big flat, a car and gave education to our children. Is it bad? Work and you will have everything. I, for example, have no nostalgia for Soviet times."

1. What problems with the Soviet-era economy does Mrs. Ospanova discuss?

2. What new business opportunity became available after independence?

3. How has life changed for the Ospanova family since independence?

4. What does Mrs. Ospanova identify as the key to success in Kazakhstan?

FOCUS ON REGIONS

Differences and Connections

In this textbook the countries of Africa are grouped together. This has been done to emphasize the region's connections. Yet any region as large as Africa has important differences from place to place. East Africa is different from West Africa, and West Africa is different from North Africa. This is also true of other large regions. In South America, for example, Brazil is different from Argentina in many important ways.

North Africa and Southwest Asia One subregion of Africa that geographers often include in another region is North Africa. These geographers see more connections between North Africa and Southwest Asia than between North Africa and the rest of the continent. For example, in both areas Arabic is the main language. The major religion is Islam. Political issues also tie North Africa to its eastern neighbors, as does physical geography. The countries of North Africa and Southwest

▲

The Muhammad Ali Mosque is one of many beautiful places of worship for Muslims in Cairo, Egypt. Although various religions, including Judaism and Christianity, are practiced in North Africa and Southwest Asia, most people in the two regions are Muslim.

Asia are part of a vast desert region. These countries face common issues such as water conservation and water management.

The African Continent There are also many reasons for placing North Africa in a region with the rest of Africa. People in Africa share some important historical, cultural, and economic ties. For example, ancient Egyptians had close contact with other peoples in Africa. In turn, cultures south of the Sahara contributed to the development of Egypt's great Nile Valley civilizations. Farther west, Mediterranean peoples have long traded with West African kingdoms south of the Sahara. Such contact helped spread

◀

This sign in Morocco is in both Arabic and French. Arabic is spoken throughout North Africa and many parts of Southwest Asia.

Regional Links

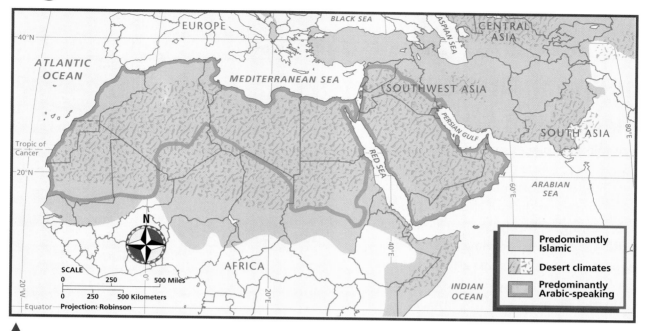

Language, religion, and climate are some of the ties between North Africa and Southwest Asia. Arabic speakers, Muslims, and desert climates are dominant throughout much of the two regions and in parts of the surrounding transition zones.

Islam among the peoples of North Africa and the rest of the continent. Today, there are mosques as far south as Nigeria and Tanzania.

North Africa also has political connections to the rest of Africa. Many African countries face similar political and economic challenges. In part, these issues arise from their shared colonial history. To resolve some of these issues, the countries of North Africa are working with other African countries. They have formed associations such as the Organization of African Unity.

Transition Zones There are many differences and connections between North Africa and the rest of the continent. Perhaps they are most evident in a band of countries that lie just south of the Sahara. These countries stretch from Mauritania in the west to Ethiopia and Sudan in the east. They form a transition zone. In other words, they resemble both North Africa and Africa south of the Sahara. In Chad and Sudan, for example, strong political and cultural differences separate north and south. The northern regions of these countries are tied closely to North Africa. The southern regions of these countries are tied closely to African countries to the south.

North Africa and the countries in the transition zone have important connections to two major world regions. Which region they are placed in depends on the geographer's point of view. Understanding the differences among countries and their connections to other areas of the world is important. It is more important than deciding where on a map a region begins or ends.

Understanding What You Read

1. What ties are there between North Africa and Southwest Asia?

2. What ties are there between North Africa and the rest of the African continent?

Building Skills for Life: Interpreting the Past

Both people and places are a product of the past. Therefore, understanding the geography of past times is important. It gives us a more complete understanding of the world today.

History and geography can hardly be separated. All historical events have to happen somewhere. These events are affected by local geography. For example, wheat and barley were domesticated in an area of Southwest Asia called the Fertile Crescent. This region received enough rainfall for these crops to grow.

Geographers who specialize in studying the past are called historical geographers. Historical geographers are interested in where things used to be and how they developed. They also try to understand how people's beliefs and values influenced historical events. In other words, why did people do what they did?

All geographers must be skilled at interpreting the past. Cultural geographers might study how old buildings and houses reflect earlier times. Physical geographers may need to reconstruct past landscapes. For example,

▲
Ancient ruins in Petra, Jordan, can provide clues to the region's past.

many rivers have changed their course. Understanding where a river used to flow could help explain its present course.

In your study of geography, think about how a place's history has shaped the way it is today. Look for clues that can tell you about its past. Ask yourself how people may have thought about a place in earlier times. No matter where you are, the evidence of the past is all around!

THE SKILL

1. Look at some of the buildings in your community. How old do you think they are? Do some look older than others? Can you describe how building styles in your community have changed over time? Why do you think styles have changed?

2. Analyze an important historical event that occurred in your state. What happened? Where did it happen? How was the event influenced by local geography?

3. Interpret the settlement history of your state or community. When was it settled? What attracted people to it? How do you think they felt about the place at the time?

HANDS on
GEOGRAPHY

One way to interpret the past is by studying old travel accounts. They often have detailed information about the people, places, and daily life of past times.

One famous travel account describes the journeys of Ibn Battuta. Ibn Battuta was one of the greatest travelers in history. During the mid-1300s he traveled about 75,000 miles (120,700 km) throughout parts of Asia and Africa. Near the end of his travels, he gave a long account of the many places he visited. This account is a valuable historical document today.

The following passage is taken from Ibn Battuta's travel account. In this passage, Ibn Battuta is visiting the Sultan of Birgi, a town in what is now western Turkey. Read the passage, and then answer the Lab Report questions.

> *In the course of this audience the sultan asked me this question: "Have you ever seen a stone that fell from the sky?" I replied, "I have never seen one, nor ever heard tell of one." "Well," he said, "a stone did fall from the sky outside this town of ours," and then called some men and told them to bring the stone. They brought in a great black stone, very hard and with a glitter in it—I reckoned its weight to amount to a hundredweight. The sultan ordered the stonebreakers to be summoned, and four of them came and on his com-mand to strike it they beat upon it as one man four times with iron hammers, but made no impression on it. I was astonished at this phe-nomenon, and he ordered it to be taken back to its place.*

▲
This painting shows Ibn Battuta during his travels in the mid-1300s.

Lab Report

1. What did the "stone that fell from the sky" look like? What do you think it was?

2. Why do you think Ibn Battuta was "astonished" by what he saw?

3. What can this story tell us about the historical geography of this region?

UNIT 7

Africa

Holding back the desert in Morocco

Cape Town, South Africa

A Physician in Sierra Leone

Dr. James Li went to Africa fresh out of medical school to work as a general practice physician. Here he describes what it was like to work at a hospital in Sierra Leone. **WHAT DO YOU THINK?** *What might Dr. Li's patients think about health care in the United States?*

Malaria, tuberculosis, and leprosy were widespread in our hospital population. We often saw patients who had walked over 100 miles for treatment. None of the patients in our area had access to clean water. Phone lines installed by the British had been cut down and the copper wires melted to make cooking pots. Our hospital was in the remote jungle, about six hours by dirt road from the nearest major city. It had 140 beds. In the clinic, we saw several hundred other patients each day. Food for the staff and patients was grown on the hospital grounds.

I came to love the people who were our patients, particularly the very young and the very old. In the midst of shortages, I met people who lived happily and suffered the tragedies of utter poverty with a dignity that would have failed me. These reflections fill me with a strange combination of awe, sadness, humility, and excitement.

Hospital in Butare, Rwanda

Masai dancers, Kenya

Understanding Primary Sources

1. What were conditions like at Dr. Li's hospital?

2. How does Dr. Li describe the culture of Sierra Leone?

Giraffe

Africa

Elevation Profile

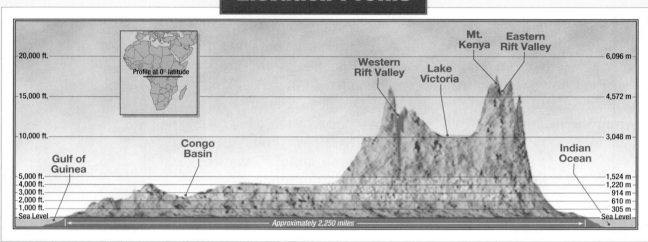

Profile at 0° latitude

20,000 ft. — 6,096 m
15,000 ft. — 4,572 m
10,000 ft. — 3,048 m
5,000 ft. — 1,524 m
4,000 ft. — 1,220 m
3,000 ft. — 914 m
2,000 ft. — 610 m
1,000 ft. — 305 m
Sea Level — Sea Level

Mt. Kenya
Eastern Rift Valley
Western Rift Valley
Lake Victoria
Congo Basin
Gulf of Guinea
Indian Ocean

Approximately 2,250 miles

The United States and Africa:
Comparing Sizes

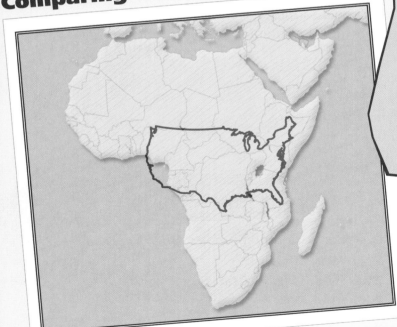

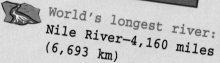

GEOSTATS:

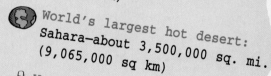

World's longest river:
Nile River—4,160 miles
(6,693 km)

World's largest hot desert:
Sahara—about 3,500,000 sq. mi.
(9,065,000 sq km)

World's highest recorded
temperature: 136°F (58°C)
in Al Azizyah, Libya on
September 13, 1992

Africa:
Physical

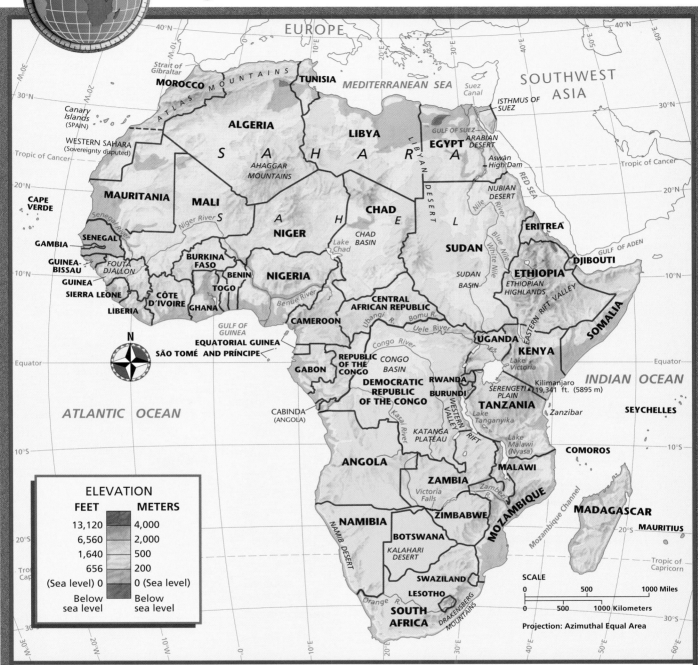

1. (Region) Which region of Africa has the high-est mountains? Which country appears to have the largest number of high mountains?

2. (Place) Which countries have areas that lie below sea level? Where is the highest point in Africa?

Critical Thinking

3. (Region) Which North African mountains might create a rain-shadow effect?

4. (Region) Compare this map to the **climate map** of the region. Which areas might have tropical rain forests?

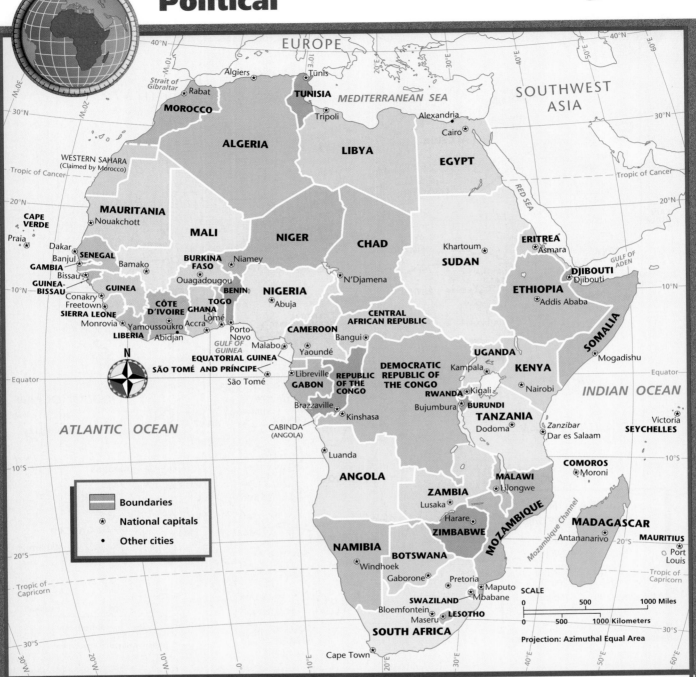

1. (*Place*) Which country is completely surrounded by another country?

2. (*Location*) Which country lies mostly on the mainland but has its capital on an island?

3. (*Place*) What is the largest African island country? What are the other island countries?

Critical Thinking

4. (*Human-Environment Interaction*) Compare this map to the **climate map** of the region. Why do you think the capitals of Algeria, Tunisia, and Libya all lie on the Mediterranean Sea?

Africa: Climate

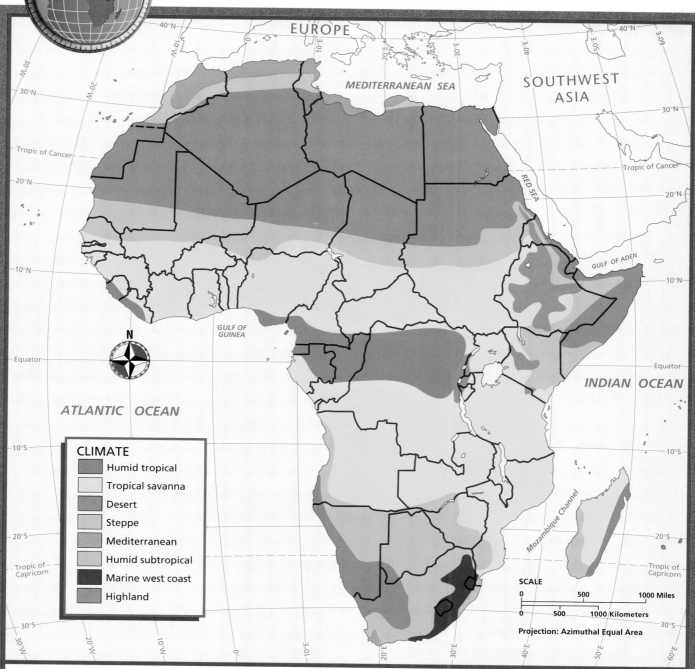

CLIMATE
- Humid tropical
- Tropical savanna
- Desert
- Steppe
- Mediterranean
- Humid subtropical
- Marine west coast
- Highland

EUROPE

MEDITERRANEAN SEA

SOUTHWEST ASIA

RED SEA

GULF OF ADEN

ATLANTIC OCEAN

GULF OF GUINEA

INDIAN OCEAN

Mozambique Channel

Tropic of Cancer

Equator

Tropic of Capricorn

SCALE
0   500   1000 Miles
0   500   1000 Kilometers
Projection: Azimuthal Equal Area

1. (Region) Where are humid tropical climates found in Africa?

2. (Region) Compare this map to the **land use and resources map** of the region. Which climate region in North Africa has limited economic activity?

Critical Thinking

3. (Human-Environment Interaction) Compare this map to the **land use and resources** and **population maps** of the region. Why might the eastern part of South Africa be more densely populated than the western part?

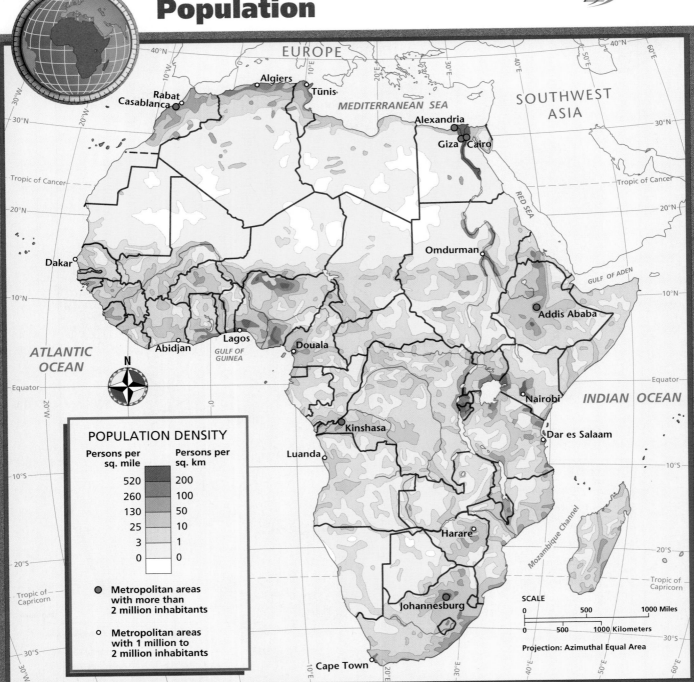

EUROPE

SOUTHWEST ASIA

MEDITERRANEAN SEA

Algiers
Tūnis
Rabat
Casablanca
Alexandria
Giza · Cairo

Tropic of Cancer

RED SEA

Dakar

Omdurman

GULF OF ADEN

Addis Ababa

ATLANTIC OCEAN

Lagos
Abidjan
Douala
GULF OF GUINEA

N

Equator

Nairobi

INDIAN OCEAN

Kinshasa

Dar es Salaam

Luanda

POPULATION DENSITY

Persons per sq. mile	Persons per sq. km
520	200
260	100
130	50
25	10
3	1
0	0

● Metropolitan areas with more than 2 million inhabitants

○ Metropolitan areas with 1 million to 2 million inhabitants

Harare

Mozambique Channel

Johannesburg

Tropic of Capricorn

SCALE

0 — 500 — 1000 Miles
0 — 500 — 1000 Kilometers

Projection: Azimuthal Equal Area

Cape Town

1. (Place) Which country has the most cities with more than 2 million people? Compare this map to the **physical map** of the region. Which river flows through or near these cities?

2. (Place) What are the two largest African cities shown south of the equator?

Critical Thinking

3. (Human-Environment Interaction) Compare this map to the **climate map** of the region. Notice that both the humid tropical climate region in central Africa and the desert regions in the north and south are areas of low population density. What is one conclusion you might draw from this?

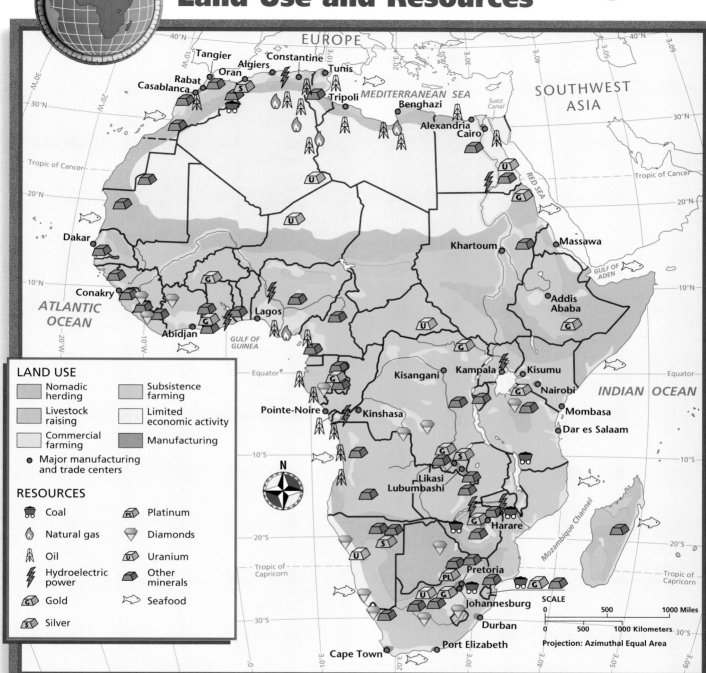

LAND USE

- Nomadic herding
- Livestock raising
- Commercial farming
- Subsistence farming
- Limited economic activity
- Manufacturing
- ● Major manufacturing and trade centers

RESOURCES

- Coal
- Natural gas
- Oil
- Hydroelectric power
- Gold
- Silver
- Platinum
- Diamonds
- Uranium
- Other minerals
- Seafood

Map labels: Tangier, Constantine, Algiers, Oran, Rabat, Casablanca, Tunis, Tripoli, MEDITERRANEAN SEA, Benghazi, Alexandria, Cairo, Suez Canal, SOUTHWEST ASIA, EUROPE, RED SEA, GULF OF ADEN, Khartoum, Massawa, Dakar, Conakry, ATLANTIC OCEAN, Abidjan, Lagos, GULF OF GUINEA, Addis Ababa, Kisangani, Kampala, Kisumu, Nairobi, INDIAN OCEAN, Mombasa, Pointe-Noire, Kinshasa, Dar es Salaam, Likasi, Lubumbashi, Harare, Mozambique Channel, Pretoria, Johannesburg, Durban, Cape Town, Port Elizabeth

Tropic of Cancer, Equator, Tropic of Capricorn

SCALE — 0 500 1000 Miles / 0 500 1000 Kilometers
Projection: Azimuthal Equal Area

1. **Region** Which region of Africa seems to have the most mineral resources?

2. **Human-Environment Interaction** What type of farming is the most common in Africa?

3. **Human-Environment Interaction** Compare this map to the **physical map** of the region. Which rivers support commercial farming in dry areas? Which river in southeastern Africa provides hydroelectric power to the region?

Critical Thinking

4. **Human-Environment Interaction** Compare this map to the **physical map** of the region. Why might mining be the only major economic activity on Namibia's western coast?

Africa

ALGERIA

CAPITAL:
Algiers

AREA:
919,590 sq. mi.
(2,381,740 sq km)

POPULATION:
32,818,500

MONEY:
Algerian dinar

LANGUAGES:
Arabic (official), French,
Berber

PEOPLE PER DOCTOR:
1,066

ANGOLA

CAPITAL:
Luanda

AREA:
481,351 sq. mi.
(1,246,700 sq km)

POPULATION:
10,766,471

MONEY:
kwanza

LANGUAGES:
Portuguese (official), Bantu
languages

PEOPLE PER DOCTOR:
data not available

BENIN

CAPITAL:
Porto-Novo

AREA:
43,483 sq. mi.
(112,620 sq km)

POPULATION:
7,041,490

MONEY:
CFAF*

LANGUAGES:
French (official), Fon, Yoruba,
other ethnic languages

PEOPLE PER DOCTOR:
14,216

BOTSWANA
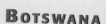

CAPITAL:
Gaborone

AREA:
231,803 sq. mi.
(600,370 sq km)

POPULATION:
1,573,267

MONEY:
pula

LANGUAGES:
English (official), Setswana

PEOPLE PER DOCTOR:
4,395

BURKINA FASO

CAPITAL:
Ouagadougou

AREA:
105,869 sq. mi.
(274,200 sq km)

POPULATION:
13,228,460

MONEY:
CFAF*

LANGUAGES:
French (official),
ethnic languages

PEOPLE PER DOCTOR:
27,158

BURUNDI

CAPITAL:
Bujumbura

AREA:
10,745 sq. mi.
(27,830 sq km)

POPULATION:
6,096,156

MONEY:
Burundi franc

LANGUAGES:
Kirundi (official), French
(official), Swahili

PEOPLE PER DOCTOR:
16,667

CAMEROON

CAPITAL:
Yaoundé

AREA:
183,567 sq. mi.
(475,440 sq km)

POPULATION:
15,746,179

MONEY:
CFAF*

LANGUAGES:
English (official), French (official), 24 ethnic language
groups

PEOPLE PER DOCTOR:
14,286

CAPE VERDE

CAPITAL:
Praia

AREA:
1,557 sq. mi. (4,033 sq km)

POPULATION:
412,137

MONEY:
Cape Verdean escudo

LANGUAGES:
Portuguese,
Crioulo

PEOPLE PER DOCTOR:
3,448

*Communaute Financiere Africaine franc

Countries not drawn to scale.

CENTRAL AFRICAN REPUBLIC

CAPITAL: Bangui

AREA:
240,534 sq. mi.
(622,984 sq km)

POPULATION: 3,683,538

MONEY: CFAF*

LANGUAGES: French (official), Sangho (national language), tribal languages

PEOPLE PER DOCTOR: 18,660

CHAD

CAPITAL:
N'Djamena

AREA:
495,752 sq. mi.
(1,284,000 sq km)

POPULATION:
9,253,493

MONEY:
CFAF*

LANGUAGES:
French (official), Arabic (official), Sara and Sango

PEOPLE PER DOCTOR: 27,765

COMOROS

CAPITAL:
Moroni

AREA:
838 sq. mi.
(2,170 sq km)

POPULATION:
632,948

MONEY:
Comoran franc

LANGUAGES:
Arabic (official), French (official), Comoran

PEOPLE PER DOCTOR:
10,000

CONGO, DEMOCRATIC REPUBLIC OF THE

CAPITAL:
Kinshasa

AREA:
905,563 sq. mi.
(2,345,410 sq km)

POPULATION:
56,625,039

MONEY:
Congolese franc

LANGUAGES:
French (official), Lingala, Kingwana, Kikongo, Tshiluba

PEOPLE PER DOCTOR:
data not available

CONGO, REPUBLIC OF THE

CAPITAL: Brazzaville

AREA:
132,046 sq. mi.
(342,000 sq km)

POPULATION: 2,954,258

MONEY: CFAF*

LANGUAGES:
French (official), Lingala, Monokutuba

PEOPLE PER DOCTOR: 3,704

CÔTE d'IVOIRE

CAPITAL:
Yamoussoukro

AREA:
124,502 sq. mi.
(322,460 sq km)

POPULATION: 16,962,491

MONEY: CFAF*

LANGUAGES:
French (official), Dioula, ethnic languages

PEOPLE PER DOCTOR:
data not available

DJIBOUTI

CAPITAL:
Djibouti

AREA:
8,494 sq. mi.
(22,000 sq km)

POPULATION:
457,130

MONEY:
Djiboutian franc

LANGUAGES:
French (official), Arabic (official), Somali, Afar

PEOPLE PER DOCTOR:
5,000

EGYPT

CAPITAL:
Cairo

AREA:
386,660 sq. mi.
(1,001,450 sq km)

POPULATION:
74,718,797

MONEY:
Egyptian pound

LANGUAGES:
Arabic (official), English, French

PEOPLE PER DOCTOR:
472

Sources: Central Intelligence Agency, *The World Factbook 2003*; United Nations Development Programme: *Health Profile*, pop. figures are 2003 estimates.

EQUATORIAL GUINEA

CAPITAL: Malabo

AREA:
10,830 sq. mi.
(28,051 sq km)

POPULATION: 510,473

MONEY: CFAF*

LANGUAGES:
Spanish (official), French
(official), Fang, Bubi, Ibo

PEOPLE PER DOCTOR: 4,762

ERITREA

CAPITAL: Asmara

AREA:
46,842 sq. mi.
(121,320 sq km)

POPULATION:
4,362,254

MONEY: nafka

LANGUAGES:
Afar, Amharic, Arabic, Tigre,
Kunama, Tigrinya

PEOPLE PER DOCTOR:
36,000

ETHIOPIA

CAPITAL: Addis Ababa

AREA:
435,184 sq. mi.
(1,127,127 sq km)

POPULATION:
66,557,553

MONEY: birr

LANGUAGES:
Amharic, Tigrinya, Orominga,
Guaraginga, Somali, Arabic

PEOPLE PER DOCTOR:
25,000

GABON

CAPITAL: Libreville

AREA:
103,346 sq. mi.
(267,667 sq km)

POPULATION:
1,321,560

MONEY: CFAF*

LANGUAGES:
French (official), Fang,
Myene, Nzebi,
Bapounou/Eschira, Bandjabi

PEOPLE PER DOCTOR: 5,263

GAMBIA

CAPITAL: Banjul

AREA:
4,363 sq. mi.
(11,300 sq km)

POPULATION:
1,501,050

MONEY: dalasi

LANGUAGES:
English (official), Mandinka,
Wolof, Fula

PEOPLE PER DOCTOR:
50,000

GHANA

CAPITAL: Accra

AREA:
92,100 sq. mi.
(238,540 sq km)

POPULATION:
20,467,747

MONEY: new cedi

LANGUAGES:
English (official), Akan,
Moshi-Dagomba, Ewe, Ga

PEOPLE PER DOCTOR:
22,970

GUINEA

CAPITAL: Conakry

AREA:
94,925 sq. mi.
(245,857 sq km)

POPULATION:
9,030,220

MONEY:
Guinean franc

LANGUAGES:
French (official),
ethnic languages

PEOPLE PER DOCTOR: 6,667

GUINEA-BISSAU

CAPITAL: Bissau

AREA:
13,946 sq. mi.
(36,120 sq km)

POPULATION: 1,360,827

MONEY: CFAF*

LANGUAGES:
Portuguese (official), Crioulo,
ethnic languages

PEOPLE PER DOCTOR: 5,556

KENYA

CAPITAL:
Nairobi

AREA:
224,961 sq. mi.
(582,650 sq km)

POPULATION: 31,639,091

MONEY:
Kenyan shilling

LANGUAGES:
English (official), Kiswahili
(official), ethnic languages

PEOPLE PER DOCTOR: 5,999

LESOTHO

CAPITAL: Maseru

AREA:
11,720 sq. mi.
(30,355 sq km)

POPULATION:
1,861,959

MONEY: loti

LANGUAGES:
English (official), Sesotho,
Zulu, Xhosa

PEOPLE PER DOCTOR:
14,306

*Communaute Financiere Africaine franc

Countries not drawn to scale.

LIBERIA

CAPITAL: Monrovia

AREA:
43,000 sq. mi.
(111,370 sq km)

POPULATION:
3,317,176

MONEY:
Liberian dollar

LANGUAGES:
English (official),
many ethnic languages

PEOPLE PER DOCTOR: 8,333

LIBYA

CAPITAL: Tripoli

AREA:
679,358 sq. mi.
(1,759,540 sq km)

POPULATION:
5,499,074

MONEY: Libyan dinar

LANGUAGES:
Arabic, Italian, English

PEOPLE PER DOCTOR:
data not available

MADAGASCAR

CAPITAL: Antananarivo

AREA:
226,656 sq. mi.
(587,040 sq km)

POPULATION:
16,979,744

MONEY:
Malagasy franc

LANGUAGES:
French (official),
Malagasy (official)

PEOPLE PER DOCTOR: 4,167

MALAWI

CAPITAL: Lilongwe

AREA:
45,745 sq. mi.
(118,480 sq km)

POPULATION:
11,651,239

MONEY:
Malawian kwacha

LANGUAGES: English (official),
Chichewa (official), many
ethnic languages

PEOPLE PER DOCTOR: 50,000

MALI

CAPITAL: Bamako

AREA:
478,764 sq. mi.
(1,240,000 sq km)

POPULATION: 11,626,219

MONEY: CFAF*

LANGUAGES:
French (official), Bambara,
many ethnic languages

PEOPLE PER DOCTOR: 25,000

MAURITANIA

CAPITAL: Nouakchott

AREA:
397,953 sq. mi.
(1,030,700 sq km)

POPULATION:
2,912,584

MONEY:
ouguiya

LANGUAGES:
Hassaniya Arabic (official),
Wolof (official), Pulaar,
Soninke, French

PEOPLE PER DOCTOR: 11,085

MAURITIUS

CAPITAL:
Port Louis

AREA:
718 sq. mi.
(1,860 sq km)

POPULATION:
1,210,447

MONEY:
Mauritian rupee

LANGUAGES:
English (official), Creole,
French, Hindi, Urdu, Hakka,
Bhojpuri

PEOPLE PER DOCTOR: 1,182

MOROCCO

CAPITAL:
Rabat

AREA:
172,413 sq. mi.
(446,550 sq km)

POPULATION:
31,689,265

MONEY:
Moroccan dirham

LANGUAGES:
Arabic (official), Berber,
French

PEOPLE PER DOCTOR: 2,923

MOZAMBIQUE

CAPITAL:
Maputo

AREA:
304,494 sq. mi.
(801,590 sq km)

POPULATION:
17,479,266

MONEY:
metical

LANGUAGES:
Portuguese (official), ethnic
languages

PEOPLE PER DOCTOR:
131,991

Sources: Central Intelligence Agency, *The World Factbook 2003*; United Nations Development Programme: *Health Profile*, pop. figures are 2003 estimates.

NAMIBIA

CAPITAL:
Windhoek

AREA:
318,694 sq. mi.
(825,418 sq km)

POPULATION:
1,927,447

MONEY:
Namibian dollar, South African rand

LANGUAGES:
English (official), Afrikaans, German, Oshivambo, Herero, Nama

PEOPLE PER DOCTOR: 4,594

NIGER

CAPITAL: Niamey

AREA:
489,189 sq. mi.
(1,267,000 sq km)

POPULATION:
11,058,590

MONEY: CFAF*

LANGUAGES:
French (official), Hausa, Djerma

PEOPLE PER DOCTOR:
35,141

NIGERIA

CAPITAL: Abuja

AREA:
356,667 sq. mi.
(923,768 sq km)

POPULATION:
133,881,703

MONEY:
naira

LANGUAGES:
English (official), Hausa, Yoruba, Ibo, Fulani

PEOPLE PER DOCTOR: 4,496

RWANDA

CAPITAL:
Kigali

AREA:
10,169 sq. mi.
(26,338 sq km)

POPULATION:
7,810,056

MONEY:
Rwandan franc

LANGUAGES:
Kinyarwanda (official), French (official), English (official), Kiswahili

PEOPLE PER DOCTOR: 50,000

SÃO TOMÉ AND PRÍNCIPE

CAPITAL: São Tomé

AREA:
386 sq. mi. (1,001 sq km)

POPULATION:
175,883

MONEY:
dobra

LANGUAGES:
Portuguese (official)

PEOPLE PER DOCTOR: 3,125

SENEGAL

CAPITAL: Dakar

AREA:
75,749 sq. mi.
(196,190 sq km)

POPULATION: 10,580,307

MONEY: CFAF*

LANGUAGES:
French (official), Wolof, Pulaar, Diola, Mandinka

PEOPLE PER DOCTOR: 14,285

SEYCHELLES

CAPITAL:
Victoria

AREA:
176 sq. mi. (455 sq km)

POPULATION: 80,469

MONEY:
Seychelles rupee

LANGUAGES: English (official), French (official), Creole

PEOPLE PER DOCTOR: 906

SIERRA LEONE

CAPITAL: Freetown

AREA:
27,699 sq. mi. (71,740 sq km)

POPULATION: 5,732,681

MONEY: leone

LANGUAGES:
English (official), Mende, Temne, Krio

PEOPLE PER DOCTOR: 10,832

SOMALIA

CAPITAL:
Mogadishu

AREA:
246,199 sq. mi.
(637,657 sq km)

POPULATION:
8,025,190

MONEY:
Somali shilling

LANGUAGES:
Somali (official), Arabic, Italian, English

PEOPLE PER DOCTOR:
data not available

SOUTH AFRICA

CAPITALS: Pretoria, Cape Town, Bloemfontein

AREA:
471,008 sq. mi.
(1,219,912 sq km)

POPULATION: 42,768,678

MONEY: rand

LANGUAGES: 11 official languages, including Afrikaans, English, Ndebele, Pedi, Sotho, Swazi, Tsonga, Tswana, Venda, Xhosa, Zulu

PEOPLE PER DOCTOR: 1,742

*Communaute Financiere Africaine franc

Countries not drawn to scale.

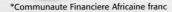

SUDAN

CAPITAL: Khartoum

AREA:
967,493 sq. mi.
(2,505,810 sq km)

POPULATION:
38,114,160

MONEY:
Sudanese dinar

LANGUAGES: Arabic (official),
Nubian, Ta Bedawie, English,
many ethnic languages

PEOPLE PER DOCTOR: 11,300

SWAZILAND

CAPITAL: Mbabane

AREA:
6,704 sq. mi. (17,363 sq km)

POPULATION:
1,161,219

MONEY: lilangeni

LANGUAGES:
English (official), siSwati

PEOPLE PER DOCTOR:
data not available

TANZANIA

CAPITALS:
Dar es Salaam and Dodoma

AREA:
364,898 sq. mi.
(945,087 sq km)

POPULATION:
35,922,454

MONEY:
Tanzanian shilling

LANGUAGES:
Kiswahili (official),
English (official), Arabic,
many ethnic languages

PEOPLE PER DOCTOR: 20,511

TOGO

CAPITAL: Lomé

AREA:
21,925 sq. mi.
(56,785 sq km)

POPULATION: 5,429,299

MONEY: CFAF*

LANGUAGES:
French (official), Ewe, Mina,
Kabye, Dagomba

PEOPLE PER DOCTOR: 16,667

TUNISIA

CAPITAL:
Tunis

AREA:
63,170 sq. mi.
(163,610 sq km)

POPULATION: 9,924,742

MONEY:
Tunisian dinar

LANGUAGES:
Arabic (official), French

PEOPLE PER DOCTOR:
1,640

UGANDA

CAPITAL:
Kampala

AREA:
91,135 sq. mi.
(236,040 sq km)

POPULATION:
25,632,794

MONEY:
Ugandan shilling

LANGUAGES:
English (official), Luganda,
Swahili, Arabic

PEOPLE PER DOCTOR:
25,000

ZAMBIA

CAPITAL:
Lusaka

AREA:
290,584 sq. mi.
(752,614 sq km)

POPULATION:
10,307,333

MONEY:
Zambian kwacha

LANGUAGES:
English (official), Bemba,
Kaonda, Lozi, Lunda, Luvale,
many ethnic languages

PEOPLE PER DOCTOR: 10,917

ZIMBABWE

CAPITAL:
Harare

AREA:
150,803 sq. mi.
(390,580 sq km)

POPULATION: 12,576,742

MONEY:
Zimbabwean dollar

LANGUAGES:
English (official), Shona,
Sindebele

PEOPLE PER DOCTOR: 6,909

internet connect

COUNTRY STATISTICS
GO TO: go.hrw.com
KEYWORD: SG5 FACTSU7
FOR: more facts about Africa

Sources: Central Intelligence Agency, *The World Factbook 2003; United Nations Development Programme: Health Profile;* pop. figures are 2003 estimates.

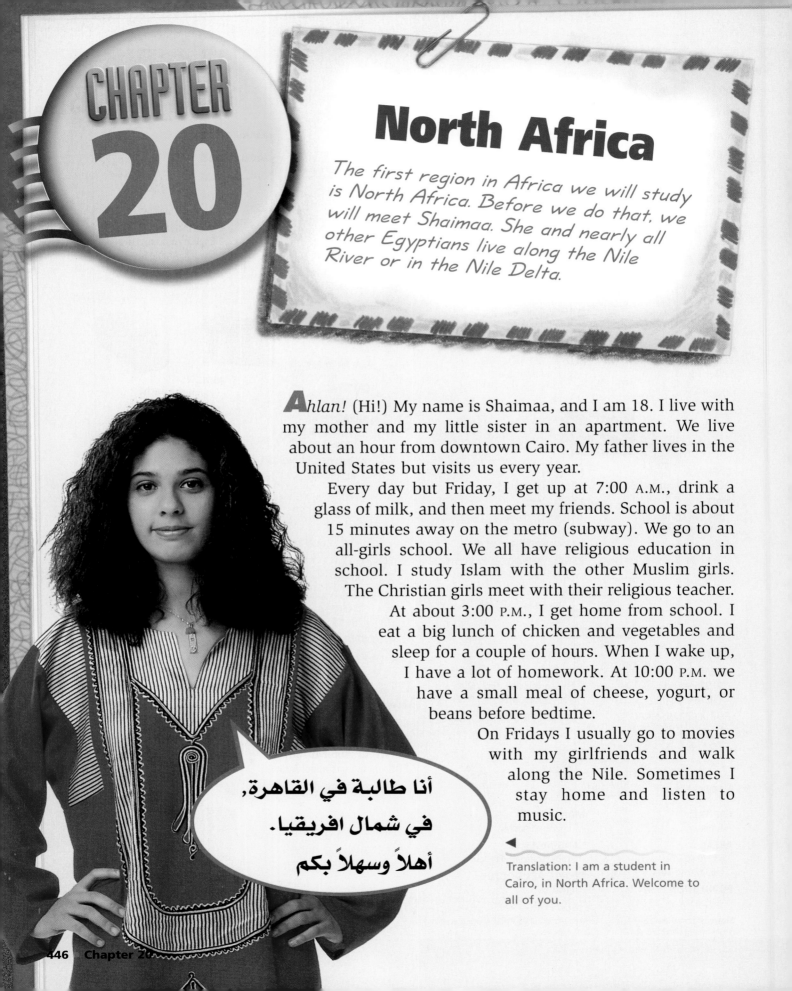

CHAPTER 20

North Africa

The first region in Africa we will study is North Africa. Before we do that, we will meet Shaimaa. She and nearly all other Egyptians live along the Nile River or in the Nile Delta.

Ahlan! (Hi!) My name is Shaimaa, and I am 18. I live with my mother and my little sister in an apartment. We live about an hour from downtown Cairo. My father lives in the United States but visits us every year.

Every day but Friday, I get up at 7:00 A.M., drink a glass of milk, and then meet my friends. School is about 15 minutes away on the metro (subway). We go to an all-girls school. We all have religious education in school. I study Islam with the other Muslim girls. The Christian girls meet with their religious teacher.

At about 3:00 P.M., I get home from school. I eat a big lunch of chicken and vegetables and sleep for a couple of hours. When I wake up, I have a lot of homework. At 10:00 P.M. we have a small meal of cheese, yogurt, or beans before bedtime.

On Fridays I usually go to movies with my girlfriends and walk along the Nile. Sometimes I stay home and listen to music.

أنا طالبة في القاهرة,
في شمال افريقيا.
أهلاً وسهلاً بكم

Translation: I am a student in Cairo, in North Africa. Welcome to all of you.

Section 1 Physical Geography

Read to Discover

1. What are the major physical features of North Africa?
2. What climates, plants, and wildlife are found in North Africa?
3. What are North Africa's major resources?

Vocabulary

ergs
regs
depressions
silt

Places

Red Sea
Mediterranean Sea
Sahara
Nile River
Sinai Peninsula
Ahaggar
  Mountains

Atlas Mountains
Qattara
  Depression
Nile Delta
Lake Nasser
Suez Canal

Reading Strategy

USING PRIOR KNOWLEDGE On a sheet of paper write the word Know on the left side. Write Learn on the right side. Look at the physical-political map of North Africa. What do you know about this region? Write your answers on the left side of the paper. As you read the section, write what you learn on the right side.

North Africa: Physical-Political

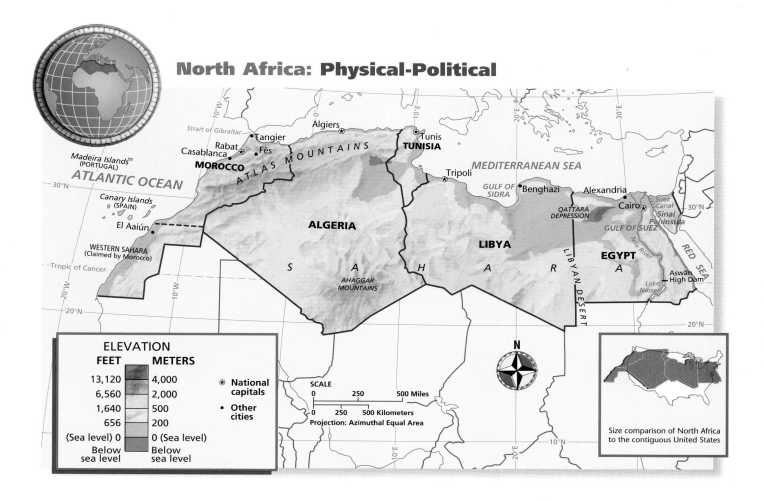

ELEVATION

FEET	METERS
13,120	4,000
6,560	2,000
1,640	500
656	200
(Sea level) 0	0 (Sea level)
Below sea level	Below sea level

⊛ National capitals
• Other cities

SCALE
0   250   500 Miles
0   250   500 Kilometers
Projection: Azimuthal Equal Area

Size comparison of North Africa to the contiguous United States

internet connect

GO TO: go.hrw.com
KEYWORD: SG5 CH20
FOR: Web sites about North Africa

Physical Features

North Africa includes Morocco, Algeria, Tunisia, Libya, and Egypt. The region stretches from the Atlantic Ocean to the Red Sea. Off the northern coast is the Mediterranean Sea. In the south is the Sahara (suh-HAR-uh), a vast desert. The region also has mountains, the northern Nile River valley, and the Sinai (SY-ny) Peninsula.

The Sahara The huge Sahara covers most of North Africa and stretches southward. The name *Sahara* comes from the Arabic word for "desert." The Sahara is the largest desert in the world. It is so big that nearly all of the United States would fit into it.

Large areas of this very dry region have few people or none at all. Great "seas" of sand dunes called **ergs** cover about a quarter of the desert. Much of the rest of the Sahara is made up of broad, windswept gravel plains. These gravel plains are called **regs**.

Mountains Do you think of deserts as flat regions? Well, the Sahara is not flat. Some sand dunes and ridges rise as high as 1,000 feet (305 m). The Sahara also has mountain ranges. For example, the Ahaggar (uh-HAH-guhr) Mountains are located in the central Sahara. Their highest peak is 9,842 feet (3,000 m). The Atlas Mountains on the northwestern side of the Sahara are higher. Mountains there rise to 13,671 feet (4,167 m).

There also are very low areas in the Sahara. These low areas are called **depressions**. The Qattara (kuh-TAHR-uh) Depression in western Egypt is 440 feet (134 m) below sea level. Other low areas often have large, dry lake beds. Water from rare rain storms collects there.

Oases like this one in Algeria are scattered throughout the vast Sahara.

Interpreting the Visual Record How do these trees survive in the desert's harsh, dry climate?

Water from the Nile River irrigates rich farmlands along the river and in its delta. You can clearly see the Nile Delta in the satellite photograph. The irrigated farmlands of the delta are shown in red.

Interpreting the Visual Record

(**Human-Environment Interaction**)

Why do you think most Egyptians live near the Nile River?

The Nile The world's longest river, the Nile, flows northward through the eastern Sahara. The Nile empties into the Mediterranean Sea. It is formed by the union of two rivers, the Blue Nile and the White Nile. They meet in Sudan, south of Egypt.

The Nile River valley is like a long oasis in the desert. Water from the Nile irrigates surrounding farmland. The Nile fans out near the Mediterranean Sea, forming a large river delta. About 99 percent of Egypt's population lives in the Nile River valley and the Nile Delta.

For centuries rain far to the south caused annual floods along the northern Nile that left rich **silt** in surrounding fields. Silt is finely ground soil good for growing crops. The Aswan High Dam, which was completed in 1971, was built to control flooding. Water trapped by the dam formed Lake Nasser in southern Egypt. However, the dam also traps silt, preventing it from being carried downriver. Today Egypt's farmers must use fertilizers to enrich the soil.

The Sinai and Suez Canal East of the Nile is the triangular Sinai Peninsula. Barren, rocky mountains and desert cover the Sinai. Between the Sinai and the rest of Egypt is the Suez Canal. The canal was built by the French in the 1860s. It is a strategic waterway that connects the Mediterranean Sea with the Red Sea.

✓ **READING CHECK:** (*Places and Regions*) What are the major physical features of North Africa?

Climate, Vegetation, and Animals

There are three main climates in North Africa. A desert climate covers most of the region. Temperatures range from mild to very hot. How hot can it get? Temperatures as high as 136°F (58°C) have been recorded in Libya! However, the humidity is very low. As a result, temperatures can drop quickly after sunset.

Our Amazing Planet

The Arabian camel has long been used for transportation in the Sahara. It can store water in the fat of its hump. Camels have survived for more than two weeks without drinking.

In some areas there has been no rain for many years. However, rare storms can cause flash floods. In places these floods as well as high winds have carved bare rock surfaces out of the land. Storms of sand and dust can also be severe.

Hardy plants and animals live in the desert. Grasses, small shrubs, and even trees grow where there is enough water. Usually this is in oases. Gazelles, hyenas, baboons, foxes, and weasels are among the region's mammals.

Much of the northern coast west of Egypt has a Mediterranean climate. Winters there are mild and moist. Summers are hot and dry. Plant life includes grasses, shrubs, and even a few forests in the Atlas Mountains. Areas between the Mediterranean climate and the Sahara have a steppe climate. Shrubs and grasses grow there.

✓ **READING CHECK:** (*Physical Systems*) How does climate affect the plants and wildlife of North Africa?

Olives like these in Morocco are an important agricultural product in North Africa. Olives and olive oil are common ingredients in many foods around the Mediterranean.

▼

Resources

Good soils and rain or river water aid farming in coastal areas and the Nile River valley. Common crops are wheat, barley, olives, grapes, citrus fruits, and cotton. The region also has good fishing waters.

Oil and gas are important resources, particularly for Libya, Algeria, and Egypt. Morocco mines iron ore and minerals used to make fertilizers. The Sahara has minerals such as copper, gold, and silver.

✓ **READING CHECK:** (*Physical Systems*) What are North Africa's major resources?

go.
hrw.
.com

Homework Practice Online

Keyword: SG5 HP20

Section Review 1

Define and explain: ergs, regs, depressions, silt

Working with Sketch Maps On a map of North Africa that you draw or that your teacher provides, label the following: Red Sea, Mediterranean Sea, Sahara, Nile River, Sinai Peninsula, Ahaggar Mountains, Atlas Mountains, Qattara Depression, Nile Delta, Lake Nasser, and the Suez Canal. In a box in the margin, identify the dam that created Lake Nasser.

Reading for the Main Idea

1. (*Places and Regions*) What two mountain ranges are found in North Africa?

2. (*Places and Regions*) What part of Egypt is east of the Suez Canal?

3. (*Environment and Society*) How did the Nile affect farming in the river valley?

Critical Thinking

4. **Drawing Inferences and Conclusions** Where would you expect to find most of North Africa's major cities?

Organizing What You Know

5. **Summarizing** Use this graphic organizer to describe the physical features of North Africa.

Climates	Plants and Animals	Resources

Section 2 History and Culture

Read to Discover

1. What are the major events in the history of North Africa?
2. What are some important facts about the people and culture of North Africa?

Vocabulary

pharaohs
hieroglyphs
Bedouins

Places

Alexandria
Cairo
Fès
Western Sahara

People

Alexander the Great
Naguib Mahfouz

Reading Strategy

FOLDNOTES: TWO-PANEL FLIP CHART Create the FoldNote titled **Two-Panel Flip Chart** described in the Appendix. Label one flap History and the other flap Culture. As you read the section, write what you learn about each topic beneath its flap.

History

The Nile River valley was home to some of the world's oldest civilizations. Sometime after 3200 B.C. lands along the northern Nile were united into one Egyptian kingdom.

The early Egyptians used water from the Nile to grow wheat, barley, and other crops. They also built great stone pyramids and other monuments. Egyptian **pharaohs**, or kings, were buried in the pyramids. How did the Egyptians build these huge monuments? See Connecting to Technology on the next page.

The Egyptians also traded with people from other places. To identify themselves and their goods, the Egyptians used **hieroglyphs** (HY-ruh-glifs). Hieroglyphs are pictures and symbols that stand for ideas or words. They were the basis for Egypt's first writing system.

West of Egypt were people who spoke what are called Berber languages. These people herded sheep and other livestock. They also grew wheat and barley in the Atlas Mountains and along the coast.

Invaders Because of North Africa's long coastline, the region was open to invaders over the centuries. Those invaders included people from the eastern Mediterranean, Greeks, and Romans. For example, one invader was the Macedonian king Alexander the Great. He founded the city of Alexandria in Egypt in 332 B.C. This city became an important seaport and trading center on the Mediterranean coast.

Beginning in the A.D. 600s, Arab armies from Southwest Asia swept across North Africa. They brought the Arabic language and Islam to the

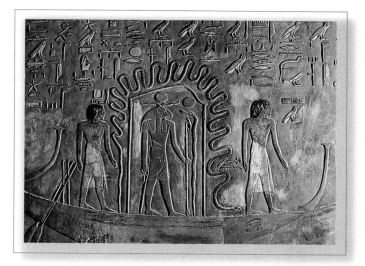

▲
The tombs of early Egyptian pharoahs were decorated with paintings, crafts, and treasures. You can see hieroglyphs across the top of this wall painting.

CONNECTING TO *Technology*

The monuments of ancient Egypt are among the wonders of the world. They are thousands of years old. These pyramids, temples, and other structures reflect the power of Egyptian rulers and the skills of Egyptian engineers.

The most famous of Egypt's monuments are the huge stone pyramids at Giza near Cairo. The pyramids there were built more than 4,000 years ago as tombs for Egyptian pharaohs. The largest structure is the Great Pyramid. At its base the pyramid's sides are each about 755 feet (230 m) long. The pyramid rises nearly 500 feet (152 m) above the desert floor.

How did the Egyptians build the pyramids? Workers cut large blocks of stone far away and rolled them on logs to the Nile. From there the blocks were moved on barges. At the building site, the Egyptians finished carving the blocks. Then they built dirt and brick ramps alongside the pyramids. They hauled the blocks up the ramps.

The average weight of each of the 2.3 million blocks in the Great Pyramid is 2.5 tons (2.25 metric tons). Building the Great Pyramid probably required from 10,000 to 30,000 workers. They finished the job in about 20 years, but the pyramid still stands thousands of years later.

BUILDING THE PYRAMIDS

Understanding What You Read

1. What kinds of monuments did the Egyptians build?
2. How did the Egyptians make up for not having wheeled vehicles?

region. Today most North Africans are Muslim and speak Arabic. Under Muslim rule, North African cities became major centers of learning, trade, and craft making. These cities included Cairo in Egypt and Fès in Morocco.

European Control In the 1800s European countries began to take over the region. By 1912 they controlled all of North Africa. In that year Italy captured Libya from the Ottoman Empire. Spain already controlled northern Morocco. France ruled the rest of Morocco as well as Tunisia and Algeria. Egypt was under British control.

Egypt gained limited independence in 1922. The British kept military bases there and maintained control of the Suez Canal until 1956. During World War II the region was a major battleground. After the war, North Africans pushed for independence. Libya, Morocco, and Tunisia each won independence in the 1950s.

Algeria was the last North African country to win independence. Many French citizens had moved to the country. They considered Algeria part of France. Algeria finally won independence in 1962, after a long, bitter war. Most French residents of Algeria then moved to France.

Modern North Africa Since independence, the countries of North Africa have tried to build stronger ties with other Arab countries. For example, Egypt led other Arab countries in several wars against Israel. However, in 1979 Egypt signed a peace treaty with Israel.

In 1976 Morocco took over the former Spanish colony of Western Sahara. Western Saharan rebels have been trying to win independence from Morocco since then.

✓ **READING CHECK:** *Places and Regions* What were some major events in the history of North Africa?

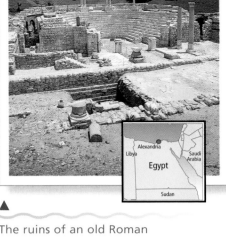

▲
The ruins of an old Roman amphitheater remain in Alexandria, Egypt.

The inset photograph shows the beautiful doors of the royal palace in Fès, Morocco.

▼

453

The floor of the beautiful Muhammad Ali mosque in Cairo is covered with carpet. Muslim men kneel and bow with their faces to the ground to pray.

Culture

As you have read, the histories of the North African countries have much in common. You will also find many cultural similarities among those countries.

Language and Religion Egyptians, Berbers, and **Bedouins** make up nearly all of Egypt's population. Bedouins are nomadic herders who travel throughout deserts of Egypt and Southwest Asia. Most people in the countries to the west are of mixed Arab and Berber ancestry. Arabic is the major language. Some people speak Berber languages.

Most ethnic Europeans left North Africa after the region's countries became independent. However, French, Italian, and English still are spoken in many areas.

Most North Africans are Muslims. Of the region's countries, Egypt has the largest number of non-Muslims. About 6 percent of Egyptians are Christians or practice other religions.

Food and Festivals What kind of food would you eat on a trip to North Africa? Grains, vegetables, fruits, and nuts are common there. Many meals include couscous (KOOS-koos). Couscous is made from wheat and looks like small pellets of pasta. It is steamed over boiling water or soup. Often it is served with vegetables or meat, butter, and olive oil. Some people mix their couscous with a fiery hot sauce called *harissa*.

A popular dish in Egypt is *fuul*. It is made from fava beans mashed with olive oil, salt, pepper, garlic, and lemons. The combination is then served with hard-boiled eggs and bread.

Important holidays in North Africa include the birthday of the prophet of Islam, Muhammad. The birthday is marked

A variety of vegetables and meat surround a large serving of couscous.

Interpreting the Visual Record What does this food tell you about agricultural products of the region?

with lights, parades, and special sweets of honey, nuts, and sugar. During the holy month of Ramadan, Muslims abstain from food and drink during the day.

Art and Literature North Africa has long been known for its beautiful architecture, wood carving, and other crafts. Women weave a variety of textiles. Among these are beautiful carpets that feature geometric designs and bright colors.

The region has also produced important writers and artists. For example, Egyptian poetry and other writing date back thousands of years. One of Egypt's most famous writers is Naguib Mahfouz. In 1988 he became the first Arab writer to win the Nobel Prize in literature. Egypt also has a growing movie industry. Egyptian films in Arabic have become popular throughout Southwest Asia and North Africa.

Many North Africans also enjoy popular music based on singing and poetry. The musical scale there has many more notes than are common in Western music. As a result, North African tunes seem to wail or waver. Musicians often use instruments such as the three-stringed *sintir* of Morocco.

▲ This Algerian woman and her daughter are using a loom to weave a rug. The loom allows a rug maker to weave horizontal and vertical threads together.

✓ **READING CHECK:** (*Human Systems*) What are some important facts about the people and culture of North Africa?

Define or identify: pharaohs, hieroglyphs, Alexander the Great, Bedouins, Naguib Mahfouz

Working with Sketch Maps On the map you drew in Section 1, label Alexandria, Cairo, Fès, and Western Sahara. In a box in the margin, identify the country that claims Western Sahara.

Reading for the Main Idea

1. (*Places and Regions*) What early civilization thrived along the northern Nile River about 3200 B.C.?

2. (*Human Systems*) How did Islam and the Arabic language come to North Africa?

3. (*Human Systems*) Which European countries controlled countries in North Africa by 1912?

Critical Thinking

4. Drawing Inferences and Conclusions Look at the world map in the textbook's Atlas. Why do you think the Suez Canal is an important waterway for world shipping?

Organizing What You Know

5. Summarizing Copy the following graphic organizer. Use it to identify at least six important facts about the languages, religions, food, festivals, art, and literature of North Africa.

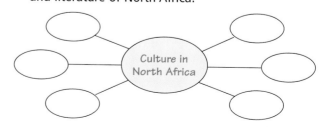

Culture in North Africa

North Africa • 455

COULD YOU SURVIVE THE SAHARA?

ONLINE EXPEDITIONS
GO TO: go.hrw.com
KEYWORD: SG5 CH20

A Land of Sun and Sand

Despite scorching heat, blinding sandstorms, scorpions, poisonous snakes, and death by starvation or thirst, people have traveled across the desert sands of the Sahara for centuries. Groups of merchants, or caravans, still travel together in the desert for protection. These merchants trade mostly in salt, or "white gold." However, water is the most important resource needed to survive the Sahara. Travelers must find a source of water every few days, or they will perish in temperatures of more than 130 degrees!

SURVIVAL CHALLENGE

You are an archaeologist working at a dig near Lake Chad. You want to find the ruins of Garama, the main city of an ancient warrior people known as the Garamantes. The city's location, in southern Libya, is not on your map. You do have a list of riddles that guided traders north during the height of the Garamantian Empire. Each riddle will lead you to the next source of water. A caravan is leaving soon for Tripoli, so jump on a camel and set out on your adventure! Remember—to survive today's environment, you'll have to solve riddles about the ancient environment. How may looking at the region's geography today shed light on its past?

Throughout the Sahara, traders travel great distances in camel caravans like this one.

Land of Change

The Sahara was not always a desert. About 8000 B.C. the region was a grassland. Stone age peoples who lived in this environment fished in large lakes and hunted giraffes, elephants, and zebras. Early peoples engraved pictures of these animals on rock walls.

By about 500 B.C. the Garamantes were powerful in the Sahara. Even though the Sahara was by this time much drier, the Garamantes grew crops. By digging miles of irrigation canals, the Garamantes tapped into billions of gallons of fossil water. From what you have learned about the importance of water in the desert, what may have caused the Garamantian civilization to decline? How do you think peoples today survive in dry environments? Can you predict what might happen to them in the future?

The Way to Garama

You are on the right path if you see the long necks who once grazed on green land not sand.

Cross the flowing waters three times but wait to drink at the well.

This lake will not quench your thirst. Gather some white gold from its edges.

Rest well in the shade of many trees. You do not have far to go.

Miles of fertile crops point you to a rich and powerful people.

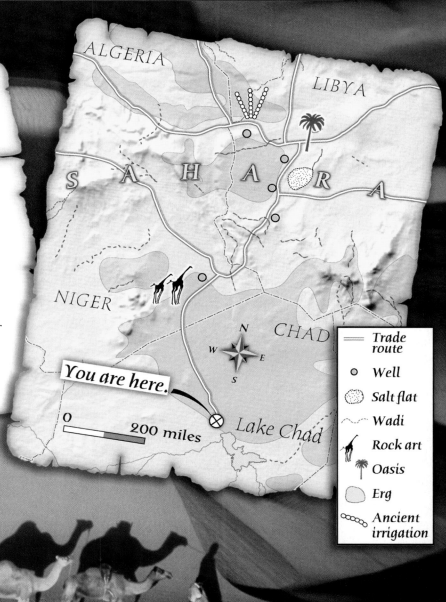

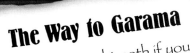
You are here.

Trade route
Well
Salt flat
Wadi
Rock art
Oasis
Erg
Ancient irrigation

Egypt Today

Read to Discover

1. What are the people and cities of Egypt like today?
2. What are Egypt's important economic activities?
3. What challenges does Egypt face today?

Vocabulary

fellahin

Places

Egypt
Cairo
Alexandria

People

Anwar Sadat

Reading Strategy

FOLDNOTES: LAYERED BOOK Create the FoldNote titled **Layered Book** described in the Appendix. Write Egypt Today on the top tab. Label the other tabs People and Cities, Economy, and Challenges. As you read this section, write what you learn about each topic above each label.

People and Cities

Egypt is North Africa's most populous country. More than 74 million people live there.

Rural Egypt More than half of all Egyptians live in small villages and other rural areas. Most rural Egyptians are farmers called **fellahin** (fel-uh-HEEN). They own very small plots of land. Most fellahin also work large farms owned by powerful families. Many also depend on money sent home by family members working abroad. Many Egyptians work in Europe or oil-rich countries in Southwest Asia.

Cities Egypt's capital and largest city is Cairo. More than 10 million people live there. Millions more live in surrounding cities.

Place A muezzin (moo-E-zuhn) calls Muslims to prayer in Cairo. A muezzin often makes his calls from the door or the minaret, or tower, of a mosque. His calls—or recordings played through speakers—can be heard throughout Islamic communities five times daily.

Place Tourist ships sit on the Nile River in Luxor. Tourists visit the ruins of a beautiful temple built there more than 2,300 years ago. These and other historical sites make tourism an important part of Egypt's economy.

Cairo was founded more than 1,000 years ago along the Nile. Its location at the southern end of the delta helped it grow. The city lies along old trading routes between Asia and Europe. Later it was connected by railroad to Mediterranean ports and the Suez Canal.

Today Cairo is a mixture of modern buildings and small, mud-brick houses. People continue to move there from rural areas. Many live in makeshift housing. Traffic and pollution are serious problems.

Alexandria has more than 4 million people. It is located in the Nile Delta along the Mediterranean coast. The city is a major seaport and home to many industries.

✓ **READING CHECK:** (*Places and Regions*) What are Egypt's people and cities like today?

Our Amazing Planet

Fish is an important food for people living along the Nile. One fish, the giant Nile perch, can grow to a weight of 300 pounds (136 kg).

Economy

To provide for its growing population, Egypt is working to expand its industries. Textiles, tourism, and oil are three of the most important industries. The Suez Canal is another source of income. Ships pay tolls to pass through it. Ships use the canal to avoid long trips around southern Africa. This makes the canal one of the world's busiest waterways.

About 30 percent of Egyptian workers are farmers. A warm, sunny climate and water for irrigation make the Nile Delta ideal for growing cotton. Farmlands along the Nile River are used for growing vegetables, grain, and fruit.

✓ **READING CHECK:** (*Places and Regions*) How does the Suez Canal affect Egypt's economy?

Egypt

Country	Population/ Growth Rate	Life Expectancy	Literacy Rate	Per Capita GDP
Egypt	74,718,797 1.9%	68, male 73, female	58%	$3,900
United States	290,342,554 0.9%	74, male 80, female	97%	$37,600

Source: Central Intelligence Agency, *The World Factbook 2003*

Interpreting the Chart **How does the growth rate of Egypt compare to that of the United States?**

BIOGRAPHY

Anwar Sadat
(1918–1981)

Character Trait: Cooperation

As Egypt's president for 11 years, Anwar Sadat was best known for negotiating peace between Egypt and Israel. During his historic visit to Israel in 1977, Sadat acknowledged Israel's existence and called for the return of Palestinian land. In 1978, Sadat received the Nobel Peace Prize along with Israel's Prime Minister Menachem Begin for both of their efforts in achieving peace. Three years later, however, an extremist group who opposed peace with Israel assassinated Sadat.

How did President Sadat cooperate with Israel?

Challenges

Egypt faces important challenges today. For example, the country's farmland is limited to the Nile River valley and delta. To keep the land productive, farmers must use more and more fertilizer. This can be expensive. In addition, overwatering has been a problem. It has brought to the surface salts that are harmful to crops. These problems and a rapidly growing population have forced Egypt to import much of its food.

In addition, Egyptians are divided over their country's role in the world. Many want their country to remain a leader among Arab countries. However, others want their government to focus more on improving life for Egyptians at home.

Many Egyptians live in severe poverty. Many do not have clean water for cooking or washing. The spread of disease in crowded cities is also a problem. In addition, about half of Egyptians cannot read and write. Still, Egypt's government has made progress. Today Egyptians live longer and are much healthier than 50 years ago.

Another challenge facing Egyptians is the debate over the role of Islam in the country. Some Muslims want to shape the country's government and society along Islamic principles. However, some Egyptians worry that such a change would mean fewer personal freedoms. Some supporters of an Islamic government have turned to violence to advance their cause. Attacks on tourists in the 1990s were particularly worrisome. A loss of tourism would hurt Egypt's economy.

✓ **READING CHECK:** (*Places and Regions*) What are some of the challenges Egypt faces today?

Section Review 3

Define or identify: fellahin, Anwar Sadat

Working with Sketch Maps On the map you drew in Section 2, label Egypt, Cairo, and Alexandria. Identify the capital of Egypt.

Reading for the Main Idea

1. (*Human Systems*) What is the relationship between religion and culture in Egypt today?

2. (*Places and Regions*) What industries and crops are important to Egypt's economy?

go.hrw.com **Homework Practice Online** Keyword: SG5 HP20

Critical Thinking

3. **Analyzing Information** Why do so many Egyptians live along the Nile and in the Nile Delta?

4. **Finding the Main Idea** How has Cairo's location shaped its development?

Organizing What You Know

5. **Summarizing** Copy the following graphic organizer. Use it to describe some of the challenges facing Egypt today.

Challenges

Read to Discover

1. What are the region's people and cities like today?
2. What are the countries' important economic activities?
3. What challenges do the countries face today?

Reading Strategy

READING ORGANIZER Create a five-column chart on a sheet of paper. Label the columns Country, People, Cities, Economy, and Challenges. In the Country column, write Libya, Tunisia, Algeria, and Morocco, skipping several lines between them. As you read the section, write what you learn about each country in the appropriate column.

Vocabulary

Casbah
souks
free port
dictator

Places

Libya
Tunisia
Algeria
Morocco
Tripoli
Benghazi
Algiers
Casablanca
Rabat
Tunis
Strait of Gibraltar

People

Mu 'ammar al-Gadhafi

People and Cities

Western Libya, Tunisia, Algeria, and Morocco are often called the Maghreb (MUH-gruhb). This Arabic word means "west" or "the direction of the setting sun." Most of the Maghreb is covered by the Sahara. There you will find sandy plains and rocky uplands. Cities and farmland are located in narrow coastal strips of land. These strips lie between the Atlantic and Mediterranean coasts in the north and the Sahara and Atlas Mountains farther inland.

Libya is almost completely desert. Fertile land is limited to small areas along the coast. Cities and most of the population are found in those coastal areas. Libya is the most urbanized country in the region. More than 85 percent of Libya's more than 5 million people live in cities. The largest cities are Benghazi and the capital, Tripoli.

Algiers is a large city and is Algeria's capital. The central part of Algiers is a maze of winding alleys and tall walls. This old district is called the **Casbah**. The Casbah is basically an old fortress. **Souks**, or marketplaces, are found there today. The centers of other North African cities also have Casbahs.

Other large cities include Casablanca and Rabat in Morocco and Tunis in Tunisia. Another Moroccan city, Tangier, overlooks the Strait of Gibraltar. This beautiful city was once a Spanish territory. Today tourists can take a quick ferry ride from Spain across the strait to Tangier, a **free port**. A free port is a city in which almost no taxes are placed on goods sold there.

✔ **READING CHECK:** *Places and Regions* What geographic factors explain the region's population patterns?

▲ With a backdrop of brightly colored mosaics, Moroccan boys enjoy a day in Tangier's Casbah.

Libya, Tunisia, Algeria, and Morocco

COUNTRY	POPULATION/ GROWTH RATE	LIFE EXPECTANCY	LITERACY RATE	PER CAPITA GDP
Algeria	32,818,500 1.65%	69, male 72, female	70%	$5,300
Libya	5,499,074 2.4%	74, male 78, female	83%	$7,600
Morocco	31,689,265 1.6%	68, male 72, female	52%	$3,900
Tunisia	9,924,742 1.7%	74, male 76, female	74%	$6,500
United States	290,342,554 0.9%	74, male 80, female	97%	$37,600

Source: Central Intelligence Agency, *The World Factbook 2003*

Interpreting the Chart **Which country is the least economically developed?**

Place Marrakech (muh-RAH-kish) is a popular tourist resort in central Morocco. It sits in the foothills of the Atlas Mountains.

▼

Economy

Oil, mining, and tourism are important industries in these countries. Oil is the most important resource, particularly in Libya and Algeria. Money from oil pays for schools, health care, other social programs, and military equipment. The region's countries also have large deposits of natural gas, iron ore, and lead.

Morocco is the only North African country with little oil. However, the country is an important producer and exporter of fertilizer.

About 20 percent of the workers in Libya, Tunisia, and Algeria are farmers. In Morocco farmers make up about half of the labor force. North Africa's farmers grow and export wheat, other grains, olives, fruits, and nuts. However, the region's desert climate and poor soils limit farming, particularly in Libya. Libya imports most of its food.

The Maghreb countries have close economic relationships with European countries. This is partly because of old colonial ties between North Africa and Europe. In addition, European countries are located nearby, lying just across the Mediterranean Sea. Formal agreements between North African countries and the European Union (EU) also have helped trade. Today about 80 percent of Tunisia's trade is with EU countries. The largest trade partners of Algeria, Libya, and Morocco are also EU members. Many European tourists visit North Africa.

✓ **READING CHECK:** *Places and Regions* How does the oil industry affect Libya's and Algeria's schools, health care, and other social programs?

Challenges

The countries of the Maghreb have made much progress in health and education. However, important challenges remain. Among these challenges is the need for more economic freedom. Each of these countries has had elements of a command economy, in which government owns and operates industry. However, in recent years the region's governments have moved to loosen that control. They have sold some government-owned businesses. They have also taken other steps to help private industry grow.

Political freedoms are limited for many North Africans. Many have little say in their governments. For example, since 1969 Libya has been ruled by a **dictator**, Mu'ammar al-Gadhafi. A dictator is someone who rules a country with complete power. Gadhafi has supported bombing, kidnapping, and other acts of violence against Israel and Israel's supporters. As a result, countries have limited their economic relationships with Libya.

As in Egypt, another challenge is conflict over the role of Islam in society. For example, in Algeria some groups want a government based on Islamic principles and laws. In 1992 the government canceled elections that many believed would be won by Islamic groups. Violence between Algeria's government and some Islamic groups has claimed thousands of lives since then.

These Islamic students at a religious school in Libya are reciting verses from the Qur'an. Religious education is important in this mostly Islamic region.

READING CHECK: *Places and Regions* What are some of the challenges the region's countries face today?

Section Review 4

Define or identify: Casbah, souks, free port, dictator, Mu'ammar al-Gadhafi

Working with Sketch Maps On the map you created in Section 3, label Libya, Tunisia, Algeria, Morocco, Tripoli, Benghazi, Algiers, Casablanca, Rabat, Tunis, and the Strait of Gibraltar. In a box in the margin, identify the national capitals of the region's countries.

Reading for the Main Idea

1. *Places and Regions* What are the old, central districts of many North African cities like?

2. *Places and Regions* What type of economy have these nations had, and how is this changing?

Critical Thinking

3. **Finding the Main Idea** Where are the region's farms and most of its people found today? Why?

4. **Analyzing Information** How are the political rights of North Africans different from those of people in the United States?

Organizing What You Know

5. **Summarizing** Copy the following graphic organizer. Use it to list industries, resources, farm products, and trade partners of the Maghreb countries.

Industries	
Resources	
Farm products	
Trade partners	

Review and Practice

Define and Identify

Identify each of the following:

1. ergs
2. regs
3. depressions
4. silt
5. pharaohs
6. hieroglyphs
7. Alexander the Great
8. Naguib Mahfouz
9. Bedouins
10. fellahin
11. Anwar Sadat
12. Casbah
13. souks
14. free port
15. dictator
16. Mu'ammar al-Gadhafi

Review the Main Ideas

17. How does geography affect settlement patterns in North Africa?
18. What are North Africa's main climates?
19. Why did many French citizens move to Algeria before 1962?
20. What are some important holidays in North Africa?
21. Which Egyptian city lies along old trading routes and was founded more than 1,000 years ago?
22. What are some important challenges facing Egypt today?

23. What are the most important industries in North Africa?
24. Which is the most urbanized country in North Africa?
25. Why do the Maghreb countries have close economic relationships with European countries?

Think Critically

26. **Finding the Main Idea** How do you think the Sahara has influenced settlement in the region?
27. **Finding the Main Idea** Why are most of North Africa's cities and population located in coastal areas?
28. **Analyzing Information** Why is the Suez Canal important to world trade?
29. **Finding the Main Idea** In what way has Islam influenced politics in North Africa?
30. **Making Generalizations and Predictions** Based on what you have read, what kinds of challenges do you think North Africans will face in coming decades? Explain your answer.

Map Activity

31. On a separate sheet of paper, match the letters on the map with their correct labels.

   Sinai Peninsula
   Ahaggar Mountains
   Atlas Mountains
   Nile Delta
   Cairo
   Western Sahara
   Tripoli
   Algiers
   Casablanca
   Strait of Gibraltar

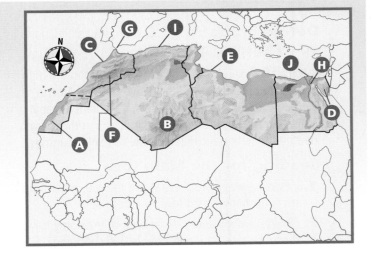

Writing Activity

Imagine that you are a Bedouin teenager in the Sahara. Write a one-paragraph journal entry about a typical day in your life. How do you cope with the desert heat? What is it like living without a permanent home? What religion do you practice? What do you eat? Use the library and other resources to help you. Be sure to use standard grammar, spelling, sentence structure, and punctuation.

⊡ internet connect

Internet Activity: **go.hrw.com**
KEYWORD: SG5 GT20

Choose a topic to explore about North Africa:
- Journey through the Sahara.
- Examine the rich history of North Africa.
- Practice using Arabic calligraphy.

Social Studies Skills Practice

Analyzing Graphs

Arable land is land that is suitable for farming. Study the following chart of the percentages of arable land in North Africa. Then answer the questions.

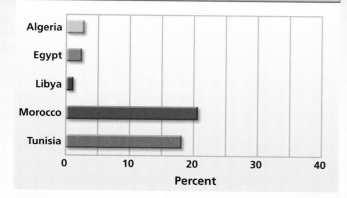

Arable Land in North Africa

1. Which country has the least land suitable for growing crops?
2. Which country has the most land suitable for growing crops?
3. Overall, do the countries of North Africa have good land for farming? Explain your answer.
4. What can you determine about the region's climate and soils from these numbers?

Analyzing Primary Sources

Read the following excerpt from Egyptian writer Naguib Mahfouz's acceptance speech after he was awarded the Nobel Prize for Literature. Then answer the questions.

"This man coming from the third world, how did he find the peace of mind to write stories? You are perfectly right. I come from a world labouring under the burden of debts whose paying back exposes it to starvation or very close to it. . . . Fortunately, art is generous and sympathetic. In the same way that it dwells with the happy ones it does not desert the wretched [unhappy]. It offers both alike the convenient means for expressing what swells up in their [heart]."

1. According to Mahfouz, what purpose does writing serve?
2. Does Mahfouz feel that everyone can become writers? Why?
3. What does Mahfouz mean when he says he comes from the third world?
4. According to Mahfouz, how are third-world countries burdened?

West Africa

We move south now to West Africa. The land becomes much wetter as we move southward. Before we continue, we meet Ousseina from Niger.

*I*na kwanna! (Good morning!) My name is Ousseina, and I am 11. I have an identical twin sister whose name is Hassana. I live in Niamey, the capital of Niger, with my sister, our grandmother, our parents, and many aunts and uncles. We have a large compound of many one- or two-room houses around a common courtyard. After breakfast, my sister and I go from door to door, greeting all the elders in our compound.

We have to walk many miles to school, but we meet all our friends along the way. Some of our friends speak Hausa like us. Others speak a different language of Niger. In the afternoon, we go home to sleep because it is so hot—more than 110°F (43°C)! Late in the afternoon we return to school for more classes.

After school, we help grandma pound spices for dinner, sweep the room, and wash the dishes. At bedtime, grandma tells us stories and sings.

**Ni Ousseina ce.
Gidana yana Nijar.**

▲
Translation: I am Ousseina.
My home is in Niger.

Section 1 Physical Geography

Read to Discover

1. What landforms and climates are found in West Africa?
2. Why is the Niger River important to the region?
3. What resources does West Africa have?

Vocabulary

zonal
Sahel
harmattan
tsetse fly
bauxite

Places

Sahara
Sahel
Niger River
Gulf of Guinea

Reading Strategy

READING ORGANIZER Create a spider map by drawing a circle on a sheet of paper. Label the circle West Africa. Create legs for Landforms, Climate, Niger River, and Resources. As you read the section, write what you learn beneath each leg.

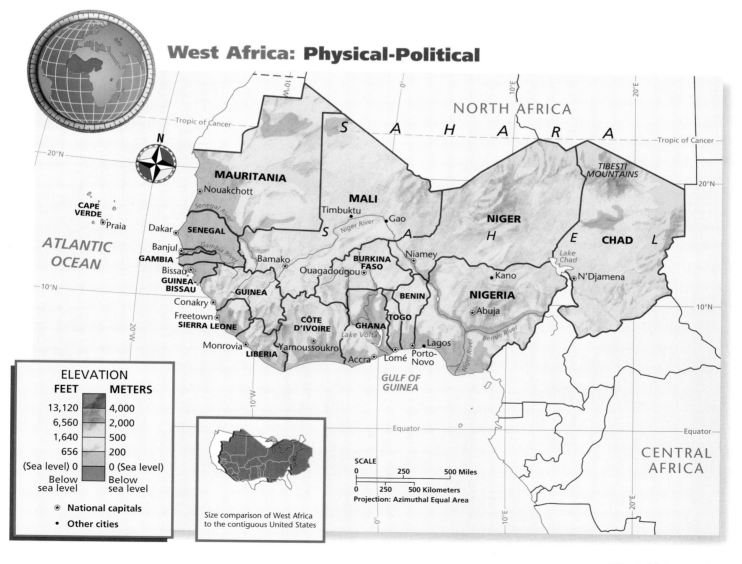

West Africa: Physical-Political

Landforms and Climate

West Africa is largely a region of plains. There are low mountains in the southwest and high mountains in the northeast. Four major climate types stretch from east to west in bands or zones. Therefore, geographers say the region's climates are **zonal**.

The Sahara The northernmost parts of the region lie within the Sahara, the first climate zone. The Sahara is the world's largest desert. It stretches across northern Africa from the Atlantic Ocean to the Red Sea. Large areas of this dry climate zone have few or no people.

The Sahel South of the Sahara is a region of dry grasslands called the **Sahel** (sah-HEL). This second climate zone has a steppe climate. Rainfall varies greatly from year to year. In some years it never rains. During winter a dry, dusty wind called the **harmattan** (hahr-muh-TAN) blows south from the Sahara.

During the late 1960s a drought began in the Sahel. Crops failed for several years, and there was not enough grass for the herds. Animals overgrazed the land, and people cut the few large trees for firewood. Wind blew away fertile soil, and the Sahara expanded southward. Without plants for food, many animals and people died. Recent years have been rainier, and life has improved.

The Savanna Farther south is the savanna zone. It contains good soil, thick grass, and scattered tall trees. Farmers can do well when the rains come regularly. However, the region is home to a dangerous insect. The **tsetse** (TSET-see) **fly** carries sleeping sickness, a deadly disease. Although insecticides can help control the flies, they are too expensive for most people to buy.

The Coast and Forest The fourth climate zone lies along the Atlantic and Gulf of Guinea coasts. Many of West Africa's largest cities lie in this coastal zone. You will find a wet, humid tropical climate there. Plentiful rain supports tropical rain forests. However, many trees

Farmers use river water to irrigate onion fields in central Mali. Farming can be difficult in the dry Sahel.

Interpreting the Visual Record

Human-Environment Interaction **How do you think economic factors have affected the use of technology in bringing water to the fields?**

have been cut to make room for growing populations. As a result, environmental damage is a serious problem.

✓ **READING CHECK:** (*Places and Regions*) What are the region's landforms and climate zones?

The Niger River

The most important river in West Africa is the Niger (NY-juhr). The Niger River starts in low mountains just 150 miles (241 km) from the Atlantic Ocean. It flows eastward and southward for 2,600 miles (4,183 km) and empties into the Gulf of Guinea.

The Niger brings life-giving water to West Africa. In the Sahel it divides into a network of channels, swamps, and lakes. This network is known as the inland delta. The Niger's true delta on the Gulf of Guinea is very wide. Half of Nigeria's coastline consists of the delta.

✓ **READING CHECK:** (*Environment and Society*) Why is the Niger River important to West Africa?

▲

The hippopotamus is just one of the many animal species living in the Niger region. Hippopotamuses are good swimmers and can stay underwater for as long as six minutes.

Resources

West Africa's mineral riches include diamonds, gold, iron ore, manganese, and **bauxite**. Bauxite is the main source of aluminum. Nigeria is a major exporter of oil. In fact, oil and related products make up about 95 percent of that country's exports.

✓ **READING CHECK:** (*Places and Regions*) What are some of the region's resources?

go.hrw.com
Homework Practice Online
Keyword: SG5 HP21

Section Review 1

Define and explain: zonal, Sahel, harmattan, tsetse fly, bauxite

Working with Sketch Maps On a map of West Africa, label the following: Sahara, Niger River, and Gulf of Guinea.

Reading for the Main Idea

1. (*Physical Systems*) What effect has drought had on West Africa's vegetation?

2. (*Places and Regions*) What natural resources are found in West Africa?

3. (*Places and Regions*) What is West Africa's most important river? Describe its two delta regions.

Critical Thinking

4. **Making Generalizations and Predictions** Where in the region would you expect to find the densest populations? Why?

Organizing What You Know

5. **Summarizing** Copy the following graphic organizer. Use it to list and describe the region's climate zones.

Zones	Characteristics

Read to Discover

1. What great African kingdoms once ruled the region?
2. How did contact with Europeans affect West Africa?
3. What challenges do the region's governments face?
4. What are some features of West African culture?

Vocabulary
archaeology
oral history
animism

Places
Timbuktu

People
Mansa Musa

Reading Strategy

READING ORGANIZER Before you read, draw eight boxes down the center of a sheet of paper. As you read this section, write what you learn in the boxes to create a chain of events in the history of West Africa.

West Africa's History

Much of what we know about West Africa's early history is based on **archaeology**. Archaeology is the study of the remains and ruins of past cultures. **Oral history**—spoken information passed down from person to person through generations—offers other clues.

Great Kingdoms Ancient artifacts suggest that the earliest trading towns developed in the Niger's inland delta. Traders brought dates and salt from the desert. People from the Sahel sold animals and hides. Other trade goods were grains, fish, kola and other tropical nuts, and metals, such as gold. (Much later, kola nuts provided the flavor for cola drinks.) This trade helped African kingdoms grow. One of the earliest West African kingdoms, Ghana (GAH-nuh), had become rich and powerful by about A.D. 800.

Place These early West African cliff paintings illustrate features from a ceremonial ritual for young people.

Some 200 years later, North African merchants began crossing the Sahara to trade in Ghana. These merchants introduced Islam to West Africa. In time, Islam became the main religion practiced in the Sahel.

Later Ghana fell to Muslim warriors from Morocco. The Muslim empire of Mali (MAH-lee) replaced the kingdom of Ghana. Mali stretched from the Niger's inland delta to the Atlantic coast. Mansa Musa was king of Mali during the early 1300s. Famous for his wealth and wise rule, Mansa Musa supported artists, poets, and scholars.

The kingdom of Songhay (SAWNG-hy) came to power as Mali declined. With a university, mosques, and more than 100 schools, the Songhay city of Timbuktu was a cultural center. By about 1600, however, Moroccan invasions had weakened the kingdom.

Forested areas south of the Sahel were also home to great civilizations. In what is now Nigeria, wealthy kings were buried with brass sculptures and other treasures.

We might think that salt is common and cheap, but it was precious to the traders of the Sahara. At one time it was worth its weight in gold.

✔ **READING CHECK:** (*Human Systems*) What are some of the great African kingdoms that once ruled the region?

The Slave Trade During the 1440s Portuguese explorers began sailing along the west coast of Africa. The Europeans called it the Gold Coast for the gold they bought there. Once they could buy gold where it was mined, the Europeans stopped buying it from Arab traders. As a result, the trans-Sahara trade and the great trade cities faded.

For a while, both Europeans and Africans profited from trade with each other. However, by the 1600s the demand for labor in Europe's American colonies changed everything. European traders met this demand by selling enslaved Africans to colonists. The slave trade was very profitable for these traders.

▲
(*Place*) There are many reminders of the slave trade and its effects on West Africans. Performers here reenact the treatment of enslaved Africans in an old slave house in Dakar, Senegal.

The slave trade had devastating effects on West African communities. Families were broken up when members were kidnapped and enslaved. Many Africans died on the voyage to the Americas. Most who survived were sent to the West Indies or Brazil. The slave trade finally ended in the 1800s. By then millions of Africans had been forced from their homes.

Colonial Era and Independence In the late 1800s, many European countries competed for colonies in West Africa. France claimed most of the region's northwest. Britain, Germany, and Portugal seized the rest.

In all of West Africa only tiny Liberia remained independent. Americans had founded it in the 1820s as a home for freed slaves. Sierra Leone, a British colony, also became a home for freed slaves.

Some Europeans moved to West Africa to run the colonies. They built roads, bridges, and railroads. Teachers and missionaries set up Christian churches and schools. After World War II, Africans increasingly worked for independence. Most of the colonies gained independence during the 1950s and 1960s. Portugal, the last European country to give up its West African colonies, did so in 1974.

✓ **READING CHECK:** (*Human Systems*) What impact did contact with Europeans have on West Africa?

Challenges

Independence brought a new set of challenges to the region. The borders that the Europeans had drawn ignored human geography. Sometimes borders separated members of one ethnic group. Other borders grouped together peoples that did not get along. As a result, many West Africans were more loyal to their ethnic groups than to their new countries. In addition, too few people had been trained to run the new governments. Dictators took control in many countries. Unrest and military rulers still trouble the region. Some countries have made progress, however. For example, in 1996 Chad created its first democratic constitution.

The governments of West African countries have several difficult problems in common. Birthrates are high. As a result, more and more people must make a living from the small amount of fertile land. In addition, many people are moving to already crowded cities even though urban jobs are few. These countries must also find ways to educate more of their people. Many families cannot afford to send their children to school.

✓ **READING CHECK:** (*Places and Regions*) What are three challenges the region faces?

Place A roadside market provides a glimpse of crowded Lagos, Nigeria's largest city. More than 10 million people live in and around Lagos. Overcrowded cities are a problem throughout much of the region.

CONNECTING TO Literature

Marriage Is a Private Affair
by Chinua Achebe

A Nigerian church carving

Chinua Achebe was born in an Ibo village in Nigeria in 1930. Many of his writings explore the changes colonialism brought to Africa. They also look at the conflict between old and new ways. In this story, Achebe looks at different views a father and son have about marriage.

"Father," began Nnaemeka suddenly, "I have come to ask for forgiveness."

"Forgiveness? For what, my son?" he asked in amazement.

"It's about this marriage question."

"Which marriage question?"

"I can't—we must—I mean it is impossible for me to marry Nweke's daughter."

"Impossible? Why?" asked his father.

"I don't love her."

"Nobody said you did. Why should you?" he asked.

"Marriage today is different . . ."

"Look here, my son," interrupted his father, "nothing is different. What one looks for in a wife are a good character and a Christian background."

Nnaemeka saw there was no hope along the present line of argument.

"Moreover," he said. "I am engaged to marry another girl who has all of Ugoye's good qualities, and who . . ."

His father did not believe his ears. "What did you say?" he asked slowly and disconcertingly[1]. . . .

"Whose daughter is she, anyway?"

"She is Nene Atang."

"What!" All the mildness was gone again. "Did you say Neneataga, what does that mean?"

"Nene Atang from Calabar. She is the only girl I can marry." This was a very rash reply and Nnaemeka expected the storm to burst.

Analyzing Primary Sources

1. What universal theme does the passage illustrate?
2. Why do you think the father and son disagree about marriage?

Vocabulary   [1]disconcertingly: disturbingly

▲
(Place) These homes in Burkina Faso are made of a mixture of mud, water, and cow dung. Trees are scarce in the Sahel and savanna zones. As a result, there is little wood for construction. Women are responsible for painting and decorating the walls of the homes.

Culture

Hundreds of ethnic groups exist in West Africa today. Hundreds of languages are spoken in the region. In some areas, using the colonial languages of French or English helps people from different groups communicate. West African languages that many people share, such as Fula and Hausa, also aid communication.

Religion The traditional religions of West Africa have often been forms of **animism**. Animism is the belief that bodies of water, animals, trees, and other natural objects have spirits. Animists also honor the memories of ancestors. In some isolated areas animism still forms the basis of most religious practices. Today most people of the Sahel practice Islam. Farther south live many Christians.

Clothing and Homes Some West Africans, particularly in cities, wear Western-style clothing. Others wear traditional robes, pants, blouses, and skirts. These are often made from colorful patterned cotton fabric. Because of the warm climate, most clothing is loose and flowing. Many women wear beautiful folded and wrapped headdresses. In the desert men often wear turbans. Both men and women may use veils to protect their faces from blowing sand.

Rural homes are small and simple. Many homes in the Sahel and savanna zones are circular. Straw or tin roofs sit atop mud, mud-brick, or straw huts. However, in cities you will find some modern buildings.

✓ **READING CHECK:** (**Human Systems**) What are some features of West African culture?

Homework Practice Online
Keyword: SG5 HP21

Section Review 2

Define or identify: archaeology, oral history, Mansa Musa, animism

Working with Sketch Maps On the map you created in Section 1, label Timbuktu. What made Timbuktu an important Songhay city?

Reading for the Main Idea

1. (**Human Systems**) How did European contact affect West Africa's people?

2. (**Human Systems**) Where in West Africa are Islam and Christianity practiced?

Critical Thinking

3. **Drawing Inferences and Conclusions** How might shared histories and challenges lead to more cooperation among the region's countries?

4. **Drawing Inferences and Conclusions** Why do you think mud bricks are used in West Africa?

Organizing What You Know

5. **Summarizing** Use the following graphic organizer to summarize challenges facing West Africa.

West Africa

Read to Discover

1. What are Mauritania, Mali, and Niger like today?
2. What challenges do Chad and Burkina Faso face?

Vocabulary

millet
sorghum
malaria
staple

Places

Nouakchott
Senegal River
Gao
Tibesti Mountains
Lake Chad
Ouagadougou

People

Moors

Reading Strategy

READING ORGANIZER Draw a three-column chart on a sheet of paper. Label the columns Country, Economic Activities, and Challenges. As you read this section, list each country and what you learn about their economic activities and challenges.

Mauritania, Mali, and Niger

Most of the people in these three large countries are Muslim. Mauritania, in fact, has laws based on Islam. These countries are also former French colonies, and French influence remains. In Mali and Niger, the official language is French. However, the people there speak more than 60 different local languages.

Today, drought and the expanding desert make feeding the people in these countries difficult. In the Sahel nomads depend on their herds of cattle, goats, and camels. In the savanna regions farmers grow **millet** and **sorghum**. These grain crops can usually survive drought.

Mauritania Many Mauritanians are Moors, people of mixed Arab and Berber origin. They speak Arabic. In the past, Moors enslaved some of the black Africans. Today, tension between the two groups continues.

Women carry goods for sale in a market in central Mali. Much of Mali's economic activity takes place in the Niger River's inland delta.

Interpreting the Visual Record

(**Human-Environment Interaction**) Why is Mali's economic activity centered around the inland delta?

Region Mud and other local materials were used to build many mosques in the Sahel. This mosque is located in Djenné [je-NAY], Mali. The majority of people living in the Sahel are Muslims.

The Tuareg (TWAH-reg) people of the Sahara and Sahel pound powdered blue dye into their flowing robes. They do this rather than dip the fabric in precious water. The blue powder wears off onto the skin, where it may help hold in moisture.

Most Mauritanians were once nomadic herders. Today, the expanding Sahara has crowded more than half of the nomads into the cities. Just 40 years ago, Nouakchott (nooh-AHK-shaht), Mauritania's capital, was a small village. More than 700,000 people live there now. About half of the population lives in shacks at the city's edges.

Throughout the country, people are very poor. Only in the far south, near the Senegal River, can farmers raise crops. Fishing in the Atlantic Ocean is another source of income.

Mali To the east of Mauritania lies landlocked Mali. The Sahara covers much of northern Mali. In the south lies a wetter farming region. About 80 percent of Mali's people fish or farm along the Niger River. Cotton is the country's main export. Timbuktu and Gao (GOW), ancient trading cities, continue to attract tourists.

Health conditions in Mali are poor. **Malaria**, a disease spread by mosquitoes, is a major cause of death among children.

Niger The Niger River flows through just the southwestern corner of landlocked Niger. Only about 3 percent of Niger's land is good for farming. All of the country's farmland lies along the Niger River and near the Nigerian border. Much of the rest of Niger lies within the Sahara. Farmers raise cotton, peanuts, beans, peas, and rice. Millet and sorghum are two of the region's **staple**, or main, food crops. The grains are cooked like oatmeal. Nomads in the desert region depend on the dairy products they get from their herds for food.

✓ **READING CHECK:** (**Places and Regions**) What is it like to live in Mauritania, Mali, and Niger?

The Sahel Countries

COUNTRY	POPULATION/ GROWTH RATE	LIFE EXPECTANCY	LITERACY RATE	PER CAPITA GDP
Burkina Faso	13,228,460 2.6%	43, male 45, female	27%	$1,080
Chad	9,253,493 3.1%	46, male 50, female	48%	$1,100
Mali	11,626,219 3%	44, male 46, female	46%	$860
Mauritania	2,912,584 2.9%	49, male 54, female	41%	$1,900
Niger	11,058,590 2.7%	42, male 42, female	17%	$830
United States	290,342,554 0.9%	74, male 80, female	97%	$37,600

Source: Central Intelligence Agency, *The World Factbook 2003*

Interpreting the Chart Based on the numbers in the chart, which two countries in the region are the least economically developed?

Chad and Burkina Faso

Drought has also affected the former French colonies of Chad and Burkina Faso (boohr-KEE-nuh FAH-soh). These countries are among the world's poorest and least developed. Most people farm or raise cattle.

Chad Chad is located in the center of Africa. The Tibesti Mountains in northern Chad rise above the Sahara. Lake Chad is in the south. Not long ago, the lake had a healthy fishing industry. It even supplied water to several other countries. However, drought has evaporated much of the lake's water. At one time, Lake Chad had shrunk to just one third its size in 1950.

The future may be better for Chad. A civil war ended in the 1990s. Also, oil reserves now being explored may help the economy.

Burkina Faso This country's name means "land of the honest people." Most of its people follow traditional religions. The country has thin soil and few mineral resources. Few trees remain in or near the capital, Ouagadougou (wah-gah-DOO-goo). They have been cut for firewood and building material. Jobs in the city are also scarce. To support their families many young men work in other countries. However, foreign aid and investment are starting to help the economy.

✓ **READING CHECK:** (*Places and Regions*) What are the challenges facing Chad and Burkina Faso?

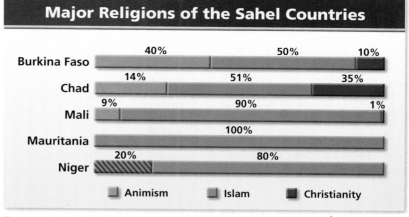

Major Religions of the Sahel Countries

Burkina Faso: 40% Animism, 50% Islam, 10% Christianity
Chad: 14% Animism, 51% Islam, 35% Christianity
Mali: 9% Animism, 90% Islam, 1% Christianity
Mauritania: 100% Islam
Niger: 20% Animism, 80% Islam

Legend: Animism, Islam, Christianity

Source: Central Intelligence Agency, *The World Factbook 2003*

Although most people in the Sahel are Muslim, some practice forms of animism and Christianity.

Interpreting the Graph (*Place*) Which country's population is entirely Muslim? Which countries have significant numbers of Christians?

Section Review 3

Homework Practice Online

Keyword: SG5 HP21

Define or identify: millet, sorghum, Moors, malaria, staple

Working with Sketch Maps On the map you created in Section 2, draw the boundaries of Mauritania, Mali, Niger, Chad, and Burkina Faso. Then label Nouakchott, Senegal River, Gao, Tibesti Mountains, Lake Chad, and Ouagadougou. In a box in the margin, describe what has happened to Lake Chad in recent decades.

Reading for the Main Idea

1. (*Places and Regions*) Why has Nouakchott grown so rapidly?

2. (*Places and Regions*) Which European language is most common in the Sahel countries? Why?

Critical Thinking

3. Drawing Inferences and Conclusions How do the typical foods of Niger relate to the country's water resources?

4. Comparing What do Chad and Burkina Faso have in common with the other Sahel countries?

Organizing What You Know

5. Comparing Copy the following graphic organizer. Label each of the star's points with one of the Section 3 countries. In the center, list characteristics the countries share.

Section 4 The Coastal Countries

Read to Discover
1. What is life in Nigeria like today?
2. What economic challenges do the region's other countries face?

Vocabulary
secede
griots
cacao

Places
Abuja
Lagos
Dakar
Monrovia
Lake Volta

People
Wole Soyinka

Reading Strategy

FOLDNOTES: TRI-FOLD Create a **Tri-Fold** FoldNote as described in the Appendix. Write what you know about West Africa's coastal countries in the column labeled "Know." Then, write what you want to know in the column labeled "Want." As you read the chapter, write what you learn about each country in the column labeled "Learn."

The faces of Nigeria are very young. About 45 percent of all Nigerians are younger than 15 years old. Only about 22 percent of all Americans are that young.

Nigeria

The largest country along West Africa's coast is Nigeria. With more than 130 million people, it has Africa's largest population.

Nigeria's People Nigeria was once an important British colony. Like many other colonies, Nigeria's borders included many ethnic groups. Today, a great variety of ethnic groups live in Nigeria. The Yoruba, Fula, Hausa, and Ibo are four of the largest ethnic groups. More than 200 languages are spoken there.

Nigeria's ethnic groups have not always gotten along. In the 1960s the Ibo tried to **secede**. That is, they tried to break away from Nigeria and form their own country. They called it Biafra (bee-AF-ruh). However, the Ibo lost the bloody war that followed.

Avoiding ethnic conflicts has continued to be an issue in Nigeria. It was important in choosing a site for a new Nigerian capital in the late 1970s. Leaders chose Abuja (ah-BOO-jah) because it was centrally located in an area of low population density.

Nigeria's Economy Nigeria has some of the continent's richest natural resources. Oil is the country's most important resource. Major oil fields are located in the Niger River delta and just off the coast. Oil accounts for 95 percent of the country's export earnings. Nigeria also

Human-Environment Interaction Oil drilling rigs like this one are common in areas of southern Nigeria. Oil accounts for about 20 percent of Nigeria's GDP.

Place The headdresses and patterned clothing worn by these women in Dakar are common in Senegal.

has good roads and railroads. Lagos (LAY-gahs), the former capital, is the country's largest city. The city is a busy seaport and trade center.

Although the country has rich resources, many Nigerians are poor. A major cause of the poverty there is a high birthrate. Nigeria can no longer feed its growing population without importing food. Another cause is the economy's dependence on oil. When prices are low, the whole country suffers. A third cause of Nigeria's poverty is a history of bad government. Corrupt government officials have used their positions to enrich themselves.

✓ READING CHECK: **Places and Regions** What are Nigeria's people and economy like today?

Other Coastal Countries

Several small West African countries lie along the Atlantic Ocean and the Gulf of Guinea. They are struggling to develop their economies.

Senegal and Gambia Senegal (se-ni-GAWL) wraps around Gambia (GAM-bee-uh). The odd border was created by French and British diplomats. Senegal, a former French colony, is larger and richer than Gambia, a former British colony. Dakar (dah-KAHR) is Senegal's capital and an important seaport and manufacturing center. Senegal and Gambia have many similarities. Peanuts are their most important crop. Common foods include chicken stew and fish with a peanut sauce. Tourism is growing slowly.

The Ashanti of Ghana

Festivals and ceremonies help the Ashanti people of Ghana keep their heritage of royal grandeur alive. The Ashanti observe the Akwasidae ceremony every six weeks. On this occasion, the Ashanti king emerges from his palace to receive the respect of his people. It is quite a sight. The king, wearing heavy gold ornaments, rides beneath immense colorful umbrellas. Drummers, dancers, musicians, and singers accompany the procession.

What does the king do during the Akwasidae ceremony?

Many of the people speak a language called Wolof (WOH-lawf). **Griots** (GREE-ohz) are important to the Wolof-speakers and other West Africans. Griots are storytellers who pass on the oral histories of their tribes or peoples. Sometimes the griots combine music with their stories, which may take hours or days to tell. Wolof women wear complex hairstyles and gold jewelry.

Guinea, Guinea-Bissau, and Cape Verde Guinea's main natural resource is a huge supply of bauxite. Its small neighbor to the east, Guinea-Bissau (GI-nee bi-SOW), has undeveloped mineral resources. Cape Verde (KAYP VUHRD) is a group of volcanic islands in the Atlantic. It is West Africa's only island country. Farming and fishing bring in the most money there.

Liberia and Sierra Leone Liberia is Africa's oldest republic. Monrovia, Liberia's capital, was named for U.S. president James Monroe. The freed American slaves who settled Liberia and their

Flowers color the countryside on Santa Antão island in Cape Verde. However, farming can be difficult because droughts are common in the island country.

descendants lived in coastal towns. They often clashed with the Africans already living there. Those Africans and their descendants were usually poorer and lived in rural areas. In the 1980s conflicts led to a bitter civil war. Sierra Leone (lee-OHN) has also experienced violent civil war. The fighting has wrecked the country's economy. Now, both Liberia and Sierra Leone must rebuild. They do have natural resources on which to build stronger economies. Liberia produces rubber and iron ore. Sierra Leone exports diamonds.

Ghana and Côte d'Ivoire The countries of Ghana and Côte d'Ivoire (koht-dee-VWAHR) have rich natural resources. Those resources may help them build strong economies. Ghana is named for the ancient kingdom, although the kingdom was northwest of the modern country. Ghana has one of the largest human-made lakes in the world—Lake Volta. Gold, timber, and **cacao** (kuh-KOW) are major products. Cocoa and chocolate are made from the seeds of the cacao tree. The tree came originally from Mexico and Central America.

Côte d'Ivoire is a former French colony whose name means "Ivory Coast" in English. It is a world leader in cacao and coffee exports. Côte d'Ivoire also boasts Africa's largest Christian church building.

Togo and Benin Unstable governments have troubled both Togo and Benin (buh-NEEN) since independence. Both have experienced periods of military rule. Their fragile economies have contributed to their unstable and sometimes violent politics. These long, narrow countries are poor. The people depend on farming and herding for income. Palm tree products, cacao, and coffee are the main crops in Togo and Benin.

✓ **READING CHECK:** (*Places and Regions*) What are characteristics of the economies of the coastal countries?

BIOGRAPHY

Wole Soyinka
(1934–)

Character Trait: Integrity

As the first black African to receive the Nobel Prize for Literature, Wole Soyinka is considered one of Africa's greatest writers. Some of Soyinka's works are based on his tribe, the Yoruba. His plays also include African dance and music. During the Nigerian civil war in the 1960s, Soyinka was jailed for 22 months for speaking out against the fighting. After his release from prison, he taught playwriting at Nigerian universities.

How did Wole Soyinka show integrity?

go.hrw.com
Homework Practice Online
Keyword: SG5 HP21

Section Review 4

Define or identify: secede, griots, cacao, Wole Soyinka

Working with Sketch Maps On the map that you drew in Section 3, draw the boundaries for the coastal countries. Label Abuja, Lagos, Dakar, Monrovia, and Lake Volta. In a box in the margin, identify the largest and most populous country on West Africa's coast.

Reading for the Main Idea

1. (*Places and Regions*) How is Cape Verde different from the other countries in the region?

2. (*Places and Regions*) What is Nigeria's most important natural resource? Why?

Critical Thinking

3. Finding the Main Idea Why must Liberia and Sierra Leone rebuild their economies?

4. Analyzing Information Why was choosing a new capital important to Nigeria's future?

Organizing What You Know

5. Summarizing Copy the following graphic organizer. Use it to list three main causes of poverty in Nigeria today.

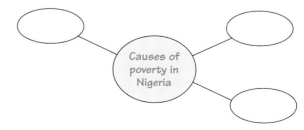

Causes of poverty in Nigeria

CHAPTER 21 Review and Practice

Define and Identify

Identify each of the following:

1. zonal
2. Sahel
3. harmattan
4. tsetse fly
5. bauxite
6. archaeology
7. oral history
8. Mansa Musa
9. animism
10. millet
11. sorghum
12. malaria
13. staple
14. secede
15. griots
16. cacao
17. Wole Soyinka

Review the Main Ideas

18. What are the four climate zones of West Africa?
19. How do the Niger River's two delta regions differ?
20. How did Islam come to West Africa?
21. What were the effects of the slave trade on West African communities?
22. How has drought affected the countries of the Sahel?
23. What religion do most people in the Sahel practice?

24. On what natural resource does Nigeria's economy depend?
25. How did the United States influence the development of Liberia?

Think Critically

26. **Drawing Inferences and Conclusions** Why are many of West Africa's largest cities located in the coastal and forest zone?
27. **Finding the Main Idea** What role did trade play in the early West African kingdoms and later European colonies in the region?
28. **Analyzing Information** What are three cultural features of West Africa influenced by Europeans?
29. **Drawing Inferences and Conclusions** How have borders set by European colonial powers led to conflicts such as Nigeria's war in Biafra in the late 1960s?
30. **Contrasting** How is Liberia's history different from that of other West African countries?

Map Activity

31. On a separate sheet of paper, match the letters on the map with their correct labels.

Niger River	Tibesti Mountains
Gulf of Guinea	Lake Chad
Timbuktu	Abuja
Nouakchott	Lagos
Senegal River	Lake Volta

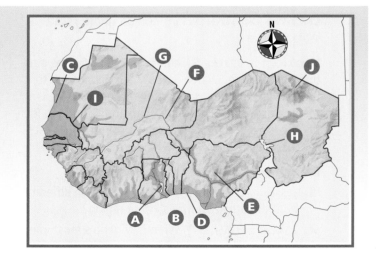

Writing Activity

Imagine that you are an economic adviser to a West African country of your choice. Use print resources to prepare a short economic report for your country's leader. Identify the country's important natural resources and what can be done with them. In addition, describe economic advantages or disadvantages of the country's climate, location, and physical features. Be sure to use standard grammar, spelling, sentence structure, and punctuation.

internet connect

Internet Activity: **go.hrw.com**
KEYWORD: SG5 GT21

Choose a topic to explore about West Africa:
- Find out about giant baobab trees.
- Meet the people of West Africa.
- Learn about the history of the slave trade.

Social Studies Skills Practice

Interpreting Graphs

Today, Nigeria relies on crude oil production for much of its wealth. However, during the 1980s the country's oil industry experienced many ups and downs. Study the graph and answer the questions.

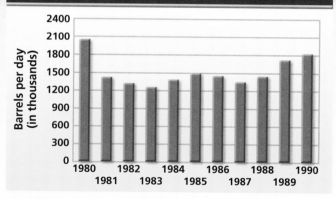

Nigeria's Crude Oil Production, 1980–1990

(y-axis: Barrels per day (in thousands), 0 to 2400; x-axis: years 1980–1990)

Source: Energy Information Administration

1. In what year did Nigeria produce the least amount of oil?

2. In what years did Nigeria produce more than 1.5 million barrels per day?

3. By approximately how much did oil production decline between 1980 and 1981?

4. Did Nigeria's oil production between 1988 and 1990 increase or decrease?

Analyzing Primary Sources

Read the following description of the kingdom of Ghana in the 1060s by the Arab geographer Al Bakri. Then answer the questions.

"The city of Ghana consists of two towns lying in a plain. One of these towns is inhabited by Muslims. It is large and possesses twelve mosques in one of which the people assemble for the Friday prayer . . . Around the town are wells of sweet water from which they drink and near which they grow vegetables. The land between the two towns is covered with houses. The houses of the inhabitants are made of stone and acacia wood. The king has a palace and a number of dome-shaped dwellings, the whole surrounded by an enclosure like the defensive wall of a city."

1. What resource may have determined the location of the two towns?

2. Why do you think the houses were made of stone and acacia wood?

3. Why were mosques in only one town within the kingdom of Ghana?

4. What is a unique feature of the king's palace?

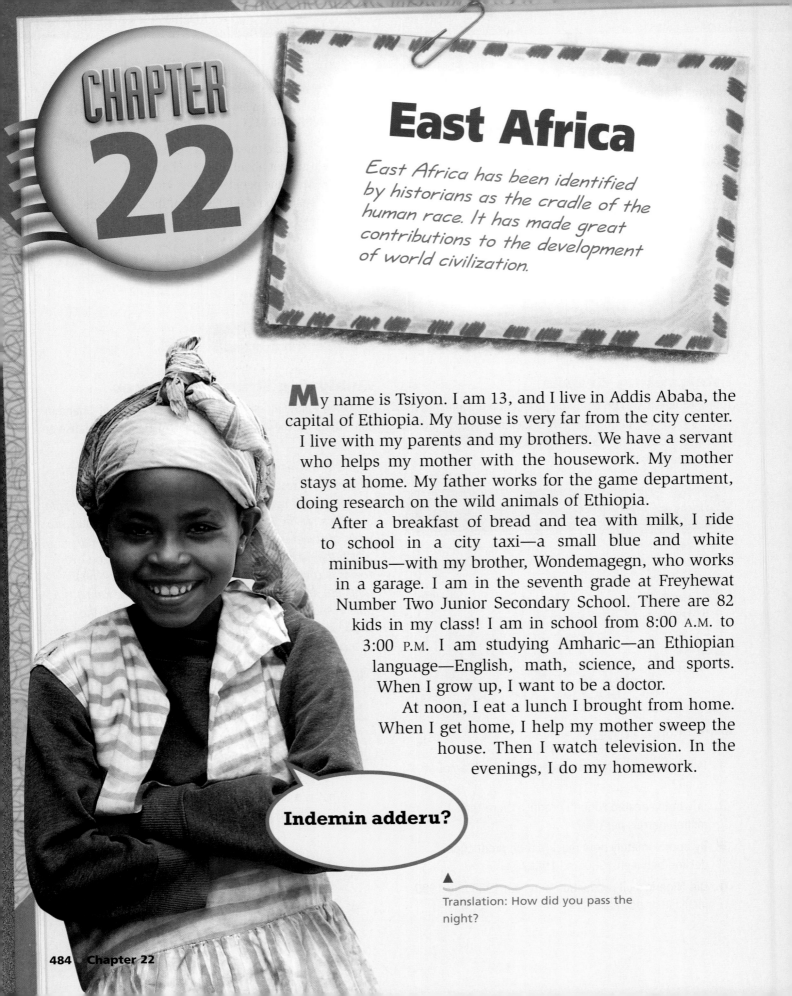

CHAPTER 22

East Africa

East Africa has been identified by historians as the cradle of the human race. It has made great contributions to the development of world civilization.

My name is Tsiyon. I am 13, and I live in Addis Ababa, the capital of Ethiopia. My house is very far from the city center. I live with my parents and my brothers. We have a servant who helps my mother with the housework. My mother stays at home. My father works for the game department, doing research on the wild animals of Ethiopia.

After a breakfast of bread and tea with milk, I ride to school in a city taxi—a small blue and white minibus—with my brother, Wondemagegn, who works in a garage. I am in the seventh grade at Freyhewat Number Two Junior Secondary School. There are 82 kids in my class! I am in school from 8:00 A.M. to 3:00 P.M. I am studying Amharic—an Ethiopian language—English, math, science, and sports. When I grow up, I want to be a doctor.

At noon, I eat a lunch I brought from home. When I get home, I help my mother sweep the house. Then I watch television. In the evenings, I do my homework.

Indemin adderu?

▲

Translation: How did you pass the night?

Section 1 Physical Geography

Read to Discover

1. What are the major landforms of East Africa?
2. Which rivers and lakes are important in this region?
3. What are East Africa's climate types and natural resources?

Vocabulary

rifts

Places

Great Rift Valley
Mount Kilimanjaro
Lake Victoria
White Nile
Blue Nile

Reading Strategy

FOLDNOTES: DOUBLE-DOOR Create the FoldNote titled **Double-Door** described in the Appendix. Label the top flap "Rivers and Lakes" and the bottom flap "Climate and Resources." Label the paper beneath the top flap "Rift Valleys" and the paper beneath the lower flap "Mountains and Plains." Then write what you learn about each topic under each label.

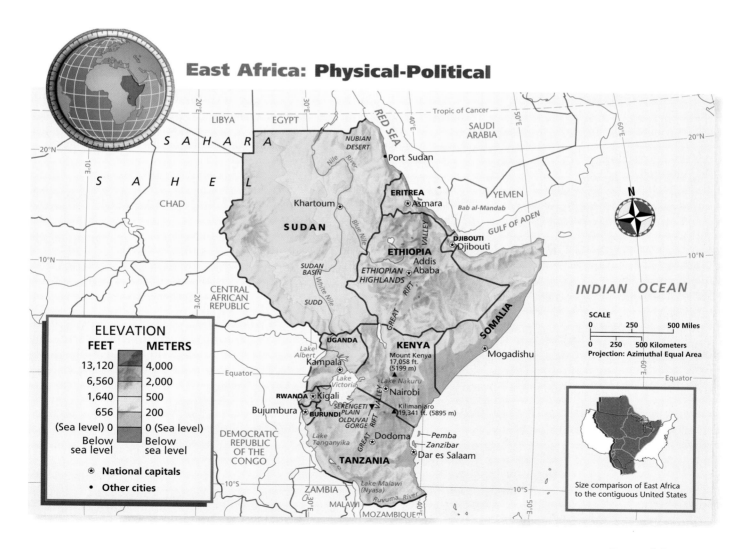

East Africa: Physical-Political

ELEVATION

FEET	METERS
13,120	4,000
6,560	2,000
1,640	500
656	200
(Sea level) 0	0 (Sea level)
Below sea level	Below sea level

⊛ National capitals
• Other cities

Mount Kenya 17,058 ft. (5199 m)
Kilimanjaro 19,341 ft. (5895 m)

SCALE
0   250   500 Miles
0   250   500 Kilometers
Projection: Azimuthal Equal Area

Size comparison of East Africa to the contiguous United States

The Land

East Africa is a land of high plains and plateaus. In the north, deserts and dry grasslands define the landscape. In the southwest, large lakes dot the plateaus. In the east, sandy beaches and beautiful coral reefs run along the coast. East Africa's most striking features are its great **rifts**. They cut from north to south across the region. Rifts are long, deep valleys with mountains or plateaus on either side. Rifts form when Earth's tectonic plates move away from each other.

The Rift Valleys Deep beneath East Africa's surface, Earth's mantle is churning. This movement causes the land to arch and split along the rift valleys. If you look at the Great Rift Valley from the air, it looks like a giant scar. The Great Rift Valley is made up of two rifts—the eastern rift and the western rift. The rift walls are usually a series of steep cliffs. These cliffs drop an average of about 9,000 feet (2,743 m) to the valley floor. The eastern rift begins north of the Red Sea. The rift continues south through Eritrea (er-uh-TREE-uh) and Ethiopia (ee-thee-OH-pee-uh) into southern Tanzania (tan-zuh-NEE-uh). The western rift extends from Lake Albert in the north to Lake Malawi (mah-LAH-wee), also known as Lake Nyasa, in the south.

Mountains and Plains East Africa also has many volcanic mountains. Mount Kilimanjaro (ki-luh-muhn-JAHR-oh), at 19,341 feet (5,895 m), is Africa's tallest mountain. Although this part of Africa is along the equator, the mountain is so high that snow covers its two volcanic cones. Plains along the eastern rift in Tanzania and Kenya are home to famous national parks.

✓ **READING CHECK:** (*Places and Regions*) What are the major landforms of East Africa?

This is a crater rim view of Mount Kilimanjaro. Another name for this volcano is Kilima Njaro—"shining mountain" in Swahili.

Rivers and Lakes

East Africa is the site of a number of rivers and large lakes. The Nile is the world's longest river. It begins in East Africa and flows north to the Mediterranean Sea. Water from small streams collects in Lake Victoria, the source of the White Nile. Waters from Ethiopia's highlands form the Blue Nile. These two rivers meet at Khartoum, Sudan, to create the mighty Nile. The Nile provides a narrow, fertile lifeline through Sudan by providing irrigation in the desert.

Lake Victoria is Africa's largest lake in area, but it is shallow. Along the western rift is a chain of great lakes. Many of the lakes along the drier eastern rift are quite different. Heat from Earth's interior makes some of these eastern lakes so hot that no human can swim in them. Others, like Lake Nakuru, are too salty for most fish. However, algae in Lake Nakuru provides food for more than a million flamingos.

✓ **READING CHECK:** (*Places and Regions*) Which rivers and lakes are most important in this region?

▲
Lake Nakuru is known in part for the many flamingos that gather there.

Climate and Resources

Northern Sudan and the northeast coast have desert and steppe climates. The climate changes to tropical savanna as you travel south. However, the greatest climate changes occur along the sides of the rift valleys. The rift floors are dry, with grasslands and thorn shrubs. In contrast, the surrounding plateaus and mountains have a humid highland climate and dense forests. Rain falls at the high elevations, but the valleys are in rain shadows.

Most East Africans are farmers or herders. However, the region does have mineral resources such as coal, copper, diamonds, gold, iron ore, and lead.

✓ **READING CHECK:** (*Places and Regions*) What are East Africa's climate types and natural resources?

Homework Practice Online
Keyword: SG5 HP22

Section Review 1

Define and explain: rifts

Working with Sketch Maps On a map of East Africa that you draw or that your teacher provides, label the following: Great Rift Valley, Mount Kilimanjaro, Lake Victoria, White Nile, and Blue Nile. How do the mountains help support the river systems?

Reading for the Main Idea

1. (*Places and Regions*) What are the major landforms of East Africa?

2. (*Places and Regions*) Which rivers and lakes are located in this part of Africa?

3. (*Physical Systems*) Why are volcanic mountains found in parts of East Africa?

Critical Thinking

4. **Drawing Inferences and Conclusions** How do you think the climate types found in East Africa influence what grows there?

Organizing What You Know

5. **Summarizing** Copy the following graphic organizer. Use it to describe what you know about East Africa's physical geography.

	Vegetation	Climates
Coasts		
Rift Valleys		
Plateaus/mountains		

Read to Discover

1. What important events and developments influenced the history of East Africa?

2. What is the culture of East Africa like?

Vocabulary
Swahili

People
Amanirenus

Reading Strategy

TAKING NOTES Use the headings in this section to create an outline. As you read the section, write what you learn about East Africa's history and culture beneath each heading.

History

Several early civilizations developed at the site known as Meroë, near where the branches of the Nile come together. These civilizations had their own forms of writing. Each controlled a major trade route. East Africans traded ivory and gold, among other things.

This statue depicts a prince from the early Nubian civilization of northern Sudan.

Christianity and Islam Like Egypt, Ethiopia was an early center of Christianity. In the A.D. 500s Christianity spread into neighboring Nubia, which is now part of Egypt and Sudan. In Nubia, Christian kingdoms lasted until about 1500. Ethiopia still has a large Christian population today.

Arab armies conquered Egypt and North Africa by about A.D. 700. However, these armies were not able to keep control of East Africa. Gradually, Arabic-speaking nomads spread into northern Sudan from Egypt. They brought their Islamic faith with them. At the same time, Islam spread to the coastal region of what is now Somalia. Christianity is believed to have been introduced in Ethiopia as early as the A.D. 300s. Christian kingdoms, particularly in Ethiopia, have fought wars with Muslim leaders. Religion continues to be a source of conflict in this East African region.

The Slave Trade The east coast slave trade dates back more than 1,000 years. Most slaves went to Islamic countries in Africa and Asia. The Portuguese had begun setting up forts and settlements on the East African coast by the early 1500s. At first, the Europeans made little

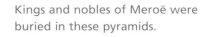
Kings and nobles of Meroë were buried in these pyramids.

effort to move into the interior. However, in the late 1700s the East African island of Zanzibar became an international slave-trading center. Later, plantations like those of the Americas were set up with slave labor to grow cloves and sugarcane.

Africa Divided In the mid-1800s European adventurers traveled into the African interior searching for the source of the Nile. Here they found rich lands well suited for agriculture. In the 1880s the European powers divided up most of the continent. Most of Africa's modern borders resulted from this process. Control over much of East Africa went to the British. Germany colonized Tanzania, Rwanda, and Burundi. After World War I, with the defeat of Germany, the British took over Tanzania. Belgium gained control of Rwanda and Burundi.

Conflict Within East Africa, just Kenya was settled by large numbers of Europeans. The colonial rulers usually controlled their countries through African deputies. Many of these deputies were traditional chiefs, who often favored their own peoples. This tended to strengthen ethnic rivalries. These ethnic divisions have made it hard for governments to create feelings of national identity.

Independence Ethiopia was never colonized. Its mountains provided natural protection, and its peoples and emperors resisted colonization. It was, however, annexed by Italy from 1936 to 1941. Most East African countries were granted independence by European colonizers in the early 1960s. More recently, East Africa has become headquarters for some international companies and organizations.

✓ **READING CHECK:** (*Human Systems*) Which European countries influenced the history of East Africa?

BIOGRAPHY

Amanirenus
(lived 20s B.C.)

Early in East Africa's history, women often ruled in the region. Those who ruled Kush used the title "Candace." Amanirenus was one of them. She led her army against invading Romans in 24 B.C. Both she and the Romans claimed that they won the fight. The Kushites were able to remove the head from a statue of Augustus Caesar. They put it under the temple stairs so everyone who entered could step on the foreigner who threatened their land.

What symbol did the Kushites use to express their pride in their land?

Afar nomads stop for rest in a desert region of northern Ethiopia.

Culture

East Africa has the world's longest history of human settlement. Gradually, the region developed the continent's greatest diversity of people and ways of life. The **Swahili** language is widely spoken in East Africa. This Bantu language has been greatly influenced by Arabic. In fact, the word Swahili comes from the Arabic word meaning "on the coast."

East Africa shares many challenges with other African regions. One challenge is that populations are growing faster than the economies that support them. Many jobless people have crowded into the cities. Another challenge is religious and ethnic conflict. Such conflict and other political problems have slowed economic progress. Often a country's wealth is spent on weapons rather than helping people.

The ethnic conflicts have roots in the region's history. Colonial borders drawn by Europeans often lumped different ethnic groups into one country. Differences between groups have led to conflict in some countries since independence.

The worst ethnic conflict has been in Rwanda and Burundi. Thousands of Tutsi were killed by the Hutu in Rwanda in the 1990s. There also has been fighting between Muslims and Christians in the northern part of the region.

✓ **READING CHECK:** (**Human Systems**) What conflicts have occurred between groups in East Africa?

Homework Practice Online
Keyword: SG5 HP22

Section Review 2

Define or identify: Amanirenus, Swahili

Working with Sketch Maps On the map you created in Section 1, highlight the location of the bodies of water you labeled. Why do you think early civilizations settled near these bodies of water?

Reading for the Main Idea

1. (**Human Systems**) Which European countries influenced the history of this area?

2. (**Human Systems**) What are the main religions practiced in East Africa?

Critical Thinking

3. **Finding the Main Idea** What conflicts have occurred because of political boundary lines?

4. **Drawing Inferences and Conclusions** Why might Swahili be a particularly important language in East Africa?

Organizing What You Know

5. **Sequencing** Create a time line listing historical events in East Africa from the A.D. 400s to the 1990s. Be sure to include the adoption of Christianity, the slave trade, exploration, colonial rule, independence, and ethnic conflict.

A.D. 400 —————————————————— 1990s

Read to Discover

1. Why did settlers come to Kenya?
2. How was Tanzania created?
3. What are Rwanda and Burundi like?
4. What is Uganda like?
5. What are the physical features of Sudan?

Vocabulary

gorge

Places

Kenya
Tanzania
Rwanda
Burundi
Uganda
Sudan

People

Kikuyu
Tutsi
Hutu

Reading Strategy

READING ORGANIZER Before you read, draw a circle in the center of a sheet of paper. Label the circle East African Countries. Draw five rays from the circle. Draw a circle at the end of each ray. Label the circles Kenya, Tanzania, Rwanda and Burundi, Uganda, and Sudan. As you read the section, write what you learn about the countries beside each circle.

Kenya

Kenya's first cities were founded along the coast of the Indian Ocean by Arab traders. Beginning in the 1500s Portugal controlled this coast for about 200 years. Arabs then recaptured it.

During the 1800s British merchants began trading on the coast. They built a railway from Mombasa to Lake Victoria. British settlers then came to take advantage of the fertile highlands. People from India and Pakistan also came to work on the Europeans' farms. Many of the local people, particularly the Kikuyu, moved out of their traditional areas. They became farmworkers or took jobs in the cities. After World War II many Africans protested British colonial rule. There were peaceful demonstrations as well as violent ones.

One conflict was over land. The British and the Kikuyu viewed land differently. The British considered land a sign of personal wealth, power, and property. The Kikuyu saw land as a source of food rather than something to be bought or sold. This caused conflict because the British wanted the land. Kenya gained independence from Britain in the 1960s, and its government has been quite stable ever since.

Kenya is a popular tourist destination. Tourism is a major source of income for the country. Kenya's greatest challenge is its rapidly increasing population. There is no empty farmland left in most areas. Much of Kenya has been set aside as national parkland.

Movement As in the rest of Africa, Europeans once ruled colonies in East Africa. Fort Jesus, founded in 1593 by the Portuguese, is a national monument in Kenya.

East Africa

Country	Population/ Growth Rate	Life Expectancy	Literacy Rate	Per Capita GDP
Burundi	6,096,156 2.2%	42, male 44, female	52%	$600
Kenya	31,639,091 1.3%	45, male 45, female	85%	$1,020
Rwanda	7,810,056 1.8%	38, male 40, female	70%	$1,200
Sudan	38,114,160 2.7%	56, male 58, female	61%	$1,420
Tanzania	35,922,454 1.7%	43, male 46, female	78%	$630
Uganda	25,632,794 2.9%	43, male 46, female	70%	$1,260
United States	290,342,554 0.9%	74, male 80, female	97%	$37,600

Source: Central Intelligence Agency, *The World Factbook 2003*

Interpreting the Chart **Which country has the lowest literacy rate?**

These giraffe feed on the tree-studded grasslands of the Serengeti. This reserve was opened in 1974 and is Kenya's most famous and popular animal reserve.

▼

Many people would like to farm these lands. If the national parks are converted to farmland, however, African wildlife would be endangered. In addition, the tourism industry would likely suffer.

✔ **READING CHECK:** (*Human Systems*) Why did settlers come to Kenya?

Tanzania

South of Kenya is the large country of Tanzania. It was created in the 1960s when Tanganyika and the island of Zanzibar united. Today many tourists come to explore numerous national parks and Mount Kilimanjaro. The mountain's southern slopes are a rich agricultural region that provides coffee and tea for exports. Also in Tanzania is the Serengeti Plain. On this plain, herds of antelope and zebras still migrate freely, following the rains. Nearby is a famous archaeological site, Olduvai Gorge. A **gorge** is a narrow, steep-walled canyon. Evidence of some of the earliest humanlike fossils have been found in Olduvai Gorge.

Tanzania is a country of mainly poor subsistence farmers. Poor soils and limited technology have restricted productivity. This country has minerals, particularly gold and diamonds. Although the Tanzanian government has tried to make the country more self-sufficient, it has not yet succeeded.

✔ **READING CHECK:** (*Places and Regions*) How was the country of Tanzania created?

Olduvai Gorge, Tanzania

Many scientists believe the human species has its origins in Africa. Archaeologists there have discovered fossil remains of humans and humanlike animals several million years old. Some of the most important finds have occurred at a site known as Olduvai Gorge.

Located in Tanzania, Olduvai is a steep-sided canyon some 30 miles (48 km) long. It is up to 300 feet (90 m) deep. The exposed sides of this gorge contain fossil deposits estimated to be more than 4 million years old. Along with the fossils, scientists found stone tools and the remains of numerous humanlike animals.

OLDUVAI GORGE

Archaeologists Louis and Mary Leakey played a key role in uncovering Olduvai's secrets. In 1931 Louis Leakey found remains of ancient tools and bones in the gorge. Then in 1959 Mary Leakey found the skeleton of an *Australopithecus*, the first humanlike creature to walk upright. Several years later, the Leakeys found the remains of a more advanced species. The new find was known as *Homo habilis*. The species could make stone tools.

These discoveries helped provide some of the missing links between humans and their ancestors. Today archaeological work at Olduvai Gorge continues to add to our understanding of human origins.

Understanding What You Read

1. What is Olduvai Gorge?
2. What part has Olduvai played in the search for human origins?

Rwanda and Burundi

These two countries in fertile highlands were once German colonies. After World War I the Belgians ruled them. In the 1960s, after they gained independence, they were divided into two countries. Both countries are mostly populated by two ethnic groups—the Tutsi and the Hutu. Violence between the groups has killed thousands. Rwanda and Burundi have the densest rural settlement in Africa. Foreign aid has helped improve farming and health care.

✓ **READING CHECK:** (**Human Systems**) Why did the creation of Rwanda and Burundi create conflict?

Red colobus monkeys of Zanzibar eat charcoal, which absorbs poisons in the fruit-tree leaves the monkeys sometimes eat.

Uganda

Uganda, another site of an ancient empire, is found on the plateau north and west of Lake Victoria. Economic progress has been slow. Foreign investment stopped as a result of a violent dictatorship. In the 1970s the country's economy collapsed. Limited peace and democracy were achieved in the late 1980s.

✓ **READING CHECK:** *(Human Systems)* What is Uganda like today?

Sudan

Sudan is Africa's largest country. It has three physical regions. The Sahara makes up the northern half of the country. Dry savannas extend across the country's center. Much of southern Sudan is taken up by a swamp called the Sudd. Sudan is mainly an agricultural country, but it is also developing some of its mineral resources. Oil reserves have not yet been developed.

Modern Sudanese culture shows influences of Arab and traditionally African cultures. Arab Muslims make up about 70 percent of the population and have political power. They dominate northern Sudan. Khartoum, the capital, is located in this area. During the last several decades there was a civil war between northern Muslims and southerners who practice Christianity or traditional African religions.

✓ **READING CHECK:** *(Human Systems)* What conflict has been occurring in Sudan?

Alfred Louis Sargent created this engraving of Khartoum, Sudan, in the 1800s.

Section Review 3

Homework Practice Online
Keyword: SG5 HP22

Define or identify: Kikuyu, gorge, Tutsi, Hutu

Working with Sketch Maps On the map you created in Section 2, label Kenya, Tanzania, Rwanda, Burundi, Uganda, and Sudan. Why are some of the countries of this region agriculturally fertile while others are not?

Reading for the Main Idea

1. *(Places and Regions)* What makes the highlands of Kenya important?

2. *(Places and Regions)* Which areas of East Africa are tourist attractions?

Critical Thinking

3. **Making Generalizations and Predictions** How might irrigation help a region's economic development?

4. **Finding the Main Idea** How has unrest hurt Rwanda and some other East African countries?

Organizing What You Know

5. **Summarizing** Copy the following graphic organizer. Use it to list each country in this section. In one column list resources important to its development, and in the next column list obstacles that could prevent the country's economic success.

Country	Resources	Obstacles

Read to Discover

1. What are the main physical features of Ethiopia?
2. What is Eritrea like?
3. What is Somalia like?
4. What are the physical and cultural characteristics of Djibouti?

Vocabulary

droughts

Places

Ethiopia
Eritrea
Somalia
Djibouti
Bab al-Mandab

People

Somali

Reading Strategy

READING ORGANIZER Before you read, draw a large square on a sheet of paper. Draw a vertical line down the center of the square. Draw a horizontal line across the center of the square. Label the boxes Ethiopia, Eritrea, Somalia, and Djibouti. As you read the section write details about each country in its box.

Ethiopia

Ethiopia is one of the world's poorest countries. The rugged mountain slopes and upland plateaus have rich volcanic soil. Agriculture is Ethiopia's chief economic activity. It exports coffee, livestock, and oilseeds. However, during the last 30 years the region has experienced serious **droughts**. Droughts are periods when little rain falls and crops are damaged. Drought, combined with war and ineffective government policies, caused the starvation of several million people in the 1980s.

Except for a time when Ethiopia was at war with Italy, the Ethiopian highlands have never been under foreign rule. The mountains protected the interior of the country from invasion. Most of the highland people are Christian, while most of the lowland people are Muslim.

✓ **READING CHECK:** *Places and Regions* What physical features are found in Ethiopia?

As Afar nomads in Ethiopia move their encampment, they are continually challenged by the environment.

Interpreting the Visual Record

Movement **How important are these camels for the Afar? What purpose do they serve?**

▼

The Horn of Africa

Country	Population/ Growth Rate	Life Expectancy	Literacy Rate	Per Capita GDP
Djibouti	457,130 2.1%	42, male 44, female	68%	$1,300
Eritrea	4,362,254 1.3%	51, male 55, female	59%	$740
Ethiopia	66,557,553 1.9%	40, male 42, female	43%	$750
Somalia	8,025,190 3.4%	45, male 49, female	38%	$550
United States	290,342,554 0.9%	74, male 80, female	97%	$37,600

Source: Central Intelligence Agency, *The World Factbook 2003*

Interpreting the Chart **Which country in the region has the highest level of economic development, and why?**

The main mosque, Khulafa el Rashidin, was built in 1937 with Italian Carrara marble in Asmara, Eritrea.

Interpreting the Visual Record **What architectural elements of this building have you seen in other regions you have studied?**

Eritrea

Eritrea, located on the Red Sea, was once part of Ethiopia. In the late 1800s the Italians made this area a colony. In the 1960s it became an Ethiopian province. After years of war, Eritrea broke away from Ethiopia in 1993. The economy has slowly improved since then. The population is made up of Muslims and Christians.

✔ **READING CHECK:** *Places and Regions* What is Eritrea like today?

Somalia

Somalia is a land of deserts and dry savannas. Most Somalis are nomadic herders. Livestock and bananas are the main exports. Somalia is less diverse than most other African countries. Most residents of Somalia are members of the Somali people. Most Somali share the same culture, religion (Islam), language (Somali), and way of life (herding). Somalia has been troubled by civil war. In the 1990s widespread starvation caused by the war and a severe drought attracted international attention. The United Nations sent aid and troops to the country. U.S. troops were sent to Somalia to assist with this operation.

✔ **READING CHECK:** *Environment and Society* How have drought and conflict affected Somalia?

Djibouti's Lake Assal has one of the lowest surface levels on the planet. It lies 515 feet (157 m) below sea level. The only way to reach this area is by use of a four-wheel drive vehicle.

Djibouti

Djibouti is a small desert country. It lies on the Bab al-Mandab. This is the narrow strait that connects the Red Sea and the Indian Ocean. The strait lies along a major shipping route. This has helped Djibouti's economy. In the 1860s Djibouti came under French control. It gained independence in 1977. The French government still contributes economic and military support to the country. Its port, which serves landlocked Ethiopia, is a major source of income. Djibouti is heavily dependent on food imports.

The people of Djibouti include the Issa and the Afar. The Issa are closely tied to the people of Somalia. The Afar are related to the people of Ethiopia. Members of both groups are Muslim. Somalia and Ethiopia have both wanted to control Djibouti. So far the country has maintained its independence.

✓ **READING CHECK:** (*Places and Regions*) What are Djibouti's physical and cultural features?

Homework Practice Online
Keyword: SG5 HP22

Section Review 4

Define or identify: droughts, Somali

Working with Sketch Maps On the map you created in Section 3, label Ethiopia, Eritrea, Somalia, Djibouti, and Bab al-Mandab. What physical features help the economies of the region?

Reading for the Main Idea

1. (*Places and Regions*) What physical features have helped protect Ethiopia from foreign invasion?

2. (*Places and Regions*) What country was part of Ethiopia until it broke away in 1993?

Critical Thinking

3. Drawing Inferences and Conclusions Why do you think France remains interested in Djibouti?

4. Finding the Main Idea Why have foreign aid agencies been involved in East Africa?

Organizing What You Know

5. Analyzing Information Copy the following graphic organizer. Use it to show the major religions of these countries. Add boxes as needed.

Country	Religion

Define and Identify

Identify each of the following:

1. rifts
2. Swahili
3. Kikuyu
4. gorge
5. droughts
6. Somali

Review the Main Ideas

7. What are East Africa's main natural resources?
8. What caused the formation of the Great Rift Valley of East Africa?
9. Why didn't Europeans ever colonize Ethiopia?
10. What is a major source of income for Kenya?
11. What was the island of Zanzibar known for in the late 1700s?
12. What factors have slowed Tanzania's economic growth?
13. How have Arabs, Portuguese, the British, and the Kikuyu affected Kenya?
14. How did the British and Kikuyu view land differently?
15. What two ethnic groups live mostly in Rwanda and Burundi?

16. How have droughts in the Horn of Africa affected its people and their relationship with the rest of the world?
17. What landform in Djibouti has helped the country's economy?

Think Critically

18. **Finding the Main Idea** What is the significance of the Nile River in this region's human history?
19. **Analyzing Information** Why are foreign investors hesitant to invest in many countries of this region?
20. **Summarizing** Why do most East Africans make their living by farming and herding?
21. **Making Generalizations and Predictions** What problems have resulted in part from the boundary lines drawn by European powers, and how might the countries of East Africa overcome these problems?
22. **Analyzing Information** How has Ethiopia avoided falling under foreign rule for most of its history?

Map Activity

23. On a separate sheet of paper, match the letters on the map with their correct labels.

Great Rift Valley	White Nile
Mount Kilimanjaro	Blue Nile
Lake Victoria	Bab al-Mandab

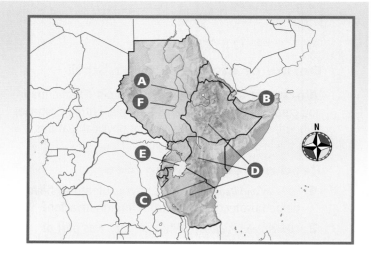

Writing Activity

Imagine that you have been awarded an all-expenses-paid vacation to East Africa. Write a letter to your travel agent explaining what you want to do on your trip. List and describe physical features you want to see and African wildlife and historical sites you would like to explore. Be sure to use standard grammar, spelling, sentence structure, and punctuation.

⏹ internet connect

Internet Activity: **go.hrw.com**
KEYWORD: SG5 GT22

Choose a topic to explore about East Africa:
- Hike Mount Kilimanjaro.
- Learn about cultural groups in East Africa.
- Travel back to ancient Nubian kingdoms.

Social Studies Skills Practice

Interpreting Charts

You have read about the role of religion in the history and culture of East Africa. Study the following chart and answer the questions below.

Religion in East Africa

Country	Christian	Muslim	Indigenous
Burundi	67%	10%	23%
Kenya	78%	10%	10%
Rwanda	94%	5%	0.1%
Sudan	5%	70%	25%
Tanzania (mainland)	30%	35%	35%
Uganda	66%	16%	18%

Source: Central Intelligence Agency, *The World Factbook 2003*

1. Where is Christianity most heavily practiced?
2. Where is Islam most heavily practiced?
3. Indigenous religions are practiced the least in which country?
4. Which two countries have the most similar patterns of religious diversity?

Analyzing Primary Sources

In "The Snows of Kilimanjaro," a short story written by Ernest Hemingway in 1938, a couple travels on safari to East Africa. Read the following passage that describes their view of the region's landscape from a small airplane. Then answer the questions.

"Then they were over the first hills and the wildebeeste were trailing up them, and then they were over the mountains with sudden depths of green-rising forest and the solid bamboo slopes, and then the heavy forest again, sculptured into peaks and hollows until they crossed, and hills sloped down and then another plain, hot now, and purple brown, bumpy with heat . . ."

1. How does an aerial view give you a sense of the region's physical geography?
2. What types of landforms, vegetation, and wildlife are described?
3. From this passage, what can you tell about the climate of the region?
4. How does the landscape described in this passage differ from other areas of East Africa?

Central Africa

The fourth region in Africa we will study includes the 10 countries of central Africa. Before we begin, meet Akalemwa Ngenda, a student living in Zambia.

Bwanji? (How are you?) This is how you say hi in Nyanja, a common language spoken by most people in my country, Zambia. At home, I would say "Mucwañi?" to my father in Lozi, my own language. My name is Akalemwa, and I am 18. *Akalemwa* means "the one you cannot outrun." I am in the twelfth grade at Choma Secondary School in Zambia's southern province. Choma is a small town. My family's house is near the hospital, about 2.5 kilometers (1.6 mi.) from town. My father is a medical assistant in charge of village health clinics for our region. My mother is a nurse. I have an older half sister, two older brothers, two younger sisters, and five younger brothers. Our house has three bedrooms and a vegetable garden.

I attend a Protestant missionary school. We sleep in a dormitory at school. Our school year has three three-month terms, starting in January. We have a month vacation after each one. I want to be a doctor, so I am studying math, physics, chemistry, biology, English, and geography.

Lumela, ni muituti mwa naha Zambia.

▲ ~~~~~~~
Translation: Hi, I am a student in Zambia.

Section 1 Physical Geography

Read to Discover

1. What are the major physical features of central Africa?
2. What climates, plants, and animals are found in the region?
3. What major natural resources does central Africa have?

Vocabulary

basin
canopy
copper belt
periodic markets

Places

Congo Basin
Western Rift Valley
Lake Tanganyika
Lake Malawi
Congo River
Zambezi River

Reading Strategy

VISUALIZING INFORMATION Look at the pictures in this section. What do they show you about Central Africa? Write your answers on a sheet of paper. As you read this section, write down the new information you learn.

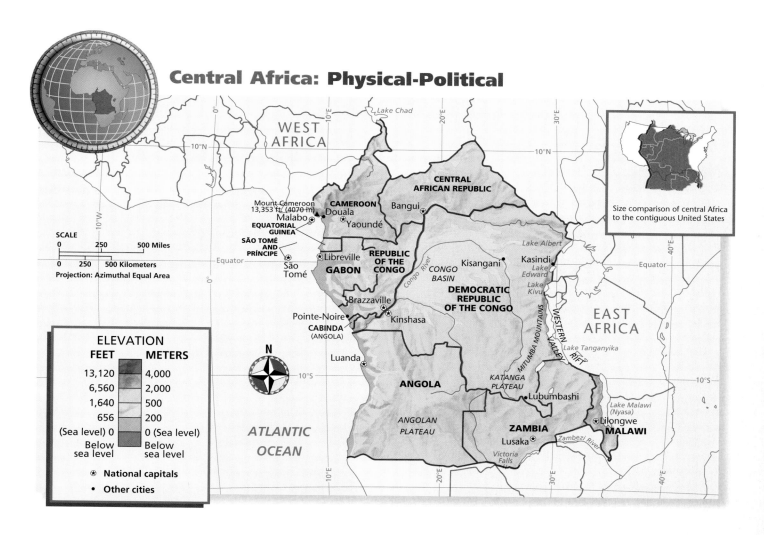

Central Africa: Physical-Political

Size comparison of central Africa to the contiguous United States

SCALE
0   250   500 Miles
0   250   500 Kilometers
Projection: Azimuthal Equal Area

ELEVATION

FEET	METERS
13,120	4,000
6,560	2,000
1,640	500
656	200
(Sea level) 0	0 (Sea level)
Below sea level	Below sea level

⊛ National capitals
• Other cities

WEST AFRICA
Lake Chad
CENTRAL AFRICAN REPUBLIC
Mount Cameroon 13,353 ft. (4070 m)
CAMEROON
Douala
Malabo
Bangui
Yaoundé
EQUATORIAL GUINEA
SÃO TOMÉ AND PRÍNCIPE
Libreville
São Tomé
GABON
REPUBLIC OF THE CONGO
Congo River
CONGO BASIN
Kisangani
Lake Albert
Kasindi
Lake Edward
Lake Kivu
DEMOCRATIC REPUBLIC OF THE CONGO
Brazzaville
Pointe-Noire
CABINDA (ANGOLA)
Kinshasa
MITUMBA MOUNTAINS
WESTERN RIFT VALLEY
EAST AFRICA
Lake Tanganyika
Luanda
ANGOLA
KATANGA PLATEAU
Lubumbashi
ANGOLAN PLATEAU
ZAMBIA
Lusaka
Lake Malawi (Nyasa)
Lilongwe
MALAWI
Zambezi River
Victoria Falls
ATLANTIC OCEAN
Equator

Our Amazing Planet

One of the Congo River's most common animals is the crocodile. This sharp-toothed reptile can grow to about 20 feet (6 m) in length. It swims by sweeping its long tail from side to side.

Location Local people call Victoria Falls *Mosi-oa-Tunya,* which means "the smoke that thunders." The Zambezi River plunges 355 feet (108 m) over a cliff between Zambia and Zimbabwe.

Physical Features

Central Africa stretches southward from Cameroon and the Central African Republic to Angola and Zambia. The Atlantic Ocean lies off the western coast.

Think of the region as a big soup bowl with a wide rim. Near the middle of the bowl is the Congo Basin. A **basin** is a generally flat region surrounded by higher land such as mountains and plateaus.

In northwestern Cameroon are volcanic mountains. The highest is 13,353 feet (4,070 m). Central Africa's highest mountains lie along the Western Rift Valley. Some of these snow-capped mountains rise to more than 16,700 feet (5,090 m). The Western Rift Valley stretches southeastward from the Democratic Republic of the Congo. Lake Tanganyika (tan-guhn-KEE-kuh) and Lake Malawi are found there.

Two major river systems drain the region. In the north the Congo River flows westward to the Atlantic Ocean. Hundreds of smaller rivers flow into the Congo. In the south the Zambezi (zam-BEE-zee) River flows eastward to the Indian Ocean. The Zambezi is famous for its great falls, hydroelectric dams, and lakes.

✓ **READING CHECK:** **Places and Regions** What are the major physical features of central Africa?

Climates, Plants, and Animals

Central Africa lies along the equator and in the low latitudes. The Congo Basin and much of the Atlantic coast have a humid tropical climate. It is wet and warm all year. This climate supports a large, dense tropical rain forest.

The many different kinds of trees in the tropical rain forest form a complete **canopy**. This is the uppermost layer of the trees where the limbs spread out. Leaves block sunlight to the ground below.

Small antelopes, hyenas, elephants, and okapis live in the rain forest region. The okapi is a short-legged relative of the giraffe. Many insects also live in the forest. However, few other plants or creatures

live on the forest floor. This is because little sunlight shines through the canopy. Many animals live in the trees. They include birds, monkeys, bats, and snakes. Large areas of the tropical rain forest are being cleared rapidly for farming and timber. This threatens the plants, animals, and people who live there.

North and south of the Congo Basin are large areas with a tropical savanna climate. Those areas are warm all year, but they have distinct dry and wet seasons. There are grasslands, scattered trees, and shrubs. Only in the high eastern mountains is there a highland climate. Dry steppe and even desert climates are found in the far south.

✓ **READING CHECK:** (*Places and Regions*) What are the region's climates, plants, and animals?

▲

Elephants have created a network of trails and clearings throughout the tropical rain forest. Many animals will gather at forest clearings.

Resources

Central Africa's rivers are among the region's most important natural resources. They are used for travel, trade, and producing hydroelectricity. Other energy resources are oil, natural gas, and coal.

Central Africa has many minerals, including copper, uranium, tin, zinc, diamonds, gold, and cobalt. Most of Africa's copper is found in an area called the **copper belt**, which includes northern Zambia and the southern Democratic Republic of the Congo.

Central African countries have mostly traditional economies. Most people in central Africa are subsistence farmers. However, an increasing number of farmers are growing crops for sale. Common crops include coffee, bananas, and corn. In rural areas, people trade their products in **periodic markets**. A periodic market is an open-air trading market. It is set up regularly at a crossroads or in a town.

✓ **READING CHECK:** (*Places and Regions*) What is central Africa's most important natural resource, and why?

go.hrw.com **Homework Practice Online** Keyword: SG5 HP23

Section Review 1

Define and explain: basin, canopy, copper belt, periodic markets

Working with Sketch Maps On a map of central Africa that you draw or that your teacher provides, label the following: Congo Basin, Western Rift Valley, Lake Tanganyika, Lake Malawi, Congo River, and Zambezi River. In a box in the margin, describe the location of the highest mountains.

Reading for the Main Idea

1. (*Places and Regions*) What major landforms and rivers are found in the region?

2. (*Physical Systems*) Why do few plants and animals live on the floor of the tropical rain forest?

3. (*Places and Regions*) For the most part, what type of economy do central African countries have?

Critical Thinking

4. **Making Generalizations and Predictions** How might central Africa become a rich region?

Organizing What You Know

5. **Summarizing** Copy the following graphic organizer. Use it to describe the region's climates, plants and animals, and major resources.

Climates	Plants and Animals	Resources

Read to Discover

1. What is the history of central Africa, and what challenges do the people there face today?
2. What are the people and cultures of central Africa like?

Vocabulary

ivory
dialects

Places

Brazzaville
Kinshasa

Reading Strategy

READING ORGANIZER Before you read, create a spider map. Draw a circle. Label the circle History and Culture. Draw seven legs and label them Early History, Modern Central Africa, Challenges, Peoples and Languages, Religion, Food, and The Arts. As you read the section, write what you learn about these topics next to each leg.

History

Early humans lived in central Africa many thousands of years ago. They had different languages and cultures. About 2,000 years ago new peoples began to move into the region from western Africa. Those new peoples spoke what are called Bantu languages. Today, Bantu languages are common in most of the region.

Early History Several early Bantu-speaking kingdoms formed in central Africa. Among the most important was the Kongo Kingdom. It was located around the mouth of the Congo River. The Kongo and other central Africans traded with peoples in western and eastern Africa.

Some of the early kingdoms used slaves. In the late 1400s, Europeans came to the region. They began to trade with some African kingdoms for slaves. The Europeans took many enslaved Africans to the Americas. Europeans also wanted the region's forest products and other resources, such as **ivory**. Ivory is a cream-colored material that comes from elephant tusks. It is used in making fine furniture, jewelry, and crafts.

Some African kingdoms became richer by trading with Europeans. However, all were gradually weakened or destroyed by the Europeans. European countries divided all of central Africa into colonies in the late 1800s. The colonial powers were France, the United Kingdom, Belgium, Germany, Spain, and Portugal.

The Europeans drew colonial borders that ignored the homelands of central Africa's ethnic groups. Many groups were lumped together in colonies. These groups spoke different languages and had different

This carved mask was created by a Bantu-speaking people called the Fang. Most live in Cameroon, Equatorial Guinea, and Gabon. Their ancestors moved there in the 1800s.

ways of life. These differences resulted in conflicts, particularly after the colonies won independence.

Modern Central Africa African colonies did not gain independence until after World War II. The largest central African colony was the Belgian Congo. It is now the Democratic Republic of the Congo. That country won independence in 1960. Angola won independence from Portugal in 1975. It was the last European colony in central Africa.

Independence for some African countries came after bloody wars. After independence, fighting between some ethnic groups continued within the new countries. The region also became a battleground in the Cold War. The United States and the Soviet Union supported their allies in small wars throughout Africa. The region's wars killed many people and caused great damage. Some fighting continues off and on in the region.

Challenges Today Ending these wars is one of central Africa's many challenges today. The region's countries must also develop their natural resources more effectively. This would help the many poor people who live there. Another great challenge is stopping the spread of diseases such as malaria and AIDS. These diseases are killing millions of people and leaving many orphans.

✓ **READING CHECK:** (*Human Systems*) What role did Europeans play in central Africa's history?

Culture

Today, about 100 million people live in central Africa. They belong to many different ethnic groups with varying customs.

Our Amazing Planet

In 1986 a cloud of carbon dioxide killed many people and animals near Cameroon's Lake Nyos. The lake is located in the center of a volcanic mountain. An earthquake may have allowed the gas to escape from deep in the lake.

Zambian women are grinding wheat to prepare it for cooking. They are using rods called pestles. The container is called a mortar. This technique is used for grinding many ingredients.

CONNECTING TO History

A headrest from early Luanda, a Bantu kingdom

BANTU LANGUAGES

About 2,000 years ago, the movement of groups of people began to change Africa. Traders, farmers, and other people moved across the southern third of Africa. Experts believe these people came from areas that are now part of Nigeria and Cameroon. Their movement across Africa lasted many centuries. During this period new languages developed. We call them Bantu languages. The grammar and root sounds of the different Bantu languages remain similar.

Some Bantu speakers moved southward along the Atlantic coast. Others moved eastward to Kenya and then turned southward. Over time they reached the tip of southern Africa. The Bantu speakers mixed with peoples who already lived in these lands.

The migration of Bantu speakers had important effects on African life. They brought new ways for growing food. They used tools made of iron, which others also began to use. The Bantu-speakers of course brought their languages. Today, many Africans speak Swahili, Zulu, and other Bantu languages.

Understanding What You Read

1. *Movement* From where did the Bantu peoples come?
2. *Movement* How did their movement shape Africa?

Peoples and Languages As you have read, many central Africans speak Bantu languages. However, those languages can be very different from each other. In fact, hundreds of different languages and **dialects** are spoken in the region. A dialect is a variation of a language.

Many people in the region speak African languages in everyday life. However, the official languages of the central African countries are European. French is the official language of the former French colonies in the north. It is also the official language of the Democratic Republic of the Congo. English is the official language in Zambia and Malawi. Portuguese is spoken in Angola and the island country of São Tomé and Príncipe. Spanish and French are the official languages of tiny Equatorial Guinea.

Religion Many people in the former French, Spanish, and Portuguese colonies are Roman Catholic. Protestant Christianity is most common in former British colonies. Many people practice traditional African religions. In some cases Christian and African practices have been combined.

Human-Environment Interaction These Cameroon juju dancers are calling attention to the destruction of the tropical rain forest. Note the headpieces that represent some of the forest's animals.

Many Muslims live near the mostly Muslim countries of the Sahel in the north. Zambia also has many Muslims as well as Hindus. The Hindus are the descendants of immigrants from southern Asia.

Food In most central African countries, corn, rice, grains, and fish are common foods. In the tropical rain forest, plantains, cassava, and various roots are important foods. For example, in Cameroon you might eat a dish called *fufu*. *Fufu*, a thick, pasty ball of mashed cassava, yams, or plantains, is served with chicken, fish, or a beef gravy.

The Arts *Makossa* dance music from Cameroon has become popular throughout Africa. It can be played with various instruments, including guitars and electric keyboards. The cities of Brazzaville and Kinshasa on the Congo River are the home of *soukous* music.

The region is also famous for carved masks, sculpture, and beautiful cotton gowns. The gowns are dyed in bright colors. They often show pictures that represent things important to the wearer.

Region The *likembe*, or thumb piano, was invented in the lower Congo region. Today its music is heard in many African countries.

✓ **READING CHECK:** (**Human Systems**) What are some characteristics of the people and culture of central Africa?

Homework Practice Online Keyword: SG5 HP23

Section Review 2

Define and explain: ivory, dialects

Working with Sketch Maps On the map you created in Section 1, label Brazzaville and Kinshasa.

Reading for the Main Idea

1. (**Human Systems**) Why are many languages that are spoken today in central Africa related?

2. (**Human Systems**) What have been some of the causes of wars in central Africa?

3. (**Human Systems**) What arts are popular in the region?

Critical Thinking

4. **Finding the Main Idea** How did Europeans influence the culture of the region?

Organizing What You Know

5. **Summarizing** Copy the following graphic organizer. Use it to identify central Africa's challenges.

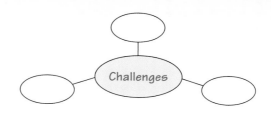

Challenges

Central Africa • 507

Read to Discover

1. What is the history of the Democratic Republic of the Congo?
2. What are the people and culture of the country like?
3. What is the economy of the country like?

Vocabulary
civil war

Places
Lubumbashi

People
Mobutu Sese Seko

Reading Strategy

READING ORGANIZER Before you read, draw a circle in the center of a sheet of paper. Label the circle Democratic Republic of the Congo. Draw three rays from the circle. Draw a circle at the end of each ray. Label the circles History, People, and Economy. As you read this section, write what you learn about these topics next to each circle.

A dancer performs in a coming-of-age ceremony for young people. Many such African traditions have survived the period of colonial rule by Europeans.

History

Portuguese sailors made contact with the Kongo Kingdom in 1482. Over time the slave trade and other problems weakened the Kongo and other African kingdoms.

A Belgian Colony In the 1870s King Leopold II of Belgium took control of the Congo Basin. The king ruled the Congo Free State as his personal colony until 1908. His soldiers treated the Africans harshly. They forced people to work in mines and on plantations. These policies brought international criticism.

The Belgian government took control of the colony from the king in 1908. Many Belgian businesses and people moved there. They mined copper and other resources. The giant colony won independence from tiny Belgium in 1960.

A New Country Many Belgians fled the country after 1960. There were few teachers, doctors, and other professionals left in the former colony. In addition, people from different areas and ethnic groups fought each other. These problems were partly to blame for keeping the country poor.

A dictator, who later changed his name to Mobutu Sese Seko, came to power in 1965. He was an ally of the United States during the Cold War. Mobutu changed the country's name to Zaire in 1971. During his rule, the country suffered from economic problems and government corruption.

A new government took over in 1997 after a **civil war**. A civil war is a war between two or more groups within a country. The new government changed the country's name to the Democratic Republic of the Congo. However, fighting between ethnic groups has continued.

✓ **READING CHECK:** (*Human Systems*) What has the history of the Democratic Republic of the Congo been like?

The Democratic Republic of the Congo

Country	Population/ Growth Rate	Life Expectancy	Literacy Rate	Per Capita GDP
Democratic Republic of the Congo	53,625,039 2.9%	47, male 51, female	65%	$600
United States	290,342,554 0.9%	74, male 80, female	97%	$37,600

Source: Central Intelligence Agency, *The World Factbook 2003*

The People

More than 50 million people live in the Democratic Republic of the Congo today. The population is very diverse. It is divided among more than 200 ethnic groups. The Kongo people are among the largest groups. These groups speak many different languages, but the official language is French. About half of the country's people are Roman Catholic. Protestant Christians, Muslims, and people who practice traditional African religions also live in the country.

More than 4 million people live in Kinshasa, the capital and largest city. Kinshasa is a river port located along the Congo River near the Atlantic coast. The crowded city has some modern buildings. However, most of the city consists of poor slums.

✓ **READING CHECK:** (*Human Systems*) What are the people and culture of the Democratic Republic of the Congo like?

Human-Environment Interaction

A family sells charcoal along a road in the northern Democratic Republic of the Congo. Charcoal is a major fuel source. In many rural areas there is no electricity.

▼

The Congo River lies in the distance in this photograph of Kinshasa.

The Economy

The Democratic Republic of the Congo is a treasure chest of minerals and tropical resources. For example, the south is part of central Africa's rich copper belt. Much of the copper from the area is shipped through the city of Lubumbashi (loo-boom-BAH-shee). The country also has gold, diamonds, and cobalt. The country's tropical rain forest also supplies wood, food, rubber, and other products.

However, the country's people are very poor. Most people live in rural areas. They must farm and trade for food. Civil war, bad government, and crime have scared many foreign businesses away. As a result, the country's rich resources have helped few of its people.

For the economy to improve, the country needs peace and a stable government. Schools must be improved and better health care provided. The country also must repair and expand roads and railways. If its challenges are met, the country's resources can make the future brighter.

✓ **READING CHECK:** *Environment and Society* How might the economy of the country improve?

Homework Practice Online

Keyword: SG5 HP23

Section Review 3

Define or identify: Mobutu Sese Seko, civil war

Working with Sketch Maps On the map you created in Section 2, label the Democratic Republic of the Congo and Lubumbashi. Why is Lubumbashi economically important?

Reading for the Main Idea

1. (Places and Regions) What European country ruled what is now the Democratic Republic of the Congo as a colony until 1960?

2. (Places and Regions) What were some problems the country faced after independence?

Critical Thinking

3. **Finding the Main Idea** In what ways is the Democractic Republic of the Congo a culturally diverse country? What ethnic group is among the largest?

4. **Drawing Inferences and Conclusions** How might better schools and transportation help the country's economy?

Organizing What You Know

5. **Sequencing** Copy the following time line. Use it to identify important groups and individuals in the history of the present-day Democratic Republic of the Congo.

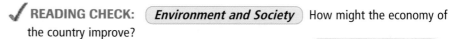

1482   2000

Section 4 The Other Central African Countries

Read to Discover

1. What are the people and economies of the northern central African countries like?
2. What are the people and economies of the southern central African countries like?

Vocabulary

exclave

Places

Douala
Yaoundé
Luanda

Reading Strategy

FOLDNOTES: TWO-PANEL FLIP CHART | Create the FoldNote **Two-Panel Flip Chart.** Label one flap Northern Central Africa and the other flap Southern Central Africa. As you read this section, write what you learn about these regions beneath each flap.

Northern Central Africa

Six countries make up northern central Africa. Four are Cameroon, the Central African Republic, Gabon, and the Republic of the Congo. They gained independence from France in 1960. Cameroon had been a German colony until after World War I. Tiny Equatorial Guinea gained independence from Spain in 1968. The island country of São Tomé and Príncipe won independence from Portugal in 1975.

The People Cameroon is by far the most populous country in this region. About 15.8 million people live there. The Central African Republic has the second-largest population, with 3.5 million. Tiny São Tomé and Príncipe has only about 165,000 people.

A large variety of ethnic groups are found in northern central Africa. Many people are moving from rural areas to cities to search for jobs. Governments are struggling to provide basic services in those crowded cities.

Douala (doo-AH-lah) and Yaoundé (yown-DAY) in Cameroon are the largest cities. Each has more than 1 million people. Douala is an important seaport on the Atlantic coast. Yaoundé is Cameroon's capital. Brazzaville, the capital of the Republic of the Congo, also has 1 million people. The city is a major Congo River port.

The Economy Most of the area's countries are very poor. Most people are farmers. Gabon has the strongest economy in central

Region Although the region's cities are growing rapidly, most people still live in rural areas. This small village is located in northern Cameroon. As in much of rural Africa, several buildings make up a family's home.

▼

Northern Central Africa

COUNTRY	POPULATION/ GROWTH RATE	LIFE EXPECTANCY	LITERACY RATE	PER CAPITA GDP
Cameroon	15,746,179 2.0%	47, male 49, female	79%	$1,700
Central African Republic	3,683,538 1.6%	40, male 43, female	51%	$1,300
Congo, Republic of the	2,954,258 1.5%	49, male 51, female	84%	$900
Equatorial Guinea	510,473 2.5%	53, male 57, female	86%	$2,700
Gabon	1,321,560 2.5%	55, male 58, female	63%	$5,700
São Tomé and Príncipe	175,883 3.2%	64, male 67, female	79%	$1,200
United States	290,342,554 0.9%	74, male 80, female	97%	$37,600

Source: Central Intelligence Agency, *The World Factbook 2003*

Interpreting the Chart Which country in the region has the smallest population? the largest?

Africa. More than half of the value of its economy comes from the oil industry. Oil is important in Cameroon as well as in the Republic of the Congo.

The mighty Congo River is also a vital trade and transportation route. As a result, it plays a major role in the region's economy. Many of the region's goods and farm products are shipped down river to Brazzaville. Brazzaville lies across the Congo River from Kinshasa. From Brazzaville, goods are shipped by railroad to a port on the Atlantic coast.

✓ **READING CHECK:** (*Human Systems*) What are the people and economies of northern central Africa like?

Southern Central Africa

Zambia, Malawi, and Angola make up the southern part of central Africa. The British gave Zambia and Malawi independence in 1964. Angola won independence from Portugal in 1975.

The People The populations of the three southern countries are nearly the same size. They range from about 10 million in Zambia to more than 11 million in Malawi. Angola and Zambia are much larger in area than Malawi. Large parts of Angola and Zambia have few people. Most people in the region live in rural areas. They grow crops and herd cattle and goats.

(*Movement*) Riverboats carry the king of Zambia's Lozi people to a dryland home during the flooding season. This event is an annual ritual for the Lozi, who live in western Zambia. As in other central African countries, many different ethnic groups live in Zambia.

Angola's capital, Luanda, is the southern region's largest city. More than 2 million people live there. Seen from the sea, Luanda looks like a modern city. The city has many high-rise buildings and factories. Unfortunately, Luanda and its people have suffered from poverty and years of war. Rebels fought the Portuguese in the 1960s and early 1970s. After independence, the country plunged into civil war. Fighting continued off and on until 2002. Many people have been killed or injured by land mines.

The Economy In peacetime, the future of Angola could be bright. There are many places with fertile soils. The country has large deposits of diamonds and oil. The oil is found offshore north of Luanda and in the exclave of Cabinda. An **exclave** is part of a country that is separated by territory of other countries. Cabinda is separated from the rest of Angola by the Democratic Republic of the Congo.

Much of Zambia's income comes from rich copper mines. However, 85 percent of Zambia's workers are farmers. Most of the country's energy comes from hydroelectric dams and power plants along rivers.

About 75 percent of Malawi's people live in rural areas. Nearly all of them are farmers. The building of factories and industries has been slow. Aid from other countries and religious missionaries has been important to the economy.

Southern Central Africa

Country	Population/ Growth Rate	Life Expectancy	Literacy Rate	Per Capita GDP
Angola	10,766,471 1.2%	36, male 38, female	42%	$1,600
Malawi	11,651,239 2.2%	37, male 38, female	62%	$670
Zambia	10,307,333 1.5%	37, male 38, female	80%	$890
United States	290,342,554 0.9%	74, male 80, female	97%	$37,600

Source: Central Intelligence Agency, *The World Factbook 2003*

Interpreting the Chart **Which country in the region has the highest literacy rate?**

✓ **READING CHECK:** (*Human Systems*) What are the people and economies of the southern central African countries like?

Homework Practice Online
Keyword: SG5 HP23

Section Review 4

Define and explain: exclave

Working with Sketch Maps On the map you created in Section 3, label the countries of northern and southern central Africa, and Douala, Yaoundé, and Luanda. In a box in the margin, describe Luanda.

Reading for the Main Idea

1. (*Places and Regions*) Which country has the strongest economy in central Africa?

2. (*Environment and Society*) What significance does oil have in the economies of many countries in the region?

3. (*Human Systems*) What has happened in Angola since that country won its independence?

Critical Thinking

4. Analyzing Information Why is Brazzaville important to the region's economy?

Organizing What You Know

5. Summarizing Copy the following graphic organizer. Divide it into nine rows below the headings. Use it to list the countries discussed in this section. Then identify the European country that colonized each central African country. Finally, list the date each country won independence.

Country	European colonial ruler	Year of independence

Define and Identify

Identify each of the following:

1. basin
2. canopy
3. copper belt
4. periodic markets
5. ivory
6. dialects
7. civil war
8. Mobutu Sese Seko
9. exclave

Review the Main Ideas

10. What two river systems are most important in central Africa?
11. Where are central Africa's highest mountains found?
12. What types of economies do central African countries practice?
13. How were the Bantu languages introduced to central Africa?
14. What challenges are the countries of central Africa facing today?
15. What religions are practiced by people in the Democratic Republic of the Congo?

16. What European countries once colonized central Africa?
17. How important has oil been to Gabon's economy?
18. How does Zambia get their energy?

Think Critically

19. **Drawing Inferences and Conclusions** Why do few large animals live on the floor of central Africa's tropical rain forests?
20. **Finding the Main Idea** How have borders drawn by European colonial powers contributed to ethnic conflicts in central Africa?
21. **Analyzing Information** How have their locations on major rivers or near important natural resources aided the growth of cities such as Brazzaville and Lubumbashi?
22. **Drawing Inferences and Conclusions** Why do you think European languages are still the official languages in the countries of central Africa?
23. **Finding the Main Idea** How did the Cold War contribute to problems in central Africa?

Map Activity

24. On a separate sheet of paper, match the letters on the map with their correct labels.

Congo Basin	Zambezi River
Western Rift Valley	Kinshasa
Lake Tanganyika	Lubumbashi
Lake Malawi	Douala
Congo River	Luanda

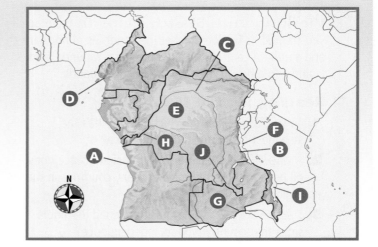

Writing Activity

Imagine that you have been hired to write a magazine article describing challenges facing central Africans. Write a descriptive headline and a brief summary for your proposed article. The article should cover the region's economic, political, and health challenges. Be sure to use standard grammar, spelling, sentence structure, and punctuation.

internet connect

Internet Activity: **go.hrw.com**
KEYWORD: **SG5 GT23**

Choose a topic to explore about central Africa:
* Identify threats to the Congo Basin.
* Visit the people of central Africa.
* Learn the importance of African cloth.

Social Studies Skills Practice

Interpreting Maps

Study the map of the Democratic Republic of Congo below. Then answer the questions.

Civil War in the Democratic Republic of Congo, 1998

1. What is the main idea of this map?
2. Which group controlled most of eastern Democratic Republic of Congo?
3. Which group controlled the Democratic Republic of Congo's capital?
4. Based on what you know about the region, why would control of Kinshasa be important?

Analyzing Primary Sources

Read the following quote from Werner Vansant, a humanitarian aid worker in the Democratic Republic of Congo during the 1998–2002 civil war. Then answer the questions.

"This is not a war of troops fighting against troops. It's a war against civil society, where infrastructures are destroyed and looted, all medicines stolen from health posts, key people like nurses are killed in villages, and agricultural fields are destroyed. So people have no food, no medical care, they don't get treated . . . They hide in the jungle for weeks and get malnourished, sick, weaker and weaker. Sometimes you see people coming out of the bush in terrible, terrible conditions, without clothes and without anything. Those are the victims of this war."

1. Why does Vansant think this civil war is different from other wars?
2. What goods and services do people in the Democratic Republic of Congo lack because of the war?
3. How did ordinary people respond to the crisis caused by the war?
4. Why does Vansant call people who are not fighting "the victims of the war"?

CHAPTER 24

Southern Africa

Southern Africa is a region going through many changes. Some people in the area have a comfortable lifestyle, but others live in severe poverty.

Abatsu! (Good morning!) My name is Kha//'an[1] and I am a San person from Namibia. I am in ninth grade at the Tsumkwe[2] Secondary School. We do not have a house, only a small shelter to store our things. We live near the gate in the fence at M'Kata. If you turn east when you arrive there, you will see our blankets under the tree. When we are seeking shade or shelter, we go and sit under the tree.

My mother and father passed away when I was five years old, and my elder brother took care of me. I live with my brother, and the government helps us survive by giving us food rations.

At school I live in a hostel. We wake up at five in the morning and have breakfast at six. Breakfast is only bread. We have maize meal, tea, and milk at noon. My favorite subjects are English, history, physical science, and mathematics. When I grow up, I want to be a doctor.

=Xai-o![3] Mi o Kha//'an.

Translation: Greetings! I am Kha//'an.

[1] The "//" is a click made by clucking the tongue at the sides of the mouth.
[2] The "k" in Tsumkwe is another kind of click. It is made by placing the tongue on the roof of the mouth and bringing it down with a "pop."
[3] The = is a click made by placing the tip of the tongue on the ridge behind the upper front teeth and bringing it down with a "pop."

Section 1 Physical Geography

Read to Discover

1. What are the major physical features and climates of southern Africa?
2. What resources are found in the region?

Vocabulary

enclaves
the veld
pans

Places

Drakensberg
Inyanga Mountains
Cape of Good Hope
Kalahari Desert

Namib Desert
Orange River
Aughrabies Falls
Limpopo River

Reading Strategy

FOLDNOTES: LAYERED BOOK Create the FoldNote titled **Layered Book** described in the Appendix. Label the layers of the book Countries, Landforms, Climates, and Resources. As you read this section, write what you learn about each topic in the appropriate layer of the book.

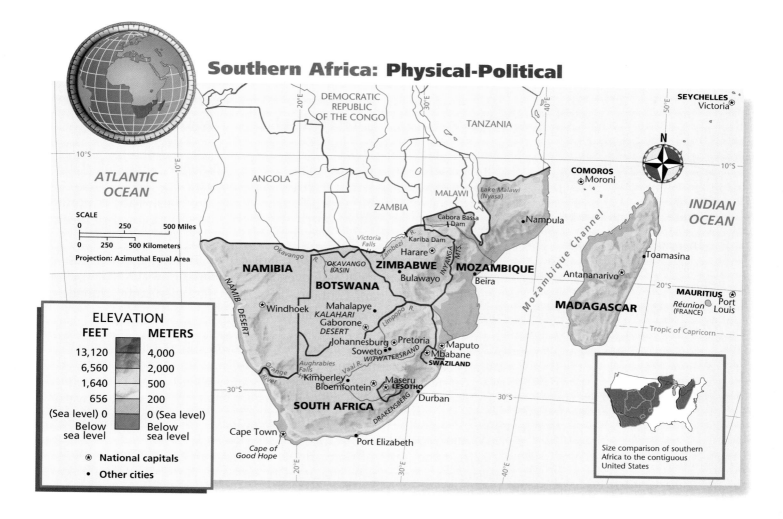

Southern Africa: Physical-Political

ELEVATION

FEET	METERS
13,120	4,000
6,560	2,000
1,640	500
656	200
(Sea level) 0	0 (Sea level)
Below sea level	Below sea level

⊛ National capitals
• Other cities

SCALE
0   250   500 Miles
0   250   500 Kilometers
Projection: Azimuthal Equal Area

ATLANTIC OCEAN

DEMOCRATIC REPUBLIC OF THE CONGO

TANZANIA

SEYCHELLES
Victoria ⊛

COMOROS
⊛ Moroni

INDIAN OCEAN

ANGOLA

ZAMBIA

MALAWI

Lake Malawi (Nyasa)

• Nampula

Cabora Bassa Dam

Victoria Falls

Kariba Dam

Harare ⊛

Okavango R.

OKAVANGO BASIN

ZIMBABWE

Bulawayo

MOZAMBIQUE

Beira

Mozambique Channel

Toamasina

Antananarivo ⊛

MADAGASCAR

MAURITIUS ⊛
Réunion (FRANCE)   Port Louis

NAMIBIA

BOTSWANA

⊛ Windhoek

Mahalapye
KALAHARI
Gaborone ⊛
DESERT

Limpopo R.

Johannesburg • ⊛ Pretoria

Soweto WITWATERSRAND

Aughrabies Falls

Vaal R.

Kimberley
Bloemfontein ⊛

Orange River

⊛ Maputo

⊛ Mbabane
SWAZILAND

Maseru ⊛ LESOTHO

Durban

DRAKENSBERG

SOUTH AFRICA

Cape Town ⊛

Cape of Good Hope

Port Elizabeth

Tropic of Capricorn

Size comparison of southern Africa to the contiguous United States

The Drakensberg range rises sharply in eastern South Africa.

Drakensberg means "dragon mountain" in the Afrikaans language. The Zulu, one of the peoples of the region, call it Kwathlamba, meaning "barrier of pointed spears" or "piled-up rocks."

Countries of the Region

Lining southern Africa's coasts are Namibia (nuh-MI-bee-uh), South Africa, and Mozambique (moh-zahm-BEEK). Botswana (bawt-SWAH-nah), Zimbabwe (zim-BAH-bway), and the two tiny countries of Lesotho (luh-SOH-toh) and Swaziland (SWAH-zee-land) are all land-locked. Lesotho and Swaziland are **enclaves**—countries surrounded or almost surrounded by another country. Madagascar (ma-duh-GAS-kuhr), off the east coast, is the world's fourth-largest island.

Physical Features and Climate

The surface of southern Africa is dominated by a large plateau. The southeastern edge of this plateau is a mountain range called the Drakensberg (DRAH-kuhnz-buhrk). The steep peaks rise as high as 11,425 feet (3,482 m) from the plains along the coast. Farther north, another mountain range, the Inyanga (in-YANG-guh) Mountains, forms the plateau's eastern edge.

The open grassland areas of South Africa are known as **the veld** (VELT). Kruger National Park covers 7,523 square miles (19,485 sq km) of the veld. The park contains lions, leopards, elephants, rhinoceroses, hippos, baboons, and antelope.

Climate The region's climates range from desert to cool uplands. Winds carry moisture from the Indian Ocean. These winds are forced upward by the Drakensberg and Inyanga Mountains. The eastern slopes are rainy, but climates are drier farther inland and westward. Most of the interior of southern Africa is semiarid and has steppe and savanna vegetation.

Near the Cape of Good Hope, winter rains and summer drought create a Mediterranean climate. Off the Cape, storms and rough seas are common.

Deserts and Rivers In the central and western parts of the region, savanna and steppe give way to two major deserts. The Kalahari (ka-luh-hahr-ee) occupies most of Botswana. Here ancient streams have drained into low, flat areas, or **pans**. Minerals left behind when the water evaporated form a glittering white layer.

The Namib (NAH-mib) Desert lies along the Atlantic coast. Inland, the Namib blends into the Kalahari and steppe. Almost no rain falls, but at night fog rolls in from the ocean. Some plants and animals survive by using the fog as a source of water.

Southern Africa has some of the world's most spectacular rivers and waterfalls. The Orange River passes through the Aughrabies (oh-KRAH-bees) Falls as it flows to the Atlantic. When the water is highest, the Aughrabies Falls are several miles wide. The water tumbles down 19 separate waterfalls. The Limpopo (lim-POH-poh) River is the region's other major river. It flows into the Indian Ocean.

✓ **READING CHECK:** (*Places and Regions*) What are southern Africa's physical features and climate?

internet connect
GO TO: go.hrw.com
KEYWORD: SG5 CH24
FOR: Web sites about southern Africa

The Orange River flows down the spectacular Aughrabies Falls. The falls are near the Namibian border in northwestern South Africa.

Resources

Southern Africa is very rich in mineral resources. Gold, diamonds, platinum, copper, uranium, coal, and iron ore are all found in the region. Where rain is plentiful or irrigation is possible, farmers can grow a wide range of crops. Ranchers raise livestock on the high plains. Some nomadic herders still live in desert areas.

✓ **READING CHECK:** (*Places and Regions*) What are the main resources of southern Africa?

go.hrw.com **Homework Practice Online**
Keyword: SG5 HP24

Section Review 1

Define and explain: enclaves, the veld, pans

Working with Sketch Maps On a map of southern Africa that you draw or that your teacher provides, label the following: Drakensberg, Inyanga Mountains, Cape of Good Hope, Kalahari Desert, Namib Desert, Orange River, Aughrabies Falls, and Limpopo River. The Orange River forms part of the border between what two countries?

Reading for the Main Idea

1. (*Places and Regions*) What are the major landforms of southern Africa?

2. (*Places and Regions*) What are the main natural resources of the region?

3. (*Physical Systems*) How do physical processes affect southern Africa's climate?

Critical Thinking

4. Drawing Inferences and Conclusions How do you think the climate off the Cape of Good Hope has affected shipping in the area?

Organizing What You Know

5. Summarizing Copy the following graphic organizer. Use it to list the landforms, climates, and resources of southern Africa.

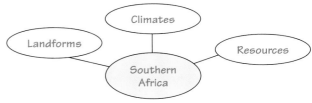

Climates

Landforms

Resources

Southern Africa

Southern Africa's History and Culture

Read to Discover

1. What was the early history of southern Africa like?

2. How did Europeans gain control of southern Africa, and what changes did this cause?

Reading Strategy

TAKING NOTES Use the headings in this section to create an outline. As you read the section, write what you learn beneath each heading.

Vocabulary

Boers

Places

Cape Town

▲

Ancient rock art of southern Africa often includes hunters and animals.

Interpreting the Visual Record What do these images suggest about the people who made them?

Early History

Southern Africa's landscape and climate have influenced the region's history. For example, monsoon winds blow from the Indian Ocean to southern Africa from November to February. From May to September the wind blows the other way, from Africa to Asia. Ancient ships used these winds to make regular trading voyages between the two continents.

The Khoisan Some of the oldest human fossils have been found in southern Africa. By about 18,000 B.C., groups of hunter-gatherers were living throughout the mainland region. They left distinctive paintings of people and animals on rock surfaces. Some descendants of these people still live in certain desert regions. They speak languages of the Khoisan language family, which share unusual "click" sounds. However, most Khoisan people were absorbed into groups that moved into the region later.

Bantu Migrations Some 1,500–2,000 years ago a different group of people spread from central Africa into southern Africa. They spoke another family of languages known as Bantu. Today, most southern Africans speak one of the more than 200 Bantu languages. Scholars believe the early Bantu people introduced the use of iron to make tools. The Bantu are also thought to have introduced cattle herding to the region.

Shona and Swahili By about A.D. 1000 one Bantu group, the Shona, had built an empire. It included much of what is now Zimbabwe and Mozambique. They farmed, raised cattle, and traded gold with other groups on the coast. They also constructed stone-walled towns called zimbabwe. The largest town, now called Great Zimbabwe, may have had 10,000 to 20,000 residents. Great Zimbabwe was abandoned in the 1400s.

Among Great Zimbabwe's trading partners were the Swahili-speaking people of the east coast. These were Africans who had adopted Islam and many Arab customs by the A.D. 1100s. The Swahili-speakers were sailors and traders. Archaeologists have found Chinese porcelain at Great Zimbabwe. This suggests that Africa and East Asia were connected by an Indian Ocean trade network.

▲

People fish with nets in the Indian Ocean. Fishing is an important industry in Mozambique and Madagascar.

Madagascar Madagascar's early history is quite different from the rest of southern Africa. Madagascar's first settlers came from Asia, rather than Africa, about A.D. 700. The island's culture shows the influence of both Africa and Asia. Malagasy, Madagascar's official language, is related to languages spoken in Indonesia. Malagasy also includes many words from the Bantu language family.

Mozambique In the early 1500s the Portuguese set up forts in Mozambique. They hoped to take over the region's gold trade from the Swahili-speakers and Arabs. The Portuguese also established large estates along the Zambezi River that used slave labor. In the 1700s and 1800s Mozambique became an important part of the slave trade. Africans were captured there and sent as slaves to Brazil and other parts of the world.

✔ **READING CHECK:** (*Human Systems*) What were some key events in the early history of southern Africa?

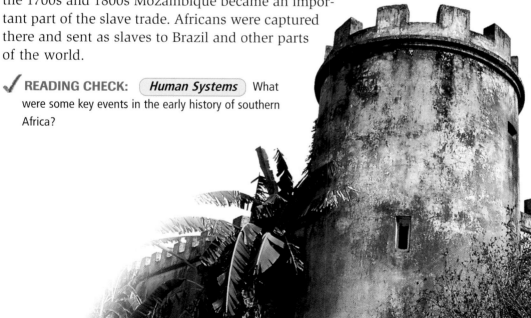

The Portuguese built this prison in Mozambique in the 1800s.

Interpreting the Visual Record

(*Movement*) **How might this architecture reflect European influences?**

◄

In this painting, British ships sail past the Cape of Good Hope. The distinctively shaped Table Mountain is visible in the distance.

Much of southern Africa was a malaria zone. Quinine, a medicine made from a South American tree, could combat malaria. Using this medicine, Europeans were able to move into lowland areas where malaria was common.

In this 1935 photograph, elephant tusks and rhino horns are inspected in a London warehouse.

The Dutch, British, and Portuguese in South Africa

The land around the Cape of Good Hope lacked the gold and copper of the Zambezi Valley. However, it had a Mediterranean climate. It also was free of the mosquitoes and tsetse flies that spread tropical diseases. In 1652 the Dutch set up a trade station at a natural harbor near the Cape. This small colony would eventually become known as Cape Town. It provided supplies to Dutch ships sailing between the Dutch East Indies and Europe. The Dutch brought in slaves to work in the colony. Some were Malays from Southeast Asia. Others were Africans bought at slave markets in other parts of Africa.

Afrikaners and Afrikaans The main language spoken in the colony was Dutch. Over time, a new language called Afrikaans emerged. Khoison, Bantu, and Malay words were added to the Dutch, together with some English vocabulary. White descendants of the original colonists are called Afrikaners. Some European men married Khoisan or Malay women. People descended from Malays, Khoisan, or a mixture of these with Europeans are called Coloureds.

A British Colony Afrikaner frontier farmers called **Boers** gradually spread out from the original colony. Then, in the early 1800s, Great Britain took over the area of the Cape. The Boers resisted the British colonial government. Many Boers packed all their belongings into wagons and moved farther east and north. This movement was called the Great Trek.

At about the same time, a Bantu-speaking group, the Zulu, became a powerful fighting force. They conquered the surrounding African peoples, creating their own empire. When the Boers moved into the northern plains, they entered Zulu territory. The two sides clashed. Eventually the Zulu were challenged by the British and defeated after a series of battles.

Trade in Slaves and Ivory The British banned slavery in their empire in 1833. The Portuguese colonies of Angola and Mozambique remained as Africa's main slave markets. The slave trade eventually ended in the late 1800s. African trade began to focus on ivory—the tusks of elephants. Hunters wiped out the entire elephant population in some parts of southern Africa.

Diamonds, Gold, and Colonies In the 1860s diamonds were discovered in the northern part of the Cape Colony. In 1886 gold was discovered in the Transvaal, an area controlled by the Boers. Thousands of British and others came to South Africa. Railroads were built to connect the interior with the coast.

As the British moved north from the Cape Colony, some Boers moved into what is now Botswana. Afraid that the Boers would take over his country, Botswana's ruler asked for British protection. In 1885 Botswana (then known as Bechuanaland) came under British control. What is now Namibia became German Southwest Africa—a German colony. In 1889 what is now Zimbabwe came under control of the British South Africa Company as part of Rhodesia. It became a self-governing British colony in 1923.

South Africa In 1899 tensions over land and mineral wealth led to war between the Boers and the British. The Boers were greatly outnumbered, but held off the British army for three years. In the end the Boers were defeated. Their territory was added to the British colony of South Africa. In 1920, following Germany's defeat in World War I, Namibia was placed under South Africa's control.

▲

This old steam train still operates in South Africa. The British built this and other railroads during the colonial period.

Interpreting the Visual Record

(*Movement*) **Why did the Europeans connect the interior with the coast?**

✓ **READING CHECK:** (*Human Systems*) How did Europeans gain control of southern Africa, and what changes did this cause?

Homework Practice Online
Keyword: SG5 HP24

Define and explain: Boers

Working with Sketch Maps On the map you created in Section 1, label Cape Town. What were the advantages of Cape Town's location?

Reading for the Main Idea

1. (*Human Systems*) How did the Bantu affect the history of southern Africa?

2. (*Human Systems*) How do archaeologists believe Chinese porcelain came to Great Zimbabwe?

Critical Thinking

3. Finding the Main Idea How did the slave trade affect southern Africa?

4. Analyzing Information What European groups settled in southern Africa? How did these groups interact with each other?

Organizing What You Know

5. Sequencing Copy the following time line. Use it to mark important events in the history of southern Africa from 18,000 B.C. to 1920.

18,000 B.C.   1920

Read to Discover

1. What was South Africa's policy of apartheid?
2. What factors led to the end of apartheid?
3. What is South Africa's economy like?
4. What are South Africa's prospects for the future?

Vocabulary

apartheid
townships
sanctions

Places

Witwatersrand
Johannesburg
Durban
Port Elizabeth

People

Nelson Mandela
Desmond Tutu

Reading Strategy

READING ORGANIZER Before you read this section, draw a large circle on a sheet of paper. Draw a vertical line and a horizontal line across the center of the circle. Label the parts Racial Divisions, Pressure against South Africa, Economy, and Future. As you read this section, write what you learn in each part of the circle.

BIOGRAPHY

Nelson Mandela
(1918–)

Character Trait: Citizenship

Because he protested against apartheid, Nelson Mandela was imprisoned for 26 years. In 1990, however, South Africa's President de Klerk released Mandela from prison. Mandela and de Klerk shared the Nobel Peace Prize in 1993. One year later, Mandela became South Africa's first black president. He wrote a new constitution and worked to improve the living conditions of black South Africans.

How did Nelson Mandela show citizenship?

Racial Divisions

In the early 1900s South Africa's government, which was dominated by Afrikaners, became increasingly racist. Some black South Africans opposed the government. They formed the African National Congress (ANC) in 1912 to defend their rights. However, the trend toward racial division and inequality continued.

After World War II South Africa became an independent country. The South African government set up a policy of separation for its different peoples. This policy was called **apartheid**, meaning "apartness." The government divided people into three groups: whites, coloureds and Asians, and blacks—the overwhelming majority. Coloureds and Asians were only allowed to live in certain areas. Each African tribe or group was given its own rural "homeland."

The whites owned most of the good farmland. They also owned the mines and other natural resources. Black Africans had no rights in white areas. Blacks' land, housing, and health care were poor compared to those for whites. Education for blacks was limited, and classes were often taught in Afrikaans. Coloureds' facilities were poor but slightly better than those for blacks. People who protested these rules were sent to prison. One of those imprisoned was a lawyer named Nelson Mandela, a leader of the ANC.

Many blacks found work in white-owned industries, mines, shops, and farms. They had to live in separate areas called **townships**. These were often crowded clusters of tiny homes. They were far from the jobs in the cities and mines.

✓ **READING CHECK:** (**Human Systems**) What was apartheid?

In townships like Kayalitsha, black workers lived in crude shacks.

Interpreting the Visual Record **How did the apartheid system affect the roles and responsibilities of South Africans?**

Pressure against South Africa

Many people around the world objected to South Africa's apartheid laws. Some countries banned trade with South Africa. Some companies in the United States and Europe refused to invest their money in South Africa. Many international scientific and sports organizations refused to include South Africans in their meetings and competitions. These penalties, called **sanctions**, were intended to force South Africa to end apartheid.

South Africa and Its Neighbors During the 1960s, 1970s, and 1980s other countries in southern Africa gained their independence from colonial rule. British colonists in Rhodesia protested Britain's decision to grant independence. They declared their own white-dominated republic in 1970. This break resulted in years of violence and civil war. Finally the white government agreed to hold elections. They turned the country over to the black majority. The new government renamed the country Zimbabwe.

Mozambique was granted independence in 1975 after 10 years of war against Portuguese rule. However, rebels backed by Rhodesia and South Africa plunged Mozambique into another long war. Despite violent resistance, Namibia continued to be ruled by South Africa until independence in 1990.

The End of Apartheid As other countries in southern Africa gained independence, South Africa became more and more isolated. Protest within the country increased. The government outlawed the ANC. Many ANC members were jailed or forced to leave the country.

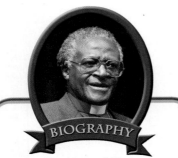
Desmond Tutu
(1931–)

Character Trait: Integrity

Black South Africans struggling for equality found an able leader in Desmond Mpilo Tutu. Educated in South Africa and England, Tutu worked his way up into the highest levels of the Anglican church. So, people around the world listened when he spoke out against apartheid. Tutu emphasized using nonviolent protest and economic pressure to gain freedom for black South Africans. In 1984, Tutu received the Nobel Peace Prize for his efforts to end apartheid peacefully.

What makes Desmond Tutu a man of integrity?

Antiapartheid protesters turned increasingly to violence. South African forces attacked suspected rebel bases in neighboring countries like Botswana and Zimbabwe.

Finally, in the late 1980s South Africa began to move away from the apartheid system. In 1990 the government released Nelson Mandela from prison. Mandela was elected president in 1994 after all South Africans were given the right to vote.

Today all races have equal rights in South Africa. Public schools and universities are open to all, as are hospitals and transportation. However, economic equality has been slow in coming. White South Africans are still wealthier than the vast majority of black South Africans. Also, divisions between different black ethnic groups have caused new tensions. Still, South Africans now hope for a better future.

✓ **READING CHECK:** (*Human Systems*) Why and how did South Africa do away with apartheid?

South Africa's Economy

South Africa's government is trying to create jobs and better conditions for black workers and farmers. However, South Africa's mineral wealth and industries are still mostly owned by white people. Even officials who favor reform are afraid that too-rapid change will weaken the economy. They fear it will drive educated and wealthy whites to leave the country. The government has avoided taking white-owned farmland to divide among black farmers.

South Africa's energy resources include coal and hydroelectric power. Rich uranium mines provide fuel for nuclear power plants. In addition to gold and diamonds, mineral resources include copper, platinum, iron ore, and chromium.

The Witwatersrand region around Johannesburg is the continent's largest industrial area. South African and foreign companies build computers, cars, televisions, and many other products needed for modern life. The major port is Durban on the Indian Ocean coast. Cape Town and Port Elizabeth are other important ports.

✓ **READING CHECK:** (*Human Systems*) How has apartheid continued to affect South Africa's economy today?

These are uncut, or rough, diamonds. Diamonds are the hardest mineral. This makes them useful for certain types of cutting and drilling.

South Africa's Future

South Africa has more resources and industry than most African countries but faces severe problems. It must begin to deliver equal education and economic opportunities to the entire population.

Place Cape Town has grown into a large industrial city. In this photograph, the harbor is visible beyond the tall buildings of the business district.

New problems have arisen since the end of apartheid. Crime has increased in the large cities. Also, South Africa, like the rest of the region, is facing a terrible AIDS epidemic.

There are 11 official languages in South Africa, although English is used in most areas. South Africa produces fine wines from the region around Cape Town. It has a unique cooking style combining Dutch, Malay, and African foods. The country also has a lively tradition of literature and the arts. Today, traditional ethnic designs are used in clothing, lamps, linens, and other products. These are sold to tourists and locals alike.

✓ READING CHECK: **Places and Regions** What are the challenges faced by South Africa?

South Africa

Country	Population/ Growth Rate	Life Expectancy	Literacy Rate	Per Capita GDP
South Africa	42,768,678 0.3%	47, male 46, female	86%	$10,000
United States	290,342,554 0.9%	74, male 80, female	97%	$37,600

Source: Central Intelligence Agency, *The World Factbook 2003*

Interpreting the Chart **What is South Africa's per capita GDP?**

Section Review 3

go. hrw .com **Homework Practice Online** Keyword: SG5 HP24

Define or identify: apartheid, Nelson Mandela, townships, sanctions, Desmond Tutu

Working with Sketch Maps On the map you created in Section 2, label Witwatersrand, Johannesburg, Durban, and Port Elizabeth.

Reading for the Main Idea

1. *Human Systems* What was the system of apartheid, and how did it affect the roles and responsibilities of South Africans?

2. *Human Systems* How did people around the world protest apartheid?

3. *Places and Regions* What challenges remain for South Africa?

Critical Thinking

4. Analyzing Information Why is South Africa the continent's most economically developed country?

Organizing What You Know

5. Summarizing Use this graphic organizer to list information about life in South Africa during apartheid and since the system ended.

During apartheid	Since apartheid ended

The Other Southern African Countries

Read to Discover

1. What groups have influenced Namibia's culture?
2. What factors have helped Botswana's economy?
3. What is Zimbabwe's economy like?
4. Why has Mozambique remained so poor?
5. What events have marked Madagascar's recent history?

Vocabulary

Organization of African Unity (OAU)

Places

Windhoek
Gaborone
Harare
Maputo

Reading Strategy

READING ORGANIZER Before you read, create a three-column chart on a sheet of paper. Label the columns Country, Resources, and Challenges. Then list each country covered in this section in the Country column. As you read this section, write what you learn about the resources and challenges of each country.

A San grandmother and child drink water from an ostrich egg. The San people traditionally lived by hunting and gathering. However, just a few live this way today.

Interpreting the Visual Record

Human-Environment Interaction **What factors do you think might lead many San people to give up their traditional way of life?**

▼

Namibia

Most Namibians live in the savannas of the north or in the cooler central highlands. Windhoek, the capital, is located in these highlands. About 6 percent of the population is white, mainly of German descent. The rest of the population is divided among several different ethnic groups. Most Namibians are Christian. English is the official language. However, schooling was in Afrikaans until recently.

At independence in 1990, white farmers held most of the productive land. Most of Namibia's income comes from the mining of diamonds, copper, lead, zinc, and uranium. Fishing in the Atlantic Ocean and sheep ranching are also important sources of income.

Namibian culture shows many different influences. In many rocky areas, ancient rock engravings and paintings of the Khoisan are preserved. Beer and pastries reflect the period of German colonization.

✓ **READING CHECK:** *Human Systems* What are Namibia's cultural influences?

Botswana

Botswana is a large, landlocked, semiarid country. Thanks to mineral resources and stable political conditions, Botswana is one of Africa's success stories. Cattle ranching and mining of copper and diamonds are the principal economic activities. Recently, international companies have set up factories here. A new capital,

Gaborone, was built after independence. Like the other countries of the region, Botswana belongs to the **Organization of African Unity (OAU)**. The OAU, founded in 1963, tries to promote cooperation between African countries.

Botswana's population is less than 1.6 million. About 79 percent belong to a single ethnic group, the Tswana. Most of the population live in the savanna and steppe areas of the east and south. The San and other minority groups mostly live in the northern swamps and the Kalahari Desert. About 15 percent of Botswana's people are Christian. The rest follow traditional African religions.

Botswana's major river, the Okavango, flows from Angola into a huge basin. The swamps of this basin are home to elephants, crocodiles, antelope, lions, hyenas, and other animals. Many tourists travel to Botswana to see these wild animals in their habitat.

Traditional crafts of Botswana include ostrich-eggshell beadwork and woven baskets with complex designs. People there also produce colorful wool tapestries and rugs.

✔ **READING CHECK:** (*Places and Regions*) Why might Botswana be considered a success story?

▲ The Okavango River spreads out to form a large swampy area. Dense vegetation allows only small boats to move through the narrow channels.

Zimbabwe

Zimbabwe's capital is Harare. Zimbabwe gained independence in 1980. Since then, the country has struggled to create a more equal distribution of land and wealth. White residents make up less than 1 percent of the population. However, they still own most of the large farms and ranches.

Zimbabwe exports tobacco, corn, sugar, and beef. It now manufactures many everyday items, including shoes, batteries, and radios. Exports of gold, copper, chrome, nickel, and tin are also important to Zimbabwe's economy.

The AIDS epidemic threatens to kill hundreds of thousands of Zimbabwe's people, leaving many orphans behind. These effects will make economic growth harder. Other diseases such as malaria and tuberculosis are often deadly. There are also tensions between the majority Shona people and the minority Ndebele.

Artists in Zimbabwe have revived the tradition of stone sculpture found at Great Zimbabwe. Some of the larger pieces are among the most striking examples of modern art in the world.

✔ **READING CHECK:** (*Places and Regions*) What is Zimbabwe's economy like?

Other Southern African Countries

COUNTRY	POPULATION/ GROWTH RATE	LIFE EXPECTANCY	LITERACY RATE	PER CAPITA GDP
Botswana	1,573,267 0.5%	32, male 32, female	79%	$9,500
Madagascar	16,979,744 3%	53, male 58, female	69%	$760
Mozambique	17,479,266 0.8%	31, male 32, female	48%	$1,000
Namibia	1,927,447 1.4%	44, male 41, female	84%	$6,900
Zimbabwe	12,576,742 0.2%	40, male 38, female	90%	$2,400
United States	290,342,554 0.9%	74, male 80, female	97%	$37,600

Source: Central Intelligence Agency, *The World Factbook 2003*

Interpreting the Chart **Which countries are the least economically developed in the region?**

CONNECTING TO History

In 1884–85, representatives of Europe's colonial countries met in Berlin. These countries included Belgium, France, Germany, Great Britain, Italy, Portugal, and Spain. Each was conquering areas in Africa. Their claims to territory were beginning to overlap. Leaders began to worry that a rivalry in Africa might trigger a war in Europe.

The Berlin conference was called to agree to boundaries for these African colonies. No Africans were invited to the conference. The European representatives divided up Africa among themselves. The new borders sometimes followed physical features, such as lakes and mountains. Many simply followed straight lines of latitude or longitude. Often people from the same ethnic group were separated by the new borders. In other places, ethnic groups hostile to each other were grouped together.

Most of the European colonies in Africa became independent after 1960. However, the leaders of the new African countries have

AFRICA'S BORDERS

Cartoon of France and Britain dividing Africa

mostly avoided drawing new boundary lines. So these countries still struggle with the borders they inherited from the Berlin Conference. These borders have made it hard for many African countries to build national loyalty among their citizens.

Understanding What You Read

1. How were Africa's borders established?
2. What consequences have these borders had for modern Africa?

Mozambique

Mozambique is one of the world's poorest countries. Its economy was badly damaged by civil war after independence from Portugal. Today, Mozambique's ports of Maputo—the capital—and Beira once again ship many products from interior Africa. The taxes collected on these shipments are an important source of revenue. Energy sources include coal and new hydroelectric dams on the Zambezi River. Plantations grow cotton, cashews, sugar, and tea.

Most of Mozambique's people belong to various Bantu ethnic groups. Each group has its own language. However, the country's official language is Portuguese. About 30 percent of the people are Christian, and 20 percent are Muslim.

Mozambique is famous for its fiery pepper or *peri-perri* sauces. They are often served on shrimp and rice.

✓ **READING CHECK:** (*Places and Regions*) What factor limited Mozambique's economic development?

Madagascar

Madagascar is a former French colony. It was ruled by a socialist dictator until the early 1990s. At that point the people demanded a new political system. The optimism that came with democracy faded as the new leaders struggled with poverty. Surprisingly, in 1996 the people voted the former dictator back into power.

Nearly all of Madagascar's people are still very poor. There is little industry. Most of the country's income comes from exports of coffee, sugar, vanilla, and cloves. Most of the people depend on subsistence farming.

Madagascar has many animals found nowhere else. This is because the island has been separated from the African mainland for millions of years. Some 40 species of lemurs, relatives of apes, live only on this island. However, destruction of the rain forests threatens many of Madagascar's animals with extinction.

Malagasy and French are spoken throughout Madagascar. About 52 percent of the people follow traditional African religions. Some 41 percent are Christian, and about 7 percent are Muslim.

✓ **READING CHECK:** (*Places and Regions*) What has Madagascar's recent history been like?

▲

Remnants of French culture can still be seen in Madagascar.

Interpreting the Visual Record

(*Movement*) **Which of these vendors' foods suggests a connection to French culture?**

Homework Practice Online

Keyword: SG5 HP24

Define and explain: Organization of African Unity (OAU)

Working with Sketch Maps On the map you created in Section 3, label Windhoek, Gaborone, Harare, and Maputo. Which cities are located on the plateau of the southern African interior?

Reading for the Main Idea

1. (*Human Systems*) How have diseases affected Zimbabwe's people and economy?

2. (*Human Systems*) How did civil war affect Mozambique?

3. (*Environment and Society*) What minerals does Namibia have, and how do they affect its economy?

Critical Thinking

4. **Drawing Inferences and Conclusions** How do you think the fact that Botswana's population is almost entirely of a single ethnic group has affected its politics?

Organizing What You Know

5. **Summarizing** Copy the following graphic organizer. Use it to list information about southern African cultures.

Country	Culture
Namibia	
Botswana	
Zimbabwe	
Mozambique	
Madagascar	

Review and Practice

Define and Identify

Identify each of the following:

1. enclaves
2. the veld
3. pans
4. Boers
5. apartheid
6. Nelson Mandela
7. townships
8. sanctions
9. Desmond Tutu
10. Organization of African Unity (OAU)

Review the Main Ideas

11. What two South African countries are enclaves?
12. What are southern Africa's two deserts like?
13. What natural resources are very plentiful in southern Africa?
14. How did traders travel between Africa and Asia?
15. What did the original Bantu migrants bring to southern Africa?
16. How have mineral resources affected South Africa?
17. What form of art have artists in Zimbabwe revived?

18. Why are some animals found only in Madagascar?
19. What three racial groups were defined and separated by apartheid? Which group made up the majority of the population?

Think Critically

20. **Drawing Inferences and Conclusions** In what parts of southern Africa do you think most farming takes place? Why?
21. **Analyzing Information** What finally motivated the South African government to end the apartheid system?
22. **Summarizing** Who were the Afrikaners, and what role did they play in the history of southern Africa?
23. **Summarizing** What factors have slowed the economic development of the countries in this region?
24. **Finding the Main Idea** How did the discovery of diamonds and gold affect the settlement of Europeans in southern Africa?

Map Activity

25. On a separate sheet of paper, match the letters on the map with their correct labels.

   Drakensberg
   Inyanga
     Mountains
   Cape of
     Good Hope

   Kalahari Desert
   Namib Desert
   Orange River
   Limpopo River
   Harare

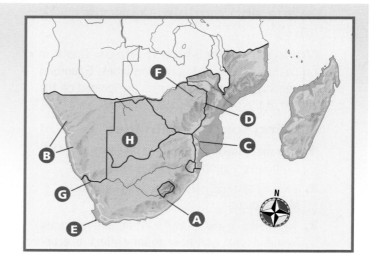

Writing Activity

Write a brief essay in which you compare and contrast Botswana and Mozambique. How are the physical features of these two countries similar or different? How do these features affect the economies of Botswana and Mozambique? What are the major industries? Be sure to use standard grammar, spelling, sentence structure, and punctuation.

internet connect

Internet Activity: **go.hrw.com**
KEYWORD: SG5 GT24

Choose a topic to explore about southern Africa:
- Explore the Namib Desert.
- Go on a South African safari.
- Investigate apartheid.

Social Studies Skills Practice

Analyzing Charts

Many people in southern Africa carry the HIV virus that causes the disease called AIDS. Study the following chart and then answer the questions.

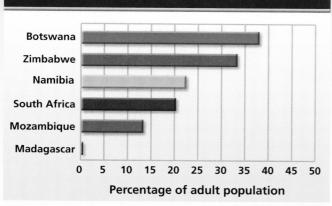

Adult Rate of HIV/AIDS

Percentage of adult population

Source: Central Intelligence Agency, *The World Factbook 2003*

1. What percentage of South Africa's adult population has HIV/AIDS?

2. Which country has the highest adult rate of HIV/AIDS?

3. Which country has the lowest adult rate of HIV/AIDS?

4. Based on the information in this chart, is AIDS a significant problem in most of southern Africa? Explain your answer.

Analyzing Primary Sources

On April 20, 1964, Nelson Mandela spoke at the opening of his trial. Read the following excerpt from his speech. Then answer the questions.

"I have fought against white domination [control], and I have fought against black domination. I have cherished the ideal of a democratic and free society in which all persons live together in harmony and with equal opportunities. It is an ideal which I hope to live for and to achieve. But if needs be, it is an ideal for which I am prepared to die."

1. What South African policy was Nelson Mandela fighting to abolish?

2. What type of government does Nelson Mandela cherish?

3. What are Nelson Mandela's goals?

4. Why might Mandela feel he must be prepared to die for his beliefs?

FOCUS ON ENVIRONMENT

Kenya's Tree Planters

Twenty million young trees scattered throughout Kenya offer new hope to farmers and families. The trees were planted by women who farm these lands. "We are planting trees to ensure our own survival," says Wangari Maathai. She is the founder of Kenya's Green Belt Movement.

Deforestation

Like many other developing countries, Kenya is a country of farmers and herders. The most productive farmlands are in the highlands. This area was once green with trees and plants. Over the past century, however, much of this land has been cleared. Today, less than 10 percent of the original forests remain. Many trees were cut for firewood, which people use for cooking.

Without tree roots to hold the soil in place, the land eroded. The land was losing its fertility.

Farmers moved to the savannas in search of better land.

Wangari Maathai recognized what was happening. "When I would visit the village where I was born," she says, "I saw whole forests had been cleared for cultivation and timber. People were moving onto hilly slopes and riverbeds and marginal areas that were only bush when I was a child." Maathai was shocked to find children suffering from malnutrition. People were no longer eating foods such as beans and corn. Instead, they were eating refined foods such as rice. They were doing this because these foods need less cooking—and thus less firewood.

The Green Belt Movement

On June 5, 1977, in honor of World Environment Day, Maathai and a few supporters planted seven trees in Nairobi, Kenya's capital. Thus began the Green Belt Movement. This movement then spread through the Kenyan highlands and captured people's attention around the world.

From the beginning, Maathai knew that the success of her efforts depended mainly on women. In Kenya, men tend cash crops such as coffee and cotton. Women collect firewood and grow corn, beans, and other food crops. It is the women who grow the food their families eat. The women were the first to see the connection between poor soil and famine.

◄

Human-Environment Interaction Many of the trees in Kenya's highlands have been cleared for crops.

The movement's workers encouraged women in Kenya to plant trees. They pointed out that women would not have to walk miles to collect firewood. They would have wood available nearby for fires, fences, and buildings. If the tree seedlings survived, the women would also be paid a small sum of money.

First, a few small nurseries were started to give out free seedlings. The nurseries are staffed by local women who are paid for their work. Nurseries also train and pay local people known as Green Belt Rangers. The Rangers visit farms, check on seedlings, and offer advice.

Before long, nurseries were appearing in communities throughout the highlands. Kenyan women talked to friends and neighbors about the benefits of planting trees. Neighbors encouraged Esther Wairimu to plant seedlings. Five years later, her fields were surrounded by mango, blue gum, and other trees. "I have learned that a tree… is life," she says.

Today, the advantages of planting trees are clear. Farmers now have fuel and shade. Even more important, the soil is being protected from

▲

Human-Environment Interaction Workers from the Green Belt Movement teach schoolchildren in Kenya how to care for tree seedlings.

erosion. The number of Green Belt nurseries has grown to about 5,000. Most are run by women.

Expanding the Movement

Maathai believes that local people must work together to protect the environment. She stresses that the Green Belt Movement relies on farmers. The movement receives little government support. Most of the money comes from small personal donations.

Now Maathai dreams of spreading her movement to other African countries. "We must never lose hope…," she says. "One person *can* make a difference."

Wangari Maathai (right) has encouraged Kenyan women to plant millions of trees. Women are paid for the seedlings they plant that survive.

▼

Your Turn

Working in small groups, think of an environmental issue facing your community or state.

1. Develop a plan that demonstrates how "one person can make a difference."

2. Present your group's plan to the rest of the class.

Building Skills for Life: Understanding Ecosystems

The plants and animals in an area, together with the nonliving parts of their environment, form an ecosystem. An important thing to remember about ecosystems is that each part is interconnected.

Life on Earth depends on the energy and nutrients flowing through ecosystems. Energy and nutrients move between plants, animals, and soils through food chains and food webs.

Most ecosystems involve three groups of organisms: producers, consumers, and decomposers. Producers make their own food. Plants are producers. They make food by combining carbon dioxide, nutrients from the soil, sunlight, and water. Consumers are unable to make food. They have to get food from producers or from other consumers. Humans are consumers. We eat plants (producers) and animals (consumers). Decomposers get food from dead organisms and wastes. Bacteria and fungi are decomposers.

Elephants have adapted to the ecosystem of Africa's Namib Desert.

Like all forms of life, humans depend on ecosystems for survival. Knowing how ecosystems work helps us understand how we are connected to both living and nonliving things. It can also help us manage, protect, and use our environments wisely.

THE SKILL

1. Describe an ecosystem in the region where you live. What plants and animals live there? How are they connected?

2. Make a table showing some of the producers, consumers, and decomposers in an ecosystem. What do you think would happen if one of these groups suddenly disappeared?

3. Try to identify some ways that human activities have changed ecosystems in your community. Have some plants or animals disappeared?

HANDS on GEOGRAPHY

Like all organisms, lions are part of an ecosystem. Lions survive by killing and eating other animals, such as zebras and gazelles. After lions have killed an animal, they eat their fill. Then other animals such as vultures and hyenas eat what is left.

The lion itself is food for other organisms. Small animals like ticks, fleas, and mosquitoes drink the lion's blood. The lion's waste serves as food for organisms that live in the soil. When the lion dies, it will be eaten by other animals.

How does the lion fit into its ecosystem? You can answer this question by drawing a connections web. These guidelines will help you get started.

1. Draw a picture of a lion.

2. Think of interactions that lions have with other parts of their environment.

3. Include these interactions in your drawing. For example, lions eat zebras, so you could add a zebra to your drawing.

4. Draw lines connecting the lion to other parts of its environment. For example, you could draw a line connecting the lion and the zebra.

5. Be sure to extend the connections to include nonliving parts of the environment as well. For example, lions eat zebras, zebras eat grass, and grass depends on sunlight.

6. Continue making connections on your diagram. When you are done, answer the Lab Report questions.

Lab Report

1. Label the producers, consumers, and decomposers on your connections web. To which group do lions belong?

2. How are lions dependent on nonliving parts of their environment?

3. Imagine there are no more lions. How do you think the ecosystem shown in your connections web would be affected?

UNIT 8

South Asia

CHAPTER 25
India

CHAPTER 26
India's Neighbors

Swayambhunath Stupa, Kathmandu, Nepal

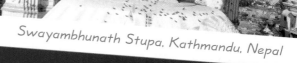
Karakoram Range, Pakistan

A Scholar in India

Emily K. Bloch coordinates educational programs at the South Asia Outreach center at the University of Chicago. Her special area of interest is South Asian children's literature. Here she describes the many types of transportation she has used in India. **WHAT DO YOU THINK?** *Which type of transportation would you enjoy the most?*

In my travels throughout India, I've had the good fortune to ride on a variety of vehicles. I've ridden in buses and cycle-rickshaws, taxis and three-wheeled scooters, on a motorcycle through Calcutta and on the crossbar of a bicycle. I rode in a howdah [seat] on the back of an elephant in a wildlife sanctuary. I even had an uncomfortable, but very welcome, lift in a bullock cart.

But my favorite mode of travel is also one of the most popular in India—riding the great trains. The railway, with more than 1.5 million employees, is the largest employer in the world. It has nearly 40,000 miles of track. Eleven thousand trains, connecting more than 7,000 stations, carry about 12 million people daily. Though the luxury of the princely rail lines beckons, and the first-class cars provide food and bed-linens, I love the crowded, second-class, wooden-benches experience and look forward to my next journey side by side with my fellow Indian and foreign travelers.

Women in festival dress, Rajasthan, India

Polo players at elephant festival, Jaipur, India

Understanding Primary Sources

1. What do Emily Bloch's transportation experiences illustrate about the use of technology in India?

2. Which method of travel does Emily Bloch prefer? Why?

White Bengal tiger

South Asia

Elevation Profile

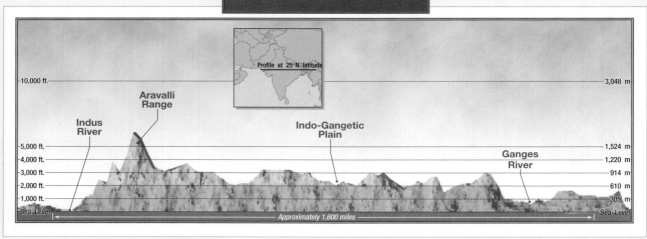

Profile at 25°N latitude

10,000 ft. — 3,048 m

Aravalli Range

Indus River

Indo-Gangetic Plain

5,000 ft. — 1,524 m
4,000 ft. — 1,220 m
3,000 ft. — 914 m

Ganges River

2,000 ft. — 610 m
1,000 ft. — 305 m
Sea Level — Sea Level

Approximately 1,600 miles

The United States and South Asia:
Comparing Sizes

GEOSTATS:

India

World's second-largest population: 1,049,700,118 (July 2003 estimate)

Predicted population in 2025: 1,415,274,000

World's most populous democracy

World's greatest recorded total rainfall in one month: 366 in. (930 cm) in Cherrapunji, in July 1861

South Asia:
Physical

UNIT **8** ATLAS

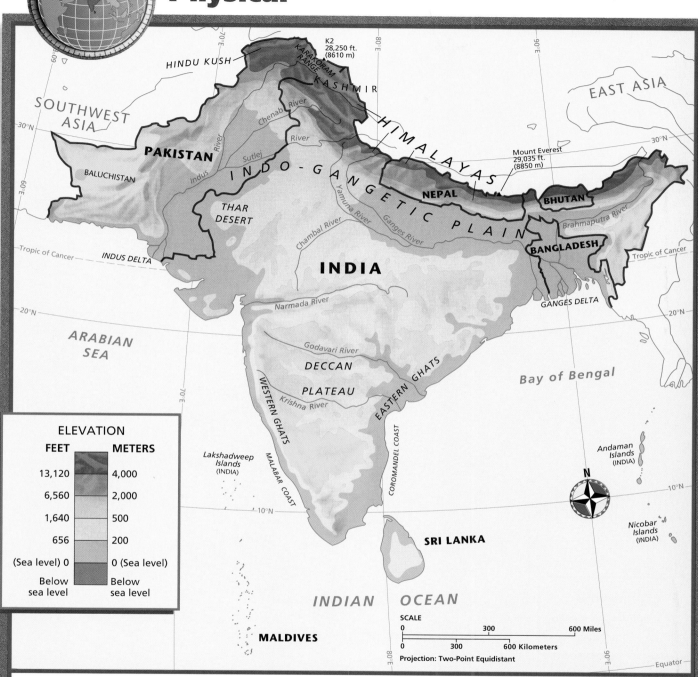

HINDU KUSH

K2
28,250 ft.
(8610 m)

KARAKORAM
RANGE

KASHMIR

EAST ASIA

SOUTHWEST
ASIA

30°N

PAKISTAN

BALUCHISTAN

Chenab River

Sutlej

Indus River

River

INDO-GANGETIC

HIMALAYAS

Mount Everest
29,035 ft.
(8850 m)

30°N

NEPAL

BHUTAN

THAR
DESERT

Yamuna River

Ganges River

Brahmaputra River

PLAIN

Tropic of Cancer

INDUS DELTA

Chambal River

INDIA

BANGLADESH

Tropic of Cancer

20°N

Narmada River

GANGES DELTA

20°N

ARABIAN
SEA

Godavari River

DECCAN

PLATEAU

EASTERN GHATS

Bay of Bengal

WESTERN GHATS

Krishna River

Andaman
Islands
(INDIA)

Lakshadweep
Islands
(INDIA)

MALABAR COAST

COROMANDEL COAST

N

10°N

ELEVATION

FEET		METERS
13,120		4,000
6,560		2,000
1,640		500
656		200
(Sea level) 0		0 (Sea level)
Below
sea level		Below
sea level

10°N

Nicobar
Islands
(INDIA)

SRI LANKA

INDIAN   OCEAN

SCALE

0   300   600 Miles

0   300   600 Kilometers

Projection: Two-Point Equidistant

MALDIVES

Equator

---

1. (Region) Which country has the lowest over-all elevation? Which countries have mountains that stretch from their western to eastern borders?

2. (Region) Which two rivers that drain the Deccan Plateau flow directly into the Bay of Bengal?

Critical Thinking

3. (Movement) Based on the map, do you think it would be easier for travelers or invaders to come to northern India by land or by sea? Why might this be the case?

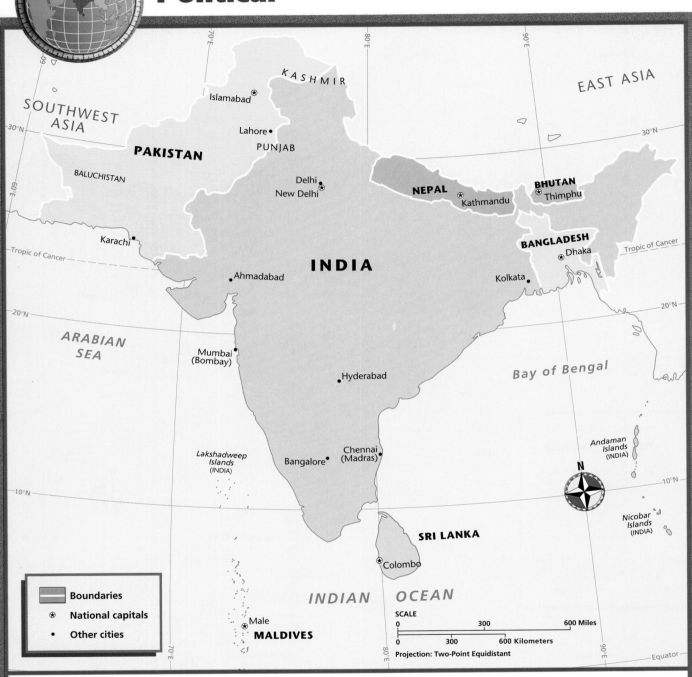

KASHMIR

SOUTHWEST
ASIA

Islamabad ✪

Lahore •

PUNJAB

PAKISTAN

BALUCHISTAN

Delhi •
New Delhi ✪

NEPAL
Kathmandu ✪

BHUTAN
✪ Thimphu

EAST ASIA

Karachi •

Tropic of Cancer

BANGLADESH
✪ Dhaka

Tropic of Cancer

INDIA

Ahmadabad •

Kolkata •

ARABIAN
SEA

Mumbai
(Bombay) •

Hyderabad •

Bay of Bengal

Lakshadweep
Islands
(INDIA)

Bangalore •

Chennai
(Madras) •

Andaman
Islands
(INDIA)

N

Nicobar
Islands
(INDIA)

SRI LANKA

• Colombo

INDIAN OCEAN

Boundaries

✪ National capitals

• Other cities

• Male
MALDIVES

SCALE

0 ——— 300 ——— 600 Miles

0 ——— 300 ——— 600 Kilometers

Projection: Two-Point Equidistant

Equator

1. (Place) What are the region's two island countries? Which is larger?

2. (Location) Which country is almost completely surrounded by India?

3. (Region) Compare this map to the **physical map**. Which small countries might be called the "Mountain Kingdoms?"

Critical Thinking

4. (Location) Bangladesh was once part of Pakistan. What role do you think Bangladesh's location may have played in its drive for independence?

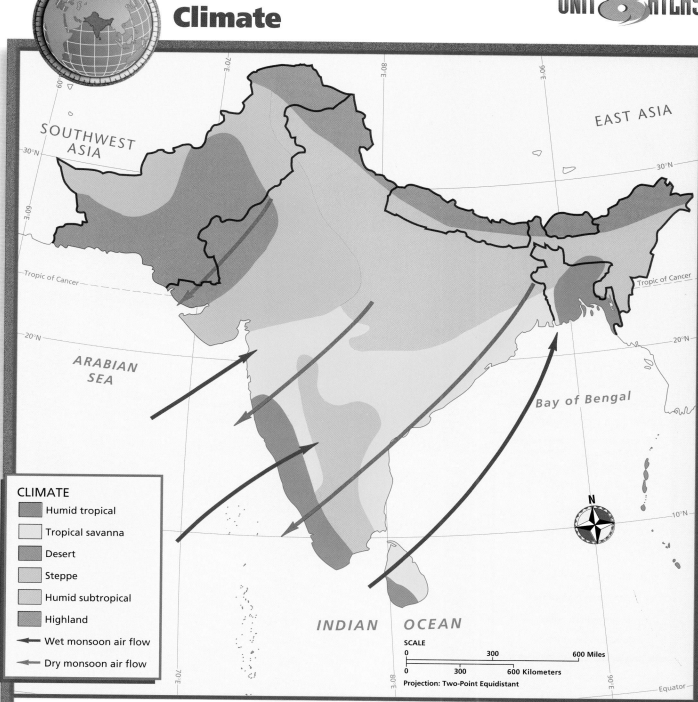

EAST ASIA

SOUTHWEST ASIA

Tropic of Cancer

ARABIAN SEA

Bay of Bengal

Tropic of Cancer

CLIMATE
- Humid tropical
- Tropical savanna
- Desert
- Steppe
- Humid subtropical
- Highland
- ← Wet monsoon air flow
- ← Dry monsoon air flow

INDIAN OCEAN

SCALE
0   300   600 Miles
0   300   600 Kilometers
Projection: Two-Point Equidistant

Equator

N

1. (Region) Compare this map to the **physical map.** Which landform in south central India has a steppe climate?

2. (Human-Environment Interaction) Compare this map to the **land use and resources map** of the region. Which climate regions have the least economic activity?

Critical Thinking

3. (Region) Compare this map to the **political map** of the region. Other than those with mainly highland climates, which country appears to be least affected by monsoons?

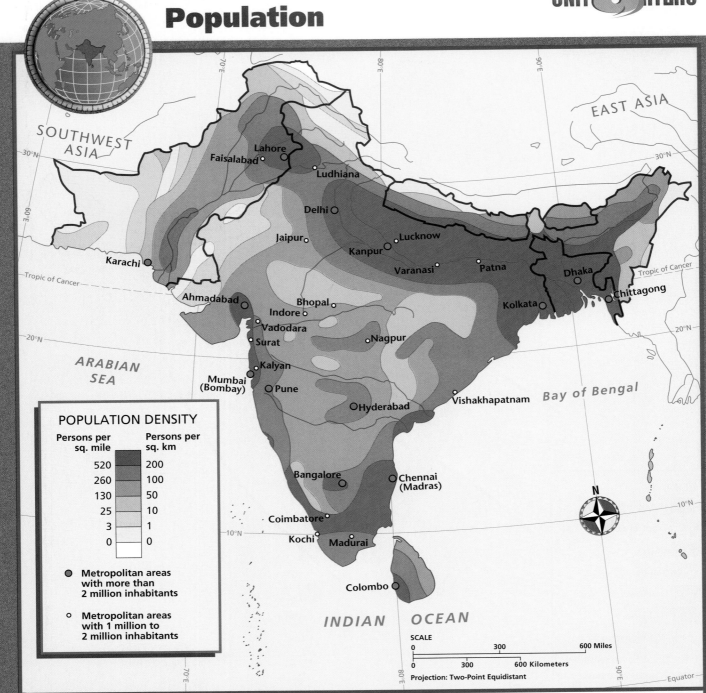

POPULATION DENSITY

Persons per sq. mile	Persons per sq. km
520	200
260	100
130	50
25	10
3	1
0	0

● Metropolitan areas with more than 2 million inhabitants

○ Metropolitan areas with 1 million to 2 million inhabitants

SCALE

0   300   600 Miles

0   300   600 Kilometers

Projection: Two-Point Equidistant

1. (Location) Compare this map to the **physical map**. Which large Indian city is located on the Ganges Delta?

2. (Region) Compare this map to the **physical map** of the region. What is the name of the large densely populated area in the northeastern part of the region?

Critical Thinking

3. (Human-Environment Interaction) Compare this map to the **climate** and **land use and resources maps**. Why do you think few people live along the western and eastern edges of Pakistan?

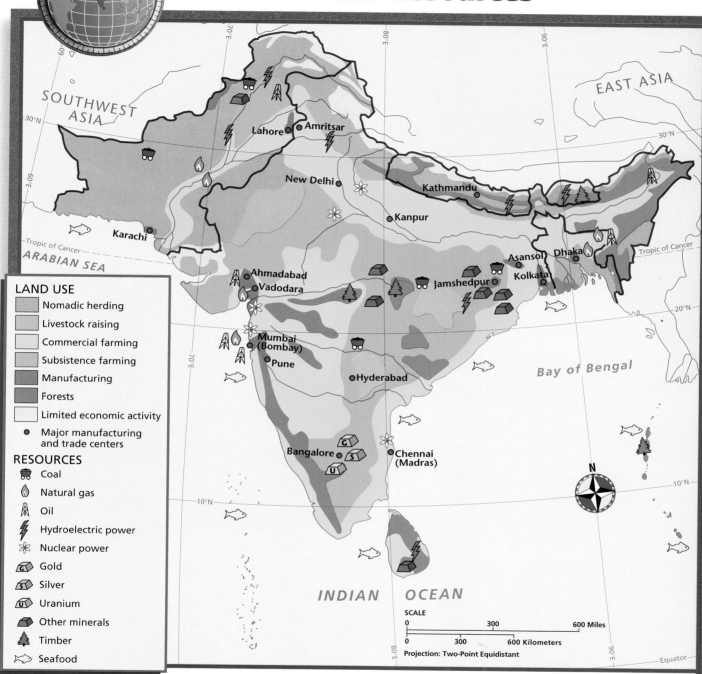

LAND USE

- Nomadic herding
- Livestock raising
- Commercial farming
- Subsistence farming
- Manufacturing
- Forests
- Limited economic activity
- • Major manufacturing and trade centers

RESOURCES

- Coal
- Natural gas
- Oil
- Hydroelectric power
- Nuclear power
- G Gold
- S Silver
- U Uranium
- Other minerals
- Timber
- Seafood

1. **Region** Which country has the largest area used for nomadic herding?

2. **Place** Which country has the largest area used for manufacturing?

3. **Location** Which city is near the region's gold, silver, and uranium mines?

4. **Human-Environment Interaction** Which country does not produce hydroelectric power?

Critical Thinking

5. **Human-Environment Interaction** Compare this map to the **climate map** of the region. Why do you think one of Bangladesh's major crops is rice?

South Asia

BANGLADESH

CAPITAL:
Dhaka

AREA:
55,598 sq. mi.
(144,000 sq km)

POPULATION:
138,448,210

MONEY:
taka

LANGUAGES:
Bangla (official), English

ARABLE LAND:
73 percent

Crystal clear waters in the Maldives

BHUTAN

CAPITAL:
Thimphu

AREA:
18,147 sq. mi.
(47,000 sq km)

POPULATION:
2,139,549

MONEY:
ngultrum, Indian rupee

LANGUAGES:
Dzongkha

ARABLE LAND:
2 percent

INDIA

CAPITAL:
New Delhi

AREA:
1,269,338 sq. mi.
(3,287,590 sq km)

POPULATION:
1,049,700,118

MONEY: Indian rupee

LANGUAGES:
Hindi (official), English (associate official), 14 other official languages, many ethnic languages

ARABLE LAND: 56 percent

MALDIVES

CAPITAL:
Male

AREA:
116 sq. mi.
(300 sq km)

POPULATION:
329,684

MONEY:
rufiyaa

LANGUAGES:
Maldivian Dhivehi, English

ARABLE LAND:
10 percent

   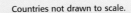

Countries not drawn to scale.

Buddhist monks in Kandy. Sri Lanka

NEPAL

CAPITAL:
Kathmandu

AREA:
54,363 sq. mi.
(140,800 sq km)

POPULATION:
26,469,569

MONEY:
Nepalese rupee

LANGUAGES:
Nepali (official), other ethnic languages

ARABLE LAND:
17 percent

SRI LANKA

CAPITAL: Colombo

AREA:
25,332 sq. mi.
(65,610 sq km)

POPULATION:
19,742,439

MONEY:
Sri Lankan rupee

LANGUAGES:
Sinhala, Tamil, English

ARABLE LAND:
14 percent

internet connect

COUNTRY STATISTICS
GO TO: go.hrw.com
KEYWORD: SG5 FactsU8
FOR: more facts about South Asia

PAKISTAN

CAPITAL:
Islamabad

AREA:
310,401 sq. mi.
(803,940 sq km)

POPULATION:
150,694,740

MONEY:
Pakistani rupee

LANGUAGES:
Punjabi, Sindhi, Siraiki, Pashtu, Urdu (official), Balochi, Hindko, Brahui, English, many ethnic languages

ARABLE LAND:
27 percent

Sources: Central Intelligence Agency, *The World Factbook 2003*;
The World Almanac and Book of Facts 2003; pop. figures are 2003 estimates.

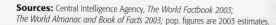

CHAPTER 25

India

India is a huge country with an ancient culture and a population of a billion people. However, you might find you have quite a bit in common with a student from India.

Hi! My name is Rojo, and I am 16. I live with my mother, father, and dog, Jacki. I live in Vaduthala, a small town outside the city of Cochin on the southern tip of India. I live in a one-floor house, with three bedrooms, two bathrooms, living area, dining area, kitchen, cooking terrace, front yard with lots of plants, and a road down to the lake. To cook, my mom usually goes outside to the cooking terrace and makes fish curry. That way, the whole house does not smell like the food.

I am a senior at the State Bank Officers Association High School. This term I am studying math, physics, chemistry, and computer science. My favorite subject is math, because I can use it in so many different ways. The computer language I am studying is based on math. We speak in English in school. At home or with friends, we speak Malayalam, the most common language of the state of Kerala.

Entha vishaisham?

◀ ～～～～～
Translation: What's new?

Section 1 Physical Geography

Read to Discover

1. What are the three main landform regions of India?
2. What are the major rivers in India?
3. What climate types does India have?
4. What natural resources does India have?

Vocabulary

teak

Places

Gangetic Plain
Deccan
Eastern Ghats
Western Ghats

Ganges River
Bay of Bengal
Brahmaputra River
Thar Desert

Reading Strategy

READING ORGANIZER Before you read, create a spider map. Draw a circle in the center of a sheet of paper. Create four legs that you label Landforms, Rivers, Climate, and Resources. As you read this section, list what you learn about each topic beneath each leg.

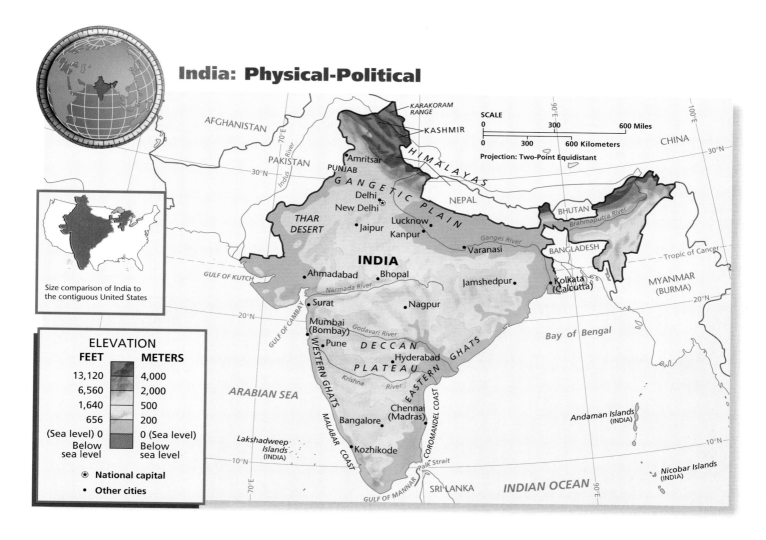

India: Physical-Political

Size comparison of India to the contiguous United States

ELEVATION

FEET	METERS
13,120	4,000
6,560	2,000
1,640	500
656	200
(Sea level) 0	0 (Sea level)
Below sea level	Below sea level

⊛ National capital

• Other cities

Landforms

India has three main landform regions: the Himalayas, the Gangetic (gan-JE-tik) Plain, and the Deccan (DE-kuhn). The Himalayas run along the country's northern border and were created when two tectonic plates collided and pushed Earth's crust up.

The vast Gangetic Plain lies to the south of the Himalayas. It stretches about 1,500 miles (2,415 km) across northern India. About half of India's population lives there.

South of the Gangetic Plain is the triangular peninsula known as the Deccan. Most of its area is a plateau, which is divided by many hills and valleys. The plateau's edges are defined by the Eastern Ghats (GAWTS) and Western Ghats. These low mountain ranges separate the plateau's eastern and western edges from narrow coastal plains.

✔ **READING CHECK:** (*Places and Regions*) What are the three main landform regions of India?

Rivers

India's most important river, the Ganges (GAN-jeez), begins on the southern slopes of the Himalayas. It then flows southeastward across northern India. It spreads into a huge delta before flowing into the Bay of Bengal. Hindus call the Ganges the "Mother River" and consider it sacred. Rich silt left by the Ganges has made the Gangetic Plain India's farming heartland.

The Brahmaputra (brahm-uh-POO-truh) River starts in the Plateau of Tibet. It flows through the far northeastern corner of India. From there the Brahmaputra flows southward through Bangladesh, where it empties into the Ganges Delta. The Narmada (nuhr-MUH-duh), Godavari (go-DAH-vuh-ree), and Krishna (KRISH-nuh) Rivers drain the Deccan. A large irrigation project along the Narmada River is under construction. It will include more than 40 branch canals.

✔ **READING CHECK:** (*Places and Regions*) What are India's most important rivers?

A farmer plows rice fields in northern India. The Himalayas rise in the distance.

Interpreting the Visual Record

(*Human-Environment Interaction*) **Why do so many of India's people live on the Gangetic Plain?**

▼

Climate

India has a variety of climate types. Areas in the Himalayas have highland climates with snow and glaciers. The Thar Desert near the border with Pakistan is hot and dry year-round. The Gangetic Plain has a humid tropical climate. Farther south in the Deccan there are tropical savanna and steppe climates.

Seasonal winds—monsoons—bring moist air from the Indian Ocean in summer. In winter the wind brings dry air from the Asian interior. The timing of the monsoons is very important to farmers in India. If the summer rains come too soon or too late, food production suffers.

✓ **READING CHECK:** (*Places and Regions*) What are India's climates?

The city of Cherrapunji (cher-uh-POOHN-jee), in northeastern India, holds the world's record for rainfall in one year: almost 87 feet (26.5 m)!

Resources

India's fertile farmlands are important to its economy. Most of India's people work in agriculture. The country also produces cash crops for export. These include cashew nuts, cotton, jute, spices, sugarcane, tea, and tobacco.

Large deposits of iron ore, bauxite, uranium, and coal are among India's mineral resources. There are some oil reserves, but not enough to meet the country's needs. Gemstones are a valuable export.

India's forests are an important resource, as well as home to wildlife. **Teak**, one of the most valuable types of wood, grows in India and Southeast Asia. Teak is very strong and durable and is used to make ships and furniture.

✓ **READING CHECK:** (*Places and Regions*) What are India's natural resources?

Homework Practice Online
Keyword: SG5 HP25

Section Review 1

Define and explain: teak

Working with Sketch Maps On a map of India that you draw or that your teacher provides, label the following: Gangetic Plain, Deccan, Eastern Ghats, Western Ghats, Ganges River, Bay of Bengal, Brahmaputra River, and Thar Desert. How would you describe the relative location of India?

Reading for the Main Idea

1. (*Places and Regions*) What is the main mountain range of India?

2. (*Places and Regions*) What are some of India's most important cash crops? What type of wood is a valuable forest product?

Critical Thinking

3. Making Generalizations and Predictions What do you think happens to India's crops if the monsoon rains come too soon? too late?

4. Summarizing How does the Ganges affect economic activities in India?

Organizing What You Know

5. Summarizing Copy the following graphic organizer. Use it to list the landforms, climates, and resources of India.

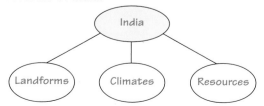

Section 2 India's History

Read to Discover

1. What outside groups affected India's history?
2. What was the Mughal Empire like?
3. How did Great Britain gain control of India?
4. Why was India divided when it became independent?

Vocabulary

Sanskrit
sepoys
boycott

Places

Delhi
Kolkata
Mumbai

People

Harappans
Akbar
Mohandas Gandhi

Reading Strategy

READING ORGANIZER Before you read, draw four large boxes down a sheet of paper. As you read this section, write what you learn in the boxes to create a chain of events in India's history.

Early Indian Civilizations

The first urban civilization on the Indian Subcontinent was centered around the Indus River valley. Its territory was mainly in present-day Pakistan but also extended into India. Scholars call this the Harappan civilization after one of its cities, Harappa. By about 2500 B.C. the people of this civilization were living in large, well-planned cities. Scholars believe the Harappans traded by sea with the peoples of Mesopotamia. The Harappans had a system of writing, but scholars have not been able to read it. As a result, very little is known about Harappan religion and customs.

Mohenjo Daro was one of the largest cities of the Harappan civilization.

Interpreting the Visual Record How might you tell from this photo that Harappan cities were well planned?

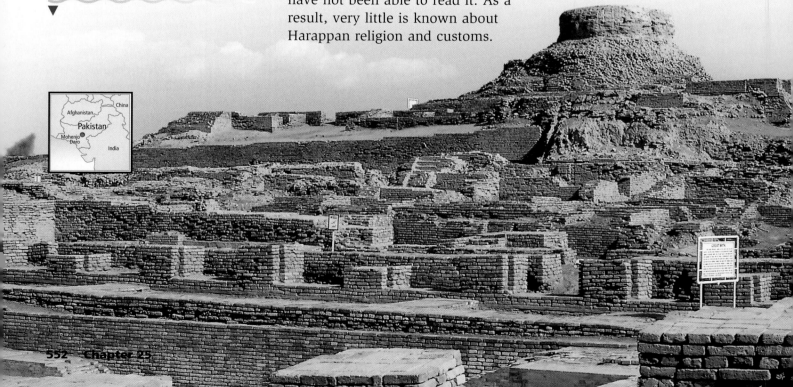

The Indo-Aryans By about 1500 B.C. a new group of people had come into northern India. Scholars call these people Indo-Aryans. Their language was an early form of **Sanskrit**. Sanskrit is still used in India in religious ceremonies.

The Indo-Aryans took control of northern India. These new arrivals mixed with Indian groups that were already living there. Their religious beliefs and customs mixed as well, forming the beginnings of the Hindu religion.

Hills and mountains prevented the Indo-Aryans from conquering southern India. However, Sanskrit and other Indo-Aryan cultural traits spread to the south.

The Coming of Islam About A.D. 1000, Muslim armies began raiding northwestern India. In the early 1200s a Muslim kingdom was established at Delhi. Because the monarch was known as a sultan, this kingdom was called the Delhi sultanate. The Delhi sultanate eventually gained control over most of northern India. It also became a leading center of Islamic art, culture, and science. Most Indians, however, kept their own religions and did not convert to Islam.

Over the next two centuries the Delhi sultanate expanded into the Deccan. However, in the early 1500s a new invasion from Central Asia swept into India. This new conquest marked the beginning of the Mughal (MOO-guhl) Empire.

✓ **READING CHECK:** (*Human Systems*) How did outside groups affect early Indian history?

◄ (*Place*) This carved-lion pillar comes from Sarnath, an ancient city in northern India. The pillar was created in the 200s B.C. and is now the state emblem of India.

The Mughal Empire

The founder of the Mughal Empire was Babur, whose name meant "the Tiger." Babur was descended from Mongol emperor Genghis Khan. He was not only a brilliant general, but also a gifted poet. Babur defeated the last sultan of Delhi and took over most of northern India. After his death, however, Babur's lands were divided among his sons. They fought each other for years.

Babur's grandson, Akbar, finally emerged to reunite the Mughal Empire. He recaptured northern India and then expanded his empire into central India. Akbar was a good ruler as well as a successful conqueror. He reorganized the government and the tax system to make them more efficient. The fertile farmland and large population of the Gangetic Plain made the Mughal Empire rich. It quickly became one of the most powerful states in the world. The reign of Akbar and his successors was a golden age of architecture, painting, and poetry.

▲ This illustration is from a book of the life of Babur, the first Mughal emperor. It shows Babur surrounded by servants and nobles.

Indian writer R.K. Narayan's My Days: A Memoir *describes the author's childhood in the early 1900s. In the following passage Narayan recalls traveling from boarding school to his parents' new home. At that time, travel was complicated and sometimes dangerous.*

At the proper time, I was awakened and put into a huge mat-covered wagon drawn by a pair of bullocks; I sat on a bed of straw covered over with a carpet; a stalwart[1] peon[2] from Hassan high school was seated beside the driver. Manja was his name . . . Part of the way as we traveled along, Manja got off and walked ahead of the caravan, carrying a staff menacingly. Some spots in that jungle and

My Days: A Memoir

mountain country were well-known retreats of highway robbers; one form of protection was to travel in a closely moving caravan with Manja waving a staff at the head of the column, uttering blood-curdling challenges. That was enough to keep off robbers in those days.

We passed along miles and miles of tree-shaded highway, gigantic mango and blueberry trees and lantana[3] shrubs in multicolored bloom stretching away endlessly. A couple of times the bullocks were rested beside a pond or a well. The road wound up and down steep slopes—the sort of country I had never known before. . . . The overpowering smell of straw in the wagon and the slow pace of the bullocks with their bells jingling made me drowsy . . . After hours of tossing on straw, we came to a bungalow[4] set in a ten-acre field. [It was my parents' new home.] . . . The moment I was received into the fold at the trellised ivy-covered porch, I totally ignored Manja, and never looked in his direction, while he carried my baggage in.

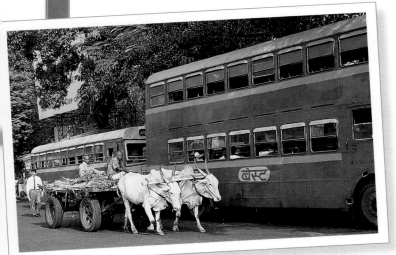

A bullock cart and a double-decker bus in India

Analyzing Primary Sources

1. What are some of the words the author uses to describe the countryside?
2. How do you think Manja's description of this journey might be different from the author's?

Vocabulary   [1]stalwart: strong and reliable   [2]peon: a menial laborer   [3]lantana: shrub with colorful flowers
[4]bungalow: one-story house with low roof that originated in Bengal, India

The ruling Mughals were Muslim, but Islam remained a minority religion in India. Most people continued to practice Hinduism. Akbar himself was tolerant and curious about other religions. He invited religious scholars and priests—including Christians, Hindus, Jains, and Muslims—to his court. He even watched them debate.

Akbar's grandson, Shah Jahan, is remembered for the impressive buildings and monuments he had built. These include the famous Taj Mahal. This grand building contains the tomb of Shah Jahan's beloved wife, Mumtaz Mahal.

In the 1600s and 1700s the Mughal Empire slowly grew weaker. Wars in the Deccan and revolts in many parts of the empire drained Mughal resources. At about this time, Europeans became an important force in Indian history.

✓ **READING CHECK:** (*Human Systems*) What was the Mughal Empire like?

Place The Taj Mahal is one of the most famous buildings in the world.

Our Amazing Planet

Construction of the Taj Mahal began in 1631 and was not completed until 1653. Almost 20,000 people worked on the building.

The British

During the 1700s and 1800s the British slowly took control of India. At first this was done by the English East India Company. This company won rights to trade in the Mughal Empire in the 1600s. The East India Company first took control of small trading posts. Later the British gained more Indian territory.

Company Rule As the Mughal Empire grew weaker, the British East India Company expanded its political power. The company also built up its own military force. This army was made up mostly of

In September 1857, British and loyal Sikh troops stormed the gate of Delhi, defended by rebel sepoys.

sepoys, Indian troops commanded by British officers. The British used the strategy of backing one Indian ruler against another in exchange for cooperation. By the mid-1800s the company controlled more than half of India. The rest was divided into small states ruled by local princes.

The British changed the Indian economy to benefit British industry. India produced raw materials, including cotton, indigo—a natural dye—and jute. These materials were then shipped to Britain for use in British factories. Spices, sugar, tea, and wheat were also grown in India for export. Railroads were built to ship the raw materials to Calcutta (now Kolkata), Bombay (now Mumbai), and other port cities. India also became a market for British manufactured goods. Indians, who had woven cotton cloth for centuries, were now forced to buy British cloth.

The Indian Mutiny British rule angered and frightened many Indians. In 1857, the sepoy troops revolted. They killed their British officers and other British residents. The violence spread across northern India. Large numbers of British troops were rushed to India. In the end the British crushed the rebellion.

The Indian Mutiny convinced the British government to abolish the British East India Company. The British government began to rule India directly, and India became a British colony.

Anti-British Protest During the late 1800s Indian nationalism took a different form. Educated, middle-class Indians led this movement. In 1885 these Indian nationalists created the Indian National Congress to organize their protests. At first they did not demand independence. Instead, they asked only for fairer treatment, such as a greater share of government jobs. The British refused even these moderate demands.

After World War I more and more Indians began demanding the end of British rule. A lawyer named Mohandas K. Gandhi became the most important leader of this Indian independence movement.

Gandhi and Nonviolence Gandhi reached out to the millions of Indian peasants. He used a strategy of nonviolent mass protest. He called for Indians to peacefully refuse to cooperate with the British. Gandhi led protest marches and urged Indians to **boycott**, or refuse to buy, British goods. Many times the police used violence against marchers. When the British jailed Gandhi, he went on hunger strikes. Gandhi's determination and self-sacrifice attracted many followers. Pressure grew on Britain to leave India.

✓ **READING CHECK:** (*Human Systems*) What role did the British play in India?

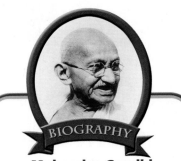

BIOGRAPHY

Mohandas Gandhi
(1869–1948)

Character Trait: Integrity

Gandhi practiced nonviolence in his struggle for Indian independence and the rights of India's lowest classes. Civil rights leaders in the United States and other countries have adopted Gandhi's nonviolent methods.

Among Gandhi's campaigns was a protest on the salt tax. To avoid having to buy salt and pay the tax, Gandhi and thousands of followers walked 200 miles to make salt from seawater.

Although he lived peacefully, violence took Gandhi's life. A radical Hindu who thought Gandhi was too kind to Muslims assassinated him.

How did Gandhi show integrity?

Independence and Division

After World War II the British government decided to give India independence. The British government and the Indian National Congress wanted India to become one country. However, India's Muslims demanded a separate Muslim state. Anger and fear grew between Hindus and Muslims. India seemed on the verge of civil war.

Finally, in 1947 the British divided their Indian colony into two independent countries, India and Pakistan. India was mostly Hindu. Pakistan, which then included what is today Bangladesh, was mostly Muslim. However, the new boundary left millions of Hindus in Pakistan and millions of Muslims in India. Masses of people rushed to cross the border. Hundreds of thousands were killed in rioting and panic.

 (*Movement*) In the chaotic days of August 1947, millions of people left their homes to cross the new border between India and Pakistan. These Muslims are preparing to leave New Delhi by train.

✔ **READING CHECK:** (*Places and Regions*) Why was India divided when it became independent?

 **Section Review 2**

Define or identify: Harappans, Sanskrit, Akbar, sepoys, Mohandas Gandhi, boycott

Working with Sketch Maps On the map you created in Section 1, label Delhi, Kolkata, and Mumbai. What bodies of water are important to each of these cities?

Reading for the Main Idea

1. (*Human Systems*) What made the Mughal Empire one of the most powerful states in the world?

2. (*Human Systems*) How did the British East India Company gain control of most of India?

 go.hrw.com **Homework Practice Online** Keyword: SG5 HP25

3. (*Human Systems*) Who was the most important leader of the Indian independence movement, and what was his strategy?

Critical Thinking

4. **Finding the Main Idea** Why was the British colony of India divided into two countries?

Organizing What You Know

5. **Sequencing** Copy the following time line. Use it to mark important events in Indian history from 2500 B.C. to A.D. 1947.

```
|————————————————————————————————————|
2500 B.C.                        A.D. 1947
```

Read to Discover

1. What four major religions originated in India?
2. What is the caste system?
3. What languages are important in India?
4. What kind of government does India have, and what is India's economy like?

Vocabulary

reincarnation
dharma
karma
nirvana
caste system

Dalits
green revolution

Places

Kashmir

People

Siddhartha
  Gautama
Mother Teresa

Reading Strategy

FOLDNOTES: FOUR-CORNER FOLD | Create the FoldNote titled **Four-Corner Fold** described in the Appendix. Label the flaps Religions, Castes, Languages, and Government and Economy. As you read this section, write what you learn beneath each flap.

Religions of India

Religion is an important part of Indian culture. Four major religions—Hinduism, Buddhism, Jainism, and Sikhism—originated in India. Christianity and Islam, both of which originated elsewhere, also have millions of followers in India. About 81 percent of India's people are Hindu. About 12 percent of Indians are Muslim, and 2.3 percent are Christian. Around 2 percent are Sikh, and 2.5 percent are Buddhist, Jain, Parsi, or followers of another religion. Remember that 1 percent of India's population is about 10 million people!

Hinduism Hinduism is one of the oldest religions in the world. It is a combination of the beliefs of the Indo-Aryans, who arrived in India in around 1750 B.C., and those of earlier Indian peoples. Hindus worship many gods. Hinduism teaches that all gods and all living beings are part of a single spirit called Brahma.

According to Hinduism, when people die their souls are reborn in new bodies. This process is called **reincarnation**. Every time a person is reborn, he or she must fulfill a moral duty, called **dharma**. A person's dharma depends upon the position he or she is born into. Hindus believe that people's actions during their lifetime have moral consequences, or **karma**, that affect how they will be reborn the next time. A person with good karma may be reborn as a person of higher status. A person with bad karma may be reborn with lower status, or as an animal or insect. People who in

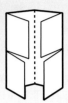

Place Cows mingle with pedestrians and bicyclists in the street of an Indian town.

each of their lifetimes fulfill their dharma may eventually break the cycle of birth and rebirth. They become one with Brahma.

Hinduism also teaches a special respect for certain plants and animals. Cows are considered sacred and are protected. Hindus do not eat beef. Even today, cows can be seen roaming cities and villages. Monkeys and some snakes are also sacred. The most sacred river is the Ganges, where millions of Hindus make a religious pilgrimage every year.

Hindus build temples for their gods and honor them with festivals at least once a year. Festivals may involve religious ceremonies, dance, and music. During the annual new year celebration, called Diwali, Hindus exchange gifts and set off fireworks.

Buddhism The founder of Buddhism, Siddhartha Gautama (sid-DAHR-tuh GOW-tuh-muh), was born a Hindu about 563 B.C. As a son of a prince, he lived a luxurious life. At age 29, Gautama left his palace and set out to learn about hunger, disease, and death.

For six years he searched for the truth. One day Gautama suddenly had a feeling of enlightenment—a state of calm and understanding. He then developed the main principles of Buddhism—the Four Noble Truths. Among these was the belief that all human life contains suffering and sadness and that desire causes suffering. By rejecting desire, people could achieve **nirvana**, or perfect peace.

Gautama rejected many of the beliefs of Hinduism, particularly that goodness and one's position in life were inherited. He also believed that priests should practice good conduct, nonviolence, and poverty.

Gautama spread his philosophy far and wide until his death about 483 B.C. His followers call him the Buddha, or "the Enlightened One." Eventually, Buddhism spread to many other parts of Asia. Buddhism is no longer widely practice in India. However, the religion is very important in Sri Lanka, China, Japan, and Southeast Asia.

▲

The Buddha is often depicted in poses of meditation.

FOCUS ON CULTURE

An Elephant-Headed God

One of the most beloved Hindu gods is Ganesh, who has the head of an elephant. Ganesh is called the Remover of Obstacles. To ensure their success, important events, such as weddings, begin with the worship of Ganesh. During Ganesh Chaturthi, a festival that honors him, Indians bring statues of Ganesh into their homes and later dip them in the sea or a river.

How do Hindus honor Ganesh?

Jainism Jainism was founded at about the same time as Buddhism. It teaches that all things in nature—animals, plants, and stones—have souls. Jains reject all forms of violence against any living thing. They are strict vegetarians. Some even cover their noses with cloth to avoid breathing in insects and thus killing them.

Jains make up only a small minority. However, they have made many contributions to Indian art, mathematics, and literature.

Sikhism Sikhism was founded in the late 1400s. It combines elements of Hinduism and Islam. Members of this religion are called Sikhs. Traditionally, many Sikh men have become soldiers. They continue to play an important role in India's army.

Most Sikhs live in the state of Punjab in northern India. Some Sikhs want to break away from India and form an independent country. The Indian government has refused to allow this, and violent clashes have resulted.

✓ **READING CHECK:** (*Human Systems*) What four religions originated in India?

▲

A Sikh guards the Golden Temple, the center of the Sikh religion, in Amritsar, India. Sikh men can be recognized by their beards and special turbans.

Interpreting the Visual Record (*Place*)
Do you know of any other religious or cultural groups whose members have a distinctive way of dressing?

Castes

Another key feature of Indian society is the **caste system**. Castes are groups of people whose birth determines their position in society. The castes are ranked in status, from highest to lowest. People from a

Many Dalits, like this woman in Goa, still perform jobs that Indians consider dirty or impure.

▼

higher caste cannot marry or even touch people of lower castes. The people at the bottom, called **Dalits**, do work that higher castes consider unclean. They wash and cremate dead bodies, process cow hides into leather goods, and sweep up trash.

Gandhi tried to improve people's attitudes toward the Dalits. He called them "Children of God." After independence, the Indian government officially ended the caste system. However, it is still a strong force in Indian society. The government also tried to improve economic conditions for the Dalits. Today some Dalits are educated and have good jobs. The majority, though, are still poor.

✓ **READING CHECK:** (*Human Systems*) How does the caste system create conflict in Indian society?

Languages

India's people speak an amazing number of different languages. There are 24 languages with a million or more speakers, plus hundreds of other languages. Hindi is the main language of about 30 percent of the people, mostly in northern India. In 1965 it became the official national language. However, the states of southern India have resisted the push to adopt Hindi. English is still commonly used in government, business, and higher education throughout India.

✓ **READING CHECK:** (*Human Systems*) What languages are important in India?

Government and Economy

India has made a great deal of economic progress since gaining independence, but the country remains poor. Rapid population growth strains the country's resources, and the divisions among India's people make it difficult to govern.

Government India is ruled by a democratic government. With more than 1 billion people, the country is the world's largest democracy. The structure of the government is based on Britain's parliamentary system. However, as in the United States, India's central government shares power with state governments.

Indian politics have sometimes been marked by violence and assassinations. The government used force to defeat Sikh rebels in 1984. There have also been outbreaks of

BIOGRAPHY

Mother Teresa
(1910–1997)

Character Trait: Kindness

Mother Teresa dedicated her life to helping people. She is best known for founding a mission for the sick and homeless in Kolkata. In 1979, Mother Teresa accepted the Nobel Peace Prize in honor of the millions of people she dedicated her life to caring for. Today, Mother Teresa's example of kindness toward the needy continues around the world at 4,500 missions she created.

How did Mother Teresa show kindness to others?

(*Place*) Parliament House, New Delhi, is the home of India's legislative branch.

India has stationed large numbers of troops in Kashmir.

Peppers are harvested in northern India.

violence between Hindus and Muslims. In 1992 a mob of Hindus tore down a mosque that stood on a Hindu holy site. Riots broke out in many parts of India as a result.

India's border with Pakistan has been in dispute since 1947. Both countries claim a mountainous region called Kashmir. Before India gained independence, Kashmir was ruled by a Hindu prince. Most of its people were Muslim, however. India and Pakistan have fought over Kashmir several times. Today, both countries have nuclear weapons, making the prospect of a future war even more frightening.

Economy India's economy is a mixture of the traditional and the modern. In thousands of villages, farmers work the fields just as they have for centuries. At the same time, modern factories and high-tech service industries demonstrate India's potential for wealth. However, the country still does not have enough good roads and telecommunications systems.

Close to 60 percent of India's workforce are farmers. Farming makes up 25 percent of India's GDP. Most farmers work on small farms less than 2.5 acres (1 hectare) in size. Many grow barely enough to feed themselves and their families. In recent years, the government has worked to promote commercial farming.

India's leading crops include rice, wheat, cotton, tea, sugarcane, and jute. Cattle and water buffalo are raised to pull plows and to provide milk.

Beginning in the 1960s, the Indian government started agricultural programs known as the **green revolution**. This effort encouraged farmers to adopt more modern methods. It promoted greater use of fertilizers, pesticides, and new varieties of wheat and rice. Crop yields increased. In years with good weather, India is self-sufficient in food and can export farm products.

India is considered a developing country. However, its economy is large enough to rank among the world's top 10 industrial countries. India's industries include textiles, jewelry, cars, bicycles, oil products, chemicals, food processing, and electronics.

India's moviemaking industry is one of the world's largest. Mumbai is a major moviemaking center. Movies are an incredibly popular form of entertainment, as millions of Indians cannot read. Many Indian movie stars have gone into politics. Indian movies have a distinctive style. They usually feature music and dancing and often draw on themes from Indian myths. Indian movies are popular in many other countries as well.

India now has a large, well-educated middle class. These people have enough money for luxuries like cable television and personal computers. Some Indians are very rich. Yet the majority of Indians are still poor.

▲
Red-hot steel is poured into molds in a foundry near Kolkata.

Interpreting the Visual Record
Which of India's industries might use the steel produced here?

✓ **READING CHECK:** *Places and Regions* What are India's government and economy like?

Section Review 3

Homework Practice Online
Keyword: SG5 HP25

Define or identify: reincarnation, dharma, karma, Siddhartha Gautama, nirvana, caste system, Dalits, Mother Teresa, green revolution

Working with Sketch Maps On the map that you created in Section 2, label the Kashmir region of India. What other country claims Kashmir?

Reading for the Main Idea

1. *Human Systems* What are the main religions practiced in India? Which religion has the largest number of followers?

2. *Environment and Society* How did India's government increase agricultural output in the 1960s?

Critical Thinking

3. Drawing Inferences and Conclusions Why might India's government find it difficult to improve the economic situation of the Dalits?

4. Finding the Main Idea Why are movies such a popular form of entertainment in India?

Organizing What You Know

5. Categorizing Copy the following graphic organizer. Use it to list the leading crops and industries of India.

Leading crops	Leading industries

Review and Practice

Define and Identify

Identify each of the following:

1. teak
2. Sanskrit
3. sepoys
4. boycott
5. reincarnation
6. karma
7. nirvana
8. caste system
9. Dalits
10. green revolution
11. Harappans
12. Mohandas Gandhi
13. Siddhartha Gautama
14. Mother Teresa

Review the Main Ideas

15. How were the Himalayas formed?
16. What is unique about the Ganges River?
17. Why are monsoons important to Indian farmers?
18. What was the first urban civilization on the Indian Subcontinent?
19. Who brought Sanskrit to India?
20. Who slowly took control of India after the Mughal Empire weakened?
21. What caused the Indian Mutiny of 1857?

22. What are the Hindu ideas of reincarnation and karma?
23. What factors divide Indian society?
24. How many languages are spoken in India?

Think Critically

25. **Drawing Inferences and Conclusions** Why do you think Hindi has not become the language of all of India?
26. **Summarizing** How do India's natural resources affect its economy?
27. **Finding the Main Idea** How did the Indian government's promotion of new farming technology affect India's farming culture?
28. **Drawing Inferences and Conclusions** Why do you think the Mughal Empire under Akbar and his successors was considered a "golden age"?
29. **Drawing Inferences and Conclusions** How might the growth of a well-educated, high-tech workforce affect India's economy?

Map Activity

30. On a separate sheet of paper, match the letters on the map with their correct labels.

    Himalayas
    Gangetic Plain
    Deccan
    Eastern Ghats
    Western Ghats
    Ganges River
    Brahmaputra River
    Thar Desert

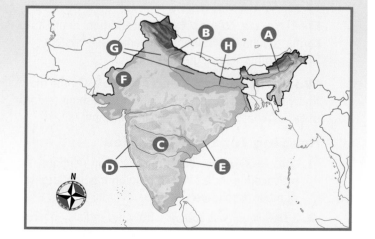

Writing Activity

Write a one- to two-page report about how religion influences life in India. List and describe India's major religions, then write about how they relate to politics, border disputes, social classes, daily life, languages, the economy, and so on. Be sure to use standard grammar, spelling, sentence structure, and punctuation.

internet connect

Internet Activity: go.hrw.com
KEYWORD: SG5 GT25

Choose a topic to explore about India:
- Tour the regions of India.
- Travel to ancient India.
- Learn about Mohandas Gandhi.

Social Studies Skills Practice

Interpreting Maps

India is divided into 28 states and 7 territories. Study the map and then answer the questions.

The States and Territories of India

1. In which state is Mumbai located?
2. If you were traveling from Kolkata to Chennai, which states would you travel through?
3. Which state or territory shares the same name as a major city in India?
4. Which states and territories border Nepal?

Analyzing Primary Sources

Using what you have learned about Gandhi, read the following quotes. Then answer the questions.

"I object to violence because when it appears to do good, the good is only temporary; the evil it does is permanent."

"An eye for an eye makes the whole world blind."

"Whether humanity will consciously follow the law of love, I do not know. But that need not disturb me. The law will work just as the law of gravitation works, whether we accept it or not."

1. What is the main idea of these statements?
2. What can you learn about Gandhi by reading these quotes?
3. How do these statements relate to Gandhi's role in achieving independence for India?
4. What is Gandhi's opinion about the "law of love"?

CHAPTER 26

India's Neighbors

The countries of this region, along with the Himalayas, help create India's border. After you meet Rehan you will learn that this land is one of majestic beauty with a rich heritage.

I am Rehan, and I am 14. I am an only child and live with my parents in Karachi, a big sprawling city like Los Angeles. On one side is the sea, on the other is the desert.

If you came to visit me in Pakistan, I would take you to the beach to watch the beautiful sunsets and ride on a camel. My parents used to take me there for camel rides when I was very little. Next I would take you to see the old colonial architecture in the city center. Then we would go and have a meal in a roadside cafe—grilled beef or lamb kabobs on a stick. I usually get up very early for school. By 7:10 A.M. I have breakfast—cereal and toast—and leave for school with my father. He is a doctor with an office near my school. I am in the second year (equivalent to grade 10) of a boys' private school styled after the British public school system.

Next year, I am going to America with my mother. My parents want me to have a chance to go to a world-class university.

السلام عليكم!

▲ Translation: God's peace be upon you!

Section 1 Physical Geography

Read to Discover

1. What major physical features are located in India's Neighbors?
2. What climates and natural resources are found in this region?
3. What are the physical features of the island countries?

Vocabulary

cyclones
storm surges

Places

Brahmaputra River
Ganges River
Himalayas
Mount Everest
Tarai
Karakoram Range

Hindu Kush
Khyber Pass
Indus River
Thar Desert

Reading Strategy

VISUALIZING INFORMATION Before you read, look at the map and pictures in this section. What environmental challenges do you think the people living in this region could face? Write your answers on a sheet of paper under the name of each country: Pakistan, Bangladesh, Bhutan, and Nepal.

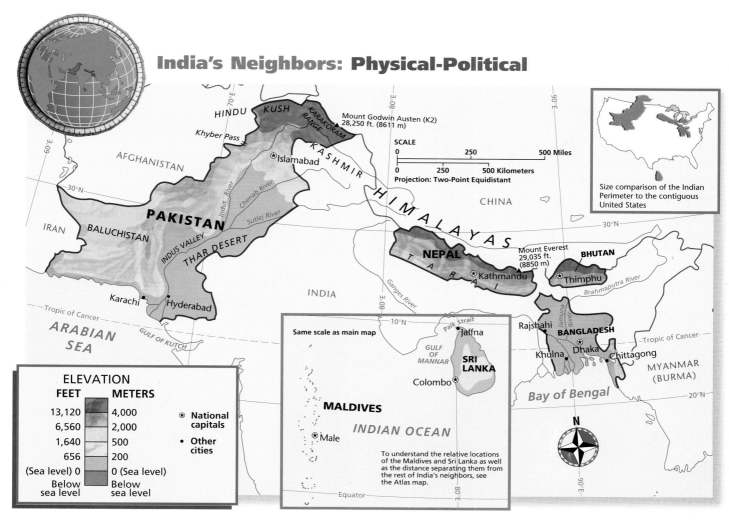

India's Neighbors: Physical-Political

HINDU KUSH
Khyber Pass
KARAKORAM RANGE
Mount Godwin Austen (K2) 28,250 ft. (8611 m)

SCALE
0 — 250 — 500 Miles
0 — 250 — 500 Kilometers
Projection: Two-Point Equidistant

AFGHANISTAN
Islamabad
KASHMIR
CHINA
IRAN
BALUCHISTAN
PAKISTAN
Indus River
Chenab River
Sutlej River
THAR DESERT
INDUS VALLEY
HIMALAYAS
NEPAL
TARAI
Kathmandu
Mount Everest 29,035 ft. (8850 m)
BHUTAN
Thimphu
Brahmaputra River
30°N

Karachi
Hyderabad
INDIA
Ganges River
Tropic of Cancer
ARABIAN SEA
GULF OF KUTCH

Size comparison of the Indian Perimeter to the contiguous United States

ELEVATION

FEET	METERS
13,120	4,000
6,560	2,000
1,640	500
656	200
(Sea level) 0	0 (Sea level)
Below sea level	Below sea level

⊛ National capitals
• Other cities

Same scale as main map
10°N
Palk Strait
Jaffna
GULF OF MANNAR
SRI LANKA
Colombo
Rajshahi
BANGLADESH
Khulna
Dhaka
Chittagong
MYANMAR (BURMA)
Tropic of Cancer
Bay of Bengal
20°N

MALDIVES
INDIAN OCEAN
Male

To understand the relative locations of the Maldives and Sri Lanka as well as the distance separating them from the rest of India's neighbors, see the Atlas map.

Equator

N

Physical Features

The broad delta formed by the Brahmaputra (brahm-uh-POO-truh) and Ganges (GAN-jeez) Rivers covers most of Bangladesh. Some 200 rivers and streams crisscross this eastern part of the Indian Subcontinent. These numerous waterways, the low elevation of the land, and heavy monsoon rains combine to bring frequent floods to Bangladesh. Although these floods cause great damage, they leave behind a layer of fertile soil.

North of Bangladesh is Bhutan. This tiny country lies high in the mountain range known as the Himalayas (hi-muh-LAY-uhz). To the west is Nepal. The Himalayas occupy some 75 percent of Nepal's land area. Mount Everest, Earth's highest mountain, is located on Nepal's border with China. The Tarai (tuh-RY) is a low plain along Nepal's southern border. It is the country's main farming area. West of the Himalayas is the Karakoram (kah-rah-KOHR-oohm) Range. To the west the Karakorams merge into another mountain range, the Hindu Kush.

On Pakistan's western border is the Khyber (KY-buhr) Pass. For centuries, invaders and traders have traveled through this high mountain pass to India. East of the Khyber Pass is the Indus River. The Indus Valley lies mostly to the east of the river. This valley is Pakistan's main farming region and its most heavily populated area. East of these fertile lands is the Thar (TAHR) Desert, or the Great Indian Desert. A barren, hilly, and dry plateau in western Pakistan joins the plateaus of Iran.

✓ **READING CHECK:** (*Places and Regions*) What are the major physical features of this region?

internet connect

GO TO: go.hrw.com
KEYWORD: SG5 CH26
FOR: Web sites about India's Neighbors

Terraced fields in the mountains of Nepal allow farmers to increase their production of millet and corn.

Interpreting the Visual Record

(*Human-Environment Interaction*) How can terracing lead to increased crop production?

▼

Climate and Resources

Bangladesh has one of the world's wettest climates. Rainfall is generally more than 60 inches (127 to 152 cm) each year. Most of the rain falls from June to October, during the wet summer monsoon. In the early and late weeks of the monsoon, **cyclones** sweep in from the Bay of Bengal. These violent storms resemble the hurricanes of the Caribbean. They bring high winds and heavy rain. Cyclones are often accompanied by **storm surges**. These are huge waves of water that are whipped up by fierce winds. The summer monsoon brings hot, wet weather to the lowland areas of Bhutan and Nepal. In the mountains, climates are generally much cooler. Much of Pakistan has a desert climate, receiving less than 10 inches (25 cm) of rain each year. Summer temperatures can reach as high as 120°F (49°C).

Bangladesh's most important resource is its fertile farmland. About 15 percent of Bangladesh is forested, so it has some timber supplies. However, severe deforestation and soil erosion have plagued the region, particularly in Nepal. Bhutan and Nepal have farmland in low-land areas. Both countries have some minerals, but few are mined. Pakistan has large natural gas reserves but limited oil supplies. It has to import oil to meet its energy needs. Pakistan's other natural resources include coal, limestone, and salt.

✓ **READING CHECK:** (*Places and Regions*) What are the natural resources of the region?

The Island Countries

India's neighbors also include Sri Lanka and the Maldives. Sri Lanka is a large island located just off the southeastern tip of India. Plains cover most of the island's northern half and coastal areas. Mountains and hills rise in the south-central part of the island.

About 1,200 tiny tropical islands in the Indian Ocean make up the Maldives. The island group stretches from south of India to the equator. Only about 200 of the islands are inhabited. None rises more than 6 feet (1.8 m) above sea level.

✓ **READING CHECK:** (*Places and Regions*) What are the physical features of the island countries?

In May 1997 a cyclone and storm surges devastated Bangladesh. More than 1.5 million people were left homeless.

Homework Practice Online
Keyword: SG5 HP26

Section Review 1

Define and explain: cyclones, storm surges

Working with Sketch Maps On a map of India and India's Neighbors that you draw or that your teacher provides, label the following: Brahmaputra River, Ganges River, Himalayas, Mount Everest, Tarai, Karakoram Range, Hindu Kush, Khyber Pass, Indus River, and Thar Desert. Where is Earth's highest mountain located? What plains area is Nepal's main farming region?

Reading for the Main Idea

1. (*Places and Regions*) Why has the Khyber Pass been important in the history of Pakistan and India?

2. (*Places and Regions*) How have erosion and defor-estation affected the region? Which country has been most affected by these problems?

3. (*Places and Regions*) What island countries are found in the region? How are they different from each other?

Critical Thinking

4. **Drawing Inferences and Conclusions** How do you think climate affects life in Pakistan and Bangladesh?

Organizing What You Know

5. **Summarizing** Copy the following graphic orga-nizer. Use it to describe the landforms, climates, and resources of the region.

	Major Landforms	Climates	Resources
Pakistan			
Bangladesh			
Bhutan			
Nepal			

Read to Discover

1. What is the history of Pakistan?
2. What are some features of Pakistan's culture?
3. What is the history of Bangladesh?
4. What challenges face Bangladesh today?

Vocabulary

cholera

Places

Pakistan
Bangladesh
Karachi
Lahore
Islamabad
Dhaka

People

Muhammad Yunus

Reading Strategy

READING ORGANIZER Create a four-column chart. Label the columns Country, History, Population, and Culture. As you read this section, write what you learn about Pakistan and Bangladesh on your chart.

▲

These tombs in Pakistan were built in the 1500s–1700s. Women's graves had floral carvings. Horses and swords decorated men's tombs.

Pakistan's History

An ancient civilization developed in the Indus River valley about 2500 B.C. Ruins of cities show that this was a large and well-organized society. The cause of the disappearance of this civilization about 1500 B.C. remains a mystery.

Over time the fertile Indus River valley was inhabited and conquered by many different groups. It has been part of the empires of Persia, Alexander the Great, and the Mughals. About A.D. 1000 Turkish invaders established Islam in the area. Islam has been the main religion there ever since.

In the early 1600s merchants from England formed the English East India Company to increase the spice trade. It later became known as the British East India Company. Although trade was only moderately successful, the company established England's power in India. It was not until 1947 that India gained independence.

Upon independence, India became two countries. The division into two countries was based on religion. India was mostly Hindu. East and West Pakistan were inhabited mainly by Muslims. Although East Pakistan and West Pakistan were mostly Muslim, they had other cultural differences. These differences led East Pakistan to break away in 1971. It became known as Bangladesh.

✔ **READING CHECK:** (*Human Systems*) What was Pakistan's early history like?

Pakistan Today

Pakistan's population is 97 percent Muslim. The country has many different languages and ethnic groups. A small number of Christians, Buddhists, and Hindus also live in Pakistan. Urdu is Pakistan's official language. However, less than 10 percent of the population speak it as their primary language. Many upper-class Pakistanis speak English.

Population Pakistan has the world's sixth largest population. The cities contain about a third of that population. The largest are the port city of Karachi (kuh-RAH-chee), Lahore (luh-HOHR), and the capital, Islamabad. Like the rest of the region, Pakistan is experiencing rapid population growth. In fact, the Indian Subcontinent accounted for about 30 percent of the world's population growth in the late 1990s. How does Pakistan support so many people? The Indus River valley has one of the world's largest irrigation systems. It allows the country to grow enough food for the large population. However, overall economic progress has been slow.

Culture In Pakistan a woman joins her husband's family at marriage. Marriages are usually arranged by parents. The young woman's parents often pay a large amount of money to the young man's family.

Pakistan celebrates many of the same Islamic festivals as other Southwest Asian countries. Festival meals are similar to those of Iran in their emphasis on rice, the region's staple food. Meals also include the grilled meat of chickens, goats, and sheep, as well as delicious breads. Pakistani foods feature strong spices and flavors.

✓ **READING CHECK:** (*Human Systems*) What is the culture of Pakistan like?

Pakistan and Bangladesh

COUNTRY	POPULATION/ GROWTH RATE	LIFE EXPECTANCY	LITERACY RATE	PER CAPITA GDP
Bangladesh	138,448,210 2.1%	61, male 61, female	43%	$1,700
Pakistan	150,694,740 2.1%	61, male 63, female	45%	$2,100
United States	290,342,554 0.9%	74, male 80, female	97%	$37,600

Source: Central Intelligence Agency, *The World Factbook 2003*

Interpreting the Chart Which country in the region has a larger population?

Place Pakistan's flag symbolizes the country's commitment to Islam and the Islamic world. The crescent and star are symbols of Islam. The vertical white stripe represents religious minorities.

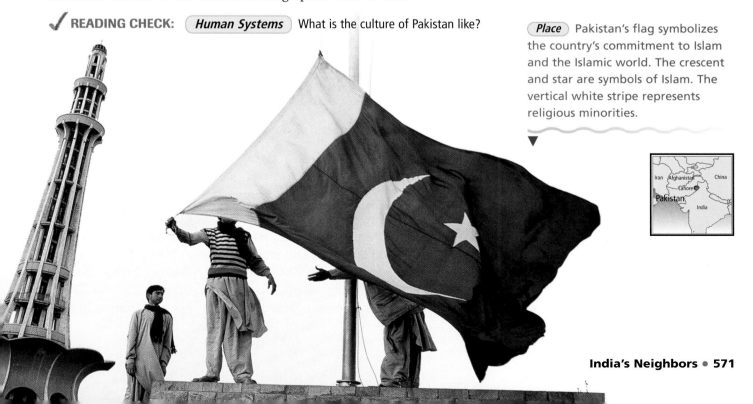

▲

(*Place*) Multan is a commercial and industrial center with several colleges and a university. The city came under Muslim control in the A.D. 700s.

Bangladesh's History

Bangladesh is part of a region known as Bengal. Bengal's many rivers are used for transporting goods. This is one reason why the area was important to Europeans in the 1500s. From the 1500s through the 1700s, the Mughal Empire combined Islam and regional Indian traditions to create a distinctive culture in this region. Eventually, the Mughal Empire weakened. The British East India Company then expanded its control over the area.

Because the British East India Company was so powerful, it could control what was traded. Therefore, British goods came into the region, but few goods other than rice and jute were exported. With a decline in trade, industry suffered. As a result, the region's economy became more agricultural in the 1800s. As you learned earlier, East Pakistan became the independent country of Bangladesh in 1971.

✓ READING CHECK: (*Places and Regions*) What has Bangladesh's history been like?

Bangladesh Today

Unlike other South Asian countries, Bangladesh has only one main ethnic group—the Bengalis. They make up 98 percent of the population. Social standing is based mostly on wealth and influence rather than on heredity or caste. Muslims may move up or down in status. Even among the country's Hindus, caste has much less importance than it does in India.

Population Bangladesh is about the same size as Wisconsin. However, it has a population nearly half the size of the entire U.S. population. Only 24 percent of Bangladesh's population lives in cities. The country's capital and largest city is Dhaka (DA-kuh). Cities and rural areas are densely populated. On average in Bangladesh there are 2,580 people per square mile (670/sq km).

Flooding and disease are two of the country's biggest challenges. Occasional violent tropical cyclones bring huge storm surges on shore. In addition, runoff from heavy rains in the distant Himalayas causes extensive flooding. When the land is flooded, sewage often washes into the water. As a result, Bangladesh has often suffered from epidemics of diseases like **cholera**. Cholera is a severe intestinal infection.

Culture Family life in Bangladesh is different from that in Pakistan. For example, many Bangladeshi women keep close ties to their own families after marriage. However, as in other South Asian countries, marriages are arranged by parents. Most couples typically do not know each other prior to their wedding.

More girls are going to secondary schools and universities than ever. Even so, the literacy rate for women remains just about half that of men. Bangladesh's official language, Bengali (Bangla), is the language spoken in schools. The country celebrates Islam's main festivals with feasts that feature fish and rice.

✓ **READING CHECK:** (*Places and Regions*) What are some challenges that Bangladesh faces today?

BIOGRAPHY

Muhammad Yunus
(1940–   )

Character Trait: Fairness

With a dream to eliminate world poverty, Muhammad Yunus founded a bank in his native Bangladesh. Since then, Yunus' Grameen Bank has lent over 3 billion dollars to poor Bangladeshis. In addition to giving out loans, Grameen Bank also teaches people how to use their money effectively. Through his fair treatment of the poor, Yunus continues to give millions an opportunity for a better future.

How does Muhammad Yunus show fairness towards poor people?

Section Review 2

Homework Practice Online
Keyword: SG5 HP26

Define or identify: cholera, Muhammad Yunus

Working with Sketch Maps On the map you created in Section 1, label Pakistan, Bangladesh, Karachi, Lahore, Islamabad, and Dhaka. What does the name of Pakistan's capital indicate about the country's dominant religion?

Reading for the Main Idea

1. (*Places and Regions*) Why were East and West Pakistan separated from India in 1947? When did East and West Pakistan split into two independent countries?

2. (*Environment and Society*) What technology allows Pakistan to grow enough food for its large population? How?

3. (*Environment and Society*) What climatic condition contributes to the high disease rate in Bangladesh? How?

Critical Thinking

4. **Contrasting/Comparing** How are marriage and married life in Pakistan different from marriage and married life in Bangladesh? How are they similar?

Organizing What You Know

5. **Comparing/Contrasting** Copy the following graphic organizer. Use it to compare and contrast Pakistan and Bangladesh.

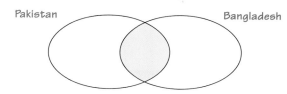

Pakistan   Bangladesh

COULD YOU SURVIVE THE FLOODS OF BANGLADESH?

A Land of Floods and Cyclones

Bangladesh is a very wet place! Some parts of the country get more than 100 inches of rain every year. Melting snow from the Himalayas combines with the heavy rain to cause disastrous floods. In addition, a cyclone can drive a wall of water, called a storm surge, inland from the ocean. People and livestock trying to escape the floods can get stranded on housetops or in trees. To make matters worse, rising waters drive poisonous snakes to the same crowded spots.

SURVIVAL CHALLENGE

What if you were a Bangladeshi farmer who lived at the location marked on the map? Your land has been flooded more than once, and your livestock have drowned. Should you abandon your farm and move to Dhaka, the capital? First, examine the chart and the map to assess the risks. Would you face the same dangers in Dhaka? Then consider what your life would be like in the city. For example, could you get a job in the city? What effect would the size of your family have on your decision?

With a partner, create a chart in which you balance the costs of remaining on the farm with the costs of moving to Dhaka. Do you have enough information yet to make your decision? If not, what kinds of information would help you?

Bangladeshis find temporary safety from floodwaters on the wreckage of houses.

Some Major Floods of Bangladesh

Year	Details
1970	Cyclones killed from 300,000 to 500,000 people.
1974	Floods ruined the grain crop, leading to 28,000 deaths. Some 2 million were left homeless.
1988	Water covered up to three-fourths of the country, and 28 million were homeless.
1991	A cyclone with 145-mile-per-hour winds hit the southeast coast with a 20-foot storm surge. Some 139,000 people and half a million animals died.
1998	Three-fourths of the country was flooded, including Dhaka.

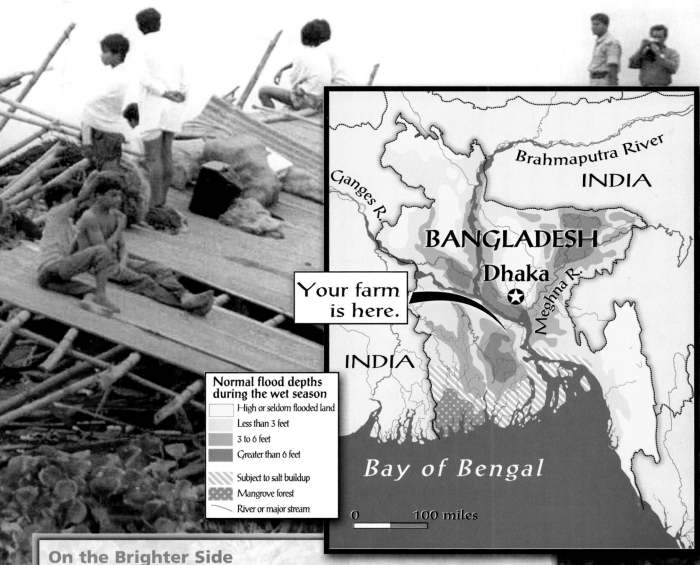

Normal flood depths
during the wet season

- High or seldom flooded land
- Less than 3 feet
- 3 to 6 feet
- Greater than 6 feet
- Subject to salt buildup
- Mangrove forest
- River or major stream

Your farm is here.

Brahmaputra River

INDIA

Ganges R.

BANGLADESH

Dhaka

Meghna R.

INDIA

Bay of Bengal

0   100 miles

On the Brighter Side

You may be wondering how Bangladesh maintains such a large population—more than 138,440,000 people in 2004. Moreover, the country usually produces enough rice to feed its population. How can this be? Here's a clue: The answer lies in the same floodwaters that cause such suffering. How may Bangladesh's floods be both a blessing and a curse?

The Himalayan and Island Countries

Read to Discover

1. What are some important features of Nepal?
2. How has Bhutan developed over time?
3. What is Sri Lanka like?
4. What are some economic activities of the Maldives?

Vocabulary

stupas
graphite
atolls

Places

Nepal
Kathmandu
Bhutan
Thimphu
Sri Lanka
Colombo
Maldives
Male

People

Tenzing Norgay

Reading Strategy

FOLDNOTES: LAYERED BOOK Create the FoldNote titled **Layered Book** described in the Appendix. Label the top layer Nepal. Label the other layers Bhutan, Sri Lanka, and the Maldives. As you read this section, write what you learn about each country above its label.

Place A temple to the Hindu god Krishna can be seen from Durban Square in Patan, near Kathmandu, Nepal. The pillar in the square honors Krishna's companion, Garuda.

Nepal

Nepal's history is linked to the early civilizations of northern India. Nepal shared its languages, culture, and economic base with peoples to the south. It was probably in Nepal that Gautama, the Buddha, was born about 563 B.C. Some of the oldest monuments to the Buddha are **stupas** in Nepal. They date back to before 300 B.C. Stupas are mounds of earth or stones covering the ashes of the Buddha or relics of Buddhist saints. Like India, Nepal adopted Buddhism at first but was mostly Hindu by A.D. 1200. About 90 percent of Nepal's people are now Hindus.

The British never formally ruled Nepal. Their army did defeat the Nepalese army in the early 1800s. As a result, the British took away the territories claimed by Nepal and sent an official to maintain indirect control. The British later recognized Nepal's independence. Nepal now is a constitutional monarchy with a king and elected parliament.

One of Nepal's ethnic groups is the Sherpa. The Sherpa guide and serve as porters for Himalayan expeditions. Tenzing Norgay, a Sherpa, and Sir Edmund Hillary, an explorer from New Zealand, climbed Mount Everest in 1953. They were the first to reach the summit.

✓ **READING CHECK:** *Places and Regions* What has the history of Nepal been like?

CONNECTING TO *Technology*

The world's highest peak, Mount Everest, sits on the border between China and Nepal. At 29,035 feet (8,850 m), it is one of the world's greatest mountaineering challenges.

After many failed attempts, two climbers—Edmund Hillary and Tenzing Norgay—finally reached the summit in 1953. One factor in their success was the use of advanced equipment. This equipment included special boots, oxygen bottles, and radio gear. Since then, technology has continued to play a key role in efforts to scale the Himalayas.

CLIMBING MOUNT EVEREST

Today's climbers use a wide range of sophisticated gear. This gear includes everything from space-age mountaineering clothes to remote sensors and satellite-tracking devices. Even so, climbing Everest remains very dangerous. In the 1990s more than 50 climbers lost their lives trying to scale the peak. Now scientists are testing new medical technologies on Mount Everest in hopes of preventing such tragedies in the future.

A joint project of the National Aeronautics and Space Administration (NASA) and Yale University has been analyzing the effects of high-altitude climbing on the human body. In 1998 this project sent a team of climbers up Mount Everest wearing "bio-packs." These packs included high-tech devices to monitor heart rate, blood oxygen, and other vital signs. This data was transmitted instantly to a base camp on Everest. There doctors could analyze the results. Scientists believe that this kind of "telemedicine" will help save lives in other extreme environments, including outer space.

Understanding What You Read

1. How do climbers use technology on Mount Everest?
2. How might climbers benefit from the use of new medical technology?

Sir Edmund Hillary (left) and Tenzing Norgay (right)

Nepal Today

Like other countries of the region, Nepal's economy is based on agriculture. More than 80 percent of the people make a living from farming. Most are subsistence farmers. The best farmland is found on the Tarai—Nepal's "breadbasket." Farmers there grow such crops as rice, other grains, and sugarcane. In the hills north of the Tarai, farmers grow fruits, grains, and vegetables. Kathmandu (kat-man-DOO), Nepal's capital and largest city, is located in this central region. For the most part, the Himalayan region is not good for

Human-Environment Interaction
Nepalese women are experts at winnowing grain. Winnowing is the process of separating chaff from grain by fanning.

Place Folk dancers in traditional dress perform near Thimphu, Bhutan.

▼

farming. Farmers graze cattle, goats, sheep, and yaks on the lower slopes. Yaks are large, longhaired oxen. In addition, some farmers grow grain and fruit trees on terraces cut into mountainsides.

With few resources and limited access to world trade routes, Nepal has developed few industries. Most of its industries are based on farm products, such as jute. Jute is a plant fiber that is used in making twine. Tourism is one of the fastest-growing and most important industries in Nepal. Tourists like to hike and climb in the mountains.

Tourism brings in much-needed income to Nepal. However, the constant stream of hikers and climbers threatens the country's environment. How? Many visitors leave behind trash. Also, their need for firewood contributes to deforestation and soil erosion. This problem is worsened as Nepalese clear woodland for farming and for wood for fuel. In response, Nepal's government has restricted access by visitors to some of the most affected areas.

✓ **READING CHECK:** **Places and Regions** What is Nepal like?

Bhutan

Little is known about the early history of Bhutan. Buddhism was practiced there as early as the A.D. 600s. Most of the people are of Tibetan origin and are Buddhist. In the 1600s a Tibetan monk helped organize Bhutan as a unified state. Then in the late 1700s the East India Company's business dealings increased British influence.

Bhutan, although very isolated, was under Indian control during British rule over that country.

Bhutan's ruler, or maharaja, declared a constitutional monarchy in 1969.

✓ **READING CHECK:** (*Places and Regions*) What has the history of Bhutan been like?

Bhutan Today

Until the mid-1970s, the government of Bhutan followed a policy of near total isolation. Even today, the country's international ties are somewhat limited.

Much of Bhutan's economy is traditional. More than 90 percent of the people make a living as subsistence farmers. Most grow rice, wheat, corn, and potatoes in fertile valleys and on mountainside terraces. A few grow fruits and spices for export. On mountain pastures, farmers raise cattle, goats, sheep, and yaks. Thimphu (thim-POO) is Bhutan's capital.

Timber and hydroelectricity are among Bhutan's most important resources. The country sells both to India, its main trading partner. Tourism is also a source of income for Bhutan. However, the government limits the number of visitors. By restricting tourism, the government hopes to protect Bhutan's way of life from outside influences and environmental damage.

✓ **READING CHECK:** (*Places and Regions*) What is Bhutan like today?

Sri Lanka

When Buddhism swept over India between the 400s and 200s B.C., Buddhist missionaries came to Sri Lanka. From Sri Lanka, traders spread Buddhism eastward to what are now Thailand and Indonesia. About 74 percent of Sri Lankans today belong to the Sinhalese ethnic group, and most are Buddhists. Sri Lanka has many dome-shaped stupas honoring the Buddha. Many are shaded by trees said to have been grown from cuttings of the original bo tree. It is believed the Buddha achieved enlightenment under this tree.

Throughout its history, Sri Lanka has been largely independent from India. In the 1500s the Portuguese established a trading post on the island. They were overthrown by the Dutch. The Dutch turned over Sri Lanka, then known as Ceylon, to the British in the late 1700s. The British granted independence in 1948. The new government made Sinhalese the official language and promoted Buddhism. An Indian and Hindu minority group, the Tamils, protested. Fighting between Tamils and the government has killed many people.

✓ **READING CHECK:** (*Places and Regions*) How have Europeans played a role in Sri Lanka's history?

Himalayan and Island Countries

COUNTRY	POPULATION/ GROWTH RATE	LIFE EXPECTANCY	LITERACY RATE	PER CAPITA GDP
Bhutan	2,139,549 2.1%	53, male 53, female	42%	$1,300
Maldives	329,684 3.0%	62, male 64, female	97%	$3,900
Nepal	26,469,569 2.3%	59, male 58, female	45%	$1,400
Sri Lanka	19,742,439 0.9%	70, male 75, female	90%	$3,700
United States	290,342,554 0.9%	74, male 80, female	97%	$37,600

Source: Central Intelligence Agency, *The World Factbook 2003*

Interpreting the Chart **Which country has the lowest literacy rate?**

▲

(*Place*) Buddhist monks prepare to pray at the top of Adam's Peak. The "yellow" robe is a symbol of Buddhism. The color of the robe varies according to the dye used.

Place The Dalada Maligawa (Temple of the Tooth) houses the sacred tooth of Buddha. Pilgrims come to pay respect to the Tooth Relic during daily ceremonies.

Human-Environment Interaction Semiprecious stones such as the sapphire, ruby, cat's eye, topaz, and garnet are mined in Sri Lanka.

Sri Lanka Today

Caste determines how Sri Lankans behave toward one another. As in India, many Sri Lankans believe associating with a member of a lower caste brings bad karma. Bad karma forces a person to undergo endless reincarnations, or rebirths. It also prevents him or her from finding nirvana, or spiritual release.

Sri Lanka has several features in common with the countries of the mainland. First, it is a mainly rural country. Less than 25 percent of Sri Lankans live in cities. Second, about 38 percent of Sri Lankans make a living from farming. They grow rice, fruits, and vegetables. Sri Lankan farmers also grow coconuts, rubber, and tea for export. Sri Lanka has a number of industries. They include food processing, textiles and apparel, telecommunications, insurance, and banking.

Mining is another important economic activity in Sri Lanka. The main resources mined are graphite and precious gems. Sri Lanka leads the world in **graphite** exports. Graphite is a form of carbon used in pencils and many other products. Recently, manufacturing—particularly of textiles and clothing—has grown in importance. Many textile and clothing factories are found in Colombo, the capital of Sri Lanka. Located on the west coast, Colombo is the country's largest city. It is also its most important commercial center and seaport. Sri Lanka's economy has grown in recent years. However, continuing ethnic conflicts between the Sinhalese majority and the Tamil minority threaten the country's progress.

✓ **READING CHECK:** **Places and Regions** What is Sri Lanka like today?

The Maldives

The Maldives were originally settled by Buddhists from Sri Lanka. Today the main religion is Islam. Education includes traditional teachings of the Qur'an. However, there are no colleges or universities.

The Maldives consists of 19 **atolls**. An atoll is a ring of coral surrounding a body of water called a lagoon. These atolls sit atop an ancient submerged volcanic plateau. Altogether, the islands cover about 115 square miles (298 sq km). The largest island, Male (MAH-lay), is home to about one fourth of the population. A city by the same name serves as the country's capital. Only about 25 percent of the people live in cities.

Tourism is the Maldives largest industry. Fishing, particularly of tuna, is another of the country's chief economic activities. Exports of fresh, dried, frozen, and canned fish account for about half the country's income. Breadfruit—a fruit that resembles bread when baked—and coconuts are the Maldives' main food crops. Most other food must be imported. A small clothing industry and boatbuilding and repair are other sources of income for this island country.

These fishers are working together to corral fish in large nets.

Interpreting the Visual Record

(*Human-Environment Interaction*) **Why must so many people be involved in catching fish in this way?**

✔ **READING CHECK:** (*Environment and Society*) What geographic factors affect the economic activities of the Maldives?

Section Review 3

Homework Practice Online
Keyword: SG5 HP26

Define or identify: stupas, Tenzing Norgay, graphite, atolls

Working with Sketch Maps On the map you created in Section 2, label Nepal, Kathmandu, Bhutan, Thimphu, Sri Lanka, Colombo, Maldives, and Male.

Reading for the Main Idea

1. (*Environment and Society*) How have the people of Nepal used the lower slopes of the Himalayas?

2. (*Human Systems*) How does the caste system affect social interaction in Sri Lanka?

3. (*Places and Regions*) What are the major economic activities of the Maldives?

Critical Thinking

4. **Comparing** In what ways have the cultures, people, and histories of India and the countries in this section been linked?

Organizing What You Know

5. **Categorizing** Copy the following graphic organizer. Use it to list the benefits and drawbacks of tourism in Nepal and Bhutan.

Tourism in Nepal and Bhutan	
Benefits	Drawbacks

CHAPTER 26 Review and Practice

Define and Identify

Identify each of the following:

1. cyclones
2. storm surges
3. cholera
4. Muhammad Yunus
5. stupas
6. Tenzing Norgay
7. graphite
8. atolls

Review the Main Ideas

9. What two rivers are important to Bangladesh?
10. What mountain is located on Nepal's border with China?
11. What brings so much rain to Bangladesh?
12. Which three of India's Neighbors are dominated by Islam? Which two are primarily Buddhist? Which one is populated mostly by Hindus?
13. How is married life for women in Bangladesh different from married life in Pakistan?
14. What are some important resources of India's Neighbors?
15. Why have so few industries developed in Nepal? What are some of Nepal's industries?

16. Why does the government of Bhutan limit tourism?
17. Why is Colombo, Sri Lanka an important commercial center?
18. What kinds of islands make up the Maldives?

Think Critically

19. **Drawing Inferences and Conclusions** What role do you think the Khyber Pass might have played in the history of this region?
20. **Finding the Main Idea** How has tourism benefited countries in the region? What problems has it caused?
21. **Analyzing Information** How did the British East India Company affect the history of this region?
22. **Analyzing Information** Is the population of India's Neighbors mostly rural or mostly urban? Explain your answer.
23. **Drawing Inferences and Conclusions** How has religion played a role in shaping the region's borders?

Map Activity

24. On a separate sheet of paper, match the letters on the map with their correct labels.

    Brahmaputra River
    Ganges River
    Himalayas
    Tarai
    Hindu Kush
    Khyber Pass
    Indus River
    Thar Desert

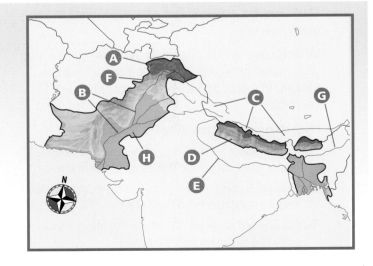

Writing Activity

Imagine that you are moving to one of India's Neighbors. In which country would you choose to live? State your choice and explain your reasons in two or three paragraphs. Explain how landforms, climate, culture, and economy influenced your decision. Be sure to use standard grammar, spelling, sentence structure, and punctuation.

internet connect

Internet Activity: **go.hrw.com**
KEYWORD: **SG5 GT26**

Choose a topic to explore about India's Neighbors.
- Climb the Himalayas.
- Learn about Sri Lanka's history.
- Visit the regions of Pakistan.

go.hrw.com

Social Studies Skills Practice

Interpreting Cartoons

Study the cartoon about Mount Everest below. Then answer the questions.

WHY ARE WE PICKING ALL THIS TRASH UP?

BECAUSE IT'S THERE.

©2000 Paul Dlugokencky (www.aDailyCartoon.com) for APS News

Source: ©2000 Paul Dlugokencky

1. What problem does this cartoon highlight?
2. How does this cartoonist show that the problem is a major one?
3. Why do you think there is trash on Mount Everest?
4. Who does the cartoonist believe should be responsible for responding to the trash problem?

Analyzing Primary Sources

Read the following quote from Sheika Hasina, who was the prime minister of Bangladesh at the time of this 2000 interview. Then answer the questions.

"We're trying to create an environment that will help us participate in globalization. . . . In 1996, Bangladesh, a country with 120 million people, had only 200,000 phones. We've undertaken major expansion and introduced cellular phones. We've withdrawn taxes on computers, all of which we import. . . . We've started computer schools to create more skilled workers. We now have more than 50 Internet service providers."

Source: *Los Angeles Times*

1. What issue does this quote focus on?
2. What is Bangladesh doing to create skilled workers?
3. What changes does Sheika Hasina see as the key to improving Bangladesh?
4. How might withdrawing taxes on computers promote economic development?

Saving Tigers

The Tiger

In the early 1800s India's tiger population was very large. By 1900, hunters had reduced the tiger population to about 40,000. To protect these tigers, India's British rulers placed strict limits on hunting them. Laws against illegal hunting were strictly enforced. After India won its independence in 1947, the hunting laws were often ignored, however. As a result, fewer than 2,000 tigers remained in India by 1972.

Why Are Tigers Endangered?

Unfortunately, laws have not kept people from hunting tigers. Tiger bones are used in traditional Chinese medicines. The bones are in high demand. International treaties now make it illegal to sell any part of an endangered species. However, the international trade in tiger bones continues.

Loss of habitat also threatens tiger survival. India's population has about doubled in the last 50 years. More land is now farmed to feed these additional people. As a result, many forests where tigers lived have been cleared for farming. As tiger habitat has decreased, so has the number of tigers.

International Efforts to Save the Tiger

Many people realized that tigers would not survive in the wild without protection. As a result, several international organizations and governments are working to ensure the tiger's future.

India's Project Tiger In 1973 the Indian government took steps to try to save its remaining tigers. With support from the World Wildlife Fund, nine tiger reserves were created as part of Project Tiger. By 2003, 27 reserves had been set up throughout India.

Each reserve has a core area. No one can enter this area without a park ranger. The core area is surrounded by a buffer zone. People can use land in these zones in ways that do not harm the environment.

Once on the verge of extinction, tigers have rebounded in India due largely to Project Tiger.

▼

Realm of the Tiger

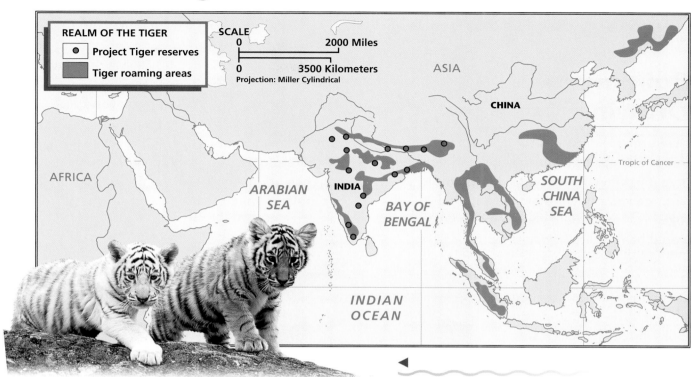

REALM OF THE TIGER
- Project Tiger reserves
- Tiger roaming areas

SCALE
0   2000 Miles
0   3500 Kilometers
Projection: Miller Cylindrical

ASIA

CHINA

AFRICA

ARABIAN SEA

INDIA

BAY OF BENGAL

Tropic of Cancer

SOUTH CHINA SEA

INDIAN OCEAN

Some rare Bengal tigers, such as this cub, are white. In the last 100 years, only about a dozen white tigers have been seen in the wild.

Some conservationists are reaching out to nearby villagers. Villagers have often felt that tigers are being protected at their expense. The conservationists want to show that tiger reserves can also help villagers. One organization has introduced new types of water buffalo that need very little grazing land. To boost the local economy, it has helped women sell their handicrafts in urban areas. The Global Environment Facility and the World Bank also helped. They spent about $10 million to aid villages around India's Ranthambhore National Park.

China's Year of the Tiger Despite these efforts, the number of tigers remains low. In 1998, the Chinese Year of the Tiger, conservationists in Hong Kong tried a new approach. They started an advertising campaign to remind people how important tigers are in traditional Chinese culture. The advertisements showed children dressed in clothes with popular tiger designs. The advertise-

ments read, "They protect your children; who will protect them?" Chinese conservationists hope their campaign will encourage people to stop using medicines made with tiger bones. They also hope it will encourage people to join the fight to save the world's tigers.

Your Turn

Imagine you are planning a worldwide campaign to save tigers in the wild. Write a short report that explains your plan and answers the following questions:

1. How would the Project Tiger reserves and the Chinese advertising campaign fit into your plan?

2. Do you think it is more important to save tiger habitat or to keep people from hunting them? why?

Building Skills for Life: Drawing Diagrams

Diagrams are drawings that explain how things work or fit together. They can be helpful in many different situations. For example, suppose you bought a bicycle and had to put it together. How would you do it? The easiest way would be to follow a diagram.

The goal of a diagram is to explain something. Diagrams are not intended to show exactly how something looks in real life. Diagrams should be easy to understand, neat, and simple.

In geography, diagrams are often used to show how different things are related. Physical geographers use diagrams to explain how sea and land breezes develop or how volcanoes form. Cultural geographers use diagrams to show settlement patterns and housing styles.

You can draw diagrams too. To draw a diagram, first decide exactly what you want it to show. Choose a short, descriptive title. Plan your diagram by making a quick sketch. How many drawings will you need? How will you arrange them? Then carefully draw your diagram. Label the important features. Use colors, patterns, and symbols if you need to. Use a ruler for straight lines and write the title at the top. Then add a short caption at the bottom that explains your diagram.

Sea and Land Breezes

Warm air

As warm air rises, it creates an area of low pressure over the land.

The cool air moves toward the land, producing a sea breeze.

Cool air

Air over the water is cooler and creates an area of high pressure.

Cool air

Air over land is cooler and creates an area of high pressure.

The cool air moves toward the water, producing a land breeze.

Warm air

Air over the water is warmer and creates an area of low pressure.

Breezes from the ocean cool the warmer land surface during the day. At night, cooler land surface breezes blow toward the ocean.

THE SKILL

1. Choose a diagram from a book, magazine, or newspaper. Write a short paragraph about the diagram. What does it show? Is it clear and easy to understand? why or why not?

2. Draw a diagram that shows how wind moves a sailboat through water.

3. Draw a diagram that shows how rocks can break off a mountain and cause a landslide.

HANDS on

The Himalayas are the highest mountains on Earth. Nine of the ten highest peaks in the world are located there. The Himalayas have 110 peaks that rise above 24,000 feet (7,315 m).

How did the Himalayas get to be so high? When were they formed? Drawing a diagram is one way to show how the Himalayas became the world's highest mountains.

Read the paragraph below. It describes how and when the Himalayas formed. Use this information to draw a diagram showing how the Himalayas became the world's highest mountains.

The Himalayas were formed long ago by the movement of Earth's tectonic plates. About 180 million years ago, the Indo-Australian plate broke off from the ancient supercontinent Gondwana and began moving north. This plate included what is now the Indian Subcontinent. About 50 million years ago, the Indo-Australian plate collided with the Eurasian plate and was forced under it. As the Indo-Australian plate was pulled under the Eurasian plate, the Himalayas began to rise. They grew slowly at first. Then, about 30 million years ago, the Himalayas began rising faster. However, they did not become the highest mountains in the world until about 500,000 years ago. The Himalayas are still rising today.

Mountain peaks rise above the clouds in the world's highest mountains.

Lab Report

1. Is your diagram clear and easy to understand? Show your diagram to another person to see if he or she can easily understand it.

2. Did you use colors or symbols in your diagram? why or why not?

3. By drawing a diagram of the Himalayas, did you learn something about diagrams in general? What did you learn?

UNIT 9

East and Southeast Asia

Shwedagon Pagoda, Yangon, Myanmar

Rice paddies near Guilin, China

A Peace Corps Volunteer in Mongolia

Matt Heller served as a Peace Corps volunteer in Mongolia. He worked as an English teacher and coordinated a greenhouse reconstruction project. **WHAT DO YOU THINK?** *What kinds of changes would you have to make in your life to live in Mongolia?*

I've been a Peace Corps volunteer in Mongolia for eighteen months. I live in a *ger*, a tent with a small wood stove in the center. It is strong and practical, perfect for a nomadic herder. I, however, am an English teacher in a small school in rural Mongolia. *Ger* life is hard. It makes twenty-year-olds look thirty-five. It makes your soul hard.

Mongolians are very proud of their history. Once, while sitting on the train going from Ulaanbaatar to my own town, Bor-Undur, a Mongolian pointed to his arm and said, "In here is the blood of Genghis Khan. Beware." There is no argument to that statement. I responded, "Yes, older brother (a respectful title addressed to elders), your country is beautiful. Mongolians are lucky."

Along with many other things, I'm learning how Mongolians live. In the steppe there is very little snow, only biting wind and dust. It gets as cold as –50 degrees, not counting the wind chill factor. If I leave tea in a mug, it will freeze by morning. I've broken three mugs that way.

A Mongolian outside his home

Festival of Ages parade, Kyoto, Japan

Understanding Primary Sources

1. What conclusion does Matt Heller make about Mongolians and their past?

2. How does Matt Heller describe the climate in Mongolia?

Giant panda

East and Southeast Asia

Elevation Profile

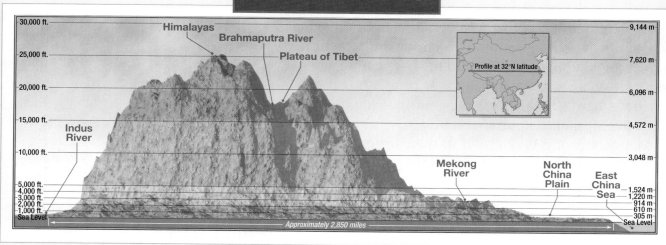

- 30,000 ft. — 9,144 m
- 25,000 ft. — 7,620 m
- 20,000 ft. — 6,096 m
- 15,000 ft. — 4,572 m
- 10,000 ft. — 3,048 m
- 5,000 ft. — 1,524 m
- 4,000 ft. — 1,220 m
- 3,000 ft. — 914 m
- 2,000 ft. — 610 m
- 1,000 ft. — 305 m
- Sea Level — Sea Level

Himalayas
Brahmaputra River
Plateau of Tibet
Indus River
Mekong River
North China Plain
East China Sea

Profile at 32°N latitude

Approximately 2,850 miles

The United States and East and Southeast Asia: Comparing Sizes

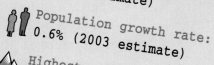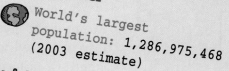

GEOSTATS:

China

🌍 World's largest population: 1,286,975,468 (2003 estimate)

👥 Population growth rate: 0.6% (2003 estimate)

⛰️ Highest point: Mount Everest—29,035 ft. (8,850 m)

🏔️ Lowest point: Turpan Depression—505 ft. (154 m) below sea level

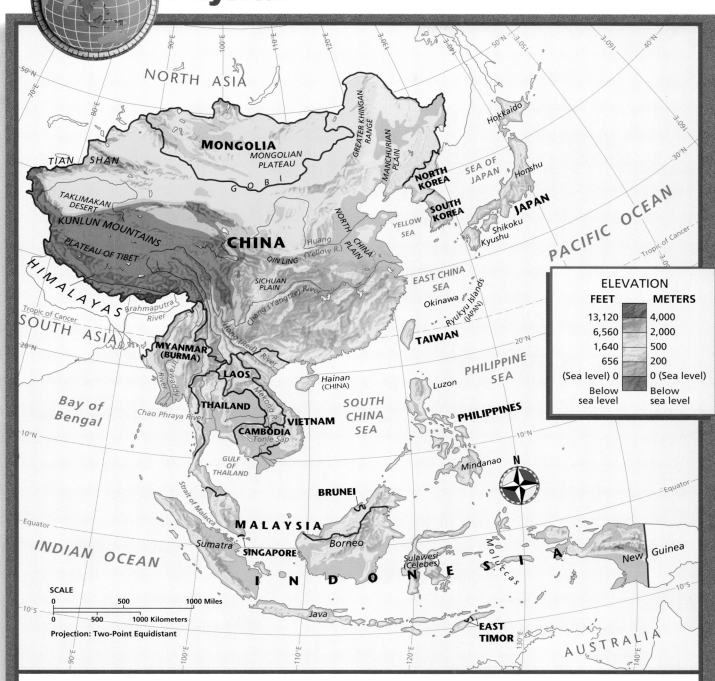

ELEVATION

FEET		METERS
13,120		4,000
6,560		2,000
1,640		500
656		200
(Sea level) 0		0 (Sea level)
Below sea level		Below sea level

SCALE

0   500   1000 Miles

0   500   1000 Kilometers

Projection: Two-Point Equidistant

1. **Movement** Which of the region's physical features could make travel and trade difficult?

2. **Region** What are the region's three largest island countries?

3. **Location** Which countries have territory on the mainland and on islands?

Critical Thinking

4. **Place** Compare this map to the **population map**. What physical features might prevent western China from becoming densely populated? Why might eastern China be so densely populated?

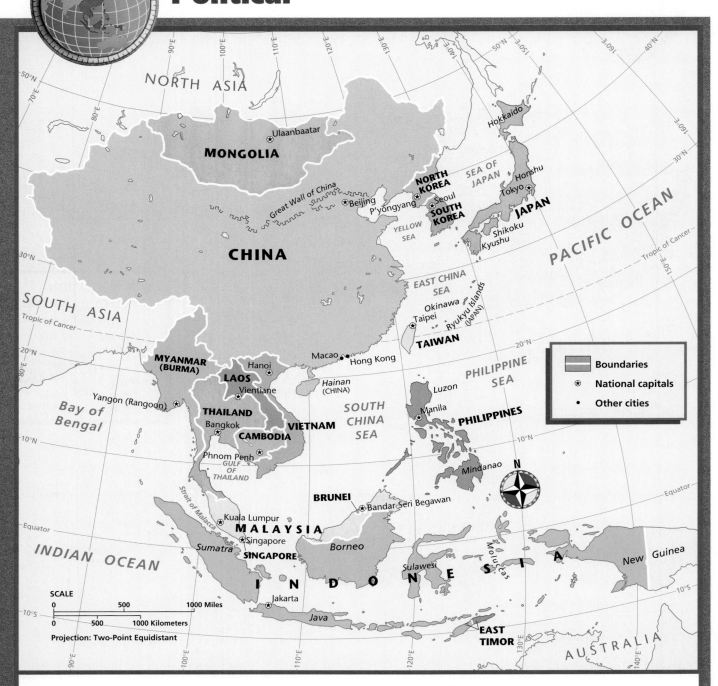

NORTH ASIA

MONGOLIA

Ulaanbaatar

Great Wall of China

CHINA

Beijing

NORTH KOREA

P'yongyang

Seoul

SOUTH KOREA

YELLOW SEA

SEA OF JAPAN

Hokkaido

Honshu

Tokyo

JAPAN

Shikoku

Kyushu

PACIFIC OCEAN

Tropic of Cancer

SOUTH ASIA

Tropic of Cancer

EAST CHINA SEA

Okinawa

Taipei

Ryukyu Islands (JAPAN)

TAIWAN

Macao

Hong Kong

MYANMAR (BURMA)

Hanoi

LAOS

Vientiane

Hainan (CHINA)

PHILIPPINE SEA

Luzon

Bay of Bengal

Yangon (Rangoon)

THAILAND

Bangkok

VIETNAM

CAMBODIA

SOUTH CHINA SEA

Manila

PHILIPPINES

Phnom Penh

GULF OF THAILAND

Mindanao

N

Strait of Malacca

Kuala Lumpur

BRUNEI

Bandar Seri Begawan

MALAYSIA

Singapore

Borneo

Equator

INDIAN OCEAN

Sumatra

SINGAPORE

I N D O N E S I A

Sulawesi

Moluccas

New Guinea

Jakarta

Java

EAST TIMOR

AUSTRALIA

Boundaries
⊛ **National capitals**
• **Other cities**

SCALE

0   500   1000 Miles

0   500   1000 Kilometers

Projection: Two-Point Equidistant

1. (Region) Which country entirely on the mainland shares a border with just one of the region's other countries?

2. (Location) What is the only landlocked country in Southeast Asia? Which country in East Asia is landlocked?

Critical Thinking

3. (Region) Compare this map to the **physical map** of the region. Which physical feature forms the border of southwestern China? Which other physical features form natural borders in the region?

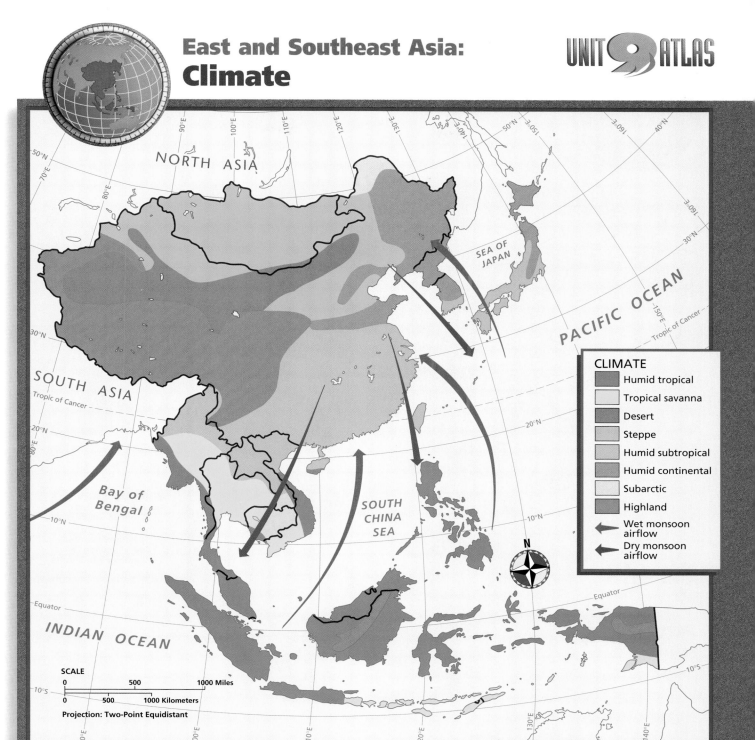

NORTH ASIA

SEA OF JAPAN

PACIFIC OCEAN

Tropic of Cancer

SOUTH ASIA

Tropic of Cancer

20°N

Bay of Bengal

SOUTH CHINA SEA

10°N

N

Equator

INDIAN OCEAN

CLIMATE
- Humid tropical
- Tropical savanna
- Desert
- Steppe
- Humid subtropical
- Humid continental
- Subarctic
- Highland
- ← Wet monsoon airflow
- ← Dry monsoon airflow

SCALE
0   500   1000 Miles
0   500   1000 Kilometers
Projection: Two-Point Equidistant

1. **Place** Compare this map to the **political map** of the region. What kind of climate does most of Mongolia have?

2. **Location** Study the monsoon airflow patterns shown on this map. In which directions do the wet and dry monsoons flow?

Critical Thinking

3. **Region** Why might this region have such a variety of climate types?

4. **Region** Why might the South China Sea be stormy?

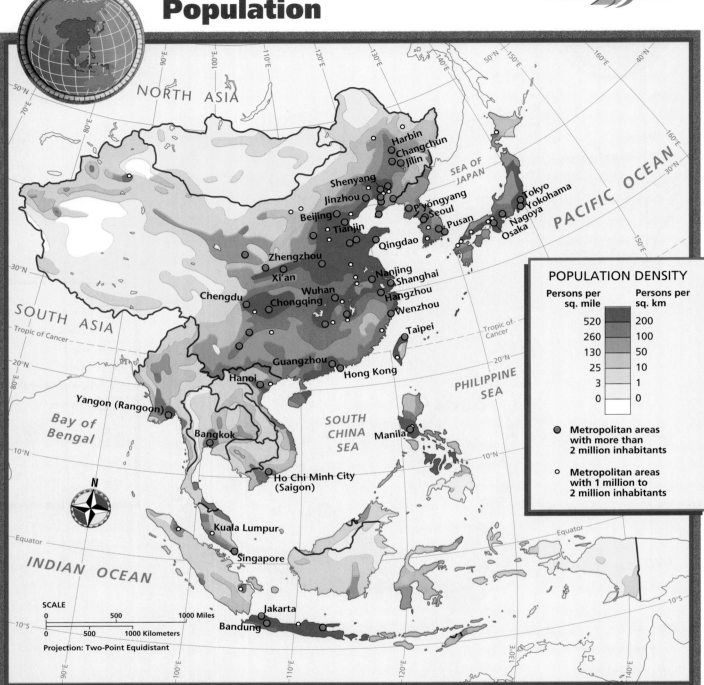

POPULATION DENSITY

Persons per sq. mile	Persons per sq. km
520	200
260	100
130	50
25	10
3	1
0	0

● Metropolitan areas with more than 2 million inhabitants

○ Metropolitan areas with 1 million to 2 million inhabitants

SCALE
0   500   1000 Miles
0   500   1000 Kilometers
Projection: Two-Point Equidistant

1. **Place** What is the population density in the area between Shanghai and Beijing?

2. **Region** Compare this map to the **physical map** of the region. Which physical features help explain the low population density in western China?

Critical Thinking

3. **Human-Environment Interaction** Compare this map to the **physical map** of the region. Which physical features help explain the high population densities near Bangkok, Ho Chi Minh City, and Yangon (Rangoon)?

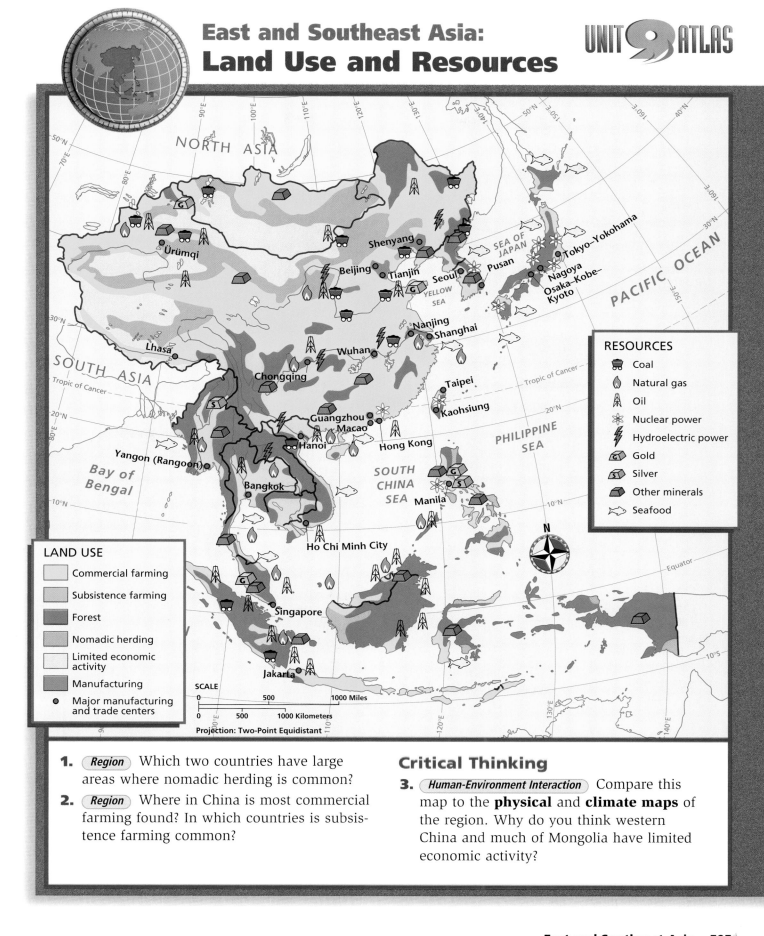

NORTH ASIA

Ürümqi

Shenyang

SEA OF JAPAN

Tokyo–Yokohama

PACIFIC OCEAN

Beijing Tianjin

Seoul Pusan

Nagoya
Osaka–Kobe–
Kyoto

YELLOW SEA

SOUTH ASIA

Tropic of Cancer

Lhasa

Nanjing
Shanghai

Wuhan

Chongqing

Taipei

Tropic of Cancer

Kaohsiung

RESOURCES

	Coal
	Natural gas
	Oil
	Nuclear power
	Hydroelectric power
	Gold
	Silver
	Other minerals
	Seafood

Guangzhou
Macao

Hanoi

Hong Kong

PHILIPPINE SEA

Yangon (Rangoon)

Bay of Bengal

Bangkok

SOUTH CHINA SEA

Manila

Ho Chi Minh City

N

Singapore

Equator

Jakarta

LAND USE

	Commercial farming
	Subsistence farming
	Forest
	Nomadic herding
	Limited economic activity
	Manufacturing
●	Major manufacturing and trade centers

SCALE
0   500   1000 Miles
0   500   1000 Kilometers
Projection: Two-Point Equidistant

1. (Region) Which two countries have large areas where nomadic herding is common?

2. (Region) Where in China is most commercial farming found? In which countries is subsistence farming common?

Critical Thinking

3. (Human-Environment Interaction) Compare this map to the **physical** and **climate maps** of the region. Why do you think western China and much of Mongolia have limited economic activity?

Fast FACTS

East and Southeast Asia

BRUNEI

CAPITAL:
Bandar Seri Begawan
AREA:
2,228 sq. mi. (5,770 sq km)
POPULATION:
358,098

MONEY:
Bruneian dollar
LANGUAGES:
Malay (official), English, Chinese
NUMBER OF INTERNET USERS: 35,000

JAPAN
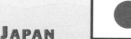

CAPITAL:
Tokyo
AREA:
145,882 sq. mi. (377,835 sq km)
POPULATION:
127,214,499

MONEY:
yen
LANGUAGES:
Japanese
NUMBER OF INTERNET USERS:
56,000,000

CAMBODIA

CAPITAL:
Phnom Penh
AREA:
69,900 sq. mi. (181,040 sq km)
POPULATION:
13,124,764

MONEY:
riel
LANGUAGES:
Khmer (official), French
NUMBER OF INTERNET USERS: 10,000

LAOS

CAPITAL:
Vientiane
AREA:
91,428 sq. mi. (236,800 sq km)
POPULATION:
5,921,545

MONEY:
kip
LANGUAGES:
Lao (official), French, English, ethnic languages
NUMBER OF INTERNET USERS: 10,000

CHINA

CAPITAL:
Beijing
AREA:
3,705,386 sq. mi. (9,596,960 sq km)
POPULATION:
1,286,975,468

MONEY:
yuan
LANGUAGES:
Mandarin, Yue, other forms of Chinese
NUMBER OF INTERNET USERS: 45,800,000

MALAYSIA

CAPITAL:
Kuala Lumpur
AREA:
127,316 sq. mi. (329,750 sq km)
POPULATION:
23,092,940

MONEY:
ringgit
LANGUAGES: Bahasa Melayu (official), English, Chinese dialects, ethnic languages
NUMBER OF INTERNET USERS: 5,700,000

INDONESIA

CAPITAL:
Jakarta
AREA:
741,096 sq. mi. (1,919,440 sq km)
POPULATION:
234,893,453

MONEY:
Indonesian rupiah
LANGUAGES:
Bahasa Indonesia (official), English, Dutch, Javanese
NUMBER OF INTERNET USERS: 4,400,000

MONGOLIA

CAPITAL:
Ulaanbaatar
AREA:
604,247 sq. mi. (1,565,000 sq km)
POPULATION:
2,712,315

MONEY:
togrog/tugrik
LANGUAGES:
Khalkha Mongol, Turkic, Russian
NUMBER OF INTERNET USERS: 40,000

Countries not drawn to scale.

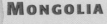

MYANMAR (Burma)

CAPITAL:
Yangon (Rangoon)

AREA:
261,969 sq. mi.
(678,500 sq km)

POPULATION:
42,510,537

MONEY:
kyat

LANGUAGES:
Burmese, many
ethnic languages

**NUMBER OF INTERNET
USERS:** 10,000

SOUTH KOREA

CAPITAL:
Seoul

AREA:
38,023 sq. mi.
(98,480 sq km)

POPULATION: 48,289,037

MONEY:
South Korean won

LANGUAGES:
Korean, English

**NUMBER OF INTERNET
USERS:** 25,600,000

NORTH KOREA

CAPITAL:
P'yŏngyang

AREA:
46,540 sq. mi.
(120,540 sq km)

POPULATION:
22,466,481

MONEY:
North Korean won

LANGUAGES:
Korean

**NUMBER OF INTERNET
USERS:** not available

TAIWAN

CAPITAL:
Taipei

AREA:
13,892 sq. mi.
(35,980 sq km)

POPULATION:
22,548,000

MONEY:
New Taiwan
dollar

LANGUAGES: Mandarin,
Taiwanese (Min), Hakka
dialects

**NUMBER OF INTERNET
USERS:** 10,100,000

PHILIPPINES

CAPITAL:
Manila

AREA:
115,830 sq. mi.
(300,000 sq km)

POPULATION:
84,619,974

MONEY:
Philippine peso

LANGUAGES:
Filipino, English

**NUMBER OF INTERNET
USERS:** 4,500,000

THAILAND

CAPITAL:
Bangkok

AREA:
198,455 sq. mi.
(514,000 sq km)

POPULATION: 64,265,276

MONEY:
baht

LANGUAGES: Thai, English,
ethnic languages

**NUMBER OF INTERNET
USERS:** 1,200,000

VIETNAM

CAPITAL:
Hanoi

AREA:
127,243 sq. mi.
(329,560 sq km)

POPULATION:
81,624,716

MONEY:
dong

LANGUAGES: Vietnamese
(official), Chinese,
English, French,
Khmer, ethnic languages

**NUMBER OF INTERNET
USERS:** 409,000

SINGAPORE

CAPITAL:
Singapore

AREA:
250 sq. mi. (648 sq km)

POPULATION:
4,608,595

MONEY:
Singapore dollar

LANGUAGES:
Chinese, Malay, Tamil,
English

**NUMBER OF INTERNET
USERS:** 2,310,000

internet connect

COUNTRY STATISTICS
GO TO: go.hrw.com
KEYWORD: SG5 FactsU9
**FOR: more facts about East
and Southeast Asia**

Sources: Central Intelligence Agency, *The World Factbook 2003*; Taipei Economic and Cultural Representative Office; pop. figures are 2003 estimates.

China, Mongolia, and Taiwan

This region of Asia with its varied landscape and cultures is home to one of the world's oldest living civilizations.

Hello! My name is Lu Hua. Lu is my family name, and Hua is my given name. In China the family name comes first. I am 16 and live in Jin Shan County, outside of Shanghai, with my parents and my brother. My father is a clerk in a Volkswagen factory. My ancestors have lived in this village for hundreds of years. All 200 people in this village are named Lu.

I am in my last year at Jin Shan County High School. To get into this school, which is the best in the county, I had to pass a very difficult exam when I was 11. I had the best score that year. The school goes from seventh to twelfth grade. Each grade has four classes with 50 kids in each class. Now I am hoping to go on to a university. In China only one or two out of a hundred kids can go to college.

Most of my friends want to be scientists. I think I would like to be a diplomat, to travel, and have adventures. My family are common people, though, not Chinese Communist Party members, so I may not get into the diplomatic college.

你好嗎?

◄ Translation: How are you?

Section 1 Physical Geography

Read to Discover

1. What are the physical features of China, Mongolia, and Taiwan?
2. What types of climate are found in China, Mongolia, and Taiwan?
3. What natural resources do China, Mongolia, and Taiwan have?

Vocabulary

dikes
arable

Places

Himalayas
Mount Everest
Kunlun Mountains
Tian Shan
Plateau of Tibet
Taklimakan Desert
Tarim Basin
Gobi
North China Plain
Huang River
Chang River
Sichuan (Red) Basin
Xi River

Reading Strategy

USING VISUAL INFORMATION Look at the map and photographs in this section. Where do you think most of China's population lives? What challenges do the people of Mongolia and Taiwan face? Write your answers on a sheet of paper. As you read this section, correct your predictions and add more details.

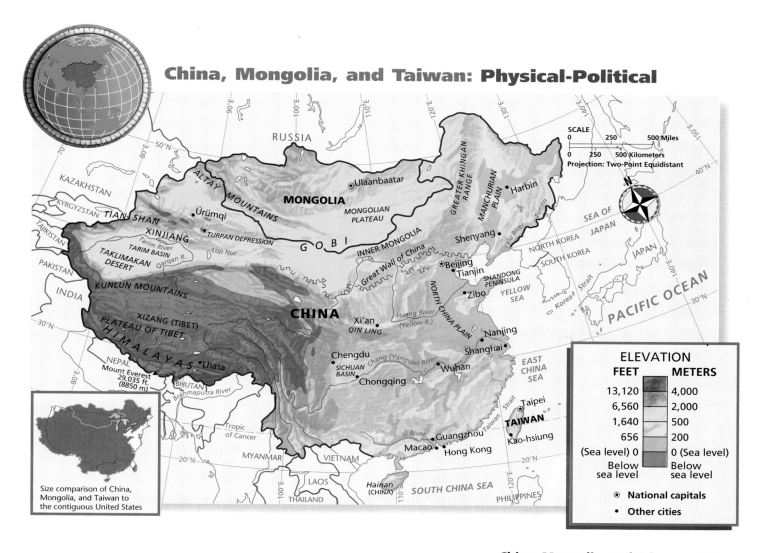

China, Mongolia, and Taiwan: Physical-Political

Size comparison of China, Mongolia, and Taiwan to the contiguous United States

ELEVATION

FEET	METERS
13,120	4,000
6,560	2,000
1,640	500
656	200
(Sea level) 0	0 (Sea level)
Below sea level	Below sea level

⊛ National capitals
• Other cities

These snow-covered mountains are in the Wolong Nature Reserve in central China.

Interpreting the Visual Record What climate types would you expect to find in this area of the reserve?

internet connect

GO TO: go.hrw.com
KEYWORD: SG5 CH27
FOR: Web sites about China, Mongolia, and Taiwan

Physical Features

China has some of the world's tallest mountains, driest deserts, and longest rivers. Mongolia (mahn-GOHL-yuh) is China's neighbor to the north. It is a large, rugged, landlocked country. Burning hot summers and bitter cold winters are common there. In contrast, Taiwan (TY-WAHN) is a green tropical island just off the coast of mainland China.

Mountains The towering Himalayas (hi-muh-LAY-uhz), the world's tallest mountain range, run along China's southwestern border. Mount Everest lies in the Himalayas on China's border with Nepal. At 29,035 feet (8,850 m), it is the world's tallest mountain. If you move north from the Himalayas, you will find several other mountain ranges. These are the Kunlun Mountains (KOON-LOON), the Tian Shan (TYEN SHAHN), and the Altay Mountains (al-TY). To the east, on Mongolia's eastern border with China, you will see the Greater Khingan (KING-AHN) Range.

Mountains stretch the length of Taiwan and cover the eastern half of the island. In some places, the mountains end in steep cliffs at the edge of the Pacific Ocean. To the west of the mountains is a fertile coastal plain.

Plateaus, Basins, and Deserts Isolated plateaus and basins separate the region's mountain ranges. The huge Plateau of Tibet lies between the Himalayas and the Kunlun Mountains. With an average elevation of 16,000 feet (4,877 m), it is the world's highest plateau. The Taklimakan (tah-kluh-muh-KAHN) Desert is a huge expanse of sand. It occupies the central part of the Tarim (DAH-REEM) Basin in western China. In the northeastern corner of the basin, the Turpan (toohr-PAHN) Depression drops about 505 feet (154 m) below sea level.

The Mongolian Plateau covers most of the country of Mongolia. The Gobi (GOH-bee) takes up much of the central and southeastern sections of the plateau. The Gobi is the coldest desert in the world and covers more than 500,000 square miles (1,295,000 sq km). Much of the Gobi is gravel and bare rock.

Plains China and Mongolia have few areas of lowlands made up of coastal and river floodplains. However, these fertile plains support the major population centers. Millions of people live in the North China Plain. It is the largest plain in China and is crossed by major rivers.

Rivers The river known as the Huang (HWAHNG) rises on the eastern edge of the Plateau of Tibet. It flows eastward through the North China Plain and empties into the Yellow Sea. It takes its name, which means "yellow river," from the yellowish mud it carries. Winds carry loess, a yellowish-brown soil, from the Gobi to northern China. The Huang picks up the loess as the river flows through the region. On its way to the sea the river dumps the loess, raising the river bottom. This can lead to flooding. Floodwaters deposit a layer of rich silt that is good for farming but also cause great damage and loss of life. As a result, the Huang has long been known as China's Sorrow. The Chinese have tried to control the Huang by building **dikes**. These high banks of earth or concrete help reduce flooding.

The Chang (CHAHNG), or Yangtze (YAHNG-TSE), River also rises in the Plateau of Tibet. It flows eastward for 3,434 miles (5,525 km) across central China through the fertile Sichuan (SEE-CHWAHN), or Red, Basin. The Chang is China's—and Asia's—longest river. In fact, its name means "long river." The Chang is one of China's most important transportation routes. It is connected to the Huang by the world's oldest and longest canal system, the Grand Canal. The Xi (SHEE) River is southern China's most important river and transportation route.

✓ **READING CHECK:** *Places and Regions* What are the major physical features of this region?

Our Amazing Planet

China has greater potential for hydroelectric power than any other country in the world. When completed in 2009, the Three Gorges Dam on the Chang River will be the world's largest dam.

The Gobi is the world's third-largest desert. Herders ride Bactrian camels.
Interpreting the Visual Record *Place*
What characteristics of a desert environment can be seen in this photo?

Climate

China, Mongolia, and Taiwan are part of a huge region with several different climates. China's precipitation varies. The southeastern coastal region is the country's most humid area. As you move northwestward the climate becomes steadily drier. The extreme northwest has a true desert climate.

Seasonal monsoon winds greatly affect the climate of the region's southern and eastern parts. In winter, winds from Central Asia bring dry, cool-to-cold weather to eastern

Russia
Mongolia
East Gobi
China

China, Mongolia, and Taiwan

Country	Population/ Growth Rate	Life Expectancy	Literacy Rate	Per Capita GDP
China	1,286,975,468 0.6%	70, male 74, female	86%	$4,400
Mongolia	2,712,315 1.4%	61, male 66, female	99%	$1,840
Taiwan	22,548,000 0.8%	74, male 80, female	94%	$17,400
United States	281,421,906 0.9%	74, male 80, female	97%	$36,200

Source: Central Intelligence Agency, *The World Factbook 2003*

Interpreting the Chart Which country has the fastest rate of population growth?

This bronze vessel dates to the A.D. 1000s. Found in a tomb, it is just over a foot long (30 cm) and is covered with detailed animal designs.

Asia. In summer, winds from the Pacific bring warm, wet air. This creates hot, rainy summers. Typhoons sometimes hit the coastal areas during the summer and fall. Typhoons are violent storms with high winds and heavy rains similar to hurricanes. They often bring flooding and cause a great deal of damage.

✓ **READING CHECK:** (*Places and Regions*) What are the climates of China, Mongolia, and Taiwan like?

Resources

China has a wide range of mineral resources. These include gold, iron ore, lead, salt, uranium, and zinc, as well as energy resources such as coal and oil. China has greater coal reserves than any other country. At the present rate of use, these reserves will last another 1,000 years. China also produces enough oil to meet most of its own needs.

Mongolia has deposits of coal, copper, gold, iron ore, and oil. Taiwan's most important natural resource is its **arable** land, or land that is suitable for growing crops.

✓ **READING CHECK:** (*Places and Regions*) What are the region's resources?

Homework Practice Online

Keyword: SG5 HP27

Section Review 1

Define and explain: dikes, arable

Working with Sketch Maps On a map of China, Mongolia, and Taiwan that you draw or that your teacher provides, label the following: the Himalayas, Mount Everest, Kunlun Mountains, Tian Shan, Plateau of Tibet, Taklimakan Desert, Tarim Basin, Gobi, North China Plain, Huang River, Chang River, Sichuan Basin, and Xi River. Where do you think the most fertile areas of the region are located?

Reading for the Main Idea

1. (*Places and Regions*) What and where is the world's largest plateau? What is the world's tallest mountain? Where is it located?

2. (*Environment and Society*) What are three major rivers in eastern and southern China? How does the Huang affect China's people?

3. (*Places and Regions*) What is the region's driest area?

Critical Thinking

4. **Drawing Inferences and Conclusions** What do you think might be the major factors that influence this region's climate?

Organizing What You Know

5. **Summarizing** Summarize the natural environments of China, Mongolia, and Taiwan.

Country	Physical Features	Climates	Resources

Read to Discover

1. What are some of the major events in the history of China?
2. What are some features of China's culture?

Vocabulary

emperor
dynasty
porcelain
martial law
pagodas

Places

China
Great Wall

People

Confucius
Genghis Khan
Sun Yat-sen
Mao Zedong
Dalai Lama

Reading Strategy

USING PRIOR KNOWLEDGE Before you read this section, list information you already know about China's history and culture. Compare your list with a partner. As you read this section, add more information to your list. Then compare your completed list with your partner's list.

History

Farmers have cultivated rice in southern China for some 7,000 years. Warm, wet weather made the region ideal for growing rice. Rice remains one of the region's main sources of food. Farmers in drier northern China grew a grain called millet and other crops. The early Chinese also grew hemp for fiber for clothing and spun silk from the cocoons of silkworms. Various cultures developed, particularly along the region's rivers.

The Qin Dynasty and the Great Wall Beginning about 2000 B.C. northern Chinese living in the Huang valley formed kingdoms. As Chinese civilization began to develop, peoples from various regions organized into large states. Each state was governed by an **emperor**—a ruler of a large empire. An emperor is often a member of a **dynasty**. A dynasty is a ruling family that passes power from one generation to the next. Beginning in about 500 B.C., the Chinese began building earthen

Place The Great Wall of China, including its branches and curves, stretches more than 2,000 miles (3,218 km).

▼

Archaeologists have discovered 6,000 of these uniquely crafted soldiers near Xi'an.

BIOGRAPHY

Confucius
(c. 551 B.C.–479? B.C.)

The philosopher's real name was K'ung Ch'iu or K'ung Fu-tzu ("Master K'ung"). We know him by the Latin version of his name—Confucius.

Few details about the life of Confucius are certain. We do know he was born about 551 B.C. in eastern China. It was a time troubled by warfare and wicked rulers. In response, Confucius argued for a different system of behavior and government. His ideas have shaped Chinese society for centuries.

How did Confucius influence Chinese society?

walls hundreds of miles long. These walls separated the kingdoms from the northern nomads and from each other. Records show that the first emperor of the Qin, also spelled Ch'in (CHIN), dynasty ordered the building of the Great Wall along China's northern border. People began to connect the sections of walls about 200 B.C.

The Qin dynasty is well known for its contributions to China's culture. It left behind many historical artifacts. For example, when the first emperor died, he was buried with thousands of life-sized warriors and horses made of clay. You might wonder why someone would want their tomb filled with clay figures. It was an ancient Chinese funeral tradition to bury masters with clay soldiers for protection. Since the Qin emperor had made many enemies during his life, he wanted protection after his death.

During the Qin dynasty the Chinese used a writing system to record their history. This system was similar to the one used in China today. China's name also dates from this time period. In Chinese, China means "Qin kingdom" or "middle kingdom." This name may refer to the Chinese belief that China was the center, or middle, of the world.

The Han Dynasty The Han dynasty came after the Qin dynasty. From the 200s B.C. to the A.D. 200s, the Han dynasty expanded its kingdom southward. The Han also extended the Great Wall westward to protect the Silk Road. This road was originally used by trading caravans taking silk and other Chinese goods to regions west of China. During the Han dynasty the Chinese invented the compass, which aided travel. The dynasties that followed the Han made China even more powerful. The Chinese continued to make important contributions to society. Later contributions include paper and **porcelain** (POHR-suh-luhn), a type of very fine pottery.

Mongols, Ming Dynasty, and the Manchu In the 1200s Mongol armies led by Genghis Khan conquered China. *Khan* is a title that means "ruler." The Mongols were feared and known for spreading terror throughout the region. Their use of horses added to their military advantage.

Within 100 years the Ming dynasty seized control of China. After several battles with the Mongols, the Ming emperors closed China to outsiders. These emperors strengthened the Great Wall and focused on the development of their own culture.

In the 1600s a group called the Manchu began expanding from their home in Manchuria. Manchuria is located in far northeastern China. The Manchus conquered Inner Mongolia, Korea, and all of northern China. Led by the Qing (CHING) dynasty, the Manchu controlled China for more than 260 years. The dynasty's strong government slowly weakened, however, and was overthrown in the early 1900s.

Outside Influences Marco Polo was one of the few Europeans to visit China before the 1500s. Europeans reached China by following the Silk Road. None came by sea before the 1500s. In the 1500s Portuguese sailors established a trade colony at Macao (muh-KOW) in south China. French and British sailors and traders followed. The Chinese believed that foreigners had little to offer other than silver in return for Chinese porcelain, silk, and tea. Even so, Europeans introduced crops like corn, hot chili peppers, peanuts, potatoes, sweet potatoes, and tobacco. By the 1800s the European countries wanted to control China's trade. A series of conflicts caused China to lose some of its independence. For example, during this period the British acquired Hong Kong. The British, Germans, and French also forced China to open additional ports. China did not regain total independence until the mid-1900s.

The Republics of China In 1912 a revolutionary group led by Sun Yat-sen (SOOHN YAHT-SUHN) forced the last emperor to abdicate, or give up power. This group formed the first Republic of China. Mongolia and Tibet each declared their independence.

After Sun Yat-sen's death the revolutionaries split into two groups, the Nationalists and the Communists. A military leader named Chiang Kai-shek (chang ky-SHEK) united China under a Nationalist government. The Communists opposed him, and a civil war began. During

The Catalan Atlas from the 1300s shows Marco Polo's family traveling by camel caravan.

Interpreting the Visual Record

(Movement) **What kind of information might this atlas provide?**

▼

This time line reviews major events in China's rich history. The last Chinese dynasty was overthrown in 1912.

Interpreting the Time Line

What events have shaped China's government in the 1900s?

▼

Historical China: A Time Line

Qin becomes China's first dynasty
200s B.C.

Rise of Ming dynasty
1368

People's Republic of China is formed under Mao Zedong
1949

The Cultural Revolution
1966–1976

| 5000 B.C. | A.D. 1 | 1000 | 1200 | 1400 | 1600 | 1800 | 2000 |

5000 B.C.
First rice farmers cultivate the area near the Chang River

206 B.C. – A.D. 220
Han dynasty dominates China

1200s
Mongols invade China

1912
Republic is established with the overthrow of the Manchu dynasty

1937
Japanese invade China

1989
Government troops crush protesters in Tiananmen Square

Mao Zedong
(1893–1976)

Mao Zedong founded a new country—the People's Republic of China. His policies, however, created disasters for his country's people.

Early in his career, Mao and 90,000 followers set off on a 6,000-mile walk to establish a new headquarters. Half of the group didn't survive the trip. Later, his economic program, The Great Leap Forward, brought widespread starvation. Some 20 million died. Mao's Cultural Revolution was supposed to make China an ideal Communist society. Instead, the country was damaged and many people were killed.

What was the result of Mao's Great Leap Forward?

Place The Potala Palace in Tibet was built in the A.D. 600s. Today, it has more than 1,000 rooms and is used for religious and political events.

World War II both groups fought the Japanese. The Communists finally defeated the Nationalists in 1949. Led by Mao Zedong (MOW ZUH-DOOHNG), the Communists set up the People's Republic of China. Mao's version of communism is known as Maoism. Only one political party—the Communist Party—was allowed.

Chiang Kai-shek and his Nationalists retreated to Taiwan. There they created a government for what they called the Republic of China. This government maintained its control through **martial law**, or military rule, for many years.

Mao's China Under Mao the government took over the country's economy. His government seized private land and organized it into large, government-run farms. Factories were also put under state control. The central government decided the amount and type of food grown on a farm. It also regulated the production of factory goods, owned all housing, and decided where people should live. Sometimes families were separated or forced to relocate. Women were given equal status and assigned equal work duties. Religious worship was prohibited. Despite the efforts to organize the economy, there were planning errors. In the 1960s a famine killed about 30 million people.

In 1966 Mao began a movement called the Cultural Revolution. The Revolution was an attempt to make everyone live a peasant way of life. Followers of Mao were known as Red Guards. They closed schools and universities. Millions of people were sent to the countryside to work in the fields. Opponents were imprisoned or executed.

Tibet Bordering the Himalayas in southwest China, the territory of Tibet is sometimes called the "Roof of the World." About two million people live in Tibet today. Tibetans see themselves as a separate nation and consider Lhasa their capital. However, Tibet is officially a part of China. The Chinese government wants Tibetans to be Chinese. In addition, China does not want Tibetans to practice their traditional Buddhist culture. For example, during China's Cultural Revolution, Chinese troops destroyed thousands of Buddhist monasteries. Many religious writings and art were demolished.

Tibetans trace their history back to the A.D. 500s when Tibet began as a Buddhist nation. In the 1400s, a religious leader called the Dalai Lama ruled Tibet. Since then there have been 14 men who have served as Dalai Lama. After a violent uprising against China in 1959, the 14th Dalai Lama sought exile in India where he lives today. In 1989, the Dalai Lama received the Nobel Peace Prize for his nonviolent protest against Chinese occupation of Tibet.

✓ **READING CHECK:** (*Human Systems*) What are some major events in China's history?

▲
The Chinese New Year is also called the Lunar New Year. This is because the cycles of the moon are the basis for the Chinese calendar.

Interpreting the Visual Record
(*Place*) **What object are parade participants carrying? What does it resemble?**

Culture

About 92 percent of China's population consider themselves Han Chinese. Almost everyone can speak one of the seven major Chinese dialects. Mandarin Chinese is the official language and the most common.

Values and Beliefs Several philosophies and religions began in China. Taoism (TOW-i-zuhm), or Daoism (DOW-i-zuhm), is an ancient Chinese religion. Taoists believe that humans should try to follow a path that agrees with nature and avoids everyday concerns. The word *dào* means "the path." Each object or natural feature is thought to have its own god or spirit that may reward good deeds or bring bad luck.

The teachings of Confucius also have been important to Chinese culture. Confucius was a philosopher who lived from 551 to 479 B.C. His teachings stressed the importance of family. Confucius believed that children should

CONNECTING TO *Literature*

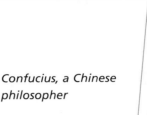

Confucius, a Chinese philosopher

This Chinese tale comes from the Hsiao Ching, *or* Book of Filial Piety—*which means "devotion to parents." A student of a follower of Confucius is believed to have written it about 400 B.C. This story encourages children to protect their parents.*

A Loving Son

Wu Meng was eight years old and very dutiful to his parents. His family was so poor that they could not afford to furnish their beds with mosquito-curtains. Every summer night thousands of mosquitoes attacked them, feasting upon their flesh and blood.

Wu Meng looked at his tired parents asleep on their bed as thousands of mosquitoes fiercely attacked them. Wu saw them sucking his parents' blood, which caused his heart to grieve.

To protect his parents, Wu decided that he would not drive the mosquitoes away from himself. Lying on the bed, he threw off his clothes, and soon feeling the pain of the mosquito attacks, he cried: "I have no fear of you, nor have you any reason to fear me. Although I have a fan, I will not use it, nor will I strike you with my hand. I will lie very quietly and let you gorge to the full." Such was his love for his parents!

Analyzing Primary Sources

1. How does this tale reflect traditional Chinese philosophical beliefs?
2. Why do you think the author of the *Hsiao Ching* wrote this story?

respect their parents and subjects should respect their ruler. He believed people should treat those under their control justly and argued that state power should be used to improve people's lives.

The religion called Buddhism also has been important in China. It was founded by an Indian prince, Siddhartha Gautama. Gautama was born in Nepal about 563 B.C. He decided to search for truth and knowledge. Enlightenment—peace and a sense of being one with the universe—came to him while he was sitting under a Bo or Bodhi tree. As a result, he was given the name Buddha, which means "awakened or enlightened one." Buddhism reached China from India about A.D. 100. It became the country's main religion between the 300s and 500s. Indian architecture also became popular in China. Chinese **pagodas**, or Buddhist temples, are based on Indian designs. Pagodas have an upward-curving roof. Some pagodas are 15 stories tall.

Lifeways Chinese culture highly values education. Chinese children are required to attend nine years of school. However, just 1 to 2 percent of students pass the difficult entrance exams to get into a university.

The Chinese government tries to control many aspects of everyday life. For example, parents are allowed to have just one child. This is because the government is trying to slow population growth.

The government also controls the newspapers and telephone system. This allows it to limit the flow of information and ideas. Satellite TV, the Internet, and e-mail are becoming more widespread, however. This makes it more difficult for the government to control communication between individuals.

Chinese food varies widely from region to region. Food in Beijing is heavily salted and flavored with garlic and cilantro. Sichuan-style cooking features hot pepper sauces. Cantonese cooking was introduced to the United States by immigrants from Guangzhou (GWAHNG-JOH).

Traditional Chinese medicine stresses herbal products and harmony with the universe. People around the world have used acupuncture. This therapy involves inserting fine needles into specific parts of the body for pain relief. Many Chinese herbal remedies have been used by American drug companies as the basis for modern medicines.

China has rich literary traditions. Painting, porcelain, sculpture, and carving of ivory, stone, and wood are also popular. Performing arts emphasize traditional folktales and stories shown in dances or operas with elaborate costumes.

▲

For more than 200 years the Beijing Opera, or Peking Opera, has been recognized worldwide for its artistic contributions. Originally performed for the royal family, it is now viewed by the public and is aired on Chinese television and radio stations.

✓ **READING CHECK:** (**Human Systems**) What is China's culture like?

Homework
Practice
Online

Keyword: SG5 HP27

Define or identify: emperor, dynasty, Confucius, porcelain, Genghis Khan, Sun Yat-sen, Mao Zedong, martial law, Dalai Lama, pagodas

Working with Sketch Maps On the map you created in Section 1, label China and the Great Wall. Why do you think the Chinese chose to build the Great Wall where they did?

Reading for the Main Idea

1. (**Human Systems**) What contributions did the Qin and Han dynasties make to Chinese history?

2. (**Human Systems**) How did Mao's rule change China?

3. (**Human Systems**) How has China changed since Mao's death in 1976?

Critical Thinking

4. **Summarizing** What are three philosophies or religions that have been important in China? Describe them.

Organizing What You Know

5. **Summarizing** Copy the following graphic organizer. Use it to describe the Ming and the Manchu.

Ming Dynasty	Manchu

Read to Discover

1. Where do most of China's people live?
2. What are the major cities in China, and what are they like?
3. What is China's economy like?
4. What challenges does China face?

Vocabulary

command economy
multiple cropping
most-favored-nation
   status

Places

Shanghai
Nanjing
Wuhan
Chongqing

Beijing
Hong Kong
Macao

Reading Strategy

READING ORGANIZER Before you read this section, create a concept map. Draw a circle in the center of a sheet of paper. Label the circle China Today. Draw four lines coming out of the circle. Then draw a circle at the end of each line. Label the circles Population, Cities, Economy, and Challenges. As you read, write what you learn about each topic beside its circle.

China's Population

China has the largest population in the world—some 1.28 billion people. That number is equal to about 20 percent of the world's population. More people live in China than in all of Europe, Russia, and the United States combined. China's population is growing rapidly—by about 11 million each year. Some years ago, China's leaders took steps to bring the growth rate under control. They encouraged people to delay getting married and starting families. The government also tried to limit couples to one child.

China's population is not evenly distributed across the land. The western half of the country, which is mostly desert and mountain ranges, is almost empty. Just 10 percent of China's people live there. The rest are crowded into the country's eastern half. In fact, more people live in the North China Plain than in the entire United States. However, this region is only about the size of Texas. Most Chinese live in the countryside. Even so, China has 40 cities with populations greater than 1 million.

✓ **READING CHECK:** (**Human Systems**) Where do most of China's people live?

COMPARING POPULATIONS

China and the United States

China

United States

= 150,000,000 people

Source: Central Intelligence Agency, *The World Factbook 2003*

Interpreting the Chart How many people does one figure on the chart represent?

China's Cities

Studying China's physical features helps explain why its residents live where they do. By locating rivers and river valleys, we can see where millions of people could best survive.

Several of China's most important cities are located on the Chang River. Shanghai, the country's largest city, lies on the Chang Delta. It serves as China's leading industrial center and is the major seaport.

Using the map in Section 1, follow the course of the Chang River inland. Locate the cities of Nanjing and Wuhan (WOO-HAHN). These two industrial centers were built around iron-ore and coal mines. If you continue to follow the river upstream, you will reach Chongqing (CHOOHNG-CHING), located in the Sichuan Basin. It is one of the few large cities in China's interior. Guangzhou, located at the mouth of the Xi River, is southern China's largest city. Long famous as a trading center, it was known in the West as Canton. Today Guangzhou is one of China's major industrial cities.

Beijing, also known as Peking, is China's capital. It was built more than 3,000 years ago as a trading center. Beijing is the largest city in northern China and is well known for its cultural heritage.

Southeast of Guangzhou is Hong Kong. With a population of 6.5 million, Hong Kong is one of the world's most densely populated places. It is only half as large as Rhode Island, but has more than seven times as many people. Hong Kong is China's major southern seaport and is a center for banking, international trade, and tourism.

The British occupied the island of Hong Kong in the 1830s. In the late 1800s Hong Kong was leased to the British for 99 years. The lease ran out in 1997, and the British left. Hong Kong then became a special administrative region of China. Hong Kong has some political independence and is allowed to maintain its free-market economy. Macao, a nearby port city, was once a Portuguese colony. At the end of 1999, it was returned to China.

✓ **READING CHECK:**　(**Places and Regions**)　What are the major cities of China?

Towering skyscrapers mark Shanghai's constantly changing skyline.

Interpreting the Visual Record　(*Place*)

How can you tell this city is growing rapidly?

▼

China's Economy

When the Chinese Communists took power in 1949 they set up a **command economy**. In this type of economy, the government owns most industries and makes most economic decisions. It set almost all production goals, prices, and wages.

Industry The Communists took over an economy that was based almost entirely on farming. Soon the Communist government introduced programs to build industry. Today, China is an industrial giant. It produces everything from satellites and rockets to toys.

In the late 1970s the government began to introduce elements of free enterprise. Now farmers can grow and market their own crops on part of their rented land. Many state-run factories are being closed or turned over to private industries. Millions of Chinese have started small businesses. A few Chinese have become wealthy. Some business owners can afford to build private homes and to buy cars and computers. However, most Chinese are poor.

Agriculture Only about 10 percent of China's land is good for farming. Nevertheless, China is a world leader in the production of many crops and can meet most of its food needs. China's huge workforce makes this possible. More than 50 percent of Chinese workers are farmers. Having many farmers means the land can be intensively worked to produce high yields. Farmers have also increased production by cutting terraces into hillsides to create new farmland.

China is divided between rice-growing and wheat-growing regions. The divide lies midway between the Huang and the Chang River. To the south, rice is the main crop. Here the warm wet weather makes **multiple cropping** possible. Multiple cropping means that two or three crops are raised each year on the same land. This practice makes southern China more prosperous than northern China.

✓ **READING CHECK:** (*Human Systems*) What kind of economy does China have?

Models of rice fields like these have been found in Han dynasty tombs.
Interpreting the Visual Record
(*Human-Environment Interaction*) **What resources appear to be necessary for growing rice in this region?**

China's Government

After Mao's death in 1976, the new Chinese communist leadership admitted some past mistakes. It tried to modernize the government.

Although the government has allowed individuals some economic freedom, it restricts political and religious freedom. In 1989 the Chinese army was called in to attack pro-democracy student demonstrators in Tiananmen Square in Beijing (BAY-JING). Many students were injured or killed. Other rebellions among China's ethnic minorities, particularly in Tibet, have been crushed.

✓ **READING CHECK:** (*Human Systems*) What freedoms does China's government restrict?

Future Challenges

China has enjoyed remarkable economic success in recent years. China's drive to industrialize has caused major problems. For example, the air and water are badly polluted by factory wastes.

Another challenge involves the government's unwillingness to match the new economic freedoms with political reforms. China's human rights record has affected its economic relations with other countries. The U.S. government has considered canceling China's **most-favored-nation status** several times. Countries with this status get special trade advantages from the United States. China's economic future might depend on its government's willingness to accept political reforms.

✓ **READING CHECK:** (*Human Systems*) What challenges does China face?

By the mid-1990s clothing, electrical equipment, footwear, textiles, and other consumer goods were among China's leading exports. Employees of the Bei Bei Shoe Factory glue soles on by hand on an assembly line in Shanghai.

▼

go.hrw.com

Homework Practice Online

Keyword: SG5 HP27

Section Review 3

Define and explain: command economy, multiple cropping, most-favored-nation status

Working with Sketch Maps On the map you created in Section 2, label Shanghai, Nanjing, Wuhan, Chongqing, Beijing, Hong Kong, and Macao. In the margin of your map, draw a box for each city. List the characteristics of each city in its box.

Reading for the Main Idea

1. (*Places and Regions*) Where do most people in China live? Why?

2. (*Places and Regions*) Along which rivers are several of China's most important cities located? Why?

3. (*Environment and Society*) What farming practices have allowed the Chinese to increase production?

Critical Thinking

4. Finding the Main Idea How has the Chinese government changed its economic policies since the late 1970s? What has been the impact of these changes?

Organizing What You Know

5. Summarizing Copy the following graphic organizer. Use it to describe the kinds of challenges facing China today. Identify specific environmental, political, and economic challenges.

Challenges

Read to Discover

1. How has Mongolia's culture developed?
2. What is Taiwan's culture like?

Vocabulary

gers

Places

Mongolia
Ulaanbaatar
Taiwan
Kao-hsiung
Taipei

People

Chiang Kai-shek

Reading Strategy

FOLDNOTES: TWO-PANEL FLIP CHART Create a **Two-Panel Flip Chart** as described in the Appendix. Label one of the flaps Mongolia and the other flap Taiwan. As you read this section, write what you learn about each country beneath its flap.

Mongolia

Mongolia is home to the Mongol people and has a fascinating history. You will learn of invaders and conquests and a culture that prizes horses.

Mongolia's History Today when people discuss the world's leading countries, they do not mention Mongolia. However, 700 years ago Mongolia was perhaps the greatest power in the world. Led by Genghis Khan, the Mongols conquered much of Asia, including China. Later leaders continued the conquests, building the greatest empire the world had seen. The Mongol Empire reached its height in the late 1200s.

It stretched from Europe's Danube River in the west to the Pacific Ocean in the east. Over time, however, the empire declined. In the late 1600s Mongolia fell under the rule of China.

In 1911, with Russian support, Mongolia declared its independence from China. Communists took control of the country 13 years later and established the Mongolian People's Republic. The country then came under the influence of the Soviet Union. Mongolia became particularly dependent on the Soviet Union for economic aid. This aid ended when the Soviet Union collapsed

This engraving shows early Mongolian soldiers.

Movement Nomads of Mongolia live in *gers* like those shown here.

in the early 1990s. Since then, Mongolians have struggled to build a democratic government and a free-market economy.

Mongolia's Culture Despite years of Communist rule and recent Western influence, the Mongolian way of life remains quite traditional. Many people still follow a nomadic lifestyle. They live as herders, driving their animals across Mongolia's vast grasslands. They make their homes in **gers** (GUHRZ). These are large, circular felt tents that are easy to raise, dismantle, and move.

Since most people live as herders, horses play an important role in Mongolian life. Mongolian children learn to ride when they are very young—often before they are even five years old. In Mongolia, the most powerful piece in the game of chess is the horse, not the queen.

Mongolia Today Mongolia is a large country—slightly larger than Alaska. Its population numbers just over 2.7 million. Some 25 percent of Mongolians live in Ulaanbaatar (oo-lahn-BAH-tawr), the capital city. Ulaanbaatar is also Mongolia's main industrial and commercial center. Mongolia's other cities are quite small. Not one has a population greater than 100,000.

✓ **READING CHECK:** (**Human Systems**) What are some elements of Mongolian culture?

Our Amazing Planet

In the Gobi, temperatures can range from -40°F (-40°C) in January to 113°F (45°C) in July. Some areas of this desert receive little more than 2 inches (5 cm) of rain each year.

Taiwan

For many years the island of Taiwan was known in the West as Formosa. This name came from Portuguese sailors who visited the island in the late 1500s. They thought the island was so lovely that they called it *Ilha Formosa*, or "beautiful island."

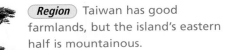

Chiang Kai-shek served in the Japanese army before returning to China to help overthrow the Manchu dynasty. He was head of the Nationalist government in China for 20 years, then moved with his followers to Taiwan.

Region Taiwan has good farmlands, but the island's eastern half is mountainous.

Taiwan's History The Chinese began settling Taiwan in the A.D. 600s. Some 600 years later the Japanese took control of eastern Taiwan. The search for spices brought European traders to Taiwan. The Dutch, Portuguese, and Spanish all tried to set up bases there. However, raiders from mainland China drove out these Europeans in the mid-1600s.

The struggle among the Chinese, Japanese, and Europeans for control of Taiwan continued until the late 1800s. In 1895 a treaty between the Chinese and the Japanese gave Taiwan to Japan. The Japanese then tried to force their way of life on the people of Taiwan. The Taiwanese rebelled against these efforts, but their revolts were crushed by the Japanese military.

After Japan's surrender at the end of World War II in 1945, China once again took command of Taiwan. In 1949 Mao Zedong established the People's Republic of China in mainland China. Chiang Kai-shek and the Nationalist Chinese government fled to Taiwan. The Nationalist government controlled Taiwan through martial law for decades. In recent years, however, the government has expanded democratic rights. China still claims that Taiwan is a province of China—not an independent country.

Taiwan's Culture Taiwan's history is reflected in its culture. Its population is about 85 percent native Taiwanese. They are descendants of people who migrated from China to Taiwan over hundreds of years. Chinese ways dominate Taiwan's culture. However, some building styles and certain foods reflect Japanese influences. European and American practices and customs have strongly influenced Taiwan's way of life in recent years. This is particularly true in the cities.

Taiwan Today Taiwan has a modern, industrial economy and a population of about 22 million. These people live on an island the size of Delaware and Maryland combined. Most people live on the western coastal plain of Taiwan. Population densities there can reach higher than 2,700 per square mile (1,042 per sq km). Taiwan's two largest cities, Kao-hsiung (KOW-SHYOOHNG) and Taipei (TY-PAY), are located on the coastal plain. Taipei is the capital city. It faces serious overcrowding and environmental problems. The thousands of cars, motorcycles, and trucks that clog Taipei's streets each day cause severe air pollution.

In the early 1950s Taiwan's economy was still largely based on agriculture. Today, however, only about 8 percent of workers make a living as farmers. Even so, Taiwan still produces enough rice—the country's chief food crop—to feed all of its people. Taiwan's farmers also grow fruits, sugarcane, tea, and vegetables.

Taiwan now has one of Asia's most successful economies. It is a world leader in the production and export of computers and sports equipment.

▲

Taipei, Taiwan, was founded in the 1700s and has developed into an important city for overseas trade.

✔ **READING CHECK:** (*Human Systems*) What are some elements of the culture of Taiwan?

Section Review 4

Define or identify: *gers,* Chiang Kai-shek

Working with Sketch Maps On the map you created in Section 3, label Mongolia, Ulaanbaatar, Taiwan, Kao-hsiung, and Taipei. In the border of your map, draw a box for each city. Describe each city in its box. How has the history of each city played a part in its growth?

Reading for the Main Idea

1. (*Human Systems*) How do most people earn a living in Mongolia?

2. (*Human Systems*) Write a brief outline of the significant individuals or groups that have influenced Taiwan's history.

3. (*Human Systems*) How has Taiwan's economy changed since the early 1950s?

Critical Thinking

4. Analyzing Information What are some problems Taiwan faces today?

Organizing What You Know

5. Summarizing Copy the following graphic organizer. Use it to design and write two postcards to a friend describing life in Mongolia. In your postcards, note how life follows traditional patterns yet is also undergoing changes.

Review and Practice

Define and Identify

Identify each of the following:

1. dikes
2. arable
3. emperor
4. Confucius
5. dynasty
6. porcelain
7. Genghis Khan
8. Sun Yat-sen
9. martial law
10. Mao Zedong
11. Dalai Lama
12. pagodas
13. command economy
14. multiple cropping
15. most-favored-nation status
16. *gers*
17. Chiang Kai-shek

Review the Main Ideas

18. What physical features separate this region's mountain ranges?
19. Why is the Huang called the Yellow River?
20. What idea did the first emperor of the Qin dynasty have that greatly affected the landscape of China?
21. What was the purpose of the Cultural Revolution in China?
22. How does Hong Kong differ from the rest of China?
23. What do more than 50 percent of China's workers do for a living?
24. What country discussed in this chapter once ruled a vast empire that stretched into Europe?
25. What are Taiwan's leading exports?

Think Critically

26. **Drawing Inferences and Conclusions** Why do you think so few Europeans reached China before the 1500s?
27. **Drawing Inferences and Conclusions** How might Chinese history have been different if Europeans had not forced trade upon the Chinese?
28. **Finding the Main Idea** What was the Cultural Revolution and how did it affect life in China?
29. **Making Generalizations and Predictions** In what ways does modern technology threaten the Chinese government's ability to control the flow of information in the country? What changes might the free flow of information bring to China?
30. **Analyzing Information** How is Taiwan's history reflected in the island's culture today?

Map Activity

31. On a separate sheet of paper, match the letters on the map with their correct labels.

    Mount Everest
    Plateau of Tibet
    North China Plain
    Huang River
    Chang River
    Great Wall
    Shanghai
    Hong Kong
    Ulaanbaatar

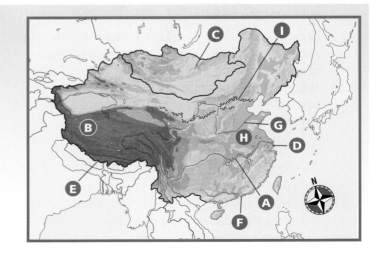

Writing Activity

Imagine that you are a Chinese university professor. Using the time line in section 2, the text, and other sources, write a brief lesson plan on China's history. You may want to include some visuals, such as photographs of artifacts, in your lesson plan. Be sure to use standard grammar, spelling, sentence structure, and punctuation.

🖩 **internet** connect

Internet Activity: **go.hrw.com**
KEYWORD: **SG5 GT27**

Choose a topic to explore about China, Mongolia, and Taiwan:
- Follow the Great Wall of China.
- Visit the land of Genghis Khan.
- See the artistic treasures of China.

Social Studies Skills Practice

Interpreting Graphs

Study the following graph and answer the questions.

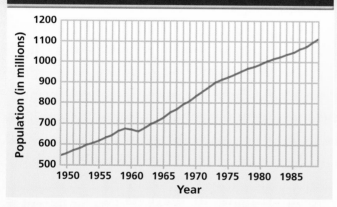

Total Population of China, 1949–1989

Population (in millions) vs. *Year*

Source: *The Cambridge Handbook of Contemporary China*, 1991

1. What was the total population of China in 1950?
2. During what period did the population decline?
3. In what year did the population reach one billion?
4. How much did the population grow between 1965 and 1985?

Analyzing Primary Sources

Read the following passage from a 1993 U.S. State Department publication on Mongolia. Then answer the questions.

"As a result of rapid urbanization and industrial growth policies under the communist regime, Mongolia's deteriorating environment has become a major concern. The burning of soft coal coupled with thousands of factories in Ulaanbaatar has resulted in severely polluted air. Deforestation, overgrazed pastures, and . . . by plowing up more virgin land has increased soil erosion. The government responded by . . . increasing publicity on environmental issues."

1. What are the two main causes of environmental problems in Mongolia?
2. What is the result of burning coal in Mongolia?
3. How has agricultural development affected the environment?
4. How might publicity help solve the problem of environmental damage?

CHAPTER 28

Japan and the Koreas

Now we continue east to North and South Korea and the island nation of Japan. First we meet Akiko, a Japanese student whose school day may be very different from yours.

Konichiwa! (Good afternoon!) I'm Akiko, and I'm in the seventh grade at Yamate school. Every morning except Sunday I put on my school uniform and eat rice soup and pickles before I leave for school. The train I take is so crowded I can't move. At school, I study reading, math, English, science, and writing. I know 1,800 Japanese characters, but I need to know about 3,000 to pass the ninth grade exams. For lunch, I eat rice and cold fish my mom packed for me. Before we can go home, we clean the school floors, desks, and windows. My dad usually isn't home until after 11:00 P.M., so my mom helps me with my homework in the "big" (8 feet by 8 feet) room of our three-room apartment. In the evenings, I go to a *juku* school to study for the ninth grade exams. If I do not do well, I will not go to a good high school, and my whole family will be ashamed. On Sundays, I sometimes go with my parents to visit my grandparents, who are rice farmers. I like rock music a lot, especially U2.

こんにちは. 私は東京に 住んでいます.

◀

Translation: Good afternoon. I live in Tokyo.

Section 1 Physical Geography

Read to Discover

1. What are the physical features of Japan and the Koreas?
2. What natural resources does the region have?
3. Which climate types are found in the region?

Vocabulary

tsunamis
Oyashio Current
Japan Current

Places

Korean Peninsula
Sea of Japan
Hokkaido

Honshu
Shikoku
Kyushu

Reading Strategy

FOLDNOTES: DOUBLE-DOOR Create a **Double-Door** FoldNote as described in the Appendix. Label the outer flaps Japan and the Koreas. As you read this section, write what you learn about the physical features, resources, and climate of Japan in the center section, North Korea in the top section, and South Korea in the bottom section.

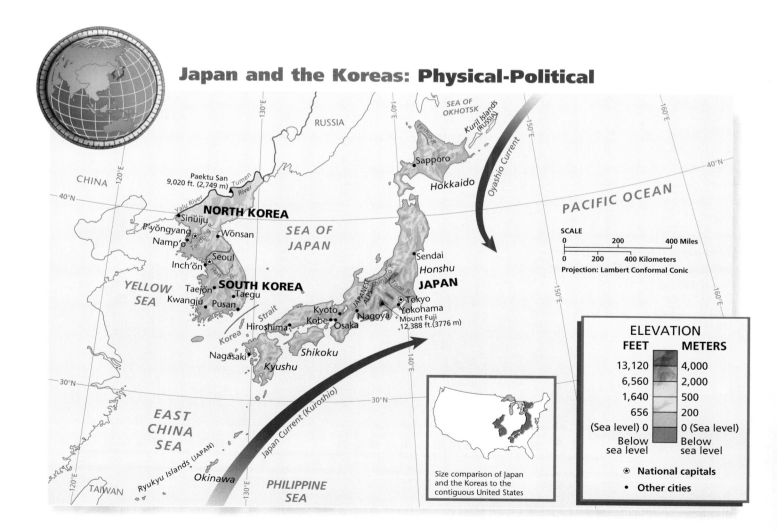

Japan and the Koreas: Physical-Political

Size comparison of Japan and the Koreas to the contiguous United States

ELEVATION

FEET	METERS
13,120	4,000
6,560	2,000
1,640	500
656	200
(Sea level) 0	0 (Sea level)
Below sea level	Below sea level

⊛ National capitals
• Other cities

SCALE
0   200   400 Miles
0   200   400 Kilometers
Projection: Lambert Conformal Conic

Physical Features

The Korean Peninsula extends southward about 600 miles (965 km) from mainland Asia. The peninsula is relatively close to southern Japan.

The Korean Peninsula is about the same size as Utah. It contains two countries, North Korea and South Korea. The Yalu and Tumen Rivers separate North Korea from China. The Tumen River also forms a short border with Russia. Off the coast of the Korean Peninsula lie more than 3,500 islands.

The Sea of Japan separates Japan from the Eurasian mainland. The narrow Korea Strait lies between South Korea and the island country of Japan. No place in Japan is more than 90 miles (145 km) from the sea. Japan is about the size of California. It is made up of four large islands called the home islands. The country also includes more than 3,000 smaller islands. The home islands from north to south are Hokkaido (hoh-KY-doh), Honshu (HAWN-shoo), Shikoku (shee-KOH-koo), and Kyushu (KYOO-shoo). South of the home islands are Japan's Ryukyu (ree-YOO-kyoo) Islands. Okinawa is the largest of these islands. Fewer than half of the Ryukyus are inhabited.

Mountains Rugged and heavily forested mountains are a common sight in the landscape of this region. Mountains cover about 75 percent of Japan. Many of Japan's mountains were formed by volcanic activity. The country's longest mountain range, the Japanese Alps, forms a volcanic spine through Honshu. The small amount of plains in these countries is found along the coasts and river valleys.

The Ring of Fire Japan lies along the Pacific Ring of Fire—a region of volcanic activity and earthquakes. Under Japan the dense

Our Amazing Planet

The world's largest crab lives off the southeastern coast of Japan. The giant spider crab can grow larger than 12 feet (3.6 m) across (from claw to claw). It can also weigh more than 40 pounds (18 kg)!

A *shinkansen*, or bullet train, speeds past Mount Fuji. This Hiroshima-to-Kokura train travels at an average 162.3 mph (261.8 kmh) but has a maximum speed of 186 mph (300 kmh).

Interpreting the Visual Record (Place)
What physical features might make building railroads in this region of Japan difficult?

Pacific plate dives beneath the lighter Eurasian and Philippine plates. This subduction zone borders the Pacific side of the Japanese islands, forming the Japan Trench. This is one of the deepest places on the ocean floor. The movement of one tectonic plate below another builds up tension in Earth's crust. The Eurasian plate buckles and pushes up, creating mountains and fractures in the crust. Magma flows up through these fractures. Where magma rises to the surface, it forms volcanoes. Today, Japan has about 40 active volcanoes. Mount Fuji (FOO-jee), Japan's highest peak, is an inactive volcano.

Because Japan lies along a subduction zone, earthquakes are also common. As many as 1,500 occur every year. Most are minor quakes. In 1995, however, an earthquake killed more than 5,000 people in Kobe.

Underwater earthquakes sometimes create huge waves called **tsunamis** (tsooh-NAH-mees). These dangerous waves can travel hundreds of miles per hour. They can also be as tall as a 10-story building when they reach shore. In 1993 a tsunami caused terrible destruction when it struck the coast of Hokkaido.

Unlike Japan, the Korean Peninsula is not located in a subduction zone. As a result, it has no active volcanoes and is dominated by eroded mountains. Earthquakes are quite rare.

✓ **READING CHECK:** (*Places and Regions*) What are the physical features of Japan and the Koreas?

Natural Resources

Except for North Korea, the region is not rich in natural resources. It has no oil or natural gas. The Korean Peninsula's mountainous terrain and rivers, however, are good for producing hydroelectric power. North Korea also has iron ore, copper, zinc, lead, and coal.

Japan lies near one of the world's best fisheries. East of Japan the cool **Oyashio** (oh-YAH-shee-oh) **Current** dives beneath the warm, less dense **Japan Current**. The cool water scours the bottom, bringing nutrients to the surface. Fish can find plentiful food to eat in this rich marine environment.

✓ **READING CHECK:**
(*Places and Regions*) What are the region's natural resources?

▲
Every hour an artificial volcano erupts at Ocean Dome, the world's largest indoor beach, at Miyazaki, Japan.

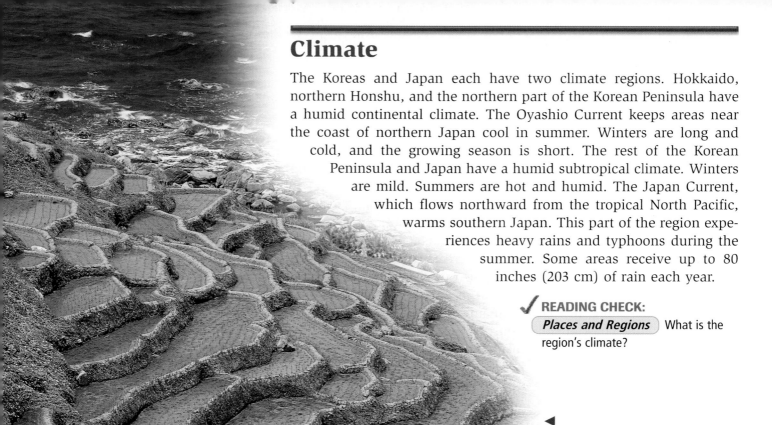

Climate

The Koreas and Japan each have two climate regions. Hokkaido, northern Honshu, and the northern part of the Korean Peninsula have a humid continental climate. The Oyashio Current keeps areas near the coast of northern Japan cool in summer. Winters are long and cold, and the growing season is short. The rest of the Korean Peninsula and Japan have a humid subtropical climate. Winters are mild. Summers are hot and humid. The Japan Current, which flows northward from the tropical North Pacific, warms southern Japan. This part of the region experiences heavy rains and typhoons during the summer. Some areas receive up to 80 inches (203 cm) of rain each year.

✓ **READING CHECK:**

Places and Regions What is the region's climate?

◄

Terracing creates more arable land for South Korean farmers.

Interpreting the Visual Record

Human-Environment Interaction

How do the terraces here hold water?

Homework Practice Online

Keyword: SG5 HP28

Section Review 1

Define and explain: tsunamis, Oyashio Current, Japan Current

Working with Sketch Maps On a map of Japan and the Koreas that you draw or that your teacher provides, label the following: the Korean Peninsula, Sea of Japan, Hokkaido, Honshu, Shikoku, and Kyushu. On what physical features might Japan and the Koreas depend for their economies?

Reading for the Main Idea

1. *Physical Systems* How has Japan's location in a subduction zone made it different from the Koreas?

2. *Physical Systems* How do ocean currents affect the climates of Japan?

Critical Thinking

3. **Drawing Inferences and Conclusions** How do you think residents are affected by this region's mountainous terrain and the nearness of the sea?

4. **Making Generalizations and Predictions** What can you predict about South Korea's and Japan's economies?

Organizing What You Know

5. **Summarizing** List the landforms, natural resources, and climates of Japan, North Korea, and South Korea.

	Landforms	Resources	Climate
Japan			
South Korea			
North Korea			

Section 2   The History and Culture of Japan

Read to Discover

1. What was Japan's early history and culture like?
2. How did the modernization of Japan take place?

Vocabulary

Shintoism
shamans
samurai
shogun
Diet

People

Murasaki Shikibu

Reading Strategy

FOLDNOTES: KEY-TERM FOLD | Create a **Key-Term Fold** FoldNote as described in the Appendix. Then write a vocabulary term from the section on each tab. Under each tab, write the definition of the term.

Early Japan

Japan's first inhabitants came from central Asia thousands of years ago. Rice farming was introduced to Japan from China and Korea about 300 B.C. As the population increased, farmers irrigated new land for growing rice. They also built dikes and canals to channel water into the rice paddies. Local chieftains organized the workers and controlled the flow of water. This control allowed the chieftains to extend their political power over larger areas.

Religion The earliest known religion of Japan, **Shintoism**, centers around the *kami*. *Kami* are spirits of natural places, sacred animals, and ancestors. Many of Japan's mountains and rivers are sacred in Shintoism. **Shamans**, or priests who communicated with the spirits, made the *kami*'s wishes known.

Buddhism and Confucianism were later introduced from China. Buddhist shrines were often located next to older *kami* shrines. Today, as in the past, most Japanese practice Shintoism and Buddhism. As you learned in an earlier chapter, the principles of Confucianism include respect for elders, parents, and rulers.

▲ Todaiji Temple in Nara, Japan, contains the largest wooden hall in the world and a statue of Buddha that is more than 48 feet (15 m) tall.

Interpreting the Visual Record ⟨*Place*⟩
What interesting features do you see in this building's architecture?

CONNECTING TO Art

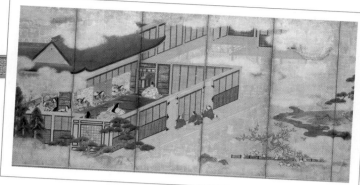

A Japanese scroll painting showing a scene from The Tale of Genji.

Japanese Scroll Paintings

Beginning in the 1100s and 1200s Japanese artists created beautifully detailed ink paintings on paper scrolls. This form of art originated in China where artists painted mostly mountain landscapes. In Japan, however, scroll paintings told stories. The themes of many scroll paintings included Buddhist teachings and historical subjects.

Many Japanese scrolls were as long as 30 feet and included text. In these paintings, artists purposely left the roofs off of buildings so they could show the interiors.

Understanding What You Read

1. Where did scroll painting originate?
2. How did Japanese artists show the interior of buildings?

BIOGRAPHY

Murasaki Shikibu
(c. 978 – c. 1026)

The women who lived at a Japanese emperor's court were educated in many areas. One of the women, Murasaki Shikibu, wrote the world's first novel—*The Tale of Genji.* The book describes court life in about A.D. 1000.

How might Murasaki Shikibu's life have compared with that of most Japanese women?

The Shoguns In the A.D. 700s Japan began to develop a political system of its own. Many small feudal domains were each ruled by a lord. **Samurai** (SA-muh-ry) were warriors who served the lords. Rivalries were put aside when a foreign threat appeared. For example, the feudal domains united against the Mongols in the 1200s. Later, power shifted from the emperor to a **shogun**. The word *shogun* means "great general" and is the highest rank for a warrior.

In the mid-1500s, Portuguese traders arrived in Japan. Spanish missionaries followed, introducing Christianity to Japan. Europeans were later forced to leave. Japanese leaders feared that foreign ideas might undermine Japanese society. Japan remained cut off from the Western world until the mid-1850s.

✓ **READING CHECK:** (*Human Systems*) What was early Japan like?

Modern Japan

In 1853 U.S. commodore Matthew Perry's warships sailed into Tokyo Bay. Perry displayed U.S. naval power and brought gifts that showed the wonders of American technology. Perry's arrival convinced the Japanese that they needed to become as politically strong as the Americans and Europeans. In the 1860s Japan began to industrialize and modernize its educational, legal, and governmental systems.

An Imperial Power Japan needed resources in order to industrialize. As a result, it began to expand its empire around 1900. Japan annexed, or took control of, Korea in 1910. Japan also took over northeastern China and its supply of coal and iron ore. Japan continued to expand in Asia during the late 1930s.

World War II During World War II Japan was an ally of Germany and Italy. Japan brought the United States into the war in 1941 by attacking the U.S. naval base at Pearl Harbor, Hawaii. Japan conquered much of Southeast Asia and many Pacific islands before being defeated by U.S. and Allied forces in 1945. With the end of World War II Japan lost its empire.

Government After World War II the United States occupied Japan until 1952. With U.S. aid, Japan began to rebuild into a major world industrial power. Japan also established a democratic government. Today, Japan is a constitutional monarchy with several political parties. The government is made up of the **Diet** (DY-uht)—an elected legislature—and a prime minister. Japan's emperor remains a symbol of the nation, but he has no political power.

Movement Commodore Matthew Perry arrives in Japan in 1853.

✓ **READING CHECK:** (**Places and Regions**) How did Japan modernize?

Homework Practice Online
Keyword: SG5 HP28

Section Review 2

Define or identify: Shintoism, shamans, Murasaki Shikibu, samurai, shogun, Diet

Working with Sketch Maps On the map you created in Section 1, label China and Korea. In a box in the margin, identify the body of water that separates Korea from Japan. Why do you think China and Korea had a strong influence on Japan's culture and history?

Reading for the Main Idea

1. (**Human Systems**) What religions have been practiced in Japan, and from where did they come?

2. (**Places and Regions**) Why did Japan decide to trade with the United States and Europe?

Critical Thinking

3. **Finding the Main Idea** How and why did rice farming develop in Japan?

4. **Analyzing Information** What influences do the principles of Confucianism have on the Japanese?

Organizing What You Know

5. **Sequencing** Copy the following graphic organizer. Use it to show important developments in modern Japanese history from the 1850s to today.

Read to Discover

1. Where do most Japanese live?
2. What are the major Japanese cities like?
3. What is life in Japan like?
4. How has the Japanese economy developed?

Vocabulary

megalopolis
kimonos
futon
intensive cultivation

work ethic
protectionism
trade surplus

Places

Inland Sea
Osaka
Tokyo
Kobe
Kyoto

Reading Strategy

FOLDNOTES: TRI-FOLD Create a **Tri-Fold** FoldNote as described in the Appendix. Write what you know about Japan in the column labeled "Know." Then write what you want to know in the column labeled "Want." As you read the section, write what you learn about Japan in the column labeled "Learn."

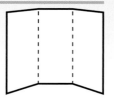

▲
Beyond Tokyo's Nijubashi Bridge is the Imperial Palace, the home of the emperor.

Where People Live

Japan is one of the world's most densely populated countries. It is slightly smaller than California but has nearly four times as many people! There are an average of 863 people per square mile (333/sq km). However, Japan is very mountainous. Within its area of livable land, population density averages 7,680 people per square mile (2,964/sq km).

Most people live on the small coastal plains, particularly along the Pacific and the Inland Sea. Japan's major cities and farms compete for space on these narrow coastal plains. Only about 11 percent of Japan's land is arable, or fit for growing crops.

The Japanese have reclaimed land from the sea and rivers. In some places, they have built dikes to block off the water. They have drained the land behind the dikes so it could be used for farming or housing. They have even built artificial islands. The airport near Osaka, for example, was built on an artificial island in the early 1990s.

✓ **READING CHECK:** (*Human Systems*) Where do most people in Japan live?

Japan's Cities

Japan's cities, like major cities everywhere, are busy, noisy, and very crowded. Almost 30 million people live within 20 miles of the Imperial Palace in Tokyo. This densely populated area forms a **megalopolis**. A megalopolis is a giant urban area that often includes more than one city as well as the surrounding suburban areas. Yokohama is Japan's major seaport.

Most of Tokyo was built recently. An earthquake in 1923 and bombings during World War II destroyed most of the old buildings.

Tokyo is the capital and the center of government. Japan's banking, communications, and education are also centered here. Tokyo is densely populated, and land is scarce. As a result, Tokyo's real estate prices are among the world's highest.

Tokyo's Ginza shopping district is the largest in the world. Some department stores sell houses and cars and provide dental care. They also offer classes on how to properly wear **kimonos**—traditional robes—and to arrange flowers.

High rents in Ginza and elsewhere in Tokyo encourage the creative use of space. Tall buildings line the streets. However, shops are also found below the streets in the subway stations. Another way the Japanese have found to maximize space is the "capsule hotel." The guests in these hotels sleep in compartments too small to stand in upright. Businesspeople often stay in these hotels rather than commuting the long distances to their homes.

So many people commute to and from Tokyo that space on the trains must also be maximized. During peak travel periods, commuters are crammed into cars. They are helped by workers hired to push as many people into the trains as possible.

Another megalopolis in Japan is located in the Kansai region. It has three major cities: Osaka (oh-SAH-kah), Kobe (KOH-bay), and Kyoto (KYOH-toh). Industrial Osaka has been a trading center for centuries. Kobe is an important seaport. Kyoto was Japan's capital for more than 1,000 years.

✓ **READING CHECK:**

Places and Regions What is life like in Japan's major cities?

	Japan			
COUNTRY	**POPULATION/ GROWTH RATE**	**LIFE EXPECTANCY**	**LITERACY RATE**	**PER CAPITA GDP**
Japan	127,214,499 0.1%	78, male 84, female	99%	$28,000
United States	290,342,554 0.9%	74, male 80, female	97%	$37,600

Source: Central Intelligence Agency, *The World Factbook 2003*

Interpreting the Chart (*Place*) **How does life expectancy in Japan compare to that of the United States?**

Japanese workers stay focused on their responsibilities on an electronics production line.

▲ (Location) The port of Kobe is located in the central part of the Japanese islands.

▲ Japanese and American all-star baseball teams compete in Yokohama.

Interpreting the Visual Record (*Place*)
How is this scoreboard different from one in the United States?

Life in Japan

Japan is a very homogeneous nation. In other words, almost everyone—more than 99 percent of the population—is ethnically Japanese and shares a common language and culture. Japanese society has traditionally been dominated by men, but this is changing. More Japanese women have jobs today than in the past, but most women are still expected to be dutiful wives and mothers. Many quit their jobs when they marry.

Many Japanese families live in suburbs, where housing is cheaper. As a result, many Japanese spend as much as three hours commuting to and from work.

Because land is so scarce, most Japanese homes do not have large yards. Most homes are also smaller than typical American homes. Rooms are usually used for more than one purpose. For example, a living room may also serve as a bedroom. During the day, people sit on cushions at low tables. At night, they sleep on the floor on a **futon** (FOO-tahn)—a lightweight cotton mattress. In the morning they put the mattress away, and the bedroom becomes a living room again.

For most occasions, people wear Western-style clothing. Many Japanese wear kimonos at festivals and weddings. Listening to music and playing video games are popular leisure activities. Baseball, golf, and skiing are also popular. On festival days, families may gather to enjoy the cherry blossoms or visit a local shrine or temple. They might also watch the ancient sport of sumo wrestling or traditional dramas on television. Many Japanese enjoy traditional arts such as the tea ceremony, flower arranging, growing dwarf potted trees called bonsai, and kite flying.

✓ **READING CHECK:** (*Human Systems*) What is life like in Japan?

Japan's Economy

Japan has few natural resources. It therefore imports many of the raw materials it uses to run its industries. Oil is one key material that Japan must import. The country produces about one third of its energy through nuclear power.

The sea is an important source of food. Japan has the world's largest fishing industry. It also imports fish from all over the world. Fish is a major part of the Japanese diet. In fact, Tokyo's largest fish market sells about 5 million pounds of seafood each day. The average Japanese eats more than 100 pounds of fish each year. In contrast, the average American eats less than 5 pounds each year.

Agriculture Most Japanese farms are located on Honshu. Many farmers own their land and live in small villages. Farms in Japan are much smaller than those in the United States. The average Japanese farm is about 2.5 acres (1 hectare). Most American farms are about 150 times larger. Japan's shortage of land means that there is little pastureland for livestock. Meat is a luxury. The Japanese get most of their protein from fish and soybeans.

Farmers make the most of their land by terracing the hillsides. This means cutting the hillside into a series of small flat fields. The terraces look like broad stair steps. The terraces give farmers more room to grow crops. Japanese farmers use **intensive cultivation**—the practice of growing food on every bit of available land. Even so, Japan must import about two thirds of its food.

Farmers are encouraged to stay on the land and to grow as much rice as possible. However, many farms are too small to be profitable. To solve this problem, the Japanese government buys the rice crop. The price is set high enough to allow farmers to support their families. The government then resells it at the same price. Because this price is much higher than the world market price, the government restricts rice imports.

Seeds of the tea plant were first brought to Japan about A.D. 800. Tea is now an important product of southern Japan. Top-quality teas are harvested by hand only. Workers pick just the tender young leaves at the plant's tip.

Interpreting the Visual Record

(*Human-Environment Interaction*)

How might using machines for harvesting leaves affect the quality of the tea?

▼

▲

A worker in this Japanese automobile factory does his job with the help of a robot.

Industry Japan imports most of its raw resources. These resources are then used to make goods to sell in other countries. For example, Japan is known for its high-quality automobiles. Japan also makes televisions, cameras, and compact disc players.

There are many reasons for Japan's economic success. Most Japanese have a strong **work ethic**. This is the belief that work in itself is worthwhile. Most Japanese work for large companies and respect their leaders. In return, employers look after workers' needs. They offer job security, exercise classes, and other benefits.

The Japanese have also benefited from investments in other countries. For example, some Japanese companies have built automobile factories in the United States. Other Japanese companies have invested in the American entertainment and real estate industries.

Japan and the Global Market Japan's economy depends on trade. In the past the government set up trade barriers to protect Japan's industries from foreign competition. This practice is called **protectionism**. This has helped Japan build up a huge **trade surplus**. A trade surplus means that a nation exports more than it imports. Other countries have objected to Japan's trade practices. Some countries have even set up barriers against Japanese goods. As a result, Japan has eased some trade barriers.

Japan has other economic problems, too. Some Asian countries that pay lower wages are able to produce goods more cheaply than Japan. The most important problem Japan—and Asia—faced in the 1990s was an economic slowdown. It threatened the country's prosperity. Japan is now in a recovery and slow-growth period.

✓ **READING CHECK:** (*Human Systems*) How have Japan's leaders tried to protect the nation's economy?

Define and explain: megalopolis, kimonos, futon, intensive cultivation, work ethic, protectionism, trade surplus

Working with Sketch Maps On the map you created in Section 2, label Inland Sea, Osaka, Tokyo, Kobe, and Kyoto. Draw a box in the margin of your map. What do the cities have in common? Write your answer in the margin box.

Reading for the Main Idea

1. (*Environment and Society*) How does Japan's physical geography affect farming?

2. (*Human Systems*) How has Japan developed its industries without plentiful raw materials?

Critical Thinking

3. Drawing Inferences and Conclusions In what ways do the daily lives of the Japanese reflect influences of Western culture?

4. Drawing Inferences and Conclusions Why do you suppose other countries might be concerned about Japan's surplus?

Organizing What You Know

5. Summarizing Copy the following graphic organizer. Use it to list the activities and services available in Tokyo.

Tokyo

The History and Culture of the Koreas

Read to Discover

1. What was Korea's ancient history like?
2. What were the major events of Korea's early modern period?
3. Why was Korea divided after World War II, and what were the effects of the division?

Vocabulary

demilitarized zone

Places

North Korea
South Korea

Reading Strategy

TAKING NOTES Use the headings in this section to create an outline. As you read, write what you learn about the history and culture of the Koreas under each heading.

Ancient Korea

Korea's earliest inhabitants were nomadic hunters from north and central Asia. About 1500 B.C. they adopted rice farming, which had been introduced from China. Then, in 108 B.C., the Chinese invaded Korea. This invasion marked the beginning of a long period of Chinese influence on Korean culture. The Chinese introduced their system of writing and their system of examinations for government jobs. They also introduced Buddhism and Confucianism to Korea.

Korea's original religion—shamanism—continued to be practiced, along with the newer traditions introduced from China. According to shamanism, natural places and ancestors have spirits. Many mountains are particularly sacred to Koreans. Shamanism is still practiced in South Korea.

Over the centuries, Korean tribes eventually recaptured most of the peninsula. In the A.D. 600s the kingdom of Silla (SI-luh) united the peninsula. Korea's golden age began. Korea became known in Asia for its architecture, painting, ceramics, and fine jewelry.

A weaver demonstrates his craft near Seoul.

This celadon vase is from the A.D. 1000s.

Heavy fencing and explosives have kept people out of the demilitarized zone for decades. As a result, this land has provided a safe home for rare animal and plant species. Some scientists hope that in the future the DMZ can be set aside as a nature preserve, which would attract tourists while protecting the wildlife.

During the Silla period Korea began using the results of examinations to award government jobs. Generally only boys who were sons of noblemen could take the examinations. People from the lower classes could not rise to important positions by studying and passing the examinations, as they could in China.

By the early 900s a new kingdom had taken power. The modern name of Korea comes from this kingdom's name, Koryo. During the Koryo dynasty, Korean artisans invented the first movable metal type. During the following dynasty, scholars developed the Hangul (HAHN-gool) alphabet, which was officially adopted in 1446. Hangul was much easier to use with the Korean language than Chinese characters had been. Because Hangul had only 24 symbols, it was easier to learn. It had previously been necessary to memorize about 20,000 Chinese characters to read the Buddhist scriptures.

✓ **READING CHECK:** (*Human Systems*) How did the Chinese influence Korea's ancient history?

Early Modern Korea

By the early 1600s China again controlled Korea. For 300 years Korea remained under Chinese control. Closed off to most other outsiders, Korea became known as the Hermit Kingdom. During this period, Catholicism was introduced into Korea through missionaries in China. Korea's Christian community was sometimes persecuted and remained small until the mid-1900s.

In the mid-1890s Japan defeated China in the Sino-Japanese War. This cleared the way for Japan to annex Korea in 1910. The Japanese ruled harshly. They took over the Korean government and many businesses and farms. Koreans were forced to take Japanese names, and

Japanese was taught in the schools. Japan ruled Korea until the end of World War II.

✔ **READING CHECK:** (*Places and Regions*) What were some major events in Korea's early modern period?

A Divided Korea

At the end of World War II, U.S. and Soviet troops oversaw the Japanese departure from Korea. Because the Soviets wanted communism to spread to other countries, they helped Communist leaders take power in the north. The United States backed a democratic government in the south. The United Nations hoped that the Koreas would reunite. However, the United States and the Soviet Union could not agree on a plan. In 1948 South Korea officially became the Republic of Korea. North Korea became the Democratic People's Republic of Korea led by Korean Communist dictator Kim Il Sung.

In 1950 North Korea tried to unify the country by invading South Korea, resulting in the Korean War. The United Nations sent troops—mostly U.S.—to defend South Korea. Communist China sent forces to North Korea. A truce was declared in 1953, but Korea remains divided. The border between North Korea and South Korea is a strip of land roughly 2.4 miles (4 km) wide called the **demilitarized zone** (DMZ). This buffer zone separates the two countries. A total of about 1 million U.S., South Korean, and North Korean soldiers patrol the DMZ. It is the world's most heavily guarded border.

In 2000, the leaders of both Koreas met to discuss the future. Also, families that had been separated for decades were briefly reunited. However, the two Koreas have not agreed on terms of reunification.

✔ **READING CHECK:** (*Places and Regions*) What were some events in Korea's history after World War II?

Our Amazing Planet

Casting bronze bells is an ancient Korean craft. The largest bell in South Korea, completed in A.D. 771, is more than 12 feet (3.6 m) tall and weighs about 25 tons (110,000 kg). When struck, it is said that the bell's tone can be heard 40 miles (64 km) away.

Section Review 4

Homework Practice Online
Keyword: SG5 HP28

Define and explain: demilitarized zone

Working with Sketch Maps On the map you created in Section 3, label North Korea and South Korea. In the margin, draw a box and include in it information that explains the significance of the DMZ. When was it established?

Reading for the Main Idea

1. (*Human Systems*) What were some of the accomplishments of the early Koreans before about 1600? What dynasty gave Korea its name?

2. (*Human Systems*) What long-lasting effect did the Korean War have on the Korean Peninsula?

Critical Thinking

3. **Analyzing Information** How has the Korean Peninsula been influenced by other countries?

4. **Making Generalizations and Predictions** What might be preventing North Korea and South Korea from reuniting?

Organizing What You Know

5. **Sequencing** Copy the following time line. Use it to list the important events of Korean history from 1500 B.C. through the 1500s.

1500 B.C. ———————————— 1500s

Japan and the Koreas • **635**

South and North Korea Today

Read to Discover

1. What are South Korea's government and society like?
2. What is South Korea's economy like?
3. What is North Korea like?
4. How has North Korea's government affected the country's development?

Vocabulary
entrepreneurs
chaebol
kimchi
famine

Places
Seoul
Pusan
P'yŏngyang

People
Kim Il Sung

Reading Strategy

READING ORGANIZER Create a spider map by drawing a circle on a sheet of paper. Label the circle South and North Korea Today. Create legs for People and Government, Society, and Economy. As you read the section, write what you learn about each country beneath each leg.

South Korea's People and Government

South Korea is densely populated. There are 1,197 people per square mile (462/sq km). Most people live in the narrow, fertile plain along the western coast of the Korean Peninsula. Travel in the peninsula's mountainous interior is difficult, so few people live there. South Korea's population is growing slowly, at about the same rate as in most industrialized countries.

South Korea's Cities Because South Korea is densely populated, space is a luxury—just as it is in Japan. Most South Koreans live in small apartments in crowded cities. Seoul (SOHL) is the country's capital and largest city. The government, the economy, and the educational system are centered there. After the Korean War, the population exploded because refugees flocked to Seoul seeking work and housing. By 1994 the city had nearly 11 million residents. Today, Seoul is one of the world's most densely populated cities. It has some 7,000 people per square mile (2,703/sq km).

South Korea's second-largest city is Pusan (POO-sahn). This major seaport and industrial center lies on the southern coast. Pusan also has an important fishing industry.

The rapid growth of South Korea's cities has brought problems. Housing is expensive. The many factories, cars, and coal-fired heating systems sometimes cause dangerous levels of air pollution. Industrial waste has also polluted the water.

Interpreting the Chart How does North Korea's per capita GDP compare to that of South Korea?

North Korea and South Korea

Country	Population/ Growth Rate	Life Expectancy	Literacy Rate	Per Capita GDP
North Korea	22,466,481 1.1%	68, male 74, female	99%	$1,000
South Korea	48,289,037 0.7%	72, male 79, female	98%	$19,400
United States	290,342,554 0.9%	74, male 80, female	97%	$37,600

Source: Central Intelligence Agency, *The World Factbook 2003*

Postwar Government South Korea is technically a democracy, but it was run by military dictators until the late 1980s. More recently, South Korea introduced a multiparty democratic government. The government controls economic development but does not own businesses and property.

✓ READING CHECK: (*Human Systems*) What kind of government does South Korea have?

South Korean Society

Like Japan's, South Korea's population is homogeneous. Most Koreans complete high school. About half go on to some form of higher education. Women are beginning to hold important jobs.

Traditional Families Most Koreans marry someone they meet through their parents. Most families still value sons. This is because only a son can take over the family name. Only a son can lead the ceremonies to honor the family's ancestors. Some couples who do not have a son adopt a boy with the same family name. This is not too difficult because there are few family names in Korea.

Religion Today, Christianity is the most common religion, followed closely by Buddhism. Whatever their religion, most Koreans take part in ceremonies to honor their ancestors. Most also follow Confucian values. Many Koreans still ask shamans for personal advice.

✓ READING CHECK: (*Human Systems*) What is South Korea's society like?

This view looks out over the busy harbor of Pusan. Travelers can take a ferry from Pusan across the Korean Strait to Japan.

Interpreting the Visual Record

(Movement) **How does this photo show the importance of shipping to this region's economy?**

South Korea's Economy

After the war, South Korea industrialized quickly, and its market economy grew. By the 1990s it had become one of the strongest economies in Asia.

Industry Koreans' strong sense of family often carries over into work. Large groups of relatives may become **entrepreneurs**. This means they use their money and talents to start and manage a business. Businesses are sometimes linked through family and personal ties into huge industrial groups called *chaebol*.

The government has encouraged the use of nuclear power. It also has encouraged the growth of high-technology industries. These industries make electronic goods for export. Other important industries are steel, shipbuilding, automobiles, and textiles. In the late 1990s South Korea, like many other Asian countries, experienced an economic slowdown. It is now making a rapid recovery.

Agriculture South Korea has the peninsula's richest agricultural land. However, less than 20 percent of the land can be farmed. The shortage of land means that South Korea must import about half of its food.

Most South Korean farms are small and lie along the western and southern coasts. The rugged terrain makes using heavy machinery difficult. As a result, farmers must do much of their work by hand and with small tractors. Since the late 1980s there has been a shortage of farmworkers.

Farmers grow rice on about half their land. Other important crops are Chinese cabbage and soybeans. Soybeans are used to make soy sauce and tofu, or bean curd. Chinese cabbage that has been spiced and pickled is called **kimchi**. This is Korea's national dish.

✓ **READING CHECK:** (*Places and Regions*) What is South Korea's economy like?

This is one of many statues of Kim Il Sung in P'yŏngyang. He led North Korea from the end of World War II until his death in 1994. Although dead, Kim Il Sung was declared the "Eternal President" of North Korea in 1998.

North Korea's People and Government

North Korea's Communist Party controls the government. Kim Il Sung's son, Kim Jong Il, took over leadership in 1998 and continued his father's strict policies.

For years, North Korea had ties mostly with other Communist countries. Since the Soviet Union's breakup, North Korea has been largely isolated from the rest of the world. In addition, many countries are worried about North Korea's ability to make nuclear weapons. In 2002 North Korea announced plans to restart a nuclear reactor. Just a year later, the government said it had enough materials to build six nuclear bombs. Negotiations have not solved the crisis.

Like South Korea and Japan, North Korea has a homogeneous population. However, North Korea is not as densely populated as South Korea.

The capital of North Korea is P'yŏngyang (pyuhng-YANG). More than 3 million people live there. North Korea's only university is in P'yŏngyang. Few private cars are on the city streets. Most residents use buses or the subway system to get around. At night, many streets are dark because the city frequently experiences shortages of electricity.

✓ **READING CHECK:** (*Places and Regions*) What is North Korea like?

North Korea's Economy

North Korea has a command economy. This means that the central government plans the economy and controls what is produced. The government also owns all the land and housing and controls access to jobs.

North Korea's best farmland is along the west coast. Only 14 percent of North Korea's land can be farmed. Most of this land is owned by the state. It is farmed by cooperatives—groups of farmers who work the land together. Some people have small gardens to grow food for themselves or to sell at local markets.

North Korea does not produce enough food to feed its people. It lost its main source of food and fertilizer when the Soviet Union collapsed. Poor harvests in the mid-1990s made the situation worse. **Famine**, or severe food shortages, resulted. The government's hostility toward the West made getting aid difficult. Thousands starved.

North Korea is rich in mineral resources. It has also developed a nuclear power industry. North Korea makes machinery, iron, and steel. However, its factories use outdated technology.

✓ **READING CHECK:** (*Human Systems*) How has North Korea's government affected the country's economic development?

▲
Rice farming requires large amounts of human energy for transplanting, weeding, and harvesting. These farmers are planting seedlings.

Section Review 5

Define or identify: entrepreneurs, *chaebol*, Kim Il Sung, kimchi, famine

Working with Sketch Maps On the map you created in Section 4, label Seoul, Pusan, and P'yŏngyang. Why do you think these cities remain important? Write your answer in a box in the margin.

Reading for the Main Idea

1. (*Places and Regions*) How did South Korea's cities change after the Korean War?

2. (*Environment and Society*) How does North Korea's physical geography affect its farmers?

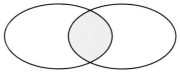
Homework Practice Online
Keyword: SG5 HP28

3. (*Places and Regions*) What kind of economies do North and South Korea have, and how are they different?

Critical Thinking

4. Finding the Main Idea How have entrepreneurs affected South Korea's economy?

Organizing What You Know

5. Sequencing List characteristics of the government, industry, and agriculture of North and South Korea since World War II. Where the circles overlap, list things the countries share.

Japan and the Koreas • 639

CHAPTER 28
Review and Practice

Define and Identify

Identify each of the following:

1. tsunamis
2. shamans
3. Murasaki Shikibu
4. samurai
5. shogun
6. Diet
7. kimonos
8. intensive cultivation
9. work ethic
10. protectionism
11. trade surplus
12. entrepreneurs
13. *chaebol*
14. Kim Il Sung
15. kimchi
16. famine

Review the Main Ideas

17. What are the main geographic features of Japan and the Koreas?
18. How are the climates of Japan and South Korea similar?
19. What kind of political system did Japan have early in its history?
20. Why did the United States go to war against Japan in 1941?
21. Japan leads the world in which industry? What key material must it import?

22. Why have other countries objected to Japan's trade practices?
23. What contributions did the Chinese make to ancient Korea?
24. What purpose does the demilitarized zone serve? What makes it unique?
25. Why are sons valued in South Korean families?
26. What are some problems that face North Koreans?

Think Critically

27. **Analyzing Information** How have geographic features affected where people live in Japan and the Korean Peninsula?
28. **Contrasting** What physical features make Japan different from the Koreas? Create a chart to organize your answer.
29. **Finding the Main Idea** How have the Japanese changed the physical landscape to meet their needs?
30. **Analyzing Information** How has Tokyo developed into a megalopolis?
31. **Contrasting** How do the economies and governments of North and South Korea differ?

Map Activity

32. On a separate sheet of paper, match the letters on the map with their correct labels.

Hokkaido	Tokyo
Honshu	Seoul
Shikoku	P'yŏngyang
Kyushu	

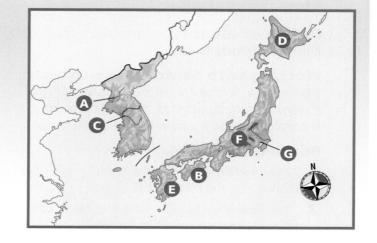

Writing Activity

Imagine that you are traveling in Japan, North Korea, or South Korea. Write a one-page letter to a friend describing the places you have visited and an adventure you have had during your stay. Be sure to use standard grammar, spelling, sentence structure, and punctuation.

internet connect

Internet Activity: **go.hrw.com**
KEYWORD: **SG5 GT28**

Choose a topic to explore Japan and the Koreas:
- Investigate volcanoes.
- Visit Japan and the Koreas.
- Compare your school to a Japanese school.

Social Studies Skills Practice

Interpreting Political Cartoons

In this chapter you have learned that North Korea caused concern among many countries with its nuclear weapons program. Study the following political cartoon that addresses the relationship between President Bush and Kim Jong Il. Then answer the questions.

Source: Daryl Cagle, Slate.com

1. What is the main idea of this cartoon?
2. Which character represents President Bush?
3. What is Kim Jong Il's character holding?
4. What is Kim Jong Il preventing President Bush from doing?

Analyzing Primary Sources

Read the following passage about young samurai warriors from *Bushido, the Warrior's Code* by Inazo Nitobe. Then answer the questions.

"The stereotype of Spartan courage and of ignoring pain was indoctrinated [taught] into the children from the time of their birth. The fledgling samurai with an empty stomach knew it was a disgrace to feel the pangs [pains] of hunger. During training they were subjected to periods of deprivation [withholding] of food and exposure to extreme cold. Endurance was the hallmark of a successful novice [beginner]."

1. When did samurai training begin for future warriors?
2. What was life like for a young samurai?
3. Why would it be a disgrace to feel hungry?
4. How might this kind of training aid a warrior in battle?

CHAPTER 29

Southeast Asia

Our study of the world now takes us to Southeast Asia. This vast region stretches from Myanmar eastward to New Guinea in the Pacific Ocean.

*S*awaddee! (May you have good fortune!) I am Chosita, and I am 14 years old. I live in Bangkok with my parents and my older sister. We get up early for school because traffic in Bangkok is very heavy. By 6:00 A.M. we are on the road. My school has an eatery where street vendors sell all kinds of food—noodles in broth with beef, stir-fried noodles with meat and greens, dessert cakes of taro, pumpkin, and sticky rice, and fruits like rambutan, mangosteen, durian, and mango.

We go to school from June to September and from November to February. Our big vacation is March through May.

Our school has 38 students and two teachers in each class. I will not learn to use the computer until next year because we are the last class under the old school policy. The new policy has all students begin learning the computer in fourth grade.

สวัสดีค่ะ ดิฉันชื่อ โชสิตา
ดิฉันอยู่ที่กรุงเทพฯ
ซึ่งเป็นเมืองหลวงของประเทศไทยค่ะ

▲
Translation: Hi! My name is Chosita. I live in Bangkok, the capital of Thailand.

Section 1 Physical Geography

Read to Discover

1. What are the major physical features of Southeast Asia?
2. What climates, vegetation, and wildlife are found in the region?
3. What resources does Southeast Asia have?

Vocabulary

mainland
archipelagos

Places

Indochina Peninsula
Malay Peninsula
New Guinea
Malay Archipelago
Philippines
Irian Jaya
Borneo
Java
Sumatra
Mekong River

Reading Strategy

MNEMONIC DEVICE Write the letters to the words Tropical down a sheet of paper. As you read this section, use each letter to write what you learn about the physical geography of Southeast Asia.

Southeast Asia: Physical-Political

ASIA

Tropic of Cancer

Mandalay
MYANMAR
(BURMA)
Irrawaddy River
Yangon
(Rangoon)
LAOS
Vientiane
Hong (Red) R.
Hanoi
GULF OF TONKIN
THAILAND
INDOCHINA PENINSULA
KHORAT PLATEAU
Chao Phraya R.
Bangkok
VIETNAM
Angkor
CAMBODIA
Tonle Sap
Phnom Penh
Ho Chi Minh City (Saigon)
SOUTH CHINA SEA
Mekong River

Mount Pinatubo 5770 ft. (1759 m)
Luzon
Quezon City
Manila
PHILIPPINE SEA
Mindoro
PHILIPPINES
Palawan
Cebu
Mindanao
Davao
Mount Apo 9692 ft. (2954 m)

INDIAN OCEAN

GULF OF THAILAND

MALAY PENINSULA

Strait of Malacca

Kuala Lumpur
Putrajaya
Singapore · SINGAPORE
Sumatra
BARISAN MOUNTAINS

Bandar Seri Begawan
BRUNEI
SABAH
MALAYSIA
SARAWAK
Borneo
KALIMANTAN

CELEBES SEA
MALAY ARCHIPELAGO

PACIFIC OCEAN

INDONESIA

Sulawesi (Celebes)
Moluccas

Jaya Peak 16,503 ft. (5030 m)
New Guinea

Jakarta
JAVA SEA
Java
Bali
Lombok
Sumbawa
Sumba
Flores
Timor
EAST TIMOR

Equator

SCALE
0   250   500 Miles
0   250   500 Kilometers
Projection: Miller

N

ELEVATION

FEET		METERS
13,120		4,000
6,560		2,000
1,640		500
656		200
(Sea level) 0		0 (Sea level)
Below sea level		Below sea level

⊛ National capitals
• Other cities
◼ Historic sites

Size comparison of Southeast Asia to the contiguous United States

internet connect

GO TO: go.hrw.com
KEYWORD: SG5 CH29
FOR: Web sites about
Southeast Asia

Physical Features

Southeast Asia is made up of two peninsulas and two large island groups. The Indochina and Malay (muh-LAY) Peninsulas lie on the Asian **mainland**. A mainland is a region's main landmass. The two large groups of islands, or **archipelagos** (ahr-kuh-PE-luh-gohs), lie between the mainland and New Guinea. They are the Malay Archipelago—made up mostly of Indonesia—and the Philippines. The Philippines are sometimes considered part of the Malay Archipelago. Western New Guinea is called Irian Jaya. It is part of Indonesia.

Landforms Southeast Asia's highest mountains are on the mainland in northern Myanmar (MYAHN-mahr). Mountain ranges fan out southward into Thailand (TY-land), Laos (LOWS), and Vietnam (vee-ET-NAHM). Between the mountains are low plateaus and river floodplains. The floodplains are rich farmlands.

Some of the large islands also have high mountains. Those islands include Borneo, Java, Sumatra, New Guinea, and some in the Philippines. They are part of the Pacific Ring of Fire. Earthquakes and volcanic eruptions often shake this part of the world.

Rivers Five major river systems drain the mainland. Many people and the largest cities are found near these rivers. The greatest river is the Mekong (MAY-KAWNG). The Mekong River flows southeast from China to southern Vietnam. You will read about the other rivers later in this chapter.

✔ **READING CHECK:** (*Places and Regions*) What are Southeast Asia's major physical features?

Climate Vegetation, and Wildlife

The warm temperatures of this tropical region generally do not change much during the year. However, northern and mountain areas tend to be cooler.

The Mekong River flows through a floodplain along the border between Thailand and Laos.

Interpreting the Visual Record What might happen to low islands and surrounding areas during the wet monsoon?

Much of the rainfall on the mainland is seasonal. Wet monsoon winds from nearby warm oceans bring heavy rains in the summer. Dry monsoons from the northeast bring drier weather in winter. Most of the islands are wet all year. Typhoons bring heavy rains and powerful winds to the island countries.

The region's tropical rain forests are home to many kinds of plants and animals. About 40,000 kinds of flowering plants grow in Indonesia alone. Rhinoceroses, orangutans, tigers, and elephants also live in the region. However, many of these plants and animals are endangered. Southeast Asia's rain forests are being cleared for farmland, tropical wood, and mining.

◀ *Orangutan* is a Malaysian word for "man of the forest." These apes once lived in jungles throughout much of Southeast Asia. Hunting by humans has thinned the orangutan population in much of the region. Most orangutans today live on Borneo and Sumatra.

✔ **READING CHECK:** (*Places and Regions*) What are the region's climates, vegetation, and wildlife like?

Resources

Southeast Asia's rain forests produce valuable wood and other products. Thailand, Indonesia, and Malaysia (muh-LAY-zhuh) are the world's largest producers of natural rubber. The rubber tree is native to South America. However, it grows well in Southeast Asia's tropical climates.

Rich volcanic soils, floodplains, and tropical climates are good for farming. Abundant water and good soils in river deltas are ideal for growing rice. Coconuts, palm oil, sugarcane, coffee, and spices are also key products. Countries here also mine tin, iron ore, oil, and gas.

✔ **READING CHECK:** (*Places and Regions*) What are the region's important resources?

go.
hrw
.com
Homework Practice Online
Keyword: SG5 HP29

Section Review 1

Define and explain: mainland, archipelagos

Working with Sketch Maps On a map of Southeast Asia that your teacher provides or that you draw, label the following: Indochina Peninsula, Malay Peninsula, New Guinea, Malay Archipelago, Philippines, Irian Jaya, Borneo, Java, Sumatra, and the Mekong River. In a box in the margin, describe the Mekong River.

Reading for the Main Idea

1. (*Places and Regions*) Where are the region's highest mountains?

2. (*Places and Regions*) Where are large cities found?

3. (*Places and Regions*) Which countries are the world's largest producers of natural rubber?

Critical Thinking

4. Making Generalizations and Predictions What do you think might happen to the region's wildlife if much of the tropical rain forests continue to be destroyed?

Organizing What You Know

5. Summarizing Copy the following graphic organizer. Use it to describe the region's climates, vegetation and wildlife, and resources.

Climates	Vegetation and wildlife	Resources

Read to Discover

1. What are some important events in the history of Southeast Asia?

2. What are the people and culture of Southeast Asia like today?

Vocabulary

refugees

Places

Angkor   Indonesia
Cambodia   Malaysia
Thailand   Timor
Vietnam   Myanmar
Laos   Singapore

Reading Strategy

TAKING NOTES Use the headings in this section to create an outline. As you read, write what you learn about the history and culture of Southeast Asia beneath each heading.

History

Southeast Asia was home to some of the world's earliest human settlements. Over time many peoples moved there from China and India. The Khmer (kuh-MER) developed the most advanced of the region's early societies. The Khmer Empire was based in Angkor in what is now Cambodia (kam-BOH-dee-uh). It controlled a large area from the early A.D. 800s to the mid-1200s.

Colonial Era Europeans began to establish colonies in Southeast Asia in the 1500s. By the end of the 1800s, the Portuguese, British, Dutch, French, and Spanish controlled most of the region. The United States won control of the Philippines from Spain after the Spanish-American War in 1898. Just Siam (sy-AM), now called Thailand, remained independent.

Japan invaded and occupied most of Southeast Asia during World War II. After Japan was defeated in 1945, the United States granted the Philippines independence a year later. European countries tried to

History Close-Up

Angkor Wat The magnificent stone towers of Angkor Wat rise from the Southeast Asian rain forest in this illustrated re-creation set in the early A.D. 1100s. Hindu priests are shown entering the temple where they will make offerings to statues of Hindu gods. To the Khmer, Angkor Wat was the center of the universe. The temple's towers symbolized mythical mountains. Reservoirs of water surrounding the temple represented the oceans. **What do you think this illustration says about Khmer society?**

regain control of their colonies in the region. Some Southeast Asians decided to fight for independence. One of the bloodiest wars was in French Indochina. The French finally left in 1954. Their former colonies of Vietnam, Laos, and Cambodia became independent. By the mid-1960s, European rule had ended in most of the region.

Modern Era Unfortunately, fighting did not end in some countries when the Europeans left. Vietnam split into two countries. In the 1960s the United States sent troops to defend South Vietnam against communist North Vietnam. Civil wars also raged in Laos and Cambodia. In 1975, communist forces took power in all the countries. As communism continued to spread throughout the region, North and South Vietnam were then united into one country.

The region's wars caused terrible destruction. Millions died, including more than 50,000 Americans. About 1 million Vietnamese **refugees** tried to escape the communist takeover in South Vietnam. Refugees are people who flee their own country, usually for economic or political reasons. Many refugees from the region came to the United States.

In Cambodia more than 1 million people died under a cruel communist government. That government ruled from 1975 to 1978. Then Vietnam invaded Cambodia in 1978, sparking another conflict. That war continued off and on until the mid-1990s. Many Cambodian refugees fled to Thailand.

Communists and other groups also fought against governments in the Philippines, Indonesia, and Malaysia. In 1975 Indonesia invaded the former Portuguese

colony of East Timor. The East Timorese demanded independence. However, the Indonesian military kept a tight grip on the region. The people of East Timor voted for independence in 1999. East Timor then plunged again into violence. The United Nations sent troops to restore peace and manage the area before independence was achieved.

Governments The region's countries have had different kinds of governments. Many have been ruled by dictators. Some countries, such as the Philippines and Indonesia, now have governments elected by the people.

In other countries, the people still have little say in their government. For example, Myanmar is ruled by a military government. That government has jailed and even killed its opponents. Vietnam and Laos are still ruled by Communist governments. Only recently have Indonesians been allowed to vote in free elections. In some countries, such as Singapore, the same party always wins elections.

✓ **READING CHECK:** (*Places and Regions*) What were some key events in Southeast Asian history?

Culture

The populations of most countries in Southeast Asia are very diverse. This is because many different peoples have moved to the area over time. Today, for example, nearly 70 percent of the people in Myanmar are Burmese. However, Chinese, Asian Indians, and many other ethnic groups also live there.

(*Place*) The Shwedagon Pagoda is a beautiful Buddhist shrine in Yangon, Myanmar. Pagodas are important parts of a Buddhist temple complex.

Many ethnic Chinese live in the largest cities of most Southeast Asian countries. In Singapore they are a majority of the population—more than 75 percent. Singapore is a tiny country at the tip of the Malay Peninsula.

Languages and Religions The peoples of Southeast Asia speak many different languages. For example, in the former Dutch colony of Indonesia, most people speak Bahasa Indonesia. However, Javanese, other local dialects, English, and Dutch are also spoken there. European and Chinese languages are spoken in many other countries.

In addition, Indians, Chinese, Arab traders, and Europeans brought different religions to the region. For example, Hinduism is practiced in the region's Indian communities. However, Buddhism is the most common religion in the mainland countries today. Islam is the major religion in Malaysia, Brunei, and Indonesia. In fact, Indonesia has the largest Islamic population in the world. Nearly 90 percent of its more than 234 million people are Muslim.

Christians are a minority in most of the former European colonies. However, more than 80 percent of people in the Philippines, a former Spanish colony, are Roman Catholic.

Food Southeast Asian foods have been influenced by Chinese, South Asian, and European cooking styles. There are many spicy, mild, and sweet varieties. Rice is the most important food in nearly all of the countries. It is served with many other foods and spices, such as curries and chili peppers. Coconut is also important. It is served as a separate dish or used as an ingredient in other foods.

▲
Women in Laos sprinkle water on Buddhist monks during a New Year festival. This custom symbolizes the washing away of the old year.

Interpreting the Visual Record
What kinds of clothes are the monks wearing?

✓ **READING CHECK:** (*Human Systems*) How have migration and cultural borrowing influenced the region's culture?

Section Review 2

Define and explain: refugees

Working with Sketch Maps On the map you created in Section 1, label the region's countries, Angkor, and Timor. In a box in the margin, describe the recent history of East Timor.

Reading for the Main Idea

1. (*Places and Regions*) What was the Khmer Empire?

2. (*Human Systems*) How did Europeans influence the region's history and culture?

go.hrw.com
Homework Practice Online
Keyword: SG5 HP29

Critical Thinking

3. Drawing Inferences and Conclusions Why do you think European countries wanted to regain their Southeast Asian colonies following World War II?

4. Finding the Main Idea What religion is most common in the mainland countries? in the island countries?

Organizing What You Know

5. Sequencing Copy the following time line. Use it to identify important people, years, periods, and events in Southeast Asia's history.

A.D. *800*   *2000*

Section 3 · Mainland Southeast Asia Today

Read to Discover

1. Where do people in the mainland countries live today?
2. What are the economies of the mainland countries like?

Vocabulary

klongs

Places

Bangkok
Yangon
Hanoi
Ho Chi Minh City
Chao Phraya River
Irrawaddy River
Hong (Red) River
Vientiane
Phnom Penh

People

Aung San Suu Kyi

Reading Strategy

READING ORGANIZER Before you read this section, draw a large five-pointed star on a sheet of paper. As you read, write what you learn about Vietnam, Laos, Cambodia, Thailand, and Myanmar in the space created by the points. In the center, write the characteristics all the countries share.

People and Cities

Most mainland Southeast Asians today live in rural areas. Many are farmers in fertile river valleys and deltas. Fewer people live in remote hill and mountain villages.

However, the region's cities have been growing rapidly. People are moving to urban areas to look for work. The cities have many businesses, services, and opportunities that are not found in rural areas. Many of the cities today are crowded, smoggy, and noisy.

Look at the chapter map. You will find that the largest cities are located along major rivers. Location near rivers places these cities near important rice-growing areas. Access to rivers also makes them key

A Vietnamese man sells incense sticks in Ho Chi Minh City.

shipping centers for farm and factory products. The largest cities are Bangkok, Yangon, Hanoi, and Ho Chi Minh City.

Bangkok The mainland's largest city is Bangkok, Thailand's capital. Bangkok lies near the mouth of the Chao Phraya (chow PRY-uh) River. More than 7 million people live there. Much of Bangkok is connected by *klongs*, or canals. The klongs are used for transportation and for selling and shipping goods. They also drain water from the city.

Other Cities The region's second-largest city is Yangon, formerly known as Rangoon. It is Myanmar's capital and major seaport. The city is located in the Irrawaddy River delta on the coast of the Andaman Sea. To the east, Vietnam's largest cities are also located in major river deltas. The capital, Hanoi (ha-NOY), is located in the Hong (Red) River delta in the north. Ho Chi Minh City is located in the Mekong River delta in the south. Ho Chi Minh City was once known as Saigon and was South Vietnam's capital. Today it is an important seaport and business center with more than 4.6 million people.

Movement Boat traffic can be heavy along Bangkok's *klongs*. These canals have been part of the city's transportation system for centuries.

✔ **READING CHECK:** (*Places and Regions*) Where do most people in mainland Southeast Asia live today and why?

Economy

War, bad governments, and other problems have slowed progress in most of the mainland countries. However, rich resources could make the future brighter for the people there.

Vietnam Vietnam's economy has been slowly recovering since the end of the war in 1975. In recent years, the Communist government has begun moving from a command economy to a more market-oriented one. Some people are now allowed to own private businesses. Most Vietnamese remain farmers.

Most of Vietnam's factories, coal, oil, and other resources are in the north. The Hong and Mekong River deltas are major farming areas. Rice is the most important crop and food. In many places it is planted twice each year.

Mainland Southeast Asia

Country	Population/ Growth Rate	Life Expectancy	Literacy Rate	Per Capita GDP
Cambodia	13,124,764 1.8%	55, male 60, female	70%	$1,500
Laos	9,921,545 2.5%	52, male 66, female	53%	$1,700
Myanmar	42,510,537 0.5%	54, male 57, female	83%	$1,500
Thailand	64,265,276 0.9%	71, male 73, female	96%	$6,900
Vietnam	81,624,716 1.3%	67, male 72, female	94%	$2,250
United States	290,342,554 0.9%	74, male 80, female	97%	$37,600

Source: Central Intelligence Agency, *The World Factbook 2003*

Interpreting the Chart **According to the data in the chart, which country in the region is the most economically developed?**

Laos This mountainous, landlocked country has few good roads, no railroads, and few telephones and televisions. Only some cities have electricity. The economy is mostly traditional—most people are subsistence farmers. They produce just enough food for themselves and their families. The Communist government in Vientiane (vyen-TYAHN), the capital, has also recently begun allowing more economic freedom.

Cambodia Economic progress in Cambodia has been particularly slow because of war and political problems. Agriculture is the most important part of the economy. The capital and largest city, Phnom Penh (puh-NAWM PEN), is located along the Mekong River. It lies in Cambodia's southern rice-growing area.

Thailand Thailand's economy has had problems but is the strongest of the mainland countries. This is partly because Thailand has rich resources. These resources include timber, natural rubber, seafood, rice, many minerals, and gems. Factories produce computers and electronics. Many Thai operate small businesses. Tourism is also important.

Myanmar This former British colony is also called Burma. It gained independence in 1948 and was officially renamed Myanmar in 1989. It has rich resources, including copper, tin, iron ore, timber, rubber, and oil. However, a harsh military government has limited political freedom. This has slowed economic progress.

✓ READING CHECK: (*Places and Regions*) What are the mainland economies like?

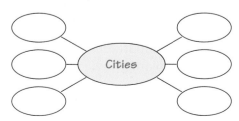

go.
hrw
.com
Homework Practice Online
Keyword: SG5 HP29

Section Review 3

Define or identify: *klongs*, Aung San Suu Kyi

Working with Sketch Maps On the map you created in Section 2, label Bangkok, Yangon, Hanoi, Ho Chi Minh City, Chao Phraya River, Irrawaddy River, Hong (Red) River, Vientiane, and Phnom Penh. Describe the mainland's largest city.

Reading for the Main Idea

1. (*Places and Regions*) Where do most mainland Southeast Asians live and why?

2. (*Human Systems*) Why are many people moving to cities?

3. (*Places and Regions*) Which country has the strongest economy and why?

Critical Thinking

4. Finding the Main Idea What kinds of problems appear to have slowed economic progress in the region?

Organizing What You Know

5. Summarizing Copy the following graphic organizer. Use it to describe the mainland's major cities. In each of its six circles, write the name of a city. In the circles, write important facts about the cities.

Cities

People and Cities

Indonesia is the largest of the island countries and the world's fourth-most-populous country. The country's more than 17,000 islands were known as the Dutch East Indies until 1949. Malaysia, Singapore, and Brunei were British colonies. The British granted independence to Malaysia in 1963. Singapore split from Malaysia in 1965. In 1984 Brunei became the region's last European colony to gain independence. As you have read, the Philippines gained independence from the United States in 1946. More than 7,000 islands make up that country.

Many people live in rural areas in the island countries. However, the island countries are more urbanized than the mainland countries. As on the mainland, many people are moving to cities in search of jobs. One country, Singapore, is simply a large city on a small island.

Modern skyscrapers tower over colonial-era buildings in Singapore. The city has one of the world's busiest ports.

Interpreting the Visual Record Place
What does Singapore's architecture tell you about its economy and culture?

CONNECTING TO Art

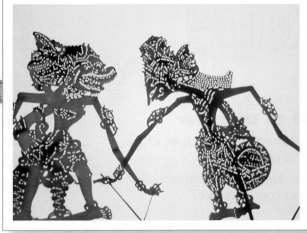

Wayang puppets

Shadow Puppets

Puppetry is an art form with roots in ancient civilizations, including Greece, Rome, China, and India. On the Indonesian island of Java, one of the world's great puppet traditions is known as *wayang*. This shadow puppet theater still entertains audiences.

Wayang puppets are beautiful works of art. The puppets are made from thin sheets of painted leather. They are pierced with holes so that light can shine through them. Then they are mounted on sticks. The performance takes place behind a screen. A light source is placed behind the puppets. The puppet's shadows fall on the screen and are visible to the audience on the other side.

Wayang performances tell stories from the *Ramayana* and the *Mahabharata*. These are two long poems of the Hindu religion. Hinduism came to Java from India hundreds of years ago. The puppets play the parts of gods, heroes, and villains. A performance usually lasts all night and includes the traditional music of Java. The music is played by an orchestra that includes gongs and other traditional instruments.

Over the years, *wayang* artists have developed other types of puppets. Some puppets are wooden forms. A new generation of artists is even creating computerized stories for *wayang* theater.

Understanding What You Read

1. Where did puppetry originate?
2. What is a *wayang* performance like?

Jakarta The region's largest city is Jakarta, Indonesia's capital. More than 11 million people live there. It is located on Java, which is by far Indonesia's most populous island. Many Indonesians live in **kampongs** around Jakarta. A kampong is a traditional village. It has also become the term for the crowded slums around large cities.

Singapore If you traveled from Jakarta to Singapore, you would find two very different cities. Singapore is one of the most modern and cleanest cities in the world. Crime rates also are very low. How has Singapore accomplished this?

Its government is very strict. For example, fines for littering are stiff. People caught transporting illegal drugs can be executed. The government even bans chewing gum and certain movies and music.

Is the lack of some individual freedoms a good trade-off for less crime, a clean city, and a strong economy? Some people in Singapore say yes. Others believe Singapore can be just as successful with less government control.

Other Cities The region's other large cities include Manila and Kuala Lumpur. More than 10 million people live in Manila, the capital of the Philippines. The city is a major seaport and industrial center on Luzon. Luzon is the country's largest and most populated island.

Kuala Lumpur is Malaysia's capital as well as its cultural, business, and transportation center. It is a modern city with two of the world's tallest buildings, the twin Petronas Towers.

✓ **READING CHECK:** *Places and Regions* What are some of the major cities of the island countries?

Island Southeast Asia

Country	Population/ Growth Rate	Life Expectancy	Literacy Rate	Per Capita GDP
Brunei	358,098 2.1%	71, male 76, female	92%	$18,600
Indonesia	234,893,453 1.5%	66, male 71, female	88%	$3,100
Malaysia	23,092,940 1.8%	69, male 74, female	89%	$9,300
Philippines	84,619,974 1.9%	66, male 72, female	96%	$4,200
Singapore	4,608,595 1.7%	77, male 83, female	93%	$24,000
United States	290,342,554 0.9%	74, male 80, female	97%	$37,600

Source: Central Intelligence Agency, *The World Factbook 2003*

Interpreting the Chart **According to the chart, which country's economic development is closest to that of the United States?**

Economy

The economies of the island countries grew rapidly until the mid-1990s. Then economic and political problems slowed growth for a while. However, rich resources are helping the economies there to recover. In addition, wages and labor costs are low in many of the countries. This means that companies there can manufacture many products more cheaply for export.

Indonesia Europeans once called Indonesia the Spice Islands because of its cinnamon, pepper, and nutmeg. Today, its rich resources include natural rubber, oil, natural gas, and timber. Indonesia also has good farmlands for rice and other crops. Busy factories turn out clothing, electronics, and furniture. Some islands, such as Bali, are popular with tourists.

(*Human-Environment Interaction*)
Farming is an important economic activity in the Philippines. In mountain areas, farmers plant rice and other crops in terraced fields. These flat terraces hold water and slow erosion along mountainsides.

▼

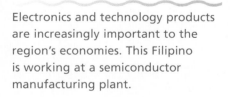

Dancers attract tourists to the island of Bali. Indonesia has many different dance styles. This *Barong* dancer uses her hands, arms, and eyes to tell a traditional story.

Large areas of Indonesia's tropical rain forests are often burned for farming. Smoke from the fires can spread for hundreds of miles. The smoke sometimes blots out sunlight, smothering cities in haze.

The Philippines The Philippines is mostly an agricultural country today. A big problem is the gap between rich and poor Filipinos. A few very rich Filipinos control most of the land and industries. Most farmers are poor and own no land.

The economy has improved in recent years. Companies sell many electronics and clothing products to overseas customers, particularly in the United States. The country also has rich resources, including tropical forests, copper, gold, silver, and oil. Farmers grow sugarcane, rice, corn, coconuts, and tropical fruits.

Singapore Singapore is by far the most economically developed country in all of Southeast Asia. The British founded the city at the tip of the Malay Peninsula in 1819. This location along major shipping routes helped make Singapore rich. Goods are stored there before they are shipped to their final stop. In addition, many foreign companies have opened banks, offices, and high-technology industries there.

Malaysia Malaysia is made up of two parts. The largest part lies on the southern Malay Peninsula. The second part lies on the northern portion of Borneo. Well-educated workers and rich resources make Malaysia's future look bright. The country produces natural rubber, electronics, automobiles, oil, and timber. The government is trying to attract more high-technology companies to the country. Malaysia is also the world's leading producer of palm oil.

Electronics and technology products are increasingly important to the region's economies. This Filipino is working at a semiconductor manufacturing plant.

Brunei Large deposits of oil have made Brunei rich. This small country on the island of Borneo is ruled by a **sultan**. A sultan is the supreme ruler of a Muslim country. Brunei shares the island of Borneo with Indonesia and Malaysia.

✔ **READING CHECK:** (*Places and Regions*) How do rich resources affect the economies of the island countries?

Homework Practice Online
Keyword: SG5 HP29

Define and explain: kampongs, sultan

Working with Sketch Maps On the map you created in Section 3, label Jakarta, Manila, Kuala Lumpur, Luzon, and Bali. In a box in the margin, identify the most heavily populated islands in Indonesia and the Philippines.

Reading for the Main Idea

1. (*Places and Regions*) What is the region's largest city? What is the importance of Manila and Kuala Lumpur to their countries?

2. (*Places and Regions*) Why was Indonesia once called the Spice Islands? What European country once controlled nearly all of Indonesia?

Critical Thinking

3. Analyzing Information Some Singaporeans say that limiting some individual freedoms is a good trade-off for less crime and a better economy. Do you agree? Why or why not?

4. Comparing/Contrasting How have Singapore and Brunei become rich countries?

Organizing What You Know

5. Summarizing Copy the following graphic organizer. Use it to list the nine Southeast Asian countries that are former European colonies. Next to each country's name, write the name of the European country that once controlled it.

Southeast Asian country	European colonial power

CASE STUDY

MULTIETHNIC INDONESIA

Indonesia is a multiethnic country—a country with many different ethnic groups. The national motto of Indonesia is *Bhinneka Tunggal Ika,* which means "the many are one." This motto comes from the many different ethnic groups that live there.

More than 300 different ethnic groups live in Indonesia. Most of these groups speak their own language and have their own way of life. No single ethnic group holds a majority. The largest are the Javanese, Sundanese, Madurese, and Coastal Malays. The country also has many smaller ethnic groups, such as the Dayaks and the Balinese. Why does Indonesia have so many different ethnic groups? Part of the answer lies in the country's diverse physical geography.

Indonesia is a very large country. It is made up of more than 17,000 islands. About 228 million people live on these islands. Indonesia's islands, mountains, and dense rain forests have served as boundaries between different ethnic groups. Many small ethnic groups lived in isolation and had very little contact with other peoples. Over time, these groups developed their own cultures, languages, and ways of life.

The modern country of Indonesia has its roots in the early 1600s. About this time, Dutch traders built forts in the area. They wanted to protect the trade routes used by Dutch ships to transport spices and other goods. The Dutch remained an important force in the region until Indonesia became independent in 1949. The long history of

Movement Most Indonesians are related to the peoples of East Asia. However, in the eastern islands, most people are of Melanesian origin. Over the centuries, many Arabs, Indians, and Europeans have added to the country's ethnic diversity.

▼

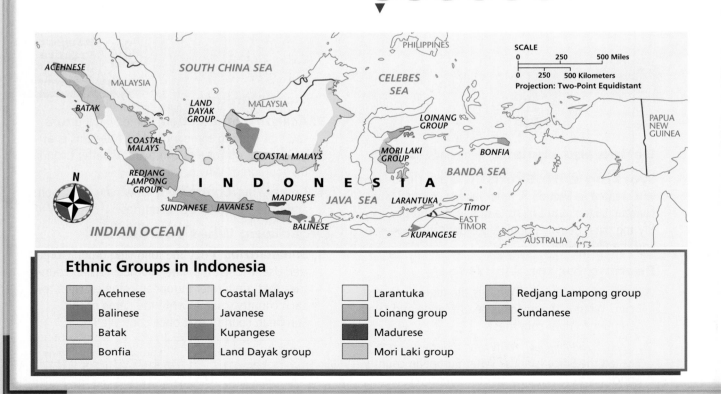

Ethnic Groups in Indonesia

- Acehnese
- Balinese
- Batak
- Bonfia
- Coastal Malays
- Javanese
- Kupangese
- Land Dayak group
- Larantuka
- Loinang group
- Madurese
- Mori Laki group
- Redjang Lampong group
- Sundanese

Dutch control helped unify the islands into the modern country of Indonesia.

In addition to this shared past, several other factors have helped unify Indonesia. For example, Indonesia's government has promoted the country's official language, Bahasa Indonesia. Although most Indonesians speak more than one language, Bahasa Indonesia is used in schools and government. The use of this language has been an important force in uniting the country. The government has also tried to develop a common Indonesian culture. It has promoted national holiday celebrations, education, popular art, and television and radio programs.

A shared history, a common education system, and an official language help give isolated ethnic groups an Indonesian identity. However, the country's multiethnic society still faces some important challenges. In certain parts of Indonesia, people want independence. For example, in 1999 people in East Timor voted for independence from Indonesia. This caused a great deal of unrest. Most people there supported the vote, but others did not. When some groups rioted, many Timorese left the area for their own safety. The Acehnese, an ethnic group on the island of Sumatra, have also been seeking independence.

Ethnic Groups in Indonesia

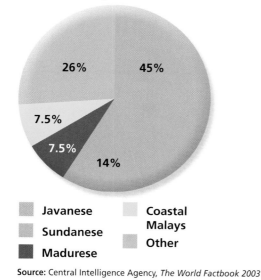

26%
45%
7.5%
7.5%
14%

Javanese
Sundanese
Madurese
Coastal Malays
Other

Source: Central Intelligence Agency, *The World Factbook 2003*

Understanding What You Read

1. How diverse is Indonesia's society? What has helped to promote cooperation among the different ethnic groups that live in the country?

2. What are some important challenges facing Indonesia today?

Review and Practice

Define and Identify

Identify each of the following:

1. mainland
2. archipelagos
3. refugees
4. *klongs*
5. Aung San Suu Kyi
6. kampongs
7. sultan

Review the Main Ideas

8. What peninsulas and archipelagos make up Southeast Asia?

9. Where will you find the highest mountains in Southeast Asia?

10. What mineral resources are found in Southeast Asia?

11. Which early society in Southeast Asia was based in Angkor?

12. What factors have slowed economic progress in mainland Southeast Asia?

13. What resources are important to the economy of Vietnam?

14. How did European countries influence Southeast Asia?

15. What is a common feature of the island countries in Southeast Asia?

16. Why do you think so many languages are spoken in Southeast Asia?

Think Critically

17. **Drawing Inferences and Conclusions** Why are some cities located near river deltas so large?

18. **Finding the Main Idea** What outside cultures have strongly influenced the development of Southeast Asian culture?

19. **Analyzing Information** How did the Philippines and Vietnam gain independence?

20. **Finding the Main Idea** How do the climates of mainland countries differ from those in the island countries? What natural disasters are a danger in the region?

21. **Analyzing Information** How do labor costs affect the island countries' economies?

Map Activity

22. On a separate sheet of paper, match the letters on the map with their correct labels.

Indochina Peninsula	Mekong River
Malay Peninsula	Timor
Malay Archipelago and the Philippines	Bangkok
Irian Jaya	Jakarta
Borneo	Manila

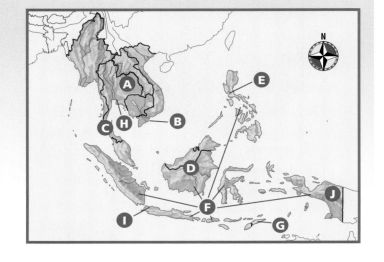

Writing Activity

Imagine that you are an economic adviser for a poor Southeast Asian country. Write a one-paragraph summary explaining how some countries in the region built stronger economies. Use the report to suggest policies your chosen country might adopt to build its economy. Be sure to use standard grammar, spelling, sentence structure, and punctuation.

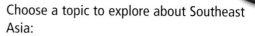

internet connect

Internet Activity: go.hrw.com
KEYWORD: SG5 GT29

Choose a topic to explore about Southeast Asia:

- Explore an Indonesian rain forest.
- Learn about shadow puppets.
- See buildings of Southeast Asia.

Social Studies Skills Practice

Interpreting Graphs

Study the graph below. Then answer the questions.

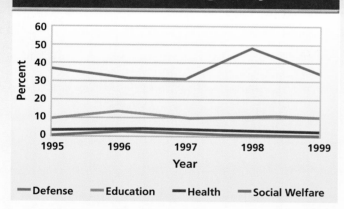

Government Spending in Myanmar

—Defense —Education —Health —Social Welfare

Source: International Monetary Fund

1. What four areas of government spending are shown in the graph?

2. In what two areas did government spending stay about the same?

3. In what area did the government spend the most? the least?

4. What percentage of government spending was devoted to defense during the period 1998–99?

Analyzing Primary Sources

Read the following quote by Cristina Pantoja-Hidalgo, a Filipino journalist who lived in Myanmar in the 1980s. Then answer the questions.

"Everything was available through the black market . . . But all these were underground. For example, if you owned a video shop, it was quite possible that the army would swoop upon you and would confiscate all your tapes. Burma is not as isolated as North Korea where the government is really efficient about keeping controls. The Burmese government cannot control the black market because of the common borders between India and Thailand . . . Thus, there's a great deal of smuggling."

1. What does Pantoja-Hidalgo mean by the term "black market"?

2. How did the government try to stop the black market?

3. Why was the government unable to control smuggling?

4. What country does Pantoja-Hidalgo say is more isolated than Burma?

ENVIRONMENT

Indonesia's Threatened Rain Forests

Why Are Rain Forests Important?

Do you know where bananas, pineapples, and oranges originally came from? Each of these plants first grew in a tropical rain forest.

Tropical rain forests are considered by many to be the most important forests in the world. It is estimated that about half of all species of plants, animals, and insects on Earth live in tropical rain forests. Rain forest trees and plants help maintain global temperatures. They also help hold rain-drenched soil in place. This prevents it from washing away and clogging rivers. About one fourth of all medicines currently found in drugstores come from tropical rain forests.

Tropical rain forests can be found in many countries along the equator and between about 20° north and south latitude. One of the largest rain forests is in Brazil's Amazon Basin. In Africa, rain forests are found in many countries, such as Gabon and the Democratic Republic of the Congo. In Southeast Asia, rain forests are found in countries such as Thailand, Vietnam, and Indonesia.

Deforestation in Indonesia

Indonesia has large areas of tropical rain forest in Borneo, Sumatra, and Irian Jaya. These areas are home to many unusual species of plants and animals. For example, the largest flower in the world, the *Rafflesia arnoldii*, is found there.

Indonesia's tropical rain forests are being rapidly cut down. About 4,700 square miles (12,170 sq km) of rain forest are lost each year. This rate of deforestation is second only to Brazil's. Some people have predicted that much of Indonesia's

▲
Found in the rain forests of Sumatra, the *Rafflesia arnoldii* is the largest known flower in the world. It can weigh up to 24 pounds (11 kg) and can measure about 3 feet (1 meter) across.

rain forests will be gone in just 10 years. When the rain forests are cleared, animals such as the endangered orangutan do not have a home.

There are many reasons that Indonesia's tropical rain forests are being cleared. Trees from tropical rain forests produce beautiful woods. They are used to make furniture, boats, and houses. The demand for special trees and wood has made logging a profitable business. Much of the logging is done by large corporations that do not replant the areas that are cut.

Deforestation in Indonesia also occurs because people need land to farm and raise animals. They also need wood for fuel. People clear the land using a method called slash-and-burn. Large trees are cut, or slashed, and left on the ground. Then the land is burned during the dry season. This clears the land of vegetation and prepares it for farming. In 1997 large areas of land in Indonesia were cleared. Huge fires burned out of control. The fires burned an area roughly the size of Denmark. Smoke filled the sky and caused some airplanes and ships to crash.

Protecting Indonesia's Rain Forests

Some people in Indonesia are trying to protect the rain forests. Parks and nature reserves have been set up that are off-limits to logging companies. Some groups are finding ways to earn money without cutting down trees. Selling fruits and nuts from the rain forest is one way. Also, international organizations such as the Rainforest Action Network are helping to protect the forests. Some environmental groups are even pressuring countries to stop buying trees that come from tropical rain forests.

▲

Much of the timber cut in Indonesia and other Southeast Asian countries is exported to Japan. Indonesia exports about 2 million tons of plywood and 145,000 tons of lumber to Japan each year.

◀

Orangutans live in the tropical rain forests of Borneo and Sumatra. Deforestation has seriously reduced their habitat. The word *orangutan* means "man of the forest."

Understanding What You Read

1. (*Human-Environment Interaction*) Why are Indonesia's tropical rain forests being cut down?

2. (*Human-Environment Interaction*) What is being done to protect Indonesia's tropical rain forests?

Geo SKILLS

Building Skills for Life: Interpreting Cultural Landscapes

Cultural landscapes are the forms put on the land by people. For example, buildings, field patterns, and roads are all a part of cultural landscapes. Cultural landscapes show a people's way of life.

Different cultures create distinctive cultural landscapes. For example, a village in China looks very different from a village in France. By comparing how the two villages look, we can begin to see how their cultures are different.

Geographers interpret cultural landscapes. They observe a landscape, describe what they see, and try to explain how it reflects the culture of the place. This is called reading the cultural landscape.

You can read cultural landscapes too. To read a cultural landscape, start by describing what you see. What kinds of buildings are there? What are they used for? What kinds of clothing are people wearing? Then, think about how what you see relates to the place's culture. What would it be like to live there? What do people there do for fun?

Cultural landscapes tell a story. By reading and interpreting these stories, you can learn a lot about people and geography.

Place Architecture is an important part of the cultural landscape at the Black Dragon Pool in southern China.

▼

THE SKILL

1. Try to read the cultural landscapes of your community. What forms have people put on the land? What do they tell you about the daily life of the people who live there?

2. Watch a television show or movie and interpret the cultural landscapes you see. What is distinctive about them? How are they different from the cultural landscapes you are used to? Can you guess where the program was filmed?

3. Look carefully at the pictures in a newspaper or magazine without reading the captions. Do the pictures tell a story? Is culture a part of this story?

HANDS on GEOGRAPHY

The photographs below show two very different cultural landscapes. What can these photographs tell us about each place's culture and way of life? Look closely at each photograph and then answer the Lab Report questions.

◄
~~~~~~
A cultural landscape in East Asia

▲
~~~~~~
A cultural landscape in Southeast Asia

Lab Report

1. What do these two photographs show? On a separate sheet of paper, write a short description of each photograph.

2. Do these two photographs tell you something about each place's culture and way of life? On a separate sheet of paper, describe what you think the culture of these two places is like.

3. Are there some things about a place's culture that you cannot learn from just looking at a photograph? What are they? If you took a trip to these two places, what else could you learn about their cultures?

UNIT 10

The Pacific World and Antarctica

CHAPTER 30
Australia and New Zealand

CHAPTER 31
The Pacific Islands and Antarctica

King penguins watching photographer, Antarctica

House in Sepik River area, Papua New Guinea

Teenagers of Melbourne, Australia

A Film Critic in New Zealand

David Gerstner is a film critic and lecturer from New York City. In 1999 he moved to New Zealand. He found the country was very different than he thought it would be. **WHAT DO YOU THINK?** *What do you know about New Zealand?*

Wellington, New Zealand

First I was surprised that New Zealand has such lively cities. I had thought it was all mountains and bush. I was also surprised by the laid-back New Zealand approach to personal interaction. Celebrities, politicians, and the "common folk" have an easier time getting together. For example, I have become friends with some of New Zealand's well-known filmmakers, writers, and fashion designers—all within a year. The social playing field is more level than in the United States.

In fact, a friend and I literally ran into Jenny Shipley, who was then New Zealand's Prime Minister, on a busy street in the capital, Wellington. She was with her daughter. There were no secret service guards with them—like there would be with the U.S. president. We even had our picture taken with her! The easy-going Kiwi style of security is refreshing. However, for a New Yorker it is sometimes unsettling.

Understanding Primary Sources

1. Why was David Gerstner surprised by New Zealand's cities?

2. What does this passage illustrate about New Zealand's culture?

Koalas

The Pacific World and Antarctica

Elevation Profile

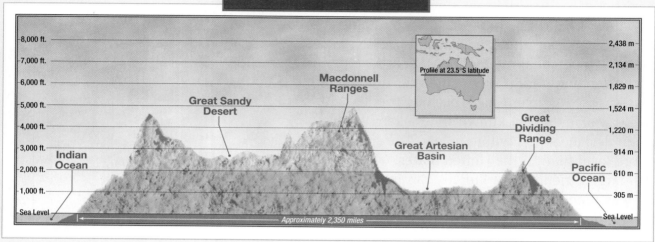

8,000 ft. — 2,438 m
7,000 ft. — 2,134 m
6,000 ft. — 1,829 m
5,000 ft. — 1,524 m
4,000 ft. — 1,220 m
3,000 ft. — 914 m
2,000 ft. — 610 m
1,000 ft. — 305 m
Sea Level — Sea Level

Profile at 23.5°S latitude

Great Sandy Desert
Macdonnell Ranges
Great Artesian Basin
Great Dividing Range
Indian Ocean
Pacific Ocean

Approximately 2,350 miles

The United States and the Pacific World and Antarctica: Comparing Sizes

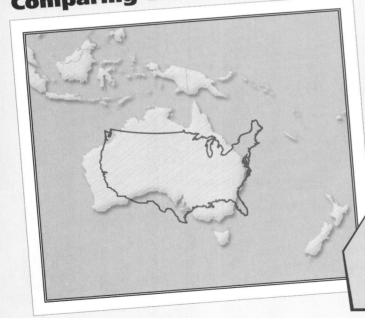

GEOSTATS:

Antarctica

World's highest, driest, coldest, and windiest continent

World's lowest recorded temperature: -129°F (-89.2°C) on July 21, 1983

Amount of the world's freshwater stored as ice in Antarctica: about 70 percent

Average thickness of ice: over 1 mile (1.6 km)

Highest mountain in Antarctica: Vinson Massif—16,066 ft. (4,897 m)

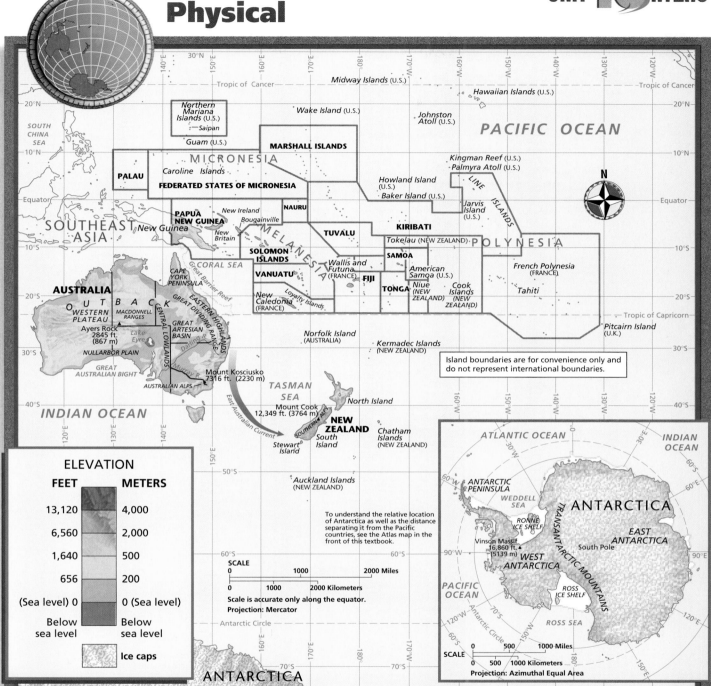

ELEVATION

FEET	METERS
13,120	4,000
6,560	2,000
1,640	500
656	200
(Sea level) 0	0 (Sea level)
Below sea level	Below sea level
	Ice caps

Island boundaries are for convenience only and do not represent international boundaries.

To understand the relative location of Antarctica as well as the distance separating it from the Pacific countries, see the Atlas map in the front of this textbook.

SCALE
0   1000   2000 Miles
0   1000   2000 Kilometers
Scale is accurate only along the equator.
Projection: Mercator

SCALE
0   500   1000 Miles
0   500   1000 Kilometers
Projection: Azimuthal Equal Area

1. (Place) What is the highest point in Australia? in the region?

2. (Location) About how far apart are Guam and Tahiti? New Zealand and Australia?

3. (Region) What physical features cover most of Australia?

Critical Thinking

4. (Region) Which country is more mountainous, Australia or New Zealand?

5. (Region) Compare this map to the **climate map** of the region. Which Australian mountain range seems to cause a rain-shadow effect?

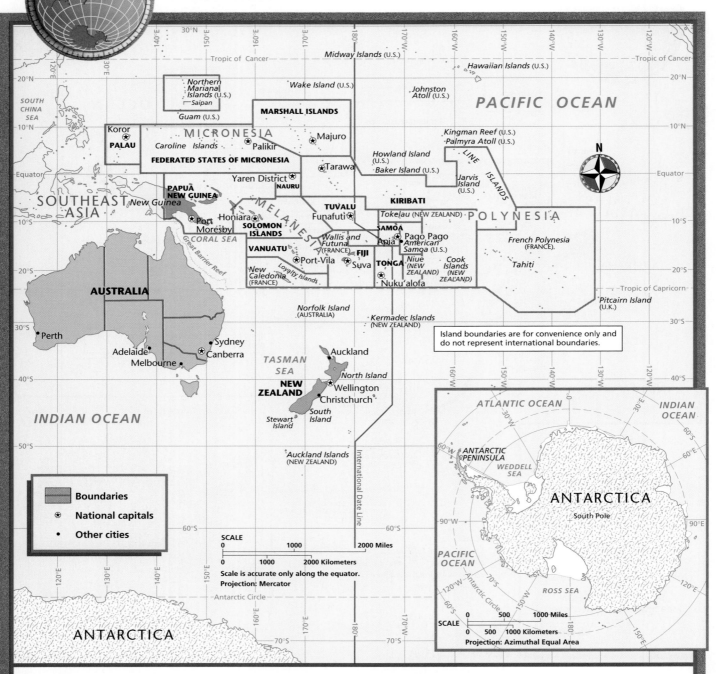

Island boundaries are for convenience only and do not represent international boundaries.

Legend:
- Boundaries
- ⊛ National capitals
- • Other cities

SCALE
0   1000   2000 Miles
0   1000   2000 Kilometers
Scale is accurate only along the equator.
Projection: Mercator

SCALE
0   500   1000 Miles
0   500   1000 Kilometers
Projection: Azimuthal Equal Area

1. (Location) Which country occupies half of a large island? Which country occupies two large islands?

2. (Location) What is the only country in the region that has a land boundary with another country?

Critical Thinking

3. (Region) What is one thing you can tell about governments in the region just by looking at the map?

4. (Region) Why do you think the international date line is not a straight line?

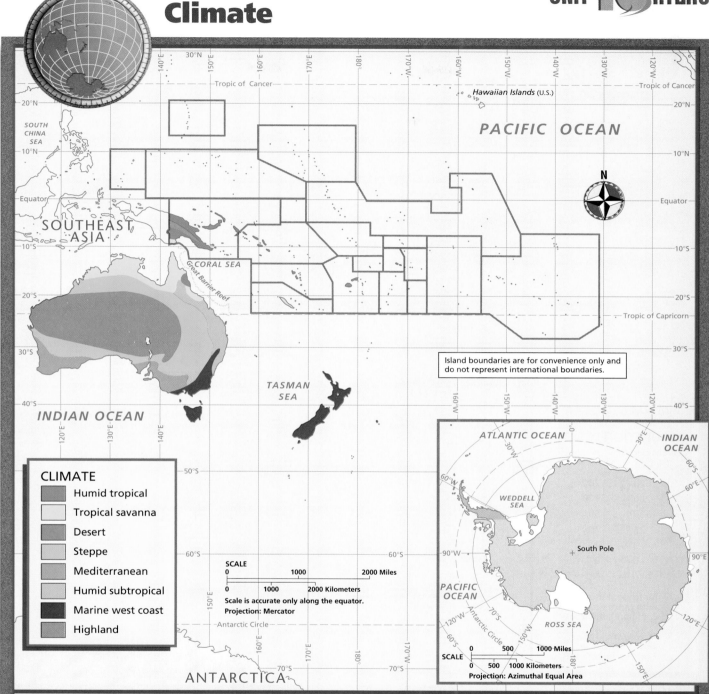

CLIMATE
- Humid tropical
- Tropical savanna
- Desert
- Steppe
- Mediterranean
- Humid subtropical
- Marine west coast
- Highland

Island boundaries are for convenience only and do not represent international boundaries.

SCALE
0   1000   2000 Miles
0   1000   2000 Kilometers
Scale is accurate only along the equator.
Projection: Mercator

SCALE
0   500   1000 Miles
0   500   1000 Kilometers
Projection: Azimuthal Equal Area

1. (Place) What type of climate does New Zealand have?

2. (Region) Which country has the greatest variety of climate types?

3. (Place) Compare this map to the **population map** of the region. What type of climate does Perth have?

Critical Thinking

4. (Region) Compare this map to the **physical map**. How might the East Australian Current affect New Zealand's weather?

5. (Human-Environment Interaction) How might climate affect Papua New Guinea's population patterns?

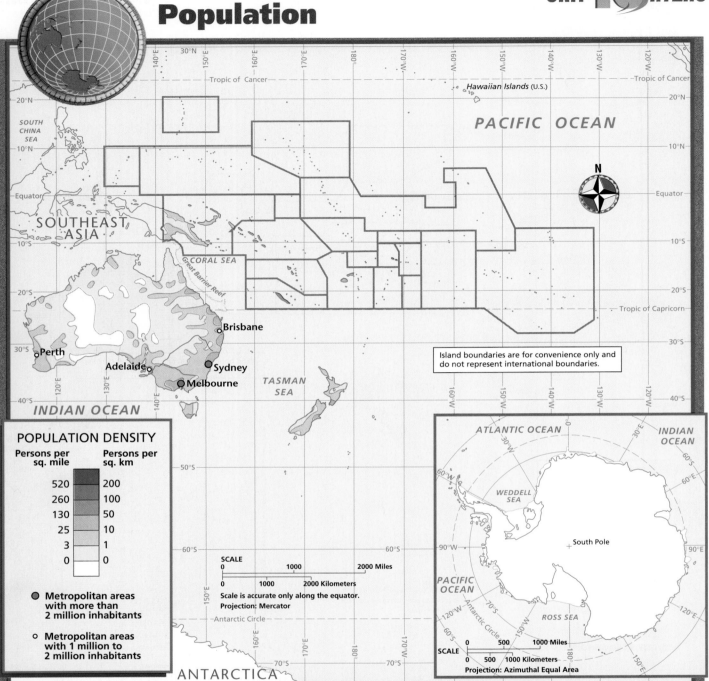

PACIFIC OCEAN

Hawaiian Islands (U.S.)

SOUTH CHINA SEA

SOUTHEAST ASIA

CORAL SEA

Great Barrier Reef

Brisbane

Perth

Adelaide

Sydney

Melbourne

TASMAN SEA

INDIAN OCEAN

Island boundaries are for convenience only and do not represent international boundaries.

POPULATION DENSITY

Persons per sq. mile	Persons per sq. km
520	200
260	100
130	50
25	10
3	1
0	0

● Metropolitan areas with more than 2 million inhabitants

○ Metropolitan areas with 1 million to 2 million inhabitants

SCALE
0   1000   2000 Miles
0   1000   2000 Kilometers
Scale is accurate only along the equator.
Projection: Mercator

Antarctic Circle

ANTARCTICA

ATLANTIC OCEAN   INDIAN OCEAN

WEDDELL SEA

South Pole

PACIFIC OCEAN

Antarctic Circle

ROSS SEA

SCALE
0   500   1000 Miles
0   500   1000 Kilometers
Projection: Azimuthal Equal Area

1. (Place) What is the only country with cities of over 2 million people?

2. (Region) What region of Australia has the highest population density?

3. (Location) Compare this map to the **physical map**. What is the densely populated island northwest of New Zealand?

Critical Thinking

4. (Region) What large landmass has no permanent population? Why?

5. (Region) From looking at this map, what is one thing that Australia and Antarctica have in common?

The Pacific World and Antarctica: Land Use and Resources

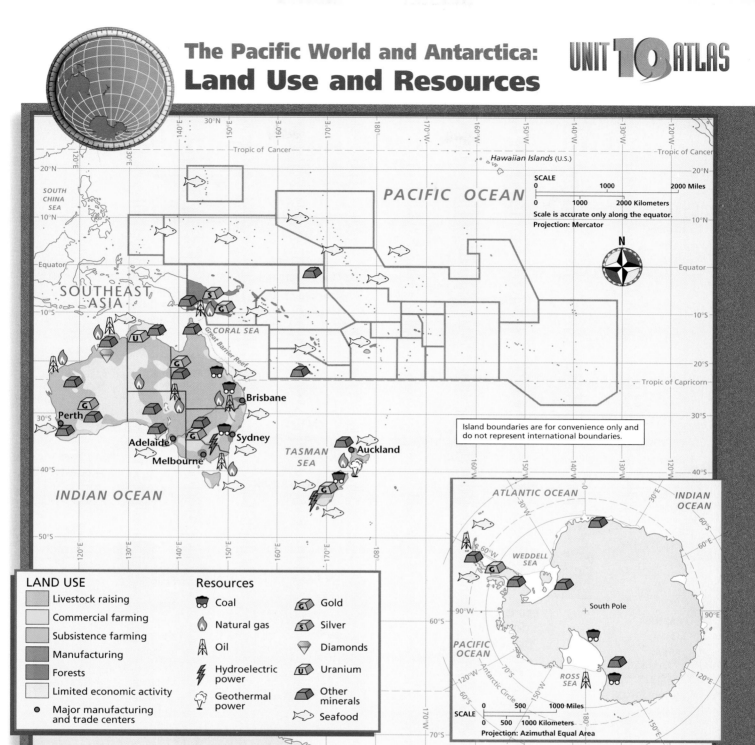

SCALE
0   1000   2000 Miles
0   1000   2000 Kilometers
Scale is accurate only along the equator.
Projection: Mercator

Island boundaries are for convenience only and do not represent international boundaries.

SCALE
0   500   1000 Miles
0   500   1000 Kilometers
Projection: Azimuthal Equal Area

LAND USE
- Livestock raising
- Commercial farming
- Subsistence farming
- Manufacturing
- Forests
- Limited economic activity
- ● Major manufacturing and trade centers

Resources
- Coal
- Natural gas
- Oil
- Hydroelectric power
- Geothermal power
- Gold
- Silver
- Diamonds
- Uranium
- Other minerals
- Seafood

1. (*Place*) What cities are part of Australia's major manufacturing and trade centers?

2. (*Human-Environment Interaction*) What resources are available in Papua New Guinea but not in Australia?

3. (*Human-Environment Interaction*) What is the main resource of most of the small Pacific islands?

Critical Thinking

4. (*Human-Environment Interaction*) Compare this map to the **physical** and **climate maps** of the region. Why would it be difficult to mine the mineral resources of Antarctica?

Fast FACTS

The Pacific World and Antarctica

Australia

CAPITAL:
Canberra

AREA:
2,967,893 sq. mi.
(7,686,850 sq km)

POPULATION:
19,731,984

MONEY:
Australian dollar

LANGUAGES:
English, ethnic languages

POPULATION AGED 0-14 YEARS:
20 percent

Marshall Islands

CAPITAL: Majuro

AREA: 70 sq. mi. (181.3 sq km)

POPULATION: 56,429

MONEY: United States dollar

LANGUAGES:
English (official), Marshallese dialects, Japanese

POPULATION AGED 0-14 YEARS: 39 percent

Federated States of Micronesia

CAPITAL: Palikir

AREA: 271 sq. mi. (702 sq km)

POPULATION: 108,143

MONEY:
United States dollar

LANGUAGES:
English (official), Trukese, Pohnpeian, Yapese, Kosrean

POPULATION AGED 0-14 YEARS: 38 percent

Nauru

CAPITAL:
no official capital

AREA:
8 sq. mi. (21 sq km)

POPULATION:
12,570

MONEY:
Australian dollar

LANGUAGES:
Nauruan (official), English

POPULATION AGED 0-14 YEARS:
40 percent

Fiji

CAPITAL:
Suva

AREA:
7,054 sq. mi.
(18,270 sq km)

POPULATION:
868,531

MONEY:
Fijian dollar

LANGUAGES:
English (official), Fijian, Hindustani

POPULATION AGED 0-14 YEARS:
32 percent

New Zealand

CAPITAL:
Wellington

AREA:
103,737 sq. mi.
(268,680 sq km)

POPULATION:
3,951,307

MONEY:
New Zealand dollar

LANGUAGES:
English (official), Maori

POPULATION AGED 0-14 YEARS:
22 percent

Kiribati

CAPITAL:
Tarawa

AREA:
277 sq. mi. (717 sq km)

POPULATION:
98,549

MONEY:
Australian dollar

LANGUAGES:
English (official), I-Kiribati

POPULATION AGED 0-14 YEARS:
40 percent

Palau

CAPITAL:
Koror

AREA:
177 sq. mi. (458 sq km)

POPULATION:
19,717

MONEY:
United States dollar

LANGUAGES:
English (official), Sonsorolese, Angaur, Japanese, Tobi, Palauan

POPULATION AGED 0-14 YEARS:
27 percent

Countries not drawn to scale.

PAPUA NEW GUINEA

CAPITAL:
Port Moresby

AREA:
178,703 sq. mi.
(462,840 sq km)

POPULATION: 5,295,816

MONEY: kina

LANGUAGES:
715 ethnic languages, pidgin English, English

POPULATION AGED 0-14 YEARS: 38 percent

SAMOA

CAPITAL:
Apia

AREA:
1,104 sq. mi. (2,860 sq km)

POPULATION:
178,173

MONEY:
tala

LANGUAGES:
Samoan (Polynesian), English

POPULATION AGED 0-14 YEARS:
29 percent

SOLOMON ISLANDS

CAPITAL:
Honiara

AREA:
10,985 sq. mi.
(28,450 sq km)

POPULATION:
509,190

MONEY:
Solomon Islands dollar

LANGUAGES:
Melanesian pidgin, 120 ethnic languages, English

POPULATION AGED 0-14 YEARS: 43 percent

TONGA

CAPITAL:
Nuku'alofa

AREA:
289 sq. mi.
(748 sq km)

POPULATION:
108,141

MONEY:
pa'anga

LANGUAGES:
Tongan, English

POPULATION AGED 0-14 YEARS:
38 percent

TUVALU

CAPITAL:
Funafuti

AREA:
10 sq. mi. (26 sq km)

POPULATION:
11,305

MONEY:
Tuvaluan dollar or Australian dollar

LANGUAGES:
Tuvaluan, English

POPULATION AGED 0-14 YEARS: 32 percent

VANUATU

CAPITAL:
Port-Vila

AREA:
4,710 sq. mi. (12,200 sq km)

POPULATION:
199,414

MONEY:
vatu

LANGUAGES:
English (official), French (official), pidgin (known as Bislama or Bichelama)

POPULATION AGED 0-14 YEARS: 35 percent

---

internet connect

COUNTRY STATISTICS
GO TO: go.hrw.com
KEYWORD: SG5 FactsU10
FOR: more facts about the Pacific World and Antarctica

Source: Central Intelligence Agency, *The World Factbook 2003;* pop. figures are 2003 estimates.

Australia and New Zealand

In this chapter we will study Australia and nearby New Zealand. First we meet Jared and Ashleigh. Their ancestors lived in Australia long before Europeans arrived.

Hi! My name is Jared. I have a twin sister, Ashleigh. We are 14 years old and live in Cooroy, Australia, which is about two hours north of Brisbane. We live with our mother in a three-bedroom house on a hill. Our land has a big creek with a dam on it. The dam forms a big pond, or a billabong. We can jump into it from the trees along the edge. Our father lives up north in the traditional lands of our people, the Djabugayndgi.

We used to speak our native language, but we've forgotten lots of it since we've been going to school. My totem, or special animal protector, is the *Ngumba,* or platypus. My sister's is the *Badgigal,* or freshwater turtle.

Since we were three years old, we have been singing and dancing in an Aboriginal dance group called *Bibayungen.* At Christmas, the whole family gathers with about 1,000 people in our traditional lands for a big dance and music festival (*warrima* in our language).

Nyurramba garran, bulmba nganydjin ngunda!

▲

Translation: Come and see our country!

Read to Discover

1. What are Australia's natural features and resources?
2. What is the history of Australia?
3. What is Australia like today?

Vocabulary

artesian wells
coral reef
endemic species
marsupials
outback
rugby
bush

Places

Eastern Highlands
Central Lowlands
Western Plateau
Great Dividing Range
Tasmania
Murray-Darling Rivers
Great Artesian Basin
Great Barrier Reef
Sydney
Melbourne
Brisbane
Perth

Reading Strategy

ANTICIPATING INFORMATION Before reading, predict whether you think the following statements are true or false.

- Australia is a mountainous continent with a cool climate.
- The seasons in Australia occur at the same time of year as those in the United States.
- Australia has a very mixed population.

Check your answers while reading. Then explain why each statement is true or false.

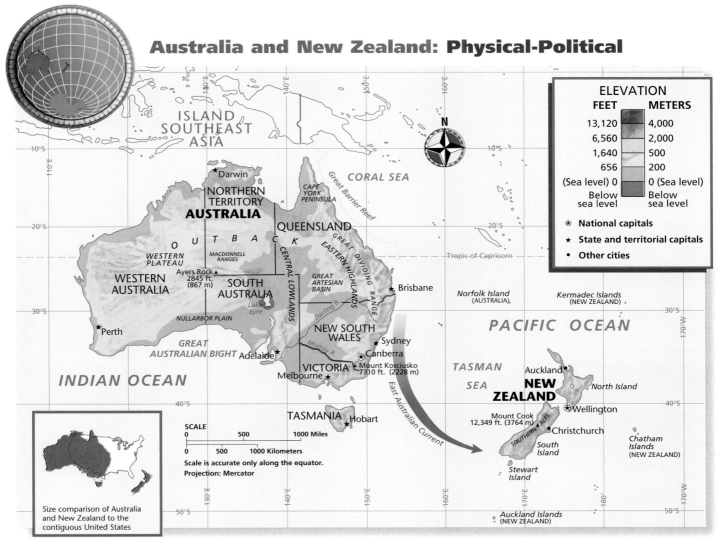

Australia and New Zealand: Physical-Political

ELEVATION

FEET		METERS
13,120		4,000
6,560		2,000
1,640		500
656		200
(Sea level) 0		0 (Sea level)
Below sea level		Below sea level

⊛ National capitals
★ State and territorial capitals
• Other cities

SCALE
0   500   1000 Miles
0   500   1000 Kilometers
Scale is accurate only along the equator.
Projection: Mercator

Size comparison of Australia and New Zealand to the contiguous United States

Natural Features

Australia is the world's smallest, flattest, and lowest continent. In addition, it is the only country that is also a continent. The country sometimes is called the Land Down Under because it lies south of the equator. Seasons there are reversed from those north of the equator. For example, when it is winter in the United States, it is summer in Australia.

Land Australia has three main landform regions. These are the Eastern Highlands, the Central Lowlands, and the Western Plateau.

The Eastern Highlands are a system of ridges, plateaus, and valleys in the eastern part of Australia. They include the Great Dividing Range. This range stretches along the eastern coast and includes the island of Tasmania. It divides Australia's rivers into those that flow eastward and those that flow westward. Australia's one major river system, the Murray-Darling, flows westward from the range.

Australia's highest mountain is in the Great Dividing Range. It rises to just 7,310 feet (2,228 m). This tells us that Australia is very old. Erosion from wind and water has lowered the continent's mountains over millions of years.

The Central Lowlands are flatter and lower than the Eastern Highlands. The Central Lowlands include the Great Artesian Basin, Australia's largest source of underground water. **Artesian wells** dot this area. Artesian wells are those in which water rises toward the surface without being pumped. The groundwater comes from rain falling on nearby mountains. As the amount of groundwater increases, some is pushed to the surface. Much of the well water here is of poor quality, so it is used mostly for watering sheep.

Our Amazing Planet

Ayers Rock in central Australia is composed of sandstone with bits of reflective minerals. The sandstone changes color as the Sun moves across the sky. At sunset Ayers Rock turns a fiery orange-red.

Ayers Rock, called Uluru by Aborigines, rises more than 1,100 feet (335 m) above the surrounding Western Plateau. It is all that is left after erosion wore away an ancient mountain.

Interpreting the Visual Record **How has erosion affected Ayers Rock?**

Australia
Ayers Rock

The Great Barrier Reef is really thousands of small reefs and tiny islands. Some rise barely above water level when the tide is low.

Farther west is the Western Plateau, which covers more than half of the continent. The treeless Nullarbor Plain stretches along the southern edge of the plateau. This plain is the flattest large area on any continent.

The Great Barrier Reef Off the northeastern coast of Australia is the Great Barrier Reef. It is the world's largest **coral reef**, stretching more than 1,250 miles (2,000 km). A coral reef is a ridge found close to shore in warm, tropical waters. It is made of rocky limestone material formed by the skeletons of tiny sea animals. You will read more about coral reefs in the next chapter.

The Great Barrier Reef and its shallow waters are home to many kinds of marine animals. They include fish, shellfish, and sea birds. Australia's government has made most of the reef a national park.

Climate Australia has been described as a desert with green edges. Dry desert and steppe climates cover most of the country. The eastern and southeastern edges and Tasmania have humid climates. Two coastal areas in the south and southwest have a Mediterranean climate. Summers there are long, dry, and sunny. Winters are mild and wet. The north has a tropical savanna climate. There monsoons bring strong wet and dry seasons.

Plants and Animals Australia has many **endemic species**. Endemic species are plants and animals that developed in one particular region of the world. Why does Australia have many endemic species? Australia has been separated from other continents for millions of years. However, over time many nonnative plants and animals have been brought to Australia. See the Case Study in this chapter.

Our Amazing Planet

The shallow ocean waters along Australia's northern coast are home to the deadly sea wasp jellyfish. Each jellyfish has as many as 60 tentacles that hang down six and a half feet (2 m). The venom from its sting can kill a human in less than five minutes.

CONNECTING TO *Literature*

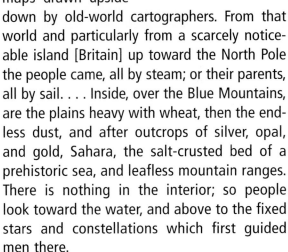

Christmas on an Australian beach

THE LAND DOWN UNDER

Europeans began settling in Australia in the late 1700s. The following selection describes what settlers found in the Land Down Under. The selection comes from Christina Stead's For Love Alone, *published in 1944.*

In the part of the world Teresa came from, winter is in July, spring brides marry in September, and Christmas is consummated[1] with roast beef [and] suckling[2] pig . . . at 100 degrees in the shade, near the tall pine tree loaded with gifts and tinsel as in the old country, and old carols have rung out all through the night.

This island continent lies in the water hemisphere. On the eastern coast, the neighboring nation is Chile, though it is far, far east, Valparaiso being more than six thousand miles away in a straight line; her northern neighbors are those of the Timor Sea, the Yellow Sea; to the south is that cold, stormy sea full of earth-wide rollers, which stretches from there without land, south to the Pole.

The other world—the old world, the land [Northern] hemisphere—is far above her as it is shown on maps drawn upside-down by old-world cartographers. From that world and particularly from a scarcely noticeable island [Britain] up toward the North Pole the people came, all by steam; or their parents, all by sail. . . . Inside, over the Blue Mountains, are the plains heavy with wheat, then the endless dust, and after outcrops of silver, opal, and gold, Sahara, the salt-crusted bed of a prehistoric sea, and leafless mountain ranges. There is nothing in the interior; so people look toward the water, and above to the fixed stars and constellations which first guided men there.

Analyzing Primary Sources

1. How does life differ from that in the "old world" in Teresa's land?
2. How does the writer give the reader a sense of Australia's isolation?

[1]consummated: completed, marked, or celebrated; [2]suckling: a young mammal that is still nursing

Two of Australia's most famous native animals are the kangaroo and the koala. Both animals are **marsupials** (mahr-SOO-pee-uhls). Marsupials are animals that carry their young in pouches. Eucalyptus (yoo-kuh-LIP-tuhs) is Australia's most common tree.

Minerals Australia's **outback**, or inland region, has many mineral resources such as gold, iron ore, and bauxite. Australia also has coal, natural gas, oil, and gemstones such as opals and diamonds.

✓ **READING CHECK:** (*Places and Regions*) What are the natural features of Australia?

A bark painting provides a glimpse of some Aborigines' spiritual beliefs. The painting shows the path taken by a soul on its journey to another world. Traditional Aboriginal culture almost disappeared after Europeans arrived in Australia.

History

The first humans to live in Australia were the Aborigines (a-buh-RIJ-uh-nees). They came from Southeast Asia at least 40,000 years ago. Early Aborigines hunted animals and gathered food from wild plants. They had many different languages, traditions, and customs. The arrival of Europeans changed life for the Aborigines.

European Settlers The British began settling colonies in Australia in 1788. Many of the first settlers were British prisoners, but other British settlers came, too. As the settlers built farms and ranches, they took over the Aborigines' lands. In addition, many Aborigines died of diseases brought unintentionally by the Europeans.

Independence The British granted independence to the Australian colonies in 1901. The colonies were united into one country within the British Commonwealth of Nations. Australia fought on the side of the British and other Allied forces in World Wars I and II.

Today Australia has six states and one large territory. The national capital is Canberra. Because Australia is part of the Commonwealth, the British monarch also is Australia's monarch. However, a prime minister and parliament make Australia's laws. Some Australians want their country to leave the Commonwealth and replace the monarch with an Australian president or other official.

✓ **READING CHECK:** (*Movement*) How has migration affected Australia's history?

States and Territories of Australia

State	Capital
New South Wales	Sydney
Victoria	Melbourne
Queensland	Brisbane
Western Australia	Perth
South Australia	Adelaide
Tasmania	Hobart

Territory	Capital
Northern Territory	Darwin
Australian Capital Territory	Canberra

Interpreting the Chart What is the capital of Tasmania?

Culture

More than 90 percent of Australians today are of British or other European ancestry. Since the 1970s Asians have been moving to

▲ The Sydney Opera House opened on the city's harbor front in 1973. It is one of Australia's most well-known buildings.

Australia in growing numbers. As a result, about 7 percent of Australia's population today is ethnic Asian. Only about 1 percent of the country's people are Aborigines. Nearly all Australians speak English, but some Aborigines also speak native languages.

Religion and Holidays Most Australians are Christians. They celebrate many of the same holidays as people in the United States. However, their traditions may be different. For example, December falls during summer in Australia. Christmas there is time for a beach party, picnic, or some other outdoor activity.

Outdoor activities are popular in sunny Australia. Many people enjoy picnics, swimming, and sports. Popular sports include the British game of cricket, sailing, horse racing, surfing, and Australian Rules football. Many Australians also enjoy **rugby**. Rugby is a British game similar to football and soccer.

The Arts Music and other arts are also popular in Australia. In fact, art by Aborigines has become popular around the world. The Australian government is an important source of money for the arts. For example, the government has built many public performance halls. One of the most famous is the Opera House in Australia's largest city, Sydney.

✓ **READING CHECK:** (*Human Systems*) What are some characteristics of Australia's people?

Australia

Country	Population/ Growth Rate	Life Expectancy	Literacy Rate	Per Capita GDP
Australia	19,731,984 0.9%	77, male 83, female	100%	$27,000
United States	290,342,554 0.9%	74, male 80, female	97%	$37,600

Source: Central Intelligence Agency, *The World Factbook 2003*

Interpreting the Chart How does Australia's literacy rate compare to that of the United States?

Australia Today

About 85 percent of Australians live in and around cities. The rest live in the **bush**, or lightly populated wilderness areas. The largest cities are Sydney and Melbourne in the southeast. Brisbane, on the eastern coast, enjoys a warm, tropical climate that attracts tourists. Towns have grown around mining and ranching areas in parts of the dry, rugged outback. Large parts of the interior have few people. The seaport of Perth is the largest city in the west.

Economy Australia is a rich, economically developed country. It is a leading producer of agricultural goods such as wool, meat, and wheat. Australia supplies nearly half of the world's wool used in clothing. One of the country's most important industries is mining, particularly in the outback. Other industries include steel, heavy machines, and computers.

Challenges Australia faces important challenges. Among these is improving the economic and political status of the Aborigines. They have only recently gained back some of the rights they lost after Europeans colonized Australia. The country also must continue to build ties with Asian and Pacific countries. At one time Australia's strongest ties were with Britain. Today, its most important trading partners are much closer Asian countries and the United States. In addition, Australia must deal with the rapid growth of its cities. It also must protect native animals and the environment.

✔ **READING CHECK:** (*Places and Regions*) What is Australia's economy like?

Major Producers of Wool

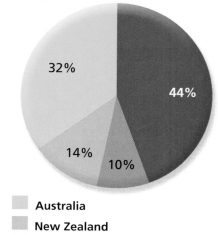

32%

44%

14%

10%

- Australia
- New Zealand
- China
- Rest of the world

Source: Based on data from The Woolmark Company

▲

Wool is produced from sheep's hair. Australia has one of the world's largest flocks of sheep.

Interpreting the Chart What nearby country is the world's second-largest wool producer?

Section Review 1

Define and explain: artesian wells, coral reef, endemic species, marsupials, outback, rugby, bush

Working with Sketch Maps On a map of Australia and New Zealand that you draw or that your teacher provides, label the following: Eastern Highlands, Central Lowlands, Western Plateau, Great Dividing Range, Tasmania, Murray-Darling Rivers, Great Artesian Basin, Great Barrier Reef, Sydney, Melbourne, Brisbane, and Perth. In a box in the margin, describe why the Great Artesian Basin is important to a dry country like Australia.

Reading for the Main Idea

1. (*Human Systems*) How has migration affected Australia's population? Which ethnic group is the largest?

2. (*Places and Regions*) What are two of Australia's most famous native marsupials?

3. (*Human Systems*) Who were the first humans to live in Australia? When did Europeans start settling there?

Critical Thinking

4. Drawing Inferences and Conclusions Why is building ties with Asian countries important for Australia today?

Organizing What You Know

5. Categorizing Copy the following graphic organizer. Use it to list Australia's climates, plants and animals, and mineral resources.

Climates	Plants and Animals	Resources

Homework Practice Online
go.hrw.com
Keyword: SG5 HP30

CASE STUDY

NONNATIVE SPECIES IN AUSTRALIA

For about the last 35 million years, Australia has been separated from the other continents by oceans. During this time Australia's plants and animals developed in isolation from the rest of the world. Eventually, a unique Australian ecosystem developed. Many interesting species of plants and animals existed only in Australia. For example, kangaroos, koalas, and eucalyptus trees were all native to Australia. They were not found anywhere else in the world.

Europeans arrived in Australia in the late 1700s. They dramatically changed the natural balance that had developed over millions of years.

Europeans brought with them many new species of plants and animals. These nonnative species have had a major impact on the environment in Australia.

European settlers turned large areas of grasslands into fields for agriculture. They set up huge wheat farms in the south and southwest. They planted sugarcane fields in the northeast. These crops had never been grown in Australia. Farmers also brought nonnative animals, such as sheep, cows, and goats, into Australia. In less than 100 years, Australia had more than 100 million sheep and 8 million cows.

Cattle are herded on the island of Tasmania in Australia.

Interpreting the Visual Record Can you see how these animals are changing the environment?

Introduced into Australia from Southeast Asia, water buffalo now eat food that Australia's native animals need to survive.

When Europeans settled in Australia they brought with them many new plants and animals. Some of these plants and animals have become pests because they damage the environment.

Many of the nonnative species that were brought into Australia spread across the continent. Some are now considered pests. These plants and animals are seriously damaging Australia's environment. For example, camels were introduced into Australia as pack animals. Now they run wild in the desert interior. Water buffalo were introduced from Southeast Asia. They trample riverbanks, killing grasses and eroding the soil. The prickly pear cactus was introduced into Australia from the United States as a garden plant. It spread across much of the country and has been very hard to control. Cane toads were introduced in the 1930s to protect Australia's sugarcane fields from cane beetles. However, they release toxic chemicals when attacked and are now threatening native species and household pets.

Of the nonnative animals introduced into Australia, rabbits have probably been the most destructive. Brought in by hunters in the 1800s, rabbits multiplied and spread quickly. With no natural predators and lots of food, their numbers increased to about 500 million. Rabbits overgrazed Australia's grasslands and caused major soil erosion.

The introduction of nonnative species into Australia has damaged the environment in several ways. Some native species have become extinct because they could not compete with nonnative species. About 13 species of mammals and one species of bird have become extinct in Australia since the late 1700s. Many more are endangered. Nonnative species such as cows, sheep, and rabbits have caused soil erosion. These animals also consume food and water that Australia's native plants and animals need to survive. As the case of Australia shows, the introduction of nonnative species into a new environment can cause serious environmental problems.

Understanding What You Read

1. How did isolation affect Australia's ecosystem?

2. What are some of the species that Europeans brought with them to Australia? How does Australia's environment now reflect their influence?

Discover

1. What are the natural features of New Zealand?
2. What are the history and culture of New Zealand?
3. What are New Zealand's cities and economy like today?

Vocabulary

kiwi

Places

Tasman Sea
South Island
North Island
Southern Alps

Wellington
Auckland
Christchurch

Reading Strategy

TAKING NOTES Taking notes while you read will help you understand and remember the information in this section. Write down the headings in the section. As you read, fill in notes under each heading. What are the most important details under each?

Natural Features

New Zealand lies southeast of Australia across the Tasman Sea. It includes two large islands—South Island and North Island. Put together, the islands are about the size of the U.S. state of Colorado.

Land The highest mountains are the Southern Alps on South Island. These rugged, glacier-capped mountains cover the western half of the island. The highest peak reaches 12,349 feet (3,764 m). A narrow coastal plain stretches along South Island's eastern side.

North Island has three major volcanic peaks separated by a volcanic plateau. Volcanic eruptions are common. Most of the rest of North Island is covered by hills and coastal plains.

The Southern Alps stretch across much of New Zealand's South Island. New Zealand's government has established large national parks throughout the mountains.

Australia
New Zealand

Autumn turns South Island's countryside golden near the city of Christchurch. New Zealand has four distinct seasons.

Climate, Wildlife, and Resources Unlike mostly dry Australia, New Zealand is humid. It has a mild marine west coast climate. Rain falls throughout the year. Winds from the west bring very heavy rain or snow to South Island's western side. The grassy plains of the drier eastern side are in a rain shadow. The north of North Island, in the lower latitudes, has a warmer, more tropical climate.

Much of New Zealand was once forested. Today, more than half is covered by pastures and farms. Sheep and other livestock graze in New Zealand's pastures. Sheep and their wool have long been important to the country's economy.

As in Australia, many animals in New Zealand are endemic species. The country's endemic species include different kinds of bats and flightless birds such as the **kiwi** (KEE-wee). The kiwi has hairlike feathers and sharp senses of smell and hearing. This bird is so linked with the country that New Zealanders are sometimes called Kiwis.

Many other species have been brought to New Zealand over time. For example, deer and trout have been introduced to provide sport for hunters and fishers.

New Zealand has fewer mineral resources than Australia. Its natural resources include gold, iron ore, natural gas, and coal.

✓ **READING CHECK:** (*Place*) What are the natural features of New Zealand?

Maori traditional art, like this carved entrance arch, survived New Zealand's colonial period.
Interpreting the Visual Record **What role does art play in Maori culture?**

▼

History and Culture

New Zealand's first settlers came from other Pacific islands more than 1,000 years ago. Their descendants, the Maori (MOWR-ee), still live in New Zealand. The early settlers' main source of food was the moa—a giant, flightless bird. However, overhunting by New Zealand's early peoples wiped out the moa. The bird was extinct by the time Europeans arrived in New Zealand.

New Zealand's All Black Rugby Union team performs a version of the Haka (HAH-kah) before international games. The Haka is a traditional Maori dance.

European Settlers A Dutch explorer in 1642 was the first European to sight New Zealand. British explorer Captain James Cook visited New Zealand in 1769. Many British settlers started to arrive after the British signed a treaty with the Maori in 1840. However, fighting broke out as British settlers took over Maori lands.

Independence The British granted New Zealand independence in 1907. Like Australia, New Zealand became a member of the British Commonwealth of Nations. New Zealanders fought alongside the British in World Wars I and II.

The government of New Zealand is led by a prime minister. An elected parliament makes the country's laws. The capital, Wellington, is located at the southern tip of North Island.

Culture Like Australia, most of New Zealand's 3.9 million people are of European ancestry. A growing number of ethnic Asians also live in the country. The Maori make up nearly 10 percent of the population. People from other Pacific islands have also come to New Zealand.

Most New Zealanders speak English. Some Maori also speak the Maori language. Most New Zealanders also are Christian. Sports, particularly rugby, are popular.

Maori culture has not disappeared. Traditional art, music, and dance remain important in Maori culture. Many Maori weddings, funerals, and other special events still are held in traditional carved houses. The Maori call these meetinghouses *whare whakairo*. Many meetinghouses are beautifully carved and decorated.

Mourners attend a funeral in a Maori-carved meeting house.

✓ **READING CHECK:** (*Human Systems*) How have conflict and cooperation affected the history of New Zealand?

New Zealand Today

Today about 75 percent of New Zealanders, including most Maori, live on North Island. Most of the country's industries and agriculture are also located there.

Cities About 85 percent of New Zealanders live in urban areas. The country's largest city and seaport, Auckland, is located in the northern part of North Island. Christchurch is South Island's largest city.

Economy New Zealand is a rich, modern country with a market economy. Its mild, moist climate helped make agriculture an important part of the economy. The country is a major producer of wool, meat, dairy products, wheat, kiwifruit, and apples.

New Zealand has become more industrialized in recent years. Factories turn out processed food, wood, paper products, clothing, and machinery. Banking, insurance, and tourism are also important industries. Australia, the United States, Japan, and the United Kingdom are the country's main trade partners.

✔ **READING CHECK:** (*Place*) What are some of New Zealand's cities, and what is its economy like?

Cable cars provide transportation for residents and visitors in Wellington.

New Zealand

COUNTRY	POPULATION/ GROWTH RATE	LIFE EXPECTANCY	LITERACY RATE	PER CAPITA GDP
New Zealand	3,951,307 1.1%	75, male 81, female	99%	$20,200
United States	290,342,554 0.9%	74, male 80, female	97%	$37,600

Source: Central Intelligence Agency, *The World Factbook 2003*

Homework Practice Online
Keyword: SG5 HP30

Section Review 2

Define and explain: kiwi

Working with Sketch Maps On the map you created in Section 1, label the Tasman Sea, South Island, North Island, Southern Alps, Wellington, Auckland, and Christchurch. In a box in the margin, identify New Zealand's capital and the country's largest city.

Reading for the Main Idea

1. (**Human Systems**) From where did the ancestors of the Maori come?

2. (**Human Systems**) Describe New Zealand's economy. How has it changed in recent years?

Critical Thinking

3. **Contrasting** How is the physical geography of North Island different from that of South Island? Describe the physical geography of each island.

4. **Drawing Inferences and Conclusions** Why do you think most New Zealanders live on North Island?

Organizing What You Know

5. **Summarizing** Copy the following graphic organizer. Use it to list the climates, plants and animals, and resources of New Zealand.

Climates	Plants and Animals	Resources

CHAPTER 30

Review and Practice

Define and Identify

Identify each of the following:

1. artesian wells
2. coral reef
3. endemic species
4. marsupials
5. outback
6. rugby
7. bush
8. kiwi

Review the Main Ideas

9. What are the three main landform regions of Australia?

10. What are the climates of the interior and the "edges" of Australia like?

11. New Zealand's North Island is known for what type of landform?

12. When did Europeans begin to settle in Australia and New Zealand?

13. What native peoples lived in Australia and New Zealand before the arrival of Europeans?

14. Australia and New Zealand are the world's two top producers of what agricultural product?

15. What country is a major trading partner with both Australia and New Zealand?

Think Critically

16. **Drawing Inferences and Conclusions** Why do you think the Great Barrier Reef would interest tourists?

17. **Drawing Inferences and Conclusions** Why do you think Australia's interior is lightly populated?

18. **Finding the Main Idea** How have humans changed the natural environments of Australia and New Zealand since the arrival of Europeans?

19. **Contrasting** How is New Zealand's climate different from Australia's? Identify the main climates in each country.

20. **Analyzing Information** What role have the arts played in Australian society?

21. **Drawing Inferences and Conclusions** How have the Maori in New Zealand kept their traditional culture?

Map Activity

22. On a separate sheet of paper, match the letters on the map with their correct labels.

Central Lowlands	Sydney
Western Plateau	Melbourne
Tasmania	Perth
Great Barrier Reef	Auckland

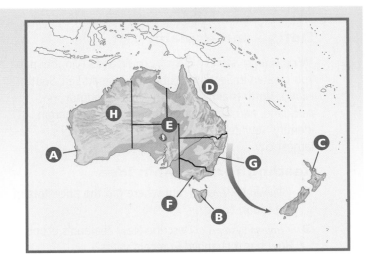

Writing Activity

Imagine that you are a European journalist in the late 1700s writing about the peoples and unique plants and animals in Australia and New Zealand. Write two paragraphs describing those peoples and endemic species. Include details that might surprise your European readers. Be sure to use standard grammar, spelling, sentence structure, and punctuation.

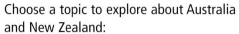

internet connect

Internet Activity: **go.hrw.com**
KEYWORD: SG5 GT30

Choose a topic to explore about Australia and New Zealand:

- Explore the Great Barrier Reef.
- Learn about the Aborigines of Australia.
- Tour New Zealand.

Social Studies Skills Practice

Interpreting Maps

Study the following map of some of Australia's cities. Then answer the questions.

1. What is the capital city of Australia?
2. What key characteristic can you determine about most of the cities in Australia?
3. Which city is located near the Great Barrier Reef?
4. Which city is far from a water source?

Analyzing Primary Sources

Read the following excerpt from the 1840 treaty between the Maori and the British government. Then answer the questions.

"Victoria, the Queen of England, in her concern to protect the chiefs and the subtribes of New Zealand and in her desire to preserve their chieftainship [trusteeship] and their lands and to maintain peace and good order considers it just to appoint [select] an administrator—one who will negotiate with the people of New Zealand to the end that their chiefs will agree to the Queen's government being established over all parts of this land . . ."

1. Does the treaty promise that the Maori will have an equal say in their government?
2. What will be the main role of the administrator?
3. Does the Queen express a desire to protect the Maori under her leadership? How?
4. What is the final goal of the treaty?

The Pacific Islands and Antarctica

In this chapter we will study the Pacific Islands and Antarctica, two very different regions.

My name is Jean Vanessa, and I am 13 years old. I live in Vabukori, a village in Port Moresby, the capital of Papua New Guinea. My mother is a journalist. My grandmother bakes our bread in a drum oven. Sometimes we sell the bread.

My house is built on stilts. It is near the village square where we have meetings and play sports. After breakfast, I take a bus to Port Moresby Grammar School. I make my own sandwiches to take for lunch.

In my society, when you are an eldest child and a girl, and if you have younger brothers and sisters, you are your mother's helper. You have to learn to cook, clean, and take care of younger children.

My favorite holidays are Christmas and New Year's. We celebrate with feasting and singing. The villagers are divided into two groups. On Christmas Day one group cooks for the other group. They sing prophet songs about Bible stories from dawn to dusk. On New Year's Day the groups exchange roles.

Daba namona!

Translation: Good morning!

Section 1 Physical Geography

Read to Discover

1. What are the physical features and resources of the Pacific Islands?
2. What are the physical features and resources of Antarctica?

Vocabulary

ice shelf
icebergs
polar desert
krill

Places

Melanesia
Micronesia
Polynesia
Tahiti
New Guinea
Papua New Guinea
Marshall Islands

New Caledonia
Transantarctic Mountains
Vinson Massif
Antarctic Peninsula

Reading Strategy

VISUALIZING INFORMATION Previewing the visuals in this section will help you understand the material you are about to read. What do the visuals on this page and the next two pages tell you about the regions you are studying? Write your answers on a sheet of paper.

The Formation of an Atoll

A A coral reef forms along the edges of a volcanic island.

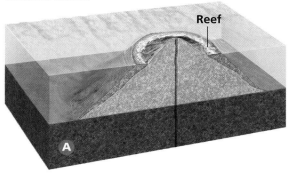

B As the island sinks into the ocean, the reef continues to grow upward. It forms a barrier reef.

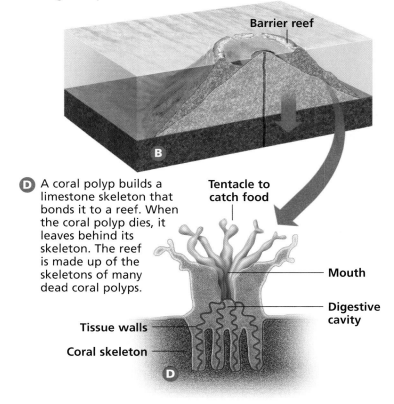

C When the island is completely underwater, the reef forms an atoll. In the middle of the ring of islands is a lagoon.

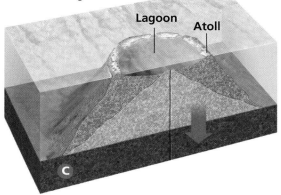

D A coral polyp builds a limestone skeleton that bonds it to a reef. When the coral polyp dies, it leaves behind its skeleton. The reef is made up of the skeletons of many dead coral polyps.

Tentacle to catch food
Mouth
Digestive cavity
Tissue walls
Coral skeleton

Place The airport on the left supports a healthy tourism industry in Bora-Bora, French Polynesia

The Pacific Islands

The Pacific Ocean covers more than one third of Earth's surface. East of Indonesia and the Philippines are thousands of large and small islands. These islands are divided into three regions: Melanesia, Micronesia, and Polynesia. These regions have high and low islands. Now we will look at these islands, their climates, and their resources.

High Islands There are two kinds of high islands: oceanic and continental. Oceanic high islands were formed by volcanoes rising from the sea floor. The Polynesian islands of Tahiti and Hawaii are examples of oceanic high islands. Many continental high islands also have volcanoes. However, these large islands were formed from continental rock. They lie on Australia's continental shelf. New Guinea, which is in Melanesia, is a continental high island.

New Guinea is the world's second-largest island. Only Greenland is larger. A long mountain chain stretches across the central part of New Guinea. The range's highest mountain lies in the western half of the island. It reaches an elevation of 16,535 feet (5,040 m). The western part of New Guinea is called Irian Jaya and is part of Indonesia. Papua New Guinea occupies the eastern half of the island.

Low Islands Most of the low islands are made of coral. They barely rise above sea level. Many are atolls. For example, the Marshall Islands include two parallel chains of coral atolls. The two chains are about 800 miles (1,287 km) long. The highest point is just 33 feet (10 m) above sea level. Measured from the ground to their roofs, many buildings in your town are probably higher!

Climates and Plants Most of the Pacific Islands lie in the tropics and have a humid tropical climate. The temperatures are warm, and rain is common all year. New Guinea's central highland regions are cooler. Rainfall there is heavy, particularly on the southern slopes of the highlands. In some years more than 300 inches (762 cm) of rain fall there. Some islands, such as New Caledonia, have a tropical savanna climate. Rain there falls mostly in the summer.

The low islands have thin soils. These islands support few trees other than the coconut palm. However, the high islands have dense tropical rain forests. In fact, Papua New Guinea is one of the world's most densely forested countries. Many peoples living in the forests and rugged mountains of the central highlands were isolated for centuries.

Resources The islands' natural beauty and pleasant climates attract many tourists. In addition, the high islands have freshwater, good soils, and forest resources. Continental high islands also have many minerals. For example, New Guinea has copper, gold, silver, and oil. However, mining these resources is difficult in the rugged highlands and dense tropical forests.

Low islands have few resources. There is little freshwater, and thin soils limit farming. Partly because of this, low islands have smaller populations than high islands. Coconut palms and the sea are important sources of food.

✓ **READING CHECK:** (**Places and Regions**) What are the physical features and resources of the Pacific Islands?

☑ internet connect

GO TO: **go.hrw.com**
KEYWORD: **SG5 CH31**
FOR: **Web sites about the Pacific Islands and Antarctica**

(*Place*) Miners search for gold along a river in Papua New Guinea. They gently wash river water over pans to separate gold particles from less dense sand.

Huge icebergs like this one are found in the ocean waters around Antarctica. Icebergs are most numerous in the spring and summer. The warmer weather causes more ice to break away from ice sheets and glaciers.

Interpreting the Visual Record **What forces do you think shaped this iceberg?**

Antarctica

In the southernmost part of the world is the continent of Antarctica. This frozen land is very different from the tropical Pacific Islands.

The Land Antarctica is larger than the United States and Mexico combined. Ice covers about 98 percent of Antarctica's 5.4 million square miles (14 mil sq km). This ice sheet contains more than 90 percent of the world's ice. On average the ice sheet is more than one mile (1.6 km) thick.

The Transantarctic Mountains divide the continent into East Antarctica and West Antarctica. Antarctica's highest mountain peak is Vinson Massif. It rises to 16,864 feet (5,140 m). The continent also includes a few dry coastal valleys and the Antarctic Peninsula. (See the map of Antarctica in Focus On Environment at the end of this chapter.)

The weight of Antarctica's ice sheet causes the ice to flow slowly off the continent. When the ice reaches the coast, it forms a ledge over the water. This ledge is called an **ice shelf**. Sometimes huge chunks of ice, called **icebergs**, break away and drift into the ocean. Some of these icebergs are larger than the state of Rhode Island.

Climate and Wildlife Antarctica is the planet's coldest, driest, highest, and windiest continent. During the Southern Hemisphere's winter, the continent is hidden from the Sun. It remains in total darkness. During Antarctica's short summer, the Sun never sets.

Antarctica's temperatures can drop below -120°F (-84°C). Less precipitation falls in this polar desert than in the Sahara in Africa. A **polar desert** is a high-latitude region that receives little precipitation. However, there is almost no evaporation or melting of ice. As a result, Antarctica's ice has built up over thousands of years.

The continent's warmest temperatures are found on the Antarctic Peninsula, which has a tundra climate. In January, during Antarctica's summer, temperatures on the coast average just below freezing.

Only tundra plant life survives in the rare ice-free areas. A few insects are the frozen land's only land animals. Antarctica has never had a permanent human population. Marine animals live in the icy waters around the continent. These animals include penguins, seals, and whales. They depend on tiny shrimplike creatures called **krill** for food.

The emperor penguin is one of the most common marine animals found in Antarctica. Penguins are flightless birds and are awkward on land. However, they are very good swimmers and are able to live in the icy climate.

Resources Antarctica has many mineral resources, including iron ore, gold, copper, and coal. However, there is debate over whether these resources should be mined. Some people worry that mining would harm the continent's environment. Others question whether mining in Antarctica would even be worthwhile for businesses.

✓ **READING CHECK:** (*Places and Regions*) What are the physical features and resources of Antarctica?

Homework Practice Online
Keyword: SG5 HP31

Define and explain: ice shelf, icebergs, polar desert, krill

Working with Sketch Maps On maps of the Pacific Islands and Antarctica that you draw or that your teacher provides, label the following: Melanesia, Micronesia, Polynesia, Tahiti, New Guinea, Papua New Guinea, Marshall Islands, New Caledonia, Transantarctic Mountains, Vinson Massif, and Antarctic Peninsula.

Reading for the Main Idea

1. (*Places and Regions*) What kinds of islands are found in the Pacific? How were they formed?

2. (*Places and Regions*) What animal life is found in Antarctica?

3. (*Places and Regions*) Which of the Pacific Islands is the second-largest island in the world?

Critical Thinking

4. Making Generalizations and Predictions What might happen if people were to begin mining Antarctica's mineral deposits on a large scale?

Organizing What You Know

5. Summarizing Copy the following graphic organizer. Use it to list physical features, climates, and resources of the Pacific Islands and Antarctica.

	Pacific Islands	Antarctica
Physical features		
Climates		
Resources		

Read to Discover

1. What is the history of the Pacific Islands?
2. What are the people and culture of the Pacific Islands like?
3. What are some challenges that Pacific Islanders face today?

Vocabulary

trust territories
Exclusive Economic Zones

Places

Guam
Northern Mariana Islands
Wake Island
French Polynesia

People

James Cook

Reading Strategy

DEVELOPING VOCABULARY Find unfamiliar words in this section. On a sheet of paper, write down what you think they might mean. Then look the words up in a dictionary. How do the words relate to the section's topics?

This map of the South Pacific was made by a European cartographer in 1798.

Interpreting the Visual Record

Compare this map to the unit map. How accurate was this 1798 map?

History

Scholars believe that people began settling the Pacific Islands at least 40,000 years ago. Most early settlers came from Southeast Asia. The large islands of Melanesia were the first islands in the region settled. Over time, people moved to the islands of Micronesia and Polynesia.

Europeans in the Pacific In the early 1500s Ferdinand Magellan became the first European to explore the Pacific. In the late 1700s British captain James Cook explored the region. He visited all the main island regions of the Pacific. By the late 1800s European countries controlled most of the Pacific Islands. These European countries included France, Germany, the Netherlands, Spain, and the United Kingdom.

Modern History The Pacific Islands were battlegrounds during several wars in the colonial era. For example, the Spanish-American War of 1898 cost Spain the Philippines and Guam. They became U.S. territories after the war. Spain then sold other island territories to Germany. After World War I ended in 1918, Japan took over Germany's territories in the Pacific.

Japan conquered many other islands in World War II. The United States and its allies eventually won them back and defeated Japan. The United Nations then made some islands **trust territories**. Trust territories are areas placed under the temporary control of another country. When the territory later sets up its own government, it gains independence. U.S. trust territories included much of Micronesia.

Most of the island countries won independence in the last half of the 1900s. Australia, France, New Zealand, the United Kingdom, and the United States still have Pacific territories. U.S. territories include the Northern Mariana Islands, Guam, and Wake Island.

✓ **READING CHECK:** (*Places and Regions*) What are some events in the history of the Pacific Islands?

Culture

About 7 million people live in Melanesia, Micronesia, and Polynesia today. Check the unit map as we look more closely at each region and its people.

Melanesia Melanesia stretches from New Guinea to Fiji. It is the most populous of the three Pacific Island regions. Papua New Guinea and Fiji have the largest populations. Nearly two thirds of all Pacific Islanders live in Papua New Guinea.

Most Melanesians live in rural areas. Many homes in Melanesia and the other regions are made of timber and thatch, or straw. Papua New Guinea's capital, Port Moresby, is Melanesia's largest city. Nearly 260,000 people live there.

Melanesia's population includes ethnic Europeans and Asians, particularly Indians and Chinese. Many ethnic Asians are descended from people brought to the islands to work on colonial plantations. In Fiji, Indians make up nearly half of the population.

Either English or French is the official language on nearly all of the islands. This is a reflection of the region's colonial history. However, hundreds of local languages also are spoken there. In fact, about 700 languages are spoken in New Guinea alone. Many Papua New Guineans live in rugged, forested areas. They have had little contact with people from other areas. These isolated peoples developed their own languages.

Europeans brought Christianity to Melanesia and the other island regions. Today, most Pacific Islanders are Christian. However, some Melanesians still practice traditional local religions.

Micronesia and Polynesia Micronesia includes more than 2,000 tiny islands north of Melanesia. It stretches from Palau in the west to Kiribati in the east. Polynesia is the largest Pacific region. Its

▲

Students learn the day's lessons at a school in Papua New Guinea. Papua New Guinea's government has struggled to make education available for all students. Many countries in Micronesia and Polynesia offer schooling for students through high school.

FOCUS ON CULTURE

Playing with the Rules

People of the South Pacific have made interesting changes to some European sports. Missionaries brought cricket, an English bat-and-ball game, to the Trobriand Islands east of New Guinea. The islanders changed cricket into more of a ritual. They added costumes, chants, and dances. They also changed almost all the rules. Up to 60 men play on a team. A regular cricket team has only 11 members. These huge matches may go on for weeks. A special dance and song celebrates each point. Even the game's basic movements are different. Players throw the ball as if they are throwing spears.

Pacific Islanders also enjoy other unusual sports. Outrigger canoe racing, underwater spearfishing, and coconut tree climbing are all popular sporting events.

Why do you think the Trobriand Islanders changed the rules for playing cricket?

corners at New Zealand, Hawaii, and Easter Island form a huge triangle.

The populations of most Micronesian and Polynesian islands are much smaller than those of Melanesia. However, towns on these small islands can be very crowded. Micronesia is the most urban of the Pacific Island regions. Most Polynesians live in rural areas.

As in Melanesia, ethnic Europeans and Asians live in Micronesia and Polynesia. Most people in these regions are Christian and speak either English or French. Some speak local languages or Japanese.

✓ **READING CHECK:** (*Human Systems*) What are some characteristics of the people and cultures of Melanesia, Micronesia, and Polynesia?

The Pacific Islands Today

Many people imagine sunny beaches and tourists when they think of the Pacific Islands today. The islands do attract many tourists. For example, Tahiti, in French Polynesia, is a popular vacation spot. Many vacationers from South Korea and Japan enjoy visiting Guam, in Micronesia. Despite the region's healthy tourism industry, however, the Pacific countries face important challenges.

Economy The Pacific Islands are trying to build stronger economies. Tourism, agriculture, and fishing are already important there. Some countries, particularly Papua New Guinea, export valuable minerals and forest products.

Each Pacific country claims control of the fishing and seabed minerals around its islands. The 200-nautical-mile (370 km) zones they claim are called **Exclusive Economic Zones** (EEZs). Most of the world's countries also claim EEZs. A country must pay fees to fish or mine in another country's EEZ.

Natural resources should help the island economies grow. However, many Pacific countries import more products from abroad than they export. Many countries rely on the United Nations, the European Union, Great Britain, Australia, and Japan for economic aid.

Environment Many Pacific Islanders are concerned about their region's environment. Many have been angered by nuclear weapons tests conducted in the region by other countries. The United States held such tests in the islands from the 1940s to the 1960s. Radiation left some islands unsafe for people for many years. France held nuclear tests in the region until the mid-1990s.

Pacific Islands				
COUNTRY	POPULATION/ GROWTH RATE	LIFE EXPECTANCY	LITERACY RATE	PER CAPITA GDP
Fiji	868,531 1.4%	66, male 71, female	93%	$5,500
Kiribati	98,549 2.3%	57, male 64, female	Not available	$840
Marshall Islands	56,429 2.3%	67, male 71, female	93%	$1,600
Micronesia, Federated States of	108,143 0.4%	67, male 70, female	89%	$2,000
Nauru	12,570 2.0%	58, male 65, female	Not available	$5,000
Palau	19,717 1.7%	66, male 72, female	92%	$9,000
Papua New Guinea	5,295,816 2.3%	62, male 66, female	66%	$2,300
Samoa	178,173 −0.2%	67, male 73, female	99%	$5,600
Solomon Islands	509,190 3.0%	69, male 74, female	Not available	$1,700
Tonga	108,141 1.9%	66, male 71, female	99%	$2,200
Tuvalu	11,305 1.4%	65, male 69, female	Not available	$1,100
Vanuatu	199,413 1.6%	60, male 63, female	53%	$2,900
United States	290,342,554 0.9%	74, male 80, female	97%	$37,600

Source: Central Intelligence Agency, *The World Factbook 2003*

Interpreting the Chart What is the literacy rate like in most of the Pacific Islands?

A fisher casts his net along the coast of New Caledonia.

▶

Place This Fijian chief's home has many traditional handicrafts. Fiji's Great Council of Chiefs has influence in the country's political system and culture.

Some people who live on islands still controlled by foreign countries want independence, which has led to outbreaks of violence. This happened in the 1980s in the French territory of New Caledonia. France has agreed to give New Caledonians more control over their local government.

Culture Many Pacific Islanders are also concerned about the loss of traditional customs and beliefs. Modern travel and communications have introduced influences from other regions. Islanders worry about the cultural effects of tourism, television, processed food, and alcohol.

✓ **READING CHECK:** *Human Systems* What are some challenges Pacific Islanders face today?

Homework Practice Online
Keyword: SG5 HP31

Section Review 2

Define or identify: James Cook, trust territories, Exclusive Economic Zones

Working with Sketch Maps On the map of the Pacific Islands that you created in Section 1, label the region's countries. Then label the territories of Guam, Northern Mariana Islands, Wake Island, and French Polynesia.

Reading for the Main Idea

1. *Human Systems* From where did the Pacific Islands' first settlers come? Which Pacific Island region was settled first?

2. *Human Systems* What colonial powers once controlled most of the Pacific Islands?

Critical Thinking

3. **Finding the Main Idea** In what ways did Europeans influence the islands' cultures?

4. **Finding the Main Idea** What are some of the challenges facing Pacific Islanders today?

Organizing What You Know

5. **Sequencing** Use this time line to explain important people and events in the region's history.

1500   2000

Early Explorers

Can you imagine a time when a large continent like Antarctica was a complete mystery? Today, orbiting satellites give us views of all of Earth's surface. Jet airliners and modern ships take people to all points on the globe. However, all of this has become possible only in the last century. For a long time, stormy ocean waters hid Antarctica from explorers. In the 1770s British explorer James Cook sighted icebergs in the waters around Antarctica. These icebergs suggested the existence of the vast, icy continent.

Other explorers followed. Some died in Antarctica's dangerous conditions while attempting to reach the South Pole and return. The huts of famous Antarctic explorers are still scattered across the continent. The first human expedition reached the South Pole in 1911.

Some countries have claimed parts of Antarctica. These countries and others agreed in 1959 to preserve the continent "for science and peace." The Antarctic Treaty of 1959 prevented more claims to the continent. It banned military activity there and set aside the whole continent for research.

✓ **READING CHECK:** *Environment and Society* How did the physical environment affect early efforts to explore Antarctica?

BIOGRAPHY

Sir Ernest Shackleton
(1874–1922)

Character Trait: Responsibility

In 1914, Ernest Shackleton and his crew of 27 men set out to be the first to cross the entire Antarctic continent. But their ship, *Endurance*, became completely frozen in ice. Using their ship's rescue boats, Shackleton and his crew sailed to a nearby deserted island. Shackleton then decided to sail another 800 miles to reach help on South Georgia Island. After surviving the dangerous journey, Shackleton then led four expeditions to rescue the rest of his crew.

What actions did Shackleton take to demonstrate responsibility?

Researchers are conducting experiments in icy waters off the coast of Antarctica.

Interpreting the Visual Record **What might these underwater researchers be trying to learn?**

Research in Antarctica

Today, researchers are the only people who live in Antarctica. They live in a number of bases or stations. U.S. stations include Palmer, on the Antarctic Peninsula, and McMurdo, on the Ross Ice Shelf. The United States also maintains a base at the South Pole. Researchers at these bases are looking for clues to Earth's past and future.

Air Pollution The researchers have made important discoveries. For example, some have studied gases trapped in old Antarctic ice. They have compared these gases with gases in Earth's atmosphere today. Their studies have shown that carbon dioxide levels in the air have risen over time. Some scientists believe high levels of carbon dioxide are responsible for global warming.

Scientists are also looking for evidence that air pollution is damaging Earth's ozone layer. The ozone layer protects living things from the harmful effects of the Sun's ultraviolet rays. Scientists have found a thinning in the ozone layer above Antarctica.

Life Other research helps us understand mysteries of life on Earth. For example, researchers have studied a kind of fish that produces a natural **antifreeze**. Antifreeze is a substance added to liquid to keep the liquid from turning to ice. Natural antifreeze in their blood protects the fish in the icy waters around Antarctica. These fish may help us understand how some animals adapt to harsh environments.

✓ **READING CHECK:** (*Environment and Society*) What can research in Antarctica tell us about our planet?

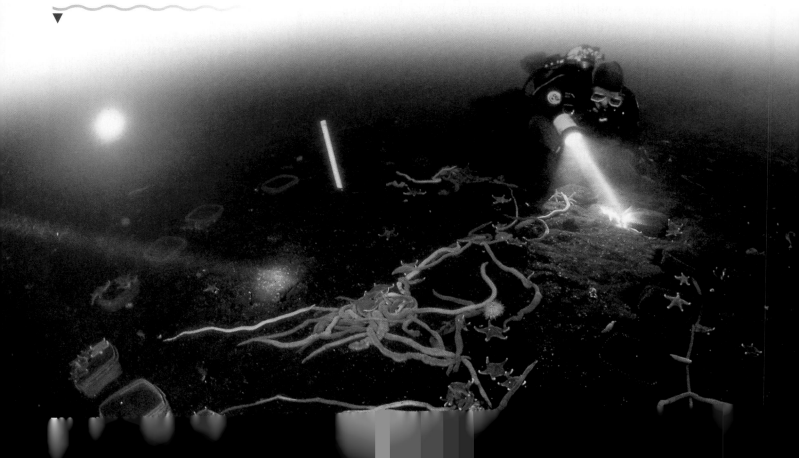

Cruise ships allow tourists to witness the icy beauty of Antarctica. About 10,000 tourists visit Antarctica during the summer months. A typical tourist trip lasts about two weeks. The only other economic activity in the region involves offshore fishing.

Interpreting the Visual Record

 Movement What potential hazards do you see for ships?

Environmental Threats

Antarctica's environment is an excellent place for research. This is because humans have disturbed little of the continent. That is changing, however. As you have read, there is already debate about whether to allow mining in Antarctica. In addition, tourists and even researchers have left behind trash, polluting the local environment. Oil spills have also caused problems.

Some people fear that mining Antarctica's resources will result in other spills and problems. To prevent this, a new international agreement was reached in 1991. This agreement forbids most activities in Antarctica that do not have a scientific purpose. It bans mining and drilling and limits tourism.

✓ **READING CHECK:** Environment and Society What are some of the problems threatening Antarctica's environment?

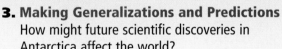
Homework Practice Online
Keyword: SG5 HP31

Define or identify: Ernest Shackleton, antifreeze

Working with Sketch Maps On the map of Antarctica you created in Section 1, label the South Pole and Ross Ice Shelf.

Reading for the Main Idea

1. (Human Systems) Who were the first Antarctic explorers to reach the South Pole, and when did they do so?

2. (Environment and Society) What did the 1959 Antarctic Treaty do? Why do you think this kind of agreement has not been made about other places on Earth?

Critical Thinking

3. **Making Generalizations and Predictions** How might future scientific discoveries in Antarctica affect the world?

4. **Finding the Main Idea** Why did many countries in 1991 agree to ban mining and to limit tourism in Antarctica?

Organizing What You Know

5. **Summarizing** Copy the following graphic organizer. Use it to describe research in Antarctica.

Research	Purpose

Review and Practice

Define and Identify

Identify each of the following:

1. ice shelf
2. icebergs
3. polar desert
4. krill
5. James Cook
6. trust territories
7. Exclusive Economic Zones
8. Ernest Shackleton
9. antifreeze

Review the Main Ideas

10. What are the three Pacific Island regions?
11. How are oceanic high islands and low islands formed?
12. Why is Antarctica covered in ice and snow even though it receives little precipitation?
13. Where are dense tropical forests found in the Pacific Islands? What trees grow on low islands?
14. Who were the first Europeans to explore the Pacific region?
15. What happened in the Pacific Islands during World War II?
16. Why are so many languages spoken by the people of Papua New Guinea?

17. Which of the Pacific Islands regions is the most urban?
18. What agreements have been made to protect Antarctica's environment?

Think Critically

19. **Drawing Inferences and Conclusions** Why would the Pacific Island countries want to keep their 200-nautical-mile Exclusive Economic Zones?
20. **Finding the Main Idea** How have Europeans influenced the languages and religions of the Pacific Islands?
21. **Understanding Cause and Effect** What could happen to the economies of the Pacific Islands countries if there is a sharp increase in the cost of airline tickets?
22. **Drawing Inferences and Conclusions** Why do you think some Pacific Islanders would not welcome the construction of a new resort even though it creates many new jobs?
23. **Making Generalizations and Predictions** Why would pollution threaten the value of research done in Antarctica?

Map Activity

24. Identify the places marked on the map.

Papua New Guinea	Guam
Fiji	French Polynesia
Marshall Islands	Palau
New Caledonia	Solomon Islands

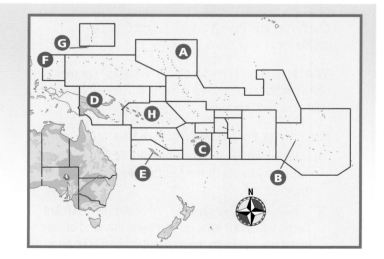

Writing Activity

Imagine that you are one of the first explorers trying to reach the South Pole. Write journal entries in which you describe what you have seen. Describe the conditions you have endured and the strategies you have used to survive. Use your textbook, the library, and the Internet to help you write your journal entries. Be sure to use standard grammar, spelling, sentence structure, and punctuation.

internet connect

Internet Activity: go.hrw.com
KEYWORD: SG5 GT31

Choose a topic to explore about the Pacific Islands and Antarctica.
- Tour the Pacific Islands.
- Explore Antarctica.
- Learn about native traditions.

Social Studies Skills Practice

Interpreting Charts

Study the chart below. Then answer the questions.

Tourism in the Pacific Islands

Country	Visitors in 2000	Visitors in 2001
Fiji	294,070	348,014
Palau	57,732	54,111
Papua New Guinea	63,448	54,235
Samoa	87,666	88,263
Solomon Islands	5,965	3,418
Tonga	34,694	32,386
Vanuatu	57,364	53,203

Source: *The Travel Industry World Yearbook 2002*

1. Which country received the most visitors in 2000? Which received the fewest?
2. Which countries experienced an increase in visitors in 2001? Which had a decrease?
3. Which country experienced more than a 40 percent decline in the number of visitors between 2000 and 2001?
4. What event took place in 2001 that might have caused many people to stay at home rather than visit another country?

Analyzing Primary Sources

Read the following quote by explorer Captain James Cook, who described the South Pacific islands that he visited. Then answer the questions.

". . . they struck into a road leading into the Country . . . several other Roads from different parts joined into this, some equally as broad and others narrower, the most of them shaded from the Scorching Sun by fruit trees. I thought I was transported into one of the most fertile plains in Europe, here was not an inch of waste ground, the roads occupied no more space than was absolutely necessary and each fence did not take up above 4 inches and even this was not wholly lost for in many of the fences were planted fruit trees and the Cloth plant, these served as support for them . . ."

1. What can you learn about the climate from Cook's account?
2. Based on your knowledge of Cook, why do you think he compared this island to Europe?
3. What conclusions can you draw about the island's economy at the time of Cook's visit?
4. What aspect of the islanders' farms impressed Cook the most?

FOCUS ON ENVIRONMENT

Preserving Antarctica

In 1912 a search party in Antarctica found the body of explorer Robert Falcon Scott. Scott had written in his diary, "Great God, what an awful place this is." He had dreamed of being the first person to reach the South Pole. However, when Scott's party arrived they found the tent and flag of Norwegian explorer Roald Amundsen. Amundsen had arrived five weeks earlier.

Almost a century later, Antarctica's modern-day explorers are research scientists. Antarctica has provided a location for international scientific research and cooperation.

A Scientific Laboratory

A wasteland to many, Antarctica is a scientific laboratory to some. Studying the continent helps scientists understand our planet. For example, the icy waters around Antarctica move north, cooling warmer waters. This movement affects ocean currents, clouds, and weather patterns. The world's climate is also affected by Antarctic sea ice. The ice acts as a shield. It keeps Earth cool by reflecting the Sun's heat energy.

Antarctic ice also provides information about the past. Buried deep within the ice are gas bubbles that are a record of Earth's air. Scientists have compared atmospheric gases trapped in Antarctic ice with atmospheric gases of today. They learned that the use of fossil fuels has raised the amount of carbon dioxide in the air. Carbon dioxide levels are now the highest in human history.

Eyes on Antarctica

Antarctica is not owned by any single country. Some countries claim parts of Antarctica, but these claims are not recognized. In 1959 the Antarctic Treaty established Antarctica as a continent for

How Antarctic Ice Affects Climate

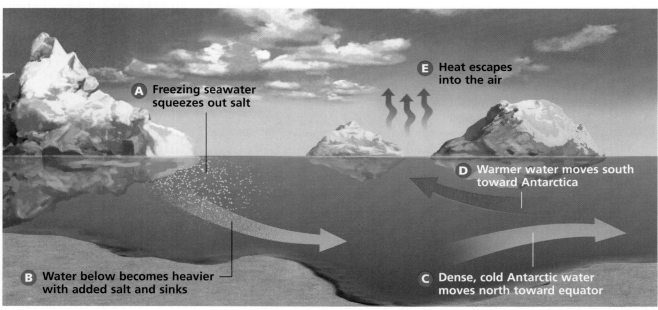

A Freezing seawater squeezes out salt

B Water below becomes heavier with added salt and sinks

C Dense, cold Antarctic water moves north toward equator

D Warmer water moves south toward Antarctica

E Heat escapes into the air

science and peace. The treaty was originally signed by 12 countries and was later agreed to by more than a dozen others. The Antarctic Treaty banned military activity in the region. It also made Antarctica a nuclear-free zone and encouraged scientific research.

However, the Antarctic Treaty did not cover mining rights on the continent. When Antarctica's mineral riches were discovered, some countries wanted rights to this new source of wealth. Geographers, scientists, and environmentalists also took notice. They feared that if mining took place, Antarctica's environment would suffer. In particular, they feared that a practical method of obtaining the offshore oil would be found. Antarctica's coastline and marine life could then be threatened by oil spills.

At the same time, evidence of environmental neglect at some of Antarctica's research stations appeared. Environmentalists voiced concern about scientists' careless disposal of trash and sewage. A U.S. Coast Guard captain who worked on icebreakers described pollution at McMurdo, a U.S. research station. "Trash was just rolled down the hill. . . . One of the jobs of the icebreakers was to break up the ice where the

Antarctica

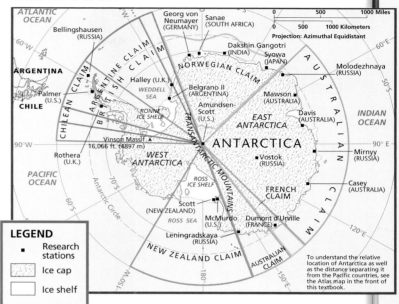

trash was and push it out to sea." In 1989, an Argentine ship ran aground in Antarctica, spilling thousands of gallons of oil. As a result, environmental concerns for the region increased.

Protecting Antarctica

In 1991, the countries that had signed the original Antarctic Treaty signed a new agreement called the Madrid Protocol. It forbids most activities on Antarctica that do not have a scientific purpose. It also bans mining and drilling and sets limits on tourism. Pollution concerns are addressed specifically.

In 50 years the agreement can be changed if enough of the signing countries agree. Then it becomes the responsibility of another generation to preserve Antarctica.

▲
Many countries have set up research stations and bases in Antarctica, such as Argentina's Camara Base on Half Moon Island.

Imagine you are helping to develop the Madrid Protocol.

1. Write a short description of the provisions you want included in the treaty.

2. Be sure to explain why you think these provisions are important.

Building Skills for Life: Making Decisions about Local Environmental Problems

Florida has named the manatee, or sea cow, its official marine mammal. The state's manatees are endangered, however. Sometimes boats hit or cut the slow-moving animals. Other dangers are pollution and fishing nets. The air-breathing animals can get tangled in the nets and drown. Some manatees get caught in underwater gates.

Imagine that you are on a committee that must decide how to protect the manatees of a coastal Florida town. How will your committee make a decision?

THE SKILL

1. **Define the problem.** First, gather information. Read printed and Internet reports. Interview environmental experts. Then narrow down the problem. For example, you may find that all the local manatee deaths were caused by boats leaving a marina.

2. **List alternatives.** Now that you have defined the problem, create possible solutions for it. Would it help to put up more signs warning boaters about the manatees? Are there ways to keep the manatees away from the marina's entrance?

3. **State the criteria.** Decide on the criteria you will use to evaluate the alternatives. For example, will you choose a plan that offers a quick solution? Is low cost more important? Maybe neither cost nor speed is as important as the solution's total success.

4. **Evaluate alternatives.** Now, evaluate your alternatives in terms of these criteria. Perhaps the committee members think that speed— doing something now!—is more important than anything else. You may find that only one plan can be started quickly.

5. **Make the decision.** Put your plan into action! Follow through and keep track of your progress. What you learn could be useful in the future.

HANDS on GEOGRAPHY

Everglades National Park in southern Florida is a beautiful wilderness with many rare plants and animals. Many of those species are now threatened with extinction. Why is this happening?

Almost 1,000 people move to Florida every day! Almost 40 million people vacation in the state every year. With more people come more roads, shopping malls, and houses. Open land has also been turned into ranches, vegetable farms, and orange groves. Developments like these take away land from wilderness areas, including the Everglades. However, rare animals that live in the Everglades, such as the Florida panther, need plenty of room to survive.

Imagine that you are an expert on the Florida panther. A town at the edge of the Everglades has asked for your help in deciding whether to allow construction of a new mall there because panthers have been seen in the area. Use the decision-making process to outline a plan for your recommendation.

Lab Report

1. What kinds of information will you need to have before you can list alternatives to solve the problem?

2. Which criteria will you use?

3. How do the alternatives fit the criteria?

FOLDNOTES APPENDIX

FoldNote Instructions

Have you ever tried to study for a test or quiz but didn't know where to start? Or have you read a chapter and found that you can remember only a few ideas? Well, FoldNotes are a fun and exciting way to help you learn and remember the ideas you encounter as you read!

FoldNotes are tools that you can use to organize concepts. By focusing on a few main concepts, FoldNotes help you learn and remember how the concepts fit together. They can help you see the "big picture." Below you will find instructions for building 10 different FoldNotes.

Pyramid

1. Place a sheet of paper in front of you. Fold the lower left-hand corner of the paper diagonally to the opposite edge of the paper.

2. Cut off the tab of paper created by the fold (at the top).

3. Open the paper so that it is a square. Fold the lower right-hand corner of the paper diagonally to the opposite corner to form a triangle.

4. Open the paper. The creases of the two folds will have created an X.

5. Using scissors, cut along one of the creases. Start from any corner, and stop at the center point to create two flaps. Use tape or glue to attach one of the flaps on top of the other flap.

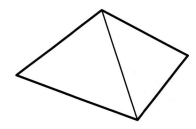

Double Door

1. Fold a sheet of paper in half from the top to the bottom. Then, unfold the paper.

2. Fold the top and bottom edges of the paper to the crease.

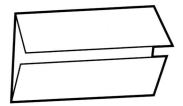

Booklet

1. Fold a sheet of paper in half from left to right. Then, unfold the paper.

2. Fold the sheet of paper in half again from the top to the bottom. Then, unfold the paper.

3. Refold the sheet of paper in half from left to right.

4. Fold the top and bottom edges to the center crease.

5. Completely unfold the paper.

6. Refold the paper from top to bottom.

7. Using scissors, cut a slit along the center crease of the sheet from the folded edge to the creases made in step 4. Do not cut the entire sheet in half.

8. Fold the sheet of paper in half from left to right. While holding the bottom and top edges of the paper, push the bottom and top edges together so that the center collapses at the center slit. Fold the four flaps to form a four-page book.

Layered Book

1. Lay one sheet of paper on top of another sheet. Slide the top sheet up so that 2 cm of the bottom sheet is showing.

2. Hold the two sheets together, fold down the top of the two sheets so that you see four 2 cm tabs along the bottom.

3. Using a stapler, staple the top of the FoldNote.

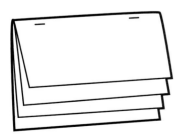

Key-Term Fold

1. Fold a sheet of lined notebook paper in half from left to right.

2. Using scissors, cut along every third line from the right edge of the paper to the center fold to make tabs.

Four-Corner Fold

1. Fold a sheet of paper in half from left to right. Then, unfold the paper.

2. Fold each side of the paper to the crease in the center of the paper.

3. Fold the paper in half from the top to the bottom. Then, unfold the paper.

4. Using scissors, cut the top flap creases made in step 3 to form four flaps.

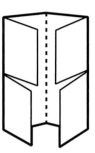

Three-Panel Flip Chart

1. Fold a piece of paper in half from the top to the bottom.

2. Fold the paper in thirds from side to side. Then, unfold the paper so that you can see the three sections.

3. From the top of the paper, cut along each of the vertical fold lines to the fold in the middle of the paper. You will now have three flaps.

Table Fold

1. Fold a piece of paper in half from the top to the bottom. Then, fold the paper in half again.
2. Fold the paper in thirds from side to side.
3. Unfold the paper completely. Carefully trace the fold lines by using a pen or pencil.

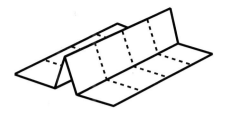

Two-Panel Flip Chart

1. Fold a piece of paper in half from the top to the bottom.
2. Fold the paper in half from side to side. Then, unfold the paper so that you can see the two sections.
3. From the top of the paper, cut along the vertical fold line to the fold in the middle of the paper. You will now have two flaps.

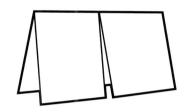

Tri-Fold

1. Fold a piece a paper in thirds from the top to the bottom.
2. Unfold the paper so that you can see the three sections. Then, turn the paper sideways so that the three sections form vertical columns.
3. Trace the fold lines by using a pen or pencil. Label the columns "Know," "Want," and "Learn."

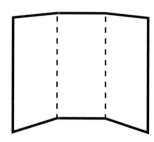

GAZETTEER

A

Abu Dhabi (24°N 54°E) capital of the United Arab Emirates, 395

Abuja (ah-BOO-jah) (9°N 7°E) capital of Nigeria, 467

Acapulco (17°N 100°W) city on the southwestern coast of Mexico, 135

Accra (6°N 0°W) capital of Ghana, 467

Addis Ababa (9°N 39°E) capital of Ethiopia, 485

Adriatic Sea sea between Italy and the Balkan Peninsula, 235, 293

Aegean (ee-JEE-uhn) **Sea** sea between Greece and Turkey, 235

Afghanistan landlocked country in central Asia, 395

Africa second-largest continent; surrounded by the Atlantic Ocean, Indian Ocean, and Mediterranean Sea, A2–A3

Ahaggar Mountains mountain range in southern Algeria, 447

Albania country in Eastern Europe on the Adriatic Sea, 293

Alberta province in Canada, 187

Aleutian Islands volcanic islands extending from Alaska into the Pacific Ocean, 81

Alexandria (31°N 30°E) city in northern Egypt, 447

Algeria country in North Africa located between Morocco and Libya, 447

Algiers (37°N 3°E) capital of Algeria, 447

Alps major mountain system in south-central Europe, 214

Altiplano broad, high plateau in Peru and Bolivia, 203

Amazon River major river in South America, 184

Amman (32°N 36°E) capital of Jordan, 377

Amsterdam (52°N 5°E) capital of the Netherlands, 253

Amu Dar'ya (uh-MOO duhr-YAH) river in Central Asia that drains into the Aral Sea, 415

Amur (ah-MOOHR) **River** river in northeast Asia forming part of the border between Russia and China, 325

Andes (AN-deez) great mountain range in South America, 168

Andorra European microstate in the Pyrenees mountains, A15

Andorra la Vella (43°N 2°E) capital of Andorra, A15

Angkor ancient capital of the Khmer Empire in Cambodia, 643

Angola country in central Africa, 501

Ankara (40°N 33°E) capital of Turkey, 377

Antananarivo (19°S 48°E) capital of Madagascar, 517

Antarctic Circle line of latitude located at 66.5° south of the equator; parallel beyond which no sunlight shines on the June solstice (first day of winter in the Southern Hemisphere), A4–A5

Antarctica continent around the South Pole, A22

Antigua and Barbuda island country in the Caribbean, 153

Antwerp (51°N 4°E) major port city in Belgium, 253

Apennines (A-puh-nynz) mountain range in Italy, 235

Apia (14°S 172°W) capital of Western Samoa, 670

Appalachian Mountains mountain system in eastern North America, 81

Arabian Peninsula peninsula in Southwest Asia between the Red Sea and Persian Gulf, 395

Arabian Sea sea between India and the Arabian Peninsula, 395

Aral (AR-uhl) **Sea** inland sea between Kazakhstan and Uzbekistan, 415

Arctic Circle line of latitude located at 66.5° north of the equator; the parallel beyond which no sunlight shines on the December solstice (first day of winter in the Northern Hemisphere), A4–A5

Arctic Ocean ocean north of the Arctic Circle; world's fourth-largest ocean, A2–A3

Argentina second-largest country in South America, 185

Armenia country in the Caucasus region of Asia; former Soviet republic, 347

Ashgabat (formerly Ashkhabad) (40°N 58°E) capital of Turkmenistan, 415

Asia world's largest continent; located between Europe and the Pacific Ocean, A3

Asmara (15°N 39°E) capital of Eritrea, 485

Astana (51°N 71°E) capital of Kazakhstan, 415

Astrakhan (46°N 48°E) old port city on the Volga River in Russia, 325

Asunción (25°S 58°W) capital of Paraguay, 185

Atacama Desert desert in northern Chile, 203

Athens (38°N 24°E) capital and largest city in Greece, 291

Atlanta (34°N 84°W) capital and largest city in the U.S. state of Georgia, 81, 114

Atlantic Ocean ocean between the continents of North and South America and the continents of Europe and Africa; world's second-largest ocean, A2

Atlas Mountains African mountain range north of the Sahara, 447

Auckland (37°S 175°E) New Zealand's largest city and main seaport, 677

Aughrabies (oh-KRAH-bees) **Falls** waterfalls on the Orange River in South Africa, 517

Australia only country occupying an entire continent (also called Australia); located between the Indian Ocean and the Pacific Ocean, A3, 677

Austria country in west-central Europe south of Germany, 253

Azerbaijan country in the Caucasus region of Asia; former Soviet republic, 347

Bab al-Mandab narrow strait that connects the Red Sea with the Indian Ocean, 485

Baghdad (33°N 44°E) capital of Iraq, 368, 395

Bahamas island country in the Atlantic Ocean southwest of Florida, 153

Bahrain country on the Persian Gulf in Southwest Asia, 395

Baja California peninsula in northwestern Mexico, 135

Baku (40°N 50°E) capital of Azerbaijan, 347

Bali island in Indonesia east of Java, 643

Balkan Mountains mountain range that rises in Bulgaria, 293

Baltic Sea body of water east of the North Sea and Scandinavia, 273

Baltimore (39°N 77°W) city in Maryland on the western shore of Chesapeake Bay, 81, 109

Bamako (13°N 8°W) capital of Mali, 467

Bandar Seri Begawan (5°N 115°E) capital of Brunei, 643

Bangkok (14°N 100°E) capital and largest city of Thailand, 643

Bangladesh country in South Asia, 567

Bangui (4°N 19°E) capital of the Central African Republic, 501

Banjul (13°N 17°W) capital of Gambia, 467

Barbados island country in the Caribbean, 153

Barcelona (41°N 2°E) Mediterranean port city and Spain's second-largest city, 235

Basel (48°N 8°E) city in northern Switzerland on the Rhine River, 253

Basseterre (17°N 63°W) capital of St. Kitts and Nevis, 153

Bay of Bengal body of water between India and the western coasts of Myanmar (Burma) and the Malay Peninsula, 549

Bay of Biscay body of water off the western coast of France and the northern coast of Spain, 253

Beijing (40°N 116°E) capital of China, 599

Beirut (34°N 36°E) capital of Lebanon, 377

Belarus country located north of Ukraine; former Soviet republic, 347

Belém (1°S 48°W) port city in northern Brazil, 185

Belfast (55°N 6°W) capital and largest city of Northern Ireland, 273

Belgium country between France and Germany in west-central Europe, 253

Belgrade (45°N 21°E) capital of Serbia and Montenegro on the Danube River, 293

Belize country in Central America bordering Mexico and Guatemala, 153

Belmopan (17°N 89°W) capital of Belize, 153

Benghazi (32°N 20°E) major coastal city in Libya, 447

Benin (buh-NEEN) country in West Africa between Togo and Nigeria, 467

Bergen (60°N 5°E) seaport city in southwestern Norway, 273

Berkshire Hills hilly region of western Massachusetts, 109

Berlin (53°N 13°E) capital of Germany, 253

Bern (47°N 7°E) capital of Switzerland, 253

Bhutan South Asian country in the Himalayas located north of India and Bangladesh, 567

Birmingham (52°N 2°W) major manufacturing center of south-central Great Britain, 273

Bishkek (43°N 75°E) capital of Kyrgyzstan, 415

Bissau (12°N 16°W) capital of Guinea-Bissau, 467

Black Sea sea between Europe and Asia, A14

Blue Nile East African river that flows into the Nile River in Sudan, 485

Bogotá (5°N 74°W) capital and largest city of Colombia, 169

Bolivia landlocked South American country, 203

Bombay see Mumbai.

Bonn (51°N 7°E) city in western Germany; replaced by Berlin as the capital of reunified Germany, 253

Borneo island in the Malay Archipelago in Southeast Asia, 643

Bosnia and Herzegovina country in Eastern Europe between Serbia and Montenegro and Croatia, 293

Bosporus a narrow strait separating European and Asian Turkey, 377

Boston (42°N 71°W) capital and largest city of Massachusetts, 81

Botswana country in southern Africa, 517

Brahmaputra River major river of South Asia that begins in the Himalayas of Tibet and merges with the Ganges River in Bangladesh, 549

Brasília (16°S 48°W) capital of Brazil, 185

Bratislava (48°N 17°E) capital of Slovakia, 293

Brazil largest country in South America, 185

Brazilian Highlands regions of old, eroded mountains in southeastern Brazil, 185

Brazilian Plateau area of upland plains in southern Brazil, 185

Brazzaville (4°S 15°E) capital of the Republic of the Congo, 501

Bridgetown (13°N 60°W) capital of Barbados, 153

Brisbane (28°S 153°E) seaport and capital of Queensland, Australia, 677

British Columbia province on the Pacific coast of Canada, 187

British Isles island group consisting of Great Britain and Ireland, A15

Brittany region in northwestern France, 253

Brunei (brooh-NY) country on the northern coast of Borneo in Southeast Asia, 643

Brussels (51°N 4°E) capital of Belgium, 253

Bucharest (44°N 26°E) capital of Romania, 293

Budapest (48°N 19°E) capital of Hungary, 293

Buenos Aires (34°S 59°W) capital of Argentina, 185

Bujumbura (3°S 29°E) capital of Burundi, 485

Bulgaria country on the Balkan Peninsula in Eastern Europe, 293

Burkina Faso (boor-KEE-nuh FAH-soh) landlocked country in West Africa, 467

Burma see Myanmar.

Burundi landlocked country in East Africa, 485

Cairo (30°N 31°E) capital of Egypt, 447

Calcutta see Kolkata.

Calgary (51°N 114°W) city in the western Canadian province of Alberta, 187

Callao (kah-YAH-oh) (12°S 77°W) port city in Peru, 203

Cambodia country in Southeast Asia west of Vietnam, 643

Cameroon country in central Africa, 501

Campeche (20°N 91°W) city in Mexico on the west coast of the Yucatán Peninsula, 135

Canada country occupying most of northern North America, 187

Canadian Shield major landform region in central Canada along Hudson Bay, 187

Canberra (35°S 149°E) capital of Australia, 677

Cancún (21°N 87°W) resort city in Mexico on the Yucatán Peninsula, 135

Cantabrian (kan-TAY-bree-uhn) **Mountains** mountains in northwestern Spain, 235

Cape Horn (56°S 67°W) cape in southern Chile; southernmost point of South America, 203

Cape of Good Hope cape of the southwest coast of South Africa, 517

Cape Town (34°S 18°E) major seaport city and legislative capital of South Africa, 517

Cape Verde island country in the Atlantic Ocean off the coast of West Africa, 467

Caracas (kuh-RAHK-uhs) (11°N 67°W) capital of Venezuela, 169

Cardiff (52°N 3°W) capital and largest city of Wales, 273

Caribbean Sea arm of the Atlantic Ocean between North and South America, A10, 153

Carpathian Mountains mountain system in Eastern Europe, 293

Casablanca (34°N 8°W) seaport city on the western coast of Morocco, 447

Cascade Range mountain range in the Northwestern United States, 81

Caspian Sea large inland salt lake between Europe and Asia, A16

Castries (14°N 61°W) capital of St. Lucia, 153

Cauca River river in western Colombia, 169

Caucasus Mountains mountain range between the Black Sea and the Caspian Sea, 325

Cayenne (5°N 52°W) capital of French Guiana, 169

Central African Republic landlocked country in central Africa located south of Chad, 501

Central America narrow southern portion of the North American continent, 153

Central Lowlands area of Australia between the Western Plateau and the Great Dividing Range, 677

Central Siberian Plateau upland plains and valleys between the Yenisey and Lena Rivers in Russia, 325

Central Valley narrow plain between the Sierra Nevada and Coast Ranges, 81

Chad landlocked country in northern Africa, 467

Chang River major river in Central China, 599

Chao Phraya (chow-PRY-uh) **River** major river in Thailand, 643

Chelyabinsk (chel-YAH-buhnsk) (55°N 61°E) manufacturing city in the Urals region of Russia, 325

Chernobyl (51°N 30°E) city in north-central Ukraine; site of a major nuclear accident in 1986, 347

Chicago (42°N 88°W) major city on Lake Michigan in northern Illinois, 81

Chile country in South America, 203

China country in East Asia; most populous country in the world, 599

Chişinău (formerly Kishinev) (47°N 29°E) capital of Moldova, 535

Chongqing (30°N 108°E) city in southern China along the Chang River, 599

Christchurch (44°S 173°E) city on the eastern coast of South Island, New Zealand, 677

Ciudad Juárez (syoo-thahth HWAHR-es) (32°N 106°W) city in northern Mexico near El Paso, 135

Coastal Plains North American landform region stretching along the Atlantic Ocean and Gulf of Mexico, 81

Cologne (51°N 7°E) manufacturing and commercial city along the Rhine River in Germany, 253

Colombia country in northern South America, 169

Colombo (7°N 80°E) capital city and important seaport of Sri Lanka, 567

Colorado Plateau uplifted area of horizontal rock layers in the western United States, 81

Columbia River river that drains the Columbia Basin in the northwestern United States, 81

Comoros island country in the Indian Ocean off the coast of Africa, 517

Conakry (10°N 14°W) capital of Guinea, 467

Congo Basin region in central Africa, 501

Congo River major navigable river in central Africa that flows into the Atlantic Ocean, 501

Congo, Democratic Republic of the largest and most populous country in central Africa, 501

Congo, Republic of the central African country located along the Congo River, 501

Constantinople (now called Istanbul) (41°N 29°E) former city in Turkey, 377

Copenhagen (56°N 12°E) seaport and capital of Denmark, 273

Córdoba (30°S 64°W) large city in Argentina northwest of Buenos Aires, 185

Cork (52°N 8°W) seaport city in southern Ireland, 273

Costa Rica country in Central America, 153

Côte d'Ivoire (KOHT-dee-VWAHR) (Ivory Coast) country in West Africa, 467

Crete largest of the islands of Greece, 235

Crimean Peninsula peninsula in Ukraine that juts southward into the Black Sea, 347

Croatia Eastern European country; former Yugoslav republic, 293

Cuba country and largest island in Caribbean, 153

Cuzco (14°S 72°W) city southwest of Lima, Peru; former capital of the Inca Empire, 203

Cyprus island republic in the eastern Mediterranean Sea, 377

Czech Republic Eastern European country and the western part of the former country in Czechoslovakia, 293

Dakar (15°N 17°W) capital of Senegal, 467

Dallas (33°N 97°W) city in northern Texas, 81

Damascus (34°N 36°E) capital of Syria and one of the world's oldest cities, 377

Danube River major river in Europe that flows into the Black Sea in Romania, 253

Dar es Salaam (7°S 39°E) capital and major seaport of Tanzania, 485

Dardanelles narrow strait separating European and Asian Turkey, 377

Dead Sea salt lake on the boundary between Israel and Jordan in southwestern Asia, 377

Deccan the southern part of the Indian subcontinent, 549

Delhi (29°N 77°E) city in India, 549

Denmark country in northern Europe, 273

Detroit (42°N 83°W) major industrial city in Michigan, 81

Devil's Island (5°N 53°W) French island off the coast of French Guiana in South America, 169

Dhaka (24°N 90°E) capital and largest city of Bangladesh, 567

Dinaric Alps mountains extending inland from the Adriatic coast to the Balkan Peninsula, 293

Djibouti (12°N 43°E) capital of Djibouti, 485

Dnieper River major river in Ukraine, 347

Dodoma (6°S 36°E) capital of Tanzania, 485

Doha (25°N 51°E) capital of Qatar, 395

Dominica Caribbean island country, 153

Dominican Republic country occupying the eastern part of Hispaniola in the Caribbean, 153

Donets Basin industrial region in eastern Ukraine, 347

Douro River river on the Iberian Peninsula that flows into the Atlantic Ocean in Portugal, 235

Drakensberg mountain range in southern Africa, 517

Dublin (53°N 6°W) capital of the republic of Ireland, 273

Durban (30°S 31°E) port city in South Africa, 517

Dushanbe (39°N 69°E) capital of Tajikistan, 415

East Timor country in Southeast Asia; former province of Indonesia, 643

Eastern Ghats mountains on the eastern side of the Deccan Plateau in southern India, 549

Eastern Highlands mountain ranges in eastern Australia, 677

Ebro River river in Spain that flows into the Mediterranean Sea, 235

Ecuador country in western South America, 203

Edmonton (54°N 113°W) provincial capital of Alberta, Canada, 187

Egypt country in North Africa located east of Libya, 447

El Salvador country on the Pacific side of Central America, 153

Elburz Mountains mountain range in northern Iran, 395

England southern part of Great Britain and part of the United Kingdom in northern Europe, 273

English Channel channel separating Great Britain from the European continent, 253

equator the imaginary line of latitude that lies halfway between the North and South Poles and circles the globe, A4–A5

Equatorial Guinea central African country, 501

Eritrea (er-uh-TREE-uh) East African country located north of Ethiopia, 485

Essen (51°N 7°E) industrial city in western Germany, 253

Estonia country located on the Baltic Sea; former Soviet republic, 293

Ethiopia East African country in the Horn of Africa, 485

Euphrates River major river in Iraq in southwestern Asia, 395

Europe continent between the Ural Mountains and the Atlantic Ocean, A3

Fergana Valley fertile valley in Uzbekistan, Kyrgyzstan, and Tajikistan, 415

Fès (34°N 5°W) city in north-central Morocco, 447

Fiji South Pacific island country in Melanesia, 669

Finland country in northern Europe located between Sweden, Norway, and Russia, 273

Flanders northern coastal part of Belgium where Dutch is the dominant language, 253

Florence (44°N 11°E) city on the Arno River in central Italy, 235

France country in west-central Europe, 253

Frankfurt (50°N 9°E) main city of Germany's Rhineland region, 253

Freetown (9°N 13°W) capital of Sierra Leone, 467

French Guiana French territory in northern South America, 169

Funafuti (9°S 179°E) capital of Tuvalu, 670

Gabon country in central Africa located between Cameroon and the Republic of the Congo, 501

Gaborone (24°S 26°E) capital of Botswana, 517

Galway (53°N 9°W) city in western Ireland, 273

Gambia country along the Gambia River in West Africa, 467

Ganges River major river in India flowing from the Himalayas southeastward to the Bay of Bengal, 549

Gangetic (gan-JE-tik) **Plain** vast plain in northern India, 549

Gao (GOW) (16°N 0°) city in Mali on the Niger River, 467

Gaza Strip area occupied by Israel from 1967 to 1994; under Palestinian self-rule since 1994, 377

Geneva (46°N 6°E) city in southwestern Switzerland, 253

Genoa (44°N 10°E) seaport city in northwestern Italy, 235

Georgetown (8°N 58°W) capital of Guyana, 169

Georgia (Eurasia) country in the Caucasus region; former Soviet republic, 347

Germany country in west-central Europe located between Poland and the Benelux countries, 253

Ghana country in West Africa, 470

Giza (30°N 31°E) Egyptian city on the west bank of the Nile, 452

Glasgow (56°N 4°W) city in Scotland, United Kingdom, 273

Gobi desert that makes up part of the Mongolian plateau in East Africa, 599

Golan Heights hilly region in southwestern Syria occupied by Israel, 377

Göteberg (58°N 12°E) seaport city in southwestern Sweden, 273

Gran Chaco (grahn CHAH-koh) dry plains region in Paraguay, Bolivia, and northern Argentina, 185

Great Artesian Basin Australia's largest source of underground well water; located in interior Queensland, 677

Great Barrier Reef world's largest coral reef; located off the northeastern coast of Australia, 677

Great Bear Lake lake in the Northwest Territories of Canada, 187

Great Britain major island of the United Kingdom, 273

Great Dividing Range mountain range of the Eastern Highlands in Australia, 677

Great Lakes largest freshwater lake system in the world; located in North America, 81

Great Plains grassland region in the central United States, 81

Great Rift Valley valley system extending from eastern Africa to Southwest Asia, 485

Great Slave Lake lake in the Northwest Territories of Canada, 187

Greater Antilles larger islands of the West Indies in the Caribbean Sea, 153

Greece country in southern Europe located at the southern end of the Balkan Peninsula, 235

Green Mountains major range of the Appalachian Mountains in Vermont, 109

Greenland self-governing province of Denmark between the North Atlantic and Arctic Oceans, 273

Grenada Caribbean island country, 153

Guadalajara (21°N 103°W) industrial city in west-central Mexico, 135

Guadalquivir (gwah-thahl-kee-VEER) **River** important river in southern Spain, 235

Guam (14°N 143°E) South Pacific island and U.S. territory in Micronesia, 669

Guatemala City (15°N 91°W) capital of Guatemala, 153

Guatemala most populous country in Central America, 153

Guayaquil (gwy-ah-KEEL) (2°S 80°W) port city in Ecuador, 203

Guiana Highlands elevated region in northeastern South America, 169

Guinea country in West Africa, 467

Guinea-Bissau (GI-nee bi-SOW) country in West Africa, 467

Gulf of Bothnia part of the Baltic Sea west of Finland, 273

Gulf of California part of the Pacific Ocean east of Baja California, Mexico, 135

Gulf of Guinea part of the Atlantic Ocean south of the West African countries, 467

Gulf of Mexico gulf of the Atlantic Ocean between Florida, Texas, and Mexico, 135

Gulf of St. Lawrence gulf between New Brunswick and Newfoundland Island in North America, 187

Guyana (gy-AH-nuh) country in South America, 169

Haiti country occupying the western third of the Caribbean island of Hispaniola, 153

Halifax (45°N 64°W) provincial capital of Nova Scotia, Canada, 187

Hamburg (54°N 10°E) seaport on the Elbe River in northwestern Germany, 253

Hanoi (ha-NOY) (21°N 106°E) capital of Vietnam, 643

Harare (18°S 31°E) capital of Zimbabwe, 517

Havana (23°N 82°W) capital of Cuba, 153

Hawaii U.S. Pacific state consisting of a chain of eight large islands and more than 100 smaller islands, 81

Helsinki (60°N 25°E) capital of Finland, 273

Himalayas mountain system in Asia; world's highest mountains, 599

Hindu Kush high mountain range in northern Afghanistan, 395

Hispaniola large Caribbean island divided into the countries of Haiti and the Dominican Republic, 153

Ho Chi Minh City (formerly Saigon) (11°N 107°E) major city in southern Vietnam; former capital of South Vietnam, 643

Hokkaido (hoh-KY-doh) major island in northern Japan, 623

Honduras country in Central America, 153

Hong (Red) River major river that flows into the Gulf of Tonkin in Vietnam, 643

Hong Kong (22°N 115°E) former British colony in East Asia; now part of China, 599

Honiara (9°S 160°E) capital of the Solomon Islands, 670

Honshu (HAWN-shoo) largest of the four major islands of Japan, 623

Houston (30°N 95°W) major port and largest city in Texas, 81

Huang River (Yellow River) one of the world's longest rivers; located in northern China, 599

Hudson Bay large bay in Canada, 187

Hungary country in Eastern Europe between Romania and Austria, 293

Iberian Peninsula peninsula in southwestern Europe occupied by Spain and Portugal, 235

Iceland island country between the North Atlantic and Arctic Oceans, 273

India country in South Asia, 549

Indian Ocean world's third-largest ocean; located east of Africa, south of Asia, west of Australia, and north of Antarctica, A3

Indochina Peninsula peninsula in southeastern Asia that includes the region from Myanmar (Burma) to Vietnam, 643

Indonesia largest country in Southeast Asia; made up of more than 17,000 islands, 643

Indus River major river in Pakistan, 567

Inland Sea body of water in southern Japan between Honshu, Shikoku, and Kyushu, 623

Interior Plains vast area between the Appalachians and the Rocky Mountains in North America, 81

Inyanga Mountains mountain region of Zimbabwe and Mozambique, 517

Iquitos (4°S 73°W) city in northeastern Peru on the Amazon River, 203

Iran country in southwestern Asia; formerly called Persia, 395

Iraq (i-RAHK) country located between Iran and Saudi Arabia, 395

Ireland country west of Great Britain in the British Isles, 273

Irian Jaya western part of the island of New Guinea and part of Indonesia, 643

Irish Sea sea between Great Britain and Ireland, 273

Irrawaddy River important river in Myanmar (Burma), 643

Islamabad (34°N 73°E) capital of Pakistan, 567

Israel country in southwestern Asia, 377

Istanbul (formerly Constantinople) (41°N 29°E) largest city and leading seaport in Turkey, 377

Italy country in southern Europe, 235

J

Jakarta (6°S 107°E) capital of Indonesia, 643
Jamaica island country in the Caribbean Sea, 153
Japan country in East Asia consisting of four major islands and more than 3,000 smaller islands, A17
Java major island in Indonesia, 643
Jerusalem (32°N 35°E) capital of Israel, 377
Johannesburg (26°S 28°E) city in South Africa, 517
Jordan River river in southwestern Asia that separates Israel from Syria and Jordan, 377
Jordan Southwest Asian country stretching east from the Dead Sea and Jordan River into the Arabian Desert, 377
Jutland Peninsula peninsula in northern Europe made up of Denmark and part of northern Germany, 273

K

Kabul (35°N 69°E) capital and largest city of Afghanistan, 395
Kalahari Desert dry plateau region in southern Africa, 517
Kamchatka Peninsula peninsula along Russia's northeastern coast, 325
Kampala (0° 32°E) capital of Uganda, 485
Kao-hsiung (23°N 120°E) Taiwan's second-largest city and major seaport, 599
Karachi (25°N 69°E) Pakistan's largest city and major seaport, 567
Karakoram Range high mountain range in northern India and Pakistan, 567
Kara-kum (kahr-uh-KOOM) desert region in Turkmenistan, 415
Kashmir mountainous region in northern India and Pakistan, 549
Kathmandu (kat-man-DOO) (28°N 85°E) capital of Nepal, 567
Kazakhstan country in Central Asia; former Soviet republic, 415
Kenya country in East Africa south of Ethiopia, 485
Khabarovsk (kuh-BAHR-uhfsk) (49°N 135°E) city in southeastern Russia on the Amur River, 325
Khartoum (16°N 33°E) capital of Sudan, 485
Khyber Pass major mountain pass between Afghanistan and Pakistan, 395
Kiev (50°N 31°E) capital of Ukraine, 347
Kigali (2°S 30°E) capital of Rwanda, 485
Kingston (18°N 77°W) capital of Jamaica, 153
Kingstown (13°N 61°W) capital of St. Vincent and the Grenadines, 153
Kinshasa (4°S 15°E) capital of the Democratic Republic of the Congo, 501
Kiribati South Pacific country in Micronesia and Polynesia, 670
Kjølen (CHUHL-uhn) **Mountains** mountain range in the Scandinavian Peninsula, 273
Kobe (KOH-bay) (35°N 135°E) major port city in Japan, 623
Kolkata (Calcutta) (23°N 88°E) giant industrial and seaport city in eastern India, 549
Korea peninsula on the east coast of Asia, 623
Koror capital of Palau, 670
Kosovo province in southern Serbia and Montenegro, 293
Kourou (5°N 53°W) city in French Guiana, 169
Kuala Lumpur (3°N 102°E) capital of Malaysia, 643
Kuril (KYOOHR-eel) **Islands** Russian islands northeast of the island of Hokkaido, Japan, 325
Kuwait City (29°N 48°E) capital of Kuwait, 395

Kuwait country on the Persian Gulf in southwestern Asia, 395
Kuznetsk Basin (Kuzbas) industrial region in central Russia, 325
Kyoto (KYOH-toh) (35°N 136°E) city on the island of Honshu and the ancient capital of Japan, 623
Kyrgyzstan (kir-gi-STAN) country in Central Asia; former Soviet republic, 415
Kyushu (KYOO-shoo) southernmost of Japan's main islands, 623
Kyzyl Kum (ki-zil KOOM) desert region in Uzbekistan and Kazakhstan, 415

L

La Paz (17°S 68°W) administrative capital and principal industrial city of Bolivia with an elevation of 12,001 feet (3,658 m); highest capital in the world, 203
Labrador region in the province of Newfoundland and Labrador, Canada, 187
Lagos (LAY-gahs) (6°N 3°E) former capital of Nigeria and the country's largest city, 467
Lahore (32°N 74°E) industrial city in northeastern Pakistan, 542
Lake Baikal (by-KAHL) world's deepest freshwater lake; located north of the Gobi in Russia, 325
Lake Chad shallow lake between Nigeria and Chad in western Africa, 467
Lake Malawi (also called Lake Nyasa) lake in southeastern Africa, 501
Lake Maracaibo (mah-rah-KY-buh) extension of the Gulf of Venezuela in South America, 169
Lake Nasser artificial lake in southern Egypt created in the 1960s by the construction of the Aswan High Dam, 447
Lake Nicaragua lake in southwestern Nicaragua, 153
Lake Poopó (poh-oh-POH) lake in western Bolivia, 203
Lake Tanganyika deep lake in the Western Rift Valley in Africa, 501
Lake Titicaca freshwater lake between Bolivia and Peru in the Andes Mountains at an elevation of 12,500 feet (3,810 m), 203
Lake Victoria large lake in East Africa surrounded by Uganda, Kenya, and Tanzania, 485
Lake Volta large artificial lake in Ghana, 467
Laos landlocked country in Southeast Asia, 643
Lapland region extending across northern Finland, Sweden, and Norway, 273
Las Vegas (36°N 115°W) city in southern Nevada, 81
Latvia country on the Baltic Sea; former Soviet republic, 293
Lebanon country in Southwest Asia, 377
Lesotho country completely surrounded by South Africa, 517
Lesser Antilles chain of volcanic islands in the eastern Caribbean Sea, 153
Liberia country in West Africa, 467
Libreville (0° 9°E) capital of Gabon, 501
Libya country in North Africa located between Egypt and Algeria, 447
Liechtenstein microstate in west-central Europe located between Switzerland and Austria, 253
Lilongwe (14°S 34°E) capital of Malawi, 501
Lima (12°S 77°W) capital of Peru, 203
Limpopo River river in southern Africa forming the border between South Africa and Zimbabwe, m517
Lisbon (39°N 9°W) capital and largest city of Portugal, 235
Lithuania European country on the Baltic Sea; former Soviet republic, 293

Ljubljana (lee-oo-blee-AH-nuh) (46°N 14°E) capital of Slovenia, 293

Lomé (6°N 1°E) capital of Togo, 467

London (52°N 0°) capital of the United Kingdom, 273

Los Angeles, California (34°N 118°W) major city in California, 81

Luanda (9°S 13°E) capital of Angola, 501

Lubumbashi (loo-boom-BAH-shee) (12°S 27°E) industrial city in the Democratic Republic of the Congo, 501

Luxembourg (50°N 7°E) capital of Luxembourg, 253

Luxembourg small European country bordered by France, Germany, and Belgium, 253

Luzon chief island of the Philippines, 643

Macao (22°N 113°E) former Portuguese territory in East Asia, now part of China, 599

Macedonia Balkan country; former Yugoslav republic, 293

Machu Picchu (13°S 73°W) ancient Inca city in the Andes of Peru, 203

Madagascar largest of the island countries off the eastern coast of Africa, 517

Madrid (40°N 4°W) capital of Spain, 235

Magdalena River river in Colombia that flows into the Caribbean Sea, 169

Magnitogorsk (53°N 59°E) manufacturing city of the Urals region of Russia, 325

Majuro (7°N 171°E) capital of the Marshall Islands, 670

Malabo (4°N 9°E) capital of Equatorial Guinea, 501

Malawi (muh-LAH-wee) landlocked country in central Africa, 501

Malay Archipelago (ahr-kuh-PE-luh-goh) large island group off the southeastern coast of Asia including New Guinea and the islands of Malaysia, Indonesia, and the Philippines, 643

Malay Peninsula peninsula in Southeast Asia, 643

Malaysia country in Southeast Asia, 643

Maldives island country in the Indian Ocean south of India, 567

Male (5°N 72°E) capital of the Maldives, 567

Mali country in West Africa, 476

Malta island country in southern Europe located in the Mediterranean Sea between Sicily and North Africa, 225

Managua (12°N 86°W) capital of Nicaragua, 153

Manama (26°N 51°E) capital of Bahrain, 395

Manaus (3°S 60°W) city in Brazil on the Amazon River, 185

Manchester (53°N 2°W) major commercial city in west-central Great Britain, 273

Manila (15°N 121°E) capital of the Philippines, 643

Manitoba prairie province in central Canada, 187

Maputo (27°S 33°E) capital of Mozambique, 517

Marseille (43°N 5°E) seaport in France on the Mediterranean Sea, 253

Marshall Islands Pacific island country in Indonesia, 670

Maseru (29°S 27°E) capital of Lesotho, 517

Masqat (Muscat) (23°N 59°E) capital of Oman, 395

Mato Grosso Plateau highland region in southwestern Brazil, 185

Mauritania African country stretching east from the Atlantic coast into the Sahara, 467

Mauritius island country located off the coast of Africa in the Indian Ocean, 517

Mazatlán (23°N 106°W) seaport city in western Mexico, 135

Mbabane (26°S 31°E) capital of Swaziland, 517

Medina (Al Madinah) (24°N 39°E) important Islamic city north of Mecca, 395

Mediterranean Sea sea surrounded by Europe, Asia, and Africa, 235

Mekong River important river in Southeast Asia, 643

Melanesia island region in the South Pacific that stretches from New Guinea to Fiji, 669

Melbourne (38°S 145°E) capital of Victoria, Australia, 677

Mexican Plateau large, high plateau in central Mexico, 135

Mexico City (19°N 99°W) capital of Mexico, 135

Mexico country in North America, 135

Miami (26°N 80°W) city in southern Florida, 81, 114

Micronesia island region in the South Pacific that includes the Mariana, Caroline, Marshall, and Gilbert island groups, 669

Micronesia, Federated States of island country in the western Pacific, 669

Milan (45°N 9°E) city in northern Italy, 235

Minsk (54°N 28°E) capital of Belarus, 347

Mississippi River major river in the central United States, 81

Mogadishu (2°N 45°E) capital and port city of Somalia, 485

Moldova Eastern European country located between Romania and Ukraine; former Soviet republic, 293

Monaco (44°N 8°E) European microstate bordered by France, 253

Mongolia landlocked country in East Asia, 599

Monrovia (6°N 11°W) capital of Liberia, 467

Monterrey (26°N 100°W) major industrial center in northeastern Mexico, 135

Montevideo (mawn-tay-bee-THAY-oh) (35°S 56°W) capital of Uruguay, 185

Montreal (46°N 74°W) financial and industrial city in Quebec, Canada, 187

Morocco country in North Africa south of Spain, 447

Moroni (12°S 43°E) capital of Comoros, 517

Moscow (56°N 38°E) capital of Russia, 325

Mount Elbrus (43°N 42°E) highest European peak (18,510 ft.; 5,642 m); located in the Caucasus Mountains, 347

Mount Everest (28°N 87°E) world's highest peak (29,035 ft.; 8,850 m); located in the Himalayas, 599

Mount Kilimanjaro (3°S 37°E) (ki-luh-muhn-JAHR-oh) highest point in Africa (19,341 ft.; 5,895 m); located in northeast Tanzania, near Kenya border, 485

Mount Orizaba (19°N 97°W) volcanic mountain (18,700 ft.; 5,700m) southeast of Mexico City; highest point in Mexico, 135

Mozambique (moh-zahm-BEEK) country in southern Africa, 517

Mumbai (Bombay) (19°S 73°E) India's largest city, 549

Munich (MYOO-nik) (48°N 12°E) major city and manufacturing center in southern Germany, 253

Murray-Darling Rivers major river system in southeastern Australia, 677

Muscat See Masqat.

Myanmar (MYAHN-mahr) (Burma) country in Southeast Asia between India, China, and Thailand, 643

N'Djamena (12°N 15°E) capital of Chad, 467

Nairobi (1°S 37°E) capital of Kenya, 485

Namib Desert Atlantic coast desert in southern Africa, 517

Namibia (nuh-MI-bee-uh) country on the Atlantic coast in southern Africa, 517

Nanjing (32°N 119°E) city along the upper Chang River in China, 599

Naples (41°N 14°E) major seaport in southern Italy, 235

Nassau (25°N 77°W) capital of the Bahamas, 153

Nauru South Pacific island country in Micronesia, 669

Negev desert region in southern Israel, 377

Nepal South Asian country located in the Himalayas, 567
Netherlands country in west-central Europe, 253
New Brunswick province in eastern Canada, 187
New Caledonia French territory of Melanesia in the South Pacific Ocean east of Queensland, Australia, 669
New Delhi (29°N 77°E) capital of India, 549
New Guinea large island in the South Pacific Ocean north of Australia, 643
New Orleans (30°N 90°W) major Gulf port city in Louisiana located on the Mississippi River, 81
New York Middle Atlantic state in the northeastern United States, 81
New Zealand island country located southeast of Australia, 677
Newfoundland and Labrador province in eastern Canada, 187
Niamey (14°N 2°E) capital of Niger, 467
Nicaragua country in Central America, 153
Nice (44°N 7°E) city in the southeastern coast in France, 253
Nicosia (35°N 33°E) capital of Cyprus, 377
Niger (NY-juhr) country in West Africa, 467
Niger River river in West Africa, 377, 467
Nigeria country in West Africa, 467
Nile Delta region in northern Egypt where the Nile River flows into the Mediterranean Sea, 447
Nile River world's longest river (4,187 miles; 6,737 km); flows into the Mediterranean Sea in Egypt, 447
Nile Valley area around the Nile River where distinct cultures developed, 449
Nizhniy Novgorod (Gorky), Russia (56°N 44°E) city on the Volga River east of Moscow, 325
North America continent including Canada, the United States, Mexico, Central America, and the Caribbean Islands, A2
North China Plain region of northeastern China, 599
North Island northernmost of two large continental islands of New Zealand, 677
North Korea country on the northern part of the Korean Peninsula in East Asia, 623
North Pole the northern point of Earth's axis, A22
North Sea major sea between Great Britain, Denmark, and the Scandinavian Peninsula, 253
Northern European Plain broad coastal plain from the Atlantic coast of France into Russia, 253
Northern Ireland the six northern counties of Ireland that remain part of the United Kingdom; also called Ulster, 273
Northern Mariana Islands U.S. commonwealth in the South Pacific, 670
Northwest Highlands region of rugged hills and low mountains in Europe, including parts of the British Isles, northwestern France, the Iberian Peninsula, and the Scandinavian Peninsula, 223
Northwest Territories division of a northern region of Canada, 187
Norway European country located on the Scandinavian Peninsula, 273
Nouakchott (nooh-AHK-shaht) (18°N 16°W) capital of Mauritania, 467
Nova Scotia province in eastern Canada, 187
Novosibirsk (55°N 83°E) industrial center in Siberia, Russia, 325
Nuku'alofa capital of Tonga, 670
Nunavut Native American territory of northern Canada, 187
Nuuk (Godthab) (64°N 52°W) capital of Greenland, 273

Ob River large river system that drains Russia and Siberia, 325
Oman country in the Arabian Peninsula; formerly known as Muscat, 395
Ontario province in central Canada, 187
Orange River river in southern Africa, 517
Orinoco River major river system in South America, 169
Osaka (oh-SAH-kuh) (35°N 135°E) major industrial center on Japan's southwestern Honshu island, 377
Oslo (60°N 11°E) capital of Norway, 273
Ottawa (45°N 76°W) capital of Canada; located in Ontario, 187
Ouagadougou (wah-gah-DOO-GOO) (12°N 2°W) capital of Burkina Faso, 467

P´yŏngyang (pyuhng-YANG) (39°N 126°E) capital of North Korea, 623
Pacific Ocean Earth's largest ocean; located between China and the Americas, A2–A3
Pakistan South Asian country located northwest of India, 567
Palau South Pacific island country in Micronesia, 670
Palestine Western edge of the Fertile Crescent bordering the Mediterranean Sea, 384
Palikir capital of the Federated States of Micronesia, 670
Pamirs mountain area mainly in Tajikistan in Central Asia, 415
Panama Canal canal allowing shipping between the Pacific Ocean and the Caribbean Sea; located in central Panama, 153
Panama City (9°N 80°W) capital of Panama, 153
Panama country in Central America, 153
Papua New Guinea country on the eastern half of the island of New Guinea, 670
Paraguay country in South America, 185
Paraguay River river that divides Paraguay into two separate regions, 185
Paramaribo (6°N 55°W) capital of Suriname in South America, 169
Paraná River major river system in southeastern South America, 185
Paris (49°N 2°E) capital of France, 253
Patagonia arid region of dry plains and windswept plateaus in southern Argentina, 185
Peloponnesus (pe-luh-puh-NEE-suhs) peninsula forming the southern part of the mainland of Greece, 235
Persian Gulf body of water between Iran and the Arabian Peninsula, 395
Perth (32°S 116°E) capital of Western Australia, 677
Peru nation on the Pacific coast of South America, 203
Philadelphia (40°N 75°W) important port and industrial center in Pennsylvania in the northeastern United States, 81
Philippines Southeast Asian island country located north of Indonesia, 643
Phnom Penh (12°N 105°E) capital of Cambodia, 643
Phoenix (34°N 112°W) capital of Arizona, 81
Plateau of Tibet high, barren plateau of western China, 599
Po River river in northern Italy, 235
Podgorica (PAWD-gawr-ett-sah) capital of Serbia and Montenegro, 304

Poland country in Eastern Europe located east of Germany, 293

Polynesia island region of the South Pacific that includes the Hawaiian and Line island groups, Samoa, French Polynesia, and Easter Island, 669

Port Elizabeth (34°S 26°E) seaport city in South Africa, 517

Port Louis (20°S 58°E) capital of Mauritius, 517

Port Moresby (10°S 147°E) seaport and capital of Papua New Guinea, 670

Port-au-Prince (pohr-toh-PRINS) (19°N 72°W) capital of Haiti, 153

Portland (46°N 123°W) seaport and largest city in Oregon, 81

Port-of-Spain (11°N 61°W) capital of Trinidad and Tobago, 153

Porto-Novo (6°N 3°E) capital of Benin, 467

Portugal country in southern Europe located on the Iberian Peninsula, 235

Port-Vila (18°S 169°E) capital of Vanuatu, 670

Prague (50°N 14°E) capital of the Czech Republic, 293

Praia (PRIE-uh) (15°N 24°W) capital of Cape Verde, 467

Pretoria (26°S 28°E) administrative capital of South Africa, 517

Prince Edward Island province in eastern Canada, 187

Pripyat (Pinsk) Marshes (PRI-pyuht) marshlands in southern Belarus and northwest Ukraine, 347

Puerto Rico U.S. commonwealth in the Greater Antilles in the Caribbean Sea, 153

Pusan (35°N 129°E) major seaport city in southeastern South Korea, 623

Pyrenees (PIR-uh-neez) mountain range along the border of France and Spain, 253

Qatar Persian Gulf country located on the Arabian Peninsula, 395

Qattara Depression lowland region (436 feet below sea level; 133 m) in western Egypt, 447

Quebec (47°N 71°W) provincial capital of Quebec, Canada, 187

Quebec province in eastern Canada, 187

Quito (0° 79°W) capital of Ecuador, 203

Rabat (34°N 7°W) capital of Morocco, 447

Rangoon See Yangon.

Red Sea sea between the Arabian Peninsula and northeastern Africa, 395

Reykjavik (RAYK-yuh-veek) (64°N 22°W) capital of Iceland, 273

Rhine River major river in Western Europe, 253

Riga (57°N 24°E) capital of Latvia, 293

Río Bravo Mexican name for the river between Texas and Mexico, 135

Rio de Janeiro (23°S 43°W) major port in southeastern Brazil, 185

Río de la Plata estuary between Argentina and Uruguay in South America, 185

Riyadh (25°N 47°E) capital of Saudi Arabia, 395

Rocky Mountains major mountain range in western North America, 81

Romania country in Eastern Europe, 293

Rome (42°N 13°E) capital of Italy, 235

Rosario (roh-SAHR-ee-oh) (33°S 61°W) city in eastern Argentina, 185

Roseau (15°N 61°W) capital of Dominica in the Caribbean, 153

Ross Ice Shelf ice shelf of Antarctica, 669

Rub' al-Khali uninhabited desert area in southeastern Saudi Arabia, 395

Russia world's largest country, stretching from Europe and the Baltic Sea to eastern Asia and the coast of the Bering Sea, 325

Rwanda country in East Africa, 485

Sahara desert region in northern Africa, 447

Sakhalin Island Russian island north of Japan, 325

Salvador (13°S 38°W) seaport city of eastern Brazil, 185

Salzburg state of central Austria, 253

Samarqand (40°N 67°E) city in southeastern Uzbekistan, 415

Samoa South Pacific island country in Polynesia, 669

San Diego (33°N 117°W) California's third largest urban area, 81

San Francisco (38°N 122°W) California's second largest urban area, 81

San José (10°N 84°W) capital of Costa Rica, 153

San Juan (19°N 66°W) capital of Puerto Rico, 153

San Marino microstate in southern Europe surrounded by Italy, 235

San Salvador (14°N 89°W) capital of El Salvador, 153

Sanaa (15°N 44°E) capital of Yemen, 395

Santa Cruz (18°S 63°W) city in south central Bolivia, 203

Santiago (33°S 71°W) capital of Chile, 203

Santo Domingo (19°N 70°W) capital of the Dominican Republic, 153

São Francisco River river in eastern Brazil, 185

São Paulo (24°S 47°W) Brazil's largest city, 185

São Tomé (1°N 6°E) capital of São Tomé and Príncipe, 501

São Tomé and Príncipe island country located off the Atlantic coast of central Africa, 501

Sarajevo (sar-uh-YAY-voh) (44°N 18°E) capital of Bosnia and Herzegovina, 293

Saskatchewan province in central Canada, 187

Saudi Arabia country occupying much of the Arabian Peninsula in southwestern Asia, 395

Scandinavian Peninsula peninsula of northern Europe occupied by Norway and Sweden, 273

Scotland northern part of the island of Great Britain, 273

Sea of Azov sea in Ukraine connected to and north of the Black Sea, 347

Sea of Japan body of water separating Japan from mainland Asia, *m325*, 535

Sea of Marmara sea between European Turkey and the Asian peninsula of Anatolia, 377

Sea of Okhotsk inlet of the Pacific Ocean on the eastern coast of Russia, 325

Seattle (48°N 122°W) largest city in the U.S. Pacific Northwest located in Washington, 81

Seine River river that flows through Paris in northern France, 253

Senegal country in West Africa, 467

Senegal River river in West Africa, 467

Seoul (38°N 127°E) capital of South Korea, 623

Serbia and Montenegro Eastern European country; former Yugoslav republics, 293

Seychelles island country located east of Africa in the Indian Ocean, 517

Shanghai (31°N 121°E) major seaport city in eastern China, 599

Shannon River river in Ireland; longest river in the British Isles, 273

Shikoku (shee-KOH-koo) smallest of the four main islands of Japan, 623

Siberia vast region of Russia extending from the Ural Mountains to the Pacific Ocean, 325

Sichuan Basin rich agriculture and mining area along the Chang (Yangtze) River in central China, 599

Sicily island region of Italy, 235

Sierra Leone West African country located northwest of Liberia, 467

Sierra Madre Occidental mountain range in western Mexico, 135

Sierra Madre Oriental mountain range in eastern Mexico, 135

Sierra Nevada located in eastern California; one of the longest and highest mountain ranges in the United States, 81

Sinai (SY-ny) **Peninsula** peninsula in northeastern Egypt, 447

Singapore island country located at the tip of the Malay Peninsula in Southeast Asia, 643

Skopje (SKAW-pye) (42°N 21°E) capital of Macedonia, 293

Slovakia country in Eastern Europe; formerly the eastern part of Czechoslovakia, 293

Slovenia country in Eastern Europe; former Yugoslav republic, 293

Sofia (43°N 23°E) capital of Bulgaria, 293

Solomon Islands South Pacific island country in Melanesia, 670

Somalia East African country located in the Horn of Africa, 485

South Africa country in southern Africa, 517

South Island the southern island of two main islands of New Zealand, 677

South Korea country occupying the southern half of the Korean Peninsula, 623

South Pole the southern point of Earth's axis, A22

Southern Alps mountain range in South Island, New Zealand, 677

Spain country in southern Europe occupying most of the Iberian Peninsula, 235

Sri Lanka island country located south of India; formerly known as Ceylon, 567

St. George's (12°N 62°W) capital of Grenada in the Caribbean Sea, 153

St. John's (17°N 62°W) capital of Antigua and Barbuda in the Caribbean Sea, 153

St. Kitts and Nevis Caribbean country in the Lesser Antilles, 153

St. Lawrence River major river linking the Great Lakes with the Gulf of St. Lawrence and the Atlantic Ocean in southeastern Canada, 187

St. Lucia Caribbean country in the Lesser Antilles, 153

St. Petersburg (formerly Leningrad; called Petrograd 1914 to 1924) (60°N 30°E) Russia's second largest city and former capital, 325

St. Vincent and the Grenadines Caribbean country in the Lesser Antilles, 153

Stockholm (59°N 18°E) capital of Sweden, 273

Strait of Gibraltar (juh-BRAWL-tuhr) strait between the Iberian Peninsula and North Africa that links the Mediterranean Sea to the Atlantic Ocean, 235

Strait of Magellan strait in South America connecting the South Atlantic with the South Pacific, 203

Sucre (19°S 65°W) constitutional capital of Bolivia, 203

Sudan East African country; largest country in Africa, 485

Suez Canal canal linking the Red Sea to the Mediterranean Sea in northeastern Egypt, 447

Sumatra large island of Indonesia, 643

Suriname (soohr-uh-NAH-muh) country in northern South America, 169

Suva (19°S 178°E) capital of Fiji, 670

Swaziland country in southern Africa, 517

Sweden country in northern Europe, 273

Switzerland country in west-central Europe located between Germany, France, Austria, and Italy, 253

Sydney (34°S 151°E) largest urban area and leading seaport in Australia, 677

Syr Dar'ya (sir duhr-YAH) river draining the Pamirs in Central Asia, 415

Syria Southwest Asian country located between the Mediterranean Sea and Iraq, 377

Syrian Desert desert region covering parts of Syria, Jordan, Iraq, and northern Saudi Arabia, 377

T'bilisi (42°N 45°E) capital of Georgia in the Caucasus region, 347

Tagus River longest river on the Iberian Peninsula in southern Europe, 235

Tahiti French South Pacific island in Polynesia, 669

Taipei (25°N 122°E) capital of Taiwan, 599

Taiwan (TY-WAHN) island country located off the southeastern coast of China, 599

Tajikistan (tah-ji-ki-STAN) country in Central Asia; former Soviet republic, 415

Taklimakan Desert desert region in western China, 599

Tampico (22°N 98°W) Gulf of Mexico seaport in central-eastern Mexico, 135

Tanzania East African country located south of Kenya, 485

Tarai (tuh-RY) region in Nepal along the border with India, 567

Tarawa capital of Kiribati, 670

Tarim Basin arid region in western China, 599

Tashkent (41°N 69°E) capital of Uzbekistan, 415

Tasman Sea part of South Pacific Ocean between Australia and New Zealand, 677

Tasmania island state of Australia, 677

Tegucigalpa (14°N 87°W) capital of Honduras, 153

Tehran (36°N 52°E) capital of Iran, 395

Tel Aviv (tehl uh-VEEV) (32°N 35°E) largest city in Israel, 377

Thailand (TY-land) country in Southeast Asia, 643

Thar (TAHR) **Desert** sandy desert of northwestern India and eastern Pakistan; also called the Great Indian Desert, 549

Thessaloníki (41°N 23°E) city in Greece, 235

Thimphu (28°N 90°E) capital of Bhutan, 567

Tian Shan (TIEN SHAHN) high mountain range separating northwestern China from Russia and some Central Asian republics, 415

Tiber River river that flows through Rome in central Italy, 235

Tibesti Mountains mountain group in northwest Chad, 467

Tierra del Fuego group of islands at the southern tip of South America, 185

Tigris River major river in southwestern Asia, 377, 395

Tijuana (33°N 117°W) city in northwestern Mexico, 135

Timbuktu (17°N 3°W) city in Mali and an ancient trading center in West Africa, *m475*

Tiranë (ti-RAH-nuh) (42°N 20°E) capital of Albania, 293

Togo West African country located between Ghana and Benin, 467

Tokyo (36°N 140°E) capital of Japan, 623

Tonga South Pacific island country in Polynesia, 670

Toronto (44°N 79°W) capital of the province of Ontario, Canada, 187

Transantarctic Mountains major mountain range that divides Antarctica into East and West, 669

Trinidad and Tobago Caribbean country in the Lesser Antilles, 153

Tripoli (33°N 13°E) capital of Libya, 447

Tropic of Cancer parallel 23.5° north of the equator; parallel on the globe at which the Sun's most direct rays strike the earth during the June solstice (first day of summer in the Northern Hemisphere), A4–A5

Tropic of Capricorn parallel 23.5° south of the equator; parallel on the globe at which the Sun's most direct rays strike the earth during the December solstice (first day of summer in the Southern Hemisphere), A4–A5

Tunis (37°N 10°E) capital of Tunisia, 447

Tunisia country in North Africa located on the Mediterranean coast between Algeria and Libya, 447

Turin (45°N 8°E) city in northern Italy, 235

Turkey country of the eastern Mediterranean occupying Anotolia and a corner of southeastern Europe, 377

Turkmenistan country in Central Asia; former Soviet republic, 415

Tuvalu South Pacific island country of Polynesia, 669

Uganda country in East Africa, 485

Ukraine country located between Russia and Eastern Europe; former Soviet republic, 347

Ulaanbaatar (oo-lahn-BAH-tawr) (48°N 107°E) capital of Mongolia, 599

United Arab Emirates country located on the Arabian Peninsula, 395

United Kingdom country in northern Europe occupying most of the British Isles; Great Britain and Northern Ireland, 273

United States North American country located between Canada and Mexico, 81

Ural Mountains mountain range in west central Russia that divides Asia from Europe, 325

Uruguay country on the northern side of the Río de la Plata between Brazil and Argentina in South America, 185

Uzbekistan country in Central Asia; former Soviet republic, 415

Vaduz (47°N 10°E) capital of Liechtenstein, A15

Valletta (36°N 14°E) capital of Malta, 226

Valparaíso (33°S 72°W) Pacific port for the national capital of Santiago, Chile, 203

Vancouver (49°N 123°W) Pacific port in Canada, 187

Vanuatu South Pacific island country in Melanesia, 669

Vatican City (42°N 12°E) European microstate surrounded by Rome, Italy, 235

Venezuela country in northern South America, 169

Victoria (1°S 33°E) capital of the Seychelles, 517

Vienna (48°N 16°E) capital of Austria, 253

Vientiane (18°N 103°E) capital of Laos, 643

Vietnam country in Southeast Asia, 643

Vilnius (55°N 25°E) capital of Lithuania, 293

Vinson Massif (78°S 87°W) highest mountain (16,066 ft.; 4,897 m) in Antarctica, 669

Virgin Islands island chain lying just east of Puerto Rico in the Caribbean Sea, 153

Vistula River river flowing through Warsaw, Poland, to the Baltic Sea, 293

Vladivostok (43°N 132°E) chief seaport of the Russian Far East, 325

Volga River Europe's longest river; located in west central Russia, 325

Wake Island (19°N 167°E) U.S. South Pacific island territory north of the Marshall Islands, 669

Wales part of the United Kingdom occupying a western portion of Great Britain, 273

Wallonia region in southern Belgium, 253

Warsaw (52°N 21°E) capital of Poland, 293

Washington, D.C. (39°N 77°W) U.S. capital; located between Virginia and Maryland on the Potomac River, 81

Wellington (41°S 175°E) capital of New Zealand, 677

West Bank area of Palestine west of the Jordan River; occupied by Israel in 1967; political status is in transition, 377

West Siberian Plain region with many marshes east of the Urals in Russia, 325

Western Ghats (GAWTS) hills facing the Arabian Sea on the western side of the Deccan Plateau, India, 549

Western Plateau large, flat plain covering more than half of Australia, 677

Western Rift Valley westernmost of two deep troughs beginning near Lake Malawi (Lake Nyasa) in eastern Africa and continuing north into the Red Sea and then into Syria, 501

Western Sahara disputed territory in northwestern Africa; claimed by Morocco, 447

White Nile part of the Nile River system in eastern Africa, 485

Windhoek (22°S 17°E) capital of Namibia, 517

Windsor (42°N 83°W) industrial city across from Detroit, Michigan, in the Canadian province of Ontario, 187

Winnipeg (50°N 97°W) provincial capital of Manitoba in central Canada, 187

Witwatersrand (WIT-wawt-uhrz-rahnd) a range of low hills in north central South Africa, 517

Wuhan (31°N 114°E) city in south central China, 599

Xi River river in southeastern China, 599

Yamoussoukro (7°N 5°W) capital of Côte d'Ivoire, 467

Yangon (Rangoon) (17°N 96°E) capital of Myanmar (Burma), 643

Yaoundé (4°N 12°E) capital of Cameroon, 501

Yekaterinburg (formerly Sverdlovsk) (57°N 61°E) city in the Urals region in Russia, 325

Yemen country located in the southwestern corner of the Arabian Peninsula, 395

Yenisey (yi-ni-SAY) major river in central Russia, 325

Yerevan (40°N 45°E) capital of Armenia, 347

Yucatán Peninsula peninsula in southeastern Mexico, 135

Yukon Territory Canadian territory bordering Alaska, 187

Zagreb (46°N 16°E) capital of Croatia, 293

Zagros Mountains mountain range of southwestern Iran, 395

Zambezi (zam-BEE-zee) **River** major river in central and southern Africa, 501

Zambia country in central Africa, 501

Zimbabwe (zim-BAH-bway) country in southern Africa, 525

Zurich (47°N 9°E) Switzerland's largest city, 253

GLOSSARY

A

abdicated Gave up the throne, **330**

absolute location The exact spot on Earth where something is found, often stated in latitude and longitude, **7**

acculturation The process of cultural changes that result from long-term contact with another society, **49**

acid rain A type of polluted rain, produced when pollution combines with water vapor, **30**

agrarian A society organized around farming, **357**

allies Friendly countries that support one another against enemies, **331**

alluvial fan A fan-shaped landform created by deposits of sediment at the base of a mountain, **21**

amber Fossilized tree sap, **295**

animism A religious belief that bodies of water, animals, trees, and other natural objects have spirits, **474**

annexed Formally adding a state or territory to a larger country, **87**

antifreeze A substance added to liquid to keep the liquid from turning to ice, **704**

apartheid The South African government policy of separation of races, which began to disappear in the 1980s, **524**

aqueducts Artificial channels for carrying water, **242**

aquifers Underground, water-bearing layers of rock, sand, or gravel, **26**

arable Land suitable for growing crops, **602**

archaeology The study of the remains and ruins of past cultures, **470**

archipelago (ahr-kuh-PE-luh-goh) A large group of islands, **154, 644**

artesian wells Wells in which water rises toward the surface without being pumped, **678**

asphalt The tar-like material used to pave streets, **379**

atmosphere Layer of gasses that surrounds Earth **31**

atolls Rings of coral surrounding lagoons, **581**

B

basins Regions surrounded by mountains or other higher land, **83, 502**

bauxite The most important aluminum ore, **155, 469**

Bedouins Nomadic herders in the deserts of Egypt and Southwest Asia, **454**

bilingual Having the ability to speak two languages, **88**

birthrate Number of births per 1,000 people in a year, **59**

Boers Afrikaner frontier farmers, white descendents of South Africa's original European colonists, **522**

bog Soft ground that is soaked with water, **284**

boycott Refuse to buy, **556**

bush Lightly populated wilderness areas, such as parts of Australia, **683**

C

cacao (kuh-KOW) A small tree on which cocoa beans grow, **158, 481**

caliph A religious and political ruler in the Muslim world, a title which means "successor to the Prophet Muhammad," **398**

calypso A type of music with origins in Trinidad and Tobago, **162**

canopy The uppermost layer of a forest's trees where limbs spread out and block out sunlight, **502**

cantons Political and administrative districts in Switzerland, **267**

caravans Groups of people who travel together for protection, **418**

cardamom A spice used in Asian foods, **159**

cartography The art and science of mapmaking, **13**

Casbah The old fortress and central part of some North African cities, **461**

cash crops Crops produced primarily to sell rather than for the farmer to eat, **147**

cassava (kuh-SAH-vuh) A tropical plant with starchy roots, **174**

caste system A system in which people's position in society is determined by their birth into a particular caste or group, **560**

caudillos (kow-THEE-yohs) Military leaders who ruled Venezuela in the 1800s and 1900s, **177**

center-pivot irrigation A method of irrigation that uses long sprinkler systems mounted on huge wheels that rotate slowly, irrigating the area within a circle, **98**

chaebol Huge industrial groups of South Korean companies, banks, and other businesses, **638**

chancellor Germany's head of government, or prime minister, **261**

chinampas (chee-NAHM-pahs) The name the Aztecs gave to raised fields on which they grew crops, **140**

cholera A life-threatening intestinal infection, **573**

city-states Self-governing cities, such as those of ancient Greece, **238**

civil war A conflict between two or more groups within a country, **159, 509**

civilization A highly complex culture with growing cities and economic activity, **52**

climate Weather conditions in an area over a long period of time, **32**

climatology The field of tracking Earth's larger atmospheric systems, **13**

cloud forest A high-elevation, very wet tropical forest where low clouds are common, **155**

coalition governments Governments in which several political parties join together to run a country, **243**

Cold War Rivalry between the United States and the Soviet Union that lasted from the 1940s to the early 1990s, **331**

colonies Territories controlled by people from a foreign land, **87**

command economy An economy in which the government owns most of the industries and makes most of the economic decisions, **56, 612**

commercial agriculture A type of farming in which farmers produce food for sale, **52**

commonwealth A self-governing territory associated with another country, **165**

condensation The process by which water changes from a gas into tiny liquid droplets, **27**

conquistadores (kahn-kees-tuh-DAWR-ez) Spanish conquerors during the era of colonization in the Americas, **141**

constitutional monarchy A government with a monarch as head of state and a parliament or other legislature that makes the laws, **279**

consumer goods Products used at home and in everyday life, **331**

contiguous Units, such as states, that connect to or border each other, **82**

Continental Divide The crest of the Rocky Mountains that divides North America's rivers into those that flow eastward and those that flow westward, **83**

cooperatives Organizations owned by their members and operated for their mutual benefit, **163**

copper belt A major copper-mining region of central Africa, **503**

coral reef A ridge made up of the skeletal remains of tiny sea animals and found close to shore in warm, tropical waters, **679**

cordillera mountain system made up of parallel ranges, **170**

cork The bark stripped from a certain type of oak tree and often used as stoppers and insulation, **249**

Corn Belt The corn-growing region in the Midwest from central Ohio to central Nebraska, **97**

cosmopolitan Having many foreign influences, **266**

Cossacks Nomadic horsemen who once lived on the Ukrainian frontier, **351**

coup (KOO) A sudden overthrow of a government by a small group of people, **211**

Creoles American-born descendents of Europeans in Spanish South America, **210**

culture A learned system of shared beliefs and ways of doing things that guide a person's daily behavior, **47**

culture region Area of the world in which people share certain culture traits, **47**

culture traits Elements of culture such as dress, food, or religious beliefs, **47**

currents Giant streams of ocean water that move from warm to cold or from cold to warm areas, **34**

cyclones Violent storms with high winds and heavy rain in South Asia, similar to hurricanes in the Caribbean, **568**

czar (ZAHR) Emperor of the Russian Empire, **330**

Dairy Belt Area including Wisconsin and most of Minnesota and Michigan which produces milk, cheese, and dairy products, **97**

Dalits People at the bottom of the Indian caste system who do the work that is considered unclean, **561**

death rate Number of deaths per 1,000 people in a year, **59**

deforestation Destruction or loss of forest area, **39**

deltas Landforms created by the deposit of sediment at the mouth of rivers, **21**

demilitarized zone A buffer zone that serves as a barrier separating two countries, such as North and South Korea, **635**

democracy A political system in which a country's people elect their leaders and rule by majority, **238**

depressions Low areas, **448**

developing countries Countries in different stages of moving toward development, **55**

dharma In Hinduism, a moral duty, **558**

dialect A variation of a language, **248, 506**

Diaspora The scattering of the Jewish population from Palestine under Roman rule, **384**

dictator One who rules a country with complete authority, **158, 463**

Diet (DY-uht) Japan's elected legislature, **627**

diffusion The movement of ideas or behaviors from one cultural region to another, **9**

dikes High banks of earth or concrete built along waterfronts to help reduce flooding, **601**

diversify For farmers, producing a variety of crops instead of just one, **94**

domestication The growing of a plant or taming of an animal by a people for their own use, **51**

dominion A territory or area of influence, **108**

droughts Periods when little rain falls and crops are damaged, **63, 495**

dynasty A ruling family that passes power from one generation to the next, **603**

earthquakes Sudden, violent movements along a fracture in the Earth's crust, **20**

ecotourism The practice of using an area's natural environment to attract tourists, **160**

ejidos (e-HEE-thohs) Lands owned and worked by groups of Mexican Indians, **142**

El Dorado (el duh-RAH-doh) "The Golden One," a legend of the early Chibcha people of Colombia, **172**

El Niño An ocean and weather pattern in the Pacific Ocean in which ocean waters become warmer, **206**

embargo A limit on trade, **407**

emigrant Person who leaves one place for another, **59**

emperor A ruler of a large empire, **603**

empire A system in which a central power controls a number of territories, **141**

enclaves Countries surrounded or almost surrounded by another country, **518**

encomienda A system in which Spanish monarchs gave land to Spanish colonists in the Americas; landowners could force Indians living there to work the land, **193**

endemic species Plants and animals that developed in one particular region of the world, **679**

entrepreneurs People who use their money and talents to start a business, **638**

epidemic Widespread outbreak, often referring to a disease, **141**

ergs Great "seas" of sand dunes in the Sahara, **448**

erosion The movement by water, ice, or wind of rocky materials to another location, **21**

estuary A partially enclosed body of water where salty seawater and freshwater mix, **187**

ethnic groups Cultural groups of people who share learned beliefs and practices, **47**

ethnocentrism Seeing differences in another culture as inferior, **49**

evaporation The process by which heated water becomes water vapor and rises into the air, **27**

exclave A part of a country that is separated by territory of other countries, **513**

Exclusive Economic Zones Areas off a country's coast within which the country claims and controls all resources, **701**

exotic rivers Rivers that begin in humid regions and then flow through dry areas, **396**

exports Products a country sells to other countries, **57**

famine A great shortage of food, **63, 282, 639**

fault A fractured surface in Earth's crust where a mass of rock is in motion, **20**

favelas (fah-VE-lahs) Huge slums that surround some Brazilian cities, **191**

fellahin (fel-uh-HEEN) Egyptian farmers who own very small plots of land, **458**

fjords (fee-AWRDS) Narrow, deep inlets of the sea set between high, rocky cliffs, **274**

floodplain A landform of level ground built by sediment deposited by a river or stream, **21**

fossil fuels Nonrenewable resources formed from the remains of ancient plants and animals, **40**

fossil water Water that is not being replaced by rainfall, **397**

free enterprise An economic system in which people, not government, decide what to make, sell, or buy, **56**

free port A city in which almost no taxes are placed on goods sold there, **461**

futon (FOO-tahn) A lightweight cotton mattress, often used in Japan, **630**

gauchos (GOW-chohz) Argentine cowboys, **193**

geography The study of Earth's physical and cultural features, **3**

geothermal energy A renewable energy resource produced from the heat of Earth's interior, **41**

gers (GURHZ) Large, circular tents that are easy to raise, dismantle, and move; used by nomadic herders in Mongolia, **615**

geysers Hot springs that shoot hot water and steam into the air, **288**

glaciers Large, slow-moving sheets or rivers of ice, **22**

glen A Scottish term for a valley, **281**

global warming A slow increase in Earth's average temperature, **30**

globalization Process in which connections around the world increase and cultures around the world share similar practices, **60**

gorge A narrow, steep-walled canyon, **492**

graphite A form of carbon used in pencils and many other products, **580**

green revolution A program, begun by the Indian government in the 1960s, that encouraged farmers to modernize their methods to produce more food, **563**

greenhouse effect Process by which Earth's atmosphere traps heat, **30**

griots (GREE-ohz) West African storytellers who pass on the oral histories of their tribes or people, **480**

gross domestic product Value of all goods and services produced within a country, **53**

gross national product Value of all goods and services that a country produces in one year within or outside the country, **53**

groundwater Water from rainfall, rivers, lakes, and melting snow that seeps into the ground, **26**

guerrilla An armed person who takes part in irregular warfare, such as raids, **163**

habitation fog A fog caused by fumes and smoke trapped over Siberian cities by very cold weather, **338**

haciendas (hah-see-EN-duhs) Huge farmlands granted by the Spanish monarch to favored people in Spain's colonies, **142**

harmattan (HAR-muh-TAN) Dry, dusty wind that blows south from the Sahara during winter, **468**

heavy industry Industry that usually involves manufacturing based on metals, **336**

hieroglyphs (HY-ruh-glifs) Pictures and symbols used to record information in ancient Egypt, **451**

Holocaust The mass murder of millions of Jews and other people by the Nazis in World War II, **261**

homogeneous Sharing the same characteristics, such as ethnicity, **357**

human geography The study of people, past or present, **11**

human-environment interaction Relationship between people and the environment, **9**

humanitarian aid Medicine, food, and shelter that international relief agencies give to people in need, **63**

hurricanes Tropical storms that bring violent winds, heavy rain, and high seas, **14**

hydroelectric power A renewable energy resource produced from dams that harness the energy of falling water to power generators, **41**

ice shelf A ledge of ice over coastal water, **696**

icebergs Large chunks of ice that break away from glaciers and ice shelves and drift into the ocean, **696**

icebreakers Ships that can break up the ice of frozen waterways, allowing other ships to pass through them, **342**

immigrant Person who arrives from another country, **59**

imports Products a country buys from other countries, **57**

impressionism A form of art that developed in France in the late 1800s and early 1900s, **259**

indentured servants People who agree to work for a certain period of time, often in exchange for travel expenses, **179**

indigo (IN-di-goh) A plant used to make a deep blue dye, **176**

Indo-European A language family that includes many languages of Europe, such as Germanic, Baltic, and Slavic languages, **296**

industrialized countries Countries that rely more on industry than agriculture, **54**

inflation The rise in prices that occurs when currency loses its buying power, **146**

intensive cultivation The practice of growing crops on every bit of available land, **631**

interdependence Depending on another country for resources or goods and services, **57**

Inuit North American Eskimos, **115**

ivory A cream-colored material that comes from elephant tusks and is used in making fine jewelry and handicrafts, **504**

Japan Current A warm ocean current east of Japan, **623**

junta (HOOHN-tuh) A small group of military officers who rule a country after seizing power, **215**

K

kampongs A traditional village in Indonesia; also the term for crowded slums around Indonesia's large cities, **654**

karma Among Hindus and Buddhists, the positive or negative force caused by a person's actions, **558**

kimchi Chinese cabbage that has been spiced and pickled; Korea's national dish, **638**

kimonos Traditional Japanese robes, **629**

kiwi (KEE-wee) A flightless bird in New Zealand; a name sometimes applied to New Zealanders, **687**

klongs Canals throughout Bangkok, Thailand, **651**

krill Tiny shrimplike marine animals that are an important food for larger Antarctic marine life, **697**

landforms The shapes of land on Earth's surface, **19**

landlocked Completely surrounded by land, with no direct access to the ocean, **198**, **416**

lava Magma that has broken through the crust to Earth's surface, **20**

light industry Industry that focuses on the production of lightweight goods, such as clothing, **336**

lignite A soft form of coal, **295**

literacy rate Percent of people who can read and write, **54**

llaneros (yah-NAY-rohs) Cowboys of the Venezuelan Llanos, **178**

Llanos (YAH-nohs) A plains region in eastern Colombia and western Venezuela, **170**

lochs Scottish lakes located in valleys carved by glaciers, **274**

loess (LES) Fine, windblown soil that is good for farming, **255**

mainland A region or country's main landmass, **236**, **644**

malaria A deadly disease spread by mosquitoes, **476**

mandate Former territories of defeated World War I countries that were placed under the control of winning countries after the war, **388**

maquiladoras (mah-kee-lah-DORH-ahs) Foreign-owned factories located along Mexico's northern border with the United States, **149**

maritime On or near the sea, such as Canada's Maritime Provinces, **112**

market economy An economy in which business owners and consumers make decisions about what to make, sell, and buy, **56**

marsupials (mahr-SOO-pee-uhls) Animals that carry their young in pouches, **680**

martial law Military rule, **606**

medieval Refers to the period from the collapse of the Roman Empire to about 1500, **257**

megalopolis A giant urban area that includes a string of cities that have grown together, **94**, **629**

Mercosur A trade organization that includes Argentina, Brazil, Paraguay, Uruguay, and two associate members (Bolivia and Chile), **196**

merengue The national music and dance of the Dominican Republic, **162**

Mesopotamia Ancient land between the Tigris and Euphrates rivers, **396**

mestizos (me-STEE-zohs) People of mixed European and American Indian ancestry, **142**

meteorology The field of forecasting and reporting rainfall, temperatures, and other atmospheric conditions, **13**

Métis (may-TEES) People of mixed European and Canadian Indian ancestry in Canada, **109**

migration Movement of people, **59**

millet A grain crop that can survive drought, **475**

missions Spanish church outposts established during the colonial era, particularly in the Americas, **142**

mixed economy An exchange of goods and services based on at least two other types of economic systems, **57**

Moors Muslim North Africans, **247**

mosaics (moh-ZAY-iks) Pictures created from tiny pieces of colored stone, **240**

mosques Islamic houses of worship, **422**

most-favored-nation status A status that grants special trade advantages from the United States, **613**

movement People and ideas moving from place to place, **9**

mulattoes (muh-LA-tohs) People of mixed European and African ancestry, **142**

multicultural A mixture of different cultures within the same country or community, **47**

multiple cropping A type of agriculture in which two or three crops are raised each year on the same land, **612**

Muslims Followers of Islam, **398**

nationalism The demand for self-rule and a strong feeling of loyalty to one's nation, **268**

NATO North Atlantic Treaty Organization, a military alliance of various European countries, the United States, and Canada, **257**

nature reserves Areas a government has set aside to protect animals, plants, soil, and water, **348**

navigable Water routes that are deep enough and wide enough to be used by ships, **254**

neutral Not taking a side in a dispute or conflict, **286**

newsprint Cheap paper used mainly for newspapers, **105**

nirvana Among Buddhists, the escape from the suffering of life, **559**

nomads People who often move from place to place, **418**

nonrenewable resources Resources, such as coal and oil, that cannot be replaced by Earth's natural processes, **38**

North Atlantic Drift A warm ocean current that brings mild temperatures and rain to parts of northern Europe, **275**

oasis A place in the desert where a spring or well provides water, **416**

oil shale Layered rock that yields oil when heated, **295**

one-crop economy Economy based on a single crop, such as bananas, sugarcane, or cacao, **57**

OPEC Organization of Petroleum Exporting Countries, which tries to influence the price of oil on world markets, **399**

oral history Spoken information passed from one generation to the next, **470**

Organization of African Unity (OAU) An organization, founded in 1963, that tries to promote cooperation among African countries, **529**

outback Australia's inland region, **680**

overpopulation More people than a region or country can self-support, **58**

Oyashio (oh-YAH-shee-oh) **Current** A cool ocean current east of Japan, **623**

ozone layer A form of oxygen in the atmosphere that helps protect Earth from harmful solar radiation, **30**

pagodas Buddhist temples, **608**

Pampas A wide, grassy plains region in central Argentina, **186**

pans Low, flat, desert areas of southern Africa into which ancient streams drained, **519**

pardos Venezuelans of mixed African, European, and South American Indian ancestry, **178**

peat Matter made from dead plants, usually mosses, **284**

periodic markets Open-air trading markets in central Africa, **503**

perspective Point of view based on a person's experience and personal understanding, **3**

Peru Current A cold ocean current off the coast of western South America, **205**

petroleum An oily liquid that can be refined into gasoline and other fuels and oils, **40**

pharaohs Ancient Egyptian kings, **451**

phosphates Mineral salts containing the element phosphorus; used to make fertilizers, **379**

physical geography The study of Earth's natural landscape and physical systems, including the atmosphere, **11**

pidgin languages Simple languages that help people who speak different languages understand each other, **179**

place Physical and human features of a specific location, **7**

plain A nearly flat area on Earth's surface, **21**

plantains A type of banana used in cooking, **164**

plantations Large farms that grow mainly one crop to sell, **87**

plate tectonics The theory that Earth's surface is divided into several major, slowly moving plates or pieces, **19**

polar desert A high-latitude region that receives little precipitation, **697**

polis Greek city-state, **238**

pope The bishop of Rome and the head of the Roman Catholic Church, **243**

popular culture Widely shared beliefs, tastes, goals, and practices, **60**

population density The average number of people living within a set area, **58**

porcelain A type of very fine pottery, **604**

potash A mineral used to make fertilizer, **105**

precipitation The process by which water falls back to Earth, **27**

prevailing winds Breezes that consistently blow in the same direction over large areas of Earth, **33**

protectionism The practice of setting up trade barriers to shield industries at home from foreign competition, **632**

provinces Administrative divisions of a country, **108**

pulp Softened wood fibers used to make paper, **105**

pyramids Huge square stone monuments with four triangular sides, **452**

Quechua (KE-chuh-wuh) The language of South America's Inca; still spoken in the region, **212**

quinoa (KEEN-wah) A native plant of South America's Andean region that yields nutritious seeds, **207**

quipu (KEE-poo) Complicated system of knots tied on strings of various colors, used by the Inca of South America to record information, **208**

Qur'an The holy book of Islam, **399**

race A group of people who share inherited physical or biological traits, **48**

rain shadow Dry area on the side of a mountain opposite the wind, **35**

reforestation The planting of trees in places where forests have been cut down, **39**

Reformation A movement in Europe to reform Christianity in the 1500s, **260**

refugees People who flee to another country, usually for economic or political reasons, **63, 163, 647**

reggae A type of music with origins in Jamaica, **162**

region Area of Earth's surface with one or more shared characteristics, **8**

regionalism The stronger connection to one's region than to one's country, **111**

regs Broad, windswept gravel plains in the Sahara, **448**

reincarnation The belief that the human soul is reborn again and again in different bodies, **558**

relative location The position of a place in relation to another place, **7**

Renaissance (re-nuh-SAHNS) French word meaning "rebirth" and referring to a new era of learning that began in Europe in the 1300s, **243**

renewable resources Materials needed and valued by people, such as soils and forests, that can be replaced by Earth's natural processes, **38**

rifts Long, deep valleys with mountains or plateaus on either side, **486**

Roma An ethnic group also known as Gypsies who are descended from people who may have migrated from India to Europe long ago, **306**

rugby A game with British origins; similar to football and soccer, **682**

rural An area of open land that is often used for farming, **4**

Sahel (sah-HEL) A dry grasslands region with a steppe climate south of the Sahara, **468**

samurai (SA-muh-ry) Warriors who served Japanese lords, **626**

sanctions An economic or political penalty, such as an embargo, used by one or more countries to force another country to cease an illegal or immoral act, **525**

Sanskrit An early language form in South Asia; used as a sacred language in India today, **553**

Santería A religion, with origins in Cuba, that mixes West African religions and traditions with those of Roman Catholicism, **162**

secede To separate from, **478**

second-growth forests The trees that cover an area after the original forest has been cut, **93**

secular Kept separate from religion, as in a secular government or state, **381**

selvas The thick tropical rain forests of eastern Ecuador, eastern Peru, and northern Bolivia, **205**

sepoys Indian troops commanded by British officers during the colonial era in India, **556**

serfs People who were bound to the land and worked for a lord, **351**

shah An ancient Persian word for king, **410**

shamans Shinto priests, **625**

Shia The second-largest branch of Islam, **398**

Shintoism The earliest known religion of Japan, **625**

shogun "Great General," the highest Japanese warrior rank, **626**

silt Finely ground soil, **449**

sinkholes A steep-sided depression formed when the roof of a cave collapses, **136**

sirocco (suh-RAH-koh) A hot, dry wind from North Africa that blows across the Mediterranean to Europe, **237**

slash-and-burn agriculture A type of agriculture in which forests are cut and burned to clear land for planting, **149**

smelters Factories that process metal ores, **337**

smog A mixture of smoke, chemicals, and fog, **148**

soil exhaustion The loss of soil nutrients needed by plants, **188**

solar power Heat and light from the Sun, **41**

sorghum A grain crop that can survive drought, **475**

souks Marketplaces in North Africa, **461**

soviet A council of Communists who governed republics and other places in the Soviet Union, **351**

spatial perspective Point of view based on looking at where something is and why it is there, **3**

staple A region or country's main food crop, **476**

steppe (STEP) A wide, flat grasslands region that stretches from Ukraine across southern Russia to Kazakhstan, **327**

storm surges Huge waves of water that are whipped up by fierce winds, particularly from cyclones, hurricanes, and other tropical storms, **568**

strait A narrow passageway that connects two large bodies of water, **204**

strip mining A process of mining by stripping away soil and rock, **98**

stupas Mounds of earth or stones covering the ashes of the Buddha or relics of Buddhist saints, **576**

subduction The movement of one of Earth's heavier tectonic plates underneath a lighter tectonic plate, **20**

subsistence agriculture A type of farming in which farmers grow just enough food to provide for themselves and their own families, **52**

sultan The supreme ruler of a Muslim country, **657**

Sunni The largest branch of Islam, **398**

superpowers Powerful countries, **331**

Swahili A Bantu language that is widely spoken in areas of Africa, **490**

symbol A word, shape, color, flag, or other sign that stands for something else, **49**

taiga (TY-guh) A forest of evergreen trees growing south of the tundra of Russia, **327**

teak A valuable type of wood that grows in India and Southeast Asia, **551**

tepuís (tay-PWEEZ) Layers of sandstone that have resisted erosion atop plateaus in the Guiana Highlands, **170**

terraces Horizontal ridges built into the slopes of steep hillsides to prevent soil loss and aid farming, **22**

textiles Cloth products, **87, 279**

theocracy A government ruled by religious leaders, **410**

third-world countries Developing countries that lack economic opportunities, **55**

topography Shape, height, and arrangement of landforms in a certain place, **19**

townships Special areas of crowded clusters of tiny homes for black South Africans living outside cities, **524**

trade deficit Value of a country's exports is lower than the value of its imports, **99**

trade surplus The value of exports is greater than the value of imports, **632**

tradition-based economy Exchange of goods or services based on custom and tradition, **56**

tributary Any smaller stream or river that flows into a larger stream or river, **26**

trust territories Areas placed under the temporary control of another country until they set up their own government, **699**

tsetse (TSET-see) **fly** A fly in Africa south of the Sahara that spreads sleeping sickness, a deadly disease, **468**

tsunamis (tsooh-NAH-mees) Huge waves created by undersea tectonic activity, such as earthquakes, **623**

U

uninhabitable Not capable of supporting human settlement, **288**

urban An area that contains a city, **4**

V

veld (VELT), **the** Open grasslands areas of South Africa, **518**

viceroy The governor of a colony, **210**

W

wadis Dry streambeds in Southwest Asia, **397**

water cycle The circulation of water from Earth's surface to the atmosphere and back, **27**

water vapor The gaseous form of water, **27**

weather The condition of the atmosphere at a given place and time, **32**

weathering The process of breaking rocks into smaller pieces through heat, water, or other means, **21**

Wheat Belt The wheat-growing area in the United States which stretches across the Dakotas, Montana, Nebraska, Kansas, Oklahoma, Colorado, and Texas, **98**

work ethic The belief that work in itself is worthwhile, **632**

Y

yurt A movable round house of wool felt mats over a wood frame, **422**

Z

Zionism The movement to establish a Jewish country or community in Palestine, **385**

zonal How climates in Africa stretch east to west in bands, **468**

SPANISH GLOSSARY

A

abdicated/abdicar Renunciar al trono, **330**

absolute location/posición exacta Lugar exacto de la tierra donde se localiza un punto, por lo general definido en términos de latitud y longitud, **7**

acculturation/aculturación Proceso de asimilación de una cultura a largo plazo por el contacto con otra sociedad, **49**

acid rain/lluvia ácida Tipo de lluvia contaminada que se produce cuando partículas de contaminación del aire se combinan con el vapor de agua de la atmósfera, **30**

agrarian/agrario Sociedad basada en la agricultura, **357**

allies/aliados Países que se apoyan entre sí para defenderse de sus enemigos, **331**

alluvial fan/abanico aluvial Accidente geográfico en forma de abanico que se origina por la acumulación de sedimentos en la base de una montaña, **21**

amber/ámbar Savia de árbol fosilizada, **295**

animism/animismo Creencia religiosa que explica que los cuerpos de agua, los animales, los árboles y otros objetos de la naturaleza tienen un espíritu, **474**

annexed/anexar Ánadir formalmente un estado o un territorio a un país más grande, **87**

antifreeze/anticongelante Sustancia que se agrega a un líquido para evitar que se congele, **704**

apartheid/apartheid Política de separación de razas aplicada por el gobierno sudafricano. Empezó a desaparecer en la década de 1980, **524**

aqueducts/acueductos Canales artificiales usados para transportar agua, **242**

aquifers/acuíferos Capas subterráneas de roca, arena y grava en las que se almacena el agua, **26**

arable/cultivable Tierra con características que favorecen el cultivo, **602**

archaeology/arqueología Estudio de los restos de culturas pasadas, **470**

archipelago/archipiélago Grupo grande de islas, **154, 644**

artesian wells/pozos artesianos Pozos en los que el agua sube a la superficie de la tierra sin ser impulsada por medios artificiales, **678**

asphalt/asfalto Material oscuro usado para pavimentar calles, **379**

atmosphere/atmósfera Capa de gases que rodea a la tierra, **31**

atolls/atolones Anillos de coral que se forman alrededor de las lagunas, **581**

B

basins/cuencas Regiones rodeadas por montañas u otras tierras altas, **83, 502**

bauxite/bauxita El mineral con contenido de aluminio más importante, **155, 469**

Bedouins/beduinos Ganaderos nómadas del desierto de Egipto y el sudoeste de Asia, **454**

bilingual/bilingüe Persona que habla dos idiomas, **88**

birthrate/índice de natalidad número de nacimientos por 1,000 personas en un año, **59**

Boers/boers Agricultores africanos de raza blanca, descendientes de los primeros colonizadores europeos de Sudáfrica, **522**

bog/ciénaga Tierra suave, humedecida por el agua, **284**

boycott/boicot Rechazo de compra, **556**

bush Zonas salvajes de escasa población, como ciertas regiones de Australia, **683**

C

cacao/cacas Árbol pequeño que produce los granos de cacao, **158, 481**

caliph/califa Líder político y religioso del mundo musulmán, **398**

calypso/calipso Tipo de música originado en Trinidad y Tobago, **162**

canopy/dosel Capa superior de un bosque espeso en el que las ramas se entrelazan, bloqueando el paso de la luz solar, **502**

cantons/cantones Distritos políticos y administrativos de Suiza, **267**

caravans/caravanas Grupos de personas que viajan juntas por razones de seguridad, **418**

cardamom/cardamomo Especia que se usa en Asia para condimentar alimentos, **159**

cartography/cartografía Arte y ciencia de la elaboración de mapas, **13**

Casbah/casbah Antigua fortaleza y centro de las ciudades del norte de África, **461**

cash crops/cultivos para la venta Cultivos producidos para su venta y no para consumo del agricultor, **147**

cassava/mandioca Planta tropical de raíces almidonadas, **174**

caste system/sistema de castas Sistema en el que la posición de una persona en la sociedad es determinada por el nivel social del grupo en el que nace, **560**

caudillos/caudillos Líderes militares que gobernaron Venezuela en los siglos XIX y XX, **177**

center-pivot irrigation/irrigación de pivote central Tipo de riego que usa aspersores montados en grandes ruedas giratorias regando un area dentro de un círculo, **98**

chaebol/chaebol Enormes grupos industriales formados por compañías, bancos y otros negocios en Corea del Sur, **638**

chancellor/canciller Jefe de gobierno o primer ministro alemán, **261**

chinampas/chinampas Nombre dado por los aztecas a los campos elevados que usaban como tierras de cultivo, **140**

cholera/cólera Infección intestinal seria que puede provocar a muerte, **573**

city-states/ciudades estado Ciudades con un sistema de autogobierno, como en la antigua Grecia, **238**

civilization/civilización Cultura altamente compleja con grandes ciudades y abundante actividad económica, **52**

civil war/guerra civil conflicto entre dos o más grupos dentro de un país, **159, 509**

climate/clima condiciones meteorológicas registradas en un periodo largo, **32**

climatology/climatología Registro de los sistemas atmosféricos de la Tierra, **13**

cloud forest/bosque nuboso Bosque tropical de gran elevación y humedad donde los bancos de nubes son muy comunes, **155**

coalition governments/gobiernos de coalición Gobiernos en los que la administración del país es regida por varios partidos políticos a la vez, **243**

Cold War/guerra fría Rivalidad entre Estados Unidos y la Unión Soviética que se extendió de la década de 1940 a la década de 1990, **331**

colonies/colonias Territorios controlados por personas de otro país, **87**

command economy/economía autoritaria Economía en la que el gobierno es propietario de la mayor parte de las industrias y toma la mayoría de las decisiones en materia de economía, **56, 612**

commercial agriculture/agricultura comercial Tipo de agricultura cuya producción es exclusiva para la venta, **52**

commonwealth/mancomunidad Territorio autogobernado que mantiene una sociedad con otro país, **165**

condensation/condensación Proceso mediante el cual el agua cambia de estado gaseoso y forma pequeñas gotas, **27**

conquistadores/conquistadores Españoles que participaron en la colonización de América, **141**

constitutional monarchy/monarquía constitucional Gobierno que cuenta con un monarca como jefe de estado y un parlamento o grupo legislador similar para la aprobación de leyes, **279**

consumer goods/bienes de consumo Productos usados en la vida cotidiana, **331**

contiguous/contiguo Unidades de territorio (como los estados) que colindan entre sí, **82**

Continental Divide/divisoria continental Cordillera que divide los ríos de Estados Unidos en dos partes: los que fluyen al este y los que fluyen al oeste, **83**

cooperatives/cooperativas Organizaciones creadas por los propietarios de una empresa y operadas para beneficio propio, **163**

copper belt/región del cobre Importante región minera de producción de cobre localizada en la parte central de África, **503**

coral reef/arrecife coralino Formaciones creadas por la acumulación de los restos de animales marinos diminutos cerca de las costas en las aguas templadas de las regiones tropicales, **679**

cordillera/cordillera Sistema montañoso de cordilleras paralelas, **170**

cork/corcho Corteza extraída de cierto tipo de roble, usada principalmente como material de bloqueo y aislante, **249**

Corn Belt/región maicera Región del medio oeste de Estados Unidos, de Ohio a Iowa, cuya actividad agrícola se basa en el cultivo del maíz, **97**

cosmopolitan/cosmopolita Que tiene influencia de muchas culturas, **266**

Cossacks/Cosacos Arrieros nómadas que habitaban en la región fronteriza de Ucrania, **351**

coup/golpe de estado Ataque repentino de un grupo reducido de personas para derrocar a un gobierno, **211**

Creoles/Criollos Personas de descendencia europea nacidas en la América colonial, **210**

culture/cultura Sistema de creencias y costumbres comunes que guía la conducta cotidiana de las personas, **47**

culture region/región cultural Región del mundo en la que se comparten ciertos rasgos culturales, **47**

culture traits/rasgos culturales Características de una cultura, como la ropa, la comida o las creencias religiosas, **47**

currents/corrientes Enormes corrientes del océano que transportan agua tibia a las regiones frías y viceversa, **34**

cyclones/ciclones Tormentas violentas con fuertes lluvias, parecidas a los huracanes del Caribe, comunes en el sur de Asia, **568**

czar/zar Emperador ruso, **330**

D

Dairy Belt/región lechera Región del medio oeste de Estados Unidos, al norte de la franja del maíz, donde la elaboración de productos lácteos es una importante actividad económica, **97**

Dalits/dalits Personas de la clase social más baja de la India, cuyas actividades son consideradas poco salubres, **561**

death rate/índice de mortalidad número de muertes por 1,000 personas en un año, **59**

deforestation/deforestación Destrucción o pérdida de un área boscosa, **39**

deltas/deltas Formaciones creadas por la acumulación de sedimentos en las desembocadura de los ríos, **21**

demilitarized zone/zona desmilitarizada Zona de protección que sirve como barrera entre dos países en conflicto, como Corea del Norte y Corea del Sur, **635**

democracy/democracia Sistema político en el que la población elige a sus líderes mediante el voto de mayoría, **238**

depressions/cavidades Zonas de elevación muy baja, **448**

developing countries/países en vías de desarrollo países que se encuentran en alguna etapa de su proceso de desarrollo, **55**

dharma/dharma En el hinduismo, un deber moral, **558**

dialect/dialecto Variación de un idioma, **248, 506**

Diaspora/Diáspora Dispersión de la población judía que emigró de territorio palestino durante el imperio romano, **384**

dictators/dictadores Personas que ejercen total autoridad sobre un gobierno, **158, 463**

Diet/Dieta Legislatura electa de Japón, **627**

diffusion/difusión Extensión de ideas o conducta de una región cultural a otra, **9**

dikes/diques Grandes muros de tierra o concreto construidos para contener a un cuerpo de agua y evitar inundaciones, **601**

diversify/diversificar En la agricultura, se refiere a la siembra de varios productos y uno solo, **94**

domestication/domesticación Cuidado de una planta o animal para uso personal, **51**

dominion/dominio Territorio en el que se ejerce una influencia, **108**

droughts/sequías Periodos en los que los cultivos sufren daños debido a la escasez de lluvia, **63, 495**

dynasty/dinastía Familia que gobierna y hereda el poder de generación en generación, **603**

earthquakes/terremotos Movimientos repentinos y fuertes que se producen en las fisuras de la superficie de la tierra, **20**

ecotourism/ecoturismo Uso de regiones naturales para atraer visitantes, **160**

ejidos/ejidos Territorios de cultivo propiedad de los indígenas de México, **142**

El Dorado/El Dorado leyenda que habla de los chibchas, antiguos habitantes de Colombia, **172**

El Niño/El Niño Patrón oceánico y climatológico del océano Pacífico que elevó la temperatura del agua en dicho océano, **206**

embargo/embargo Límite impuesto a las relaciones comerciales, **407**

emigrant/emigrante persona que sale de un lugar para otro, **59**

emperor/emperador Gobernante supremo de vastos territorios, **603**

empire/imperio Sistema cuyo gobierno central controla diversos territorios, **141**

enclaves/enclaves Países rodeados en su mayor parte o en su totalidad por otro país, **518**

encomienda/encomienda Sistema mediante el cual los monarcas españoles cedían territorios de América a los colonizadores de su país, quienes obligaban a los indígenas de esas dichas tierras a trabajar para ganarse el sustento, **193**

endemic species/especies endémicas Plantas y animales que se desarrollan en una región particular del planeta, **679**

entrepreneurs/empresarios Personas que usan su dinero y su talento para iniciar un negocio, **638**

epidemic/epidemia Expansión vasta, por general de una enfermedad, **141**

ergs/ergs Grandes "mares" de arena formados por las dunas del desierto del Sahara, **448**

erosion/erosión Desplazamiento de agua, hielo, viento o minerales a otro lugar, **21**

estuary/estuario Cuerpo de agua parcialmente cerrado en el que el agua de mar se combina con agua dulce, **187**

ethnic groups/grupos étnicos Grupos culturales que comparten creencias y prácticas comunes, **47**

ethnocentrism/etnocentrismo ver diferencias en otra cultura como inferior, **49**

evaporation/evaporación Proceso mediante el cual el agua se convierte en vapor y se eleva en el aire, **27**

exclave/exclave Parte de un país separada por el territorio de uno o más países, **513**

Exclusive Economic Zones/zonas de exclusividad económica Zonas costeras de un país en las que éste tiene derecho a extraer y controlar los recursos existentes, **701**

exotic rivers/ríos exóticos Ríos originados en regiones húmedas que fluyen a zonas más secas, **396**

exports/exportaciones productos que un país vende a otros países, **57**

famine/hambruna Gran escasez de alimento, **63, 282, 639**

fault/falla Fractura de la superficie de la tierra que causa el movimiento de grandes masas de rocas, **20**

favelas/favelas Grandes poblaciones localizadas en los alrededores de algunas ciudades brasileñas, **191**

fellahin/fellahin agricultores egipcios dueños de pequeñas porciones de terreno, **458**

fjords/fiordos Grietas estrechas y profundas localizadas entre altos acantilados donde se acumula el agua de mar, **274**

floodplain/llanura aluvial Especie de plataforma a nivel de la tierra, formada por la acumulación de los sedimentos de una corriente de agua, **21**

fossil fuels/combustibles fósiles Recursos no renovables formados por restos muy antiguos de plantas y animales, **40**

fossil water/aguas fósiles Agua que no es reemplazada por el agua de lluvia, **397**

free enterprise/libre empresa Sistema económico en el que las personas, y no el gobierno, deciden qué productos fabrican, venden y compran, **56**

free port/puerto libre Ciudad en la que casi no se aplican impuestos a los productos que allí se adquieren, **461**

futon/futón Especie de sofá ligero, también usado como cama, muy común en Japón, **630**

gauchos/gauchos Arrieros argentinos, **193**

geography/geografía Estudio de las características físicas y culturales de la Tierra, **3**

geothermal energy/energía geotérmica Fuente energética no renovable producida por el calor del interior de la tierra, **41**

gers/gers Grandes tiendas circulares que son fáciles de armar, desarmar y transportar; usadas por los ganaderos nómadas de Mongolia, **615**

geysers/géiseres Manantiales que lanzan chorros de agua caliente y vapor a gran altura, **288**

glaciers/glaciares Grandes bloques de hielo que se desplazan con lentitud sobre el agua, **22**

glen/glen Término de origen escocés que es sinónimo de valle, **281**

globalization/globalización Proceso mediante el que as comunicaciones alrededor del mundo se han incrementado haciendo a las culturas más oarecidas, **60**

global warming/calentamiento global Aumento lento y constante de la temperatura de la Tierra, **30**

gorge/garganta Cañón estrecho y muy profundo, **492**

graphite/grafito Tipo de carbón usado para fabricar puntas de lápices y muchos otros productos, **580**

greenhouse effect/efecto invernadero Proceso mediante el cual la atmósfera terrestre atrapa el calor de su superficie, **30**

green revolution/revolución verde Programa iniciado por el gobierno de la India en la década de 1960 para modernizar los métodos y producir mayor cantidad de alimento, **563**

griots/griots Narradores de historias de África Occidental que pasan sus tradiciones tribales de manera oral, **480**

gross domestic product/producto interno bruto Valor de todos los bienes y servicios producidos en un país, **53**

gross national product/producto nacional bruto valor de todos los bienes y servicios producidos en un año por un país, dentro o fuera de sus límites, **53**

groundwater/agua subterránea Agua de lluvia, ríos, lagos y nieve derretida que se filtra al subsuelo, **26**

guerrilla/guerrillero Persona armada que participa en una lucha armada irregular (los ataques sorpresa, por ejemplo), **163**

habitation fog/humo residente Especie de niebla producida por el humo atrapado en la atmósfera de las ciudades siberianas debido al intenso frío, **338**

haciendas/haciendas Granjas de gran tamaño cedidas por los monarcas españoles a los colonizadores de América, **142**

harmattan/harmattan Viento seco y polvoso que sopla con fuerza hacia el sur durante el invierno en el desierto del Sahara, **468**

heavy industry/industria pesada Industria basada en la manufactura de metales, **336**

hieroglyphs/jeroglíficos imágenes y símbolos usados para registrar información en el antiguo Egipto, **451**

Holocaust/holocausto Asesinato masivo de millones de judíos y personas de otros grupos a manos de los nazis durante la Segunda Guerra Mundial, **261**

homogeneous/homogéneo Agrupamiento que comparte ciertas características, como el origen étnico, **357**

human-environment interaction/ interacción humano-ambiente relación entre personas y el medio ambiente, **9**

human geography/geografía humana estudio del pasado y presente de la humanidad, **11**

humanitarian aid/ayuda humanitaria medicina, comida, y cobertizo que las agencias de ayuda internacional dan a las personas con necesidades, **63**

hurricanes/huracanes Tormentas tropicales con intensos vientos, fuertes lluvias y altas mareas, **14**

hydroelectric power/energía hidroeléctrica Fuente energética renovable producida en generadores impulsados por caídas de agua, **41**

icebergs/icebergs Grandes bloques de hielo que se separan de los glaciales y flotan a la deriva en el océano, **696**

icebreakers/rompehielos Barcos que rompen la capa de hielo que se forma en la superficie de algunos cuerpos de agua para permitir el paso de otras embarcaciones, **342**

ice shelf/capa de hielo Cubierta de hielo que se forma en aguas costeras, **696**

immigrant/inmigrante persona que llega de otro país, **59**

imports/importaciones productos que un país compra de otros paises, **57**

impressionism/impresionismo Forma de arte desarrollada en Francia a finales del siglo XIX y principios del siglo XX, **259**

indentured servants/trabajadores por contrato Personas que trabajan por un tiempo determinado, en la mayoría de los casos a cambio de gastos de viaje, **179**

indigo/índigo Planta que se usa para fabricar un tinte de color azul oscuro, **176**

Indo-European/Indoeuropeo Familia que incluye muchos idiomas europeos como el germánico, el báltico y los dialectos eslavos, **296**

industrialized countries/paises industrializados paises que depende más en la industria que en la agricultura, **54**

inflation/inflación Aumento de los precios que ocurre cuando la moneda de un país pierde poder adquisitivo, **146**

intensive cultivation/cultivo intenso Cultivo de productos en cualquier terreno disponible, **631**

interdependence/interdependencia Depender en otro país para recursos o productos y servicios, **57**

Inuit/inuit Tribu esquimal de América del norte, **115**

ivory/marfil Material de color crema extraído de los colmillos de los elefantes que se usa para fabricar joyería y artículos decorativos, **504**

Japan Current/Corriente de Japón corriente oceánica de aguas tibias que fluye al este de Japón, **623**

junta/junta Grupo de oficiales militares que asumen el control de un país al derrocar al poder anterior, **215**

kampongs/kampongs Aldea tradicional de Indonesia; el término también se usa para referirse a las grandes poblaciones humanas establecidas en los alrededores de las ciudades de Indonesia, **654**

karma/karma Para los hinduistas y budistas, es la fuerza positiva o negativa generada por las acciones de una persona, **558**

kimchi/kimchi Especie de col china aderezada y avinagrada que se sirve como plato tradicional en Corea, **638**

kimonos/kimonos vestidos tradicionales japoneses, **629**

kiwi/kiwi Ave que no vuela, originaria de Nueva Zelanda; a veces, este término se usa para referirse a los neozelandeses, **687**

klongs/klongs Canales de Bangkok, una ciudad de Tailandia, **651**

krill/krill Animales marinos diminutos que son una importante fuente alimenticia para otras especies marinas del Océano Atlántico, **697**

landforms/accidentes geográficos Forma de la tierra en diferentes partes de la superficie, **19**

landlocked/sin salida al mar Zona rodeada de agua por completo y sin acceso directo al océano, **198, 416**

lava/lava Magma que emerge del interior de la tierra por un orificio de la corteza, **20**

light industry/industria ligera Industria que se enfoca en la manufactura de objetos ligeros como la ropa, **336**

lignite/lignita Tipo de carbón suave, **295**

literacy rate/índice de alfabetismo Procentaje de personas que puenden leer y escribir, **54**

Llaneros/llaneros Vaqueros de los llanos de Venezuela, **178**

Llanos/llanos Planicies localizadas al este de Colombia y al oeste de Venezuela, **170**

lochs/lagos Lagos escoceses enclavados en valles labrados por los glaciales, **274**

loess/limo Suelo fino de arenisca, excelente para la agricultura, **255**

mainland/región continental Región donde se localiza la mayor porción de terreno de un país, **236, 644**

malaria/malaria Enfermedad mortal que se difunde por medio de los mosquitos, **476**

mandate/mandato Territorios que formaban parte de los países derrotados en la Primera Guerra Mundial, y que pasaron a control de los países vencedores, **388**

maquiladoras/maquiladoras Fábricas extranjeras establecidas en la frontera de México con Estados Unidos, **149**

maritime/marítimo En o cerca del mar, como las provincias marítimas de Canadá, **112**

market economy/economía de mercado Tipo de economía en la que los consumidores ayudan a determinar qué productos se fabrican al comprar o rechazar ciertos bienes y servicios, **56**

marsupials/marsupiales Animales que transportan a sus crías en un saco, **680**

martial law/ley marcial Ley militar, **606**

medieval/medieval Periodo de colapso del imperio romano, aproximadamente en el año 1,500 de nuestra era, **257**

megalopolis/megalópolis Enorme zona urbana que abarca una serie de ciudades que se han desarrollado juntas, **94, 629**

Mercosur/Mercosur Organización comercial en la que participan Argentina, Brasil, Paraguay, Uruguay y dos países asociados (Bolivia y Chile), **196**

merengue/merengue Tipo de música y baile nacional en la República Dominicana, **162**

Mesopotamia/Mesopotamia Tierra antigua entre los ríos Tigris y Eufrates, **396**

mestizos/mestizos Personas cuyo origen combina las razas europeas y las razas indígenas de América, **142**

meteorology/meteorología Predicción y registro de lluvias, temperaturas y otras condiciones atmosféricas, **13**

Métis/Métis Personas cuyo origen combina las razas europeas y las razas indígenas de Canadá, **109**

migration/migración movimiento de personas, **59**

millet/mijo Tipo de cultivo resistente a las sequías, **475**

missions/misiones Puestos españoles de evangelización establecidos en la época colonial, especialmente en América, **142**

mixed economy/economía mixta Intercambio de bienes y servicios basado en al menos dos otros sistemas, **57**

Moors/moros Musulmanes del norte de África, **247**

mosaics/mosaicos Imágenes creadas con pequeños fragmentos de piedras coloreadas, **240**

mosques/mezquitas Casas de adoración islámica, **422**

most-favored-nation status/estatus de nación favorecida Estatus que otorga privilegios de intercambio comercial entre Estados Unidos y otros países, **613**

movement/movimiento El ir y venir de gente e ideas, **9**

mulattoes/mulatos Personas cuyo origen combina las razas europeas y las razas indígenas de África, **142**

multicultural Mezcla de culturas en un mismo país o comunidad, **47**

multiple cropping/cultivo múltiple Tipo de agricultura en la que se producen dos o tres cultivos cada año en las mismas tierras, **612**

Muslims/Mulsulmanes Seguidores del Islam, **398**

nationalism/nacionalismo Demanda de autogo-bierno y fuerte sentimiento de lealtad hacia una nación, **268**

NATO/OTAN (Organización del Tratado del Atlántico Norte); alianza militar formada por varios países europeos, Estados Unidos y Canadá, **257**

nature reserves/reservas naturales Zonas asignadas por el gobierno para la protección de animales, plantas, suelo y agua, **348**

navigable/navegable Rutas acuáticas de profundidad suficiente para la navegación de barcos, **254**

neutral/neutral Que no toma ningún partido en una disputa o conflicto, **286**

newsprint/papel periódico Papel económico usado para imprimir publicaciones periódicas, **105**

nirvana/nirvana Para los budistas, es el escape de los sufrimientos de la vida, **559**

nomads/nómadas Personas que se mudan frecuentemente de un lugar a otro, **418**

nonrenewable resources/recursos no renova-bles Recursos, como el carbón mineral y el petróleo, que no pueden reemplazarse a corto plazo por medios naturales, **38**

North Atlantic Drift/Corriente del Atlántico Norte corriente de aguas tibias que aumenta la temperatura y genera lluvias en el norte de Europa, **275**

oasis/oasis Lugar del desierto donde un manantial proporciona una fuente natural de agua, **416**

oil shale/pizarra petrolífera Capa de roca que al calentarse produce petróleo, **295**

one-crop economy/economía de un cultivo Economía basada en un solo cultivo, como las bananas, la caña de azúcar o el cacao, **57**

OPEC/OPEP Organización de países exportadores de petróleo; grupo formado para ejercer influencia en el precio de los mercados petroleros mundiales, **399**

oral history/historia oral Información oral transmitida de una persona a otra y de generación en generación, **470**

Organization of African Unity (OAU)/Organización África Unida (OAU) Grupo fundado en 1963 para promover la cooperación entre los países africanos, **529**

outback/*Outback* (Interior) Región interior de Australia, **680**

overpopulation/superpoblación más personas que una región o un país puede mantener por sus propios medios, **58**

Oyashio Current/Corriente Oyashio Corriente de aguas frías que fluye al este de Japón, **623**

ozone layer/ozonosfera Forma del oxígeno en la atmósfera que ayuda a proteger a la Tierra de los daños que produce la radiación solar, **30**

pagodas/pagodas Templos budistas, **608**

Pampas/pampas Región extensa cubierta de hierba en la zona central de Argentina, **186**

pans/pans Regiones desérticas del sur de África, de terreno bajo y plano, en las que desaguaban corrientes antiguas, **519**

pardos/pardos Venezolanos descendientes de la unión entre africanos, europeos e indígenas sudamericanos, **178**

peat/turba Sustancia formada por plantas muertas, por lo general musgos, **284**

periodic markets/mercados periódicos Mercados al aire libre en el África central, **503**

perspective/perspectiva Punto de vista basado en la experiencia y la comprensión de una persona, **3**

Peru Current/corriente de Perú Corriente oceánica fría del litoral oeste de América del Sur, **205**

petroleum/petróleo Líquido graso que al refinarse produce gasolina y otros combustibles y aceites, **40**

pharaohs/faraones Reyes del antiguo Egipto, **451**

phosphates/fosfatos Sales minerales que contienen el elemento fósforo; se usa para hacer fertilizantes, **379**

physical geography/geografía física Estudio del paisaje natural y los sistemas físicos de la Tierra, entre ellos la atmósfera, **11**

pidgin languages/lenguas francas Lenguajes sencillos que ayudan a entenderse a personas que hablan idiomas diferentes, **179**

place/lugar Rasgos físicos y humanos de una ubicación específica, **7**

plain/planicie Área casi plana de la superficie terrestre, **21**

plantains/banano Tipo de plátano que se usa para cocinar, **164**

plantations/plantaciones Granjas muy grandes en las que se produce un solo tipo de cultivo para vender, **87**

plate tectonics/tectónica de placas Teoría de que la superficie terrestre está dividida en varias placas enormes que se mueven lentamente, **19**

polar desert/desierto polar Región de latitudes altas donde cae muy poca precipitación, **697**

polis/polis Ciudad estado griega, **238**

pope/papa Obispo de Roma y líder de la Iglesia católica romana, **243**

popular culture/cultura popular Creencias, gustos, metas y practicas generalmente compartidos, **60**

population density/densidad de población Número promedio de personas que viven en una milla cuadrada o un kilómetro cuadrado, **58**

porcelain/porcelana Tipo de vajilla muy fina, **604**

potash/potasa Mineral que se usa para hacer fertilizantes, **105**

precipitation/precipitación Proceso por el que el agua vuelve de regreso a la Tierra, **27**

prevailing winds/vientos predominantes Brisas que sopla consistentemente en la misma dirección sobre grandes regiones de la Tierra, **33**

protectionism/proteccionismo Práctica de poner barreras comerciales para proteger a las industrias nacionales de la competencia de las industrias extranjeras, **632**

provinces/provincias Divisiones administrativas de un país, **108**

pulp/pulpa Fibras reblandecidas de madera para hacer papel, **105**

pyramids/pirámides Enormes monumentos de piedra cuadrados y con cuatro lados triangulares, **452**

Quechua/quechua Idioma de los incas de América del Sur; todavía se habla en esta región, **212**

quinoa/quinua Planta nativa de la región sudamericana de los Andes que da semillas muy nutritivas, **207**

quipus/quipus Complicados sistemas de cuerdas de varios colores con nudos, que usaron los incas de América del Sur para registrar información, **208**

Qur'an/Corán El libro sagra do del Islam, **399**

race/raza Grupo de personas que comparten características físicas o biológicas heredadas, **48**

rain shadow/barrera montañosa Área seca en el sotavento de una montaña o de una cordillera, **35**

reforestation/reforestación Plantación de árboles donde los bosques han sido talados, **39**

Reformation/Reforma Movimiento europeo del siglo XVI para reformar el cristianismo, **260**

refugees/refugiados Personas que han escapado a otro país, generalmente por razones económicas o políticas, **163, 647**

reggae/reggae Tipo de música que tiene sus orígenes en Jamaica, **162**

region/región Área de la superficie de la Tierra con una o más características compartidas, **8**

regionalism/regionalismo Conexión más fuerte con la región a la que se pertenece que con el propio país, **111**

regs/regs Extensas planicies de grava azotadas por el viento, en el Sahara, **448**

reincarnation/reencarnación Creencia de que el alma humana vuelva a nacer una y otra vez en diferentes cuerpos, **558**

relative location/ubicación relativa Posición de un lugar en relación con otro, **7**

Renaissance/Renaissance Palabra francesa que significa "renacimiento" y se refiere a una nueva era de conocimiento que empieza en Europa en el siglo XIV, **243**

renewable resources/recursos renovables Recursos, como el suelo y los bosques, que pueden reemplazarse por medio de procesos naturales de la Tierra, **38**

rifts/hendeduras Valles largos y profundos con montañas o mesetas a cada lado, **486**

Roma/Roma Grupo étnico, también conocido como gitanos, que pudo haber migrado de la India a Europa hace mucho tiempo, **306**

rugby/rugby Juego de origen británico similar al fútbol, **682**

rural/rural Área de terreno abierto que se usa para la agricultura, **4**

Sahel/sahel Región de pastizales secos con clima estepario del sur del Sahara, **468**

samurai/samurai Guerreros al servicio de señores japoneses, **626**

sanctions/sanciones Penalidad económica o política, como un embargo, que uno o más países usan para obligar a otro país a dejar de cometer un acto ilegal o inmoral, **525**

Sanskrit/sánscrito Idioma antiguo del sur de Asia; en la actualidad se usa en la India como lengua sagrada en la, **553**

Santería/santería Religión originaria de Cuba que mezcla religiones del oeste de África y otras tradiciones, entre otras del catolicismo romano, **162**

secede/separar Dividir un país para formar otro, **478**

second-growth forests/bosques reforestados Árboles que cubren una región después de que el bosque original ha sido talado, **93**

secular/seglar Que está separado de la religión, como un gobierno o estado secular, **381**

selvas/selvas Bosques tropicales exuberantes del oeste de Ecuador y Perú, y del norte de Bolivia, **205**

sepoys/cipayos Tropas indias dirigidas por oficiales británicos durante el periodo colonial de la India, **556**

serfs/siervos Personas que, en Rusia, estaban atados a una tierra y trabajaban para un señor, **351**

shah/sha Rey de Irán, **410**

shamans/shaman Monje sintoísta, **625**

Shia/Shia La segunda más grande rama del Islam, **398**

Shintoism/shintoismo Religión más antigua conocida de Japón, **625**

shogun/shogún "Gran general" el más alto rango entre los guerreros japoneses, **626**

silt/cieno Tierra de granos muy finos, **449**

sinkholes/sumideros agujero profundo de pendiente empinada que se forma cuando el techo de una cueva se hunde, **136**

sirocco/siroco Viento seco y caliente del norte de África que viaja por el mar Mediterráneo hacia Europa, **237**

slash-and-burn agriculture/agricultura de corte y quema Tipo de agricultura en que los bosques se talan y se queman para limpiar el terreno y plantarlo, **149**

smelters/fundidoras Fábricas que procesan menas de metal, **337**

smog/smog Mezcla de humo, sustancias químicas y niebla, **148**

soil exhaustion/agotamiento del suelo Pérdida de los nutrientes del suelo que necesitan las plantas, **188**

solar power/energía solar calor y luz del sol, **41**

sorghum/sorgo Grano de cultivo que puede sobrevivir a las sequías, **475**

souks/souks Mercados del norte de África, **461**

soviet/soviet supremo Consejo comunista que gobernó la república y otras regiones de la Unión Soviética, **351**

spatial perspective/perspectiva espacial Punto de vista basado o visto en relación con el lugar en que se encuentra un objeto, así como la razón por la que está ahí, **3**

staple/producto básico Cultivo principal de una región o un país, **476**

steppe/estepario Gran llanura de pastos altos que se extiende desde Ucrania, pasa por el sur de Rusia y llega hasta Kazajistan, **327**

storm surges/mareas de tormenta Grandes ondas de agua que se elevan por la fuerza del viento, en particular de los ciclones, huracanes y otras tormentas tropicales, **568**

strait/estrecho Paso angosto que une dos grandes cuerpos de agua, **204**

strip mining/minería a cielo abierto Tipo de minería en que se retiran la tierra y las rocas para extraer carbón y otros recursos que están bajo la superficie terrestre, **98**

stupas/stupas Montículos de tierra o piedras que cubren las cenizas del Buda o las reliquias de los santos budistas, **576**

subduction/subducción Movimiento en el que una placa tectónica terrestre más gruesa se sumerge debajo de una más delgada, **20**

subsistence agriculture/agricultura de subsistencia Tipo de agricultura en que los campesinos siembran sólo lo necesario para mantenerse a ellos mismos y a sus familias, **52**

sultan/sultán Gobernante supremo de un país musulmán, **567**

Sunni/sunita La rama más grande del Islam, **398**

superpowers/superpotencias Países poderosos, **331**

Swahili/suahili Idioma bantú que se habla extensamente en África, **490**

symbol/símbolo Palabra, forma, color, estandarte o cualquier otra cosa que se use en representación de algo, **49**

taiga/taiga Bosque de árboles siempre verdes que existen en el sur de la tundra en Rusia, **327**

teak/teca Tipo de madera preciosa que crece en la India y al sudeste de Asia, **551**

tepuís/tepuís Capas de roca arenisca resistentes a la erosión en las mesetas de los altiplanos de las Guyanas, **170**

terraces/terrazas Crestas horizontales que se construyen sobre las laderas de las colinas para prevenir la pérdida de suelo y favorecer la agricultura, **22**

textiles/textiles Productos para fabricar ropa, **87, 279**

theocracy/teocracia Gobierno regido por líderes religiosos, **410**

third-world countries/países del tercer mundo países en desarrollo que faltan oportunidades económicas, **55**

topography/topografía forma, altura y arreglo de la tierra en un cierto lugar, **19**

townships/municipios Regiones de multitudes de pequeñas casas apiñadas que habitan los sudafricanos de raza negra en las afueras de las ciudades, **524**

trade deficit/deficit comercial Valor de las exportaciones de un país es más bajo que el valor de sus importaciones, **99**

trade surplus/excedente comercial Ocurre cuando el valor de las importaciones es mayor que el de las importaciones, **632**

tradition-based economy/economía tradicional Economía basada en las costumbres y las tradiciones, **56**

tributary/tributario Cualquier corriente pequeña o río que fluye hacia un río o una corriente más grande, **26**

trust territories/territorios bajo administración fiduciaria Regiones que están bajo el control temporal de otro país hasta que establezca su propio gobierno, **699**

tsetse fly/mosca tse tse Mosca africana del sur del Sahara que transmite el mal del sueño, una enfermedad mortal, **468**

tsunamis/tsunamis Olas muy grandes que se forman por la actividad submarina de las placas tectónicas, tales como los terremotos, **623**

uninhabitable/inhabitable Que no es propicio para el establecimiento de seres humanos, **288**

urban/urbano Área en que se encuentra una ciudad, **4**

veld, the/el veld regiones de pastos altos en el sur de África, **518**

viceroy/virrey Gobernador de una colonia, **210**

wadis/wadis Lechos secos de corrientes en el sudoeste de Asia, **397**

water cycle/ciclo del agua Circulación del agua del la superficie de la Tierra a la atmósfera y su regreso, **27**

water vapor/vapor de agua Estado gaseoso del agua, **27**

weather/tiempo Condiciones de la atmósfera en un tiempo y un lugar determinados, **32**

weathering/desgaste Proceso de desintegración de las rocas en pedazos pequeños por la acción del calor, el agua y otros medios, **21**

Wheat Belt/región triguera Zona de la región de las Grandes Planicies en Estados Unidos en la que la actividad principal es el cultivo del trigo, **98**

work ethic/ética laboral Creencia de que el trabajo es un mérito en sí mismo, **632**

yurt/yurta Tienda redonda y portátil de lana tejida que se coloca sobre una armazón de madera, **422**

Zionism/sionismo Movimiento que trata de establecer un país o comunidad judía en Palestina, **385**

zonal/zonal Clima del este de África que se extiende en franjas de este a oeste, **468**

INDEX

Belgium, 264–65; Benelux countries, 264–66; climate and waterways, 254–55; culture, 252; France, 256–59; Germany, 260–63; Luxembourg, 264–65; Netherlands, 264–66; physical features, 254; resources, 255; student profile, 252, *p252*; Switzerland, 267–68. *See also* specific countries

Western Ghats, *m549*, 550
Western Hemisphere, S3, *gS3*
Western New Guinea *See* Irian Jaya
Western Plateau (Australia), *m677*, 678
Western Rift Valley, *m501*, 502
Western Sahara, *m447*, 453
wheat, 98, 171, 353, *g353*
Wheat Belt (U.S.), 98
White Nile, 449, *m485*, 486
wind: as energy resource, 41; sirocco, 237, land breezes, 586; monsoons, 601, 551; sea breezes, 586; typhoons, 602
wind turbines, *p40*
Windhoek, Namibia, *m517*, 528
Windsor, Ontario, *m103*, 112
Winnipeg, Manitoba, *m103*, 115
Wisconsin, *m81*; climate, 84; economy, 95, 97; natural resources, 85; physical features, 82; statistics, 79
Witwatersrand, *m517*, 526
Wolong Nature Reserve, *p600*
work ethic, 632

world population growth, *gS10*; issues, 58–59
World War I: Belgium, 264; Eastern Europe, 298, 303; France, 257; Germany, 261; U.S., 88
World War II, Austria, 268; France, 257; Germany, 261, *p261*; Japan, 627; North Africa, 453; Poland, 300; U.S., 88
World Wildlife Fund, 584
writing: Sanskrit, 553
Wuhan, China, *m599*, 611
Wyoming, *m81*; climate, 84–85; economy, 97–98; natural resources, 85; physical features, 83–84; statistics, 79

Xi River, *m599*, 601

Yalta, Ukraine, *p352*
Yalu River, 622
Yangon, Myanmar, *m643*, *p648*, 651
Yangtze River *See* Chang River
Yaoundé, Cameroon, *m501*, 511
Yekaterinburg, Russia, *m325*, 337
Yellow Sea, 601
Yellowstone National Park (Wyoming, Montana, and Idaho), *p98*

Yemen, *m395*, 400, 403, *p403*; climate, 396–97; physical features, 396; resources, 397; statistics, 375, *g402*
Yenisey River, *m325*, 339
yerba mate, *p199*
Yucatán Peninsula, *m135*, 136, 149
Yugoslavia *See* Serbia and Montenegro
Yukon Territory, Canada, *m103*, 115
Yunus, Muhammad, 573, *p573*
yurt, 422, 424–25, *p425*

Zagreb, Croatia, *m293*, 305
Zaire, *m501*, 508. *See also* Democratic Republic of the Congo
Zambezi River, *m501*, 502
Zambia, *m501*, 512–13; climate, plants, animals, 502–03; culture, 505–07, *p512*; history, 504–05; physical features, 502; resources, 503; statistics, 445, *g513*
Zanzibar, 489, 492. *See also* Tanzania
Zimbabwe, *m517*, 529; ancient history, 520–21; HIV/AIDS rate, *g533*; European colonization in, 522–23; physical features and climate, 518–19; resources, 519; statistics, 445, *g529*
Zionism, 385
zonal, 468
Zurich, Switzerland, *m253*, 269

ACKNOWLEDGMENTS

...mission to reproduce copyrighted material, ...eful acknowledgment is made to the following sources:

Doubleday, a division of Random House, Inc.; electronic format by permission of Harold Ober Associates Incorporated: From "Marriage Is a Private Affair" from *Girls at War and Other Stories* by Chinua Achebe. Copyright © 1972, 1973 by Chinua Achebe.

FocalPoint f/8: From "October 5—Galtai" from "Daily Chronicles" and from "Buddhist Prayer Ceremony" from "Road Stories" by Gary Matoso and Lisa Dickey from *The Russian Chronicles* from *FocalPoint f/8*, accessed October 14, 1999, at http://www.f8.com/FP/Russia.

HarperCollins Publishers, Inc.; electronic format by permission of Wallace Literary Agency: From *My Days* by R. K. Narayan. Copyright © 1973, 1974 by R. K. Narayan.

International Rescue Committee: From "IRC Staff Members Talk About 'The Biggest Humanitarian Crisis on the Planet'" by Werner Vansant from *International Rescue Committee* Web site, accessed October 19, 2003, at **http://www.theirc.org/index.cfm?section = where&wwwID = 1708**. Copyright © 2003 by International Rescue Committee.

Professor Hugh Kawharu: From "Treaty of Waitangi, 1840," translated by Prof. Sir Hugh Kawharu from *Government of New Zealand* Web site, accessed October 30, 2003, at **http://www.govt.nz/en/aboutnz/?d = a3217d70e71e9632aad1016cb343f900**.

James Li, M.D.: From "Africa" by James Li, M.D from *eMedicine*, accessed October 11, 1999, at http://www.emedicine.com/emerg/topic726.htm. Copyright © 1999 by James Li.

Ms. Magazine: From "Foresters Without Diplomas" by Wangari Maathai from *Ms.*, vol. 1, no. 5, March/April 1991. Copyright © 1991 by *Ms.* Magazine.

National Geographic Society: From "El Niño/La Niña" by Curt Suplee from *National Geographic*, vol. 195, no. 3, March 1999. Copyright © 1999 by National Geographic Society.

National Public Radio: Quote by Schwarma from *National Public Radio*, August 31, 2003. Copyright © 2003 by National Public Radio.

Penguin Books Ltd.: From *The Epic of Gilgamesh*, translated by N. K. Sandars (Penguin Classics 1960, Third Edition, 1972). Copyright © 1960, 1964, 1972 by N. K. Sandars.

Time, Inc.: From "Coco Chanel" by Ingrid Sischy from *Time*, June 8, 1998. Copyright © 1998 by Time, Inc.

Writer's House, Inc. c/o The Permissions Company: From *For Love Alone* by Christina Stead. Copyright © 1944 by Harcourt, Inc.; copyright renewed © 1972 by Christina Stead.

Sources Cited:

"B. Ospanova, a citizen of Almaty, 50 years old, December 1998" from *President of the Republic of Kazakhstan* Web site, accessed December 2, 2003, at **http://www.president.kz/articles/Sover_Kaz.asp?lng = ng = en&art = kazakh_10**. Published by the Analysis and Strategic Research Center of the Administration of the President of the Republic of Kazakhstan, 1998.

From "Dinner with Attila the Hun, c. AD 450" by Priscus from *Historici Graeci Minores*, translated by B. K. Workman. Published in *They Saw It Happen in Classical Times* by Blackwell, Oxford, UK, 1964.

From "Weekender: Woman of Courage (Tales of the Century: A Filipino writer recalls an interview with Aaung San Suu Kyi" from *Businessworld*, Manila, March 5, 1999, pg. 1.

From "Where We Stand Today: Overview of Nunavut" by Stephen Vail and Graeme Clinton from *Nunavut Economic Outlook*, May 2001. Published by The Conference Board of Canada, 2001.

From "President Khatami's Interview with the NY Times" from *The New York Times*, November 9, 2001.

From "Courage, the Spirit of Daring" from *Bushido: The Warrior's Code* by Inazo Nitobe. Published by Ohara Publications, Inc. Burbank, CA, 1979.

From "Ancient Ghana and the Customs of Its Inhabitants" by Al Bakri from *Africa in the Days of Exploration*, edited by Roland Oliver and Caroline Oliver. Published by Prentice-Hall, Inc., Englewood Cliffs, NJ, 1965.

From "Industrial Wasteland" from *Siberian Odyssey: A Voyage into the Russian Soul* by Frederick Kempe. Published by G. P. Putnam's Sons, New York, NY, 1992.

From "The Wild Irish West" from *The Irish: Portrait of a People* by Richard O'Connor. Published by G. P. Putnam's Sons, New York, NY, 1971.

From "The Aztecs in 1519" from *The Discovery and Conquest of Mexico* by Bernal Díaz. Published by Routledge and Kegan Paul, London, 1938.

Quote by Sergei Ling from *Chernobyl Legacy* by Paul Fusco and Magdalena Caris. Published by de.MO, Millbrook, NY, 2001.

ART CREDITS

Abbreviated as follows: (t) top, (b) bottom, (l) left, (r) right, (c) center.

Unit flags of United States created by One Mile Up, Inc. Unit flags of Canadian provinces created by EyeWire, Inc. Other flags, country silhouettes, feature maps and atlas maps created by MapQuest.com., Inc. All other illustrations, unless otherwise noted, contributed by Holt, Rinehart and Winston.

Atlas: Page A2, MapQuest.com, Inc.; A4, MapQuest.com, Inc.; A6, MapQuest.com, Inc.; A8, MapQuest.com, Inc.; A10, MapQuest.com, Inc.; A11, MapQuest.com, Inc.; A12, MapQuest.com, Inc.; A13, MapQuest.com, Inc.; A14, MapQuest.com, Inc.; A15, MapQuest.com, Inc.; A16, MapQuest.com, Inc.; A17, MapQuest.com, Inc.; A18, MapQuest.com, Inc.; A19, MapQuest.com, Inc.; A20, MapQuest.com, Inc.; A21, MapQuest.com, Inc.; A22, MapQuest.com, Inc.

Geography and Map Skills Handbook: Page S2, MapQuest.com, Inc.; S3, MapQuest.com, Inc.; S4 (cl, bl), MapQuest.com, Inc.; S5, MapQuest.com, Inc.; S6, MapQuest.com, Inc.; S7, MapQuest.com, Inc.; S8, MapQuest.com, Inc.; S9, MapQuest.com, Inc.; S10 (tr), MapQuest.com, Inc.; S11 (t), Leslie Kell; S11 (b), Ortelius Design; S12 (b), Leslie Kell; S13, Uhl Studios, Inc.; S14, MapQuest.com, Inc.; S16, Robert Hynes.

Chapter 1: Page 5, MapQuest.com, Inc.; 6 (bl), MapQuest.com, Inc.; 8 (l, bc), MapQuest.com, Inc.; 9 (tr), MapQuest.com, Inc.; 11 (bc), MapQuest.com, Inc.; 14 (b), MapQuest.com, Inc.; 16 (b), MapQuest.com, Inc.; 17, MapQuest.com, Inc.

Chapter 2: Page 19, MapQuest.com, Inc.; 26, Uhl Studios, Inc.; 27, Uhl Studios, Inc.; 28, MapQuest.com, Inc.; 29, HRW art; 31, Uhl Studios, Inc.; 32, MapQuest.com, Inc.; 33, Uhl Studios, Inc.; 34, MapQuest.com, Inc.; 35 (tl), Uhl Studios, Inc.; 37, MapQuest.com, Inc.; 38, MapQuest.com, Inc.; 41, MapQuest.com, Inc; 42 (t), MapQuest.com, Inc.; 42 (t, b), MapQuest.com, Inc.; 44, MapQuest.com, Inc.; 45, Leslie Kell.

Chapter 3: Page 48 (t, b), MapQuest.com, Inc.; 49 (tr), MapQuest.com, Inc.; 50 (bl), MapQuest.com, Inc.; 53, MapQuest.com, Inc.; 54, MapQuest.com,

Inc.; 55 (t), MapQuest.com, Inc.; 58, MapQuest.com, Inc.; 64, MapQuest.com, Inc.: 67, MapQuest.com, Inc.

Unit 2: Page 72 (t, bl), Ortelius Design; 73, MapQuest.com, Inc.; 74, MapQuest.com, Inc.; 75, MapQuest.com, Inc.; 76, MapQuest.com, Inc.; 77, MapQuest.com, Inc.; 78–79, MapQuest.com, Inc.

Chapter 4: Page 81, MapQuest.com, Inc.; 82, MapQuest.com, Inc.; 83, MapQuest.com, Inc.; 86, MapQuest.com, Inc.; 87, MapQuest.com, Inc.; 88, MapQuest.com, Inc.; 89, MapQuest.com, Inc.; 92, MapQuest.com, Inc.; 93, MapQuest.com, Inc.; 94, MapQuest.com, Inc.; 95 (t), MapQuest.com, Inc.; 95 (b), Uhl Studios, Inc.; 96 (t), The John Edwards Group; 96 (b), MapQuest.com, Inc.; 97, MapQuest.com, Inc.; 98, MapQuest.com, Inc.; 100, MapQuest.com, Inc.; 101, MapQuest.com, Inc.

Chapter 5: Page 103, MapQuest.com, Inc.; 104, MapQuest.com, Inc.; 105, MapQuest.com, Inc.; 107, MapQuest.com, Inc.; 108, MapQuest.com, Inc.; 109, MapQuest.com, Inc.; 110, MapQuest.com, Inc.; 112, MapQuest.com, Inc.; 116, MapQuest.com, Inc.; 117, MapQuest.com, Inc.; 118 (t), MapQuest.com, Inc.; 118 (b), Russ Charpentier; 119 (t, b), Jack Scott/line art; 119 (t, b), Joe LeMonnier/paper graphic.

Unit 3: Page 124 (t, bl), Ortelius Design; 125, MapQuest.com, Inc.; 126, MapQuest.com, Inc.; 127, MapQuest.com, Inc.; 128, MapQuest.com, Inc.; 129, MapQuest.com, Inc.; 130–133, MapQuest.com, Inc.

Chapter 6: Page 135, MapQuest.com, Inc.; 136, MapQuest.com, Inc.; 137 (t, br), MapQuest.com, Inc.; 140, MapQuest.com, Inc.; 142, MapQuest.com, Inc.; 144, Leslie Kell; 145, MapQuest.com, Inc.; 147, MapQuest.com, Inc.; 148, MapQuest.com, Inc.; 150, MapQuest.com, Inc.; 151, Leslie Kell.

Chapter 7: Page 153, MapQuest.com, Inc.; 154, MapQuest.com, Inc.; 156, MapQuest.com, Inc.; 157, MapQuest.com, Inc.; 161, MapQuest.com, Inc.; 163 (t, b), MapQuest.com, Inc.; 165, MapQuest.com, Inc.; 166, MapQuest.com, Inc.

Chapter 8: Page 169 (b), MapQuest.com, Inc.; 170 Uhl Studios, Inc.; 172, MapQuest.com, Inc.; 173 (br), MapQuest.com, Inc.; 175 (tr), MapQuest.com, Inc.; 176 (bl), MapQuest.com, Inc.; 179 (br) MapQuest.com, Inc.; 180 (bl) MapQuest.com, Inc.; 181, MapQuest.com, Inc.; 182 MapQuest.com, Inc.

Chapter 9: Page 185 MapQuest.com, Inc.; 186, MapQuest.com, Inc.; 191, MapQuest.com, Inc.; 192, Leslie Kell; 196 (t), MapQuest.com, Inc.; 197, MapQuest.com, Inc.; 198, MapQuest.com, Inc.; 200, MapQuest.com, Inc.; 201, Leslie Kell.

Chapter 10: Page 203, MapQuest.com, Inc.; 205, MapQuest.com, Inc.; 208, MapQuest.com, Inc.; 210, MapQuest.com, Inc.; 212, MapQuest.com, Inc.; 213, MapQuest.com, Inc.; 216, MapQuest.com, Inc.; 217, MapQuest.com, Inc.; 218; MapQuest.com, Inc.; 219 (t), MapQuest.com, Inc.; 219 (b), Elizabeth Wolf.

Unit 4: Page 224 (t, bl), Ortelius Design; 225, MapQuest.com, Inc.; 226, MapQuest.com, Inc.; 227, MapQuest.com, Inc.; 228, MapQuest.com, Inc.; 229, MapQuest.com, Inc.; 230–233, MapQuest.com, Inc.

Chapter 11: Page 235 (b), MapQuest.com, Inc.; 236 (t), Leslie Kell; 236 (b), MapQuest.com, Inc.; 237, MapQuest.com, Inc.; 238, MapQuest.com, Inc.; 239, MapQuest.com, Inc.; 242, MapQuest.com, Inc.; 243, MapQuest.com, Inc.; 244, MapQuest.com, Inc.; 246, MapQuest.com, Inc.; 247, MapQuest.com, Inc.; 249, MapQuest.com, Inc.; 250, MapQuest.com, Inc.; 251, MapQuest.com, Inc.

Chapter 12: Page 253, MapQuest.com, Inc.; 254 (t, b), MapQuest.com, Inc.; 255, MapQuest.com, Inc.; 258, MapQuest.com, Inc.; 260, MapQuest.com, Inc.; 261, MapQuest.com, Inc.; 262, MapQuest.com, Inc.; 264, MapQuest.com, Inc.; 268, MapQuest.com, Inc.; 270, MapQuest.com, Inc.; 271, MapQuest.com, Inc.

Chapter 13: Page 273 (b), MapQuest.com, Inc.; 274 (bl), MapQuest.com, Inc.; 278 (bl), MapQuest.com, Inc.; 279, MapQuest.com, Inc.; 281, Leslie Kell; 282, MapQuest.com, Inc.; 286, MapQuest.com, Inc.; 288 (tl), MapQuest.com, Inc.; 290, MapQuest.com, Inc.

Chapter 14: Page 293 (b), MapQuest.com, Inc.; 294, MapQuest.com, Inc.; 298, MapQuest.com, Inc.; 300, MapQuest.com, Inc.; 301, MapQuest.com, Inc.; 302, MapQuest.com, Inc.; 303, MapQuest.com, Inc.; 304 MapQuest.com, Inc.; 305 (t, b), MapQuest.com, Inc.; 308, MapQuest.com, Inc.; 309, Leslie Kell; 311, MapQuest.com, Inc.

Unit 5: Page 316 (t, bl), Ortelius Design; 317, MapQuest.com, Inc.; 318, MapQuest.com, Inc.; 319, MapQuest.com, Inc.; 320, MapQuest.com, Inc.; 321, MapQuest.com, Inc.; 322–323, MapQuest.com, Inc.

Chapter 15: Page 325 (b), MapQuest.com, Inc.; 330 (t), MapQuest.com, Inc.; 331, MapQuest.com, Inc.; 333, MapQuest.com, Inc.; 335, MapQuest.com, Inc.; 336 (t,b), MapQuest.com, Inc.; 337, MapQuest.com, Inc.; 338, MapQuest.com, Inc.; 339, MapQuest.com, Inc.; 340, MapQuest.com, Inc.; 342, MapQuest.com, Inc.; 343, MapQuest.com, Inc.; 344, MapQuest.com, Inc.

Chapter 16: Page 347, MapQuest.com, Inc.; 348, MapQuest.com, Inc.; 351, MapQuest.com, Inc.; 352, MapQuest.com, Inc.; 353, Uhl Studios, Inc.; 356, MapQuest.com, Inc.; 358, MapQuest.com, Inc.; 359, MapQuest.com, Inc.; 361, MapQuest.com, Inc.

Unit 6: Page 366 (bl, t), Ortelius Design; 367, MapQuest.com, Inc.; 368, MapQuest.com, Inc.; 369, MapQuest.com, Inc.; 370, MapQuest.com, Inc.; 371, MapQuest.com, Inc.; 372–375, MapQuest.com, Inc.

Chapter 17: Page 377, (b) MapQuest.com, Inc.; 378 (bl), MapQuest.com, Inc.; 379 (t), MapQuest.com, Inc.; 380 (b), MapQuest.com, Inc.; 383 (t), MapQuest.com, Inc.; 384, (bl) MapQuest.com, Inc.; 386, MapQuest.com, Inc.; 387, MapQuest.com, Inc.; 388 (bc), MapQuest.com, Inc.; 389 (b), MapQuest.com, Inc.

Chapter 18: Page 395, MapQuest.com, Inc.; 396, MapQuest.com, Inc.; 398, MapQuest.com, Inc.; 399, MapQuest.com, Inc.; 400, MapQuest.com, Inc.; 403, MapQuest.com, Inc.; 404 MapQuest.com, Inc.; 406, MapQuest.com, Inc.; 409, Uhl Studios, Inc.; 410 MapQuest.com, Inc.; 412 MapQuest.com, Inc.; 413, Leslie Kell.

Chapter 19: Page 415, MapQuest.com, Inc.; 417, MapQuest.com, Inc.; 418, MapQuest.com, Inc.; 419, MapQuest.com, Inc.; 422, MapQuest.com, Inc.; 425, Leslie Kell; 426, MapQuest.com, Inc.; 429, MapQuest.com, Inc.

Unit 7: Page 434 (bl, t), Ortelius Design; 435, MapQuest.com, Inc.; 436, MapQuest.com, Inc.; 437, MapQuest.com, Inc.; 438, MapQuest.com, Inc.; 439, MapQuest.com, Inc.; 440–445, MapQuest.com, Inc.

Chapter 20: Page 447, MapQuest.com, Inc.; 448, MapQuest.com, Inc.; 449, MapQuest.com, Inc.; 452, Ralph Voltz; 453, MapQuest.com, Inc.; 454, MapQuest.com, Inc.; 455, MapQuest.com, Inc.; 456, MapQuest.com, Inc.; 457 (r,l), Joe LeMonnier; 458, MapQuest.com, Inc.; 459 (tr), MapQuest.com, Inc.; 462, MapQuest.com, Inc.; 464, MapQuest.com, Inc.; 465, Leslie Kell.

Chapter 21: Page 467 (b), MapQuest.com, Inc.; 468 (bl), MapQuest.com, Inc.; 470 (bl), MapQuest.com, Inc.; 471 (br), MapQuest.com, Inc.; 472 (bl), MapQuest.com, Inc.; 474 (tl), MapQuest.com, Inc.; 475 (br), MapQuest.com, Inc.; 476 (tl), MapQuest.com, Inc.; 477 (tr), Leslie Kell; 478 (bl), MapQuest.com, Inc.; 479 (t), MapQuest.com, Inc.; 480, MapQuest.com, Inc.; 482, MapQuest.com, Inc.; 483, Leslie Kell.

Chapter 22: Page 485 (b), MapQuest.com, Inc.; 486 (br), MapQuest.com, Inc.; 487 (tr), MapQuest.com, Inc.; 491 (br), MapQuest.com, Inc.; 492 (bl), MapQuest.com, Inc.; 496 (br), MapQuest.com, Inc.; 497 (tr), MapQuest.com, Inc.; 498, MapQuest.com, Inc.

Chapter 23: Page 501 (b), MapQuest.com, Inc.; 502 (bl), MapQuest.com, Inc.; 505 (br), MapQuest.com, Inc.; 507 (tr), MapQuest.com, Inc.; 510, MapQuest.com, Inc.; 511, MapQuest.com, Inc.; 514, MapQuest.com, Inc.; 515, MapQuest.com, Inc.

Chapter 24: Page 517, MapQuest.com, Inc.; 518 (tl), MapQuest.com, Inc.; 519 (tr), MapQuest.com, Inc.; 522 (tl), MapQuest.com, Inc.; 528, MapQuest.com, Inc.; 531 (tr), MapQuest.com, Inc.; 532, MapQuest.com, Inc.; 533, Leslie Kell.

Unit 8: Page 540 (bl, t), Ortelius Design; 541, MapQuest.com, Inc.; 542, MapQuest.com, Inc.; 543, MapQuest.com, Inc.; 544, MapQuest.com, Inc.; 545, MapQuest.com, Inc.; 546–547, MapQuest.com, Inc.

Chapter 25: Page 549, MapQuest.com, Inc.; 550 (bl), MapQuest.com, Inc.; 552, MapQuest.com, Inc.; 555 (tr), MapQuest.com, Inc.; 558 (bl), MapQuest.com, Inc.; 560, MapQuest.com, Inc.; 561, MapQuest.com, Inc.; 564, MapQuest.com, Inc.; 565, MapQuest.com, Inc.

Chapter 26: Page 567 (b), MapQuest.com, Inc.; 570 (t), MapQuest.com, Inc.; 571, Joe LeMonnier; 572 (bl), MapQuest.com, Inc.; 573 (br), MapQuest.com, Inc.; 574 (tl), MapQuest.com, Inc.; 576, MapQuest.com, Inc.; 578, MapQuest.com, Inc.; 579, MapQuest.com, Inc.; 580, MapQuest.com, Inc.; 581, MapQuest.com, Inc.; 582, MapQuest.com, Inc.; 585, MapQuest.com, Inc.; 586, Stephen Durke/Washington Artists; 587 (l), Ortelius Design.

Unit 9: Page 590 (bl, t), Ortelius Design; 591, MapQuest.com, Inc.; 592, MapQuest.com, Inc.; 593, MapQuest.com, Inc.; 594, MapQuest.com, Inc.; 595, MapQuest.com, Inc.; 596–597, MapQuest.com, Inc.

Chapter 27: Page 599 (b), MapQuest.com, Inc.; 600 (tl), MapQuest.com, Inc.; 601 (br), MapQuest.com, Inc.; 604 (tl), MapQuest.com, Inc.; 605 (b), Leslie Kell; 607 (br, tr), MapQuest.com, Inc.; 609 (tr), MapQuest.com, Inc.; 610 (bl), Rosa + Wesley; 611 (br), MapQuest.com, Inc.; 612 (bl), MapQuest.com, Inc.; 613 (tr), MapQuest.com, Inc.; 615 (tl), MapQuest.com, Inc.; 616 (bl), MapQuest.com, Inc.; 618, MapQuest.com, Inc.; 619, Leslie Kell.

Chapter 28: Page 621 (b), MapQuest.com, Inc.; 622 (bl), MapQuest.com, Inc.; 623 (br), MapQuest.com, Inc.; 625, MapQuest.com, Inc.; 630 (tl, bl), MapQuest.com, Inc.; 633 (br), MapQuest.com, Inc.; 634 (tl), MapQuest.com, Inc.; 637 (br), MapQuest.com, Inc.; 638 (bl), MapQuest.com, Inc.; 640, MapQuest.com, Inc.

Chapter 29: Page 643, MapQuest.com, Inc.; 644 (bl), MapQuest.com, Inc.; 646, Dave Henderson; 649 (tr), MapQuest.com, Inc.; 650 (bl), MapQuest.com, Inc.; 651 (tr), MapQuest.com, Inc.; 653 (br), MapQuest.com, Inc.; 655 (br), MapQuest.com, Inc.; 656 (tl), MapQuest.com, Inc.; 657 (tr), MapQuest.com, Inc.; 658, MapQuest.com, Inc.; 659, Leslie Kell; 660, MapQuest.com, Inc.; 661, Leslie Kell; 663 (tr), MapQuest.com, Inc.

Unit 10: Page 668 (bl, t), Ortelius Design; 669, MapQuest.com, Inc.; 670, MapQuest.com, Inc.; 671, MapQuest.com, Inc.; 672, MapQuest.com, Inc.; 673, MapQuest.com, Inc.; 674–675, MapQuest.com, Inc.

Chapter 30: Page 677 (b), MapQuest.com, Inc.; 678 (bl), MapQuest.com, Inc.; 682 (tl), MapQuest.com, Inc.; 683, Leslie Kell; 685, Nenad Jakesevic; 686 (bl), MapQuest.com, Inc.; 687 (bl), MapQuest.com, Inc.; 688, MapQuest.com, Inc.; 689, MapQuest.com, Inc.; 690, MapQuest.com, Inc.; 691, MapQuest.com, Inc.

Chapter 31: Page 693 (b), Uhl Studios, Inc.; 694 (tr), MapQuest.com, Inc.; 695 (bl), MapQuest.com, Inc.; 701 (br), MapQuest.com, Inc.; 702 (tl), MapQuest.com, Inc.; 706, MapQuest.com, Inc.; 708, Uhl Studios, Inc.; 709, MapQuest.com, Inc.

PHOTO CREDITS

Cover and Title Page: (child image) AlaskaStock Images; (bkgd) Image Copyright © 2003 PhotoDisc, Inc./HRW

Table of Contents: Page iv, SuperStock; v (t), S. Sherbell/Corbis SABA; v (b), © Richard Paisley/Viesti Collection; vi (t), © STONE/Robert Frerck/Getty Images; vii (t), © STONE/William J. Hebert/Getty Images; vi (b), © Robert Frerck/Odyssey/Chicago; vii (b), Rosenback/ZEFA/Index Stock Imagery; viii (t), © Travelpix/FPG International/Getty Images; viii (b), © The State Russian Museum/CORBIS; ix (t), Steve Raymer/National Geographic Society Image Collection; ix (b), © Marc Riboud/Magnum; x (t), Ed Kashi © 1995; x (b), © Alex Wasinski/FPG International/Getty Images; xi (b), Daniel J. Cox/Natural Exposures; xi (tl), Giraudon/Art Resource, NY; xii (bl), © C. Rennie/Art Directors & TRIP Photo Library; xii (t), Richard Bickel/CORBIS; xiii (b), Ric Ergenbright; xiii (c), CORBIS; xiv (b), Digital Stock Corp; xiv (t), © Frans Lanting/Minden Pictures; **Geography and Map Skills:** Page S1 (tr), HRW photo by Sam Dudgeon: S1 (br), HRW photo by Sam Dudgeon; S4 (tr), Andy Christiansen/HRW Photo; **Unit 1:** Page 0 (cl), © Joe Viesti/The Viesti Collection; 0 (t), © Norbert Wu/www.norbertwu.com; 0–1 (b), Photo © Transdia/Panoramic Images, Chicago 1998; 1 (tr), Francois Gohier/Photo Researchers, Inc.; 1 (br), Steven David Miller/Animals Animals/Earth Scenes; **Chapter 1:** Page 2 (cl), © STONE/Philip & Karen Smith/Getty Images; 2 (bl), Sam Dudgeon/HRW Photo; 2 (tr), CORBIS Images; 2 (c), © Joseph Sohm; ChromoSohm Inc./CORBIS; 3 (b), © STONE/Ken McVey/Getty Images; 4, Luca Turi/AP/Wide World Photos; 5 (l), Jose Fuste Raga/Corbis Stock Market; 5 (r), NASA; 6 (l), Robert Caputo/Aurora; 7 (br), © Bob Daemmrich Photo, Inc.; 8, © Bob Daemmrich Photo, Inc.; 8 (b), K.D. Frankel/Bilderberg/Aurora; 9 (b), Wolfgang Kaehler Photography; 10, © Nik Wheeler/CORBIS; 11 (cr), © Ilene Perlman/Stock, Boston; 12, CORBIS/Roger Ressmeyer; 13, © Chris Rainier/CORBIS; **Chapter 2:** Page 18 (tc), © STONE/Glenn Christianson/Getty Images; 18 (tr), © STONE/A. Witte/C. Mahaney/Getty Images; 18, Image Copyright © 2002 PhotoDisc, Inc./HRW: 18 (tr), Image © copyright Digital Stock Imagery Inc.; 20, © Galen Rowell/CORBIS; 21, Wendell Metzen/Bruce Coleman, Inc.; 21 (b), 1996 CORBIS; Original image courtesy of NASA/CORBIS; 22, Nenad Jakesevic/HRW Art & Stone/Denis Waugh; 23, HRW; 24, The Granger Collection, New York; 25, Carr Clifton/Minden Pictures; 26 (t), Grant Heilman/Grant Heilman Photography; 26, Joseph Hutchins Colton, Johnson's New Illustrated Family Atlas with Physical Geography ... (New York, 1864), pp. 10-11; 27, © STONE/Martin Puddy/Getty Images; 28 (b), Boll/Liaison Agency/Getty Images; 28, Wolfgang Kaehler Photography; 30 (b), Steven Burr Williams; 31, HRW Art; 32, © Darrell Gulin/CORBIS; 34, Rosentiel School of Marine and Atmospheric Science, University of Miami; 35, © John Elk III; 35, David Madison/Bruce Coleman, Inc.; 38, © Michael Busselle/CORBIS; 39 (c), © Kevin Schafer/kevinschafer.com; 39, L. Linkhart/Visuals Unlimited; 40 (b), © STONE/Mike Abrahams/Getty Images; 40, © Telegraph Colour Library/FPG International/Getty Images; 41, B. Brander/Photo Researchers, Inc.; 41, David R. Frazier Photolibrary; 42, © Ernest Manewal/FPG International/Getty Images; 42, CORBIS/AFP Photo/Vanderlei Almeida; 43, David Hiser/Photographers/Aspen; **Chapter 3:** Page 46 (t), © Gerald Brimacombe/International Stock Photography/Image State; 46 (cr), © Bob Firth/International Stock Photography/Image State; 46 (c), © Wally McNamee/CORBIS; 46-47 (b), © Ahu Tongariki/Bruce Coleman, Inc.; 47 (b), © Bob Daemmrich/Stock, Boston; 48 (b), © Bohdam Hrynewch/Stock, Boston/PNI; 49 (b), © STONE/Ron Sherman/ Getty Images; 49 (t), © STONE/Rich La Salle/Getty Images; 50 (b), Bruno Barbey/Magnum Photos; 50 (t), S. Sherbell/Corbis SABA; 51 (c), © Werner Forman/CORBIS; 52, © Eric and David Hosking/CORBIS; 53 (b), © Rich Iwasaki/AllStock/STONE/Getty Images; 54 (tr), © Michelle Gabel/The Image Works; 54 (tc), © Richard Hamilton Smith/CORBIS; 54 (cr), Henry Friedman; 54 (br), © Stephen Frisch/Stock, Boston/PNI; 54 (bl), © Glen Allison/Getty Images/Stone; 55, John Elk III/Bruce Coleman, Inc.; 56 (b), Carolyn Schaefer/SCHAE/Bruce Coleman, Inc.; 57 (t), Martin Rogers/CORBIS; 58, © Sally Mayman/Getty Images/Stone; 59, Alon Reininger/Woodfin Camp & Associates; 60 (b), Richard T. Nowitz/CORBIS; 61 (b), Dave G. Houser/CORBIS; 61 (t), © Ulrike Welsch; 62 (b), Reuters/CORBIS; 63 (t), Peter Turnley/Black Star; 65, Martin Guhl; **Unit 2:** Page 70 (bl), © Walter Bibikow/FPG International/Getty Images; 70 (t), SuperStock; 70 (bc), Lawrence Migdale; 71 (cr), © STONE/Zigy Kaluzny/Getty Images; 71 (br), Alan Nelson/Animals Animals/Earth Scenes; **Chapter 4:** Page 80, Steve Ewert Photography; 82, SuperStock; 83, ©Robert Frerck/Odyssey/Chicago; 84 (tl), Jay Malonson/AP/Wide World Photos; 84 (bl), Jim Schwabel/Southern Stock/PNI; 84 (tr), SuperStock; 84 (br), Image Copyright © 2002 PhotoDisc, Inc.; 86 (b), © Laurence Parent; 87 (t), The Metropolitan Museum of Art, Gift of Edgar William and Bernice Chrysler Garbish, 1963.; 87 (b), © Lee Snider/CORBIS; 88 (b), © David Frazier/The Image Works; 88 (cl), The Granger Collection, New York; 89 (t), © Bob Daemmrich/The Image Works; 92 (l), © Joe Sohm/The Image Works; 93, STONE/Jake Rajs/Getty Images; 94, © Ron Thomas/FPG International/Getty Images; 95, © Annie Griffiths Belt/CORBIS; 97, CORBIS/Layne Kennedy; 98 (b), © Vladamir Pcholkin/FPG International/Getty Images; 98 (t), © 1991 Bill Lach/Nawrocki Stock Photo; **Chapter 5:** Page 102, Steve Ewert Photography; 104, © Carr Clifton/Minden Pictures; 105 (b), © STONE/Gordon Fisher/Getty Images; 105 (t), © Walter Bibikow/

Viesti Collection; 106 (b), Henry E. Huntington Library and Art Gallery; 107, © Bill Terry/Viesti Collection, Inc.; 107 (r), Hulton Archive/Getty Images; 108, © STONE/Bob Herger/Getty Images; 109, © Robert Winslow/Viesti Collection; 110, © Mark E. Gibson; 111 (b), © Nazima Kowall/CORBIS; 112, © Nik Wheeler/CORBIS; 113, Sam Dudgeon/HRW Photo; 114 (b), © STONE/George Hunter/Getty Images; 114 (t), © STONE/Cosmo Condine/Getty Images; 115 (t), © Richard Pasley/Viesti Collection; 118-119, Kennan Ward/CORBIS; 120, © Planet Art; 121, © Landiscor Aerial Information; 121, © Landiscor Aerial Information; **Unit 3:** Page 122 (b), Francois Gohier/Photo Researchers, Inc.; 122 (t), George Holton/Photo Researchers, Inc.; 122-123 (c), Cliff Hollenbeck/International Stock Photography/Image State; 123 (cr), Stephen J. Krasemann/Nature Conservancy/Photo Researchers, Inc; 123 (b), C.K. Lorenz/Photo Researchers, Inc; **Chapter 6:** Page 134, Steve Ewert Photography; 135 (b), MapQuest.com, Inc;. 135 (cr), MapQuest.com, Inc.; 135 (cl), MapQuest.com, Inc.; 135 (br), MapQuest .com, Inc; 136 (t), © Robert Frerck/Odyssey/Chicago; 136 (cl), © STONE/George Lepp/Getty Images; 136 (b), Image copyright © 2001 PhotoDisc, Inc;. 136 (tc), MapQuest.com, Inc;. 137 (b), © Robert Frerck/Odyssey/Chicago; 137 (t), MapQuest.com, Inc; 137, MapQuest.com, Inc;. 139 (b), Dallas and John Heaton/CORBIS; 140 (b), © STONE/Richard A. Cooke III/Getty Images; 140 (t), The Bodleian Library, Oxford, MS Arch. Selden A. 1, fol 37R; 140 (br), MapQuest.com, Inc; 141 (c), Library of Congress; 142, © Robert Frerck/Odyssey/Chicago; 142 (cl), MapQuest.com, Inc.; 142 (tl), CORBIS; 143, © Danny Lehman/CORBIS;144 (tr), Leslie Kell; 144, Alex S. MacLean/Landslides; 145 (t), MapQuest.com, Inc.; 145, © Bob Daemmrich Photo, Inc.; 146 (bl), Rosa + Wesley; 147 (b), © Danny Lehman/CORBIS; 147 (bl), MapQuest.com, Inc.; 147 (t), © Jan Butchofsky-Houser/CORBIS; 148 (b), John Neubauer; 148 (br), MapQuest.com, Inc.; 149 (t), © STONE/David Hiser/Getty Images; 150 (tr), MapQuest.com, Inc.; **Chapter 7:** Page 152, Steve Ewert Photography; 154 (b), Bruce Dale/National Geographic Society Image Collection; 155 (tr), K.M. Westermann/CORBIS; 156 (c), © Frank Staub/Index Stock Imagery, Inc.; 156 (inset), ©Kevin Schafer/kevinschafer.com; 157, © Robert Frerck/Odyssey/Chicago; 158, Ancient Art and Architecture Collection Ltd.; 159, © Robert Frerck/Odyssey/Chicago; 161 (b), © Carol Lee/Index Stock Imagery; 163 (t), © STONE/Doug Armand/Getty Images; 163 (b), © Jose Azel/Aurora,; 164 (bc), Nik Wheeler/CORBIS; 165, Terry Eggers 1998/Corbis Stock Market; **Chapter 8:** Page 168, Steve Ewert Photography; 171, © Kevin Schafer/kevinschafer.com; 172 (b), Patrick Rouillard/Latin Stock/CORBIS Stock Market; 173, © Dave G. Houser/CORBIS; 174 (t), © Gianni Dagli Orti/CORBIS; 175, © Jeremy Horner/CORBIS; 176 (b), James Marshall/Corbis Stock Market; 178, © Kevin Schafer/CORBIS; 179 (b), Chip and Rosa Maria Peterson; 180, © Nicole Duplaix/CORBIS; 181 (t), © Bruno Barbey/Magnum Photos; **Chapter 9:** Page 184, Steve Ewert Photography; 186, © STONE/Robert Van Der Hilst/Getty Images; 187, © Gail Shumway/FPG International/Getty Images; 188, © Carlos Humberto T.D.C./Contact Press Images/PNI; 189 (b), © Archivo Iconografico, S.A./CORBIS; 190, David Leah/Allsport/Getty Images; 191, © STONE/Chad Ehlers/Getty Images; 193 (b), Sepp Seitz/Woodfin Camp & Associates; 194, © STONE/Robert Frerck/Getty Images; 194 (tl), CORBIS; 195, © Yann Arthus-Bertrand/CORBIS; 196, © Johnny Stockshooter/International Stock Photography/Image State; 197 (b), RAGA/Corbis Stock Market; 198, © Daniel Rivademar/Odyssey/Chicago; 199, © Alex Webb/Magnum Photos; **Chapter 10:** Page 202, Steve Ewert Photography; 204, © STONE/William J. Hebert/Getty Images; 205, © Robert Frerck/Odyssey/Chicago; 206, Mirielle Vautier/Woodfin Camp & Associates/PNI; 207 (br), Don Mason 1986/Corbis Stock Market; 207 (bl), Don Mason 1989/Corbis Stock Market; 208 (b), © Robert Frerck/Odyssey/Chicago; 208 (t), © Robert Frerck/Odyssey/Chicago; 209, © Robert Frerck/Odyssey/Chicago; 210 (t), © Robert Frerck/Odyssey/Chicago; 211, EPA/Diario El Tiempo de Piura PERU; 212 (b), © Kevin Schafer/kevinschafer.com; 213 (t), © Robert Frerck/Odyssey/Chicago; 213 (b), © Index Stock Imagery, Inc.; 214, Daniel Rivadamar/Odyssey/Chicago; 218-219, Kennan Ward/CORBIS; 220 (t), Nair Benedicto/f4/DDB Stock Photo; 220 (b), Nair Benedicto/f4/DDB Stock Photo; 221, Bruce Coleman Inc; **Unit 4:** Page 222 (bl), Alfredo Venturi/Masterfile; 222 (t), © Walter Bibikow/Viesti Collection; 222-223, (c), SuperStock; 223 (t), FPG International/Getty Images; 223 (b), Robert Maier/Animals Animals/Earth Scenes; **Chapter 11:** Page 234, Steve Ewert Photography; 236, Photo © Earl Bronsteen 1/Panoramic Images, Chicago 1998; 237, © Gary Braasch/CORBIS; 238 (b), © Travelpix/FPG International/Getty Images; 239 (b), © Joe Viesti/The Viesti Collection; 239 (t), Steve Vidler/eStock Photo; 240 (br), © Araldo de Luca/CORBIS; 240 (bl), Museo di Cipro/Art Resource, NY; 240, University at Buffalo Science & Engineering Library; 241, Bettmann/CORBIS; 242 (b), © Archivo Iconografico, S.A./CORBIS; 243 (t), © Louis Goldman/FPG International/Getty Images; 243 (b), © Gianni Dagli Orti/CORBIS; 244 (b), Siegfried Tauqueur/eStock Photo; 246 (b), Rosenback/ZEFA/Index Stock Imagery, Inc; 247, © Jean Kugler/FPG International/Getty Images; 248, Patrick Ward/CORBIS; 249 (t), © Sitki Tarlan/Panoramic Images, Chicago 1998; **Chapter 12:** Page 252, Steve Ewert Photography; 254 (t), J. Messerschmidt/eStock Photo; 254 (b), Photographers Consortium/eStock Photo; 255, H.P. Merton/Corbis Stock Market; 256 (l), Castres, Musee Goya/Art Resource, NY; 257 (t), The Art Archive; 257 (b), Scala/Art Resource, NY; 258 (tl), Pierre Witt/Rapho Agency; 258 (r), Photographers Consortium/eStock Photo; 259 (cl), Francis G. Mayer/CORBIS; 260 (b), Wolfgang Kaehler Photography; 261 (t), CORBIS/Bettmann; 261 (c), Archive Photos/Getty Images; 261. (b), AKG Photo, London; 262, Gisela Damm/eStock Photo; 262 (tl), Archivo Iconografico, S.A./CORBIS; 264 (l), Sigfried Tuaqueur/eStock Photo; 265 (t), Wolfgang Kaehler Photography; 267 (b), © Ken Ross/FPG International/Getty Images; 268 (b), © G. Wagner/Viesti Collection; 268 (t), © STONE/Siegfried Layda/Getty Images; **Chapter 13:** Page 272, Steve Ewert Photography; 274, © Walter Bibikow/Viesti Collection; 274 (t), © E. Nagele/FPG International/Getty Images; 274, Roger Ressmeyer/CORBIS; 276-277, Bettman/CORBIS; 278 (b), British Museum, London, UK/Bridgeman Art Library, London/New York; 278 (c), © Yann Arthus-Bertrand/CORBIS; 279 (t), Private Collection/Bridgeman Art Library, London/New York; 279 (b), © STONE/Ed Pritchard/Getty Images; 280 (t), Popperfoto; 282 (b), © Joe Englander/Viesti Collection 283 (tr), AP Photo/Donald Stampfli; 285 (b), Index Stock Imagery, Inc; 286, © Walter Bibikow/FPG International/Getty Images; 286 Chris Lisle/CORBIS; 287, © Index Stock Photography, Inc; 288, Tom Stewart/Corbis Stock Market; 289, © Bryan & Cherry Alexander; **Chapter 14:** Page 292, Steve Ewert Photography; 294, © Figaro Magazine/Robert Tixador/Gamma Presse; 296 (b), © Paul Almasy/CORBIS; 297, Aldo Pavan/Gamma Presse; 298, © David Bartruff/FPG International/Getty Images; 299 (t), Image Copyright © 2001 PhotoDisc, Inc.; 300 (b), © Fergus O'Brien/FPG International/Getty Images 300 (tl), Getty News Services; 301, © Garbor Feher/Corbis Sygma; 302 (l), © Francois de Mulder/CORBIS; 303 (b), Krpan Jasmin/Gamma Presse; 303 (t), © Michael S. Yamashita/CORBIS; 304, Daniels Marleen/Gamma Presse; 305 (b), Francis Li/Liaison International/Getty Images; 305 (t), Patrick Chauvel/Corbis Sygma; 306 (b), Bogdan Cristel/Corbis; 310, Bill Ross/CORBIS; 312 (t), AKG Photo, London; 313, © STONE/Getty Images; 337 (tr), © European Communities; **Unit 5:** Page 314 (bl), SuperStock; 314 (br), Ed Kashi; 314 (c), Mark Wadlow/Russia and Eastern Images; 314 (bl), SuperStock; 315 (t), Bruce Coleman Inc; 315 (br), Gerard Lacz/Peter Arnold, Inc; 322, Robert S. Semeniuk/Black Star; **Chapter 15:** Page 324, Steve Ewert Photography; 326, Tass/Sovfoto/Eastfoto; 328, © 1996 Hans J. Burkard/AURORA; 329 (b), Tretyakov Gallery, Moscow, Russia/Bridgeman Art Library, New York/London330Bettman/CORBIS; 331, © Steve Raymer/CORBIS; 332 (t), © Wally McNamee/CORBIS; 333, © Steve Raymer/CORBIS; 334, Image © copyright Digital Stock Imagery Inc;. 335 (b), © Vladamir Pcholkin/FPG International/Getty Images; 336 (t), © Steve McCurry/Magnum Photos; 336 (b), Steve Raymer/CORBIS-Bettmann; 337, Claus Meyer/Black Star/PNI; 338 (b), © Bryan & Cherry Alexander; 339 (t), Sovfoto/Eastfoto; 340, © Dean Conger/CORBIS; 341 (b), © Planet Earth Pictures 1998/FPG International/Gettty Images; 342 (b), © Wolfgang Kaehler/CORBIS; 343, © Michael S. Yamashita/CORBIS; 345, Roger Harvell/The Greenville News; 345 (br), Peter Turnley/CORBIS; **Chapter 16:** Page 346, Steve Ewert Photography; 348, © Dean Conger/CORBIS; 350 (b), AKG Photo, London; 351 (b),Steve Raymer/National Geographic Society Image Collection; 351 (t), AKG Photo, London; 352, Steve Raymer/National Geographic Society Image Collection; 353, Randall Hyman; 355 (b), © Charles Lenars/CORBIS; 356 (b), Sovfoto/Eastfoto; 356 (t), CORBIS/Stephanie Maze; 360, © 1990 Abbas/Magnum Photos; 361 (c), Marc Garanger/CORBIS; 362 (t), BIOS/M. Gunther/Peter Arnold, Inc.; 363, Sovfoto/Eastfoto; **Unit 6:** Page 364 (br), Kevin Rushby; 364 (c), © Beryl Goldberg; 365 (cr), Annie Griffiths Belt/National Geographic Society Image Collection; 365 (b), Hill, M. Osf/Animals Animals/Earth Scenes; **Chapter 17:** Page 376, © 2000 Zafer KIZILKAYA; 378, © Robert Frerck/Odyssey/Chicago; 379, © Robert Frerck/Odyssey/Chicago; 380 (l), © Robert Frerck/Odyssey/Chicago; 381 (b), © Robert Frerck/Odyssey/Chicago; 381 (t), © AFP/CORBIS; 382, Ruenion des Musees Nationaux/Bridgeman Art Library, New York/London; 383, © Robert Frerck/Odyssey/Chicago; 384 (b), © Bill Curtsinger/National Geographic Society Image Collection; 385, 386, © Alexandra Avakian/Contact Press Images; 387, © Richard T. Nowitz/CORBIS; 388 (b), Ed Kashi © 1995; 389 (b), Maynard Owen Wiliams/National Geographic Society Image Collection; 389 (t), © 1993 Ed Kashi; 390, © Wolfgang Kaehler/CORBIS; 390 (tl), © Thomas Muscionico/Contact Press Images; 391 (t), Bettmann/CORBIS; **Chapter 18:** Page 394, Steve Ewert Photography; 396, © Marc Riboud/Magnum Photos; 397, © Stephen Frink/CORBIS; 398 (b), © Abbas/Magnum Photos; 399, © Adam Woolfitt/CORBIS; 400, NASA; 401, University Library Istanbul/The Art Archive; 402, © H Rogers/Art Directors & TRIP Photo Library; 403, © Abbie Enock/Travel Ink/CORBIS; 405 (t), © Burnett H. Moody/Bruce Coleman, Inc.; 405 (b), © Burnett H. Moody/Bruce Coleman, Inc.; 406 (l), Stephen Wallace/Black Star; 407, © Alexandra Avakian/Contact Press Images; 408, © Nik Wheeler/CORBIS; 410, © Alexandra Avakian/Contact Press Images; 410, ODD ANDERSEN/AFP/Getty Images; **Chapter 19:** Page 414, Steve Ewert Photography; 416 (t), Tass/Sovfoto/Eastfoto; 416 (b), © Hans Reinhard/Bruce Coleman, Inc;. 417, © Yann Arthus-Bertrand/CORBIS; 418 (b), © K.M. Westermann/CORBIS; 419, © Wolfgang Kaehler/CORBIS; 420, © Nevada Wier/CORBIS; 421 (b), © Wolfgang Kaehler/CORBIS; 422, © Dean Conger/CORBIS; 423-424, Alain Le Garsmeur/Panos Pictures; 425 (t), Chris Stowers/Panos Pictures; 428 (bl), Roger Antrobus/CORBIS; 428 (tr), Pictor Uniphoto; 430 (tr), Robert O'Dea/AKG Photo, London; 431 (cr), Burt Silverman/National Geographic Society Image Collection; **Unit 7:** 432 (bl), © STONE/Theo Allofs/Getty Images; 432 (tr), © Robert Frerck/Odyssey/Chicago; 432-433 (c), Herb Zulpier/Masterfile; 433 (cr), © Charles Henneghien/Bruce Coleman, Inc.; 433 (br), S. Michael Bisceglie/Animals Animals/Earth Scenes; **Chapter 20:** Page 446 (bl), Steve Ewert Photography; 448 (b), Guiseppe Bizzarri/Panos Pictures; 449 (tl), © Staffan Widstrand/CORBIS; 449 (tr), Photo Researchers, Inc.; 450 (cl), © Roger Tidman/CORBIS; 451 (br), Kenneth Garrett/National Geographic Society Image Collection; 452 (br), STONE/Hugh Sitton/Getty Images; 453 (tr), © M. Timothy O'Keefe/Bruce Coleman, Inc.; 453 (b), © Carmen Redondo/CORBIS; 453 (inset), © Sharon Smith/Bruce Coleman, Inc.; 454 (t), Frank and Helen Schreider/Photo Researchers, Inc.; 454 (bl), Jean-Léo Dugast/Panos Pictures; 455 (tr), Kazuyoshi Nomachi/Photo Researchers, Inc.; 456-457, Yann Arthus-Bertrand/CORBIS; 458 (b), © Christine Osborne/CORBIS; 459 (tl), © Yann Arthus-Bertrand/CORBIS; 460 (tl), Wally McNamee/CORBIS; 462 (b), J. PH. Charbonnier/Photo Researchers, Inc.; 463 (cr), James L. Stanfield/National Geographic Society Image Collection; **Chapter 21:** Page 466 (bl), Steve Ewert Photography; 468 (b), Wolfgang Kaehler Photography; 469 (tr), © Gail Shumway/FPG International/Getty Images; 470 (b), Wolfgang Kaehler Photography; 471 (cr), Wolfgang Kaehler Photography; 472 (b), © STONE/Will Curtis/Getty Images; 473 (tr), M & E Bernheim/Woodfin Camp & Associates; 474 (tl), © Peter Guttman/LIFE Magazine; 475 (br), Wolfgang Kaehler Photography; 476 (tr), © John Elk/Bruce Coleman, Inc.; 478 (cl), © STONE/Sally Mayman/Getty Images; 479 (br), © Alex Wasinski/FPG International/Getty Images; 479 (t), © STONE/James Nelson/Getty Images; 480 (br), SuperStock; 480, Daniel Lainé/CORBIS; 481, PELLETIER MICHELINE/CORBIS SYGMA; **Chapter 22:** Page 484 (bl), Neil Cooper/Panos Pictures; 486 (b), Gerald Cubitt; 487 (tr), M. Denis-Huot/HOA-QUI; 488 (bl), Giraudon/Art Resource, NY; 489 (t), Jonathan Blair/CORBIS; 490 (tl), Victor Englebert; 491 (br), Dave G. Houser; 492 (b), Daniel J. Cox/Natural Exposures; 493 (tr), Wolfgang Kaehler Photography; 494 (tl), Private Collection/Bridgeman Art Library, New York/London; 495 (b), Victor Englebert; 496 (b), Betty Press/Woodfin Camp & Associates; 497 (t), Maya Kardum/Panos Pictures; **Chapter 23:** Page 500 (bl), Steve Ewert Photography; 502 (b), Gerald Cubitt; 503 (tr), Michael Nichols/National Geographic Society Image Collection; 504 (bl), Christie's Images; 505 (b), © STONE/Ian Murphy/Getty Images; 506 (tr), M. & E. Bernheim/Woodfin Camp & Associates; 507 (tl), M. Edwards/Still Pictures/Peter Arnold, Inc.; 507 (cr), © David Reed/CORBIS; 508 (bl), Jose Azel/Aurora; 509 (b), SuperStock; 510 (tr), Robert Caputo/Aurora; 511 (br), M & E Bernheim/Woodfin Camp & Associates; 512 (br), Jason Lauré/Lauré Communications; **Chapter 24:** Page 516 (bl), Trygve Bolstad/Panos Pictures; 518 (t), © STONE/John Lamb/Getty Images;